THE DEDUCTIVE FOUNDATIONS
OF
COMPUTER PROGRAMMING

A One-Volume Version of
**"The Logical Basis for
Computer Programming"**

THE DEDUCTIVE FOUNDATIONS

OF

COMPUTER PROGRAMMING

A One-Volume Version of
**"The Logical Basis for
Computer Programming"**

ZOHAR MANNA
Computer Science Department
Stanford University
and
Computer Science Department
Weizmann Institute of Science

RICHARD WALDINGER
Artificial Intelligence Center
SRI International
and
Computer Science Department
Stanford University

▲

ADDISON-WESLEY PUBLISHING COMPANY

Reading, Massachusetts • Menlo Park, California • New York
Don Mills, Ontario • Wokingham, England • Amsterdam • Bonn
Sydney • Singapore • Tokyo • Madrid • San Juan • Milan • Paris

Library of Congress Cataloging-in-Publication Data

Manna, Zohar.
  The deductive foundations of computer programming / Zohar
Manna, Richard Waldinger.
     p. 717   cm.
  Includes bibliographical references (p. 673) and indexes.
  ISBN 0-201-54886-0
  1. Electronic digital computers – Programming. 2. Logic, Symbolic
and mathematical. I. Waldinger, Richard. II. Title.
QA76.6.M35595 1993
519.7–dc20
                                                        90-1235
                                                          CIP

Reproduced by Addison-Wesley from camera-ready copy supplied
by the authors.

1 2 3 4 5 6 7 8 9 10 – MA – 95949392

Preface

In recent years, mathematical logic has developed from a theoretical activity to a practical tool, playing a fundamental role for computer science similar to that played by calculus for physics and traditional engineering. Once studied only by philosophers and mathematicians, logic is now becoming a standard part of the computer science curriculum. This book is a basic introduction to the logical concepts and techniques underlying computer programming.

Goals

The language of logic has been found to be the natural tool for expressing the purposes or intended behavior of computer programs, in the same way that programming languages express the algorithms that achieve these purposes. Logical techniques play a central role in work leading to the automation of computer programming, including program synthesis, verification, debugging, and transformation. Methods derived from logic are valuable in many branches of artificial intelligence, including planning, knowledge representation, and natural-language understanding. Computer languages (such as LISP and PROLOG) that use logical sentences as programs have been more and more widely applied. A knowledge of logic is now a daily necessity for the computer professional.

This book is intended to make logical concepts accessible to intelligent readers without any special background in mathematics or computer programming. We require no knowledge of mathematical logic, but only an intuitive grasp of basic mathematical concepts at the level of a good high school course. Nor do we require knowledge of any programming language; the book presents the reasoning that is fundamental to all computer programming, regardless of the particular programming language employed.

The One-Volume Version

The original version of *The Logical Basis for Computer Programming* was a two-volume work, each more than 600 pages long. The first volume, subtitled *Deductive Reasoning*, gave a general introduction to logic, emphasizing theories of importance to computer science and presenting methods for the informal but rigorous and intuitively convincing proof of theorems within these theories. The methods are "human-oriented," that is, they are intended to be used by people proving theorems by hand. The second volume, *Deductive Systems*, presented a formal *deductive-tableau* system for proving such theorems; the system is "machine-oriented," that is, it is suitable for implementation in an automatic or interactive computer theorem-proving program.

Each volume was the subject of a separate one-semester or one-quarter course. We found, however, that there was a demand for a single, more accessible course that combined subjects from both volumes. Consequently, we assembled a one-volume version, whose manuscript served as the text for a new course. The condensation was accomplished by concentrating on the most important theories of Volume I, nonnegative integers, tuples, and trees, and by giving a brisker and more informal treatment of some of the topics in Volume II (in particular, well-founded induction and unification). Many results are given here without proof. In this simplified version, the division between intuitive reasoning and formal proof is not maintained. The formal system for proving theorems in each theory is presented immediately after the theory has been introduced informally.

Intentions

There are many textbooks presenting deductive systems as an object of study for the logician. The author of such a book will attempt to use a few simple deduction rules to make it easier to study the systems' properties and limitations. Although such a system may be elegant and concise, a proof expressed within the system may be painfully detailed; it is common that intuitively evident sentences are quite difficult to prove.

Our primary concern here is that the system be useful: proofs of evident theorems should be easy to discover, perhaps automatically, and should reflect the intuitions behind them. We choose to give several rather high-level rules, designed so that proofs within the system will reflect the underlying commonsense arguments.

In discussing a theorem-proving program, we can distinguish between the *logical* component, which tells us what legal inferences can be made in a given theory, and the *strategic* (or heuristic) component, which tells us what inferences are advantageous to make in searching for a proof of a given sentence. (The same distinction can be made between the rules for playing a game and the strategy for winning one.) The logical component of a theorem-proving program is provided by a deductive system. Designing the strategic component is still something of a black art, and our emphasis in this book is on the logical component.

Nevertheless, our system is intended to assist in the discovery of the proof, in the sense that it will forbid some inferences that are logically sound but that can never contribute to the proof. In restricting logical inference, the system allows us to consider fewer alternatives. In this way, the system is more amenable to implementation than a system that allows unlimited logical freedom.

We give only cursory treatment to some of the topics that occur in more philosophically oriented logic books, such as the completeness and undecidability results for predicate logic or the incompleteness of the theory of the nonnegative integers. While we believe that these topics are of great interest, to computer scientists as well as to mathematicians, we have focused this book on the use of logic as a practical tool.

Applications

Automated theorem-proving systems have begun to be of interest to mathematicians because of their recent success in settling certain previously unsolved problems. Proving such mathematical theorems is a demanding application, however, because the system must be capable of finding a proof that has somehow eluded the human mathematician. There are many uses for theorem-proving systems that do not require such superhuman logical abilities.

In software engineering, for instance, theorem provers have assisted in the construction, verification, and transformation of computer programs. Logic-programming languages (such as PROLOG) may be understood as special-purpose theorem-proving systems. Artificial-intelligence researchers have been applying theorem-proving systems for natural-language understanding, commonsense reasoning, and robotic planning. Expert systems may be regarded as rudimentary theorem provers, and application of better deductive techniques is expected to lead to more sophisticated expert systems. Theorem-proving methods have also been used to give inferential abilities to database systems.

Topics

Let us give a brief summary of the contents of this book.

We first, in Part I, introduce the basic notions of propositional logic and the deductive-tableau system for proving propositional-logic theorems.

We then, in Part II, introduce the corresponding notions for predicate logic. To extend the deductive-tableau system to prove predicate-logic theorems, we introduce the ideas of skolemization and unification.

Next, in Part III, we introduce the notion of an axiomatic theory, that is, one defined by a collection of axioms. We present the theory of equality and add a new inference rule to the deductive-tableau system to treat the equality relation.

Of the greatest interest to computer science are the theories with induction, in Part IV. We present three: the theories of nonnegative integers, tuples (arrays), and trees. Algorithms operating on these structures are expressed not as conventional programs but as program-like definitions of functions and relations. The correctness of such algorithms is established by proving theorems about the corresponding functions and relations.

We finally present, in Part V, a single *well-founded* induction principle that combines the separate stepwise-induction principles of the theories with induction. In a final chapter, we give a brief survey of the completeness and decidability aspects of all the theories we have studied.

Presentation and Conventions

We have been serious about making this book understandable by the general reader, including the beginning student, programmer, and computer professional. Our presentation is laced with examples, so that the reader develops the intuition behind the formal notions. In presenting logical arguments, we have been especially careful that the gaps between steps are not too large, so that the reading will be smooth. Logical sentences are presented in a two-dimensional format, in which some information may be conveyed by indentation.

Mathematical works commonly enumerate the definitions and results and refer to them later by number. We have chosen to give them mnemonic names rather than numbers, so that the reader will not need to turn back so frequently. The names of all definitions and results are included in the index.

Many of the problems at the end of each chapter present new, supplementary, material. To indicate which problems pertain to a given portion of the text, we annotate the text with references to the appropriate problems in a bold typefont, and we provide a page reference with each problem. These back-references are useful not only to identify what reading is relevant to solve each problem, but also to indicate which results from the text may be used in the solution. This is described in more detail at the beginning of the problem section of Chapter 1.

Solutions to all the problems are available from the publisher to instructors who adopt the book as a class text.

Differences between the one- and two-volume versions of this text are indicated in remarks enclosed by brackets "⟦" and "⟧".

Curriculum

For several years, successive versions of the manuscript for this book have been used as texts in a sequence of courses taught at Stanford University. Our classes have been attended by undergraduate and graduate students, as well as some computer professionals from industry. We believe that this material should be introduced quite early in the computer science curriculum. It does not require any familiarity with programming, but rather provides the intellectual foundation for the study of programming. We believe that logic is more appropriate than calculus as a requirement for undergraduate computer-science majors.

The book provides a conceptual basis for most computer science courses, including data structures, algorithms, and programming languages. The material on theorem proving, in particular, constitutes the logical basis for courses in software engineering, artificial intelligence, database theory, and the theory of computation.

The Tableau Deductive System

Many of the students in our classes have used an interactive system, implemented on the Macintosh computer, for proving theorems in the deductive-tableau framework. This system accepts direction to decide what inferences to attempt at each stage, but it will never allow the student to perform an erroneous step. For information about how to obtain the system, write to

> Tableau Deductive Systems
> P.O. Box 9779
> Stanford, California 94309.

For information about educational site licenses, instructors should write to

> Addison-Wesley Publishing Company
> Attn: Computer Science and Engineering Marketing Department
> Jacob Way
> Reading, Massachusetts 01867.

Acknowledgments

We have continually revised the manuscript for this book based on our teaching experience and the comments and suggestions of our students and colleagues, including Martín Abadi, Luca de Alfaro, Marianne Baudinet, Tomás Feder, David Gries, Wolfgang Heinle, Pat Lincoln, Yoni Malachi, Narciso Marti-Oliet, Eric Muller, Amir Pnueli, Bill Scherlis, Henny Sipma, Mark Stickel, Carolyn Talcott, Jonathan Traugott, Pierre Wolper, and Frank Yellin. Special thanks are due to Eddie Chang and Tom Henzinger, who did a detailed reading, made particularly extensive suggestions, devised some of the problems, and prepared the booklet of solutions. Tom Henzinger, Peter Ladkin, John Mitchell, and Benjamin Wells have taught courses based upon our original volumes and have given us many comments and criticisms that have been very helpful to us in our revision. The implementors of the interactive Tableau Deductive System, Ron Burback (project director), Hugh McGuire, Michael Winstandley, and Jeff Smith, with assistance from Scott Fraser, have actively contributed to the design of the formal system; we have benefited from their unique perspective and their insights.

We would like to thank our colleagues at Stanford University, the Weizmann Institute, and SRI International for providing a supportive and encouraging environment. For support of the research behind this book, we thank the Air Force Office of Scientific Research, the Defense Advanced Research Projects Agency, the National Science Foundation, and the Office of Naval Research. Evelyn Eldridge-Diaz and Phyllis Winkler have done a magnificent job of typesetting the many versions of the manuscript. Joe Weening's detailed technical knowledge and expertise has been essential in using the TEX document-preparation system of Donald Knuth.

Stanford University   Z. M.
SRI International   R. W.

Contents

PART II: PREDICATE LOGIC

PART III: AXIOMATIC THEORIES

PART IV: THEORIES WITH INDUCTION

Propositional

Logic

1

Foundations

1.1   INTRODUCTION

Even if we do not know whether there is life on the planet Jupiter, we know that the sentence

> There are monkeys on Jupiter
>> or
> there are no monkeys on Jupiter

is true. The truth of the sentence can be determined from its structure alone, without knowing whether its constituents are true or false. Similarly, we can determine that the sentence

> Boise, Idaho, has fewer than 200,000 inhabitants
>> or
> Boise, Idaho, does not have fewer than 200,000 inhabitants

is true without consulting an almanac. In fact, both sentences are instances of the abstract sentence

> P
>> *or*
> (*not P*)

and any sentence of this form is true, regardless of whether P is a true or a false proposition.

We shall say that an abstract sentence is *valid* if it is true regardless of the truth or falsehood of its constituent propositions. By establishing the validity of such an abstract sentence, we can conclude the truth of all its infinitely many concrete instances. For example, if we know that the abstract sentence

$$not \ \big(P \ \ and \ \ (not \ P)\big)$$
$$or$$
$$Q$$

is valid, we can conclude immediately that the concrete sentence

$$not \ \big([x < 0] \ \ and \ \ (not \ [x < 0])\big)$$
$$or$$
$$y \geq 0$$

is true, taking P to be $x < 0$ and Q to be $y \geq 0$, regardless of whether $x < 0$ and $y \geq 0$ are true or false.

On the other hand, any instance of an abstract sentence such as

$$P \ \ and \ \ (not \ P)$$

is false independently of whether P is true or false; such a sentence is called *contradictory.*

Many abstract sentences, such as

$$P \ \ or \ \ Q \qquad and \qquad not \ P,$$

are neither valid nor contradictory; they have both true and false instances.

Certain pairs of abstract sentences, such as

$$if \ \ P \ \ then \ \ Q \qquad and \qquad if \ \ (not \ Q) \ \ then \ \ (not \ P),$$

are *equivalent,* in the sense that a concrete instance of either of them is true if and only if the corresponding instance of the other is true. For example, the two concrete sentences

If it is raining, then the streets are wet

and

If the streets are not wet, then it is not raining

are instances of the pair above, taking P to be "it is raining" and Q to be "the streets are wet," and are both true. Neither abstract sentence of the pair is valid.

The purpose of this chapter is to present a language of abstract sentences, called *propositional logic,* and to introduce techniques for determining whether a given abstract sentence is valid or contradictory and whether two given abstract sentences are equivalent. By the methods of propositional logic, we shall be able to determine the truth or falsehood of many concrete sentences merely by examining their form.

1.2   THE LANGUAGE

We first introduce the basic symbols and show how they are combined to form the (abstract) sentences of propositional logic. We present *syntactic rules*, which say what combinations of symbols are taken to be sentences in the language. We shall not yet consider what these sentences mean.

Definition (propositions)

The sentences of propositional logic are made up of the following symbols, called *propositions*:

- The *truth symbols*

    true   and   *false.*

- The *propositional symbols*

    $P, \ Q, \ R, \ S, \ P_1, \ Q_1, \ R_1, \ S_1, \ P_2, \ Q_2, \ R_2, \ S_2, \ \ldots$

    (the capital letters P, Q, R, or S, possibly with a numerical subscript). ◢

In our informal discussion, we use script letters, such as $\mathcal{E}$, $\mathcal{F}$, $\mathcal{G}$, and $\mathcal{H}$, possibly with a numerical subscript, to stand for sentences. However, these symbols are not part of the language of propositional logic, but are only in our informal "metalanguage," the language in which we speak about propositional logic.

Definition (sentences)

The *sentences* of propositional logic are built up from the propositions by application of the *propositional connectives*:

    not,   and,   or,   if-then,   ≡,   and   if-then-else.

The sentences are formed according to the following rules:

- Every proposition, i.e., a truth symbol or a propositional symbol, is a sentence.
- If $\mathcal{F}$ is a sentence, then so is its *negation*

    $(not \ \mathcal{F})$.

- If $\mathcal{F}$ and $\mathcal{G}$ are sentences, then so is their *conjunction*

    $(\mathcal{F} \ and \ \mathcal{G})$.

    We call $\mathcal{F}$ and $\mathcal{G}$ the *conjuncts* of $(\mathcal{F} \ and \ \mathcal{G})$.

- If $\mathcal{F}$ and $\mathcal{G}$ are sentences, then so is their *disjunction*

    $(\mathcal{F} \ or \ \mathcal{G})$.

    We call $\mathcal{F}$ and $\mathcal{G}$ the *disjuncts* of $(\mathcal{F} \ or \ \mathcal{G})$.

- If $\mathcal{F}$ and $\mathcal{G}$ are sentences, then so is the *implication*

  (*if* $\mathcal{F}$ *then* $\mathcal{G}$).

  We call $\mathcal{F}$ the *antecedent* and $\mathcal{G}$ the *consequent* of (*if* $\mathcal{F}$ *then* $\mathcal{G}$). The sentence (*if* $\mathcal{G}$ *then* $\mathcal{F}$) is called the *converse* of the sentence (*if* $\mathcal{F}$ *then* $\mathcal{G}$).

- If $\mathcal{F}$ and $\mathcal{G}$ are sentences, then so is the *equivalence*

  ($\mathcal{F} \equiv \mathcal{G}$).

  We call $\mathcal{F}$ the *left side* and $\mathcal{G}$ the *right side* of the equivalence ($\mathcal{F} \equiv \mathcal{G}$).

- If $\mathcal{F}$, $\mathcal{G}$, and $\mathcal{H}$ are sentences, then so is the *conditional*

  (*if* $\mathcal{F}$ *then* $\mathcal{G}$ *else* $\mathcal{H}$).

  We call $\mathcal{F}$, $\mathcal{G}$, and $\mathcal{H}$ the *if-clause*, *then-clause*, and *else-clause*, respectively, of the conditional (*if* $\mathcal{F}$ *then* $\mathcal{G}$ *else* $\mathcal{H}$).

In each case, the sentences $\mathcal{F}$, $\mathcal{G}$, and $\mathcal{H}$ used to construct the more complex sentence, by one of the above rules, will be called its *components*. Thus the components of (*if* $\mathcal{F}$ *then* $\mathcal{G}$) are its antecedent $\mathcal{F}$ and its consequent $\mathcal{G}$.

Every intermediate sentence we use in building up a sentence $\mathcal{E}$, including $\mathcal{E}$ itself, is a *subsentence* of $\mathcal{E}$. Thus the subsentences of $\mathcal{E}$ are $\mathcal{E}$ itself and the subsentences of the components of $\mathcal{E}$. The subsentences of $\mathcal{E}$ other than $\mathcal{E}$ itself are the *proper subsentences* of $\mathcal{E}$.

Example.   The expression

$$\mathcal{E}: \quad \Big((not\ (P\ or\ Q))\ \equiv\ ((not\ P)\ and\ (not\ Q))\Big)$$

is a sentence. For

$$P \qquad and \qquad Q$$

are sentences; hence

$$(P\ or\ Q), \quad (not\ P), \quad and \quad (not\ Q)$$

are sentences; hence

$$\big(not\ (P\ or\ Q)\big) \quad and \quad \big((not\ P)\ and\ (not\ Q)\big)$$

are also sentences; hence the given expression $\mathcal{E}$,

$$\Big((not\ (P\ or\ Q))\ \equiv\ ((not\ P)\ and\ (not\ Q))\Big),$$

is a sentence. Each of the above eight sentences (including $\mathcal{E}$) is a subsentence of $\mathcal{E}$; each of the first seven sentences (excluding $\mathcal{E}$) is a proper subsentence of $\mathcal{E}$.

Note that there may be more than one *occurrence* of the same subsentence in a given sentence. For example, the above sentence $\mathcal{E}$ has two occurrences of the subsentence P and two occurrences of the subsentence Q.

NOTATION

We may omit the parentheses from sentences when they are not necessary to indicate the structure of the sentence. For example, the sentence

$$\big(not\ (P\ \ and\ \ (not\ Q))\big)$$

can be written as

$$not\ (P\ \ and\ \ not\ Q),$$

without ambiguity.

For clarity, we shall sometimes use pairs of square brackets, [and], or braces, { and }, instead of some of the parentheses. Also we often use indentation rather than parentheses to indicate the structure of a sentence. Thus the sentence $\mathcal{E}$ of the above example may be written as

$$not\ (P\ \ or\ \ Q)$$
$$\equiv$$
$$(not\ \ P)\ \ and\ \ (not\ \ Q).$$

The sentence

$$\mathcal{F}:\quad \big(if\ \ ((P\ \ or\ \ Q)\ \ and\ \ (if\ Q\ \ then\ \ R))\ \ then\ \ (if\ \ (P\ \ and\ \ R)\ then\ \ (not\ \ R))\big)$$

may be written as

$$if\ \ \begin{bmatrix} P\ \ or\ \ Q \\ and \\ if\ Q\ \ then\ \ R \end{bmatrix}$$
$$then\ \ if\ \ (P\ \ and\ \ R)$$
$$then\ \ not\ \ R.$$

The reader should be aware that the English-like notation we use for the propositional connectives (other than $\equiv$) is not the conventional one. Some of the most common notations are as follows:

Our notation	Conventional notation
and	$\wedge$ or $\&$
or	$\vee$
not	$\neg$ or $\sim$
if-then	$\supset$ or $\rightarrow$

(The *if-then-else* connective is generally not included in conventional logical systems.) To distinguish them from ordinary usages of English words, we always italicize the connectives.

We have chosen to use the English-like notation for clarity in the text; the reader may prefer to use a more concise mathematical notation in writing. For example, the sentence $\mathcal{E}$ from the earlier example can be written as

$$\Big(\big(\neg(P \vee Q)\big) \equiv \big((\neg P) \wedge (\neg Q)\big) \Big).$$

The sentence $\mathcal{F}$ can be written as

$$\Big(\big((P \vee Q) \wedge (Q \supset R)\big) \supset \big((P \wedge R) \supset (\neg R)\big) \Big).$$

1.3   THE MEANING OF A SENTENCE

So far we have presented the syntax or form of the sentences of propositional logic without assigning them any semantics or meaning. We now show how to assign a *truth-value*,

true   or   false,

to a propositional-logic sentence. (We sharply distinguish between the truth symbols *true* and *false*, which may occur within a sentence and which are always italicized, and the truth-values true and false, which are the possible meanings of a sentence and which are never italicized.) It is meaningful to talk about whether the truth-value of a sentence such as $\big(P \ or \ (not \ Q)\big)$ is true or false if we know whether the truth-values of the propositional symbols P and Q themselves are true or false. This information is provided by an "interpretation."

INTERPRETATIONS

Let us now define more precisely the notion of an interpretation.

Definition (interpretation)
> An *interpretation* is an assignment of a truth-value, either true or false, to all the propositional symbols.   ◢

We use the script letters $\mathcal{I}$ and $\mathcal{J}$, possibly subscripted, for interpretations.

For example, one interpretation $\mathcal{I}_1$ might assign true to all the propositional symbols; another interpretation $\mathcal{I}_2$ might assign false to all propositional symbols; some interpretations assign true to some symbols and false to others.

SEMANTIC RULES

Once we have provided an interpretation, we can determine the truth-value of a sentence under that interpretation by applying certain rules.

Definition (semantic rules)

Let $\mathcal{E}$ be a sentence and $\mathcal{I}$ an interpretation. Then the *truth-value of $\mathcal{E}$* (and all of its subsentences) *under $\mathcal{I}$* is determined by applying repeatedly the following *semantic rules*:

- *proposition rule*

  The truth-value of each propositional symbol P, Q, R, ... in $\mathcal{E}$ is the same as the truth-value assigned to it by $\mathcal{I}$.

- *true rule*

  The sentence *true* is true.

- *false rule*

  The sentence *false* is false.

- *not rule*

  The negation (*not $\mathcal{F}$*) is true if $\mathcal{F}$ is false, and false if $\mathcal{F}$ is true.

- *and rule*

  The conjunction (*$\mathcal{F}$ and $\mathcal{G}$*) is true if $\mathcal{F}$ and $\mathcal{G}$ are both true, and false otherwise (that is, if $\mathcal{F}$ is false or if $\mathcal{G}$ is false).

- *or rule*

  The disjunction (*$\mathcal{F}$ or $\mathcal{G}$*) is true if $\mathcal{F}$ is true or if $\mathcal{G}$ is true, and false otherwise (that is, if $\mathcal{F}$ and $\mathcal{G}$ are both false).

- *if-then rule*

  The implication (*if $\mathcal{F}$ then $\mathcal{G}$*) is true if $\mathcal{F}$ is false or if $\mathcal{G}$ is true, and false otherwise (that is, if $\mathcal{F}$ is true and $\mathcal{G}$ is false).

- $\equiv$ *rule*

  The equivalence (*$\mathcal{F} \equiv \mathcal{G}$*) is true if the truth-value of $\mathcal{F}$ is the same as the truth-value of $\mathcal{G}$ (that is, if $\mathcal{F}$ and $\mathcal{G}$ are both true or if $\mathcal{F}$ and $\mathcal{G}$ are both false), and false otherwise (that is, if $\mathcal{F}$ is true and $\mathcal{G}$ is false, or if $\mathcal{F}$ is false and $\mathcal{G}$ is true).

- *if-then-else rule*

  The truth-value of the conditional (*if $\mathcal{F}$ then $\mathcal{G}$ else $\mathcal{H}$*) is the truth-value of $\mathcal{G}$ if $\mathcal{F}$ is true and the truth-value of $\mathcal{H}$ if $\mathcal{F}$ is false. ◢

The semantic rules for the connectives may be summarized in the following *truth tables*:

$\mathcal{F}$	*not* $\mathcal{F}$
true	false
false	true

Here, if the truth-value of $\mathcal{F}$ under $\mathcal{I}$ is as given by the first column, the truth-value of $(not\ \mathcal{F})$ is as shown in the second column.

$\mathcal{F}$	$\mathcal{G}$	$\mathcal{F}\ and\ \mathcal{G}$	$\mathcal{F}\ or\ \mathcal{G}$	$if\ \mathcal{F}\ then\ \mathcal{G}$	$\mathcal{F} \equiv \mathcal{G}$
true	true	true	true	true	true
true	false	false	true	false	false
false	true	false	true	true	false
false	false	false	false	true	true

Here, if the truth-values of $\mathcal{F}$ and $\mathcal{G}$ under $\mathcal{I}$ are as given in the first two columns, the truth-values of the sentences $(\mathcal{F}\ and\ \mathcal{G})$, $(\mathcal{F}\ or\ \mathcal{G})$, ... are as shown in the appropriate columns.

$\mathcal{F}$	$\mathcal{G}$	$\mathcal{H}$	$if\ \mathcal{F}\ then\ \mathcal{G}\ else\ \mathcal{H}$
true	true	true	true
true	true	false	true
true	false	true	false
true	false	false	false
false	true	true	true
false	true	false	false
false	false	true	true
false	false	false	false

Observe that according to the *or* rule, the *or* connective is "inclusive" in the sense that $(P\ or\ Q)$ is true in the case in which both P and Q are true. Intuitively speaking, in the concrete sentence

> John is married
> or
> John is over forty-five,

we allow the possibility that both components of the disjunction are true.

Note also that, according to the *if-then* rule, the sentence $(if\ \mathcal{F}\ then\ \mathcal{G})$ is true whenever its antecedent $\mathcal{F}$ is false or its consequent $\mathcal{G}$ is true, even if there is no causal relation between $\mathcal{F}$ and $\mathcal{G}$. For example, the concrete sentence

> If California is the capital of Washington,
> then the moon is made of green cheese

is regarded as a true sentence among logicians, because its antecedent is false.

To determine the truth-value of a complex sentence under a given interpretation, we first apply the semantic rules to determine the truth-value of each of its components; we then apply the appropriate semantic rule to determine the truth-value of the entire sentence.

Example.   Consider the sentence

$$\mathcal{F}: \quad \begin{array}{l} \textit{if } \big(P \ \textit{ and } \ (\textit{not } Q)\big) \\ \textit{then } \big((\textit{not } P) \ \textit{ or } \ R\big) \end{array}$$

and an interpretation $\mathcal{I}$ under which

P is true,
Q is false,
R is false.

We speak of "an" interpretation $\mathcal{I}$ because there are infinitely many interpretations $\mathcal{I}$ that make these three assignments, but make different assignments to other propositional symbols.

Then we can use the semantic rules to determine the truth-value of the sentence $\mathcal{F}$ under this interpretation as follows: Because Q is false, we know (by the *not* rule) that

$(\textit{not } Q)$ is true.

Because P is true and $(\textit{not } Q)$ is true, we know (by the *and* rule) that

$\big(P \textit{ and } (\textit{not } Q)\big)$ is true.

Because P is true, we know (by the *not* rule) that

$(\textit{not } P)$ is false.

Because $(\textit{not } P)$ is false and R is false, we know (by the *or* rule) that

$\big((\textit{not } P) \textit{ or } R\big)$ is false.

Because $\big(P \textit{ and } (\textit{not } Q)\big)$ is true and $\big((\textit{not } P) \textit{ or } R\big)$ is false, we know (by the *if-then* rule) that the entire sentence $\mathcal{F}$,

$$\begin{array}{l} \textit{if } \big(P \ \textit{ and } \ (\textit{not } Q)\big) \\ \textit{then } \big((\textit{not } P) \ \textit{ or } \ R\big), \end{array}$$

is false.   ◢

〚In the two-volume version of this book, we have adopted a slightly different notion of interpretation. In that version, an interpretation assigns truth-values to some, but not necessarily all, propositional symbols. We have introduced this change to simplify the exposition.〛

1.4   VALIDITY AND EQUIVALENCE

Recall that we have said that a sentence is valid if it is true, and contradictory if it is false, regardless of the truth or falsehood of its constituent propositional symbols. Also, two sentences are equivalent if they are either both true or both false, regardless of the truth or falsehood of their constituent propositional symbols. Now we can define these notions precisely.

Definition (valid, contradictory, implies, equivalent).

A sentence $\mathcal{F}$ is *valid* if $\mathcal{F}$ is true under every interpretation. Valid sentences of propositional logic are sometimes called *tautologies*.

A sentence $\mathcal{F}$ is *contradictory* if $\mathcal{F}$ is false under every interpretation.

A sentence $\mathcal{F}$ *implies* a sentence $\mathcal{G}$ if, for any interpretation $\mathcal{I}$, if $\mathcal{F}$ is true under $\mathcal{I}$ then $\mathcal{G}$ is also true under $\mathcal{I}$.

Two sentences $\mathcal{F}$ and $\mathcal{G}$ are *equivalent* if, under every interpretation, $\mathcal{F}$ has the same truth-value as $\mathcal{G}$. ◢

Let us illustrate these notions with some simple examples.

Examples.   The sentence

$$P \ or \ (not \ P)$$

is valid, because it is true under any interpretation $\mathcal{I}$, regardless of whether $\mathcal{I}$ assigns P to be true or false.

The sentence

$$P$$

is true under any interpretation that assigns P to be true; however, the sentence is not valid, because it is false under any interpretation that assigns P to be false.

The sentence

$$P \ and \ Q$$

implies the sentence

$$P,$$

because, under any interpretation for which $(P \ and \ Q)$ is true, P is also true.

However, the sentence

$$P$$

does not imply the sentence

$$P \ and \ Q,$$

because, under the interpretation that assigns P to be true and Q to be false, P is true but $(P \ and \ Q)$ is false.

The two sentences

$$P \quad and \quad not \ (not \ P)$$

are equivalent, because they are each true under any interpretation that assigns P to be true, and false under any interpretation that assigns P to be false.

The two sentences

$$P \quad and \quad Q$$

are not equivalent, because they have different truth-values under any interpretation that assigns different values to P and Q. ◢

The notions above are all related. To explain this, we introduce some informal terminology. For ordinary English sentences α and β we say that

> α if and only if β

to indicate that α is true if β is and β is true if α is. We emphasize that "if and only if," in contrast with $\equiv$, is not a connective of propositional logic and that α and β are themselves English sentences, not propositional-logic sentences.

Remark (contradictory and valid).   For any sentence $\mathcal{F}$,

> $\mathcal{F}$ is contradictory
>   if and only if
> the sentence (*not* $\mathcal{F}$) is valid.

For we have

> $\mathcal{F}$ is contradictory

if and only if (by the definition of contradictory)

> $\mathcal{F}$ is false under any interpretation $\mathcal{I}$

if and only if (by the *not* rule)

> (*not* $\mathcal{F}$) is true under any interpretation $\mathcal{I}$

if and only if (by the definition of validity)

> (*not* $\mathcal{F}$) is valid.   ∎

Remark (implies and valid).   For two sentences $\mathcal{F}$ and $\mathcal{G}$,

> $\mathcal{F}$ implies $\mathcal{G}$
>   if and only if
> the sentence (*if* $\mathcal{F}$ *then* $\mathcal{G}$) is valid.

For we have

> $\mathcal{F}$ implies $\mathcal{G}$

if and only if (by the definition of implication)

> for any interpretation $\mathcal{I}$,
>   if $\mathcal{F}$ is true under $\mathcal{I}$ then $\mathcal{G}$ is also true under $\mathcal{I}$
>   (that is, $\mathcal{F}$ is false under $\mathcal{I}$ or $\mathcal{G}$ is true under $\mathcal{I}$)

if and only if (by the *if-then* rule)

> (*if* $\mathcal{F}$ *then* $\mathcal{G}$) is true under any interpretation $\mathcal{I}$

if and only if (by the definition of validity)

> (*if* $\mathcal{F}$ *then* $\mathcal{G}$) is valid.   ∎

Remark (equivalent and valid).   For two sentences $\mathcal{F}$ and $\mathcal{G}$,

> $\mathcal{F}$ and $\mathcal{G}$ are equivalent
>> if and only if
> the sentence $(\mathcal{F} \equiv \mathcal{G})$ is valid.

For we have

> $\mathcal{F}$ and $\mathcal{G}$ are equivalent

if and only if (by the definition of equivalence)

> $\mathcal{F}$ and $\mathcal{G}$ have the same truth-value under any interpretation

if and only if (by the $\equiv$ rule)

> $(\mathcal{F} \equiv \mathcal{G})$ is true under any interpretation

if and only if (by the definition of validity)

> $(\mathcal{F} \equiv \mathcal{G})$ is valid.   ⌟

Remark (equivalent and implies).   For two sentences $\mathcal{F}$ and $\mathcal{G}$,

> $\mathcal{F}$ and $\mathcal{G}$ are equivalent
>> if and only if
> $\mathcal{F}$ implies $\mathcal{G}$ and $\mathcal{G}$ implies $\mathcal{F}$.

For we have

> $\mathcal{F}$ and $\mathcal{G}$ are equivalent

if and only if (by the definition of equivalence)

> $\mathcal{F}$ and $\mathcal{G}$ have the same truth-value under any interpretation $\mathcal{I}$

if and only if

> for any interpretation $\mathcal{I}$,
>> if $\mathcal{F}$ is true under $\mathcal{I}$ then $\mathcal{G}$ is true under $\mathcal{I}$ and
>> if $\mathcal{G}$ is true under $\mathcal{I}$ then $\mathcal{F}$ is true under $\mathcal{I}$

if and only if

> for any interpretation $\mathcal{I}$,
>> if $\mathcal{F}$ is true under $\mathcal{I}$ then $\mathcal{G}$ is true under $\mathcal{I}$
> and
> for any interpretation $\mathcal{I}$,
>> if $\mathcal{G}$ is true under $\mathcal{I}$ then $\mathcal{F}$ is true under $\mathcal{I}$

if and only if (by the definition of implication)

> $\mathcal{F}$ implies $\mathcal{G}$
> and
> $\mathcal{G}$ implies $\mathcal{F}$,

as we wanted to show.   ⌟

We now introduce two propositions relating implication, equivalence, and validity.

Proposition (implication and validity)

For any two sentences $\mathcal{F}$ and $\mathcal{G}$,

> if $\mathcal{F}$ implies $\mathcal{G}$
> then if $\mathcal{F}$ is valid
> then $\mathcal{G}$ is valid. ◢

Proof.   Suppose

> $\mathcal{F}$ implies $\mathcal{G}$ and $\mathcal{F}$ is valid;

we would like to show that then

> $\mathcal{G}$ is valid.

To show that $\mathcal{G}$ is valid, it suffices to show that, for an arbitrary interpretation $\mathcal{I}$,

> $\mathcal{G}$ is true under $\mathcal{I}$.

Because we have supposed that $\mathcal{F}$ is valid, we know that

> $\mathcal{F}$ is true under $\mathcal{I}$.

Because we have supposed that $\mathcal{F}$ implies $\mathcal{G}$, we can infer (by the definition of implies) that

> $\mathcal{G}$ is true under $\mathcal{I}$,

as we wanted to show. ◢

The converse of the above proposition is not true: It is possible to find sentences $\mathcal{F}$ and $\mathcal{G}$ such that if $\mathcal{F}$ is valid then $\mathcal{G}$ is valid, but $\mathcal{F}$ does not imply $\mathcal{G}$. This can occur when $\mathcal{F}$ is not valid but there is an interpretation under which $\mathcal{F}$ is true and $\mathcal{G}$ is false. For example, the validity of the sentence P implies the validity of the sentence Q, because the sentence P is not valid; but P does not imply Q, because there are interpretations under which P is true but Q is false.

We now show a similar property of the equivalence relation. We have already shown in earlier remarks that

> two sentences $\mathcal{F}$ and $\mathcal{G}$ are equivalent
> if and only if
> the sentence $(\mathcal{F} \equiv \mathcal{G})$ is valid

and

> two sentences $\mathcal{F}$ and $\mathcal{G}$ are equivalent
> if and only if
> $\mathcal{F}$ implies $\mathcal{G}$ and $\mathcal{G}$ implies $\mathcal{F}$.

We also have the following result:

Proposition (equivalence and validity)

For any two sentences $\mathcal{F}$ and $\mathcal{G}$,

> if $\mathcal{F}$ and $\mathcal{G}$ are equivalent,
> then $\mathcal{F}$ is valid
> > if and only if
> > $\mathcal{G}$ is valid. ⌙

Proof.   Suppose that

> $\mathcal{F}$ and $\mathcal{G}$ are equivalent;

then

> $\mathcal{F}$ implies $\mathcal{G}$ and $\mathcal{G}$ implies $\mathcal{F}$.

Therefore (by the previous *implication-and-validity* proposition)

> if $\mathcal{F}$ is valid,   if $\mathcal{G}$ is valid,
>   and
> then $\mathcal{G}$ is valid   then $\mathcal{F}$ is valid.

In other words,

> $\mathcal{F}$ is valid
> > if and only if
> > $\mathcal{G}$ is valid,

as we wanted to show.   ⌙

The converse of the above proposition, like that of the *implication-and-validity* proposition, is not true: It is possible to find sentences $\mathcal{F}$ and $\mathcal{G}$ such that $\mathcal{F}$ is valid if and only if $\mathcal{G}$ is valid, but $\mathcal{F}$ and $\mathcal{G}$ are not equivalent. This can occur when $\mathcal{F}$ and $\mathcal{G}$ are not valid but are false under different interpretations. For example, the sentence P is valid if and only if the sentence Q is valid, because neither sentence is valid; but P and Q are certainly not equivalent, because there are interpretations under which one is true and the other is false.

We have seen that each of the notions we have considered can be paraphrased in terms of the validity of a propositional-logic sentence. Therefore we concentrate on methods of determining whether a given sentence is valid or not.

It is not always easy to see whether a sentence is valid; for example, consider the sentence

$$
\textit{if}
\begin{bmatrix}
\begin{bmatrix} \textit{if } P_1 \textit{ then } (P_2 \textit{ or } P_3) \\ \textit{else } (P_3 \textit{ or } P_4) \end{bmatrix} \textit{ and} \\
\begin{bmatrix} \begin{bmatrix} \textit{if } P_3 \textit{ then } (\textit{not } P_6) \\ \textit{else } (\textit{if } P_4 \textit{ then } P_1) \end{bmatrix} \textit{ and} \\ \begin{bmatrix} \textit{not } (P_2 \textit{ and } P_5) \textit{ and} \\ (\textit{if } P_2 \textit{ then } P_5) \end{bmatrix} \end{bmatrix}
\end{bmatrix}
$$

$$\textit{then not } (\textit{if } P_3 \textit{ then } P_6).$$

This sentence is actually valid, although it is difficult to recognize its validity at first glance.

1.5   TRUTH TABLES

The most straightforward way to determine whether a sentence is valid is by a complete case analysis of the possible truth-values assigned to its propositional symbols. Thus if a sentence contains only the propositional symbols P and Q, we distinguish between two cases, assigning P the truth-values true and false, respectively. In each case we distinguish between two further subcases, assigning Q the truth-values true and false, respectively.

Thus for a sentence containing only the propositional symbols P and Q there are four possible assignments to P and Q that an interpretation can make:

P is true and Q is true;

P is true and Q is false;

P is false and Q is true;

P is false and Q is false.

(It does not matter what truth-values are assigned to propositional symbols other than P and Q.) If the given sentence turns out to have the truth-value true under the interpretation in each of the four cases, the sentence is valid. Such a process is facilitated by a *truth table*. Suppose, for example, our given sentence is

$$\mathcal{F}: \quad \begin{array}{c} not\ (P\ \ or\ \ Q) \\ \equiv \\ (not\ P)\ \ and\ \ (not\ Q). \end{array}$$

The corresponding truth table is

P	Q	$P\ or\ Q$	not $(P\ or\ Q)$	$not\ P$	$not\ Q$	$(not\ P)$ and $(not\ Q)$	$\mathcal{F}$
true	true	true	false	false	false	false	true
true	false	true	false	false	true	false	true
false	true	true	false	true	false	false	true
false	false	false	true	true	true	true	true

In the two leftmost columns of the table we record the four possible assignments of truth-values to P and Q. For each interpretation we enter in successive columns the truth or falsehood of each subsentence of $\mathcal{F}$. The truth-value in each column is determined from the truth-values in the previous columns by applying the semantic rule for the corresponding connective. For example, the truth-values in the column headed $not\ (P\ or\ Q)$ are obtained from the truth-values in the column headed (P *or* Q) by applying the *not* rule. The final column exhibits the truth-value of the entire sentence; because $\mathcal{F}$ is true in each case, we have determined that $\mathcal{F}$ is valid.

On the other hand, if we are given the sentence

$$\mathcal{G}: \quad \begin{array}{l} \textit{if } (\textit{if } P \textit{ then } Q) \\ \textit{then } (\textit{if } (\textit{not } P) \textit{ then } (\textit{not } Q)), \end{array}$$

the corresponding truth table is

P	Q	*if P then Q*	*not P*	*not Q.*	*if (not P) then (not Q)*	$\mathcal{G}$
true	true	true	false	false	true	true
true	false	false	false	true	true	true
false	true	true	true	false	false	false
false	false	true	true	true	true	true

We can see from the final column of the truth table that the sentence $\mathcal{G}$ is not valid; it is true in three cases, but false in the case in which P is false and Q is true.

The same technique can be used to determine whether two sentences are equivalent by computing the truth table for each sentence separately, including in each table all the propositional symbols that occur in either sentence. The two sentences are equivalent if the corresponding entries in the final columns of the two tables are all identical.

Thus we can determine that the sentences

$$\textit{not } (P \textit{ or } Q) \qquad \text{and} \qquad (\textit{not } P) \textit{ and } (\textit{not } Q)$$

are equivalent by comparing the final columns of their truth tables

P	Q	*P or Q*	*not (P or Q)*
true	true	true	false
true	false	true	false
false	true	true	false
false	false	false	true

and

P	Q	$not\ P$	$not\ Q$	$(not\ P)$ and $(not\ Q)$
true	true	false	false	false
true	false	false	true	false
false	true	true	false	false
false	false	true	true	true

Alternatively, by the earlier remark relating equivalence and validity, we can determine if two sentences $\mathcal{F}$ and $\mathcal{G}$ are equivalent by checking whether the sentence $(\mathcal{F} \equiv \mathcal{G})$ is valid. Thus since we have shown earlier that the sentence

$$not\ (P\ or\ Q)$$
$$\equiv$$
$$(not\ P)\ and\ (not\ Q)$$

is valid, this also establishes the equivalence of the two sentences

$$not\ (P\ or\ Q) \qquad and \qquad (not\ P)\ and\ (not\ Q).$$

1.6   PROOF BY FALSIFICATION

An alternative method for testing the validity of a sentence, which is convenient to apply by hand, is called *proof by falsification*. As usual, we illustrate the technique with an example.

Example.   We want to establish the validity of the sentence

$$\mathcal{E}: \quad \begin{aligned} &if\ \big((not\ P)\ or\ (not\ Q)\big) \\ &then\ \big(not\ (P\ and\ Q)\big). \end{aligned}$$

Suppose, to the contrary, that $\mathcal{E}$ is false under some interpretation; we indicate this by annotating the *if* with the letter F:

$$\underset{\text{F}}{if}\ \big((not\ P)\ or\ (not\ Q)\big)\ then\ \big(not\ (P\ and\ Q)\big).$$

We attempt to derive a contradiction, i.e., to show that this cannot occur.

By the *if-then* rule, the antecedent $\big((not\ P)\ or\ (not\ Q)\big)$ and the consequent $\big(not\ (P\ and\ Q)\big)$ must have truth-values true and false, respectively, under this interpretation; that is,

$$\underset{\text{F}}{if}\ \big(\underset{\text{T}}{(not\ P)\ or\ (not\ Q)}\big)\ then\ \big(\underset{\text{F}}{not\ (P\ and\ Q)}\big).$$

Again, we put T and F, respectively, under the main connectives of the antecedent and consequent.

The truth of the antecedent $\big((not\ P)\ or\ (not\ Q)\big)$ does not allow us to determine the truth-values of its subsentences $(not\ P)$ and $(not\ Q)$ uniquely: $(not\ P)$ could be true, $(not\ Q)$ could be true, or they both could be true. To avoid treating these cases separately, we focus our attention first on the consequent.

Because the consequent $\big(not\ (P\ and\ Q)\big)$ is false, its subsentence $(P\ and\ Q)$ must be true, and hence its subsentences P and Q are both true:

$$if\ \ \big((not\ P)\ \ or\ \ (not\ Q)\big)\ \ then\ \ \big(not\ (P\ \ and\ \ Q)\big).$$
$$\text{F}\qquad\text{T}\quad\text{T}\qquad\text{T}\qquad\quad\text{F}\ \ \text{T}\ \ \text{T}\ \ \text{T}$$

Note that when we discover the truth-value of a symbol or subsentence we label all of its occurrences. Thus we have labeled each occurrence of P and Q with its truth-value indication T.

At this stage, we return our attention to the antecedent. Because P and Q are both true, $(not\ P)$ and $(not\ Q)$ are both false. By the *or* rule, this requires that the antecedent $\big((not\ P)\ or\ (not\ Q)\big)$ is also false. However, we have determined earlier that this subsentence is true, as the annotation reveals:

$$if\ \ \big((not\ P)\ \ or\ \ (not\ Q)\big)\ \ then\ \ \big(not\ (P\ \ and\ \ Q)\big).$$
$$\text{F}\qquad\text{F}\ \ \text{T}\ \ \text{T}_{\text{F}}\quad\text{F}\ \ \text{T}\qquad\quad\text{F}\ \ \text{T}\ \ \text{T}\ \ \text{T}$$

We have given a conflicting annotation T_{F} (that is, T and F together) to the subsentence $\big((not\ P)\ or\ (not\ Q)\big)$. Consequently, we have contradicted our original supposition, that the sentence $\mathcal{E}$ is false under some interpretation. In other words, $\mathcal{E}$ is valid. ∎

By postponing the treatment of the antecedent in the above example, we avoided any case analysis. In general, however, we shall not always be so fortunate; it may be necessary to consider several possibilities separately, as is illustrated next.

Example. Suppose we want to establish the validity of the sentence

$$\mathcal{F}:\quad\begin{array}{c}(if\ \ P\ \ then\ \ Q)\\ \equiv\\ \big((not\ P)\ \ or\ \ Q\big).\end{array}$$

We derive a contradiction by assuming that $\mathcal{F}$ is false under some interpretation.

According to the $\equiv$ rule, $\mathcal{F}$ may be false for two possible reasons: Either the left subsentence, $(if\ P\ then\ Q)$, is true and the right subsentence, $\big((not\ P)\ or\ Q\big)$, is false, or vice versa. We therefore split the annotation into two cases, corresponding to the two possibilities. In each case we must obtain a conflicting annotation.

Case: (*if P then Q*) is true and ((*not P*) *or Q*) is false

This case corresponds to the annotation

$$(if \ \ P \ \ then \ \ Q) \ \equiv \ ((not \ P) \ \ or \ \ Q).$$
$$\text{T} \text{F} \text{F}$$

There are two ways in which the left subsentence, (*if P then Q*), could be true; therefore we consider first the right subsentence, ((*not P*) *or Q*). Because ((*not P*) *or Q*) is false, both (*not P*) and *Q* must be false, and hence *P* must be true. We have

$$(if \ \ P \ \ then \ \ Q) \ \equiv \ ((not \ P) \ \ or \ \ Q).$$
$$\text{T} \ \text{T} \text{F} \ \ \text{F} \text{F} \ \ \text{T} \ \ \text{F} \ \ \text{F}$$

Because *P* is true and *Q* is false, (*if P then Q*) must also be false, contradicting our annotation for this case:

$$(if \ \ P \ \ then \ \ Q) \ \equiv \ ((not \ \ P) \ \ or \ \ Q).$$
$$\text{T}_\text{F} \ \ \text{T} \text{F} \ \ \text{F} \text{F} \ \ \text{T} \ \ \text{F} \ \ \text{F}$$

Case: (*if P then Q*) is false and ((*not P*) *or Q*) is true

This case corresponds to the annotation

$$(if \ \ P \ \ then \ \ Q) \ \equiv \ ((not \ P) \ \ or \ \ Q).$$
$$\text{F} \text{F} \text{T}$$

Because the left subsentence, (*if P then Q*), is false, we have that *P* is true and *Q* is false. Hence (*not P*) is false, and we have

$$(if \ \ P \ \ then \ \ Q) \ \equiv \ ((not \ P) \ \ or \ \ Q).$$
$$\text{F} \ \ \text{T} \text{F} \ \ \text{F} \text{F} \ \ \text{T} \ \ \text{T} \ \ \text{F}$$

However, because (*not P*) and *Q* are both false, it follows that ((*not P*) *or Q*) is also false, contradicting the annotation we have assumed for this case:

$$(if \ \ P \ \ then \ \ Q) \ \equiv \ ((not \ P) \ \ or \ \ Q).$$
$$\text{F} \ \ \text{T} \text{F} \ \ \text{F} \text{F} \ \ \text{T} \ \ \text{T}_\text{F} \ \ \text{F}$$

We have shown in each case that no interpretation can falsify $\mathcal{F}$; therefore $\mathcal{F}$ is true for any interpretation, that is, $\mathcal{F}$ is valid. ◢

Although it was not possible to avoid a case split, the above analysis still examined fewer cases than the truth-table analysis of the same sentence.

In the preceding example we were forced into a case split at the very beginning. In the next example, we are forced into a case split at a later stage.

Example.   Suppose we want to establish the validity of the sentence

$$\mathcal{G}: \quad \begin{array}{l} if \ \big(if \ (not \ P) \ \ then \ \ Q\big) \\ then \ \big(if \ (not \ Q) \ \ then \ \ P\big) \ \ and \ (P \ \ or \ Q). \end{array}$$

We assume that $\mathcal{G}$ is false under some interpretation. According to the *if-then* rule, this implies that the antecedent is true and the consequent is false. We annotate $\mathcal{G}$ accordingly:

$$if \ \big(if \ (not \ P) \ then \ Q \big)$$
$$\text{F} \qquad \text{T}$$
$$then \ \big(if \ (not \ Q) \ then \ P \big) \ and \ (P \ or \ Q).$$
$$\text{F}$$

The antecedent $\big(if \ (not \ P) \ then \ Q \big)$ of $\mathcal{G}$ is itself an implication. According to the *if-then* rule, it may be true in two ways: if its antecedent $(not \ P)$ is false or if its consequent Q is true (or both). If we focus on the antecedent, we cannot proceed without a case analysis.

On the other hand, the consequent of $\mathcal{G}$ is a conjunction. According to the *and* rule, it may be false for two reasons: either its first conjunct $\big(if \ (not \ Q) \ then \ P \big)$ is false or its second conjunct $(P \ or \ Q)$ is false (or both). We thus cannot focus on the consequent without a case analysis either.

We arbitrarily decide to focus on the antecedent of $\mathcal{G}$ and consider separately the two possibilities according to whether $(not \ P)$ is false or Q is true. We split the annotation into two cases, one for each possibility.

Case: $(not \ P)$ is false

We have

$$if \ \big(if \ (not \ P) \ then \ Q \big)$$
$$\text{F} \qquad \text{T} \qquad \text{F}$$
$$then \ \big(if \ (not \ Q) \ then \ P \big) \ and \ (P \ or \ Q).$$
$$\text{F}$$

By the *not* rule, because $(not \ P)$ is false, P is true. We have

$$if \ \big(if \ (not \ P) \ then \ Q \big)$$
$$\text{F} \qquad \text{T} \qquad \text{F} \ \text{T}$$
$$then \ \big(if \ (not \ Q) \ then \ P \big) \ and \ (P \ or \ Q).$$
$$\text{T} \qquad \text{F} \qquad \text{T}$$

Because P is true, we know (by the *if-then* and *or* rules) that the subsentences $\big(if \ (not \ Q) \ then \ P \big)$ and $(P \ or \ Q)$ of the consequent are both true, obtaining

$$if \ \big(if \ (not \ P) \ then \ Q \big)$$
$$\text{F} \qquad \text{T} \qquad \text{F} \ \text{T}$$
$$then \ \big(if \ (not \ Q) \ then \ P \big) \ and \ (P \ or \ Q).$$
$$\text{T} \qquad \qquad \text{T} \quad \text{F} \quad \text{T} \ \text{T}$$

But because both conjuncts of the consequent are true, the consequent itself is true, contradicting the previous annotation of the consequent (under the connective *and*):

$$if \ \big(if \ (not \ P) \ then \ Q \big)$$
$$\text{F} \qquad \text{T} \qquad \text{F} \ \text{T}$$
$$then \ \big(if \ (not \ Q) \ then \ P \big) \ and \ (P \ or \ Q).$$
$$\text{T} \qquad \qquad \text{T} \quad \text{T}_\text{F} \quad \text{T} \ \text{T}$$

Now let us consider the second case.

Case: Q is true

We have

$$\begin{array}{l} if \ \Big(if \ (not \ P) \ then \ Q \Big) \\ \ \ \text{F} \quad\quad \text{T} \quad\quad\quad\quad \text{T} \\ then \ \Big(if \ (not \ Q) \ then \ P \Big) \ and \ (P \ or \ Q). \\ \ \ \text{T} \quad\quad\quad\quad\quad \text{F} \quad\quad \text{T} \end{array}$$

Because Q is true, the subsentence $(not \ Q)$ of the consequent is false (by the *not* rule) and the second conjunct $(P \ or \ Q)$ of the consequent is true (by the *or* rule). Because $(not \ Q)$ is false, the first conjunct $\big(if \ (not \ Q) \ then \ P\big)$ of the consequent is true (by the *if-then* rule); we have

$$\begin{array}{l} if \ \Big(if \ (not \ P) \ then \ Q \Big) \\ \ \ \text{F} \quad\quad \text{T} \quad\quad\quad\quad \text{T} \\ then \ \Big(if \ (not \ Q) \ then \ P \Big) \ and \ (P \ or \ Q). \\ \ \text{T} \quad\quad \text{F} \ \ \text{T} \quad\quad\quad \text{F} \quad\quad \text{T} \ \ \text{T} \end{array}$$

Finally, because both conjuncts of the consequent are true, the consequent itself is true (by the *and* rule), contradicting the previous annotation of the consequent:

$$\begin{array}{l} if \ \Big(if \ (not \ P) \ then \ Q \Big) \\ \ \ \text{F} \quad\quad \text{T} \quad\quad\quad\quad \text{T} \\ then \ \Big(if \ (not \ Q) \ then \ P \Big) \ and \ (P \ or \ Q). \\ \ \text{T} \quad\quad \text{F} \ \ \text{T} \quad\quad\quad \text{T}_{\text{F}} \quad\quad \text{T} \ \ \text{T} \end{array}$$

We have shown in each case that no interpretation can falsify $\mathcal{G}$. Therefore $\mathcal{G}$ is true under any interpretation, that is, $\mathcal{G}$ is valid. ∎

Finally, let us see what happens if we attempt to prove by the falsification method a sentence that is not valid.

Example. Consider the sentence

$$\mathcal{H}: \quad \begin{array}{l} if \ (if \ P \ then \ Q) \\ then \ \big(if \ (not \ P) \ then \ (not \ Q) \big), \end{array}$$

and suppose that $\mathcal{H}$ is false under some interpretation. According to the *if-then* rule, this implies that the antecedent is true and the consequent is false; we have

$$\begin{array}{l} if \ (if \ P \ then \ Q) \\ \ \text{F} \quad \text{T} \\ then \ \big(if \ (not \ P) \ then \ (not \ Q) \big). \\ \ \text{F} \end{array}$$

To avoid a case analysis we postpone treatment of the antecedent and focus on the consequent.

Because the consequent, $\big(if \ (not \ P) \ then \ (not \ Q) \big)$, is false, we know (by the *if-then* rule) that its antecedent, $(not \ P)$, is true and its consequent, $(not \ Q)$, is false. Hence (by the *not* rule) P is false and Q is true, and we have

$$\begin{array}{l} if \ (if \ P \ then \ Q) \\ \ \text{F} \quad \text{T} \ \text{F} \quad\quad \text{T} \end{array}$$

$$then \ \bigl(if \ (not \ P) \ then \ (not \ Q)\bigr).$$
$$ \text{F} \quad \text{T} \quad \text{F} \text{F} \quad \text{T}$$

Because P is false and Q is true, the antecedent, $(if \ P \ then \ Q)$, is true (by the *if-then* rule), confirming our previous annotation.

We have finished the annotation without deriving a contradiction. In fact, we have found that $\mathcal{H}$ is false under an interpretation that assigns

> P to be false
> Q to be true.

Therefore $\mathcal{H}$ is not valid. ⌟

In some cases, the discrepancy between the truth-table and the proof-by-falsification methods is dramatic. For example, to show the validity of the sentence

$$\bigl((\dots(P_1 \ or \ P_2) \ or \ \dots) \ or \ P_{20}\bigr) \ or \ true,$$

which contains 20 propositional symbols, requires a truth table of $2^{20} = 1,048,576$ rows. The corresponding proof by falsification contains only a single step: By the *or* rule, because the entire sentence is assumed to be false, the subsentence *true* is also false; that is,

$$\bigl((\dots(P_1 \ or \ P_2) \ or \ \dots) \ or \ P_{20}\bigr) \ or \ true.$$
$$ \text{F} \text{F} \quad \text{T}_\text{F}$$

But this is a contradiction.

In **Problems 1.1** and **1.2**, the reader is requested to establish the validity (or nonvalidity) of some propositional-logic sentences.

In the next section, we discuss "sentence schemata," which are abstract sentences that stand for entire classes of concrete propositional-logic sentences.

1.7 VALID SENTENCE SCHEMATA

Up to now we have presented particular propositional-logic sentences and introduced methods of establishing their validity. Although we can establish the validity of a particular sentence, such as

> $P \ or \ (not \ P),$

we cannot immediately conclude that similar sentences, such as

> $Q \ or \ (not \ Q)$

and

> $(P \ and \ Q) \ or \ \bigl(not \ (P \ and \ Q)\bigr),$

are also valid.

We would prefer to be able to discuss such classes of sentences as a unit. For this purpose, we introduce "sentences" containing script symbols $\mathcal{E}$, $\mathcal{F}$, $\mathcal{G}$, $\mathcal{H}$, ..., instead of the ordinary propositional symbols P, Q, R, ... Such script symbols may stand for any sentences of propositional logic. For example, we shall say

$\mathcal{F}$ or $(not\ \mathcal{F})$

is valid, to imply that the sentences

P or $(not\ P)$,

Q or $(not\ Q)$,

$(P\ and\ Q)$ or $\big(not\ (P\ and\ Q)\big)$,

and infinitely many other sentences are all valid. Informally we shall refer to such a "sentence" as a *sentence schema*; because it contains script symbols it is not itself a legal sentence of propositional logic, but it represents an infinite class of legal sentences. These sentences are called the *instances* of the schema.

A sentence schema is said to be *valid* if all of its instances are valid. We may check the validity of a sentence schema by any of the methods we have introduced, treating the script symbols the way we treat propositional symbols. For example, to show that the sentence schema

$\mathcal{F}$ or $(not\ \mathcal{F})$

is valid by the falsification method, we assume that the sentence schema is false under some interpretation and annotate it accordingly:

$\mathcal{F}$ or $(not\ \mathcal{F})$.
F

By the *or* rule, both $\mathcal{F}$ and $(not\ \mathcal{F})$ must be false:

$\mathcal{F}$ or $(not\ \mathcal{F})$.
F   F   F   F

By the *not* rule, because the subsentence schema $(not\ \mathcal{F})$ is false, its subsentence schema $\mathcal{F}$ must then be true:

$\mathcal{F}$ or $(not\ \mathcal{F})$.
T$_F$ F   F   T$_F$

We have developed contradictory annotations for the two occurrences of $\mathcal{F}$. This shows that the given sentence schema cannot be false under any interpretation; i.e., it is valid. Because the same reasoning can be carried out regardless of what sentence takes the place of $\mathcal{F}$, each instance of the schema is valid.

A CATALOG OF VALID SENTENCE SCHEMATA

We present a catalog of some of the most important valid sentence schemata.

- Basic

$$\mathcal{F} \equiv \mathcal{F}$$

$\mathcal{F}$ or (not $\mathcal{F}$)   if $\mathcal{F}$ then $\mathcal{F}$

if ($\mathcal{F}$ and $\mathcal{G}$) then $\mathcal{F}$ if $\mathcal{F}$ then ($\mathcal{F}$ or $\mathcal{G}$)

- True-false

true   not false

$\mathcal{F}$ or true   not ($\mathcal{F}$ and false)

if false then $\mathcal{F}$ if $\mathcal{F}$ then true

($\mathcal{F}$ or false) $\equiv$ $\mathcal{F}$ ($\mathcal{F}$ and true) $\equiv$ $\mathcal{F}$

(if true then $\mathcal{F}$) $\equiv$ $\mathcal{F}$

(if true then $\mathcal{F}$ else $\mathcal{G}$) $\equiv$ $\mathcal{F}$ (if false then $\mathcal{F}$ else $\mathcal{G}$) $\equiv$ $\mathcal{G}$

(true $\equiv$ $\mathcal{F}$) $\equiv$ $\mathcal{F}$ (false $\equiv$ $\mathcal{F}$) $\equiv$ (not $\mathcal{F}$)

- Commutativity

($\mathcal{F}$ and $\mathcal{G}$) $\equiv$ ($\mathcal{G}$ and $\mathcal{F}$)   ($\mathcal{F}$ or $\mathcal{G}$) $\equiv$ ($\mathcal{G}$ or $\mathcal{F}$)

($\mathcal{F}$ $\equiv$ $\mathcal{G}$) $\equiv$ ($\mathcal{G}$ $\equiv$ $\mathcal{F}$)

- Associativity

(($\mathcal{F}$ and $\mathcal{G}$) and $\mathcal{H}$)   (($\mathcal{F}$ or $\mathcal{G}$) or $\mathcal{H}$)
$\equiv$ $\equiv$
($\mathcal{F}$ and ($\mathcal{G}$ and $\mathcal{H}$))   ($\mathcal{F}$ or ($\mathcal{G}$ or $\mathcal{H}$))

(($\mathcal{F}$ $\equiv$ $\mathcal{G}$) $\equiv$ $\mathcal{H}$) $\equiv$ ($\mathcal{F}$ $\equiv$ ($\mathcal{G}$ $\equiv$ $\mathcal{H}$))

- Reduction

($\mathcal{F}$ and $\mathcal{F}$) $\equiv$ $\mathcal{F}$ ($\mathcal{F}$ or $\mathcal{F}$) $\equiv$ $\mathcal{F}$

($\mathcal{F}$ and ($\mathcal{F}$ or $\mathcal{G}$)) $\equiv$ $\mathcal{F}$ ($\mathcal{F}$ or ($\mathcal{F}$ and $\mathcal{G}$)) $\equiv$ $\mathcal{F}$

(if $\mathcal{F}$ then $\mathcal{G}$ else $\mathcal{G}$) $\equiv$ $\mathcal{G}$

- Transitivity

$$if \begin{bmatrix} if\ \mathcal{F}\ then\ \mathcal{G} \\ and \\ if\ \mathcal{G}\ then\ \mathcal{H} \end{bmatrix}$$
then if $\mathcal{F}$ then $\mathcal{H}$

$$if \begin{bmatrix} \mathcal{F} \equiv \mathcal{G} \\ and \\ \mathcal{G} \equiv \mathcal{H} \end{bmatrix}$$
then $\mathcal{F}$ $\equiv$ $\mathcal{H}$

- Contrapositive

$$(\textit{if } \mathcal{F} \textit{ then } \mathcal{G})$$
$$\equiv$$
$$(\textit{if } (\textit{not } \mathcal{G}) \textit{ then } (\textit{not } \mathcal{F}))$$

$$(\mathcal{F} \equiv \mathcal{G})$$
$$\equiv$$
$$((\textit{not } \mathcal{F}) \equiv (\textit{not } \mathcal{G}))$$

- Distributivity

$$(\mathcal{F} \textit{ and } (\mathcal{G} \textit{ or } \mathcal{H}))$$
$$\equiv$$
$$((\mathcal{F} \textit{ and } \mathcal{G}) \textit{ or } (\mathcal{F} \textit{ and } \mathcal{H}))$$

$$(\mathcal{F} \textit{ or } (\mathcal{G} \textit{ and } \mathcal{H}))$$
$$\equiv$$
$$((\mathcal{F} \textit{ or } \mathcal{G}) \textit{ and } (\mathcal{F} \textit{ or } \mathcal{H}))$$

$$(\textit{if } (\mathcal{F} \textit{ or } \mathcal{G}) \textit{ then } \mathcal{H})$$
$$\equiv$$
$$\begin{bmatrix} (\textit{if } \mathcal{F} \textit{ then } \mathcal{H}) \\ \textit{and} \\ (\textit{if } \mathcal{G} \textit{ then } \mathcal{H}) \end{bmatrix}$$

$$(\textit{if } \mathcal{F} \textit{ then } (\mathcal{G} \textit{ or } \mathcal{H}))$$
$$\equiv$$
$$\begin{bmatrix} (\textit{if } \mathcal{F} \textit{ then } \mathcal{G}) \\ \textit{or} \\ (\textit{if } \mathcal{F} \textit{ then } \mathcal{H}) \end{bmatrix}$$

$$(\textit{if } (\mathcal{F} \textit{ and } \mathcal{G}) \textit{ then } \mathcal{H})$$
$$\equiv$$
$$\begin{bmatrix} (\textit{if } \mathcal{F} \textit{ then } \mathcal{H}) \\ \textit{or} \\ (\textit{if } \mathcal{G} \textit{ then } \mathcal{H}) \end{bmatrix}$$

$$(\textit{if } \mathcal{F} \textit{ then } (\mathcal{G} \textit{ and } \mathcal{H}))$$
$$\equiv$$
$$\begin{bmatrix} (\textit{if } \mathcal{F} \textit{ then } \mathcal{G}) \\ \textit{and} \\ (\textit{if } \mathcal{F} \textit{ then } \mathcal{H}) \end{bmatrix}$$

$$(\textit{if } (\mathcal{F} \textit{ and } \mathcal{G}) \textit{ then } \mathcal{H})$$
$$\equiv$$
$$(\textit{if } \mathcal{F} \textit{ then } (\textit{if } \mathcal{G} \textit{ then } \mathcal{H}))$$

- Negation

$$\textit{not } (\textit{not } \mathcal{F})$$
$$\equiv$$
$$\mathcal{F}$$

$$\textit{not } (\mathcal{F} \textit{ and } \mathcal{G})$$
$$\equiv$$
$$((\textit{not } \mathcal{F}) \textit{ or } (\textit{not } \mathcal{G}))$$

$$\textit{not } (\mathcal{F} \textit{ or } \mathcal{G})$$
$$\equiv$$
$$((\textit{not } \mathcal{F}) \textit{ and } (\textit{not } \mathcal{G}))$$

$$\textit{not } (\textit{if } \mathcal{F} \textit{ then } \mathcal{G})$$
$$\equiv$$
$$(\mathcal{F} \textit{ and } (\textit{not } \mathcal{G}))$$

$$\textit{not } (\textit{if } \mathcal{F} \textit{ then } \mathcal{G} \textit{ else } \mathcal{H})$$
$$\equiv$$
$$(\textit{if } \mathcal{F} \textit{ then } (\textit{not } \mathcal{G}) \textit{ else } (\textit{not } \mathcal{H}))$$

$$\textit{not } (\mathcal{F} \equiv \mathcal{G})$$
$$\equiv$$
$$(\mathcal{F} \equiv (\textit{not } \mathcal{G}))$$

- Connective elimination

$$(\textit{if } \mathcal{F} \textit{ then } \mathcal{G})$$
$$\equiv$$
$$((\textit{not } \mathcal{F}) \textit{ or } \mathcal{G})$$

$(if\ \mathcal{F}\ then\ \mathcal{G}\ else\ \mathcal{H})$

$\equiv$

$$\left[\begin{array}{l} (\mathcal{F}\ and\ \mathcal{G}) \\ or \\ ((not\ \mathcal{F})\ and\ \mathcal{H}) \end{array}\right]$$

$(if\ \mathcal{F}\ then\ \mathcal{G}\ else\ \mathcal{H})$

$\equiv$

$$\left[\begin{array}{l} (if\ \mathcal{F}\ then\ \mathcal{G}) \\ and \\ (if\ (not\ \mathcal{F})\ then\ \mathcal{H}) \end{array}\right]$$

$(\mathcal{F} \equiv \mathcal{G})$

$\equiv$

$$\left[\begin{array}{l} (\mathcal{F}\ and\ \mathcal{G}) \\ or \\ ((not\ \mathcal{F})\ and\ (not\ \mathcal{G})) \end{array}\right]$$

$(\mathcal{F} \equiv \mathcal{G})$

$\equiv$

$$\left[\begin{array}{l} (if\ \mathcal{F}\ then\ \mathcal{G}) \\ and \\ (if\ \mathcal{G}\ then\ \mathcal{F}) \end{array}\right]$$

EQUIVALENT SENTENCE SCHEMATA

Two sentence schemata are said to be *equivalent* if each instance of one is equivalent to the corresponding instance of the other. Note that many of the valid sentences above are of the form

$$\mathcal{A} \equiv \mathcal{B}.$$

By an earlier remark this establishes that $\mathcal{A}$ and $\mathcal{B}$ are equivalent. Thus since the sentence schema

$$not\ (not\ \mathcal{F}) \equiv \mathcal{F},$$

which is one of the negation schemata from the catalog, is valid, we know that the sentence schemata

$$not\ (not\ \mathcal{F}) \qquad and \qquad \mathcal{F}$$

are equivalent. In other words, any sentence of the form $\big(not\ (not\ \mathcal{F})\big)$ is equivalent to the corresponding sentence of the form $\mathcal{F}$. In particular, the sentences

$$not\ \big(not\ (P\ or\ Q)\big) \qquad and \qquad P\ or\ Q$$

are equivalent.

We shall say that the sentence schema $\big(if\ (not\ \mathcal{G})\ then\ (not\ \mathcal{F})\big)$ is the *contrapositive* of the implication $(if\ \mathcal{F}\ then\ \mathcal{G})$. Thus the schema

$$(if\ \mathcal{F}\ then\ \mathcal{G})$$
$$\equiv$$
$$\big(if\ (not\ \mathcal{G})\ then\ (not\ \mathcal{F})\big)$$

in the catalog may be rephrased as saying that an implication is equivalent to its contrapositive.

In **Problem 1.3** the reader is asked to show that each of the connectives can be paraphrased in terms of the conditional connective *if-then-else* and the truth symbols *true* and *false*.

MULTIPLE CONJUNCTION AND DISJUNCTION

The reader may note that, because of the associativity sentence schema from the catalog,

$$((\mathcal{F} \ and \ \mathcal{G}) \ and \ \mathcal{H})$$
$$\equiv$$
$$(\mathcal{F} \ and \ (\mathcal{G} \ and \ \mathcal{H})),$$

sentences such as

$$((P \ and \ Q) \ and \ R) \ and \ S,$$

$$P \ and \ (Q \ and \ (R \ and \ S)),$$

$$P \ and \ ((Q \ and \ R) \ and \ S),$$

and so forth are equivalent. For this reason, we will sometimes write any of these sentences without parentheses, as

$$P \ and \ Q \ and \ R \ and \ S.$$

To be definite, we regard the multiple conjunction

$$\mathcal{F}_1 \ and \ \mathcal{F}_2 \ and \ \mathcal{F}_3 \ and \ \ldots \ and \ \mathcal{F}_n$$

as an abbreviation for

$$\big((\ldots((\mathcal{F}_1 \ and \ \mathcal{F}_2) \ and \ \mathcal{F}_3) \ and \ \ldots) \ and \ \mathcal{F}_n\big).$$

Similarly, the multiple disjunction

$$\mathcal{F}_1 \ or \ \mathcal{F}_2 \ or \ \mathcal{F}_3 \ or \ldots or \ \mathcal{F}_n$$

is an abbreviation for

$$\big((\ldots((\mathcal{F}_1 \ or \ \mathcal{F}_2) \ or \ \mathcal{F}_3) \ or \ \ldots) \ or \ \mathcal{F}_n\big).$$

We can derive the following semantic rules for these multiple connectives, to be added to the other rules for determining the truth-value of a sentence under an interpretation:

- A multiple conjunction

$$\mathcal{F}_1 \ and \ \mathcal{F}_2 \ and \ \ldots \ and \ \mathcal{F}_n$$

is true if and only if each of its conjuncts $\mathcal{F}_1, \mathcal{F}_2, \ldots, \mathcal{F}_n$ is true.

- A multiple disjunction

$$\mathcal{F}_1 \ or \ \mathcal{F}_2 \ or \ \ldots \ or \ \mathcal{F}_n$$

is true if and only if at least one of its disjuncts $\mathcal{F}_1, \mathcal{F}_2, \ldots, \mathcal{F}_n$ is true.

Problems 1.4, 1.5, and **1.6** present some puzzles to be solved with the help of propositional-logic techniques for establishing validity.

1.8   SUBSTITUTION

Let us introduce some notation for the operation of replacing subsentences of a given sentence with other subsentences. We shall use this notation throughout the book. We distinguish between "total substitution," in which all occurrences of a subsentence are replaced, and "partial substitution," in which zero, one, or more, but not necessarily all, occurrences of the subsentence are replaced.

TOTAL SUBSTITUTION

Total substitution allows us to replace all occurrences of a subsentence of a given sentence with another subsentence.

Definition (total substitution)

Suppose $\mathcal{F}$, $\mathcal{G}$, and $\mathcal{H}$ are sentences. In preparation for replacing occurrences of $\mathcal{G}$ in $\mathcal{F}$, let us write $\mathcal{F}$ as

$$\mathcal{F}[\mathcal{G}].$$

Then we denote by

$$\mathcal{F}[\mathcal{H}]$$

the sentence obtained by replacing every occurrence of $\mathcal{G}$ in $\mathcal{F}[\mathcal{G}]$ with $\mathcal{H}$. ◢

For example, if $\mathcal{F}[P]$ is

> P *and*
> $(Q$ *or* $P)$

then the result $\mathcal{F}[if\ R\ then\ S]$ of a total substitution is the sentence

> $(if\ R\ then\ S)\ and$
> $\big(Q\ or\ (if\ R\ then\ S)\big).$

Note that we can make substitutions for entire subsentences, not only for propositional symbols. Thus, if $\mathcal{F}[Q\ and\ R]$ is

> *if* P
> *then* $(Q\ and\ R),$

then $\mathcal{F}[true]$ is the sentence

> *if* P
> *then* $true.$

The substitution is performed in one stage. Thus if $\mathcal{F}[P]$ is

> $P\ and\ R,$

then $\mathcal{F}\big[P \text{ and } Q\big]$ is

> $(P \;\; and \;\; Q) \;\; and \;\; R.$

We do not then go on to replace the newly introduced occurrence of P with $(P \text{ and } Q)$.

Note also that we may write $\mathcal{F}$ as $\mathcal{F}\big[\mathcal{G}\big]$ and apply substitution even if $\mathcal{G}$ does not occur in $\mathcal{F}\big[\mathcal{G}\big]$. In this case, $\mathcal{F}\big[\mathcal{H}\big]$ will be the same as $\mathcal{F}\big[\mathcal{G}\big]$. Thus, if $\mathcal{F}\big[R\big]$ is

> $P \;\; and \;\; Q\,,$

which has no occurrence of R, $\mathcal{F}\big[S\big]$ is also

> $P \;\; and \;\; Q.$

Finally note that the order in which we mention $\mathcal{F}[\mathcal{P}]$ and $\mathcal{F}[\mathcal{Q}]$ is significant. If we mention $\mathcal{F}[\mathcal{P}]$ first, then $\mathcal{F}[\mathcal{Q}]$ is obtained from $\mathcal{F}[\mathcal{P}]$ by replacing every occurrence of $\mathcal{P}$ with $\mathcal{Q}$. On the other hand, if we mention $\mathcal{F}[\mathcal{Q}]$ first, then $\mathcal{F}[\mathcal{P}]$ is obtained from $\mathcal{F}[\mathcal{Q}]$ by replacing every occurrence of $\mathcal{Q}$ with $\mathcal{P}$.

Remark (multiple conjunction and disjunction). In applying a substitution, we must recall that the multiple conjunction

> $\mathcal{F}_1 \;\; and \;\; \mathcal{F}_2 \;\; and \;\; \ldots \;\; and \;\; \mathcal{F}_n$

is an abbreviation for the sentence

> $(\ldots(\mathcal{F}_1 \;\; and \;\; \mathcal{F}_2) \;\; and \;\; \ldots \;\; and \;\; \mathcal{F}_n).$

Therefore, if $\mathcal{F}\big[P \text{ and } Q\big]$ is

> $P \;\; and \;\; Q \;\; and \;\; R\,,$

that is,

> $(P \;\; and \;\; Q) \;\; and \;\; R\,,$

then $\mathcal{F}\big[S\big]$ denotes the sentence

> $S \;\; and \;\; R.$

But if $\mathcal{F}\big[Q \text{ and } R\big]$ is

> $P \;\; and \;\; Q \;\; and \;\; R\,,$

that is,

> $(P \;\; and \;\; Q) \;\; and \;\; R\,,$

then $\mathcal{F}\big[S\big]$ is the sentence

> $(P \;\; and \;\; Q) \;\; and \;\; R$

itself.

A similar remark applies to the multiple disjunction

> $\mathcal{F}_1 \;\; or \;\; \mathcal{F}_2 \;\; or \;\; \ldots \;\; or \;\; \mathcal{F}_n.$

The substitution operation can be distributed over the components of a sentence. More precisely, if $\mathcal{F}[\mathcal{G}]$ is

$$not \; \mathcal{F}'[\mathcal{G}]$$

then $\mathcal{F}[\mathcal{H}]$ is

$$not \; \mathcal{F}'[\mathcal{H}].$$

Similarly, if $\mathcal{F}[\mathcal{G}]$ is

$$\mathcal{F}_1[\mathcal{G}] \; and \; \mathcal{F}_2[\mathcal{G}],$$

then $\mathcal{F}[\mathcal{H}]$ is

$$\mathcal{F}_1[\mathcal{H}] \; and \; \mathcal{F}_2[\mathcal{H}].$$

Similarly for the other connectives.

PARTIAL SUBSTITUTION

The partial substitution operation allows us to replace some, but not necessarily all, occurrences of a subsentence of a given sentence with another sentence.

Definition (partial substitution)

Suppose $\mathcal{F}$, $\mathcal{G}$, and $\mathcal{H}$ are sentences. In preparation for replacing occurrences of $\mathcal{G}$ in $\mathcal{F}$, let us write $\mathcal{F}$ as

$$\mathcal{F}\langle\mathcal{G}\rangle.$$

Then we denote by

$$\mathcal{F}\langle\mathcal{H}\rangle$$

any one of the sentences obtained by replacing zero, one, or more occurrences of $\mathcal{G}$ in $\mathcal{F}\langle\mathcal{G}\rangle$ with $\mathcal{H}$. ◢

Thus in contrast to a total substitution, a partial substitution does not necessarily result in a particular sentence, but may result in any of several sentences.

For example, if $\mathcal{F}\langle P \rangle$ is

$$P \; or \; P$$

then the result $\mathcal{F}\langle Q \rangle$ of a partial substitution may be any of the following sentences:

$P \;\; or \;\; P$	(replacing zero occurrences of P);
$Q \;\; or \;\; P$	(replacing the first occurrence of P);
$P \;\; or \;\; Q$	(replacing the second occurrence of P);
$Q \;\; or \;\; Q$	(replacing both occurrences of P).

Thus, the partial substitution above could result in any of four sentences. If we wish to specify further which occurrences are to be replaced, we must do so in words.

Note that we may write $\mathcal{F}$ as $\mathcal{F}\langle\mathcal{G}\rangle$ and apply a partial substitution even if $\mathcal{G}$ does not occur in $\mathcal{F}\langle\mathcal{G}\rangle$. In this case, $\mathcal{F}\langle\mathcal{H}\rangle$ will be the same as $\mathcal{F}\langle\mathcal{G}\rangle$. This is similar to total substitution.

Remark. For given sentences $\mathcal{F}$, $\mathcal{G}$, and $\mathcal{H}$, let us compare the results of a total and a partial substitution. For this purpose, let us write $\mathcal{F}$ as both $\mathcal{F}[\mathcal{G}]$ and $\mathcal{F}\langle\mathcal{G}\rangle$. Then the result $\mathcal{F}[\mathcal{H}]$ of a total substitution is one of the possible results $\mathcal{F}\langle\mathcal{H}\rangle$ of a partial substitution. This is because the sentence obtained by replacing all occurrences of $\mathcal{G}$ in $\mathcal{F}$ with $\mathcal{H}$ is one of the sentences obtained by replacing zero, one, or more occurrences of $\mathcal{G}$ in $\mathcal{F}$ with $\mathcal{H}$. ◢

MULTIPLE SUBSTITUTION

The above notions may be extended to allow us to replace more than one subsentence of a given sentence at the same time.

Definition (multiple substitution)

Suppose $\mathcal{F}$, $\mathcal{G}_1$, $\ldots$, $\mathcal{G}_n$, and $\mathcal{H}_1$, $\ldots$, $\mathcal{H}_n$ are sentences, where $\mathcal{G}_1$, $\ldots$, $\mathcal{G}_n$ are distinct.

- *Total substitution*

  In preparation for replacing occurrences of $\mathcal{G}_i$ in $\mathcal{F}$, let us write $\mathcal{F}$ as

  $$\mathcal{F}[\mathcal{G}_1, \ldots, \mathcal{G}_n].$$

  Then we denote by

  $$\mathcal{F}[\mathcal{H}_1, \ldots, \mathcal{H}_n]$$

  the sentence obtained by replacing simultaneously every occurrence of each subsentence $\mathcal{G}_i$ in $\mathcal{F}[\mathcal{G}_1, \ldots, \mathcal{G}_n]$ with the corresponding sentence $\mathcal{H}_i$.

- *Partial substitution*

  In preparation for replacing occurrences of $\mathcal{G}_i$ in $\mathcal{F}$, let us write $\mathcal{F}$ as

  $$\mathcal{F}\langle\mathcal{G}_1, \ldots, \mathcal{G}_n\rangle.$$

  Then we denote by

  $$\mathcal{F}\langle\mathcal{H}_1, \ldots, \mathcal{H}_n\rangle$$

  any of the sentences obtained by replacing simultaneously zero, one, or more occurrences of some of the subsentences $\mathcal{G}_i$ in $\mathcal{F}\langle\mathcal{G}_1, \ldots, \mathcal{G}_n\rangle$ with the corresponding sentence $\mathcal{H}_i$. ◢

Example.   If $\mathcal{F}[P,\ Q \ or \ R]$ is

>   *if P*
>   *then if (Q or P)*
>   *then (Q or R)*,

then the result $\mathcal{F}[R,\ not\ R]$ of a multiple total substitution is the sentence

>   *if R*
>   *then if (Q or R)*
>   *then (not R)*.

The two occurrences of P were replaced by R and the occurrence of $(Q \ or \ R)$ is replaced by $(not \ R)$.

   If $\mathcal{F}\langle P,\ Q \ or \ R \rangle$ is

>   *if P*
>   *then if (Q or P)*
>   *then (Q or R)*,

then the result $\mathcal{F}\langle R,\ not\ R \rangle$ of a multiple partial substitution may be any of several sentences, including

>   *if R*
>   *then if (Q or P)*   (replacing the first occurrence of P)
>   *then (Q or R)*

>   *if P*
>   *then if (Q or P)*   (replacing the occurrence of $(Q \ or \ R)$)
>   *then (not R)*

>   *if R*
>   *then if (Q or P)*   (replacing the first occurrence of P
>   *then (not R)*   and the occurrence of $(Q \ or \ R)$)

>   *if R*
>   *then if (Q or R)*   (replacing both occurrences of P
>   *then (not R)*   and the occurrence of $(Q \ or \ R)$).

Altogether, this partial substitution may result in any of eight sentences.   ⌐

   Note that the replacements of a multiple substitution are performed simultaneously in a single stage. Thus, if $\mathcal{F}[P,\ Q]$ is the sentence P then the result $\mathcal{F}[Q,\ R]$ of a total substitution is the sentence Q rather than the sentence R. Though the occurrence of P is replaced by Q, the newly introduced occurrence of Q is not subsequently replaced by R.

   If $\mathcal{F}[P,\ P \ or \ Q]$ is $(P \ or \ Q)$, the reader may wonder what is meant by $\mathcal{F}[R,\ S]$. Here, the subsentence P occurs in the subsentence $(P \ or \ Q)$, and both subsentences are to be replaced. By convention, the outer subsentence, in this case $(P\ or\ Q)$, is actually the one to be replaced. Thus, the result of the above total substitution is the sentence S rather than the sentence $(R\ or\ Q)$.

On the other hand, if $\mathcal{F}\langle P,\ P\ or\ Q\rangle$ is $(P\ or\ Q)$, then the result $\mathcal{F}\langle R,\ S\rangle$ of the partial substitution will be either S, when the outer subsentence $(P\ or\ Q)$ is replaced, or $(R\ or\ Q)$, when the inner subsentence P is replaced.

The reader is requested to apply total and partial substitution in **Problem 1.7**.

SUBSTITUTIVITY OF EQUIVALENCE

The equivalence relationship has the property that two sentences that are equivalent may in some sense be treated interchangeably. This is expressed in terms of the substitution notation in the following result:

Proposition (substitutivity of equivalence)

> For any sentences $\mathcal{G}$, $\mathcal{H}$, and $\mathcal{F}\langle\mathcal{G}\rangle$, the sentence
>
> $$if\ (\mathcal{G}\ \equiv\ \mathcal{H})$$
> $$then\ \left(\mathcal{F}\langle\mathcal{G}\rangle\ \equiv\ \mathcal{F}\langle\mathcal{H}\rangle\right)$$
>
> is valid. ⏌

In other words, the sentence

$$\mathcal{G}\ \equiv\ \mathcal{H}$$

implies the sentence

$$\mathcal{F}\langle\mathcal{G}\rangle\ \equiv\ \mathcal{F}\langle\mathcal{H}\rangle.$$

In particular (by the *implication-and-validity* proposition),

> if $(\mathcal{G}\ \equiv\ \mathcal{H})$ is valid,
> then $\left(\mathcal{F}\langle\mathcal{G}\rangle\ \equiv\ \mathcal{F}\langle\mathcal{H}\rangle\right)$ is valid.

Thus (by an earlier remark), we have the following result:

Corollary (substitutivity of equivalence).

> For any sentences $\mathcal{G}$, $\mathcal{H}$, and $\mathcal{F}\langle\mathcal{G}\rangle$,
>
> > if $\mathcal{G}$ and $\mathcal{H}$ are equivalent,
> > then $\mathcal{F}\langle\mathcal{G}\rangle$ and $\mathcal{F}\langle\mathcal{H}\rangle$ are equivalent. ⏌

Thus if two sentences are equivalent, we may replace zero, one, or more occurrences of one of them with the other, obtaining an equivalent sentence.

The proposition itself is intuitively clear, because, for any interpretation $\mathcal{I}$ such that

$$(\mathcal{G} \equiv \mathcal{H}) \text{ is true under } \mathcal{I},$$

we know (by the $\equiv$ rule) that

$$\mathcal{G} \text{ and } \mathcal{H} \text{ have the same truth-value under } \mathcal{I}.$$

But $\mathcal{F}\langle\mathcal{G}\rangle$ and $\mathcal{F}\langle\mathcal{H}\rangle$ differ only in that certain occurrences of $\mathcal{G}$ in $\mathcal{F}\langle\mathcal{G}\rangle$ have been replaced by $\mathcal{H}$. Therefore in determining the truth-value of $\mathcal{F}\langle\mathcal{G}\rangle$ and $\mathcal{F}\langle\mathcal{H}\rangle$ under $\mathcal{I}$, we obtain the same result in each case. The sentences $\mathcal{G}$ and $\mathcal{H}$ have the same truth-value and thus may be used interchangeably. The precise proof of the proposition is omitted here.

As an important special case of the proposition, we may conclude that the corresponding sentence for total substitution,

$$\begin{aligned} &\textit{if } (\mathcal{G} \equiv \mathcal{H}) \\ &\textit{then } (\mathcal{F}[\mathcal{G}] \equiv \mathcal{F}[\mathcal{H}]), \end{aligned}$$

is valid. This is because the result of a total substitution is one of the possible results of a partial substitution.

Example.   We know that the sentence

$$\mathcal{G}: \quad \textit{not } (P \textit{ and } Q)$$

is equivalent to the sentence

$$\mathcal{H}: \quad (\textit{not } P) \textit{ or } (\textit{not } Q).$$

Therefore, by the above corollary, the sentence

$$\mathcal{F}\langle\mathcal{G}\rangle: \quad \begin{aligned} &\textit{not } (P \textit{ and } Q) \\ &\textit{or} \\ &R \textit{ and } \textit{not } (P \textit{ and } Q) \end{aligned}$$

is equivalent to the sentence

$$\mathcal{F}\langle\mathcal{H}\rangle: \quad \begin{aligned} &(\textit{not } P) \textit{ or } (\textit{not } Q) \\ &\textit{or} \\ &R \textit{ and } \textit{not } (P \textit{ and } Q), \end{aligned}$$

obtained by replacing the first occurrence of $\mathcal{G}$ in $\mathcal{F}\langle\mathcal{G}\rangle$ with $\mathcal{H}$. Note that we did not replace the second occurrence of $\mathcal{G}$ in $\mathcal{F}\langle\mathcal{G}\rangle$, although we could have. ⌐

1.9   SIMPLIFICATION

Simplification allows us to replace every occurrence of a subsentence $\mathcal{E}$ of a given sentence $\mathcal{S}[\mathcal{E}]$ with an equivalent, simpler subsentence $\mathcal{E}'$, obtaining an equivalent, simpler sentence $\mathcal{S}[\mathcal{E}']$.

For example, we know that any sentence of form
$$\mathcal{E}: \quad not \ (not \ \mathcal{F})$$
is equivalent to the corresponding sentence of form
$$\mathcal{E}': \quad \mathcal{F}.$$
By the *substitutivity-of-equivalence* corollary, this means that if $\mathcal{E}$ occurs as a subsentence of some sentence $\mathcal{S}[\mathcal{E}]$, then the sentence $\mathcal{S}[\mathcal{E}']$, obtained by replacing every occurrence of $\mathcal{E}$ with $\mathcal{E}'$, is equivalent to $\mathcal{S}[\mathcal{E}]$. We will say that $\mathcal{S}[\mathcal{E}']$ is obtained from $\mathcal{S}[\mathcal{E}]$ by applying the *simplification*
$$not \ (not \ \mathcal{F}) \quad \Rightarrow \quad \mathcal{F}.$$

In particular, applying the preceding simplification to the sentence
$$\mathcal{S}: \quad P \ or \ not \ (not \ Q),$$
we obtain the sentence
$$\mathcal{S}': \quad P \ or \ Q,$$
because $\mathcal{S}'$ is obtained from $\mathcal{S}$ by replacing the subsentence $\mathcal{E}$: $not \ (not \ Q)$, which is of the form $not \ (not \ \mathcal{F})$, with the equivalent sentence $\mathcal{E}'$: Q, which is the corresponding sentence of the form $\mathcal{F}$.

This motivates the following definition.

Definition (simplification).

Suppose that any sentence of the form $\mathcal{E}$ is equivalent to the corresponding sentence of the form $\mathcal{E}'$, and that
$$\mathcal{E} \Rightarrow \mathcal{E}'$$
is a *simplification* (see the following catalogs).

The result of *applying* the simplification to a sentence $\mathcal{S}$ is the sentence obtained by replacing every occurrence of a subsentence of the form $\mathcal{E}$ in $\mathcal{S}$ with the corresponding sentence of the form $\mathcal{E}'$.

The result of *simplifying* $\mathcal{S}$ is the sentence $\mathcal{S}'$ obtained by successively applying all possible simplifications to $\mathcal{S}$ until no more can be applied. We shall also say that $\mathcal{S}$ *reduces to $\mathcal{S}'$ under simplification.* ⌐

For each simplification $\mathcal{E} \Rightarrow \mathcal{E}'$ in our catalog, the schemata $\mathcal{E}$ and $\mathcal{E}'$ are equivalent. In other words, every instance of one is equivalent to the corresponding instance of the other. In applying a simplification, we thus replace subsentences with equivalent sentences. Therefore, by the *substitutivity-of-equivalence* corollary, the result of applying a simplification is equivalent to the original sentence.

Each simplification in our catalog reduces the length of the sentence to which it is applied. Therefore we can be sure that we cannot apply simplifications to a given sentence indefinitely.

Example. Consider the sentence

$$\mathcal{S}: \quad not \left(not \begin{bmatrix} if & \boxed{not\,(not\,P)} & or & Q \\ then & \boxed{not\,(not\,P)} & \end{bmatrix} \right).$$

By a single application of the simplification

$$not\,(not\,\mathcal{F}) \quad \Rightarrow \quad \mathcal{F},$$

replacing the two occurrences of the subsentence $not\,(not\,P)$, annotated with boxes, with the equivalent sentence P, we obtain the new sentence

$$\mathcal{S}': \quad not \left(not \begin{bmatrix} if\ P\ or\ Q \\ then\ P \end{bmatrix} \right),$$

which is equivalent to $\mathcal{S}$.

We can now apply the same simplification to the new sentence

$$\mathcal{S}': \quad \boxed{not \left(not \begin{bmatrix} if\ P\ or\ Q \\ then\ P \end{bmatrix} \right)}$$

obtaining the sentence

$$\mathcal{S}'': \quad \begin{matrix} if\ P\ or\ Q \\ then\ P, \end{matrix}$$

which is also equivalent to $\mathcal{S}$. Since no more simplifications can be applied, $\mathcal{S}''$ is the result of simplifying $\mathcal{S}$.

Note that, alternatively, we could first apply the simplification to the entire sentence, obtaining

$$\begin{matrix} if & \boxed{not\,(not\,P)} & or & Q \\ then & \boxed{not\,(not\,P)}, & \end{matrix}$$

and then apply the simplification to the two occurrences of $not\,(not\,P)$. The result would be the same. ◢

Simplification will be part of our deductive system for proving the validity of sentences. In this system, only simplifications from the following catalog may be applied, and only in the specified $\Rightarrow$ (left-to-right) direction. Many other simplifications could have been included in this catalog; we have chosen only the most basic ones.

CATALOG OF TRUE-FALSE SIMPLIFICATIONS

Certain of the simplifications contain occurrences of the truth symbols *true* and *false* on their left-hand sides; we will call them *true-false simplifications*. For example,

$$\mathcal{F}\ and\ true \quad \Rightarrow \quad \mathcal{F} \qquad and \qquad if\ false\ then\ \mathcal{G} \quad \Rightarrow \quad true$$

are both *true-false* simplifications.

Because of their importance, we list all the *true-false* simplifications here.

- Negation

$$not\ true \quad \Rightarrow \quad false \qquad\qquad (not\ true)$$

$$not\ false \quad \Rightarrow \quad true \qquad\qquad (not\ false)$$

- Conjunction

$$\mathcal{F}\ and\ true \quad \Rightarrow \quad \mathcal{F} \qquad\qquad (and\ true)$$

$$true\ and\ \mathcal{F} \quad \Rightarrow \quad \mathcal{F} \qquad\qquad (true\ and)$$

$$\mathcal{F}\ and\ false \quad \Rightarrow \quad false \qquad\qquad (and\ false)$$

$$false\ and\ \mathcal{F} \quad \Rightarrow \quad false \qquad\qquad (false\ and)$$

- Disjunction

$$\mathcal{F}\ or\ true \quad \Rightarrow \quad true \qquad\qquad (or\ true)$$

$$true\ or\ \mathcal{F} \quad \Rightarrow \quad true \qquad\qquad (true\ or)$$

$$\mathcal{F}\ or\ false \quad \Rightarrow \quad \mathcal{F} \qquad\qquad (or\ false)$$

$$false\ or\ \mathcal{F} \quad \Rightarrow \quad \mathcal{F} \qquad\qquad (false\ or)$$

- Implication

$$if\ true\ then\ \mathcal{G} \quad \Rightarrow \quad \mathcal{G} \qquad\qquad (if\ true)$$

$$if\ false\ then\ \mathcal{G} \quad \Rightarrow \quad true \qquad\qquad (if\ false)$$

$$if\ \mathcal{F}\ then\ true \quad \Rightarrow \quad true \qquad\qquad (then\ true)$$

$$if\ \mathcal{F}\ then\ false \quad \Rightarrow \quad not\ \mathcal{F} \qquad\qquad (then\ false)$$

- Equivalence

$$\mathcal{F} \equiv true \quad \Rightarrow \quad \mathcal{F} \qquad\qquad (iff\ true)$$

$$true \equiv \mathcal{F} \quad \Rightarrow \quad \mathcal{F} \qquad\qquad (true\ iff)$$

$$\mathcal{F} \equiv false \quad \Rightarrow \quad not\ \mathcal{F} \qquad\qquad (iff\ false)$$

$$false \equiv \mathcal{F} \quad \Rightarrow \quad not\ \mathcal{F} \qquad\qquad (false\ iff)$$

- Conditional

$$if\ true\ then\ \mathcal{G}\ else\ \mathcal{H} \quad \Rightarrow \quad \mathcal{G} \qquad\qquad (cond\ if\ true)$$

$$if\ false\ then\ \mathcal{G}\ else\ \mathcal{H} \quad \Rightarrow \quad \mathcal{H} \qquad\qquad (cond\ if\ false)$$

$$if\ \mathcal{F}\ then\ true\ else\ \mathcal{H} \quad \Rightarrow \quad \mathcal{F}\ or\ \mathcal{H} \qquad\qquad (cond\ then\ true)$$

$$if\ \mathcal{F}\ then\ false\ else\ \mathcal{H} \quad \Rightarrow \quad (not\ \mathcal{F})\ and\ \mathcal{H} \qquad\qquad (cond\ then\ false)$$

$$if\ \mathcal{F}\ then\ \mathcal{G}\ else\ true \quad \Rightarrow \quad if\ \mathcal{F}\ then\ \mathcal{G} \qquad\qquad (cond\ else\ true)$$

$$if \ \mathcal{F} \ then \ \mathcal{G} \ else \ false \ \Rightarrow \ \mathcal{F} \ and \ \mathcal{G} \qquad (cond \ else \ false)$$

CATALOG OF OTHER SIMPLIFICATIONS

We present some additional simplifications:

- Negation

$$not \ (not \ \mathcal{F}) \ \Rightarrow \ \mathcal{F} \qquad\qquad (not \ not)$$

$$not \ ((not \ \mathcal{F}) \ and \ (not \ \mathcal{G})) \ \Rightarrow \ \mathcal{F} \ or \ \mathcal{G} \qquad (not \ and)$$

$$not \ ((not \ \mathcal{F}) \ or \ (not \ \mathcal{G})) \ \Rightarrow \ \mathcal{F} \ and \ \mathcal{G} \qquad (not \ or)$$

$$not \ (if \ \mathcal{F} \ then \ (not \ \mathcal{G})) \ \Rightarrow \ \mathcal{F} \ and \ \mathcal{G} \qquad (not \ if)$$

$$not \ ((not \ \mathcal{F}) \equiv \mathcal{G}) \ \Rightarrow \ \mathcal{F} \equiv \mathcal{G} \qquad (not \ iff \ left)$$

$$not \ (\mathcal{F} \equiv (not \ \mathcal{G})) \ \Rightarrow \ \mathcal{F} \equiv \mathcal{G} \qquad (not \ iff \ right)$$

$$not \ (if \ \mathcal{F} \ then \ (not \ \mathcal{G}) \ else \ (not \ \mathcal{H})) \ \Rightarrow \ if \ \mathcal{F} \ then \ \mathcal{G} \ else \ \mathcal{H} \quad (not \ cond)$$

- Conjunction

$$\mathcal{F} \ and \ \mathcal{F} \ \Rightarrow \ \mathcal{F} \qquad (and \ two)$$

$$\mathcal{F} \ and \ (not \ \mathcal{F}) \ \Rightarrow \ false \qquad (and \ not)$$

$$(not \ \mathcal{F}) \ and \ \mathcal{F} \ \Rightarrow \ false \qquad (not \ and)$$

- Disjunction

$$\mathcal{F} \ or \ \mathcal{F} \ \Rightarrow \ \mathcal{F} \qquad (or \ two)$$

$$\mathcal{F} \ or \ (not \ \mathcal{F}) \ \Rightarrow \ true \qquad (or \ not)$$

$$(not \ \mathcal{F}) \ or \ \mathcal{F} \ \Rightarrow \ true \qquad (not \ or)$$

- Implication

$$if \ \mathcal{F} \ then \ \mathcal{F} \ \Rightarrow \ true \qquad (if \ two)$$

$$if \ (not \ \mathcal{F}) \ then \ \mathcal{F} \ \Rightarrow \ \mathcal{F} \qquad (if \ not)$$

$$if \ \mathcal{F} \ then \ (not \ \mathcal{F}) \ \Rightarrow \ not \ \mathcal{F} \qquad (then \ not)$$

$$if \ (not \ \mathcal{G}) \ then \ (not \ \mathcal{F}) \ \Rightarrow \ if \ \mathcal{F} \ then \ \mathcal{G} \qquad (contrapositive)$$

- Equivalence

$$\mathcal{F} \equiv \mathcal{F} \ \Rightarrow \ true \qquad (iff \ two)$$

$$\mathcal{F} \equiv (not \ \mathcal{F}) \ \Rightarrow \ false \qquad (iff \ not)$$

$$(not \ \mathcal{F}) \equiv \mathcal{F} \ \Rightarrow \ false \qquad (not \ iff)$$

• Conditional

$$if \ \mathcal{F} \ then \ \mathcal{G} \ else \ \mathcal{G} \ \Rightarrow \ \mathcal{G} \qquad\qquad (cond \ two)$$

$$if \ (not \ \mathcal{F}) \ then \ \mathcal{G} \ else \ \mathcal{H} \ \Rightarrow \ if \ \mathcal{F} \ then \ \mathcal{H} \ else \ \mathcal{G} \qquad (cond \ not)$$

In **Problem 1.8**, the reader is requested to simplify several sentences.

1.10 POLARITY

Polarity is a syntactic indicator as to how the truth of a subsentence contributes to the truth of the sentence as a whole. The notion will be of strategic value when we attempt to prove the validity of a sentence. We shall assign a polarity, positive (+) or negative (−), to each occurrence of a subsentence $\mathcal{E}$ of a given sentence $\mathcal{S}$. Roughly, an occurrence of $\mathcal{E}$ is positive [negative] in $\mathcal{S}$ if it is in the scope of an even [odd] number of *not*'s (negations).

POLARITY OF OCCURRENCES

We define the polarity of each individual occurrence of a subsentence of a given sentence.

Definition (polarity of occurrences).

If $\mathcal{S}$ is a sentence, we assign a *polarity in* $\mathcal{S}$,

positive (+), or negative (−), or both (±),

to every occurrence of a subsentence of $\mathcal{S}$, according to the following *polarity-assignment rules.*

In stating these rules, we say that two subsentences are of *opposite polarity* if one of them is positive and the other is negative, even if one or the other has both polarities. Also, π indicates a polarity (+ or − or ±) and $-\pi$ indicates the opposite polarity (− or + or ±, respectively).

• *top rule*

The sentence $\mathcal{S}$ itself is positive in $\mathcal{S}$; that is,

$\mathcal{S}^{+}$.

• *not rule*

If a subsentence $\mathcal{E}$ of $\mathcal{S}$ is of form (*not* $\mathcal{F}$), then its component $\mathcal{F}$ has polarity in $\mathcal{S}$ opposite to that of $\mathcal{E}$. We shall express this rule with the notation

$[not \ \mathcal{F}]^{\pi} \ \Rrightarrow \ not \ \mathcal{F}^{-\pi}$.

- *and/or rules*

  If a subsentence $\mathcal{E}$ of $\mathcal{S}$ is of form $(\mathcal{F} \ and \ \mathcal{G})$ or $(\mathcal{F} \ or \ \mathcal{G})$, then its components $\mathcal{F}$ and $\mathcal{G}$ have the same polarity as $\mathcal{E}$ in $\mathcal{S}$; that is,

  $$[\mathcal{F} \ and \ \mathcal{G}]^{\pi} \ \Rightarrow \ \mathcal{F}^{\pi} \ and \ \mathcal{G}^{\pi}$$

  $$[\mathcal{F} \ or \ \mathcal{G}]^{\pi} \ \Rightarrow \ \mathcal{F}^{\pi} \ or \ \mathcal{G}^{\pi}.$$

- *if-then rule*

  If a subsentence $\mathcal{E}$ of $\mathcal{S}$ is of form $(if \ \mathcal{F} \ then \ \mathcal{G})$, then its consequent $\mathcal{G}$ has the same polarity as $\mathcal{E}$ in $\mathcal{S}$, but its antecedent $\mathcal{F}$ has polarity in $\mathcal{S}$ opposite to that of $\mathcal{E}$; that is,

  $$[if \ \mathcal{F} \ then \ \mathcal{G}]^{\pi} \ \Rightarrow \ if \ \mathcal{F}^{-\pi} \ then \ \mathcal{G}^{\pi}.$$

- $\equiv$ *rule*

  If a subsentence $\mathcal{E}$ of $\mathcal{S}$ is of form $(\mathcal{F} \equiv \mathcal{G})$, then its components $\mathcal{F}$ and $\mathcal{G}$ have both positive and negative polarity in $\mathcal{S}$ (independent of the polarity of $\mathcal{E}$ in $\mathcal{S}$); that is,

  $$[\mathcal{F} \equiv \mathcal{G}]^{\pi} \ \Rightarrow \ \mathcal{F}^{\pm} \equiv \mathcal{G}^{\pm}.$$

- *if-then-else rule*

  If a subsentence $\mathcal{E}$ of $\mathcal{S}$ is of form $(if \ \mathcal{F} \ then \ \mathcal{G} \ else \ \mathcal{H})$, then its *then*-clause $\mathcal{G}$ and its *else*-clause $\mathcal{H}$ have the same polarity as $\mathcal{E}$ in $\mathcal{S}$, and its *if*-clause $\mathcal{F}$ has both positive and negative polarity in $\mathcal{S}$; that is,

  $$[if \ \mathcal{F} \ then \ \mathcal{G} \ else \ \mathcal{H}]^{\pi} \ \Rightarrow \ if \ \mathcal{F}^{\pm} \ then \ \mathcal{G}^{\pi} \ else \ \mathcal{H}^{\pi}.$$

Starting with $\mathcal{S}$ itself, we can assign a polarity to each of its components by applying one of the preceding rules. Thus, step by step, we can assign a polarity to each occurrence of each subsentence of $\mathcal{S}$.

Example (polarity assignment).   Let us gradually annotate the sentence

$$if \ \big((not \ P) \ or \ Q\big)$$
$$then \ \Big(Q \ and \ \big(P \equiv (not \ Q)\big)\Big)$$

with the polarities of each of its subsentences. We use the preceding *polarity-assignment* rules to obtain each row from the preceding row (the boxes indicate the subsentences being considered at each stage).

By the *top* rule, the sentence itself has a positive polarity:

$$\boxed{\begin{array}{l} if \ ((not \ P) \ or \ Q) \\ \\ then \ \begin{bmatrix} Q \\ and \\ P \equiv (not \ Q) \end{bmatrix} \end{array}}^{+}.$$

By the *if-then* rule, the consequent is positive and the antecedent is negative:

$$
\left[
\begin{array}{l}
\textit{if} \quad \boxed{(not\ P)\ \ or\ \ Q}^{-} \\[4pt]
\textit{then} \quad \boxed{\begin{array}{l} Q \\ and \\ P \equiv (not\ Q) \end{array}}^{+}
\end{array}
\right]^{+}.
$$

By the *and* and *or* rules, the connectives *and* and *or* do not change polarity:

$$
\left[
\begin{array}{l}
\textit{if} \quad \left[\ \boxed{not\ P}^{-}\ \ or\ \ \boxed{Q}^{-}\ \right]^{-} \\[6pt]
\textit{then} \quad \left[\ \boxed{Q}^{+} \ and\ \ \boxed{P \equiv (not\ Q)}^{+}\ \right]^{+}
\end{array}
\right]^{+}.
$$

Applying the *not* rule to the antecedent and the $\equiv$ rule to the consequent:

$$
\left[
\begin{array}{l}
\textit{if} \quad \left[\left[not\ \boxed{P}^{+}\right]^{-}\ or\ \ Q^{-}\right]^{-} \\[6pt]
\textit{then} \quad \left[\begin{array}{l} Q^{+} \\ and \\ \left[\boxed{P}^{\pm} \equiv \boxed{not\ Q}^{\pm}\right]^{+} \end{array}\right]^{+}
\end{array}
\right]^{+}.
$$

Finally, by the *not* rule, if the subsentence *not Q* has both polarities, *Q* itself has both polarities:

$$
\left[
\begin{array}{l}
\textit{if} \quad \left[\left[not\ P^{+}\right]^{-}\ or\ \ Q^{-}\right]^{-} \\[6pt]
\textit{then} \quad \left[\begin{array}{l} Q^{+} \\ and \\ \left[P^{\pm} \equiv \left[not\ \boxed{Q}^{\pm}\right]^{\pm}\right]^{+} \end{array}\right]^{+}
\end{array}
\right]^{+}.
$$

Thus, as a result of this annotation process, we obtain the full polarity annotation:

$$
\left[
\begin{array}{l}
\textit{if} \quad \left[\left[not\ P^{+}\right]^{-}\ or\ \ Q^{-}\right]^{-} \\[6pt]
\textit{then} \quad \left[\begin{array}{l} Q^{+} \\ and \\ \left[P^{\pm} \equiv \left[not\ Q^{\pm}\right]^{\pm}\right]^{+} \end{array}\right]^{+}
\end{array}
\right]^{+}.
$$

Note that different occurrences of the same subsentence may have different polarities. For instance, one occurrence of the subsentence Q is negative, one is positive, and one has both polarities. ◢

In **Problem 1.9**, the reader is requested to annotate the polarity of a sentence in the same way.

Remark (implicit negation). Roughly, the polarity of a subsentence indicates whether it is enclosed in an even or odd number of negation connectives; here, we include "implicit" as well as "explicit" negations. The *polarity-assignment* rules for the *if-then*, $\equiv$, and *if-then-else* connectives take into consideration implicit negations.

if-then rule: $[if \; \mathcal{F} \; then \; \mathcal{G}]^{\pi} \;\Rightarrow\; if \; \mathcal{F}^{-\pi} \; then \; \mathcal{G}^{\pi}$

The implication

$$if \; \mathcal{F} \; then \; \mathcal{G}$$

can be regarded as an abbreviation for

$$(not \; \mathcal{F}) \; or \; \mathcal{G}.$$

Thus the antecedent $\mathcal{F}$ is enclosed within an additional implicit negation connective, and therefore has polarity opposite to that of the implication.

$\equiv$ *rule*: $\left[\mathcal{F} \equiv \mathcal{G}\right]^{\pi} \;\Rightarrow\; \mathcal{F}^{\pm} \equiv \mathcal{G}^{\pm}$

The equivalence

$$\mathcal{F} \equiv \mathcal{G}$$

can be regarded as an abbreviation for

$\mathcal{F}$ *and* $\mathcal{G}$		*if* $\mathcal{F}$ *then* $\mathcal{G}$
or	*or*	*and*
$(not \; \mathcal{F}) \; and \; (not \; \mathcal{G})$		*if* $\mathcal{G}$ *then* $\mathcal{F}$.

Thus, if the polarity of the equivalence is π, the polarity of the subsentences is

$\mathcal{F}^{\pi}$ *and* $\mathcal{G}^{\pi}$		*if* $\mathcal{F}^{-\pi}$ *then* $\mathcal{G}^{\pi}$
or		*and*
$(not \; \mathcal{F}^{-\pi}) \; and \; (not \; \mathcal{G}^{-\pi})$		*if* $\mathcal{G}^{-\pi}$ *then* $\mathcal{F}^{\pi}$.

That is, there are actually two occurrences of $\mathcal{F}$ and of $\mathcal{G}$ buried in the formula $\mathcal{F} \equiv \mathcal{G}$, one enclosed within an additional implicit negation connective. Therefore $\mathcal{F}$ and $\mathcal{G}$ in the equivalence are each considered to have both polarities.

if-then-else rule: $\left[if \; \mathcal{F} \; then \; \mathcal{G} \; else \; \mathcal{H}\right]^{\pi} \;\Rightarrow\; if \; \mathcal{F}^{\pm} \; then \; \mathcal{G}^{\pi} \; else \; \mathcal{H}^{\pi}$

The conditional

$$if \; \mathcal{F} \; then \; \mathcal{G} \; else \; \mathcal{H}$$

can be regarded as an abbreviation for

$\mathcal{F}$ *and* $\mathcal{G}$		*if* $\mathcal{F}$ *then* $\mathcal{G}$
or	*or*	*and*
$(not \; \mathcal{F}) \; and \; \mathcal{H}$		*if* $(not \; \mathcal{F})$ *then* $\mathcal{H}$.

Thus, if the polarity of the conditional is π, the polarity of the subsentences is

$$\mathcal{F}^{\pi} \ and \ \mathcal{G}^{\pi} \qquad\qquad\qquad if \ \mathcal{F}^{-\pi} \ then \ \mathcal{G}^{\pi}$$
$$or \qquad\qquad\qquad\qquad\qquad and$$
$$(not \ \mathcal{F}^{-\pi}) \ and \ \mathcal{H}^{\pi} \qquad\quad if \ (not \ \mathcal{F}^{\pi}) \ then \ \mathcal{H}^{\pi}.$$

That is, $\mathcal{F}$ is considered to have both polarities, but $\mathcal{G}$ and $\mathcal{H}$ have the same polarity as the conditional.

Note that, by repeated application of the *polarity-assignment* rules, every proper subsentence of an equivalence, and every proper subsentence of the *if*-clause of a conditional, has both polarities. ⌐

Definition (strict polarity of occurrences)

An occurrence of a subsentence $\mathcal{E}$ in a sentence S has *strictly positive polarity* in S if $\mathcal{E}$ has positive but not negative polarity in S; that is,

$$\mathcal{E}^{+} \quad but \ not \ \mathcal{E}^{\pm}.$$

Similarly, an occurrence of $\mathcal{E}$ has *strictly negative polarity* in S if $\mathcal{E}$ has negative but not positive polarity in S; that is,

$$\mathcal{E}^{-} \quad but \ not \ \mathcal{E}^{\pm}. ⌐$$

Thus each occurrence of a subsentence has strictly positive polarity, strictly negative polarity, or both polarities, in the enclosing sentence.

PARTIAL SUBSTITUTION

We will need an extension of partial substitution to allow us to replace only strictly positive, or only strictly negative, occurrences of one subsentence with another.

Definition (partial substitution with polarity)

Suppose that $\mathcal{E}$, $\mathcal{F}$, and $S\langle \mathcal{E}^{+} \rangle$ are sentences; then $S\langle \mathcal{F}^{+} \rangle$ denotes the result of replacing zero, one, or more strictly positive occurrences of $\mathcal{E}$ in $S\langle \mathcal{E}^{+} \rangle$ with $\mathcal{F}$.

Similarly, suppose that $\mathcal{E}$, $\mathcal{F}$, and $S\langle \mathcal{E}^{-} \rangle$ are sentences; then $S\langle \mathcal{F}^{-} \rangle$ denotes the result of replacing zero, one, or more strictly negative occurrences of $\mathcal{E}$ in $S\langle \mathcal{E}^{-} \rangle$ with $\mathcal{F}$. ⌐

Here we write $S\langle \mathcal{E} \rangle$ as $S\langle \mathcal{E}^{+} \rangle$ so that later, when we refer to $S\langle \mathcal{F}^{+} \rangle$, it is clear that we are replacing only strictly positive occurrences of $\mathcal{E}$ with $\mathcal{F}$. (When we write $S\langle \mathcal{E}^{+} \rangle$, we may imagine that we have already selected zero, one, or more strictly positive occurrences of $\mathcal{E}$ to be replaced.) Similarly, we write $S\langle \mathcal{E} \rangle$ as $S\langle \mathcal{E}^{-} \rangle$ so that later, when we refer to $S\langle \mathcal{F}^{-} \rangle$, it is clear that we are replacing only strictly negative occurrences of $\mathcal{E}$ with $\mathcal{F}$.

Example.   Consider the sentence

$$S\langle P^+\rangle: \quad \textit{if } P^\pm \textit{ then } P^+ \textit{ else } (\textit{not } P^-).$$

This sentence contains three occurrences of the propositional symbol P, with positive, negative, and both polarities.

Then $S\langle Q^+\rangle$ denotes either of the sentences

$$\textit{if } P \textit{ then } P \textit{ else } (\textit{not } P),$$

that is, S itself (zero replacements), or

$$\textit{if } P \textit{ then } Q \textit{ else } (\textit{not } P),$$

that is, the result of replacing the only strictly positive occurrence of P with Q. ⌐

A similar extension can be defined for total substitution, but we will not need it here.

THE POLARITY PROPOSITION

The relation of polarity to the truth of a sentence is elucidated by the following proposition.

Proposition (polarity)
Suppose that $\mathcal{E}$, $\mathcal{F}$, and $S\langle \mathcal{E}^+\rangle$ are sentences. Then the sentence

$$\textit{if } (\textit{if } \mathcal{E} \textit{ then } \mathcal{F})$$
$$\textit{then } (\textit{if } S\langle \mathcal{E}^+\rangle \textit{ then } S\langle \mathcal{F}^+\rangle) \qquad\qquad (\textit{positive})$$

is valid.
Suppose that $\mathcal{E}$, $\mathcal{F}$, and $S\langle \mathcal{E}^-\rangle$ are sentences. Then the sentence

$$\textit{if } (\textit{if } \mathcal{E} \textit{ then } \mathcal{F})$$
$$\textit{then } (\textit{if } S\langle \mathcal{F}^-\rangle \textit{ then } S\langle \mathcal{E}^-\rangle) \qquad\qquad (\textit{negative})$$

is valid. ⌐

If a subsentence of the form $(\textit{if } \mathcal{E} \textit{ then } \mathcal{F})$ is true, we say informally that $\mathcal{F}$ is "truer" than $\mathcal{E}$, and that $\mathcal{E}$ is "falser" than $\mathcal{F}$. For, according to the semantic rule for implication, it is impossible for $\mathcal{E}$ to be true and $\mathcal{F}$ to be false in this case.

The proposition says, roughly, that the truth of a sentence is directly related to the truth of its strictly positive subsentences, but inversely related to the truth of its strictly negative subsentences. In other words, if we replace some strictly positive occurrences of a subsentence with a "truer" sentence (i.e., one that it implies), the entire sentence becomes "truer" (i.e., the resulting sentence is implied by the original). On the other hand, if we replace some strictly negative occurrences of a subsentence with a "truer" sentence, the entire sentence becomes "falser" (i.e., the resulting sentence implies the original). The proof of the proposition is omitted.

The reader is asked to use the *polarity* proposition in **Problem 1.10**.

PROBLEMS

As mentioned in the preface, in solving a problem, the reader may use any result or technique that appears in the text prior to the page reference for the problem. For example, in solving Problem 1.1, one may use any result or technique that appears before the boldface problem reference on page 24 or earlier. Also, the reader may use the results of any previous problem, and the results of previous parts of the same problem. For example, in solving Problem 2.2(b) of Chapter 2, the reader may use the results of Problems 2.1 and 2.2(a), as well as any of the results of the problems of Chapter 1.

Problem 1.1 (validity)   page 24

Consider the following sentences:

(a) $(if \ P \ then \ Q) \ or \ (if \ Q \ then \ P)$

(b) $(not \ Q) \ or \ not \ \begin{bmatrix} if \ P \ then \ (not \ Q) \\ and \\ P \end{bmatrix}$

(c) $(if \ P \ then \ (not \ Q)) \ \equiv \ not \ (P \ and \ Q)$

(d) $\begin{bmatrix} if \ (P \ or \ Q) \\ then \ R \end{bmatrix} \ \equiv \ \begin{bmatrix} if \ P \ then \ R \\ and \\ if \ Q \ then \ R \end{bmatrix}$

(e) $\begin{bmatrix} if \ P \\ then \ (Q \ and \ R) \end{bmatrix} \ \equiv \ \begin{bmatrix} if \ P \ then \ Q \\ or \\ if \ P \ then \ R \end{bmatrix}$

(f) $\begin{bmatrix} if \ P \\ then \ (if \ Q \ then \ R) \end{bmatrix} \ \equiv \ \begin{bmatrix} if \ (P \ and \ Q) \\ then \ R \end{bmatrix}$

(g) $\begin{bmatrix} if \ P \\ then \ (Q \ or \ R) \end{bmatrix} \ \equiv \ \begin{bmatrix} if \ (P \ and \ (not \ Q)) \\ then \ R \end{bmatrix}$

(h) $\begin{bmatrix} P \ and \\ if \ Q \ then \ R \end{bmatrix} \ \equiv \ \begin{bmatrix} if \ ((not \ P) \ or \ Q) \\ then \ (P \ and \ R) \end{bmatrix}$

(i)
$$\begin{bmatrix} P \\ \equiv \\ (Q \ \equiv \ R) \end{bmatrix} \ \equiv \ \begin{bmatrix} (P \ \equiv \ Q) \\ \equiv \\ R \end{bmatrix}$$

(j)
$$\begin{bmatrix} \textit{if } P \\ \textit{then } Q \ \textit{and } R \\ \textit{else } (\textit{not } Q) \ \textit{and } S \end{bmatrix} \ \equiv \ \begin{bmatrix} \textit{if } Q \\ \textit{then } P \ \textit{and } R \\ \textit{else } (\textit{not } P) \ \textit{and } S \end{bmatrix}$$

Some of these sentences are valid; some are not. Find which sentences are not valid and produce interpretations under which they are false. Prove the validity of the other sentences, using one of the two methods: truth tables and proof by falsification. Use each method at least once.

Problem 1.2 (frightful sentence) page 24

Establish the validity of the following sentence:

$$\textit{if } \begin{bmatrix} \begin{bmatrix} \textit{if } P_1 \ \textit{then} \ (P_2 \ \textit{or} \ P_3) \\ \textit{else} \ (P_3 \ \textit{or} \ P_4) \end{bmatrix} \ \textit{and} \\[2mm] \begin{bmatrix} \begin{bmatrix} \textit{if } P_3 \ \textit{then} \ (\textit{not } P_6) \\ \textit{else} \ (\textit{if } P_4 \ \textit{then} \ P_1) \end{bmatrix} \ \textit{and} \\[2mm] \begin{bmatrix} \textit{not} \ (P_2 \ \textit{and} \ P_5) \ \textit{and} \\ (\textit{if } P_2 \ \textit{then} \ P_5) \end{bmatrix} \end{bmatrix} \end{bmatrix}$$

$$\textit{then} \ \textit{not} \ (\textit{if } P_3 \ \textit{then} \ P_6).$$

Problem 1.3 (paraphrasing connectives) page 28

(a) The valid sentence schema

$$(\textit{not } \mathcal{F})$$
$$\equiv$$
$$(\textit{if } \mathcal{F} \ \textit{then false else true})$$

suggests that the negation connective *not* can be "paraphrased" in terms of the conditional connective *if-then-else*. Show that the other connectives (i.e., *and*, *or*, *if-then*, and $\equiv$) can be paraphrased in the same way in terms of the conditional connective. In other words, any sentence is equivalent to one whose only connective is *if-then-else*.

*(b) Show that the connectives cannot all be paraphrased in terms of the connectives *and* and *or* alone. In particular, find a sentence $\mathcal{F}$ that is equivalent to no sentence $\mathcal{G}$ whose only connectives are *and* and *or*. Say why.

Problem 1.4 (tardy bus) page 29

Suppose the following three statements are given:

A_1: If Bill takes the bus, then if the bus is late, Bill misses his appointment.

A_2: If Bill misses his appointment and Bill feels downcast, Bill shouldn't go home.

A_3: If Bill doesn't get the job, then Bill feels downcast and Bill should go home.

Assuming these statements are all true, which of the following statements are also true?

G_1: If Bill takes the bus and the bus is late, then Bill does get the job.

G_2: If Bill misses his appointment and Bill should go home, then Bill does get the job.

G_3: If the bus is late, then either Bill does not take the bus or Bill does not miss his appointment.

G_4: If the bus is late or if Bill misses his appointment, then Bill feels downcast.

G_5: If Bill should go home and Bill takes the bus, then Bill does not feel downcast if the bus is late.

Let P_1 stand for "Bill takes the bus," P_2 for "the bus is late," P_3 for "Bill misses his appointment," P_4 for "Bill feels downcast," P_5 for "Bill gets the job," and P_6 for "Bill should go home." For each of the sentences G_i ($i = 1, 2, 3, 4, 5$), consider the sentence

$$\text{if } (A_1 \text{ and } A_2 \text{ and } A_3) \text{ then } G_i,$$

expressed in propositional logic in terms of the propositional symbols P_1, P_2, P_3, P_4, P_5, and P_6. If the sentence is valid, give a proof. Otherwise, give an interpretation under which it is false.

Note the difference between the inclusive "or" and the exclusive "either-or." The inclusive or is (P or Q), and is true in particular in the case in which both P and Q are true; the exclusive either-or is

$$\big((P \text{ or } Q) \quad \text{and} \quad \text{not } (P \text{ and } Q)\big)$$

and is false in particular in the case in which both P and Q are true.

Problem 1.5 (love)   page 29

Use propositional logic to answer the following questions. (This problem is due to R. Smullyan.)

(a) Suppose the following two statements are true:

(1)   I love Pat or I love Quincy.

(2)   If I love Pat, then I love Quincy.

Does it necessarily follow that I love Pat? Does it necessarily follow that I love Quincy?

(b) Suppose someone asks me,

"Is it really true that if you love Pat, then you also love Quincy?"

I reply,

"If it is true, then I love Pat."

Does it follow that I love Pat? Does it follow that I love Quincy?

(c) Suppose someone asks me,

"Is it really true that if you love Pat, then you also love Quincy?"

I reply,

"If it is true, then I love Pat, and if I love Pat, then it is true."

Which do I necessarily love?

(d) This time we are given three people, Pat, Quincy, and Ray. Suppose the following facts are given:

(1) I love at least one of the three.

(2) If I love Pat but not Ray, then I also love Quincy.

(3) I love both Ray and Quincy or I love neither one.

(4) If I love Ray, then I also love Pat.

Which of the three do I love?

Hint: Let P stand for "I love Pat," Q for "I love Quincy," and R for "I love Ray." Then determine the validity of the appropriate propositional-logic sentences. For example, in part (a) we are actually asked if the sentences

$$if \begin{bmatrix} P & or & Q \\ & and & \\ if & P & then & Q \end{bmatrix} \quad and \quad if \begin{bmatrix} P & or & Q \\ & and & \\ if & P & then & Q \end{bmatrix}$$
$$then \ \ P \qquad\qquad\qquad\qquad then \ \ Q$$

are valid.\

Problem 1.6 (the land of the liars and truth tellers) page 29

Use propositional logic to solve the following problem.

A certain country is inhabited entirely by people who either always tell the truth or always tell lies and who will respond to questions with only a yes or a no.

A tourist comes to a fork in the road, where one branch leads to a restaurant and the other does not. There is no sign indicating which branch to take, but there is an inhabitant, Mr. X, standing at the fork.

What single yes/no question can the hungry tourist ask to find the way to the restaurant?

Hint: Let P stand for "Mr. X always tells the truth" and Q stand for "The left-hand branch leads to the restaurant." We must find a propositional-logic sentence $\mathcal{F}$ in terms of P and Q such that, whether or not Mr. X tells the truth, his answer to the question "Is $\mathcal{F}$ true?" will be yes if and only if Q is true. Construct the truth table that $\mathcal{F}$ must have, in terms of P and Q, and then design an appropriate sentence $\mathcal{F}$ accordingly.

Problem 1.7 (substitution)   page 35

Let $\mathcal{F}$ be the sentence
$$\mathcal{F}: \begin{bmatrix} P \ \text{and} \ Q \\ \text{or} \\ \text{if} \ R \ \text{then} \ (P \ \text{and} \ Q \ \text{and} \ R) \end{bmatrix}.$$

Apply the following substitutions. (Give three possible results of applying each partial substitution.)

(a) If $\mathcal{F}$ is $\mathcal{F}[P \ \text{and} \ Q]$, what is $\mathcal{F}[P]$?

(b) If $\mathcal{F}$ is $\mathcal{F}\langle P \ \text{and} \ Q\rangle$, what is $\mathcal{F}\langle P\rangle$?

(c) If $\mathcal{F}$ is $\mathcal{F}[P, \ P \ \text{and} \ Q]$, what is $\mathcal{F}[S, \ P]$?

(d) If $\mathcal{F}$ is $\mathcal{F}\langle P, \ P \ \text{and} \ Q\rangle$, what is $\mathcal{F}\langle S, \ P\rangle$?

Problem 1.8 (simplification)   page 41

Simplify the following sentences as much as possible:

(a) $not \ \big(if \ true \ then \ (not \ P)\big)$

(b) $P \ or \ \big(if \ true \ then \ (true \ or \ Q)\big)$

(c) $\begin{bmatrix} if \ not \ (P \ or \ P) \\ then \ (not \ Q) \ or \ false \end{bmatrix}$

(d) $\begin{bmatrix} P \ and \ P \\ and \\ not \ \big(not \ (Q \ or \ false)\big) \end{bmatrix} \ or \ not \ \begin{bmatrix} if \ true \ then \ P \\ and \\ if \ R \ then \ Q \ else \ Q \end{bmatrix}.$

Problem 1.9 (polarity annotation)   page 44

Annotate all the subsentences of the following sentence according to their polarity:

$$(not \ P) \ and \ \begin{bmatrix} if \ \begin{bmatrix} if \ Q \ then \ R \ else \ P \\ or \\ Q \ \equiv \ (P \ or \ R) \end{bmatrix} \\ then \ (not \ R) \end{bmatrix}.$$

*Problem 1.10 (polarity proposition)   page 46

Let
$$\mathcal{E}_1: \ if \ P \ then \ (not \ Q)$$

$$\mathcal{S}_1[\mathcal{E}_1]: \quad (not\ Q)\ or\ not \begin{bmatrix} if\ P\ then\ (not\ Q) \\ and \\ P \end{bmatrix}$$

and

$$\mathcal{E}_2: \quad not\ Q$$

$$\mathcal{S}_2[\mathcal{E}_2]: \quad if\ P\ then\ (not\ Q).$$

Determine which of the following sentences are valid. For each valid sentence, either use the *polarity* proposition (and simplification) to prove its validity, or indicate that the *polarity* proposition does not apply.

(a)   *if* $\mathcal{S}_1[\mathcal{E}_1]$ *then* $\mathcal{S}_1[true]$ (e)   *if* $\mathcal{S}_2[\mathcal{E}_2]$ *then* $\mathcal{S}_2[true]$

(b)   *if* $\mathcal{S}_1[\mathcal{E}_1]$ *then* $\mathcal{S}_1[false]$ (f)   *if* $\mathcal{S}_2[\mathcal{E}_2]$ *then* $\mathcal{S}_2[false]$

(c)   *if* $\mathcal{S}_1[true]$ *then* $\mathcal{S}_1[\mathcal{E}_1]$ (g)   *if* $\mathcal{S}_2[true]$ *then* $\mathcal{S}_2[\mathcal{E}_2]$

(d)   *if* $\mathcal{S}_1[false]$ *then* $\mathcal{S}_1[\mathcal{E}_1]$ (h)   *if* $\mathcal{S}_2[false]$ *then* $\mathcal{S}_2[\mathcal{E}_2].$

2

Deductive Tableaux

One of our central concerns is in developing methods for establishing the validity of sentences. If our only interest were in propositional logic, we might be happy with the truth-table or proof-by-falsification methods. Our main reason for studying propositional logic, however, is to introduce techniques that we can later extend to more expressive logics. The truth-table or proof-by-falsification methods, unfortunately, apply only to propositional logic.

In this chapter, we introduce a formal deductive system for proving the validity of propositional-logic sentences. This *deductive-tableau* system will be extended to deductive systems for predicate logic and the axiomatic theories, which we shall introduce later. It can also serve as the foundation for computer theorem-proving programs.

2.1 TABLEAUX: NOTATION AND MEANING

The fundamental structure of our deductive system is the *tableau*, which consists of a collection of *rows* of two *columns* each. Each row contains a sentence, either an *assertion* $\mathcal{A}$ or a *goal* $\mathcal{G}$. The assertions appear in the first column and the goals in the second column. An assertion and a goal may not both appear in the same row.

For example, the tableau $\mathcal{T}_1$ has two assertions and two goals.

assertions	goals
	G1. Q
A2. P or Q	
A3. if P then R	
	G4. R

Tableau T_1

MEANING OF A TABLEAU

For a given interpretation of its propositional symbols, a tableau will be either true or false according to the following semantic rule for tableaux.

Definition (semantic rule for tableaux)

A tableau with the assertions A_1, A_2, ..., A_m and the goals G_1, G_2, ..., G_n is *true under* an interpretation I if the following condition holds:

if all the assertions A_i are true under I,
then at least one of the goals G_j is true under I.

On the other hand, the tableau is *false under I* if the following condition holds:

all the assertions A_i are true under I and
all the goals G_j are false under I.   ◢

Example.   Consider the tableau T_2:

assertions	goals
	G1. *not P*
A2. Q or R	
	G3. if P then Q

Tableau T_2

This tableau is true under any interpretation in which

- Q and R are false, because then the assertion A2 is false, or
- P is false, because then the goal G1 is true (and also the goal G3 is true), or

- Q is true, because then the goal G3 is true.

On the other hand, the tableau T_2 is false under any interpretation in which

- P is true, Q is false, and R is true, because then the assertion is true but both goals are false. In fact, these are the only interpretations under which T_2 is false. ⌐

Note that the order in which the rows occur in the tableau has no significance. In other words, we can reorder the rows without changing the truth of the tableau. Similarly, the multiplicity of the rows has no significance. That is, we can add new copies of any assertion or goal without changing the truth of the tableau.

Remark (semantic rule). By the semantic rule for tableaux and propositional logic, a tableau T is true under an interpretation I if and only if

> at least one of the assertions A_i is false under I or
> at least one of the goals G_j is true under I.

We shall regard this as an alternative form of the rule. ⌐

THE ASSOCIATED SENTENCE

The meaning of a given tableau can be characterized in terms of a single propositional-logic sentence.

Definition (associated sentence)

> If a tableau contains the assertions
>
> $$A_1, A_2, \ldots, A_m$$
>
> and the goals
>
> $$G_1, G_2, \ldots, G_n,$$
>
> its *associated sentence* is
>
> > *if* $\begin{bmatrix} A_1 & and & A_2 & and & \ldots & and & A_m \end{bmatrix}$
> > *then* $\begin{bmatrix} G_1 & or & G_2 & or & \ldots & or & G_n \end{bmatrix}.$ ⌐

Example. The associated sentence of the tableau T_2 is

$$if \ (Q \ or \ R) \ then \ \begin{bmatrix} not \ P \\ or \\ if \ P \ then \ Q \end{bmatrix}.$$

The associated sentence of the earlier tableau T_1 is

$$if \ \begin{bmatrix} P \ or \ Q \\ and \\ if \ P \ then \ R \end{bmatrix} \ then \ (Q \ or \ R). \ ⌐$$

Remark (no assertions or no goals).   In the special case in which a tableau has no assertions (i.e., if $m = 0$), the conjunction

> $\mathcal{A}_1$ *and* $\mathcal{A}_2$ *and* ... *and* $\mathcal{A}_m$

is taken to be the truth symbol *true*, and the associated sentence is

> *if true*
> *then* $\begin{bmatrix} \mathcal{G}_1 & or & \mathcal{G}_2 & or & ... & or & \mathcal{G}_n \end{bmatrix}$,

which is equivalent to

> $\mathcal{G}_1$ *or* $\mathcal{G}_2$ *or* ... *or* $\mathcal{G}_n$.

If furthermore there is only one goal $\mathcal{G}_1$ (i.e., if $m = 0$ and $n = 1$), the disjunction

> $\mathcal{G}_1$ *or* $\mathcal{G}_2$ *or* ... *or* $\mathcal{G}_n$

is taken to be

> $\mathcal{G}_1$

itself, and the associated sentence is simply $\mathcal{G}_1$.

On the other hand, in the special case in which the tableau has no goals (i.e., if $n = 0$), the disjunction

> $\mathcal{G}_1$ *or* $\mathcal{G}_2$ *or* ... *or* $\mathcal{G}_n$

is taken to be the truth symbol *false*, and the associated sentence is

> *if* $\begin{bmatrix} \mathcal{A}_1 & and & \mathcal{A}_2 & and & ... & and & \mathcal{A}_m \end{bmatrix}$
> *then false*,

which is equivalent to

> *not* $\begin{bmatrix} \mathcal{A}_1 & and & \mathcal{A}_2 & and & ... & and & \mathcal{A}_m \end{bmatrix}$. ◣

The importance of the associated sentence follows from the following property.

Proposition (truth of a tableau)

> A tableau is true under an interpretation $\mathcal{I}$
>   if and only if
> its associated sentence is true under $\mathcal{I}$. ◣

Proof.   For an arbitrary interpretation $\mathcal{I}$,

> a tableau is true under $\mathcal{I}$

if and only if (by the semantic rule for tableaux)

> if all the assertions $\mathcal{A}_i$ are true under $\mathcal{I}$
> then at least one of the goals $\mathcal{G}_j$ is true under $\mathcal{I}$

if and only if (by the semantic rules for *and* and *or*)

>if $[\mathcal{A}_1 \ \textit{and} \ \mathcal{A}_2 \ \textit{and} \ \ldots \ \textit{and} \ \mathcal{A}_m]$ is true under $\mathcal{I}$
>then $[\mathcal{G}_1 \ \textit{or} \ \mathcal{G}_2 \ \textit{or} \ \ldots \ \textit{or} \ \mathcal{G}_n]$ is true under $\mathcal{I}$

if and only if (by the semantic rule for *if-then*)

>the associated sentence is true under $\mathcal{I}$. ⌐

VALIDITY

The notion of validity for a tableau is analogous to that for a sentence.

Definition (validity of a tableau)

>A tableau is said to be *valid* if it is true under every interpretation.

>Equivalently, a tableau is *valid* if its associated sentence is valid. ⌐

Example. The tableau $\mathcal{T}_2$ is not valid; we have already seen that it is false under an interpretation for which P is true, Q is false, and R is true.

On the other hand, the tableau $\mathcal{T}_1$ is valid. We shall give later a formal method for proving the validity of tableaux; however, we can informally demonstrate the validity of $\mathcal{T}_1$ by an extension of the proof-by-falsification method, as follows:

Suppose $\mathcal{T}_1$ is false under some interpretation; then

- Each of its assertions is true and each of its goals is false.

- In particular, the goals Q and R are both false.

- Because the assertion $(P \ or \ Q)$ is true and Q is false, we know that P must be true.

- Because the assertion $(if \ P \ then \ R)$ is true and P is true, we know that R must be true. But this contradicts our previous conclusion that R is false. Hence $\mathcal{T}_1$ cannot be false under any interpretation; that is, $\mathcal{T}_1$ is valid.

Alternatively, one can demonstrate the validity of the associated sentence

$$if \quad \begin{bmatrix} P \ or \ Q \\ and \\ if \ P \ then \ R \end{bmatrix} \quad then \quad (Q \ or \ R)$$

using one of the techniques presented in Chapter 1. ⌐

Remark (special cases). A tableau is automatically valid if one of its assertions is the truth symbol *false* or if one of its goals is the truth symbol *true*, that is,

false	

or

	true

This is because the corresponding associated sentences of form

$$\begin{array}{l} \textit{if } [\ldots \ \textit{and false and } \ldots] \\ \textit{then } \ldots \end{array} \quad \text{and} \quad \begin{array}{l} \textit{if } \ldots \\ \textit{then } [\ldots \ \textit{or true or } \ldots] \end{array}$$

are valid. These two special cases will be important to remember later.

EQUIVALENCE

The notion of equivalence for tableaux is again analogous to that for sentences.

Definition (equivalence of tableaux)

> Two tableaux are said to be *equivalent* if, under every interpretation, they have the same truth-value.

> Alternatively, two tableaux are *equivalent* if their associated sentences are equivalent.

Example. The following tableau T_2' is equivalent to the preceding tableau T_2. For, this tableau is false only under an interpretation in which P is true, Q is false, and R is true. These are also the only interpretations under which T_2 is false.

assertions	goals
	G1′. Q
A2′. P	
	G3′. *not* (*if* (*not* R) *then* Q)

Tableau T_2'

IMPLIED-ROW PROPERTY

The *implied-row* property gives a simple condition under which we may add or remove assertions or goals from a given tableau while *preserving its equivalence*. In other words, the tableau obtained is equivalent to the given tableau.

Proposition (implied row)

Assertion part

Suppose a sentence $\mathcal{A}$ is implied by all the assertions $\mathcal{A}_1, \ldots, \mathcal{A}_m$ of a tableau $\mathcal{T}$, that is,

$$(\dagger) \quad \begin{array}{l} \textit{if } [\mathcal{A}_1 \textit{ and } \ldots \textit{ and } \mathcal{A}_m] \\ \textit{then } \mathcal{A} \end{array}$$

is valid. Then $\mathcal{T}$ is equivalent to the tableau $\mathcal{T}_A$ obtained from $\mathcal{T}$ by introducing the new assertion

$\mathcal{A}$	

Goal part

Similarly, suppose a sentence $\mathcal{G}$ implies some of the goals $\mathcal{G}_1, \ldots, \mathcal{G}_n$ of the tableau $\mathcal{T}$, that is,

$$(\ddagger) \quad \begin{array}{l} \textit{if } \mathcal{G} \\ \textit{then } [\mathcal{G}_1 \textit{ or } \ldots \textit{ or } \mathcal{G}_n] \end{array}$$

is valid. Then $\mathcal{T}$ is equivalent to the tableau $\mathcal{T}_G$ obtained by introducing the new goal

	$\mathcal{G}$

Proof.   By ($\dagger$), it follows that

$$\mathcal{A}_1 \textit{ and } \ldots \textit{ and } \mathcal{A}_m$$

is equivalent to

$$[\mathcal{A}_1 \textit{ and } \ldots \textit{ and } \mathcal{A}_m] \textit{ and } \mathcal{A}.$$

Therefore, the sentence associated with $\mathcal{T}$, that is,

$$\begin{array}{l} \textit{if } [\mathcal{A}_1 \textit{ and } \ldots \textit{ and } \mathcal{A}_m] \\ \textit{then } [\mathcal{G}_1 \textit{ or } \ldots \textit{ or } \mathcal{G}_n] \end{array}$$

is equivalent to the sentence associated with $\mathcal{T}_A$,

$$\begin{array}{l} \textit{if } [\mathcal{A}_1 \textit{ and } \ldots \textit{ and } \mathcal{A}_m] \textit{ and } \mathcal{A} \\ \textit{then } [\mathcal{G}_1 \textit{ or } \ldots \textit{ or } \mathcal{G}_n]. \end{array}$$

The sentence associated with $\mathcal{T}$ is also equivalent, by (‡), to the sentence associated with $\mathcal{T}_\mathcal{G}$, that is,

> *if* $[\mathcal{A}_1$ *and* ... *and* $\mathcal{A}_m]$
> *then* $[\mathcal{G}_1$ *or* ... *or* $\mathcal{G}_n]$ *or* $\mathcal{G}$.   ⌐

Remark (valid assertions and contradictory goals).   By the *implied-row* property, any valid sentence $\mathcal{A}$ may be added to a tableau as an assertion, preserving the equivalence of the tableau, because then the sentence (†) is automatically valid. In other words, the tableau before $\mathcal{A}$ is added is equivalent to the tableau after $\mathcal{A}$ is added.

Applying the property in reverse, for any valid sentence $\mathcal{A}$, the assertion

$\mathcal{A}$	

may be dropped from a tableau, preserving its equivalence. In particular, the assertion

true	

may always be dropped, because the truth symbol *true* is valid. We shall refer to this as the *trivial assertion*.

Similarly, if $\mathcal{G}$ is a contradictory sentence (i.e., one that is false under any interpretation), the goal

	$\mathcal{G}$

may be added to or dropped from any tableau, preserving equivalence, because then the sentence (‡) of the *implied-row* property is automatically valid. In particular, the goal

	false

may be dropped from any tableau, because the truth symbol *false* is contradictory. We shall refer to this as the *trivial goal*.   ⌐

Remark (initial tableau).   In our deductive system, presented in the next section, we use as our *initial tableau* a special tableau that consists of m assertions $\mathcal{A}_1, \ldots, \mathcal{A}_m$ and a single goal $\mathcal{G}$

assertions	goals
$\mathcal{A}_1$	
$\vdots$	
$\mathcal{A}_m$	
	$\mathcal{G}$

where each assertion $\mathcal{A}_i$ is a sentence known to be valid. (We admit the possibility that $m = 0$.)

This tableau is equivalent (by repeated application of the *implied-row* property) to the tableau

assertions	goals
	$\mathcal{G}$

in which $\mathcal{G}$ is the only goal. The sentence associated with this tableau is simply $\mathcal{G}$. Hence the initial tableau is valid if and only if $\mathcal{G}$ is valid. ⌐

DUALITY PROPERTY

The *duality property* states that we can move sentences freely between the assertion and goal columns simply by negating them, obtaining an equivalent tableau.

Proposition (duality)

> A tableau containing an assertion $\mathcal{A}$
> is equivalent to
> the tableau containing instead the goal (*not* $\mathcal{A}$).
>
> (*assertion-to-goal*)
>
> A tableau containing a goal $\mathcal{G}$
> is equivalent to
> the tableau containing instead the assertion (*not* $\mathcal{G}$).
>
> (*goal-to-assertion*) ⌐

Proof.   To prove the *assertion-to-goal* part, observe that, under a given interpretation,

> the original tableau (containing $\mathcal{A}$ as an assertion) is false

if and only if (by the semantic rule for tableaux)

    $\mathcal{A}$ is true, the other assertions are all true, and the goals are all false

if and only if (by the semantic rule for *not*)

    the other assertions are all true, (*not* $\mathcal{A}$) is false, and the goals are all false

if and only if (by the semantic rule for tableaux, again)

    the new tableau (containing (*not* $\mathcal{A}$) as a goal) is false.

Thus the original tableau (containing $\mathcal{A}$ as an assertion) is false under a given interpretation $\mathcal{I}$ if and only if the new tableau (containing (*not* $\mathcal{A}$) as a goal) is false under $\mathcal{I}$; that is, the two tableaux are equivalent.

The *goal-to-assertion* part is proved similarly.　◢

By the *duality* property, assertions and goals may be moved freely from one column to the other simply by negating them. Thus the distinction between assertions and goals is artificial and does not increase the "logical power" of the system. In particular, any tableau is equivalent to a tableau with only assertions and no goals and to a tableau with only goals and no assertions. Nevertheless, distinguishing between assertions and goals makes proofs easier to understand.

Remark (replacing versus adding rows). The *duality* property allows us to replace an assertion $\mathcal{A}$ with a goal (*not* $\mathcal{A}$), maintaining the equivalence of the tableau. We could also add the new goal (*not* $\mathcal{A}$) to the original tableau without replacing the assertion $\mathcal{A}$, and still maintain the equivalence of the tableau. To see this, we first note that the original tableau is equivalent to one with two copies of the assertion $\mathcal{A}$; we may then (by the *duality* property) replace only one of them with the goal (*not* $\mathcal{A}$), obtaining an equivalent tableau.

In the same way, any property that allows us to replace one row with another also allows us to add the new row without removing the original one.　◢

SUBTABLEAUX

It will be useful for us to think of a tableau as a set of rows, and to apply to tableaux some notions about sets.

Definition (subtableau)

    A tableau $\mathcal{T}'$ is a *subtableau* of a tableau $\mathcal{T}$, written $\mathcal{T}' \subseteq \mathcal{T}$, if every row of $\mathcal{T}'$ is also a row of $\mathcal{T}$.　◢

Proposition (subtableau)

For any tableaux T and T',

if $T' \subseteq T$
then, for any interpretation $\mathcal{I}$,
if T' is true under $\mathcal{I}$
then T is true under $\mathcal{I}$. ⌐

Proof. Suppose T' is true under $\mathcal{I}$. Then (by the alternative form of the semantic rule for tableaux) at least one assertion of T' is false under $\mathcal{I}$ or at least one goal of T' is true under $\mathcal{I}$. But since (by the definition of a subtableau) every row of T' is also a row of T, this means that at least one assertion of T is false under $\mathcal{I}$ or at least one goal of T is true under $\mathcal{I}$; that is (by the semantic rule, again), T is true under $\mathcal{I}$. ⌐

Definition (union of tableaux)

The *union* $T_1 \cup T_2$ of two tableaux T_1 and T_2 is the tableau whose rows are all the rows of T_1 and all the rows of T_2. ⌐

In other words, the assertions of $T_1 \cup T_2$ are the assertions of T_1 and the assertions of T_2, and the goals of $T_1 \cup T_2$ are the goals of T_1 and the goals of T_2.

Proposition (union tableau)

For any tableaux T_1 and T_2 and any interpretation $\mathcal{I}$,

$T_1 \cup T_2$ is true under $\mathcal{I}$
if and only if
T_1 is true under $\mathcal{I}$ or
T_2 is true under $\mathcal{I}$. ⌐

The proof of this proposition is requested in **Problem 2.1(a)**.

Proposition (intermediate tableau)

For any tableaux T_1, T_2, and T_3,

if $T_1 \subseteq T_2 \subseteq T_3$
then if T_1 is equivalent to T_3
then T_1 is equivalent to T_2 and T_2 is equivalent to T_3. ⌐

As a consequence of this *intermediate-tableau* property, we observe that if we can add a certain number of rows to a tableau while preserving its equivalence, we can add instead any portion of those rows and still preserve equivalence. The proof is requested in **Problem 2.1(b)**.

2.2   THE DEDUCTIVE PROCESS

In the deductive system for propositional logic we are about to describe, we establish the validity of a tableau by applying *deduction rules* that add new rows to the tableau in such a way that equivalence is preserved; in other words, the new tableau (after applying the rule) is equivalent to the old tableau (before applying the rule). Hence at each stage the new tableau is equivalent to the initial tableau. The process continues until we obtain a tableau that is clearly valid; in this case, we know that the initial tableau is valid too.

Simplification is a fundamental part of the operation of the deductive system.

SIMPLIFICATION

We have already discussed simplification as applied to sentences, in which a sub-sentence is replaced by an equivalent but simpler sentence. An assertion or goal introduced into a tableau is first automatically subjected to all the simplifications of the catalog in Section 1.9. This applies to the rows of the initial tableau as well as rows introduced subsequently by deduction rules. In other words, the deductive system will never deal with a tableau with unsimplified rows.

Example.   In the deductive system, we shall never derive a tableau containing the assertion

$$P \ or \ \boxed{not \ \big(not \ (Q \ and \ R)\big)}$$

The boxed subsentence would automatically be replaced with $(Q \ and \ R)$, by application of the simplification

$$not \ (not \ \mathcal{F}) \ \Rightarrow \ \mathcal{F},$$

yielding the assertion

$P \ or \ (Q \ and \ R)$	

OUTLINE OF THE DEDUCTIVE SYSTEM

In the deductive system, to *prove* that a given sentence $\mathcal{S}$ is valid, we form an initial tableau and then apply deduction rules successively until we arrive at the final tableau.

Initial Tableau

We form the *initial tableau*, whose sole goal is the (simplified) sentence $\mathcal{S}$. We may (by the *implied-row* property) include as assertions $\mathcal{A}_1, \ldots, \mathcal{A}_m$ any sentences that have previously been proved (by this deductive system) to be valid.

assertions	goals
$\mathcal{A}_1$	
$\vdots$	
$\mathcal{A}_m$	
	$\mathcal{S}$

Therefore,

$\mathcal{S}$ is valid if and only if the initial tableau is valid.

Applying Deduction Rules

The tableau is developed by applying *deduction rules* successively; each rule adds one or more rows to the tableau in such a way that equivalence is preserved, that is,

the new tableau (after the rows are added)
is equivalent to
the old tableau (before the rows are added).

Hence each tableau produced by applying another deduction rule is equivalent to the initial tableau.

Each new row contains either an assertion or a goal, which is simplified before being introduced into the tableau.

We shall say that a rule that preserves equivalence is *sound*.

Final Tableau

The process continues until one of the new rows contains the goal *true*, that is,

	true

or the assertion *false*, that is,

false	

We know that

the final tableau is valid.

Because the final tableau is valid and the deduction rules preserve equivalence, this means that the initial tableau, and hence the given sentence S, are also valid. We shall say that the final tableau is a *proof* of both the initial tableau and of the sentence S. Any sentence that has a proof will be called a *theorem* of propositional logic. Any theorem S may be added as an assertion in the initial tableaux of subsequent proofs. This is because S has been proved to be valid, and we may add a valid sentence as an assertion to any tableau, while preserving the equivalence of the tableau.

THE DEDUCTION RULES

The deduction rules we will employ are divided into four groups:

- The *rewriting* rule, which replaces a subsentence with an equivalent sentence.

- The *splitting* rules, which break a row down into its logical components.

- The *resolution* rule, which performs a case analysis on the truth of a subsentence.

- The *equivalence* rule, which facilitates our handling of the equivalence connective $\equiv$.

Of these groups, only the *resolution* rule is essential. In other words, if a sentence is valid, it can be proved using the *resolution* rule alone.

Each deduction rule requires that certain *required rows* already be present in the tableau and introduces certain *generated rows* into the tableau. For simplicity, in applying a deduction rule, we always add rows, never delete rows.

In the tableau notation, we write a rule in the form

	assertions	goals
T_r:		
T_g:		

where the required rows are those that appear above the double line, and the generated rows are those that appear below the double line.

The required rows form the *required subtableau,* denoted by $\mathcal{T}_r$, and the generated rows form the *generated subtableau,* denoted by $\mathcal{T}_g$.

The deduction rule is applied only if the required subtableau $\mathcal{T}_r$ occurs as part of the old tableau. The new tableau is obtained by adding the generated subtableau $\mathcal{T}_g$ to the old tableau. That is, we require that $\mathcal{T}_r$ be a subtableau of the old tableau $\mathcal{T}$ (that is, $\mathcal{T}_r \subseteq \mathcal{T}$), and obtain the new tableau $\mathcal{T} \cup \mathcal{T}_g$.

We shall ensure that all of our deduction rules are sound, that is, that they preserve equivalence.

2.3   REWRITING RULE

Simplification is applied automatically because it always reduces the complexity of the tableau and never makes it more difficult to prove. There is another category of equivalent sentences that can be used to manipulate a tableau, such as *and-or distributivity,*

$$\mathcal{F} \ and \ (\mathcal{G} \ or \ \mathcal{H}) \ \Leftrightarrow \ (\mathcal{F} \ and \ \mathcal{G}) \ or \ (\mathcal{F} \ and \ \mathcal{H}),$$

which are not regarded as simplifications. Replacing subsentences with equivalent sentences from this category does not necessarily make the tableau simpler, but it may sometimes make it easier to prove. We call this operation *rewriting.*

We do not apply rewriting automatically; we regard it as a deduction rule, to be applied only at our discretion. (In this respect, we deviate from the usual use of the term "rewriting" in the literature.) Also, we do not replace the rewritten assertion or goal; both the original row and the rewritten row are included in the new tableau because we are not sure which will be used in the proof. This is another way in which rewriting differs from simplification.

Rewritings may be applied in either direction; for this reason, they are written with a double-headed arrow ($\Leftrightarrow$). Only one occurrence of a subsentence can be replaced with each application of the rule. For example, *and* associativity,

$$\mathcal{F} \ and \ (\mathcal{G} \ and \ \mathcal{H}) \ \Leftrightarrow \ (\mathcal{F} \ and \ \mathcal{G}) \ and \ \mathcal{H},$$

can be used right-to-left to replace a single subsentence occurrence of the form $\big((\mathcal{F} \ and \ \mathcal{G}) \ and \ \mathcal{H}\big)$ with the corresponding sentence of the form $\big(\mathcal{F} \ and \ (\mathcal{G} \ and \ \mathcal{H})\big)$, as well as in the other direction.

Justification of the *rewriting* rule, that is, showing that it is sound, is straightforward because we are always replacing a subsentence with an equivalent sentence. By the *substitutivity-of-equivalence* and *implied-row* propositions, the new tableau contains an additional row equivalent to one of the given rows.

Rewriting is never an essential step; it is always possible to do without it. It can, however, give us simpler and more natural proofs.

Example.   Let us apply left-to-right the *and-or* distributivity rewriting,

$$\mathcal{F} \ and \ (\mathcal{G} \ or \ \mathcal{H}) \ \Leftrightarrow \ (\mathcal{F} \ and \ \mathcal{G}) \ or \ (\mathcal{F} \ and \ \mathcal{H}),$$

to a tableau containing the goal

	$P \ and \ \boxed{(Q \ and \ (R \ or \ S))}$

(As usual, we enclose the subsentence to be replaced in a box.) We obtain the
new goal

	$P \ and \ ((Q \ and \ R) \ or \ (Q \ and \ S))$

which is added to the tableau without dropping the given goal. ⌙

CATALOG OF REWRITINGS

We present several rewritings, to be used at our discretion. Note that this catalog
does not include simplifications, which are performed automatically. A catalog of
simplifications is contained in Section 1.9.

- Negation

$$not \ (\mathcal{F} \ and \ \mathcal{G}) \ \Leftrightarrow \ (not \ \mathcal{F}) \ or \ (not \ \mathcal{G}) \qquad (not \ and)$$

$$not \ (\mathcal{F} \ or \ \mathcal{G}) \ \Leftrightarrow \ (not \ \mathcal{F}) \ and \ (not \ \mathcal{G}) \qquad (not \ or)$$

$$not \ (if \ \mathcal{F} \ then \ \mathcal{G}) \ \Leftrightarrow \ \mathcal{F} \ and \ (not \ \mathcal{G}) \qquad (not \ if)$$

$$not \ (\mathcal{F} \equiv \mathcal{G}) \ \Leftrightarrow \ \mathcal{F} \equiv (not \ \mathcal{G}) \qquad (not \ iff)$$

$$not \ (if \ \mathcal{F} \ then \ \mathcal{G} \ else \ \mathcal{H}) \ \Leftrightarrow \ if \ \mathcal{F} \ then \ (not \ \mathcal{G}) \ else \ (not \ \mathcal{H}) \quad (not \ cond)$$

- Elimination

$$if \ \mathcal{F} \ then \ \mathcal{G} \ \Leftrightarrow \ (not \ \mathcal{F}) \ or \ \mathcal{G} \qquad (if \ or)$$

$$\mathcal{F} \equiv \mathcal{G} \ \Leftrightarrow \ (if \ \mathcal{F} \ then \ \mathcal{G}) \ and \ (if \ \mathcal{G} \ then \ \mathcal{F}) \qquad (iff \ and)$$

$$\mathcal{F} \equiv \mathcal{G} \ \Leftrightarrow \ (\mathcal{F} \ and \ \mathcal{G}) \ or \ ((not \ \mathcal{F}) \ and \ (not \ \mathcal{G})) \qquad (iff \ or)$$

$$if \ \mathcal{F} \ then \ \mathcal{G} \ else \ \mathcal{H} \ \Leftrightarrow \ (if \ \mathcal{F} \ then \ \mathcal{G}) \ and \ (if \ (not \ \mathcal{F}) \ then \ \mathcal{H}) \ (cond \ and)$$

$$if \ \mathcal{F} \ then \ \mathcal{G} \ else \ \mathcal{H} \ \Leftrightarrow \ (\mathcal{F} \ and \ \mathcal{G}) \ or \ ((not \ \mathcal{F}) \ and \ \mathcal{H}) \qquad (cond \ or)$$

- Commutativity

$$\mathcal{F} \ and \ \mathcal{G} \ \Leftrightarrow \ \mathcal{G} \ and \ \mathcal{F} \qquad (and)$$

$$\mathcal{F} \ or \ \mathcal{G} \ \Leftrightarrow \ \mathcal{G} \ or \ \mathcal{F} \qquad (or)$$

$$\mathcal{F} \equiv \mathcal{G} \ \Leftrightarrow \ \mathcal{G} \equiv \mathcal{F} \qquad (iff)$$

- Associativity

$$(\mathcal{F} \ and \ \mathcal{G}) \ and \ \mathcal{H} \ \Leftrightarrow \ \mathcal{F} \ and \ (\mathcal{G} \ and \ \mathcal{H}) \qquad (and)$$

$$(\mathcal{F} \ or \ \mathcal{G}) \ or \ \mathcal{H} \ \Leftrightarrow \ \mathcal{F} \ or \ (\mathcal{G} \ or \ \mathcal{H}) \qquad (or)$$

$$(\mathcal{F} \equiv \mathcal{G}) \equiv \mathcal{H} \ \Leftrightarrow \ \mathcal{F} \equiv (\mathcal{G} \equiv \mathcal{H}) \qquad (i\!f\!f)$$

- Distributivity

$$\mathcal{F} \ and \ (\mathcal{G} \ or \ \mathcal{H}) \ \Leftrightarrow \ (\mathcal{F} \ and \ \mathcal{G}) \ or \ (\mathcal{F} \ and \ \mathcal{H}) \qquad (and \ or)$$

$$\mathcal{F} \ or \ (\mathcal{G} \ and \ \mathcal{H}) \ \Leftrightarrow \ (\mathcal{F} \ or \ \mathcal{G}) \ and \ (\mathcal{F} \ or \ \mathcal{H}) \qquad (or \ and)$$

2.4   SPLITTING RULES

The splitting rules decompose a row (assertion or goal) into its logical components. We first describe the splitting rules and then show their soundness, i.e., that they preserve the equivalence of the tableaux to which they are applied.

There are three splitting rules.

AND-SPLIT RULE

If a tableau contains an assertion of the form

$$\mathcal{A}_1 \ and \ \mathcal{A}_2,$$

we may add the corresponding sentences $\mathcal{A}_1$ and $\mathcal{A}_2$ to the tableau as new assertions. This *and-split* rule is expressed in our tableau notation as follows:

assertions	goals
$\mathcal{A}_1 \ and \ \mathcal{A}_2$	
$\mathcal{A}_1$	
$\mathcal{A}_2$	

In other words, if an instance of the row above the double line (the required row) is present in the tableau, then we may add the corresponding instances of the rows below the double line (the generated rows). Intuitively, if we know that the conjunction ($\mathcal{A}_1 \ and \ \mathcal{A}_2$) is true, we also know that each of the conjuncts $\mathcal{A}_1, \mathcal{A}_2$ is true.

In using the preceding notation, we do not restrict the location of the row containing the assertion

$$\mathcal{A}_1 \ and \ \mathcal{A}_2$$

in the given tableau. In particular, it need not be the first or the last row; the order of the rows is not significant. As usual, we do not delete the required assertion when we apply the deduction rule.

OR-SPLIT RULE

If the tableau contains a goal of form

$$\mathcal{G}_1 \ or \ \mathcal{G}_2,$$

we may add the corresponding sentences $\mathcal{G}_1$ and $\mathcal{G}_2$ as new goals; that is,

assertions	goals
	$\mathcal{G}_1 \ or \ \mathcal{G}_2$
	$\mathcal{G}_1$
	$\mathcal{G}_2$

Intuitively, if we want to prove the disjunction ($\mathcal{G}_1 \ or \ \mathcal{G}_2$), it suffices to establish any one of the disjuncts $\mathcal{G}_1, \mathcal{G}_2$.

Note that there is no *or-split* rule for assertions or *and-split* rule for goals.

IF-SPLIT RULE

If the tableau contains a goal of form

$$if \ \mathcal{A} \ then \ \mathcal{G},$$

then we may add the corresponding sentence $\mathcal{A}$ as a new assertion and $\mathcal{G}$ as a new goal; that is,

assertions	goals
	$if \ \mathcal{A} \ then \ \mathcal{G}$
$\mathcal{A}$	
	$\mathcal{G}$

Intuitively, if we want to prove the implication ($if \ \mathcal{A} \ then \ \mathcal{G}$), it suffices to assume that the antecedent $\mathcal{A}$ is true and to establish that then the consequent $\mathcal{G}$ is also true.

Let us consider a simple example of the use of all three splitting rules.

Example. Suppose we have the initial tableau

assertions	goals
	G1. *if* (*P and Q*) *then* (*Q or R*)

Then we can apply the *if-split* rule to goal G1, obtaining the new assertion and the new goal

A2. *P and Q*	
	G3. *Q or R*

We can then apply the *and-split* rule to assertion A2, yielding the new assertions

A4. *P*	
A5. *Q*	

We can also apply the *or-split* rule to goal G3, yielding the new goals

	G6. *Q*
	G7. *R*

The tableau we obtain is then

assertions	goals
	G1. *if* (*P and Q*) *then* (*Q or R*)
A2. *P and Q*	
	G3. *Q or R*
A4. *P*	
A5. *Q*	
	G6. *Q*
	G7. *R*

We have not yet proved the sentence G1 because we have not derived the final goal *true* or the final assertion *false*. ◢

Remark (multiple conjunction and disjunction).   The *and* and *or* connectives apply to two arguments. In Section 1.7, we extended these connectives to apply to several arguments as well. We defined the multiple conjunction

$$\mathcal{F}_1 \ and \ \mathcal{F}_2 \ and \ \mathcal{F}_3 \ and \ \ldots \ and \ \mathcal{F}_k$$

to be an abbreviation for

$$(\ldots((\mathcal{F}_1 \ and \ \mathcal{F}_2) \ and \ \mathcal{F}_3)\ldots) \ and \ \mathcal{F}_k,$$

and the multiple disjunction

$$\mathcal{F}_1 \ or \ \mathcal{F}_2 \ or \ \mathcal{F}_3 \ or \ \ldots or \ \mathcal{F}_k$$

to be an abbreviation for

$$(\ldots((\mathcal{F}_1 \ or \ \mathcal{F}_2) \ or \ \mathcal{F}_3)\ldots) \ or \ \mathcal{F}_k.$$

Therefore, from a multiple-conjunction assertion

assertions	goals
$\mathcal{A}_1 \ and \ \mathcal{A}_2 \ and \ \ldots \ and \ \mathcal{A}_k$	

we can deduce, by $k-1$ applications of the *and-split* rule, the assertions

$\mathcal{A}_1$	
$\mathcal{A}_2$	
$\vdots$	
$\mathcal{A}_k$	

Similarly, from a multiple-disjunction goal

	$\mathcal{G}_1 \ or \ \mathcal{G}_2 \ or \ \ldots \ or \ \mathcal{G}_k$

we can deduce, by $k-1$ applications of the *or-split* rule, the goals

	$\mathcal{G}_1$
	$\mathcal{G}_2$
	$\vdots$
	$\mathcal{G}_k$

◢

2.5 JUSTIFICATION OF DEDUCTION RULES

When we introduce a new deduction rule we must show that it is sound, i.e., that it actually does preserve the equivalence of any tableau to which it is applied. We now introduce a *justification* proposition, which will facilitate such proofs.

Recall that we called those rows (assertions and goals) that must be present in the tableau for a deduction rule to be applied the *required rows*, forming the *required subtableau* $\mathcal{T}_r$, and those that are added to the tableau by the rule the *generated rows*, forming the *generated subtableau* $\mathcal{T}_g$. Thus the required rows are those that appear above the double line in the tableau form of the rule, and the generated rows are those that appear below the double line.

Proposition (justification)

A deduction rule is sound (i.e., preserves equivalence) if the following *justification condition* holds:

For every interpretation $\mathcal{I}$,

if the required subtableau $\mathcal{T}_r$ is false under $\mathcal{I}$,
then the generated subtableau $\mathcal{T}_g$ is false under $\mathcal{I}$. ◢

In other words, the *justification* condition states that

if all the required assertions are true and
all the required goals are false under $\mathcal{I}$,
then all the generated assertions are true and
all the generated goals are false under $\mathcal{I}$.

Equivalently (taking the contrapositive), the *justification* condition says that

if the generated subtableau $\mathcal{T}_g$ is true under $\mathcal{I}$,
then the required subtableau $\mathcal{T}_r$ is also true under $\mathcal{I}$.

The *justification* proposition states that, if the *justification* condition holds, the new tableau (produced by adding the generated assertions and goals) is equivalent to the old tableau (before the generated assertions and goals are added). Hence, to justify a rule, we need not consider any of the assertions and goals of the tableau other than those required or generated by the rule.

Before we prove the proposition, let us apply it to justify one of our splitting rules.

Justification (*if-split* rule).   The *if-split* rule requires a goal

	if A then G

and generates the assertion and goal

A	
	G

To justify this deduction rule, we need only consider an arbitrary interpretation under which the required goal (*if A then G*) is false, and show that, under this interpretation, the generated assertion A is true and the generated goal G is false. But this follows from the semantic rule for the *if-then* connective. ◢

The other splitting rules can be justified in the same way.

Remark (**deleting rows**).   Recall that in applying a deduction rule, we do not delete the required rows from the tableau. In fact, in the case of the splitting rules, we could have deleted the required assertion or goal and still preserved the equivalence of the tableau. For some rules, however, deleting a required row may cause us to lose validity. That is, the old tableau may be valid, but the new tableau may not be valid. ◢

Let us now prove the *justification* proposition.

Proof (justification).   Suppose a deduction rule is applied to a tableau $\mathcal{T}$ and the *justification* condition holds. We want to show that the new tableau $\mathcal{T} \cup \mathcal{T}_g$ is equivalent to $\mathcal{T}$, the old tableau. We show that, if either tableau is true under some interpretation, then the other is true under the same interpretation. We treat each direction separately.

Old tableau is true $\Rightarrow$ new tableau is true

This direction does not depend on the *justification* condition. The old tableau $\mathcal{T}$ is a subtableau of the new tableau $\mathcal{T} \cup \mathcal{T}_g$. It follows, by the *subtableau* property, that if the old tableau is true for a given interpretation, the new tableau is also true under the same interpretation.

New tableau is true $\Rightarrow$ old tableau is true

Suppose that, for a given interpretation $\mathcal{I}$, the new tableau $\mathcal{T} \cup \mathcal{T}_g$ is true. Then, by the *union* property, $\mathcal{T}$ is true or $\mathcal{T}_g$ is true (under $\mathcal{I}$). In the first case, the old tableau, $\mathcal{T}$ itself, is true. In the other case, if $\mathcal{T}_g$ is true then (by the *justification* condition) $\mathcal{T}_r$ is true. But $\mathcal{T}_r$ is a subtableau of $\mathcal{T}$; therefore (by the *subtableau* property) the old tableau, $\mathcal{T}$ itself, is true. ◢

In **Problem 2.2** the reader is requested to formulate and prove a more ambitious *justification* proposition.

2.6 RESOLUTION RULE

The *resolution* rule allows us to perform a case analysis on the truth of any sentence that occurs as a common subsentence of two rows.

There are four different versions of the *resolution* rule: *AA-resolution* (applied to two assertions), *GG-resolution* (applied to two goals), *AG-resolution* (applied to an assertion and a goal), and *GA-resolution* (applied to a goal and an assertion). We present first the *AA-resolution* rule, which is considered to be the basic form.

THE BASIC FORM

The basic form of the *resolution* rule is expressed as follows.

Rule (**AA-resolution**)

assertions	goals
$\mathcal{A}_1[\mathcal{P}]$	
$\mathcal{A}_2[\mathcal{P}]$	
$\mathcal{A}_1[\mathit{false}]$ *or* $\mathcal{A}_2[\mathit{true}]$	

where $\mathcal{P}$ is a sentence that occurs as a subsentence of both $\mathcal{A}_1$ and $\mathcal{A}_2$. ◢

In other words, to apply the rule to a tableau, we do the following:

- Choose any two assertions $\mathcal{A}_1[\mathcal{P}]$ and $\mathcal{A}_2[\mathcal{P}]$ with a common subsentence $\mathcal{P}$.

- Replace every occurrence of $\mathcal{P}$ in $\mathcal{A}_1[\mathcal{P}]$ with the truth symbol *false*, and every occurrence of $\mathcal{P}$ in $\mathcal{A}_2[\mathcal{P}]$ with the truth symbol *true*, obtaining $\mathcal{A}_1[false]$ and $\mathcal{A}_2[true]$, respectively.

- Take the disjunction $(\mathcal{A}_1[false]$ *or* $\mathcal{A}_2[true])$ and apply to it all possible simplifications.

- Add the simplified disjunction to the tableau as a new assertion.

We will say that the new assertion is a *resolvent*, obtained by *applying* the *resolution* rule to the assertions $\mathcal{A}_1[\mathcal{P}]$ and $\mathcal{A}_2[\mathcal{P}]$, *matching* $\mathcal{P}$.

Although the total substitution notation does not require that the subsentence $\mathcal{P}$ occur in $\mathcal{A}_1[\mathcal{P}]$ or $\mathcal{A}_2[\mathcal{P}]$, we intend here that $\mathcal{P}$ occur at least once in each assertion.

Note that $\mathcal{A}_1[\mathcal{P}]$ and $\mathcal{A}_2[\mathcal{P}]$ may be chosen to be any two assertions in the tableau; their location in the tableau is completely irrelevant. Normally, in describing a step in a proof, we mention the sentence $\mathcal{A}_1[\mathcal{P}]$, whose subsentence is replaced by *false*, before the sentence $\mathcal{A}_2[\mathcal{P}]$, whose subsentence is replaced by *true*. This is not necessarily the actual order of the assertions in the tableau. Nor need the assertions be adjacent in the tableau.

Example. Suppose our tableau contains the assertions

$$\mathcal{A}_1[\mathcal{P}]:\ P\ or\ Q$$

$$\mathcal{A}_2[\mathcal{P}]:\ if\ (P\ or\ Q)\ then\ R.$$

Let $\mathcal{P}$ be $(P\ or\ Q)$. Both of the assertions contain $(P\ or\ Q)$ as a subsentence. The required rows are therefore

assertions	goals
$\mathcal{A}_1[\mathcal{P}]:$ $\boxed{P\ or\ Q}$	
$\mathcal{A}_2[\mathcal{P}]:$ $if\ \boxed{P\ or\ Q}\ then\ R$	

We use the boxes to indicate the subsentences about to be matched in applying the rule.

Replacing every occurrence of $(P\ or\ Q)$ in $\mathcal{A}_1[\mathcal{P}]$ with the truth symbol *false*, we obtain

$$\mathcal{A}_1[false]:\quad false.$$

Replacing every occurrence of $(P \ or \ Q)$ in $\mathcal{A}_2[\mathcal{P}]$ with the truth symbol *true*, we obtain

$\mathcal{A}_2[true]:$ *if true then R.*

Therefore, matching $(P \ or \ Q)$, we can apply the *resolution* rule to $\mathcal{A}_1[\mathcal{P}]$ and $\mathcal{A}_2[\mathcal{P}]$, replacing $(P \ or \ Q)$ with *false* and *true*, respectively, and add to our tableau as a new assertion the resolvent

$\mathcal{A}_1[false] \ or \ \mathcal{A}_2[true],$

that is,

> *false*
>> *or*
> *if true then R.*

This assertion can be reduced (by means of the *false-or* and *if-true* simplifications) to the assertion

R	

The *resolution* rule is asymmetric in the sense that, if we reverse the roles of $\mathcal{A}_1[\mathcal{P}]$ and $\mathcal{A}_2[\mathcal{P}]$ in applying the rule, we may get different results.

Example (reversing the order).   In the preceding example, suppose we reverse $\mathcal{A}_1[\mathcal{P}]$ and $\mathcal{A}_2[\mathcal{P}]$:

assertions	goals
$\mathcal{A}_1[\mathcal{P}]:$ *if* $\boxed{P \ or \ Q}$ *then R*	
$\mathcal{A}_2[\mathcal{P}]:$ $\boxed{P \ or \ Q}$	

Then, again matching the subsentence $(P \ or \ Q)$, we obtain the assertion

$\mathcal{A}_1[false] \ or \ \mathcal{A}_2[true],$

that is,

> *if false then R*
>> *or*
> *true.*

This assertion can be reduced (by *or-true* simplification) to the trivial assertion

true	

By interchanging the two assertions in applying the *resolution* rule, we have obtained a different result. The results of both examples are legal consequences of applying the rule to the two given assertions. The second result is not useful, however, as we explain later.

Note that we do not exclude the possibility of applying the *resolution* rule to an assertion and itself, that is, taking both $\mathcal{A}_1[\mathcal{P}]$ and $\mathcal{A}_2[\mathcal{P}]$ to be the same assertion.

Example (assertion and itself).   Suppose we apply the *resolution* rule, taking both $\mathcal{A}_1[\mathcal{P}]$ and $\mathcal{A}_2[\mathcal{P}]$ to be the assertion

assertions	goals
if $\left(P \ \ or \ \ \boxed{Q} \right) \ \ then \ \ \left(\boxed{Q} \ \ and \ \ R \right)$	

that is,

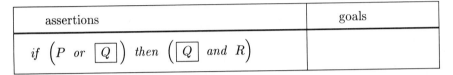

$$\mathcal{A}_1[\mathcal{P}]: \quad if \ \left(P \ \ or \ \ \boxed{Q} \right) \ \ then \ \ \left(\boxed{Q} \ \ and \ \ R \right)$$

$$\mathcal{A}_2[\mathcal{P}]: \quad if \ \left(P \ \ or \ \ \boxed{Q} \right) \ \ then \ \ \left(\boxed{Q} \ \ and \ \ R \right),$$

taking $\mathcal{P}$ to be Q (matching the subsentence Q). Our unsimplified resolvent is the assertion

$$\mathcal{A}_1[false] \quad or \quad \mathcal{A}_2[true],$$

that is,

$$if \ (P \ \ or \ \ false) \ \ then \ \ (false \ \ and \ \ R)$$
$$or$$
$$if \ (P \ \ or \ \ true) \ \ then \ \ (true \ \ and \ \ R),$$

which is reduced (by *or-false, false-and, then-false, or-true, true-and,* and *if-true* simplifications) to the assertion

$(not \ P) \ \ or \ \ R$	

Remark (at least one replacement).   Although our substitution notation admits the possibility that the subsentence $\mathcal{P}$ does not occur in the assertions $\mathcal{A}_1$ or $\mathcal{A}_2$, the wording of the rule requires that the subsentence occur at least once in each of the assertions. Otherwise, the assertion we derive would be weaker than the ones we were given. ◢

Let us justify the basic *resolution* rule, showing that the old tableau, before applying the rule, is equivalent to the new tableau, obtained by adding the resolvent.

Justification (AA-resolution).   First we make an observation. Suppose a sentence $\mathcal{F}[\mathcal{P}]$ is true under some interpretation. By the *substitutivity-of-equivalence* proposition, we do not alter the truth of a sentence by replacing one of its subsentences with another having the same truth-value under this interpretation. Thus, if $\mathcal{P}$ is false under the interpretation, then $\mathcal{F}[false]$ is true under the same interpretation. And, if $\mathcal{P}$ is true under the interpretation, then $\mathcal{F}[true]$ is true under the same interpretation.

Suppose the required assertions $\mathcal{A}_1[\mathcal{P}]$ and $\mathcal{A}_2[\mathcal{P}]$ both contain $\mathcal{P}$ as a subsentence. Consider an interpretation $\mathcal{I}$ under which the required subtableau $\mathcal{T}_r$ is false, that is, $\mathcal{A}_1[\mathcal{P}]$ and $\mathcal{A}_2[\mathcal{P}]$ are both true under $\mathcal{I}$. By the *justification* proposition, it suffices to establish that the generated subtableau $\mathcal{T}_g$ is false under $\mathcal{I}$, that is, the assertion generated by the rule, the simplified disjunction

$$\mathcal{A}_1[false] \quad or \quad \mathcal{A}_2[true],$$

is also true under $\mathcal{I}$.

We distinguish between two subcases.

Case: $\mathcal{P}$ is false under $\mathcal{I}$

Then, by our initial observation, because $\mathcal{P}$ and *false* have the same truth-values, and because $\mathcal{A}_1[\mathcal{P}]$ is true under $\mathcal{I}$, we know that

$$\mathcal{A}_1[false]$$

is also true under $\mathcal{I}$. By the semantic rule for the *or* connective, the disjunction

$$\mathcal{A}_1[false] \quad or \quad \mathcal{A}_2[true]$$

is true under $\mathcal{I}$. The simplified disjunction is true under $\mathcal{I}$ as well.

Case: $\mathcal{P}$ is true under $\mathcal{I}$

Then, because $\mathcal{P}$ and *true* have the same truth-values, and because $\mathcal{A}_2[\mathcal{P}]$ is true under $\mathcal{I}$, we know that

$$\mathcal{A}_2[true]$$

is also true under $\mathcal{I}$, and (by the semantic rule for *or*) the disjunction

$$\mathcal{A}_1[false] \quad or \quad \mathcal{A}_2[true]$$

is true under $\mathcal{I}$. The simplified disjunction is true under $\mathcal{I}$ as well.

Because, in each case, the conclusion of the *AA-resolution* rule is true under $\mathcal{I}$, the *justification* condition for the rule is established. ◢

DUAL FORMS

The basic form of the *resolution* rule derives a conclusion from two assertions; we therefore called this form *AA-resolution*. Because of the duality between assertions and goals, there exist different forms of the rule applied to two goals (*GG-resolution*), an assertion and a goal (*AG-resolution*), and a goal and an assertion (*GA-resolution*). Because all these forms of the rule can be justified by duality, we call them *dual forms*.

The form that applies to two goals is as follows.

Rule (GG-resolution).

assertions	goals
	$\mathcal{G}_1[\mathcal{P}]$
	$\mathcal{G}_2[\mathcal{P}]$
	$\mathcal{G}_1[\mathit{false}]$ *and* $\mathcal{G}_2[\mathit{true}]$

where $\mathcal{P}$ is a sentence that occurs as a subsentence of both $\mathcal{G}_1$ and $\mathcal{G}_2$. ◢

Note that the GG-form of the rule introduces a conjunction rather than a disjunction.

Justification (GG-resolution).   This form, like *AA-resolution*, can be justified directly by establishing the appropriate *justification* condition. It is more instructive, however, to derive *GG-resolution* from *AA-resolution* by appeal to the *duality* property. The relationship between the two forms then becomes clear.

A tableau with the goals required by *GG-resolution*,

assertions	goals
	$\mathcal{G}_1[\mathcal{P}]$
	$\mathcal{G}_2[\mathcal{P}]$

is equivalent (by the *duality* property) to a tableau with the additional assertions

not $\mathcal{G}_1[\mathcal{P}]$	
not $\mathcal{G}_2[\mathcal{P}]$	

This tableau is equivalent (by the soundness of *AA-resolution*) to the tableau to which we add the simplified assertion

$$\begin{array}{|l|l|}
\hline
\begin{array}{c}
not\ (\mathcal{G}_1[false]) \\
or \\
not\ (\mathcal{G}_2[true])
\end{array} & \\
\hline
\end{array}$$

or, equivalently (by one of the *negation* valid sentence schemata of Section 1.7),

$$\begin{array}{|l|l|}
\hline
not\ \begin{bmatrix}\mathcal{G}_1[false] \\ and \\ \mathcal{G}_2[true]\end{bmatrix} & \\
\hline
\end{array}$$

But (by the *duality* property, again, and simplification) a tableau with this assertion is equivalent to a tableau with the additional goal

$$\begin{array}{|l|c|}
\hline
 & \begin{array}{c}\mathcal{G}_1[false] \\ and \\ \mathcal{G}_2[true]\end{array} \\
\hline
\end{array}$$

This is precisely the goal generated by *GG-resolution*.

We have shown that we can add to the tableau the preceding goal and the intermediate assertions, maintaining the equivalence of the tableau. Therefore, by the *intermediate-tableau* property, we may add only the goal and still maintain equivalence. ⌙

Remark (properties are not rules). In justifying the *GG-resolution* rule, we used the *duality* property to justify introducing a new row into the tableau. The reader is not to get the impression that we may use duality as if it were a deduction rule, to add new rows to a tableau during a proof. The reason for not including duality as a deduction rule is that it never helps the proof; for, whatever deduction rule that can be applied to the added goal $\mathcal{A}$, there is a dual version that can be applied directly to the given assertion (*not* $\mathcal{A}$). The *duality* property is useful in justifying the dual versions but is not itself necessary in the proof. A similar remark applies to the *implied-row* property. ⌙

Let us illustrate the *GG-resolution* rule.

Example. Suppose we are given a tableau containing the two goals

assertions	goals
	$\mathcal{G}_1[\mathcal{P}]:$ *if* $\boxed{P}$ *then* Q
	$\mathcal{G}_2[\mathcal{P}]:$ $\boxed{P}$

Then, taking $\mathcal{P}$ to be the sentence P, which occurs as a subsentence of both goals, we can apply the *GG-resolution* rule to obtain the new goal

> *if false then* Q
>   *and*
> *true*,

which reduces (by the *if-false* and *and-true* simplifications) to

	true

The two other dual forms of the *resolution* rule apply to an assertion and a goal and to a goal and an assertion.

Rule (AG-resolution)

assertions	goals
$\mathcal{A}[\mathcal{P}]$	
	$\mathcal{G}[\mathcal{P}]$
	not $\mathcal{A}[false]$ *and* $\mathcal{G}[true]$

where $\mathcal{P}$ is a sentence that occurs as a subsentence of both $\mathcal{A}$ and $\mathcal{G}$.

Rule (GA-resolution)

assertions	goals
	$\mathcal{G}[\mathcal{P}]$
$\mathcal{A}[\mathcal{P}]$	
	$\mathcal{G}[false]$ *and* *not* $\mathcal{A}[true]$

where $\mathcal{P}$ is a sentence that occurs as a subsentence of both $\mathcal{A}$ and $\mathcal{G}$.

These *AG-* and *GA-resolution* rules are not identical because of the asymmetric role of the assertion and the goal in each case. In *AG-resolution*, a subsentence of the assertion is replaced by *false*; in *GA-resolution*, a subsentence of the goal is replaced by *false*. By the *duality* property, each of these forms is equivalent to *AA-resolution*. The justification of these two forms resembles the justification of *GG-resolution* and is omitted.

Example.   Suppose we are given a tableau that contains the assertion $\mathcal{A}[\mathcal{P}]$ and the goal $\mathcal{G}[\mathcal{P}]$:

assertions	goals
$\mathcal{A}[\mathcal{P}]:$ *if* P *then* $\boxed{if\ \ Q_1\ \ then\ \ Q_2}$	
	$\mathcal{G}[\mathcal{P}]:$ $\boxed{if\ \ Q_1\ \ then\ \ Q_2}$ *and* R

Then, taking $\mathcal{P}$ to be the sentence (*if* Q_1 *then* Q_2), which occurs as a subsentence of both $\mathcal{A}[\mathcal{P}]$ and $\mathcal{G}[\mathcal{P}]$, we can apply *AG-resolution* to obtain the new goal

$$not\ \begin{bmatrix} if\ \ P \\ then\ \ false \end{bmatrix}$$
$$and$$
$$true\ \ and\ \ R,$$

which reduces (by *then-false*, *not-not*, and *true-and* simplifications) to

	$P\ \ and\ \ R$

In **Problem 2.3** the reader is requested to justify the *hyper-resolution* rule, which is a variant of the *resolution* rule.

COMMON EXAMPLES

Certain special applications of the *resolution* rule occur frequently enough that it is worthwhile to recognize them. We illustrate these applications with a few examples.

The first three applications establish the final goal *true* or the final assertion *false*.

Identity

Suppose P is both an assertion and a goal:

assertions	goals
$\boxed{P}$	
	$\boxed{P}$

Then we can derive (by *AG-resolution*, matching P) the goal

> *not false*
>   *and*
> *true,*

which reduces (by *not-false* and *true-and* simplifications) to the final goal

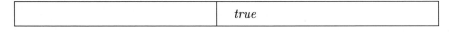

	true

In other words, if we want to show P and P is known to be true, we are done.

Contradiction

Suppose we are given two assertions that contradict each other:

assertions	goals
$\boxed{P}$	
not $\boxed{P}$	

Then we can derive (by *AA-resolution*) the assertion

> *false*
>   *or*
> *not true*,

which reduces (by *false-or* and *not-true* simplifications) to the final assertion

false	

In other words, from two contradictory assertions, every goal can be proved.

Excluded middle

Suppose our problem is to establish either of two complementary goals (*not P*) or *P*.

assertions	goals
	not $\boxed{P}$
	$\boxed{P}$

Then we can derive (by *GG-resolution*) the goal

> *not false*
>   *and*
> *true*,

which reduces (by *not-false* and *true-and* simplifications) to the final goal

	true

In other words, if it suffices to establish either P or its negation, the proof is complete.

Forward chaining (modus ponens)

Suppose we are given the two assertions P and (*if P then Q*).

assertions	goals
$\boxed{P}$	
if $\boxed{P}$ *then* Q	

Then, we can derive (by *AA-resolution*, matching P) the assertion

> *false*
>   *or*
> *if true then* Q,

which reduces (by *false-or* and *if-true* simplifications) to the assertion

Q	

In other words, from P and (*if P then Q*) we can conclude Q.

Backward chaining

Suppose we know (*if P then Q*) and want to show Q:

assertions	goals
if P then $\boxed{Q}$	
	$\boxed{Q}$

Then (by *AG-resolution*, matching Q) we obtain the goal

> *not* (*if P then false*)
>   *and*
> *true*,

which reduces (by *then-false, not-not*, and *and-true* simplifications) to the goal

	P

In other words, if we know (*if P then Q*) and want to show Q, then it suffices to show P.

Clausal resolution

Suppose we know both (*P or Q*) and ((*not P*) *or R*):

assertions	goals
$\boxed{P}$ *or* Q	
$\left(not \ \boxed{P} \right)$ *or* R	

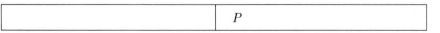

Then (by *AA-resolution*, matching P) we obtain the goal

> *false or Q*
>   *or*
> (*not true*) *or R*,

which reduces (by *false-or* and *not-true* simplifications) to the assertion

Q *or* R	

In **Problem 2.4** the reader is asked to apply the *resolution* rule in several other common cases.

A SAMPLE PROOF

Although we will later present another rule, for dealing with equivalence (Section 2.8), we already have enough rules to prove any valid propositional sentence, as we remarked. (This will be shown in general in Chapter 14.) Let us now consider an example of a complete proof of the validity of a propositional-logic sentence.

We let $\mathcal{S}$ be the sentence

$$\mathcal{S}: \quad \begin{array}{l} \textit{if } (P \ \textit{and}\ Q) \\ \textit{then } (Q \ \textit{or}\ R), \end{array}$$

which was discussed in an earlier example. We present three different proofs of the validity of $\mathcal{S}$, depending on the extent to which the splitting rules are applied.

Proof 1:   full splitting

Consider the initial tableau in which $\mathcal{S}$ is the only goal:

assertions	goals
	G1. *if* $(P \ and\ Q)$ *then* $(Q \ or\ R)$

Applying the *if-split* rule to goal G1, we obtain the assertion and the goal

A2. $P \ and\ Q$	
	G3. $Q \ or\ R$

Applying the *and-split* rule to assertion A2, we obtain the assertions

A4. P	
A5. $\boxed{Q}$	

Applying the *or-split* rule to goal G3, we obtain the goals

	G6. $\boxed{Q}$
	G7. R

Now we can apply *AG-resolution* to assertion A5 and goal G6, matching Q, obtaining the goal

> *not false*
> *and*
> *true,*

which reduces (by *not-false* and *true-and* simplifications) to the final goal

	G8. *true*

Because we have obtained the final goal *true*, it follows that the given sentence $\mathcal{S}$ is valid.

Proof 2:   partial splitting

The preceding proof is not the only possible proof of $\mathcal{S}$. For example, suppose we have developed the first three rows as before, that is,

assertions	goals
	G1. *if* $(P$ *and* $Q)$ *then* $(Q$ *or* $R)$
A2. P *and* $\boxed{Q}$	
	G3. $\boxed{Q}$ *or* R

Then, if (instead of applying the splitting rules to rows A2 and G3) we apply *AG-resolution* to assertion A2 and goal G3, matching Q, we obtain the goal

> *not* (*P and false*)
>   *and*
> *true or R*,

which reduces (by *and-false*, *not-false*, *true-and*, and *true-or* simplifications) to the final goal

	G4. *true*

Proof 3:   no splitting

In fact, still another proof can be obtained. Suppose we begin with the same initial tableau:

assertions	goals
	G1. *if* $\left(P \;\; and \;\; \boxed{Q}\right)$ *then* $\left(\boxed{Q} \;\; or \;\; R\right)$

If (instead of applying the *if-split* rule) we apply *GG-resolution* to goal G1 and itself, matching *Q*, we obtain the goal

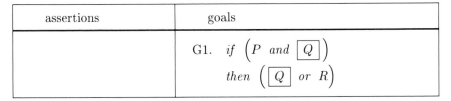

which reduces (by *and-false*, *if-false*, *true-and*, *true-or*, and *then-true* simplifications) to

	G2. *true*

In fact, as will be shown later, any valid propositional-logic sentence can always be proved by applying only *GG-resolution* and *true-false* simplifications. Proofs often become more readable, however, if we do use the splitting rules, the rewriting rule, the other simplifications, and the other forms of the *resolution* rule.

2.7   POLARITY STRATEGY

Between two rows of a tableau, there may be many ways to apply the *resolution* rule.

Example.   Suppose our tableau contains the following assertion and goal:

assertions	goals
if *P* *then* $\boxed{Q}$	
	P *and* $\boxed{Q}$

Then there are four different ways to apply the *resolution* rule to these two rows.

AG-resolution, matching Q

     We can apply *AG-resolution*, matching the subsentence Q, obtaining the new goal

> *not* (*if*   *P*   *then*   *false*)
>   *and*
> *P*   *and*   *true*,

which reduces (by *then-false*, *not-not*, *and-true*, and *and-two* simplifications) to the goal

	P

AG-resolution, matching P

     From the same assertion and goal,

assertions	goals
if $\boxed{P}$ *then* *Q*	
	$\boxed{P}$ *and* *Q*

however, we can apply *AG-resolution*, matching P instead of Q, to obtain the new goal

> *not* (*if*   *false*   *then*   *Q*)
>   *and*
> *true*   *and*   *Q*,

which reduces (by *if-false*, *not-true*, and *false-and* simplifications) to the trivial goal

	false

GA-resolution, matching P

If we consider the goal and the assertion

assertions	goals
	$\boxed{P}$ *and* Q
if $\boxed{P}$ *then* Q	

we can apply *GA-resolution*, matching P, to obtain the new goal

> *false and* Q
>   *and*
> *not* (*if true then* Q),

which reduces (by *false-and* simplification) to the trivial goal

	false

GA-resolution, matching Q

If we consider again the goal and the assertion

assertions	goals
	P *and* $\boxed{Q}$
if P *then* $\boxed{Q}$	

we can apply *GA-resolution*, matching Q this time, to obtain the new goal

> P *and false*
>   *and*
> *not* (*if* P *then true*),

which reduces (by *and-false* and *false-and* simplifications) to the trivial goal

	false

Thus, in the preceding example, there are four possible ways to apply the *resolution* rule to the given assertion and goal, three of which produce the trivial goal *false*, which is of no use in any proof. Only one of them (*AG-resolution*, matching Q) produces a nontrivial resolvent. In this section, we employ the notion of polarity to detect many fruitless applications of resolution before actually applying the rule. The three trivial applications of the rule in the example will be detected in advance.

POLARITY IN A TABLEAU

We have already defined (in Section 1.11) the notion of the polarity of a subsentence of a given sentence. We now extend that notion to tableaux.

Definition (polarity in a tableau)

If $\mathcal{T}$ is a tableau, we assign a *polarity*, positive ($+$), negative ($-$), or both ($\pm$), to every occurrence of a subsentence of the assertions and goals of $\mathcal{T}$, according to the following *polarity-assignment rules*:

- Each goal has positive polarity in $\mathcal{T}$.

- Each assertion has negative polarity in $\mathcal{T}$.

- The polarity of a proper subsentence of an assertion or goal in $\mathcal{T}$ is determined by the *polarity-assignment* rules for a proper subsentence of a sentence.

An occurrence of a subsentence of a tableau is said to have *strict polarity* in the tableau if it does not have both polarities. ◢

The polarity of a subsentence in a tableau is the same as the polarity of the corresponding subsentence in the associated sentence. Indeed, the assertions $\mathcal{A}_i$ have negative polarity and the goals $\mathcal{G}_j$ have positive polarity in the associated sentence

$$\text{if } \left(\boxed{\mathcal{A}_1}^{\,-} \text{ and } \boxed{\mathcal{A}_2}^{\,-} \text{ and } \ldots \text{ and } \boxed{\mathcal{A}_m}^{\,-} \right)$$

$$\text{then } \left(\boxed{\mathcal{G}_1}^{\,+} \text{ or } \boxed{\mathcal{G}_2}^{\,+} \text{ or } \ldots \text{ or } \boxed{\mathcal{G}_n}^{\,+} \right).$$

Example.   The subsentences of the goals and assertions of the following tableaux are annotated according to their polarities.

Annotated goals

assertions	goals
	$\left[if\ \ P^-\ \ then\ \ Q^+\right]^+$
	$\left[not\ P^-\right]^+$
	$\left[\begin{array}{l}\left[not\ \left[P^-\ \ or\ \ [not\ Q^+]^-\right]^-\right]^+ \\ and \\ P^+\end{array}\right]^+$

Annotated assertions

$\left[not\ P^+\right]^-$	
$\left[\begin{array}{l}[P^-\ \ or\ \ Q^-]^- \\ and \\ [not\ [P^+\ \ or\ \ Q^+]^+]^-\end{array}\right]^-$	
$\left[\begin{array}{l}if\ [not\ P^-]^+ \\ then\ \ Q^-\end{array}\right]^-$	

Here, for instance, the last assertion is negative in the tableau because all assertions are negative in a tableau; therefore (by a *polarity-assignment* rule), the antecedent [*not P*] is positive and the consequent Q is negative in the tableau; therefore P is negative in the tableau.

Occurrences of both polarities

	$\left[not\ \left[P^\pm \equiv [not\ Q^\pm]^\pm\right]^-\right]^+$
$\left[\begin{array}{l}if\ \ [not\ P^\pm]^\pm \\ then\ \ Q^- \\ else\ \ [not\ R^+]^-\end{array}\right]^-$	

Remark (polarity and duality).   Note that if a sentence is pushed (by the *duality* property) from one column to the other and negated, its polarity does not change. For example, a tableau with the goal

	$\boxed{P}^{+}$

is by duality equivalent to the tableau containing instead the assertion

$\left[not\ \boxed{P}^{+}\right]^{-}$	

The polarity of the occurrence of P in the goal is positive in the tableau; the polarity of the occurrence of P in the assertion is also positive in the tableau because it is within the scope of both an implicit and an explicit negation. ◢

The polarity of an occurrence of a subsentence of an assertion or goal in a tableau, as in a sentence, indicates whether the occurrence has a positive or a negative impact on the truth of the tableau; that is, the truth of a tableau is directly related to the truth of its strictly positive subsentences, but inversely related to the truth of its strictly negative subsentences. For instance, replacing a strictly negative subsentence of the tableau with a "truer" sentence (i.e., one that it implies) can only make the entire tableau "falser."

POLARITY STRATEGY

Now let us use the notion of polarity to restrict the application of the *resolution* rule; this restriction will avoid many fruitless applications of the rule.

Strategy (polarity)
> Suppose that $\mathcal{F}_1[\mathcal{P}]$ and $\mathcal{F}_2[\mathcal{P}]$ are two assertions or goals in a tableau with a matching subsentence $\mathcal{P}$.
> Assume that the *resolution* rule has been applied to $\mathcal{F}_1[\mathcal{P}]$ and $\mathcal{F}_2[\mathcal{P}]$, replacing every occurrence of $\mathcal{P}$ in $\mathcal{F}_1[\mathcal{P}]$ with *false* and replacing every occurrence of $\mathcal{P}$ in $\mathcal{F}_2[\mathcal{P}]$ with *true*.
> Then we will say that the rule has been applied in accordance with the *polarity strategy* if
>> at least one occurrence of $\mathcal{P}$ in $\mathcal{F}_1[\mathcal{P}]$ is negative in the tableau
>
> and
>> at least one occurrence of $\mathcal{P}$ in $\mathcal{F}_2[\mathcal{P}]$ is positive in the tableau. ◢

In other words, according to the *polarity* strategy, we may apply the *resolution* rule to a tableau only if at least one of the occurrences of the subsentence that are replaced by *false* is negative, and at least one of the occurrences that are replaced by *true* is positive, in the tableau. These polarities need not be strict.

Let us see how the *polarity* strategy applies to the example we considered at the beginning of this section.

Example.   Assume a tableau has the assertion and the goal

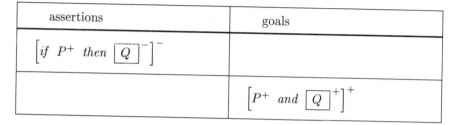

assertions	goals
$\left[if\ \ P^+\ \ then\ \ \boxed{Q}^{\ -}\right]^{\ -}$	
	$\left[P^+\ \ and\ \ \boxed{Q}^{\ +}\right]^{+}$

We have annotated each subsentence of this assertion and goal with its po-larity in the tableau. Note that the only subsentence that has both a positive occurrence and a negative occurrence is Q. Therefore, if resolution is to be ap-plied to these rows according to the *polarity* strategy, the matching subsentence must be Q.

Thus the only application of resolution to these rows that obeys the *polarity* strategy is *AG-resolution*, replacing the occurrence of Q in the assertion, which is negative in the tableau, with *false*, and the occurrence of Q in the goal, which is positive in the tableau, with *true*. This application yields the new goal

> *not* (*if P then false*)
> *and*
> *P and true*,

which reduces (by *then-false, not-not, and-true,* and *and-two* simplifications) to the nontrivial goal

	P

Each of the three other applications of the rule, which yield trivial goals, is forbidden by the *polarity* strategy. ◢

Remark (rationale for the polarity strategy).   Any valid sentence can be proved using only applications of the *resolution* rule that are in accordance with the *polarity* strategy. As it turns out, if we apply the rule in violation of the strategy, we always derive a row we can do without. In particular, if the improperly derived row is an assertion (obtained by *AA-resolution*), it will always be implied by one of the two given assertions and we could use that given assertion in place of the derived one in any proof. ◢

COMPLETE EXAMPLE

Let us give another complete example: the proof of the validity of the sentence

$$\mathcal{S}: \quad if \quad \begin{bmatrix} if \ P \ then \ R \\ and \\ if \ Q \ then \ R \end{bmatrix} \quad then \quad \begin{bmatrix} if \ (P \ or \ Q) \\ then \ R \end{bmatrix}.$$

We begin with the tableau

assertions	goals
	G1. $if \ \begin{bmatrix} if \ P \ then \ R \\ and \\ if \ Q \ then \ R \end{bmatrix} \ then \ \begin{bmatrix} if \ (P \ or \ Q) \\ then \ R \end{bmatrix}$

We first apply the splitting rules in succession.

Applying the *if-split* rule yields

A2.   *if P then R*
      and
      if Q then R	

	G3. *if (P or Q)* *then R*

We now present two alternative ways to complete the proof.

Proof 1

Applying the *and-split* rule to assertion A2 yields

Applying the *if-split* rule to goal G3 produces

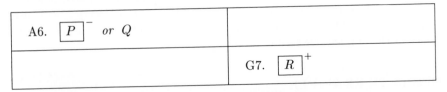

Applying the *AG-resolution* rule twice, to assertion A4 and goal G7, and to assertion A5 and goal G7, matching R, yields the goals

$$\begin{array}{ccc}
not \ (if \ P \ then \ false) & & not \ (if \ Q \ then \ false) \\
and & and & and \\
true & & true,
\end{array}$$

which reduce (by the *then-false*, *not-not*, and *and-true* simplifications) to

	G8. $\boxed{P}$ $^+$
	G9. $\boxed{Q}$ $^+$

respectively.

Applying *AG-resolution* to assertion A6 and goal G8, matching P, yields the goal

$$not \ (false \ or \ Q)$$
$$and$$
$$true,$$

which reduces (by the *false-or* and *and-true* simplifications) to

	G10. $not \ \boxed{Q}$ $^-$

Finally, we can apply *GG-resolution* to goals G9 and G10, matching Q, to yield the goal

$$not \ false$$
$$and$$
$$true,$$

which reduces (by *not-false* and *true-and* simplifications) to the final goal

	G11. *true*

Thus the given sentence S is valid.

Note that each application of the *resolution* rule has been in accordance with the *polarity* strategy.

Proof 2

Let us again apply splitting rules to assertion A2 and goal G3, obtaining

A4. *if* $\boxed{P}^{+}$ *then* R	
A5. *if* $\boxed{Q}^{+}$ *then* R	
A6. $\boxed{P}^{-}$ *or* Q	
	G7. $\boxed{R}^{+}$

The rows are the same as before, but the polarity annotations reflect the application of the *resolution* rule in Proof 2.

Applying *AA-resolution* to assertions A6 and A4, matching P, we obtain the assertion

false or Q
   or
if true then R,

which reduces (by the *false-or* and *if-true* simplifications) to

A8′. Q *or* $\boxed{R}^{-}$	

Applying *AG-resolution* to assertion A8′ and goal G7, matching R, yields the goal

not (Q or false)
   and
true,

which reduces (by *or-false* and *and-true* simplifications) to

	G9′. *not* $\boxed{Q}^{-}$

Applying *GA-resolution* to goal G9′ and assertion A5, matching Q, we obtain

not false
   and
not (if true then R),

which reduces (by *not-false, true-and,* and *if-true* simplifications) to

	G10'. *not* $\boxed{R}^{\,-}$

By *GG-resolution*, applied to goal G10' and goal G7, matching R, we obtain the goal

not false
   and
true,

which reduces (by *not-false* and *true-and* simplifications) to the final goal,

	G11'. *true*

We have thus proved in two different ways the validity of the sentence

$$if \quad \begin{bmatrix} if \ P \ then \ R \\ and \\ if \ Q \ then \ R \end{bmatrix} \quad then \quad \begin{bmatrix} if \ (P \ or \ Q) \\ then \ R \end{bmatrix}.$$

We can also prove the converse of this sentence, that is,

$$if \quad \begin{bmatrix} if \ (P \ or \ Q) \\ then \ R \end{bmatrix} \quad then \quad \begin{bmatrix} if \ P \ then \ R \\ and \\ if \ Q \ then \ R \end{bmatrix}.$$

The proof is requested in **Problem 2.5(a)**.

Remark (implicit simplification). In deriving a new row we always simplify the result before adding it to the tableau. Up to now, we have been scrupulous in mentioning that simplification has taken place, and we have specified exactly which simplifications have occurred. Henceforth we shall usually apply simplification automatically as part of each deduction rule, not mentioning exactly which simplifications have been used. ⏌

In **Problem 2.5(b)–(f)** the reader is requested to use the deductive-tableau system to prove the validity of several sentences.

USE OF VALID SENTENCES

Once we have proved the validity of a sentence, we may add it as an initial assertion in proofs of subsequent theorems. Let us illustrate this.

Example.   Suppose we would like to show the validity of the equivalence

$$\begin{bmatrix} if \ P \ then \ R \\ and \\ if \ Q \ then \ R \end{bmatrix} \ \equiv \ \begin{bmatrix} if \ (P \ or \ Q) \\ then \ R \end{bmatrix}.$$

We begin with the initial tableau

assertions	goals
	G1. $\begin{bmatrix} if \ P \ then \ R \\ and \\ if \ Q \ then \ R \end{bmatrix} \ \equiv \ \begin{bmatrix} if \ (P \ or \ Q) \\ then \ R \end{bmatrix}$

Because we proved the validity of the sentence

$$if \ \begin{bmatrix} if \ P \ then \ R \\ and \\ if \ Q \ then \ R \end{bmatrix} \ then \ \begin{bmatrix} if \ (P \ or \ Q) \\ then \ R \end{bmatrix}$$

in an earlier example, and requested as an exercise to prove its converse,

$$if \ \begin{bmatrix} if \ (P \ or \ Q) \\ then \ R \end{bmatrix} \ then \ \begin{bmatrix} if \ P \ then \ R \\ and \\ if \ Q \ then \ R \end{bmatrix},$$

we may add these sentences as new assertions in our initial tableau:

A2.	$if \ \begin{bmatrix} if \ P \ then \ R \\ and \\ if \ Q \ then \ R \end{bmatrix} \ then \ \begin{bmatrix} if \ (P \ or \ Q) \\ then \ R \end{bmatrix}^{-}$	
A3.	$if \ \begin{bmatrix} if \ (P \ or \ Q) \\ then \ R \end{bmatrix} \ then \ \begin{bmatrix} if \ P \ then \ R \\ and \\ if \ Q \ then \ R \end{bmatrix}^{-}$	

By the *iff-and* elimination rewriting (left-to-right)

$$\mathcal{F} \equiv \mathcal{G} \quad \Leftrightarrow \quad \begin{bmatrix} if \ \mathcal{F} \ then \ \mathcal{G} \\ and \\ if \ \mathcal{G} \ then \ \mathcal{F} \end{bmatrix},$$

we decompose the equivalence in goal G1 into a conjunction of implications, that is,

G4. $\quad$ if $\begin{bmatrix} if\ P\ then\ R \\ and \\ if\ Q\ then\ R \end{bmatrix}$ $\quad$ then $\begin{bmatrix} if\ (P\ or\ Q) \\ then\ R \end{bmatrix}^{+}$

and

$\quad$ $\begin{bmatrix} if\ \begin{bmatrix} if\ (P\ or\ Q) \\ then\ R \end{bmatrix}\ then\ \begin{bmatrix} if\ P\ then\ R \\ and \\ if\ Q\ then\ R \end{bmatrix} \end{bmatrix}$

The two conjuncts of goal G4 are identical to the assertions A2 and A3. We may drop the first conjunct of goal G4 by *AG-resolution* applied to assertion A2 and goal G4, leaving the second conjunct:

G5. $\quad$ if $\begin{bmatrix} if\ (P\ or\ Q) \\ then\ R \end{bmatrix}$ $\quad$ then $\begin{bmatrix} if\ P\ then\ R \\ and \\ if\ Q\ then\ R \end{bmatrix}^{+}$

By *AG-resolution* applied to assertion A3 and goal G5, we obtain the final goal,

G6. $\quad$ *true*

We could have proved the equivalence of the preceding example even if we had not previously proved the two implications, but the proof would have been more cumbersome.

In general, if we are given an equivalence of form

$$\mathcal{F} \equiv \mathcal{G}$$

to prove, we may find it convenient first to prove separately the corresponding two implications

$$if\ \mathcal{F}\ then\ \mathcal{G} \quad\quad and \quad\quad if\ \mathcal{G}\ then\ \mathcal{F},$$

and then to add these implications as assertions in the proof of the equivalence.

In **Problem 2.5(g)** the reader is requested to prove the validity of such an equivalence.

PROOFS MAY RUN ON FOREVER

As we have mentioned, many different sequences of deduction rules can be applied
to a given sentence. Even if the tableau is valid and the *polarity* strategy is
observed, not all of these possible paths will lead to a proof. Special care must
be taken with the *rewriting* rule, as illustrated in the following example.

Example.   Consider the valid sentence

$$\mathcal{S}: \quad \begin{array}{c} (not\ P)\ \ or\ \ (not\ Q) \\ or \\ P\ \ and\ \ Q. \end{array}$$

First, let us give a successful proof of this sentence.

Successful proof

  We begin with the tableau

assertions	goals
	G1. $(not\ P)\ \ or\ \ (not\ Q)$ or $P\ \ and\ \ Q$

Applying the *or-split* rule (twice), we decompose goal G1 into

	G2. $not\ \boxed{P}^{\,-}$
	G3. $not\ \boxed{Q}^{\,-}$
	G4. $\boxed{P}^{\,+}\ and\ Q$

By *GG-resolution* applied to goals G2 and G4, matching P, we obtain

	G5. $\boxed{Q}^{\,+}$

Then, by the *GG-resolution* rule applied to goals G3 and G5, we obtain the
final goal,

	G6. *true*

This shows that there is a sequence of deduction rules that does lead to a proof.

Failed attempt

Now let us exhibit a sequence of deduction rules that continues endlessly but fails to lead to a proof of $\mathcal{S}$.

We begin with the same initial tableau:

assertions	goals	
	G1.	$\begin{array}{l} (not\ P)\ \ or\ \ (not\ Q) \\ \quad or \\ P\ \ and\ \ Q \end{array}$

By the *or-and* distributivity rewriting (left-to-right),

$$\mathcal{F}\ \ or\ \ (\mathcal{G}\ \ and\ \ \mathcal{H})\quad\Leftrightarrow\quad(\mathcal{F}\ \ or\ \ \mathcal{G})\ \ and\ \ (\mathcal{F}\ \ or\ \ \mathcal{H}),$$

we obtain the goal

	goals	
	G2.	$\begin{array}{l} ((not\ P)\ \ or\ \ (not\ Q))\ \ or\ \ P \\ \quad and \\ ((not\ P)\ \ or\ \ (not\ Q))\ \ or\ \ Q \end{array}$

By the *and-or* distributivity rewriting (left-to-right),

$$\mathcal{F}\ \ and\ \ (\mathcal{G}\ \ or\ \ \mathcal{H})\quad\Leftrightarrow\quad(\mathcal{F}\ \ and\ \ \mathcal{G})\ \ or\ \ (\mathcal{F}\ \ and\ \ \mathcal{H}),$$

we obtain the goal

	goals	
	G3.	$\begin{bmatrix} ((not\ P)\ \ or\ \ (not\ Q))\ \ or\ \ P \\ \quad and \\ (not\ P)\ \ or\ \ (not\ Q) \end{bmatrix}$ or $\begin{bmatrix} ((not\ P)\ \ or\ \ (not\ Q))\ \ or\ \ P \\ \quad and \\ Q \end{bmatrix}$

The form of this goal enables us to apply *or-and* distributivity rewriting again. Afterwards, we will be able to apply the *and-or* distributivity rewriting again, and so on, indefinitely. In other words, even though the original sentence was valid, it is possible to apply the infinite sequence *or-and, and-or, or-and, and-or, ...* of distributivity rewritings without ever discovering a proof. ⏺

2.8   EQUIVALENCE RULE

If some of the assertions and goals of our tableau contain the equivalence connective $\equiv$, we can treat it like any other connective. Some proofs can be made shorter, easier to find, and more readable, however, if we use the special *equivalence* rule that we introduce in this section. The *equivalence* rule enables us to replace subsentences of the tableau with equivalent sentences. This rule does not increase the logical power of the system, in the sense that it does not allow us to prove the validity of any new sentences that cannot be proved by the *resolution* rule alone; it does, however, make the system easier to use.

THE BASIC FORM

The basic form of the *equivalence* rule is expressed as follows.

Rule (AA-equivalence, left-to-right)

Note that, because the replacement of $(\mathcal{P} \equiv \mathcal{Q})$ with *false* simplifies

assertions	goals
$\mathcal{A}_1[\mathcal{P} \equiv \mathcal{Q}]$	
$\mathcal{A}_2\langle \mathcal{P} \rangle$	
$\mathcal{A}_1[\textit{false}]$ *or* $\mathcal{A}_2\langle \mathcal{Q} \rangle$	

where $\mathcal{A}_1$ contains at least one occurrence of a subsentence $(\mathcal{P} \equiv \mathcal{Q})$ and $\mathcal{A}_2$ contains at least one occurrence of the subsentence $\mathcal{P}$. ◢

More precisely, to apply the rule to a tableau, we do the following:

- Choose an assertion $\mathcal{A}_1[\mathcal{P} \equiv \mathcal{Q}]$ with a subsentence of the form $(\mathcal{P} \equiv \mathcal{Q})$, where $\mathcal{P}$ and $\mathcal{Q}$ are distinct.
- Choose an assertion $\mathcal{A}_2\langle \mathcal{P} \rangle$ with a subsentence $\mathcal{P}$.
- Replace every occurrence of $(\mathcal{P} \equiv \mathcal{Q})$ in $\mathcal{A}_1[\mathcal{P} \equiv \mathcal{Q}]$ with the truth symbol *false*, obtaining $\mathcal{A}_1[\textit{false}]$.
- Replace some (one or more) of the occurrences of $\mathcal{P}$ in $\mathcal{A}_2\langle \mathcal{P} \rangle$ with $\mathcal{Q}$, obtaining $\mathcal{A}_2\langle \mathcal{Q} \rangle$.
- Take the disjunction $(\mathcal{A}_1[\textit{false}] \textit{ or } \mathcal{A}_2\langle \mathcal{Q} \rangle)$ and apply to it all possible simplifications.

- Add the simplified disjunction to the tableau as a new assertion.

We will say that we have applied the *AA-equivalence* rule to $\mathcal{A}_1[\mathcal{P} \equiv \mathcal{Q}]$ and $\mathcal{A}_2\langle \mathcal{P} \rangle$, *replacing* $\mathcal{P}$ *with* $\mathcal{Q}$.

Note that, because the replacement of $(\mathcal{P} \equiv \mathcal{Q})$ with *false* simplifies the sentence, the rule is defined to replace every occurrence of $(\mathcal{P} \equiv \mathcal{Q})$ in $\mathcal{A}_1[\mathcal{P} \equiv \mathcal{Q}]$ with *false*. On the other hand, because in some proofs we want to replace certain occurrences of $\mathcal{P}$ with $\mathcal{Q}$, but leave others intact, the rule is defined to replace some (at least one) but not necessarily all occurrences of $\mathcal{P}$ in $\mathcal{A}_2\langle \mathcal{P} \rangle$ with $\mathcal{Q}$.

The preceding left-to-right version of the *AA-equivalence* rule replaces occurrences of the left-hand side $\mathcal{P}$ of the equivalence with the right-hand side $\mathcal{Q}$. By the symmetry of the $\equiv$ connective, i.e., because $(\mathcal{P} \equiv \mathcal{Q})$ and $(\mathcal{Q} \equiv \mathcal{P})$ are themselves equivalent, we can apply the rule right-to-left to replace occurrences of the right-hand side $\mathcal{Q}$ with the left-hand side $\mathcal{P}$ instead.

Rule (AA-equivalence, right-to-left)

assertions	goals
$\mathcal{A}_1[\mathcal{P} \equiv \mathcal{Q}]$	
$\mathcal{A}_2\langle \mathcal{Q} \rangle$	
$\mathcal{A}_1[\textit{false}]$ *or* $\mathcal{A}_2\langle \mathcal{P} \rangle$	

where $\mathcal{A}_1$ contains at least one occurrence of a subsentence $(\mathcal{P} \equiv \mathcal{Q})$ and $\mathcal{A}_2$ contains at least one occurrence of the subsentence $\mathcal{Q}$. ⌟

EXAMPLES

Before we justify the rule, let us illustrate it with two examples.

Example. Suppose that our tableau contains the assertions

assertions	goals
$\mathcal{A}_1$: $\big[\,\boxed{P} \equiv Q\,\big]$ *or* R	
$\mathcal{A}_2$: *if* $\Big(\boxed{P}$ *and* $S\Big)$ *then* P	

Here, taking $\mathcal{P}$ to be P and $\mathcal{Q}$ to be Q, the assertion $\mathcal{A}_1[\mathcal{P} \equiv \mathcal{Q}]$ contains a subsentence $(P \equiv Q)$, and the assertion $\mathcal{A}_2\langle\mathcal{P}\rangle$ contains a subsentence P.

We annotate with brackets the equivalence and with boxes the subsentences that are matched in applying the rule. Replacing every occurrence of $(P \equiv Q)$ in $\mathcal{A}_1[\mathcal{P} \equiv \mathcal{Q}]$ with the truth symbol *false*, we obtain

$\quad\quad\mathcal{A}_1[false]: \quad$ *false or R*.

Replacing the first occurrence of P in $\mathcal{A}_2\langle\mathcal{P}\rangle$ with Q, we obtain

$\quad\quad\mathcal{A}_2\langle\mathcal{Q}\rangle: \quad$ *if (Q and S) then P*.

By the *AA-equivalence* rule (left-to-right version), we may add the disjunction

$$\mathcal{A}_1[false] \;\; or \;\; \mathcal{A}_2\langle\mathcal{Q}\rangle: \quad \begin{array}{c} \textit{false or R} \\ \textit{or} \\ \textit{if (Q and S) then P} \end{array}$$

as a new assertion, which reduces (by *false-or* simplification) to

R or *if (Q and S) then P*	

In the preceding example, we replaced only the first occurrence of P in $\mathcal{A}_2$ with Q. We could have replaced only the second occurrence of P, ultimately obtaining the assertion

R or *if (P and S) then Q*	

Alternatively, we could have replaced both occurrences of P in $\mathcal{A}_2$ with Q, ultimately obtaining the assertion

R or *if (Q and S) then Q*	

Each of the three assertions was obtained by different applications of the *equivalence* rule to the same two assertions $\mathcal{A}_1$ and $\mathcal{A}_2$. ⌁

Example.   Suppose our tableau contains the assertions

assertions	goals
$\mathcal{A}_1:$ *if* S *then* $\Big[(Q \ or \ R) \ \equiv \ \boxed{not \ P} \Big]$	
$\mathcal{A}_2:$ $\boxed{not \ P}$ *and* Q	

Then we can apply the right-to-left version of the *AA-equivalence* rule to the assertions, replacing $\mathcal{Q}: (not \ P)$ in assertion $\mathcal{A}_2$ with $\mathcal{P}: (Q \ or \ R)$, to obtain the new assertion

if S *then* *false*
   or
$(Q \ or \ R)$ *and* $Q,$

which reduces (by *then-false* simplification) to

not S *or* $(Q \ or \ R)$ *and* Q	

This cannot be simplified further because we have chosen not to include the possible simplification

$$(\mathcal{F} \ or \ \mathcal{G}) \ and \ \mathcal{F} \ \Rightarrow \ \mathcal{F}$$

in our catalog.

Note that in this example we replaced the subsentence $(not \ P)$, not just a single propositional symbol. ◢

Remark (at least one replacement). Although our substitution notation admits the possibility that the subsentence $\mathcal{P} \equiv \mathcal{Q}$ does not occur in the assertion $\mathcal{A}_1$, the wording of the rule requires that it occur at least once. Otherwise, the assertion we derive would be weaker than $\mathcal{A}_1$. Similarly, we require in words that at least one occurrence of $\mathcal{P}$ in $\mathcal{A}_2$ be replaced by $\mathcal{Q}$; otherwise, there would be little point in applying the rule. ◢

JUSTIFICATION

Now let us justify the *AA-equivalence* rule.

Justification (AA-equivalence).   The justification for the *AA-equivalence* rule is analogous to that for the *AA-resolution* rule. We consider the left-to-right version; the proof of the right-to-left version is similar.

Consider an interpretation $\mathcal{I}$ under which the required subtableau $\mathcal{T}_r$ is false, i.e., the required assertions $\mathcal{A}_1[\mathcal{P} \equiv \mathcal{Q}]$ and $\mathcal{A}_2\langle \mathcal{P} \rangle$ are both true under $\mathcal{I}$. By the *justification* proposition, it suffices to establish that the generated subtableau $\mathcal{T}_g$ is false under $\mathcal{I}$, that is, that the assertion generated by the rule, the simplified disjunction

$$\mathcal{A}_1[false] \quad or \quad \mathcal{A}_2\langle \mathcal{Q} \rangle,$$

is true under $\mathcal{I}$.

We distinguish between two subcases.

Case: $(\mathcal{P} \equiv \mathcal{Q})$ is false under $\mathcal{I}$

Then (by the semantic rule for $\equiv$), the equivalence $\big((\mathcal{P} \equiv \mathcal{Q}) \equiv false\big)$ is true under $\mathcal{I}$. Thus (by the substitutivity of equivalence), because $\mathcal{A}_1[\mathcal{P} \equiv \mathcal{Q}]$ is true under $\mathcal{I}$, $\mathcal{A}_1[false]$ is also true under $\mathcal{I}$. By the semantic rule for the *or* connective, the disjunction

$$\mathcal{A}_1[false] \quad or \quad \mathcal{A}_2\langle \mathcal{Q} \rangle$$

is true under $\mathcal{I}$. The simplified disjunction is true under $\mathcal{I}$ as well.

Case: $(\mathcal{P} \equiv \mathcal{Q})$ is true under $\mathcal{I}$

Then (by the substitutivity of equivalence), because $\mathcal{A}_2\langle \mathcal{P} \rangle$ is true, $\mathcal{A}_2\langle \mathcal{Q} \rangle$ is also true under $\mathcal{I}$, and (by the semantic rule for the *or* connective) the disjunction

$$\mathcal{A}_1[false] \quad or \quad \mathcal{A}_2\langle \mathcal{Q} \rangle$$

is true under $\mathcal{I}$. The simplified disjunction is true under $\mathcal{I}$ as well.

Because, in each case, the conclusion of the *AA-equivalence* rule is true under $\mathcal{I}$, the *justification* condition for the rule is established. ⌙

DUAL FORMS

The form of the *AA-equivalence* rule we have just introduced applies to two assertions. By the duality between assertions and goals, we can establish the following alternative forms.

Rule (GG-equivalence, left-to-right)

assertions	goals
	$\mathcal{G}_1[\mathcal{P} \equiv \mathcal{Q}]$
	$\mathcal{G}_2\langle\mathcal{P}\rangle$
	$\mathcal{G}_1[\mathit{false}]$ *and* $\mathcal{G}_2\langle\mathcal{Q}\rangle$

where $\mathcal{G}_1$ and $\mathcal{G}_2$ satisfy the same requirements as $\mathcal{A}_1$ and $\mathcal{A}_2$, respectively, in the *AA-equivalence* rule. ◢

Rule (AG-equivalence, left-to-right)

assertions	goals
$\mathcal{A}[\mathcal{P} \equiv \mathcal{Q}]$	
	$\mathcal{G}\langle\mathcal{P}\rangle$
	not $(\mathcal{A}[\mathit{false}])$ *and* $\mathcal{G}\langle\mathcal{Q}\rangle$

where $\mathcal{A}$ and $\mathcal{G}$ satisfy the same requirements as $\mathcal{A}_1$ and $\mathcal{A}_2$, respectively, in the *AA-equivalence* rule. ◢

Rule (GA-equivalence, left-to-right)

assertions	goals
	$\mathcal{G}[\mathcal{P} \equiv \mathcal{Q}]$
$\mathcal{A}\langle\mathcal{P}\rangle$	
	$\mathcal{G}[\mathit{false}]$ *and* *not* $(\mathcal{A}\langle\mathcal{Q}\rangle)$

where $\mathcal{G}$ and $\mathcal{A}$ satisfy the same requirements as $\mathcal{A}_1$ and $\mathcal{A}_2$, respectively, in the *AA-equivalence* rule. ◢

The right-to-left versions of these rules are analogous. The reader is requested to justify related rules in **Problems 2.6** and **2.7**.

We have remarked that the *equivalence* rule gives no additional power to our propositional-logic system, in the sense that no sentences can be proved with the rule that cannot be proved without it. The rule does, however, make some deductions shorter, easier to find, and more readable.

Example. Suppose we would like to prove the validity of the sentence

$$if \begin{bmatrix} P \ \equiv \ Q \\ and \\ (P \ and \ R) \ or \ S \end{bmatrix}$$

then $(Q \ and \ R) \ or \ S$.

We first give a proof that uses the *equivalence* rule. Later, we prove the same sentence without using the rule.

Proof (with equivalence rule)

We begin with the initial tableau

assertions	goals
	G1. *if* $\begin{bmatrix} P \ \equiv \ Q \\ and \\ (P \ and \ R) \ or \ S \end{bmatrix}$ *then* $(Q \ and \ R) \ or \ S$

Applying the *if-split* and *and-split* rules, we decompose goal G1 to obtain the rows

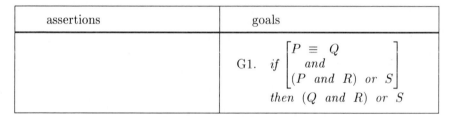

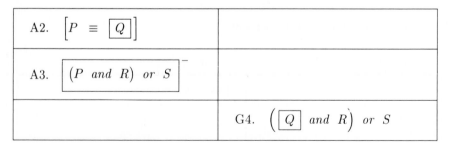

Applying the *AG-equivalence* rule (right-to-left) with assertion A2, we may replace Q with P in goal G4, to obtain

> *not false*
>   *and*
> $(P \ and \ R) \ or \ S,$

which reduces (by *not-false* and *true-and* simplifications) to

	G5. $\boxed{(P \ \ and \ \ R) \ \ or \ \ S}^{+}$

Then, by *AG-resolution* applied to assertion A3 and goal G5, we obtain the final goal

	G6. *true*

We now prove the same sentence without using the *equivalence* rule.

Proof (*without equivalence rule*)

We begin with the initial tableau

assertions	goals
	G1. *if* $\begin{bmatrix} P \ \equiv \ Q \\ and \\ (P \ \ and \ \ R) \ \ or \ \ S \end{bmatrix}$ *then* $(Q \ \ and \ \ R) \ \ or \ \ S$

Applying the *if-split* and *and-split* rules, we decompose goal G1 to obtain

A2. $P \ \equiv \ \boxed{Q}^{\pm}$	
A3. $(P \ \ and \ \ R) \ \ or \ \ \boxed{S}^{-}$	
	G4. $(Q \ \ and \ \ R) \ \ or \ \ S$

Applying the *or-split* rule, we may decompose goal G4 into

	G5. $Q \ \ and \ \ \boxed{R}^{+}$
	G6. $\boxed{S}^{+}$

By *AG-resolution*, applied to assertion A3 and goal G6, matching S, we obtain the goal

	G7. $not \left(P \;\; and \;\; \boxed{R}^{-} \right)$

(To understand the rest of the proof it is helpful to observe that, by *duality*, G7 is equivalent to an assertion $(P \; and \; R)$.)

By *GG-resolution*, applied to goals G7 and G5, matching R, we obtain the goal

	G8. $\boxed{Q}^{+}$

By *AG-resolution*, applied to assertion A2 and goal G8, matching Q, we obtain the goal

	G9. $\boxed{P}^{+}$

(Note that the preceding application of the *resolution* rule is in accordance with the polarity strategy, because the occurrence of Q in A2 has both polarities, while the occurrence of Q in G8 is positive, in the tableau.)

By *GG-resolution*, applied to our earlier goal G7,

	$not \left(\boxed{P}^{-} and \;\; R \right)$

and goal G9, we obtain the goal

	G10. *true*

The reader may confirm that the proof without the *equivalence* rule is somewhat longer. ◢

POLARITY STRATEGY

We can be guided in applying the *equivalence* rule by a strategy that is analogous to the *polarity* strategy for the *resolution* rule and allows us to avoid many fruitless applications of the *equivalence* rule.

Strategy (polarity)

> Consider an application of the *equivalence* rule in which every occurrence
> of a subsentence $(\mathcal{P} \equiv \mathcal{Q})$ in the assertion or goal $\mathcal{F}[\mathcal{P} \equiv \mathcal{Q}]$ is replaced
> by the truth symbol *false*.
>
> Then we will say that the rule has been applied in accordance with the
> *polarity strategy* if
>
> > at least one occurrence of $(\mathcal{P} \equiv \mathcal{Q})$ in $\mathcal{F}[\mathcal{P} \equiv \mathcal{Q}]$ is negative in
> > the tableau. ◢

Note again that the negative polarity of $(\mathcal{P} \equiv \mathcal{Q})$ need not be strict. The polarity
of the occurrences of $\mathcal{P}$ in $\mathcal{G}\langle\mathcal{P}\rangle$ is not restricted by the strategy at all.

All the examples of the application of the *equivalence* rule in this section
have been in accordance with the *polarity* strategy. For instance, in one of the
examples we applied the rule to the assertions

$\mathcal{A}_1:$	*if* S *then* $\Big[(Q \ or \ R) \ \equiv \ \boxed{not \ P}\Big]^{\,-}$	
$\mathcal{A}_2:$	$\boxed{not \ P} \ and \ Q$	

This application was in accordance with the *polarity* strategy because one occurrence (the only occurrence) of

$$(Q \ or \ R) \ \equiv \ \boxed{not \ P}$$

in assertion $\mathcal{A}_1$ is negative in the tableau.

Now let us see how a violation of the strategy can lead in a fruitless direction.

Example (violating the strategy).   Suppose our tableau contains the assertion and goal

assertions	goals
$not \ \Big[\boxed{P} \equiv Q\Big]^{\,+}$	
	$\boxed{P} \ and \ S$

Note that the assertion contains no negative occurrences of the equivalence $(P \equiv Q)$. If we apply the *AG-equivalence* rule (left-to-right) to replace P with Q in the
goal, in violation of the *polarity* strategy, we obtain the new goal

> *not* (*not false*)
>   *and*
> *Q and S*,

which reduces (by simplification) to the trivial goal

	false

This goal cannot help us in any proof. ◢

In **Problem 2.8**, the reader is requested to prove a sentence in two different ways: with and without the *equivalence* rule.

PROBLEMS

Problem 2.1 (tableaux as sets)   page 63

(a) *Union of tableaux*

Prove the *union-tableau* proposition:

For any tableaux T_1 and T_2 and interpretation $\mathcal{I}$,

$T_1 \cup T_2$ is true under $\mathcal{I}$
  if and only if
T_1 is true under $\mathcal{I}$ or T_2 is true under $\mathcal{I}$.

(b) *Intermediate tableau*

Prove the *intermediate-tableau* proposition:

For any tableaux T_1, T_2, and T_3,

if $T_1 \subseteq T_2 \subseteq T_3$,
  then if T_1 is equivalent to T_3,
    then T_1 is equivalent to T_2 and T_2 is equivalent to T_3.

Problem 2.2 (extended justification proposition)   page 75

(a) The *justification* proposition allows us to establish the soundness of rules that add new rows to a tableau without deleting any old rows. Suppose we want to justify rules that may both add new rows and delete old ones. Formulate a *justification* condition, analogous to the one given in the proposition, for this extended class of rules. Show that, if its *justification* condition holds, a rule is sound, i.e., it preserves the equivalence of the tableau.

(b) Suppose the extended *and-split* rule deletes the assertion ($\mathcal{A}_1$ *and* $\mathcal{A}_2$) as well as adding the two new assertions $\mathcal{A}_1$ and $\mathcal{A}_2$. Use your extended *justification* proposition to establish the soundness of this rule.

Problem 2.3 (hyper-resolution rule)   page 84

Justify the following extension of the *resolution* rule:

assertions	goals
$\mathcal{A}_1[\mathcal{P}]$	
$\mathcal{A}_2[\mathcal{Q}]$	
$\mathcal{A}_3[\mathcal{P}, \mathcal{Q}]$	
$\mathcal{A}_1[true]$ or $\mathcal{A}_2[false]$ or $\mathcal{A}_3[false,\ true]$	

Here $\mathcal{P}$ has at least one occurrence in $\mathcal{A}_1[\mathcal{P}]$, $\mathcal{Q}$ has at least one occurrence in $\mathcal{A}_2[\mathcal{Q}]$, and $\mathcal{P}$ and $\mathcal{Q}$ each have at least one occurrence in $\mathcal{A}_3[\mathcal{P}, \mathcal{Q}]$.

Problem 2.4 (common examples of the resolution rule)   page 87

Apply the *resolution* rule to the following rows:

(a)   *Transitivity of implication*

assertions	goals
if P then Q	
if Q then R	

(b)   *Double backward chaining*

assertions	goals
if P_1 then (if P_2 then Q)	
	Q

Problem 2.5 (tableau proofs of valid sentences)   page 99, 101

Use the deductive-tableau technique to prove the validity of the following sentences:

(a)   *if* $\begin{bmatrix} if\ (P\ or\ Q) \\ then\ R \end{bmatrix}$ *then* $\begin{bmatrix} if\ P\ then\ R \\ and \\ if\ Q\ then\ R \end{bmatrix}$

(b)   *if* $\big(if\ (not\ P)\ then\ Q\big)$
     then $\big(if\ (not\ Q)\ then\ P\big)$

(c) *if* $\begin{bmatrix} if\ (if\ P\ then\ Q) \\ then\ P \end{bmatrix}$ *then* *P*

(d) *if P*
    then $(P\ and\ (P\ or\ Q))$

(e) *if* $\begin{bmatrix} if\ (not\ P)\ then\ (not\ Q) \\ and \\ if\ (not\ P)\ then\ Q \end{bmatrix}$ *then* *P*

(f) *if* $\begin{bmatrix} (P\ or\ Q)\ and \\ (if\ P\ then\ R)\ and \\ if\ Q\ then\ R \end{bmatrix}$ *then* *R* .

(g) *if P then* $(Q\ or\ R)$
       $\equiv$
    if $(P\ and\ (not\ Q))$ *then* *R*.

Problem 2.6 (equivalence matching rule)   page 110

   Consider the following *AA-equivalence matching* rule:

assertions	goals
$\mathcal{A}_1[\mathcal{P}]$	
$\mathcal{A}_2[\mathcal{Q}]$	
if $(\mathcal{P} \equiv \mathcal{Q})$ *then* $(\mathcal{A}_1[false]\ or\ \mathcal{A}_2[true])$	

where $\mathcal{A}_1$ and $\mathcal{A}_2$ contain at least one occurrence of $\mathcal{P}$ and $\mathcal{Q}$, respectively.

(a) Justify the rule.

(b) Give the *GG-equivalence matching* rule and its justification.

Problem 2.7 (implication rule)   page 110

   Justify the following two special rules for the implication connective *if-then*:

(a) *Left-to-right version*

assertions	goals
$\mathcal{A}_1[\textit{if } \mathcal{P} \textit{ then } \mathcal{Q}]$	
$\mathcal{A}_2\langle\mathcal{P}^-\rangle$	
$\mathcal{A}_1[\textit{false}] \;\;\textit{or}\;\; \mathcal{A}_2\langle\mathcal{Q}^-\rangle$	

where $\mathcal{A}_1$ has at least one occurrence of the subsentence $(\textit{if } \mathcal{P} \textit{ then } \mathcal{Q})$, and $\mathcal{A}_2$ has
at least one occurrence of the subsentence $\mathcal{P}$ that is strictly negative in the tableau.
Here $\mathcal{A}_2\langle\mathcal{Q}^-\rangle$ indicates the result of replacing with $\mathcal{Q}$ one or more occurrences of
$\mathcal{P}$ in $\mathcal{A}_2\langle\mathcal{P}^-\rangle$ that are strictly negative in the tableau.

(b) *Right-to-left version*

assertions	goals
$\mathcal{A}_1[\textit{if } \mathcal{P} \textit{ then } \mathcal{Q}]$	
$\mathcal{A}_2\langle\mathcal{Q}^+\rangle$	
$\mathcal{A}_1[\textit{false}] \;\;\textit{or}\;\; \mathcal{A}_2\langle\mathcal{P}^+\rangle$	

where $\mathcal{A}_1$ has at least one occurrence of the subsentence $(\textit{if } \mathcal{P} \textit{ then } \mathcal{Q})$, and $\mathcal{A}_2$
has at least one occurrence of the subsentence $\mathcal{Q}$ that is strictly positive in the
tableau. As before, $\mathcal{A}_2\langle\mathcal{P}^+\rangle$ indicates the result of replacing with $\mathcal{P}$ one or more
occurrences of $\mathcal{Q}$ in $\mathcal{A}_2\langle\mathcal{Q}^+\rangle$ that are strictly positive in the tableau.

Problem 2.8 (transitivity of equivalence)   page 114

Use the deductive-tableau system to prove the validity of the sentence

$$\textit{if}\; \begin{bmatrix} P \;\equiv\; Q \\ \textit{and} \\ Q \;\equiv\; R \end{bmatrix} \;\textit{then}\; (P \;\equiv\; R)$$

in two different ways:

(a) Using the *equivalence* rule.

(b) Without using the *equivalence* rule.

Predicate

Logic

3

Foundations

3.1 INTRODUCTION

By our study of propositional logic we have determined that a sentence such as

The monkeys on Jupiter are red
or
the monkeys on Jupiter are not red

is true without needing to investigate Jovian biology: The sentence is an instance of the valid propositional-logic sentence

$$P \ \ or \ \ (not \ P),$$

taking P to be the proposition "The monkeys on Jupiter are red."

There are some sentences, however, that we can tell to be true by their form, but that are not instances of any valid sentences in propositional logic. For example, we can tell that the sentences

There are red rocks on Jupiter
or
all the rocks on Jupiter are not red

and

There is an odd perfect number
or
all perfect numbers are not odd

are true without launching a spacecraft or even knowing the definition of a perfect number. The propositional-logic language is too coarse and primitive to express the concept of an object, a property of an object (such as being a rock or a perfect number), or a relationship between several objects.

The predicate-logic language we are about to introduce extends propositional logic by enabling us to speak about objects and the relationships between them. In this language, the two sentences above can both be regarded as instances of the abstract sentence

$$\mathcal{F}: \quad \begin{array}{l} (\exists x)\big[p(x) \ \ and \ \ q(x)\big] \\ or \\ (\forall x)\big[if \ \ p(x) \ \ then \ \ not \ q(x)\big]. \end{array}$$

Here, for a given domain of objects, $(\exists x)$ means "there exists an object x" and $(\forall x)$ means "for every object x."

For the "rocks" sentence, we take the domain of objects to be the rocks, $p(x)$ to be "x is on Jupiter," and $q(x)$ to be "x is red." Under this interpretation, the intuitive meaning of the abstract sentence $\mathcal{F}$ becomes

> There exists a rock x such that x is on Jupiter and x is red
>
> or
>
> for every rock x, if x is on Jupiter then x is not red,

which is an awkward rewording of the original rock sentence.

For the "numbers" sentence, we take the domain of objects to be the numbers, $p(x)$ to be "x is a perfect number," and $q(x)$ to be "x is odd." Under this interpretation, the intuitive meaning of the abstract sentence $\mathcal{F}$ becomes

> There exists a number x such that x is a perfect number and x is odd
>
> or
>
> for every number x, if x is a perfect number then x is not odd.

Both of the interpreted sentences are true; in fact, any instance of the abstract sentence $\mathcal{F}$ is true regardless of the choice of a domain of objects or the meaning assigned to $p(x)$ and $q(x)$.

On the other hand, not every instance of the abstract sentence

$$\mathcal{G}: \quad \begin{array}{l} (\forall x)p(x) \\ or \\ (\forall x)[not \ p(x)] \end{array}$$

is true. For example, if we take the domain of objects to be the animals and $p(x)$ to be "x is a rhesus monkey," the intuitive meaning of the sentence $\mathcal{G}$ becomes

> For every animal x, x is a rhesus monkey
>
> or
>
> for every animal x, x is not a rhesus monkey;

that is,

> Every animal is a rhesus monkey
>
> or
>
> every animal is not a rhesus monkey.

Since it is not true that every animal is a rhesus monkey, but it is also not true that every animal is not a rhesus monkey (in fact, there actually do exist some animals that are rhesus monkeys), the entire sentence is false.

The purpose of this section is to adapt the propositional-logic language to speak of objects and the relationships between them and to extend the notion of validity accordingly. The new language, along with the extended notion of validity, is called *predicate logic*. We then extend the deductive-tableau system to show the validity of predicate-logic sentences.

3.2   THE LANGUAGE

We begin by introducing the language of predicate logic. We present *syntactic rules*, which say what the predicate-logic sentences are without saying what these sentences mean.

THE SENTENCES

We begin by introducing the symbols of predicate logic.

Definition (symbols)

The sentences of predicate logic are made up of the following symbols:

- The *truth symbols*

    true   and   *false*

- The *constant symbols* (or *constants*)

    a, b, c, a', b', c', a_1, b_1, c_1, a_2, b_2, c_2, $\ldots$

    (i.e., the letters a, b, and c, possibly with a prime or a numerical subscript)

- The *variable symbols* (or *variables*)

    u, v, w, x, y, z, u', v', w', x', y', z', u_1, v_1, $\ldots$

- The *function symbols*

    f, g, h, f_1, g_1, h_1, f_2, $\ldots$

    Each function symbol has an associated positive integer called its *arity*, indicating how many arguments the function symbol should take.

- The *predicate symbols*

    p, q, r, p_1, q_1, r_1, p_2, $\ldots$

    Each predicate symbol also has an associated *arity*.   ⌟

A function or predicate symbol of arity n will also be called an *n-ary* function or predicate symbol. Also, 1-ary, 2-ary, and 3-ary symbols are called *unary*, *binary*, and *ternary*, respectively.

Intuitively, the constants and variables will denote objects, and the function and predicate symbols will denote functions and relations, respectively, on these objects.

We build the language from these symbols in three stages: First we define the terms of the language, then we define its propositions, and finally we define its sentences.

Definition (terms)

The *terms* of predicate logic are the expressions that denote objects. They are built up according to the following rules:

- The constants a, b, c, ... are terms.

- The variables u, v, w, ... are terms.

- If t_1, t_2, ..., t_n are terms, where $n \geq 1$ and f is a function symbol of arity n, then the *application*

  $$f(t_1, t_2, \ldots, t_n)$$

  is a term.

- If $\mathcal{F}$ is a sentence and s and t are terms, then the *conditional*

  if $\mathcal{F}$ then s else t

  is a term. Note that this rule depends on the concept of "sentence," which has not yet been defined. The operator *if-then-else* is known as the *conditional term constructor*. ⌙

Example.   Assume the function symbol f is binary, i.e., of arity 2, and the function symbol g is ternary, i.e., of arity 3. Then

a is a term (since a is a constant);

x is a term (since x is a variable);

$f(a, x)$ is a term (since a and x are terms and f is a binary function symbol);

$g(x, f(a, x), a)$ is also a term (since x, $f(a, x)$, and a are terms and g is a ternary function symbol). ⌙

An example of a conditional term is postponed until after the definition of "sentence."

Note that it is impossible for $f(a, x)$ and $f(y)$ both to be terms, because f must have a unique arity. However, it is possible that in one discussion we will assume that f has arity 2 and in another discussion assume that f has arity 1, if there is no chance of confusion. Alternatively, one might have introduced superscripts to indicate the arity; thus, f^1 would be a function symbol of arity 1 and f^2 would be a different function symbol, of arity 2.

Definition (propositions)

The *propositions* of predicate logic are intended to represent relations between objects. They are constructed according to the following rules:

- The truth symbols

    true   and   *false*

    are propositions.

- If t_1, t_2, ..., t_n are terms, where $n \geq 1$ and p is a predicate symbol of arity n, then

    $p(t_1, t_2, \ldots, t_n)$

    is a proposition. ⌐

For example, if p is a ternary predicate symbol, then

$$p(a,\ x,\ f(a,x))$$

is a proposition (since a, x, and $f(a, x)$ are terms and p is a ternary predicate symbol).

Definition (sentences)

The *sentences* of predicate logic are built from its propositions, just as in propositional logic, according to the following rules:

- Every proposition is a sentence.
- If $\mathcal{F}$ is a sentence, then so is its *negation*

    (*not* $\mathcal{F}$).

- If $\mathcal{F}$ and $\mathcal{G}$ are sentences, then so are their *conjunction*,

    ($\mathcal{F}$ *and* $\mathcal{G}$),

    and their *disjunction*,

    ($\mathcal{F}$ *or* $\mathcal{G}$).

- If $\mathcal{F}$ and $\mathcal{G}$ are sentences, then so are the *implication*,

    (*if* $\mathcal{F}$ *then* $\mathcal{G}$),

and the *equivalence*,

$(\mathcal{F} \equiv \mathcal{G})$.

- If $\mathcal{F}$, $\mathcal{G}$, and $\mathcal{H}$ are sentences, then so is the *conditional*,

    (*if* $\mathcal{F}$ *then* $\mathcal{G}$ *else* $\mathcal{H}$).

- If x is any variable and $\mathcal{F}$ is a sentence, then

    $((\forall x)\mathcal{F})$

    and

    $((\exists x)\mathcal{F})$

    are sentences. The prefixes "$\forall$" and "$\exists$" are called the *universal quantifier* and the *existential quantifier*, respectively; the occurrence of $\mathcal{F}$ is said to be the *scope* of the corresponding quantifier; the quantifier is said to *surround* its scope. ⌐

We read $(\forall x)\mathcal{F}$ as "for all x, $\mathcal{F}$" and $(\exists x)\mathcal{F}$ as "for some x, $\mathcal{F}$." ⟦In the first volume of the two-volume version of this book, we write $(\forall x)\mathcal{F}$ as (*for all x*)$\mathcal{F}$ and $(\exists x)\mathcal{F}$ as (*for some x*)$\mathcal{F}$.⟧

We illustrate the definition with an example.

Example.   Assume the function symbols f and g and the predicate symbol q are binary, i.e., of arity 2, and the predicate symbol p is ternary, i.e., of arity 3. Then

$p(a,\, x,\, f(a, x))$

is a sentence (since it is a proposition);

$q(g(b, x),\, y)$

is a sentence (since it is a proposition);

$((\exists y)q(g(b, x),\, y))$

is a sentence (since the scope of the existential quantifier $(\exists y)$ is a sentence);

$\big(p(a,\, x,\, f(a, x)) \ \ and \ \ ((\exists y)q(g(b, x),\, y))\big)$

is a sentence (since both conjuncts are sentences);

$((\forall x)\big(p(a,\, x,\, f(a, x)) \ \ and \ \ ((\exists y)q(g(b, x),\, y))\big))$

is a sentence (since the scope of the universal quantifier $(\forall x)$ is a sentence). ⌐

In conventional logical writings, sentences are known as "formulas." For clarity, we shall display sentences with brackets, braces, two dimensions, and indentation. We omit parentheses when they are not necessary to indicate the structure of a sentence. These are merely informal conventions that do not really extend the language of predicate logic.

Example.   The sentence
$$((\forall x)(p(a,\ x,\ f(a,x))\ \textit{and}\ ((\exists y)q(g(b,x),\ y))))$$
may be written informally as
$$(\forall x)\begin{bmatrix}p(a,\ x,\ f(a,x))\\ \textit{and}\\ (\exists y)q(g(b,x),\ y)\end{bmatrix}.$$

The sentence
$$((\forall y)((\forall x)((\forall z)(\textit{if}\ \ q(y,z)\ \textit{then}\ \ (\textit{if}\ \ r(x)\ \textit{then}$$
$$((\exists u)p(y,z,u))))))))$$
may be written informally as
$$(\forall y,\ x,\ z)\begin{bmatrix}\textit{if}\ \ q(y,z)\\ \textit{then}\ \ \textit{if}\ \ r(x)\\ \qquad\textit{then}\ \ (\exists u)p(y,z,u)\end{bmatrix}.$$

Here $(\forall y,\ x,\ z)$ is an abbreviation for $(\forall y)(\forall x)(\forall z)$.   ⌐

Remark (0-ary function and predicate symbols).   We have required that
the arities of function and predicate symbols be positive integers. It is common
to allow function symbols $a, b, c, \dots$ of arity 0 and to identify the applications
$a(\ ), b(\ ), c(\ ), \dots$ with the constants $a, b, c, \dots$. One might also allow predicate
symbols $P, Q, R, \dots$ of arity 0 and to identify the propositions $P(\ ), Q(\ ), R(\ ), \dots$
with the propositional symbols $P, Q, R, \dots$ of propositional logic.

In our formulation here, for pedagogical reasons, we distinguish between
constants and applications and we do not include propositional symbols in the
language of predicate logic.   ⌐

Note that we have defined *and* and *or* to apply to two arguments. As in
propositional logic, we may extend these connectives to apply to several arguments.

On some occasions we need a phrase that includes both terms and sentences.

Definition (expressions).

An *expression* of predicate logic is either a sentence or a term.   ⌐

Thus both x and $p(x)$ are expressions.

Now that we have defined sentences, the terms employing the *if-then-else*
term constructor are completely characterized. For example, the conditional
$$\begin{aligned}&\textit{if}\ \ (\forall x)p(a,b,x)\\ &\textit{then}\ \ f(a,x)\\ &\textit{else}\ \ g(b,y)\end{aligned}$$
is a term, since $(\forall x)p(a,b,x)$ is a sentence and $f(a,x)$ and $g(b,y)$ are terms.

Remark (*if-then-else*).   We have used the same *if-then-else* operator as a
term constructor to construct conditional terms and as a connective to construct
conditional sentences. Which meaning we intend will be apparent from the *then*
and *else* clauses of the expression. For example,

> *if* $(\forall x)p(a, b, x)$
> *then* $f(a, x)$
> *else* $g(b, y)$

is a term, because $f(a, x)$ and $g(b, y)$ are terms, while

> *if* $(\forall x)p(a, b, x)$
> *then* $(\exists y)q(x, y)$
> *else* $r(y)$

is a sentence, because $(\exists y)q(x, y)$ and $r(y)$ are sentences. ⌐

As in propositional logic, we introduce terminology for the components of an
expression.

Definition (subterms, subsentences, subexpressions).

Every intermediate term we use in building up a term t (including t
itself) or a sentence $\mathcal{F}$ is called a *subterm* of t or $\mathcal{F}$, respectively.

Also, every intermediate sentence we use in building up a term t or a
sentence $\mathcal{F}$ (including $\mathcal{F}$ itself) is called a *subsentence* of t or $\mathcal{F}$, respectively.

Together the subterms and subsentences of a term t (including t itself)
are called the *subexpressions* of t. Similarly, the subterms and subsentences of a sentence $\mathcal{F}$ (including $\mathcal{F}$ itself) are called the *subexpressions*
of $\mathcal{F}$.

A *proper* subterm, *proper* subsentence, or *proper* subexpression of an
expression $\mathcal{E}$ is one that is distinct from $\mathcal{E}$ itself. ⌐

A single subexpression of a given expression may have more than one occurrence in the given expression.

Example.   In the conditional term

> $t:$
> *if* $(\forall x)q\big(x, f(a)\big)$
> *then* $f(a)$
> *else* b

the subterms are

> $x,$ $a,$ $f(a),$ $b,$ and t itself.

The subsentences are

> $q\big(x, f(a)\big)$ and $(\forall x)q\big(x, f(a)\big).$

Here t has two occurrences of the subterm x, two occurrences of the subterm a, and two occurrences of the subterm $f(a)$. All of these subterms and subsentences are subexpressions of t.

In the sentence

$$\mathcal{F}: \quad \begin{array}{l} p\big(a,\ x,\ f(a,x)\big) \\ \quad and \\ (\exists y)q\big(g(b,x),\ y\big), \end{array}$$

the subterms are

$$a, \quad x, \quad f(a,x), \quad b, \quad g(b,x), \quad and \quad y.$$

The subsentences are

$$p\big(a,\ x,\ f(a,x)\big), \quad q\big(g(b,x),\ y\big), \quad (\exists y)q\big(g(b,x),\ y\big),$$

and $\mathcal{F}$ itself.　◢

FREE AND BOUND VARIABLES

We have now introduced the terms and sentences of predicate logic. Before we can begin to consider the meanings of these expressions, however, we must introduce the technical notions of "bound" and "free" variable. In the next section we shall introduce interpretations for predicate logic and discuss how to determine the value of a predicate-logic expression under a given interpretation, just as we did earlier for propositional logic. The distinction between free and bound occurrences of variables will then become very important, because the values of the free occurrences will be assigned by the interpretation, while the values of the bound occurrences will be independent of the interpretation.

Because the definitions of bound and free variables can be confusing at first, we begin with an example.

In the sentence

$$(\forall x) \begin{bmatrix} p(x,y) \\ and \\ (\exists y)q(y,x) \end{bmatrix}$$

there are two occurrences of x in the scope of the universal quantifier $(\forall x)$; these occurrences of x are said to be "bound" by the quantifier $(\forall x)$. On the other hand, the first occurrence of y, in $p(x,y)$, is not within the scope of any quantifier of form $(\forall y)$ or $(\exists y)$; it is said to be a "free" occurrence of y. The final occurrence of y, in $q(y,x)$, is a bound occurrence, because it is within the scope of the quantifier $(\exists y)$. The occurrences of the symbols x and y within the quantifiers $(\forall x)$ and $(\exists y)$ themselves are considered to be neither bound nor free.

Note that the same occurrence of a variable x can be within the scope of more than one quantifier $(\forall x)$ or $(\exists x)$. For example, in the sentence

$$(\forall x) \begin{bmatrix} p(x,y) \\ and \\ (\exists x)(\forall y)q(y,x) \end{bmatrix}$$

the final occurrence of x, in $q(y,x)$, is in the scope of both the inner quantifier $(\exists x)$ and the outer quantifier $(\forall x)$. However, we do not regard x as being bound by both quantifiers, but only by the inner quantifier $(\exists x)$. Again, the occurrences of the symbols x and y within the quantifiers $(\forall x)$, $(\exists x)$, and $(\forall y)$ themselves are considered to be neither bound nor free.

Now let us be more precise.

Definition (bound and free occurrences).

Let x be a variable and $\mathcal{E}$ be an expression (i.e., a sentence or term) of predicate logic. The occurrences of x in the quantifiers $(\forall x)$ and $(\exists x)$ themselves are neither bound nor free. Consider an occurrence of x in $\mathcal{E}$ that is not in a quantifier.

The occurrence of x is *bound in* $\mathcal{E}$ if it is within the scope of a quantifier $(\forall x)$ or $(\exists x)$ in $\mathcal{E}$; it is *bound by* the innermost quantifier $(\forall x)$ or $(\exists x)$ that contains the occurrence of x within its scope.

The occurrence of x is *free in* $\mathcal{E}$ if it is not within the scope of any quantifier $(\forall x)$ or $(\exists x)$ in $\mathcal{E}$. ⌐

Example.   Consider the sentence

$$\mathcal{E}: \quad (\forall x) \begin{bmatrix} p(x,y) \\ and \\ (\exists y)q(y,z) \end{bmatrix}.$$

The occurrence of x in $p(x,y)$ is bound in $\mathcal{E}$, by the quantifier $(\forall x)$. The occurrence of z, in $q(y,z)$, is free in $\mathcal{E}$. The occurrence of y in $p(x,y)$ is free, while the occurrence of y in $q(y,z)$ is bound, by the quantifier $(\exists y)$. ⌐

Note that an occurrence of a variable is always free in an expression with no quantifiers. Also, note that it is quite possible for an occurrence of a variable x to be bound in a term, because we admit conditional terms (*if $\mathcal{F}$ then s else t*), where $\mathcal{F}$ is a sentence which may contain quantifiers $(\forall x)$ or $(\exists x)$.

Remark.   If $\mathcal{F}$ is a subexpression of an expression $\mathcal{E}$, an occurrence of a variable in $\mathcal{F}$ can be free in $\mathcal{F}$ but bound in $\mathcal{E}$. For example, if $\mathcal{E}$ is the sentence

$$\mathcal{E}: \quad (\forall x)(\exists y)p(x,y)$$

and $\mathcal{F}$ is its subsentence

$$\mathcal{F}: \quad (\exists y)p(x,y),$$

the occurrence of x is free in $\mathcal{F}$, because it is within the scope of no quantifier $(\forall x)$ or $(\exists x)$ in $\mathcal{F}$. The same occurrence of x, however, is bound in $\mathcal{E}$, because it is within the scope of the quantifier $(\forall x)$ in $\mathcal{E}$. ⌐

The preceding definition (of bound and free occurrences) determines whether a particular occurrence of a variable is bound or free in an expression. We now define whether the variable itself is bound or free in the expression, independent of any particular occurrence of the variable.

Definition (bound and free variables)

The variable x is *bound in* an expression $\mathcal{E}$ if there is at least one bound occurrence of x in $\mathcal{E}$, and *free in $\mathcal{E}$* if there is at least one free occurrence of x in $\mathcal{E}$. ⏌

Note that a variable will be both bound and free in an expression $\mathcal{E}$ if it has at least one bound occurrence and at least one free occurrence in $\mathcal{E}$.

Example.   Consider the sentence $\mathcal{E}$,

$$(\forall x) \begin{bmatrix} p(x,y) \\ and \\ (\exists y)q(y,z) \end{bmatrix},$$

of the preceding example. The variable x is bound in $\mathcal{E}$, because it has a bound occurrence, in $p(x,y)$; the variable z is free in $\mathcal{E}$, because it has a free occurrence, in $q(y,z)$; the variable y is both bound and free in $\mathcal{E}$, because it has a bound occurrence, in $q(y,z)$, and a free occurrence, in $p(x,y)$. ⏌

Definition (closed sentence)

A sentence is *closed* if it has no free occurrences of any variable. ⏌

Example.   The sentence

$$(\forall x)p(x,y)$$

is not closed, because the occurrence of y is free. On the other hand, the sentence

$$(\forall x)(\exists y)p(x,y)$$

is closed. ⏌

3.3   THE MEANING OF A SENTENCE

In defining validity for propositional logic, we first defined the notion of the truth of a sentence under an interpretation, which assigned truth-values to all the propositional symbols of the sentence. In this section, we will extend this notion to the sentences of predicate logic in an analogous way. But since these sentences involve terms, an interpretation must include a "domain," a set of objects that provides a meaning for the terms.

The precise notion of an interpretation will be defined shortly, but first we give an informal preview of the meaning of predicate-logic sentences.

MOTIVATION

An interpretation assigns a meaning to each constant, function, and predicate symbol. It will assign domain elements (i.e., objects) to the constants and the variables, functions (over the domain) to the function symbols, and relations (over the domain) to the predicate symbols.

For example, consider the closed sentence

$$\mathcal{G}: \quad \begin{aligned} &\text{if } \ (\forall x)(\exists y)p(x,\, y) \\ &\text{then } \ p(a,\, f(a)). \end{aligned}$$

Any interpretation specifies a domain and assigns meanings to each symbol and, in particular, to the constant a, the unary function symbol f, and the binary predicate symbol p.

Consider an interpretation $\mathcal{I}$ in which we take the domain D to be the integers and under which

a is 0;

f is the "successor" function,
   that is, the function $f_{\mathcal{I}}$ such that $f_{\mathcal{I}}(d)$ is $d+1$;

p is the "greater-than" relation,
   that is, the relation $p_{\mathcal{I}}$ such that $p_{\mathcal{I}}(d_1, d_2)$ is $d_1 > d_2$.

The intuitive meaning of the consequent $p(a, f(a))$ of $\mathcal{G}$ under this interpretation is the inequality

$$0 > 0 + 1.$$

Because $0+1$ is 1, and because $0 > 1$ is false, the value of the consequent $p\big(a, f(a)\big)$ under this interpretation is false.

If we could determine the truth-value of the antecedent

$$(\forall x)(\exists y)p(x,\, y),$$

we could apply the *if-then* semantic rule of propositional logic to determine the truth-value of the whole sentence. However, the antecedent contains quantifiers; to determine its truth-value we must introduce new semantic rules for the universal and existential quantifier.

According to one of these rules, a sentence of form $(\forall x)\mathcal{F}$ will be true under a given interpretation if the subsentence $\mathcal{F}$ is true under the interpretation for every possible assignment of a domain element d to x. According to the other rule, a sentence of the form $(\exists x)\mathcal{F}$ will be true under a given interpretation if there exists an assignment of a domain element d to x such that $\mathcal{F}$ is true under the interpretation.

Thus the antecedent

$$(\forall x)(\exists y)p(x, y)$$

will be given the intuitive meaning

> For every integer d,
>> there exists an integer d'
>>> such that $d > d'$.

This is true (e.g., for any d, we could take d' to be $d - 1$).

Thus under the above interpretation $\mathcal{I}$, the entire sentence $\mathcal{G}$ will be given the intuitive meaning

> If for every integer d,
>> there exists an integer d'
>>> such that $d > d'$,
> then $0 > 0 + 1$.

Because its antecedent is true and its consequent is false, the entire sentence

> *if* $(\forall x)(\exists y)p(x, y)$
> *then* $p(a, f(a))$

is false under $\mathcal{I}$.

On the other hand, suppose we consider the interpretation $\mathcal{J}$, which differs from $\mathcal{I}$ only in that, under $\mathcal{J}$,

> f is the "predecessor" function,
>> that is, the function $f_{\mathcal{J}}$ such that $f_{\mathcal{J}}(d)$ is $d - 1$;

> p is the "inequality" relation,
>> that is, the relation $p_{\mathcal{J}}$ such that $p_{\mathcal{J}}(d_1, d_2)$ is $d_1 \neq d_2$.

Under the interpretation $\mathcal{J}$, the intuitive meaning of the sentence $\mathcal{G}$ is

> If, for every integer d,
>> there exists an integer d'
>>> such that $d \neq d'$,
> then $0 \neq 0 - 1$.

This is a true statement about the integers: Its antecedent

> For every integer d,
>> there exists an integer d'
>>> such that $d \neq d'$

is true again (e.g., for any d, take d' to be $d + 1$), but its consequent

$$0 \neq 0 - 1$$

is also true; therefore (by the *if-then* rule) the entire implication is true under $\mathcal{J}$.

To be valid, a closed sentence must be true under every possible interpretation. Thus although the above sentence $\mathcal{G}$ is true under the interpretation $\mathcal{J}$, it is not valid, because it is false under the interpretation $\mathcal{I}$.

Next consider the sentence

$$\mathcal{H}: \quad \begin{array}{l} \textit{if} \ \ (\forall x)p(x, \, f(x)) \\ \textit{then} \ \ (\exists y)p(a, \, y). \end{array}$$

This sentence is true under both of the above interpretations, $\mathcal{I}$ and $\mathcal{J}$.

Under $\mathcal{I}$, the intuitive meaning of the sentence $\mathcal{H}$ is

> If, for every integer d,
> $\quad d > d + 1$,
> then there exists an integer d'
> $\quad$ such that $0 > d'$.

Here the antecedent is false and the consequent is true, and therefore (by the *if-then* rule) the entire sentence is true under $\mathcal{I}$.

Under $\mathcal{J}$, the intuitive meaning of the sentence $\mathcal{H}$ is

> If, for every integer d,
> $\quad d \neq d - 1$,
> then there exists an integer d'
> $\quad$ such that $0 \neq d'$.

Here both the antecedent and the consequent are true, so the entire sentence is also true, under $\mathcal{J}$.

In fact, this sentence is valid: It is true under every interpretation, as we shall see in a later section.

INTERPRETATIONS

Let us now define the notion of interpretation for predicate logic more precisely.

Definition (interpretation)

Let D be an arbitrary nonempty set of elements.

An *interpretation $\mathcal{I}$ over the domain D* assigns values to each constant, variable, function, and predicate symbol, as follows:

- To each constant a, an element $a_{\mathcal{I}}$ of D.
- To each variable x, an element $x_{\mathcal{I}}$ of D.
- To each function symbol f of arity n, an n-ary function $f_{\mathcal{I}}(d_1, d_2, \ldots, d_n)$; the function $f_{\mathcal{I}}$ is defined on arguments $d_1, d_2, \ldots, d_n$ in D, and its value $f_{\mathcal{I}}(d_1, d_2, \ldots, d_n)$ belongs to D.
- To each predicate symbol p of arity n, an n-ary relation $p_{\mathcal{I}}(d_1, d_2, \ldots, d_n)$; the relation $p_{\mathcal{I}}$ is defined on arguments $d_1, d_2, \ldots, d_n$ in D, and its value $p_{\mathcal{I}}(d_1, d_2, \ldots, d_n)$ is either true or false. ◢

We have required that the domain of an interpretation be a nonempty set; otherwise we would not be able to assign any values to the constants and variables of an expression.

Example.   Consider the sentence

$$\mathcal{E}: \quad \begin{array}{l} if \ \ p(x, \ f(x)) \\ then \ \ (\exists y)p(a, \ y). \end{array}$$

Note that $\mathcal{E}$ has a free variable x.

Let $\mathcal{I}$ be an interpretation over the domain of the real numbers under which

$a_{\mathcal{I}}$ is $\sqrt{2}$,

$x_{\mathcal{I}}$ is π,

$f_{\mathcal{I}}$ is the "division by 2" function (that is, $f_I(d)$ is $d/2$), and

$p_{\mathcal{I}}$ is the "greater than or equal" relation (that is, $p_I(d_1, d_2)$ is $d_1 \geq d_2$).

Then the intuitive meaning of the sentence under $\mathcal{I}$ is

If $\pi \geq \pi/2$,
then there exists a real number d
    such that $\sqrt{2} \geq d$.

Note that the value assigned to the variable y, which occurs bound but not free in $\mathcal{E}$, does not affect the meaning of the sentence.

Now let $\mathcal{J}$ be an interpretation over the set of all people under which

$a_{\mathcal{J}}$ is Queen Elizabeth,

$x_{\mathcal{J}}$ is George Washington,

$f_{\mathcal{J}}$ is the "mother" function (that is, $f_{\mathcal{J}}(d)$ is the mother of d), and

$p_{\mathcal{J}}$ is the "child" relation (that is, $p_{\mathcal{J}}(d_1, d_2)$ is "d_1 is the child of d_2").

Then the intuitive meaning of the sentence under $\mathcal{J}$ is

If George Washington is the child of George Washington's mother,
then there exists a person y
    such that Queen Elizabeth is the child of y. ⏌

Henceforth we shall drop the subscripts $\mathcal{I}$, $\mathcal{J}$, etc., and just write $a, x, \ldots$ rather than $a_{\mathcal{I}}, x_{\mathcal{I}}, \ldots$ when the context makes our meaning clear.

Definition (agree)
Let s be a constant, variable, function, or predicate symbol. Two interpretations $\mathcal{I}$ and $\mathcal{J}$ over the same domain *agree on* s if $\mathcal{I}$ and $\mathcal{J}$ make the same assignment to s. ⏌

For example, if $\mathcal{I}$ assigns 1 to a and 2 to x, and $\mathcal{J}$ assigns 1 to a and 3 to x, then $\mathcal{I}$ and $\mathcal{J}$ agree on a but not on x.

3.4   SEMANTIC RULES

Once we have provided an interpretation $\mathcal{I}$ for an expression (i.e., a sentence or term) $\mathcal{E}$, we can determine its value. For a sentence, this value is a truth-value, either true or false; for a term, this value is an object in the domain D of the interpretation. As in propositional logic, the association of a value with an expression is done "recursively"; i.e., the value of the expression is determined from the values of its components, by applying the following semantic rules.

BASIC RULES

We first present the rules that apply to symbols other than quantifiers.

Definition (basic semantic rules)

Let $\mathcal{E}$ be an expression and $\mathcal{I}$ an interpretation over a domain D. Then the *value of $\mathcal{E}$ under $\mathcal{I}$* is determined by applying repeatedly the following *semantic rules*:

- *constant rule*
  The value of a constant a is the domain element $a_{\mathcal{I}}$.
- *variable rule*
  The value of a variable x is the domain element $x_{\mathcal{I}}$.
- *application rule*
  The value of an application $f(t_1, t_2, \ldots, t_n)$ is the domain element $f_{\mathcal{I}}(d_1, d_2, \ldots, d_n)$, where $f_{\mathcal{I}}$ is the function assigned to f and $d_1, d_2, \ldots, d_n$ are the values of the terms $t_1, t_2, \ldots, t_n$, under $\mathcal{I}$.
- *if-then-else term rule*
  The value of a conditional term (*if $\mathcal{F}$ then s else t*) is the value of the term s if the sentence $\mathcal{F}$ is true and the value of the term t if $\mathcal{F}$ is false, under $\mathcal{I}$.
- *true and false rules*
  The values of the truth symbols *true* and *false* are the truth-values true and false, respectively.
- *proposition rule*
  The value of a proposition $p(t_1, t_2, \ldots, t_n)$ is the truth-value $p_{\mathcal{I}}(d_1, d_2, \ldots, d_n)$, either true or false, where $p_{\mathcal{I}}$ is the relation assigned to p and $d_1, d_2, \ldots, d_n$ are the values of the terms $t_1, t_2, \ldots, t_n$, under $\mathcal{I}$.

The rules for the logical connectives are the same as for propositional logic:

- *not rule*
  The value of the negation (*not $\mathcal{F}$*) is true if the sentence $\mathcal{F}$ is false and false if $\mathcal{F}$ is true, under $\mathcal{I}$.

We omit the rules for the other logical connectives *and, or, if-then, $\equiv$,* and *if-then-else.*   ⌐

Before we give the semantic rules for the two quantifiers $(\forall x)$ and $(\exists x)$, which are somewhat more complex, let us give an example that does not include quantifiers.

Example.   Consider the sentence

$$\mathcal{E}: \quad \begin{array}{c} not\ p(y,\ f(y)) \\ or \\ p(a,\ f(f(a))) \end{array}$$

and let $\mathcal{I}$ be an interpretation over the domain of nonnegative integers under which

a is 0,

y is 2,

f is the successor function (that is, $f_{\mathcal{I}}(d)$ is $d+1$), and

p is the less-than relation (that is, $p_{\mathcal{I}}(d_1, d_2)$ is $d_1 < d_2$).

In other words, the interpretation $\mathcal{I}$ gives $\mathcal{E}$ the intuitive meaning

not $(2 < 2 + 1)$
or
$0 < (0 + 1) + 1$.

We can use the semantic rules to determine the value of the first disjunct $not\ p(y, f(y))$ under this interpretation as follows: We know (by the *variable* rule) that

the value of y is 2.

Because y is 2 and f is the successor function, we know (by the *application* rule) that

the value of $f(y)$ is 2+1, that is, 3.

Because y is 2, $f(y)$ is 3, and p is the less-than relation $<$, we know (by the *proposition* rule) that

the value of $p(y,\ f(y))$ is $2 < 3$, that is, true.

Because $p(y,\ f(y))$ is true, we know (by the *not* rule) that

the value of $not\ p(y,\ f(y))$ is false.

On the other hand, we can determine the value of the second disjunct $p(a, f(f(a)))$ under the interpretation $\mathcal{I}$ as follows: We know (by the *constant* rule) that

the value of a is 0.

Because a is 0 and f is the successor function, we know (by the *application* rule) that

the value of $f(a)$ is $0 + 1$, that is, 1.

Because $f(a)$ is 1 and f is the successor function, we know (by the *application* rule) that

<blockquote>the value of $f(f(a))$ is $1 + 1$, that is, 2.</blockquote>

Because a is 0, $f(f(a))$ is 2, and p is the less-than relation $<$, we know (by the *proposition* rule) that

<blockquote>the value of $p\big(a,\ f(f(a))\big)$ is $0 < 2$, that is, true.</blockquote>

Finally, because under the interpretation $\mathcal{I}$ the first disjunct $not\ p\big(y, f(y)\big)$ is false and the second disjunct $p\big(a, f(f(a))\big)$ is true, we know (by the *or* rule) that

<blockquote>the value of the entire sentence $\mathcal{E}$, that is,

$not\ p\big(y,\ f(y)\big)$

$\quad or$

$p\big(a,\ f(f(a))\big),$

is true.</blockquote>

A problem arises when we attempt to express the value of a quantified sentence, of the form $(\forall x)\mathcal{F}$ or $(\exists x)\mathcal{F}$, in terms of the value of its component $\mathcal{F}$, analogously to the other semantic rules. For example, if $\mathcal{E}$ is the sentence

$$(\forall x)p(x,y),$$

an interpretation $\mathcal{I}$ will assign a domain element to y and a relation to p. Although the interpretation also assigns some domain element to the variable x, we would like to ignore this assignment and to say that the sentence is true if $p(x,y)$ is true no matter what domain element is assigned to x. To make this idea precise requires that we introduce the notion of a "modified interpretation" for predicate logic. This interpretation assigns new values to symbols of a given interpretation.

MODIFIED INTERPRETATION

We show how to extend an interpretation by assigning a new value to a symbol.

Definition (modified interpretation)

> Let $\mathcal{I}$ be any interpretation over a domain D.
>
> For any variable x and element d of the domain D, the *modification*
>
> $$\langle x \leftarrow d \rangle \circ \mathcal{I}$$
>
> of $\mathcal{I}$ is the interpretation over D under which:
>
> - The variable x is assigned the domain element d.
> - Each variable y other than x is assigned the domain element $y_{\mathcal{I}}$, its original value under $\mathcal{I}$.
> - Each constant a, function symbol f, and predicate symbol p are assigned their original values $a_{\mathcal{I}}$, $f_{\mathcal{I}}$, and $p_{\mathcal{I}}$, respectively, under $\mathcal{I}$.

Note that the original interpretation $\mathcal{I}$ has already assigned some value to the symbol x. This assignment is superseded under the modified interpretation. The modified interpretation agrees with $\mathcal{I}$ on all symbols other than x.

Example.   Suppose that $\mathcal{I}$ is an interpretation over the domain of integers under which

$$x \text{ is } 1$$
$$y \text{ is } 2.$$

Then the modified interpretation

$$\langle x \leftarrow 3 \rangle \circ \mathcal{I}$$

will still assign 2 to y but will now assign 3 to x; in other words, under $\langle x \leftarrow 3 \rangle \circ \mathcal{I}$,

$$x \text{ is } 3$$
$$y \text{ is } 2. \quad \lrcorner$$

We may extend an interpretation several times in succession. For an interpretation $\mathcal{I}$ over a domain D, variables $x_1, x_2, \ldots, x_n$, and domain elements $d_1, d_2, \ldots, d_n$ in D, the notation

$$\langle x_1 \leftarrow d_1 \rangle \circ \langle x_2 \leftarrow d_2 \rangle \circ \ldots \circ \langle x_n \leftarrow d_n \rangle \circ \mathcal{I}$$

is an abbreviation for the *multiply modified interpretation*

$$\langle x_1 \leftarrow d_1 \rangle \circ \big(\langle x_2 \leftarrow d_2 \rangle \circ \ldots \circ (\langle x_n \leftarrow d_n \rangle \circ \mathcal{I}) \ldots \big).$$

Note that, if x and y are distinct variables, the multiply modified interpretations

$$\langle x \leftarrow d \rangle \circ \langle y \leftarrow e \rangle \circ \mathcal{I} \qquad \text{and} \qquad \langle y \leftarrow e \rangle \circ \langle x \leftarrow d \rangle \circ \mathcal{I}$$

are identical for any domain elements d and e. On the other hand, if d and e are distinct domain elements, the multiply modified interpretations

$$\langle x \leftarrow d \rangle \circ \langle x \leftarrow e \rangle \circ \mathcal{I} \qquad \text{and} \qquad \langle x \leftarrow e \rangle \circ \langle x \leftarrow d \rangle \circ \mathcal{I}$$

are different; the former is identical to

$$\langle x \leftarrow d \rangle \circ \mathcal{I},$$

while the latter is identical to

$$\langle x \leftarrow e \rangle \circ \mathcal{I}.$$

RULES FOR QUANTIFIERS

We are finally ready to present the semantic rules that determine the truth-values of sentences of the form $(\forall x)\mathcal{F}$ and $(\exists x)\mathcal{F}$ under an interpretation $\mathcal{I}$. In each case, the value of the sentence under $\mathcal{I}$ is determined from the values of its component $\mathcal{F}$, not under $\mathcal{I}$ but under certain modifications of $\mathcal{I}$.

Definition (semantic rules for quantifiers)

   • ∀ *rule*

Let $\mathcal{I}$ be an interpretation over a domain D.

Then the value of a universally quantified sentence

$$(\forall x)\mathcal{F}$$

is true under $\mathcal{I}$ if

> for every domain element d in D,
> the value of $\mathcal{F}$ is true under the modified interpretation
> $$\langle x \leftarrow d \rangle \circ \mathcal{I}.$$

On the other hand, the value of the sentence is false under $\mathcal{I}$ if

> there exists a domain element d in D
> such that the value of $\mathcal{F}$ is false under the modified interpretation
> $$\langle x \leftarrow d \rangle \circ \mathcal{I}.$$

   • ∃ *rule*

Let $\mathcal{I}$ be an interpretation over a domain D.

Then the value of an existentially quantified sentence

$$(\exists x)\mathcal{F}$$

is true under $\mathcal{I}$ if

> there exists a domain element d in D
> such that the value of $\mathcal{F}$ is true under the modified interpretation
> $$\langle x \leftarrow d \rangle \circ \mathcal{I}.$$

On the other hand, the value of the sentence is false under $\mathcal{I}$ if

> for every domain element d in D,
> the value of $\mathcal{F}$ is false under the modified interpretation
> $$\langle x \leftarrow d \rangle \circ \mathcal{I}. \quad \blacksquare$$

Example.   Consider the sentence

$$\mathcal{G}: \quad (\exists x)p(x, y)$$

and let $\mathcal{I}$ be the interpretation over the positive integers under which

> y is 2
> p is the less-than relation $<$.

We claim that $\mathcal{G}$ is true under $\mathcal{I}$.

To show this, we must show (by the ∃ rule) that

> there exists a domain element d in D
> such that the value of
> $$p(x, y)$$
> is true under the modified interpretation $\langle x \leftarrow d \rangle \circ \mathcal{I}$.

To show this, let us take d to be 1. Then, because p is the less-than relation, x is 1, and y is 2 under the modified interpretation $\langle x \leftarrow 1 \rangle \circ \mathcal{I}$, we know (by the *proposition* rule) that

> the value of
> $$p(x, \, y)$$
> is $1 < 2$, that is, true, under $\langle x \leftarrow 1 \rangle \circ \mathcal{I}$,

as we wanted to show.

Therefore, the given sentence $\mathcal{G}$ is true under $\mathcal{I}$. ◢

Example. Consider the sentence

$$\mathcal{H} : \quad \begin{array}{l} if \;\; (\forall x)(\exists y)p(x, \, y) \\ then \;\; p(a, \, f(a)), \end{array}$$

and let $\mathcal{I}$ be the interpretation over the positive real numbers under which

> a is 1
> f is the square-root function $\sqrt{\;}$
> p is the inequality relation $\neq$.

We claim that the sentence $\mathcal{H}$ is false under this interpretation. To show this, we show that, under $\mathcal{I}$, the antecedent

$$(\forall x)(\exists y)p(x, \, y)$$

is true and the consequent

$$p(a, \, f(a))$$

is false.

To show that the antecedent is true under $\mathcal{I}$, we must show (by the $\forall$ rule) that

> for every domain element d in D,
> the value of the subsentence
> $$(\exists y)p(x, \, y)$$
> is true under the modified interpretation $\langle x \leftarrow d \rangle \circ \mathcal{I}$.

For this purpose, we show (by the $\exists$ rule) that

> for every domain element d in D,
> there exists a domain element d' in D
> such that the value of
> $$p(x, \, y)$$
> is true under the modified interpretation $\langle y \leftarrow d' \rangle \circ \langle x \leftarrow d \rangle \circ \mathcal{I}$.

For an arbitrary domain element d, let us take d' to be $d + 1$. Then because p is the inequality relation $\neq$, x is d, and y is $d + 1$, we know (by the *proposition* rule) that

> the value of
> $$p(x, \, y)$$
> is $d \neq d + 1$, that. is, true, under $\langle y \leftarrow d + 1 \rangle \circ \langle x \leftarrow d \rangle \circ \mathcal{I}$,

as we wanted to show. Therefore

> the value of the antecedent
> $$(\forall x)(\exists y)p(x, y)$$
> is true under $\mathcal{I}$.

On the other hand, because p is the inequality relation $\neq$, a is 1, and f is the square-root function, we know (by the *proposition* rule) that

> the value of the consequent
> $$p(a, f(a))$$
> is $1 \neq \sqrt{1}$, that is, false, under $\mathcal{I}$.

Since the antecedent is true and the consequent is false, the entire implication $\mathcal{H}$ is false under $\mathcal{I}$. ◢

In **Problem 3.1**, the reader is requested to determine the truth-values of several sentences under particular interpretations.

The following proposition relates the value of an expression to the notion of agreement.

Proposition (agreement)

If two interpretations $\mathcal{I}$ and $\mathcal{J}$ agree on all the constant, function, and predicate symbols of an expression $\mathcal{E}$, and on all its free variables, then the value of $\mathcal{E}$ under $\mathcal{I}$ is the same as the value of $\mathcal{E}$ under $\mathcal{J}$. ◢

The proposition is intuitively straightforward: We apply the same semantic rules in determining the value of $\mathcal{E}$ under each interpretation, yielding the same value at each stage.

Remark (modified interpretation).   Suppose the variable x does not occur free in the sentence $\mathcal{G}$. Then, for an interpretation $\mathcal{I}$ and domain element d, $\mathcal{I}$ and $\mathcal{J}: \langle x \leftarrow d \rangle \circ \mathcal{I}$ agree on all the constant, function, and predicate symbols of $\mathcal{G}$ and on all its free variables. Therefore, by the *agreement* proposition, the truth-value of $\mathcal{G}$ under $\mathcal{I}$ is the same as the truth-value of $\mathcal{G}$ under $\mathcal{J}$. ◢

3.5   VALIDITY

In predicate logic, we define validity only for closed sentences, i.e., sentences without free variables. The definition is the same as it is for propositional-logic sentences.

Definition (valid)

A closed sentence $\mathcal{F}$ is *valid* if it is true under every interpretation. ◢

ESTABLISHING VALIDITY

In this chapter, we do not introduce the deductive-tableau system for proving the validity of closed sentences of predicate logic; this system is presented in subsequent chapters. However, we can use the semantic rules and common sense to convince ourselves that these sentences are valid.

Example.   Suppose we want to show the validity of the following *duality-of-quantifiers* sentence

$$\mathcal{E}: \quad \begin{matrix} not\ (\forall x)p(x) \\ \equiv \\ (\exists x)[not\ p(x)]. \end{matrix}$$

By the $\equiv$ rule, it suffices to show that

$$not\ (\forall x)p(x)$$

and

$$(\exists x)[not\ p(x)]$$

have the same truth-value under any interpretation, i.e., that the former sentence is true if and only if the latter sentence is true.

Consider an arbitrary interpretation $\mathcal{I}$. We have that

$$not\ (\forall x)p(x) \text{ is true under } \mathcal{I}$$

if and only if (by the *not* rule)

$$(\forall x)p(x) \text{ is false under } \mathcal{I}$$

if and only if (by the $\forall$ rule)

> there exists a domain element d
> such that $p(x)$ is false under $\langle x \leftarrow d \rangle \circ \mathcal{I}$

if and only if (by the *not* rule)

> there exists a domain element d
> such that $\bigl(not\ p(x)\bigr)$ is true under $\langle x \leftarrow d \rangle \circ \mathcal{I}$

if and only if (by the $\exists$ rule)

$$(\exists x)[not\ p(x)] \text{ is true under } \mathcal{I},$$

as desired. ◢

This sentence and the similar valid sentence

$$not \ (\exists x)p(x)$$
$$\equiv$$
$$(\forall x)[not \ p(x)]$$

are said to express the *duality* between the universal and existential quantifiers.

Example.   Suppose we would like to show the validity of the sentence

$$\mathcal{F}: \quad \begin{array}{l} if \ (\exists x)\big[p(x) \ \ and \ \ r(x)\big] \\ then \ \ \big[(\exists x)p(x) \ \ and \ \ (\exists x)r(x)\big]. \end{array}$$

It suffices (by the *if-then* rule) to show that, for any interpretation $\mathcal{I}$, if the antecedent

$$(\exists x)[p(x) \ \ and \ \ r(x)]$$

is true under $\mathcal{I}$, then the consequent

$$(\exists x)p(x) \ \ and \ \ (\exists x)r(x)$$

must also be true under $\mathcal{I}$.

Consider an arbitrary interpretation $\mathcal{I}$ and assume that the antecedent

$$(\exists x)[p(x) \ and \ r(x)]$$

is true under $\mathcal{I}$. Then (by the $\exists$ rule)

there exists a domain element d such that
    $p(x) \ \ and \ \ r(x)$
is true under $\langle x \leftarrow d \rangle \circ \mathcal{I}$.

Hence (by the *and* rule)

there exists a domain element d such that
    $p(x)$
and
    $r(x)$
are both true under $\langle x \leftarrow d \rangle \circ \mathcal{I}$.

Hence (by common sense)

there exists a domain element d such that
    $p(x)$
is true under $\langle x \leftarrow d \rangle \circ \mathcal{I}$
  and
there exists a domain element d such that
    $r(x)$
is true under $\langle x \leftarrow d \rangle \circ \mathcal{I}$.

Hence (by the ∃ rule, applied twice)

> the subsentence
> > $(\exists x)p(x)$
> is true under $\mathcal{I}$

> and

> the subsentence
> > $(\exists x)r(x)$
> is true under $\mathcal{I}$.

Hence (by the *and* rule)

> the consequent of $\mathcal{F}$,
> > $(\exists x)p(x)$ *and* $(\exists x)r(x)$,
> is true under $\mathcal{I}$,

as desired. ◢

The reader may be surprised that the commonsense principles applied in establishing the validity of simple predicate-logic sentences are the same as the intuitive meanings of the sentences themselves. This circularity is only apparent. In these arguments, we are not establishing the correctness of the commonsense principles, but only that the abstract symbols we have devised behave in accordance with our intuition. Otherwise we would have no way of knowing, for instance, that the symbol *and* in predicate language has anything to do with the "and" of ordinary thought.

Let us illustrate an indirect approach to showing the validity of a sentence. In this approach, we assume that the sentence is not valid and derive a contradiction.

Example.   Suppose we want to show the validity of the sentence

> $\mathcal{G}:$ *if* $(\exists y)(\forall x)q(x,\, y)$
> *then* $(\forall x)(\exists y)q(x,\, y)$.

Assume that $\mathcal{G}$ is not valid, i.e., that it is false under some interpretation $\mathcal{I}$. We try to derive a contradiction.

We have (by the *if-then* rule) that the antecedent,

> $(\exists y)(\forall x)q(x,\, y)$,

is true under $\mathcal{I}$ and the consequent,

> $(\forall x)(\exists y)q(x,\, y)$,

is false under $\mathcal{I}$.

Because the antecedent is true under $\mathcal{I}$, we have (by the ∃ rule) that there exists a domain element e such that

> (1) $(\forall x)q(x,\, y)$
> is true under $\langle y \leftarrow e \rangle \circ \mathcal{I}$.

Because the consequent is false under $\mathcal{I}$, we have (by the $\forall$ rule) that there exists a domain element d such that

(2) $(\exists y)q(x, y)$
         is false under $\langle x \leftarrow d \rangle \circ \mathcal{I}$.

From (1) above, we can conclude (by the $\forall$ rule) that

     for every domain element e'

(3) $q(x, y)$
         is true under $\langle x \leftarrow e' \rangle \circ \langle y \leftarrow e \rangle \circ \mathcal{I}$.

From (2) above, we can conclude (by the $\exists$ rule) that

     for every domain element d'

(4) $q(x, y)$
         is false under $\langle y \leftarrow d' \rangle \circ \langle x \leftarrow d \rangle \circ \mathcal{I}$.

In particular, in (3) above we can take the domain element e' to be d; and in (4) above, we can take the domain element d' to be e. We obtain, respectively,

(5) $q(x, y)$
         is true under $\langle x \leftarrow d \rangle \circ \langle y \leftarrow e \rangle \circ \mathcal{I}$

and

(6) $q(x, y)$
         is false under $\langle y \leftarrow e \rangle \circ \langle x \leftarrow d \rangle \circ \mathcal{I}$.

Because x and y are distinct, the interpretations

$$\langle x \leftarrow d \rangle \circ \langle y \leftarrow e \rangle \circ \mathcal{I}$$

and

$$\langle y \leftarrow e \rangle \circ \langle x \leftarrow d \rangle \circ \mathcal{I}$$

are identical, and hence (5) and (6) contradict each other.

We have show that our original assumption, that the sentence $\mathcal{G}$,

if $(\exists y)(\forall x)\, q(x, y)$
then $(\forall x)(\exists y)\, q(x, y)$,

is false under some interpretation $\mathcal{I}$, leads to a contradiction; therefore the sentence is valid. ◢

ESTABLISHING NONVALIDITY

To be valid, a sentence must be true under any interpretation. Consequently, to show that a sentence is not valid, it suffices to discover a single interpretation under which the sentence is false.

Example.   Let us show that the sentence

$$\mathcal{F}' : \quad \begin{array}{l} if \ \big[(\exists x)p(x) \ and \ (\exists x)r(x)\big] \\ then \ (\exists x)[p(x) \ and \ r(x)], \end{array}$$

which is the converse of the sentence $\mathcal{F}$ from a previous example, is not valid.

To show this, we need only discover a single interpretation $\mathcal{I}$ under which $\mathcal{F}'$ is false. Let $\mathcal{I}$ be the interpretation over all the integers under which

p is the "positive" relation   (that is, $p_{\mathcal{I}}(d)$ is $d > 0$)
r is the "negative" relation   (that is, $r_{\mathcal{I}}(d)$ is $d < 0$).

The intuitive meaning of the sentence $\mathcal{F}'$ under $\mathcal{I}$ is

If there exists an integer x such that $x > 0$ and
there exists an integer x such that $x < 0$,
then there exists an integer x such that $x > 0$ and $x < 0$.

In other words, the sentence asserts that the existence of a positive integer x and the existence of a negative integer x guarantee the existence of a single integer x that is both positive and negative.

In fact, $\mathcal{F}'$ is false under the interpretation $\mathcal{I}$. To show this, it suffices (by the *if-then* rule and the *and* rule) to show that

$(\exists x)p(x)$ is true under $\mathcal{I}$,

$(\exists x)r(x)$ is true under $\mathcal{I}$,

but

$(\exists x)\big[p(x) \ and \ r(x)\big]$ is false under $\mathcal{I}$.

We have (by the *proposition* rule) that

$p(x)$ is true under $\langle x \leftarrow 1 \rangle \circ \mathcal{I}$

and

$r(x)$ is true under $\langle x \leftarrow -1 \rangle \circ \mathcal{I}$.

Therefore (by the $\exists$ rule)

$(\exists x)p(x)$ is true under $\mathcal{I}$

and

$(\exists x)r(x)$ is true under $\mathcal{I}$.

On the other hand, for any integer d we know that d cannot be both positive and negative. Therefore

$\big(p(x) \ and \ r(x)\big)$ is false under $\langle x \leftarrow d \rangle \circ \mathcal{I}$, for every integer d,

and hence (by the $\exists$ rule)

$(\exists x)\big[p(x) \ and \ r(x)\big]$ is false under $\mathcal{I}$,

as we wanted to show.   ⌐

Example (beloved of us all).   Let us show that the sentence

$$\mathcal{G}' : \quad \begin{array}{l} \textit{if } (\forall x)(\exists y)\, q(x,\,y) \\ \textit{then } (\exists y)(\forall x)\, q(x,\,y), \end{array}$$

which is the converse of the sentence $\mathcal{G}$ of a previous example, is not valid.

Let $\mathcal{I}$ be the interpretation over the set of all people under which

> q is the "loves" relation
> (that is, $q_I(d_1, d_2)$ is "d_1 loves d_2").

The intuitive meaning of the sentence under this interpretation is

> if for every person x,
>> there exists a person y
>> such that x loves y,
>> then there exists a person y
>>> such that for every person x,
>>> x loves y,

that is,

> if everybody loves somebody,
> then there is somebody that everybody loves.

By applying the semantic rules for predicate logic, as in the previous example, we can establish that the antecedent of $\mathcal{G}'$ is true and the consequent of $\mathcal{G}'$ is false under $\mathcal{I}$; therefore the entire sentence $\mathcal{G}'$ is false under $\mathcal{I}$. Because we have found an interpretation $\mathcal{I}$ under which $\mathcal{G}'$ is false, we can conclude that $\mathcal{G}'$ is not valid. ⏌

Example.   Suppose we want to show that the sentence

$$\mathcal{H} : \quad (\forall x,\, y) \left[\begin{array}{l} \textit{if } p(x,x) \\ \textit{then } \textit{if } p(x,y) \\ \qquad \textit{then } p(y,y) \end{array} \right]$$

is not valid. To establish this, it suffices to discover an interpretation $\mathcal{I}$ such that $\mathcal{H}$ is false under $\mathcal{I}$. For this purpose, we must (by two applications of the $\forall$ rule) find domain elements d and e such that the quantifier-free subsentence

$$\mathcal{H}' : \quad \begin{array}{l} \textit{if } p(x,x) \\ \textit{then } \textit{if } p(x,y) \\ \qquad \textit{then } p(y,y) \end{array}$$

is false under the modified interpretation

$$\mathcal{I}' : \quad \langle x \leftarrow d \rangle \circ \langle y \leftarrow e \rangle \circ \mathcal{I}.$$

It suffices (by two applications of the *if-then* rule) to construct $\mathcal{I}$ and find domain elements d and e such that

$$p(x,x) \text{ and } p(x,y) \text{ are true under } \mathcal{I}'$$

and

      $p(y, y)$ is false under $\mathcal{I}'$.

    Let $\mathcal{I}$ be the interpretation over the set $\{A, B\}$ of two elements under which p is the relation $p_\mathcal{I}$ such that

      $p_\mathcal{I}(A, A)$ and $p_\mathcal{I}(A, B)$ are true

and

      $p_\mathcal{I}(B, A)$ and $p_\mathcal{I}(B, B)$ are false.

This relation can be illustrated by the following diagram:

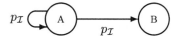

    In this representation each node corresponds to a domain element. An arc labeled $p_\mathcal{I}$ leading from one node to another indicates that the binary relation $p_\mathcal{I}$ holds between the corresponding domain elements; the absence of an arc indicates that the relation does not hold. A circular arc, leading from the node to itself, indicates that the relation $p_\mathcal{I}$ holds between the corresponding element and itself. This diagram notation is a convenient way to describe a binary relation over a finite set.

    Let d and e be the domain elements A and B, respectively. Then the modified interpretation $\mathcal{I}'$ is

      $\langle x \leftarrow A \rangle \circ \langle y \leftarrow B \rangle \circ \mathcal{I},$

and the truth-values of

      $p(x, x), \quad p(x, y), \quad \text{and} \quad p(y, y)$

under $\mathcal{I}'$ are

      $p_\mathcal{I}(A, A), \quad p_\mathcal{I}(A, B), \quad \text{and} \quad p_\mathcal{I}(B, B),$

respectively. Therefore

      $p(x, x)$ and $p(x, y)$ are true under $\mathcal{I}'$

and

      $p(y, y)$ is false under $\mathcal{I}'$,

as we wanted to show.   ◢

Remark.   Note that we could not have used an interpretation over a domain $\{A\}$ of a single element to show that the sentence $\mathcal{H}$ of the previous example is not valid. In fact, $\mathcal{H}$ is true under any such interpretation.

    To show this, it suffices (by two applications of the $\forall$ rule) to establish that, for any domain elements d and e, the quantifier-free subsentence

                if $p(x, x)$
$\mathcal{H}':$ *then if* $p(x, y)$
                    then $p(y, y)$

is true under the modified interpretation $\mathcal{I}' : \langle x \leftarrow d \rangle \circ \langle y \leftarrow e \rangle \circ \mathcal{I}$. But since we have only one element in our domain, we are forced to take d and e to be the same element A. Therefore, the truth-values of $p(x, x)$, $p(x, y)$, and $p(y, y)$ under $\mathcal{I}'$ are all identical to $p_{\mathcal{I}}(\text{A}, \text{A})$. Hence (by two applications of the *if-then* rule, whether or not $p_{\mathcal{I}}(\text{A}, \text{A})$ is true), $\mathcal{H}'$ is true under $\mathcal{I}'$, as we wanted to show. ⌐

EXAMPLES OF VALID SENTENCES

We present some examples of valid sentences, dividing them into separate categories.

- Removal and introduction of quantifiers

  if $(\forall x)p(x)$ *if* $p(a)$
  then $p(a)$ *then* $(\exists y)p(y)$

- Renaming of variables

  $(\forall x)p(x)$ $(\exists x)p(x)$

  $\equiv$ $\equiv$

  $(\forall y)p(y)$ $(\exists y)p(y)$

- Reversal of quantifiers

  $(\forall x, y)q(x, y)$ $(\exists x, y)q(x, y)$

  $\equiv$ $\equiv$

  $(\forall y, x)q(x, y)$ $(\exists y, x)q(x, y)$

  $$\textit{if}\ (\exists y)(\forall x)q(x, y)$$
  $$\textit{then}\ (\forall x)(\exists y)q(x, y)$$

- Redundant quantifiers

  $(\forall x, x)p(x)$ $(\exists x, x)p(x)$

  $\equiv$ $\equiv$

  $(\forall x)p(x)$ $(\exists x)p(x)$

- Duality of quantifiers

  not $(\forall x)p(x)$ *not* $(\exists x)p(x)$

  $\equiv$ $\equiv$

  $(\exists x)[\textit{not}\ p(x)]$ $(\forall x)[\textit{not}\ p(x)]$

- Distribution of quantifiers

  $(\forall x)[p(x)\ \textit{and}\ r(x)]$ $(\exists x)[p(x)\ \textit{or}\ r(x)]$

  $\equiv$ $\equiv$

  $(\forall x)p(x)\ \textit{and}\ (\forall x)r(x)$ $(\exists x)p(x)\ \textit{or}\ (\exists x)r(x)$

$$(\exists x)[if \ p(x) \ then \ r(x)]$$
$$\equiv$$
$$if \ (\forall x)p(x) \ then \ (\exists x)r(x)$$

• Distribution of conditionals

$$(\forall x) \begin{bmatrix} p\big(if \ r(x) \ then \ a \ else \ b\big) \\ \equiv \\ if \ r(x) \ then \ p(a) \ else \ p(b) \end{bmatrix} \qquad (\forall x) \begin{bmatrix} p\big(f\big(if \ r(x) \ then \ a \ else \ b\big)\big) \\ \equiv \\ p\big(if \ r(x) \ then \ f(a) \ else \ f(b)\big) \end{bmatrix}$$

The validity of some of these sentences has been established earlier.

The reader is requested to establish the validity or nonvalidity of several sentences in **Problem 3.2**. The relationship between the truth of a sentence under an interpretation and the number of elements in the interpretation's domain is discussed in **Problems 3.3** and **3.4**.

3.6   UNIVERSAL AND EXISTENTIAL CLOSURE

We have defined validity and the other logical concepts only for closed sentences. We now define two operations that add quantifiers to a given sentence to produce a closed sentence.

Definition (closure)

Suppose that $x_1, x_2, \ldots, x_n$ is a complete list of the distinct free variables of a sentence $\mathcal{F}$ (in the order in which they first occur). Then:

• The *universal closure of* $\mathcal{F}$, denoted by $(\forall *)\mathcal{F}$, is the closed sentence

$$(\forall x_1, x_2, \ldots, x_n)\mathcal{F}.$$

• The *existential closure of* $\mathcal{F}$, denoted by $(\exists *)\mathcal{F}$, is the closed sentence

$$(\exists x_1, x_2, \ldots, x_n)\mathcal{F}. \quad \lrcorner$$

Here again $(\forall x_1, x_2, \ldots, x_n)$ is an abbreviation for $(\forall x_1)(\forall x_2) \ldots (\forall x_n)$ and $(\exists x_1, x_2, \ldots, x_n)$ is an abbreviation for $(\exists x_1)(\exists x_2) \ldots (\exists x_n)$.

Example.   The free variables of the sentence

$$\mathcal{F}: \quad (\exists z) \begin{bmatrix} q(y, z) \ or \ r(x) \\ and \\ (\forall w)p(y, z, w) \end{bmatrix},$$

in order of first occurrence, are y and x; therefore the universal closure of $\mathcal{F}$, that is, $(\forall *)\mathcal{F}$, is

$$(\forall\, y, x)(\exists\, z) \begin{bmatrix} q(y, z) & or & r(x) \\ & and & \\ (\forall\, w)p(y, z, w) & & \end{bmatrix},$$

and the existential closure of $\mathcal{F}$, that is, $(\exists *)\mathcal{F}$, is

$$(\exists\, y, x)(\exists\, z) \begin{bmatrix} q(y, z) & or & r(x) \\ & and & \\ (\forall\, w)p(y, z, w) & & \end{bmatrix}.$$

⌐

Although the closure operators, $(\forall *)$ and $(\exists *)$, are merely abbreviations and not legitimate symbols of predicate logic, they may be shown to obey semantic rules resembling those for quantifiers. We present each rule in a separate proposition.

Proposition (semantic rule for universal closure)

Suppose $\mathcal{F}$ is a sentence and $\mathcal{I}$ is an interpretation over a domain $\mathcal{D}$.

Let x_1, x_2, $\ldots$, x_n be a complete list of the distinct free variables of $\mathcal{F}$, in order of occurrence.

Then

the value of the universal closure
$(\forall *)\mathcal{F}$
is true under $\mathcal{I}$ (*closure*)

if and only if

for any domain elements d_1, d_2, $\ldots$, d_n of D,
the value of $\mathcal{F}$ is true under the modified interpretation
$\langle x_1 \leftarrow d_1\rangle \circ \langle x_2 \leftarrow d_2\rangle \circ \ldots \circ \langle x_n \leftarrow d_n\rangle \circ \mathcal{I}$ (*modification*)

if and only if

for every interpretation $\mathcal{J}$ that agrees with $\mathcal{I}$ on
the constant, function, and predicate symbols of $\mathcal{F}$,
the value of $\mathcal{F}$ is true under $\mathcal{J}$ (*agreement*)   ⌐

Recall that when we say that two interpretations agree on a symbol, we mean that they both assign the same value to that symbol.

We have named the three conditions of the rule for ease in referring to them later.

Example.   Consider the sentence

$\mathcal{F}:$ $q(x_1, x_2)$ *or* *not* $q(x_1, x_2).$

The free variables of $\mathcal{F}$, in order of first occurrence, are x_1 and x_2. The universal closure of $\mathcal{F}$ is

$$(\forall *)\mathcal{F}: \quad (\forall x_1,\, x_2)\big[q(x_1, x_2) \ \ or \ \ not \ q(x_1, x_2)\big].$$

According to the proposition,

$(\forall *)\mathcal{F}$ is true under $\mathcal{I}$

if and only if

> for any domain elements d_1 and d_2 of D,
> $\mathcal{F}$ is true under $\langle x_1 \leftarrow d_1 \rangle \circ \langle x_2 \leftarrow d_2 \rangle \circ \mathcal{I}$

if and only if

> for any interpretation $\mathcal{J}$ that agrees with $\mathcal{I}$ on the predicate symbol q,
> $\mathcal{F}$ is true under $\mathcal{J}$. ⏌

The semantic rule for the existential closure is analogous.

Proposition (semantic rule for existential closure)

Suppose $\mathcal{F}$ is a sentence and $\mathcal{I}$ is an interpretation over a domain D.

Let $x_1,\, x_2,\, \ldots,\, x_n$ be a complete list of the distinct free variables of $\mathcal{F}$, in order of first occurrence.

Then

> the value of the existential closure
> $(\exists *)\mathcal{F}$
> is true under $\mathcal{I}$ (*closure*)

if and only if

> there exist domain elements $d_1,\, d_2,\, \ldots,\, d_n$ of D such that
> the value of $\mathcal{F}$ is true under the modified interpretation
> $\langle x_1 \leftarrow d_1 \rangle \circ \langle x_2 \leftarrow d_2 \rangle \circ \ldots \circ \langle x_n \leftarrow d_n \rangle \circ \mathcal{I}$ (*modification*)

if and only if

> there exists an interpretation $\mathcal{J}$ that agrees with $\mathcal{I}$ on
> the constant, function, and predicate symbols of $\mathcal{F}$,
> such that the value of $\mathcal{F}$ is true under $\mathcal{J}$ (*agreement*) ⏌

The propositions may be justified by appealing to the semantic rules for the universal and existential quantifiers.

We have defined validity for closed sentences only. If a sentence is not closed, we may consider the validity of its universal or existential closure. For the universal closure, we have the following proposition:

Proposition (universal closure)

> For any sentence $\mathcal{F}$
>
>> the universal closure $(\forall *)\mathcal{F}$ is valid
>>> if and only if
>> $\mathcal{F}$ is true under every interpretation.   ⌙

Proof (universal closure).   Let $x_1, x_2, \ldots, x_n$ be a complete list of the distinct free variables in $\mathcal{F}$, in order of first occurrence. We establish each direction separately. In the "forward" direction, indicated by $\Rightarrow$, we show that if $\mathcal{F}$ is true under every interpretation, then $(\forall *)\mathcal{F}$ is valid. In the "backward" direction, indicated by $\Leftarrow$ and presented first, we show that if $(\forall *)\mathcal{F}$ is valid then $\mathcal{F}$ is true under every interpretation.

$(\Leftarrow)$

Suppose $\mathcal{F}$ is true under every interpretation; we would like to show that its universal closure $(\forall *)\mathcal{F}$ is valid, i.e., true under any interpretation.

Consider an arbitrary interpretation $\mathcal{I}$. To show that $(\forall *)\mathcal{F}$ is true under $\mathcal{I}$, it suffices (by the *universal-closure* rule) to show that $\mathcal{F}$ is true under the modified interpretation

$$\langle x_1 \leftarrow d_1 \rangle \circ \langle x_2 \leftarrow d_2 \rangle \circ \ldots \circ \langle x_n \leftarrow d_n \rangle \circ \mathcal{I}$$

for any domain elements $d_1, d_2, \ldots, d_n$; but this follows from our assumption that $\mathcal{F}$ is true under any interpretation.

$(\Rightarrow)$

Suppose $(\forall *)\mathcal{F}$ is valid; we would like to show that $\mathcal{F}$ is true under every interpretation.

Consider an arbitrary interpretation $\mathcal{J}$ and suppose that it assigns the domain elements $d_1, d_2, \ldots, d_n$ to $x_1, x_2, \ldots, x_n$, respectively. Then the interpretation

$$\mathcal{J}' : \quad \langle x_1 \leftarrow d_1 \rangle \circ \langle x_2 \leftarrow d_2 \rangle \circ \ldots \circ \langle x_n \leftarrow d_n \rangle \circ \mathcal{J}$$

and $\mathcal{J}$ itself are identical. Because $(\forall *)\mathcal{F}$ is valid, it is true under $\mathcal{J}$. Therefore (by the *universal-closure* rule) $\mathcal{F}$ is also true under $\mathcal{J}'$, that is $\mathcal{J}$, as we wanted to show.   ⌙

So far, we introduced methods for establishing validity and other properties of particular predicate-logic sentences. It is often more convenient to treat an entire class of sentences as a single unit, or "schema." This is the subject of the following sections.

3.7   VALID SENTENCE SCHEMATA

We have given examples of particular valid sentences of predicate logic such as

$$not \ (\forall x)p(x)$$
$$\equiv$$
$$(\exists x)[not \ p(x)].$$

We cannot directly conclude from the above sentence that a different sentence of the same form, such as

$$not \ (\forall x)\big[(\exists y)q(x,y)\big]$$
$$\equiv$$
$$(\exists x)\big[not \ (\exists y)q(x,y)\big],$$

is also valid.

It is more useful to establish at once that entire classes of sentences are valid. For example, in a single argument we can establish that, for any sentence $\mathcal{F}$, the universal closure of the sentence

$$not \ (\forall x)\mathcal{F}$$
$$\equiv$$
$$(\exists x)[not \ \mathcal{F}]$$

is valid. This accomplished, we can immediately infer that the above two particular sentences are valid: In the first case, we take $\mathcal{F}$ to be $p(x)$; in the second, we take $\mathcal{F}$ to be $(\exists y)q(x,y)$. As in propositional logic, we shall refer to such a "sentence," containing script symbols $\mathcal{E}$, $\mathcal{F}$, $\mathcal{G}$, $\mathcal{H}$, ..., as a *sentence schema*; we shall refer to the particular sentences it represents as *instances* of the schema.

Note that we generally speak about establishing the validity of the universal closure of a sentence schema, rather than of the schema itself, because a particular sentence $\mathcal{F}$, $\mathcal{G}$, or $\mathcal{H}$ may have some free variables, and we have only defined validity for closed sentences. We shall say that the universal closure of a schema is *valid* if the universal closure of its predicate-logic instances is valid.

VALIDITY OF SENTENCE SCHEMA

We can establish the validity of a sentence schema by the same style of argument we used for particular sentences.

Example.   Suppose we want to show the validity of the universal closure of the sentence schema

$$not \ (\forall x)\mathcal{F}$$
$$\equiv$$
$$(\exists x)[not \ \mathcal{F}].$$

In other words, we would like to show that

$$(\forall *) \quad \begin{bmatrix} not\ (\forall x)\mathcal{F} \\ \equiv \\ (\exists x)[not\ \mathcal{F}] \end{bmatrix}$$

is valid. It suffices (by the *universal-closure* proposition) to show that the subsentence

$$\mathcal{E}: \quad \begin{array}{c} not\ (\forall x)\mathcal{F} \\ \equiv \\ (\exists x)[not\ \mathcal{F}] \end{array}$$

is true under every interpretation. For this purpose, we may (by the $\equiv$ rule) show that

$$not\ (\forall x)\mathcal{F}$$

and

$$(\exists x)[not\ \mathcal{F}]$$

have the same truth-value under any interpretation, i.e., that the former sentence is true if and only if the latter sentence is true.

Consider an arbitrary interpretation $\mathcal{I}$. We have that

$$not\ (\forall x)\mathcal{F} \text{ is true under } \mathcal{I}$$

if and only if (by the *not* rule)

$$(\forall x)\mathcal{F} \text{ is false under } \mathcal{I}$$

if and only if (by the $\forall$ rule)

there exists a domain element d such that
$\mathcal{F}$ is false under $\langle x \leftarrow d \rangle \circ \mathcal{I}$

if and only if (by the *not* rule)

there exists a domain element d such that
$(not\ \mathcal{F})$ is true under $\langle x \leftarrow d \rangle \circ \mathcal{I}$

if and only if (by the $\exists$ rule)

$$(\exists x)[not\ \mathcal{F}] \text{ is true under } \mathcal{I},$$

as desired. ◢

The reader may have noticed that the proof of the validity of the sentence schema in the above example resembles the earlier proof of the validity of the particular sentence

$$not\ (\forall x)p(x)$$
$$\equiv$$
$$(\exists x)\big[not\ p(x)\big],$$

which is an instance of the sentence schema.

CATALOG OF VALID SENTENCE SCHEMATA

By similar methods, we can establish the validity of the universal closures of the following sentence schemata.

- Reversal of quantifiers

$$(\forall x)(\forall y)\mathcal{F} \qquad\qquad (\exists x)(\exists y)\mathcal{F}$$
$$\equiv \qquad\qquad\qquad \equiv$$
$$(\forall y)(\forall x)\mathcal{F} \qquad\qquad (\exists y)(\exists x)\mathcal{F}$$

$$\text{if } (\exists y)(\forall x)\mathcal{F}$$
$$\text{then } (\forall x)(\exists y)\mathcal{F}$$

- Duality of quantifiers

$$\text{not } (\forall x)\mathcal{F} \qquad\qquad \text{not } (\exists x)\mathcal{F}$$
$$\equiv \qquad\qquad\qquad \equiv$$
$$(\exists x)[\text{not } \mathcal{F}] \qquad\qquad (\forall x)[\text{not } \mathcal{F}]$$

- Distribution of quantifiers (equivalences)

$$(\forall x)[\mathcal{F} \text{ and } \mathcal{G}] \qquad\qquad (\exists x)[\mathcal{F} \text{ or } \mathcal{G}]$$
$$\equiv \qquad\qquad\qquad \equiv$$
$$(\forall x)\mathcal{F} \text{ and } (\forall x)\mathcal{G} \qquad\qquad (\exists x)\mathcal{F} \text{ or } (\exists x)\mathcal{G}$$

$$(\exists x)[\text{if } \mathcal{F} \text{ then } \mathcal{G}]$$
$$\equiv$$
$$\text{if } (\forall x)\mathcal{F} \text{ then } (\exists x)\mathcal{G}$$

- Distribution of quantifiers (implications)

$$\text{if } (\exists x)[\mathcal{F} \text{ and } \mathcal{G}] \qquad\qquad \text{if } [(\forall x)\mathcal{F} \text{ or } (\forall x)\mathcal{G}]$$
$$\text{then } [(\exists x)\mathcal{F} \text{ and } (\exists x)\mathcal{G}] \qquad\qquad \text{then } (\forall x)[\mathcal{F} \text{ or } \mathcal{G}]$$

$$\text{if } [\text{if } (\exists x)\mathcal{F} \text{ then } (\forall x)\mathcal{G}] \qquad\qquad \text{if } (\forall x)[\text{if } \mathcal{F} \text{ then } \mathcal{G}]$$
$$\text{then } (\forall x)[\text{if } \mathcal{F} \text{ then } \mathcal{G}] \qquad\qquad \text{then } [\text{if } (\forall x)\mathcal{F} \text{ then } (\forall x)\mathcal{G}]$$

$$\text{if } (\forall x)[\mathcal{F} \equiv \mathcal{G}]$$
$$\text{then } (\forall x)\mathcal{F} \equiv (\forall x)\mathcal{G}$$

The reader is requested in **Problem 3.5** to establish the validity of some of these schemata.

Note that under the headings *reversal of quantifiers* and *distribution of quantifiers*, certain of the sentences are implications rather than equivalences. In fact, the universal closures of the converses of each of these implications are not valid.

For example, consider the implication under the heading *reversal of quanti-fiers,*

> *if* $(\exists y)(\forall x)\mathcal{F}$
> *then* $(\forall x)(\exists y)\mathcal{F}.$

The converse is the sentence schema

> *if* $(\forall x)(\exists y)\mathcal{F}$
> *then* $(\exists y)(\forall x)\mathcal{F}.$

In a previous example (the *beloved-of-us-all* example), we have discussed a particular instance of this schema,

> *if* $(\forall x)(\exists y)q(x,y)$
> *then* $(\exists y)(\forall x)q(x,y).$

We have seen that this sentence is not valid; e.g., it is false under the interpretation over the domain of all people under which the predicate symbol q is taken to be the "loves" relation.

The reader is requested in **Problem 3.5** to construct such interpretations for the converses of some other implications in this section.

VALID PROPOSITIONAL-LOGIC SCHEMATA

A useful if obvious class of valid sentences is the class of the universal closures of predicate-logic sentences that are instances of valid propositional-logic schemata. For example, consider the valid propositional-logic schema

> *if* $\mathcal{F}$
> *then* $(\mathcal{F} \ or \ \mathcal{G}).$

An instance of this schema in predicate logic is obtained by replacing the script symbols $\mathcal{F}$ and $\mathcal{G}$ with arbitrary predicate-logic sentences. Thus, taking $\mathcal{F}$ and $\mathcal{G}$ to be $p(x)$ and $(\exists y)q(x,y)$, respectively, we obtain the predicate-logic sentence

> *if* $p(x)$
> *then* $\big(p(x) \ or \ (\exists y)q(x,y)\big).$

This sentence is not closed (it has the free variable x), but its universal closure is the valid predicate-logic sentence

$$(\forall x)\left[\begin{array}{l} if \ p(x) \\ then \ \big(p(x) \ or \ (\exists y)q(x,y)\big) \end{array}\right].$$

Additional examples of instances of valid propositional-logic schemata are

$$(\forall x)p(x)$$
$$or$$
$$not \ (\forall x)p(x)$$

$$(\forall y)\left[\begin{array}{l} if \ (\exists x)q(x,y) \\ then \ (\exists x)q(x,y) \end{array}\right]$$

The validity of such predicate-logic sentences is established in the following result:

Proposition (instances of valid propositional-logic schemata)

If a propositional-logic schema $\mathcal{E}$ is valid,
then the universal closure of a predicate-logic instance of $\mathcal{E}$ is valid. ⏌

Proof. Let $\mathcal{E}$ be a valid propositional-logic schema, let $\mathcal{E}_0$ be the instance of $\mathcal{E}$ obtained by replacing the symbols $\mathcal{F}, \mathcal{G}, \mathcal{H}, \ldots$ of $\mathcal{E}$ with propositional symbols $P_0, Q_0, R_0, \ldots$, respectively, and let $\mathcal{E}_1$ be the instance of $\mathcal{E}$ obtained by replacing $\mathcal{F}, \mathcal{G}, \mathcal{H}, \ldots$ with predicate-logic sentences $\mathcal{F}_1, \mathcal{G}_1, \mathcal{H}_1, \ldots$, respectively. Because $\mathcal{E}$ is a valid schema, we know that $\mathcal{E}_0$ is valid in propositional logic. We would like to show that $(\forall *)\mathcal{E}_1$ is valid in predicate logic.

To show that $(\forall *)\mathcal{E}_1$ is valid in predicate logic, it suffices (by the *universal-closure* proposition) to show that $\mathcal{E}_1$ is true under every predicate-logic interpretation. Consider an arbitrary interpretation $\mathcal{I}_1$ for $\mathcal{E}_1$; we would like to show that $\mathcal{E}_1$ is true under $\mathcal{I}_1$.

Consider the truth-values of the subsentences $\mathcal{F}_1, \mathcal{G}_1, \mathcal{H}_1, \ldots$ of $\mathcal{E}_1$ under $\mathcal{I}_1$, and let $\mathcal{I}_0$ be a propositional-logic interpretation that assigns the same truth-values to the corresponding propositional symbols $P_0, Q_0, R_0, \ldots$ of $\mathcal{E}_0$. Then the truth-value of $\mathcal{E}_0$ under $\mathcal{I}_0$ is the same as the truth-value of $\mathcal{E}_1$ under $\mathcal{I}_1$, because the semantic rules for the logical connectives *not, and, or,* $\ldots$ are the same in propositional logic and predicate logic. Since $\mathcal{E}_0$ is valid, $\mathcal{E}_0$ is true under $\mathcal{I}_0$; therefore $\mathcal{E}_1$ is also true under $\mathcal{I}_1$, as we wanted to show. ⏌

VALIDITY UNDER SIDE CONDITIONS

Certain sentence schemata are not valid in general but are valid if particular conditions hold. The universal closures of the following sentence schemata are valid under the following side condition:

The variable x does not occur free in the sentence $\mathcal{G}$.

- Redundant quantifiers

$$(\forall x)\mathcal{G} \;\equiv\; \mathcal{G}$$

$$(\exists x)\mathcal{G} \;\equiv\; \mathcal{G}$$

- Distribution of quantifiers

$$(\forall x)[\mathcal{F} \ and \ \mathcal{G}]$$
$$\equiv$$
$$(\forall x)\mathcal{F} \ and \ \mathcal{G}$$

$$(\exists x)[\mathcal{F} \ or \ \mathcal{G}]$$
$$\equiv$$
$$(\exists x)\mathcal{F} \ or \ \mathcal{G}$$

$$(\forall x)[\mathcal{F} \ or \ \mathcal{G}]$$
$$\equiv$$
$$(\forall x)\mathcal{F} \ or \ \mathcal{G}$$

$$(\exists x)[\mathcal{F} \ and \ \mathcal{G}]$$
$$\equiv$$
$$(\exists x)\mathcal{F} \ and \ \mathcal{G}$$

$$(\forall x)[if\ \mathcal{F}\ then\ \mathcal{G}]$$
$$\equiv$$
$$if\ (\exists x)\mathcal{F}\ then\ \mathcal{G}$$

$$(\exists x)[if\ \mathcal{F}\ then\ \mathcal{G}]$$
$$\equiv$$
$$if\ (\forall x)\mathcal{F}\ then\ \mathcal{G}$$

$$(\forall x)[if\ \mathcal{G}\ then\ \mathcal{F}]$$
$$\equiv$$
$$if\ \mathcal{G}\ then\ (\forall x)\mathcal{F}$$

$$(\exists x)[if\ \mathcal{G}\ then\ \mathcal{F}]$$
$$\equiv$$
$$if\ \mathcal{G}\ then\ (\exists x)\mathcal{F}$$

$$(\forall x)[if\ \mathcal{G}\ then\ \mathcal{E}\ else\ \mathcal{F}]$$
$$\equiv$$
$$[if\ \mathcal{G}\ then\ (\forall x)\mathcal{E}\ else\ (\forall x)\mathcal{F}]$$

$$(\exists x)[if\ \mathcal{G}\ then\ \mathcal{E}\ else\ \mathcal{F}]$$
$$\equiv$$
$$[if\ \mathcal{G}\ then\ (\exists x)\mathcal{E}\ else\ (\exists x)\mathcal{F}]$$

The side condition that x does not occur free in $\mathcal{G}$, which we imposed in asserting the validity of the above sentences, is essential. Let us illustrate this point for the first *redundant-quantifiers* sentence.

Example (necessity for side condition).   The universal closure of the *redundant-quantifiers* sentence

$$(\forall x)\mathcal{G}\ \equiv\ \mathcal{G}$$

is asserted to be valid under the side condition that the variable x does not occur free in the sentence $\mathcal{G}$. Thus, taking $\mathcal{G}$ to be the sentence

$$(\exists y)q(z, y),$$

in which x does not occur free, we can conclude that the universal closure of

$$(\forall x)(\exists y)q(z, y)\ \equiv\ (\exists y)q(z, y)$$

is valid.

On the other hand, taking $\mathcal{G}$ to be the sentence

$$p(x),$$

in which the variable x is free, violating the side condition, we cannot conclude that the universal closure of

$$(\forall x)p(x)\ \equiv\ p(x)$$

is valid; indeed, it is not.

To show this, it suffices (by the *universal-closure* proposition) to exhibit a single interpretation under which the sentence is false. Let $\mathcal{I}$ be an interpretation over the set $\{A, B\}$ of two elements such that

$$p_{\mathcal{I}}(A)\ \text{is true}$$
$$p_{\mathcal{I}}(B)\ \text{is false}$$
$$x_{\mathcal{I}}\ \text{is A}.$$

Because $p_{\mathcal{I}}(B)$ is false, we have that

$$p(x)\ \text{is false under the modified interpretation}\ \langle x \leftarrow B\rangle \circ \mathcal{I}$$

and therefore (by the $\forall$ rule) that

$(\forall x)p(x)$ is false under $\mathcal{I}$.

Because $p_{\mathcal{I}}(\mathrm{A})$ is true and $x_{\mathcal{I}}$ is A, we have that

$p(x)$ is true under $\mathcal{I}$.

Therefore (by the $\equiv$ rule)

$$\big[(\forall x)p(x) \ \equiv \ p(x)\big] \quad \text{is false under } \mathcal{I},$$

as we wanted to show. ◢

Note that, for any sentence $\mathcal{G}'$, the variable x is not free in $(\forall x)\mathcal{G}'$. Therefore, taking $\mathcal{G}$ to be $(\forall x)\mathcal{G}'$ in the above *redundant-quantifiers* sentence, we have, as a special case, that the universal closure of the sentence schema

$$(\forall x)(\forall x)\mathcal{G}' \ \equiv \ (\forall x)\mathcal{G}'$$

is valid, without side conditions.

Let us illustrate how the side conditions come into play in showing the validity of the above sentences.

Example. Suppose we would like to show that the universal closure of the *distribution-of-quantifiers* equivalence

$$(\exists x)[\mathcal{F} \ and \ \mathcal{G}]$$
$$\equiv$$
$$(\exists x)\mathcal{F} \ and \ \mathcal{G}$$

is valid, where x is not free in $\mathcal{G}$. By the *universal-closure* proposition, it suffices to show that the equivalence itself is true under any interpretation $\mathcal{I}$. However,

the left-hand side of the equivalence, that is,
$(\exists x)[\mathcal{F} \ and \ \mathcal{G}]$,
is true under $\mathcal{I}$

if and only if (by the $\exists$ rule)

there exists a domain element d such that the subsentence
$\mathcal{F} \ and \ \mathcal{G}$
is true under the modified interpretation $\langle x \leftarrow d \rangle \circ \mathcal{I}$

if and only if (by the *and* rule)

there exists a domain element d such that
$\mathcal{F}$
is true under $\langle x \leftarrow d \rangle \circ \mathcal{I}$
and
$\mathcal{G}$
is true under $\langle x \leftarrow d \rangle \circ \mathcal{I}$

if and only if (because x does not occur free in $\mathcal{G}$)

> there exists a domain element d such that
>> $\mathcal{F}$
>
> is true under $\langle x \leftarrow d \rangle \circ \mathcal{I}$
> and
>> $\mathcal{G}$
>
> is true under $\mathcal{I}$

if and only if (by the $\exists$ rule)

>> $(\exists x)\mathcal{F}$
>
> is true under $\mathcal{I}$
> and
>> $\mathcal{G}$
>
> is true under $\mathcal{I}$

if and only if (by the *and* rule)

>> $(\exists x)\mathcal{F}$ *and* $\mathcal{G}$,
>
> that is, the right-hand side of the equivalence, is true under $\mathcal{I}$.

We have shown that the left-hand side of the equivalence is true under $\mathcal{I}$ if and only if the right-hand side is true under $\mathcal{I}$; therefore (by the $\equiv$ rule) the equivalence

> $(\exists x)[\mathcal{F}$ *and* $\mathcal{G}]$
> $\equiv$
> $(\exists x)\mathcal{F}$ *and* $\mathcal{G}$

is true under $\mathcal{I}$, as we wanted to show.

In showing the validity of the above sentence, we have used the fact that

> $\mathcal{G}$ is true under $\langle x \leftarrow d \rangle \circ \mathcal{I}$

if and only if

> $\mathcal{G}$ is true under $\mathcal{I}$,

which holds because we have assumed the side condition that x does not occur free in $\mathcal{G}$. By the remark that follows the *agreement* proposition, this implies that $\mathcal{G}$ has the same truth-value under the two interpretations. ◢

The reader is requested to establish the validity of some of the above sentence schemata in **Problem 3.6** and to illustrate that the side condition is essential in each case.

PROPERTIES OF CLOSURES

The universal and existential closures exhibit the following properties, which reflect the properties of the corresponding quantifiers.

Proposition (equivalences of closures)

For any sentences $\mathcal{F}$ and $\mathcal{G}$ the following sentences are valid:

- Duality

$$not\ (\forall *)\mathcal{F}$$
$$\equiv$$
$$(\exists *)[not\ \mathcal{F}]$$

$$not\ (\exists *)\mathcal{F}$$
$$\equiv$$
$$(\forall *)[not\ \mathcal{F}]$$

- Distribution

$$(\forall *)[\mathcal{F}\ and\ \mathcal{G}]$$
$$\equiv$$
$$(\forall *)\mathcal{F}\ and\ (\forall *)\mathcal{G}$$

$$(\exists *)[\mathcal{F}\ or\ \mathcal{G}]$$
$$\equiv$$
$$(\exists *)\mathcal{F}\ or\ (\exists *)\mathcal{G}$$

$$(\exists *)[if\ \mathcal{F}\ then\ \mathcal{G}]$$
$$\equiv$$
$$if\ (\forall *)\mathcal{F}\ then\ (\exists *)\mathcal{G}$$
⌐

Proof.   To prove the first duality equivalence, let $\mathcal{F}$ be a sentence and $\mathcal{I}$ be an arbitrary interpretation. Let $x_1, x_2, \ldots, x_n$ be the free variables of $\mathcal{F}$.

Then

$$not\ (\forall *)\mathcal{F}\ \text{is true under}\ \mathcal{I}$$

if and only if (by the *not* rule)

$$(\forall *)\mathcal{F}\ \text{is false under}\ \mathcal{I}$$

if and only if (by the *universal-closure* rule)

there exist domain elements $d_1, d_2, \ldots, d_n$ such that
$\mathcal{F}$ is false under $\langle x_1 \leftarrow d_1 \rangle \circ \langle x_2 \leftarrow d_2 \rangle \circ \ldots \circ \langle x_n \leftarrow d_n \rangle \circ \mathcal{I}$

if and only if (by the *not* rule)

there exist domain elements $d_1, d_2, \ldots, d_n$ such that
$(not\ \mathcal{F})$ is true under $\langle x_1 \leftarrow d_1 \rangle \circ \langle x_2 \leftarrow d_2 \rangle \circ \ldots \circ \langle x_n \leftarrow d_n \rangle \circ \mathcal{I}$

if and only if (by the *existential-closure* rule)

$$(\exists *)[not\ \mathcal{F}]\ \text{is true under}\ \mathcal{I}.$$

In short, for an arbitrary interpretation $\mathcal{I}$, $not\ (\forall *)\mathcal{F}$ is true under $\mathcal{I}$ if and only if $(\exists *)[not\ \mathcal{F}]$ is true under $\mathcal{I}$. Thus the sentence $[not\ (\forall *)\mathcal{F}] \equiv (\exists *)[not\ \mathcal{F}]$ is valid. ⌐

The proofs of the other equivalences are similar, and are requested in **Problem 3.7**.

3.8   EQUIVALENCE

The notions of implication and equivalence for predicate logic are the same as those for propositional logic.

Definition (implication, equivalence)

A sentence $\mathcal{F}$ *implies* a sentence $\mathcal{G}$ if, for any interpretation $\mathcal{I}$, if $\mathcal{F}$ is true under $\mathcal{I}$, then $\mathcal{G}$ is true under $\mathcal{I}$.

Two sentences $\mathcal{F}$ and $\mathcal{G}$ are *equivalent* if, under every interpretation, $\mathcal{F}$ has the same truth-value as $\mathcal{G}$.   ◢

Note that we do not require $\mathcal{F}$ and $\mathcal{G}$ to be closed sentences.

IMPLICATION, EQUIVALENCE, AND VALIDITY

A simple relationship between implication and validity and between equivalence and validity is expressed by the following observations:

Remark.   For any two sentences $\mathcal{F}$ and $\mathcal{G}$ in predicate logic

$$\mathcal{F} \text{ implies } \mathcal{G}$$
if and only if
$$(\forall *)[if \;\; \mathcal{F} \;\; then \;\; \mathcal{G}] \text{ is valid.}$$

Also

$$\mathcal{F} \text{ is equivalent to } \mathcal{G}$$
if and only if
$$(\forall *)[\mathcal{F} \equiv \mathcal{G}] \text{ is valid.}$$

Consider the first observation. We have

$$\mathcal{F} \text{ implies } \mathcal{G}$$
if and only if (by the definition)
> for any interpretation $\mathcal{I}$,
>> if $\mathcal{F}$ is true under $\mathcal{I}$
>> then $\mathcal{G}$ is true under $\mathcal{I}$

if and only if (by the *if-then* rule)
> for any interpretation $\mathcal{I}$,
>> (*if $\mathcal{F}$ then $\mathcal{G}$*) is true under $\mathcal{I}$

if and only if (by the *universal-closure* proposition)
$$(\forall *)[if \;\; \mathcal{F} \;\; then \;\; \mathcal{G}] \text{ is valid,}$$
as we wanted to show.

The proof of the second observation is similar and uses the $\equiv$ rule.   ◢

Example.   We have mentioned that the closed sentence

$$not\ (\forall x)p(x)$$
$$\equiv$$
$$(\exists x)[not\ p(x)],$$

which expresses part of the duality of quantifiers, is valid. This implies (by the above remark) that the sentences

$$not\ (\forall x)p(x) \quad \text{and} \quad (\exists x)[not\ p(x)]$$

are equivalent.

Similarly, because the universal closure of

$$not\ (\forall x)q(x,y)$$
$$\equiv$$
$$(\exists x)\big[not\ q(x,y)\big]$$

is valid, the two sentences

$$not\ (\forall x)q(x,y) \quad \text{and} \quad (\exists x)[not\ q(x,y)]$$

are equivalent.

In fact, we have determined that the universal closure of the corresponding schema

$$not\ (\forall x)\mathcal{F}$$
$$\equiv$$
$$(\exists x)[not\ \mathcal{F}]$$

is valid. Therefore for any sentence $\mathcal{F}$, the two sentences

$$not\ (\forall x)\mathcal{F} \quad \text{and} \quad (\exists x)[not\ \mathcal{F}]$$

are equivalent.   ◢

We now consider a further connection between implication and validity and between equivalence and validity.

Proposition (implication and validity)

For any two sentences $\mathcal{F}$ and $\mathcal{G}$,

> if $\mathcal{F}$ implies $\mathcal{G}$,
> then   if $(\forall *)\mathcal{F}$ is valid,
> then $(\forall *)\mathcal{G}$ is valid.   ◢

Proposition (equivalence and validity)

For any two sentences $\mathcal{F}$ and $\mathcal{G}$,

> if $\mathcal{F}$ is equivalent to $\mathcal{G}$,
> then $(\forall *)\mathcal{F}$ is valid

$$\text{if and only if}$$
$$(\forall *)\mathcal{G} \text{ is valid.} \quad \lrcorner$$

The proofs of these propositions are analogous to the proofs of the corresponding results in propositional logic and are requested in **Problem 3.8**. The converses do not hold.

EQUIVALENT PROPOSITIONAL-LOGIC SCHEMATA

We have observed that the universal closure of any instance of a valid propositional-logic schema is valid in predicate logic. It is also true that corresponding instances of equivalent propositional-logic schemata are equivalent in predicate logic. This is expressed more precisely as follows.

Proposition (instances of equivalent propositional-logic schemata)

> If two propositional-logic schemata $\mathcal{E}$ and $\mathcal{E}'$ are equivalent,
> then corresponding predicate-logic instances of $\mathcal{E}$ and $\mathcal{E}'$
> are equivalent. $\lrcorner$

Before proving the proposition we consider an example.

Example. We have seen that the schemata

$$\begin{array}{cc} if \ \mathcal{F} & \\ then \ \mathcal{G} & \end{array} \quad \text{and} \quad \begin{array}{c} if \ not \ \mathcal{G} \\ then \ not \ \mathcal{F} \end{array}$$

are equivalent in propositional logic; the latter is the contrapositive of the former. The proposition therefore implies that the predicate-logic instances of these sentences,

$$\begin{array}{c} if \ p(x) \\ then \ (\exists y)q(x, y) \end{array} \quad \text{and} \quad \begin{array}{c} if \ not \ (\exists y)q(x, y) \\ then \ not \ p(x) \end{array}$$

(obtained by replacing $\mathcal{F}$ and $\mathcal{G}$ with $p(x)$ and $(\exists y)q(x, y)$, respectively), are equivalent in predicate logic. $\lrcorner$

Now let us prove the proposition.

Proof. Suppose $\mathcal{E}$ and $\mathcal{E}'$ are equivalent propositional-logic schemata, and let $\mathcal{E}_0$ and $\mathcal{E}_0'$ be corresponding predicate-logic instances of $\mathcal{E}$ and $\mathcal{E}'$. We want to show that $\mathcal{E}_0$ is equivalent to $\mathcal{E}_0'$.

Because $\mathcal{E}$ and $\mathcal{E}'$ are equivalent, the propositional-logic schema

$$\mathcal{E} \equiv \mathcal{E}'$$

is valid (in propositional logic). Consequently, the universal closure of its predicate-logic instance,

$$\mathcal{E}_0 \equiv \mathcal{E}_0',$$

is valid (in predicate logic). Therefore (by our earlier remark)

   $\mathcal{E}_0$ is equivalent to $\mathcal{E}'_0$.   ◢

REPLACEMENT OF EQUIVALENT SENTENCES

If two sentences are equivalent, they may be used interchangeably, in a sense made precise in the following proposition.

Proposition (replacement of equivalence)

For any sentences $\mathcal{G}$, $\mathcal{H}$, and $\mathcal{F}$, let $\mathcal{F}'$ be the result of replacing one or more occurrences of $\mathcal{G}$ in $\mathcal{F}$ with $\mathcal{H}$. Then

   if $\mathcal{G}$ and $\mathcal{H}$ are equivalent,

   then $\mathcal{F}$ and $\mathcal{F}'$ are equivalent.   ◢

The intuitive justification is straightforward. In determining the truth-values of $\mathcal{F}$ and $\mathcal{F}'$ under a given interpretation $\mathcal{I}$, the respective results will be the same at each stage. Although $\mathcal{F}'$ may have occurrences of $\mathcal{H}$ where $\mathcal{F}$ has occurrences of $\mathcal{G}$, the corresponding subsentences $\mathcal{G}$ and $\mathcal{H}$ are themselves equivalent, and hence yield the same truth-values under any interpretation.

Let us illustrate the proposition with an example.

Example.   Consider the sentences

   $\mathcal{G}:$ $p(x)$ *and* $p(x)$ and $\mathcal{H}':$ $p(x)$.

Then, because $\mathcal{G}$ and $\mathcal{H}$ are instances of the equivalent propositional-logic sentences $(P \ and \ P)$ and P,

   $\mathcal{G}$ and $\mathcal{H}$ are equivalent.

Consider now the sentence

$$\mathcal{F}: \quad (\forall x)(\exists y) \begin{bmatrix} p(x) \ \ and \ \ p(x) \\ or \\ r(y, \, z) \end{bmatrix}$$

and the sentence

$$\mathcal{F}': \quad (\forall x)(\exists y) \begin{bmatrix} p(x) \\ or \\ r(y, \, z) \end{bmatrix},$$

obtained by replacing one occurrence of $\mathcal{G}$ in $\mathcal{F}$ with $\mathcal{H}$. Then, according to the proposition,

   $\mathcal{F}$ and $\mathcal{F}'$ are equivalent.   ◢

RENAMING OF BOUND VARIABLES

A consequence of the semantic rule for quantifiers is that the variable x in a
quantified sentence $(\forall x)\mathcal{G}$ or $(\exists x)\mathcal{G}$ is a "dummy," in the sense that we can
systematically replace it with a new variable, i.e., one not occurring in $\mathcal{G}$, without
changing the meaning of the sentence. For example, the two sentences

$$(\forall x)p(x) \quad \text{and} \quad (\forall y)p(y)$$

are equivalent: Whether we choose to use x or y has no effect on the meaning of
the sentence. Because the variables x and y are quantified, the truth-values of
the sentences under an interpretation do not depend on which domain element is
assigned to these variables by the interpretation.

In contrast, the two sentences

$$p(x) \quad \text{and} \quad p(y),$$

in which x and y occur free, are not equivalent. If the two variables x and y are
assigned different elements under an interpretation $\mathcal{I}$, the two sentences $p(x)$ and
$p(y)$ may have different truth-values under $\mathcal{I}$.

We can rename the variable x of quantifiers $(\forall x)$ or $(\exists x)$ even if these quantifiers do not occur at the top level of the sentence. Let us explain this with an
example.

Example.   The sentence

$$\mathcal{F}: \quad \begin{array}{l} (\forall z)\big[p(z) \ \ and \ \ r(x)\big] \\ \qquad and \\ if \ \ p(u) \ \ then \ \ (\forall x)\big[p(u) \ \ and \ \ r(x)\big] \end{array}$$

is equivalent to the sentence

$$\mathcal{F}': \quad \begin{array}{l} (\forall z)\big[p(z) \ \ and \ \ r(x)\big] \\ \qquad and \\ if \ \ p(u) \ \ then \ \ (\forall y)\big[p(u) \ \ and \ \ r(y)\big], \end{array}$$

obtained by renaming the variable x of the quantifier $(\forall x)$ to y. ⌐

It is important that, in renaming the variable of a quantifier, we choose a
new variable, i.e., one that does not already occur in the replaced subsentence $\mathcal{G}$.
The reason for this will be illustrated in the following two examples.

Example.   Consider the sentence

$$\mathcal{F}: \quad (\forall x)p(x, y).$$

This sentence is not equivalent to the sentence

$$\mathcal{F}': \quad (\forall y)p(y, y),$$

obtained by renaming the variable x of the quantifier $(\forall x)$ to the variable y, which
already occurs free in the replaced subsentence.

In particular, under any interpretation that assigns p to be the equality relation over a domain with two or more elements, $\mathcal{F}$ is given the intuitive meaning

for every x, $x = y$,

which is false, while $\mathcal{F}'$ is given the intuitive meaning

for every y, $y = y$,

which is true. ⌐

In the example above, we renamed the quantified variable to a variable that already has a free occurrence in the sentence. Similar problems may occur if we rename the quantified variable to a variable that occurs bound in the sentence.

Example.   Consider the sentence

$$\mathcal{F}: \quad (\forall x)(\forall y)p(x, y);$$

this sentence is not equivalent to the sentence

$$\mathcal{F}': \quad (\forall y)(\forall y)p(y, y),$$

obtained by renaming the variable x of the quantifier $(\forall x)$ to the variable y, which already occurs bound in the replaced subsentence.

In particular, under any interpretation over a domain with two or more elements that assigns p to be the equality relation, $\mathcal{F}$ is given the intuitive meaning

for every x and y, $x = y$,

which is false, while $\mathcal{F}'$, which is equivalent to

$$(\forall y)p(y, y),$$

is given the intuitive meaning

for every y, $y = y$,

which is true. ⌐

We summarize the notion of renaming in the following proposition.

Proposition (renaming of bound variables)

Let $\mathcal{F}$ be a sentence with a subsentence $(\ldots x)\mathcal{G}$, where $(\ldots x)$ is a quantifier, either $(\forall x)$ or $(\exists x)$.

Let x' be a variable that does not occur in $(\ldots x)\mathcal{G}$ and let $\mathcal{G}'$ be the result of replacing every free occurrence of x in $\mathcal{G}$ with x'.

Let $\mathcal{F}'$ be the result of replacing one or more occurrences of $(\ldots x)\mathcal{G}$ in $\mathcal{F}$ with $(\ldots x')\mathcal{G}'$.

Then $\mathcal{F}$ and $\mathcal{F}'$ are equivalent. ⌐

Remark (nested quantifiers).   It is often confusing when a sentence contains nested quantifiers over the same variable. For example, in the sentence

$$\mathcal{F}: \quad (\forall x)\big[p(x) \ and \ (\exists x)q(x, \, y)\big],$$

the second quantifier, $(\exists x)$, is within the scope of the first quantifier, $(\forall x)$. Consequently the occurrence of the variable x in $p(x)$ is bound by the first quantifier, $(\forall x)$, but the occurrence of x in $q(x, y)$ is bound by the second quantifier, $(\exists x)$.

We can rename the variable x of the second quantifier $(\exists x)$ to x', obtaining the equivalent sentence

$$\mathcal{F}': \quad (\forall x)\big[p(x) \ and \ (\exists x')q(x', \, y)\big].$$

Although $\mathcal{F}$ and $\mathcal{F}'$ are equivalent, $\mathcal{F}'$ may be easier to understand, because it is clearer which quantifier binds which variable in $\mathcal{F}'$.   ◢

3.9   SAFE SUBSTITUTION

We now introduce a notion of substitution for predicate logic analogous to the one we used for propositional logic. Because this notion is surprisingly complex, we begin with examples showing that more straightforward definitions of substitution do not exhibit the desired properties.

BOUND AND FREE SUBEXPRESSIONS

In our chapter on propositional logic, we observed that the equivalence connective $\equiv$ has the substitutivity property: For any propositional-logic sentences $\mathcal{G}$, $\mathcal{H}$, and $\mathcal{F}\langle\mathcal{G}\rangle$, the sentence

$$if \ \mathcal{G} \equiv \mathcal{H}$$
$$then \ \mathcal{F}\langle\mathcal{G}\rangle \equiv \mathcal{F}\langle\mathcal{H}\rangle$$

is valid, where $\mathcal{F}\langle\mathcal{H}\rangle$ is the result of replacing zero, one, or more occurrences of $\mathcal{G}$ in $\mathcal{F}\langle\mathcal{G}\rangle$ with $\mathcal{H}$.

We would like to extend the substitution operation to predicate logic so that the universal closure of the corresponding predicate-logic sentence

$$(*) \quad \begin{aligned} & if \ \mathcal{G} \equiv \mathcal{H} \\ & then \ \mathcal{F}\langle\mathcal{G}\rangle \equiv \mathcal{F}\langle\mathcal{H}\rangle \end{aligned}$$

is valid. Unfortunately, if we naively adopt the propositional-logic definition of substitution, this is not the case, as is illustrated by the following examples.

Our first observation will lead us to distinguish between "bound" and "free" subexpressions of a given expression and to define the substitution operation so that only "free" subexpressions are replaced.

Example (replacing bound subexpressions).   Consider the sentences

$$\mathcal{G} : p(x), \quad \mathcal{H} : q(x), \quad \text{and} \quad \mathcal{F}\langle \mathcal{G}\rangle : (\forall x)p(x).$$

Suppose we define predicate-logic substitution so that $\mathcal{F}\langle \mathcal{H}\rangle$ may denote

$$(\forall x)q(x),$$

that is, the result of replacing the occurrence of $p(x)$ in $(\forall x)p(x)$ with $q(x)$. Then, according to the desired substitutivity-of-equivalence property $(*)$ above, the universal closure of the implication

> *if* $p(x) \equiv q(x)$
> *then* $(\forall x)p(x) \equiv (\forall x)q(x)$

should be valid; but this is not the case.

To show this, it suffices, by the *universal-closure* proposition, to exhibit a single interpretation under which the implication itself is false.

Consider the interpretation $\mathcal{I}$ over all the integers under which

x is 0

p is the nonnegative relation; that is,
    for every integer z, $p(z)$ is true if and only if $z \geq 0$

q is true for all integers; that is,
    for every integer z, $q(z)$ is true.

Under this interpretation, the antecedent,

$$p(x) \equiv q(x),$$

is true. Its left and right sides are both true under $\mathcal{I}$ because 0 is nonnegative and $q(x)$ is always true.

The consequent,

$$(\forall x)p(x) \equiv (\forall x)q(x),$$

on the other hand, is false under $\mathcal{I}$. It has been given the intuitive meaning "Every integer is nonnegative if and only if true," that is, "Every integer is nonnegative," which does not hold.   ⌐

In the above example, the problem was that the variable x, which is free in $p(x)$, is bound in $(\forall x)p(x)$ and thus has a different meaning in $p(x)$ and in $(\forall x)p(x)$.

To phrase the definition of substitution for predicate logic to avoid the sort of mishap illustrated in the above example, we need to introduce some special terminology. We extend the notions of bound and free to subexpressions, either terms or sentences.

Definition (bound subexpressions)

Consider an occurrence of a subexpression $\mathcal{E}'$ in an expression $\mathcal{E}$.

The occurrence of $\mathcal{E}'$ is *bound in* $\mathcal{E}$ if

some occurrence of a variable x is free in the occurrence of $\mathcal{E}'$,
but the same occurrence of x is bound in $\mathcal{E}$. ⌐

In other words, the occurrence of x is not within the scope of any quantifier $(\dots x)$ in $\mathcal{E}'$, but the occurrence of $\mathcal{E}'$ is within the scope of some quantifier $(\dots x)$ in $\mathcal{E}$.

Example.   Consider the subsentence

$\qquad \mathcal{E}': \quad p(x)$

of the sentence

$\qquad \mathcal{E}: \quad (\forall x)p(x).$

The occurrence of $p(x)$ is bound in $(\forall x)p(x)$, because $p(x)$ has a free occurrence of x that is bound in $(\forall x)p(x)$. ⌐

A sentence may have bound occurrences in a term if the sentence occurs in the *if*-clause of a conditional term.

Example.   Consider the subsentence

$\qquad \mathcal{E}': \quad p(x)$

of the conditional term

$$\mathcal{E}: \quad \begin{array}{l} if \ \ (\forall x)p(x) \\ then \ \ a \\ else \ \ f(x). \end{array}$$

The occurrence of $p(x)$ is bound in $\mathcal{E}$, because the free occurrence of x in $p(x)$ is bound in $\mathcal{E}$, by the quantifier $(\forall x)$. ⌐

Definition (free subexpressions)

Consider an occurrence of a subexpression $\mathcal{E}'$ in an expression $\mathcal{E}$.

The occurrence of $\mathcal{E}'$ is *free in* $\mathcal{E}$ if,

in that occurrence of $\mathcal{E}'$,
every free occurrence of a variable is also free in $\mathcal{E}$. ⌐

In other words, if the occurrence of a variable x is not within the scope of any quantifier $(\dots x)$ in the occurrence of $\mathcal{E}'$, then it is also not within the scope of any quantifier $(\dots x)$ in $\mathcal{E}$.

Example.   Consider the subsentence

$\qquad \mathcal{E}': \quad q(y, z)$

of the sentence

$\qquad \mathcal{E}: \quad q(y, z) \ \ and \ \ (\forall y)q(u, y).$

The occurrence of $q(y, z)$ is free in $\mathcal{E}$, because the free occurrences of y and z in $q(y, z)$ are also free in $\mathcal{E}$. ⌐

A subexpression may have both bound and free occurrences in the same expression.

Example.   Consider the subterm

$$\mathcal{E}' : \quad f(y)$$

of the sentence

$$\mathcal{E} : \quad \begin{array}{c} (\exists y)p\big(f(y)\big) \\ or \\ q\big(f(y)\big). \end{array}$$

The first occurrence of the term $f(y)$, in $p\big(f(y)\big)$, is bound in $\mathcal{E}$, because the free occurrence of y in this occurrence of $f(y)$ is bound in $\mathcal{E}$, by the quantifier $(\exists y)$.

The second occurrence of the term $f(y)$, in $q\big(f(y)\big)$, is free in $\mathcal{E}$, because the free occurrence of y in this occurrence of $f(y)$ is also free in $\mathcal{E}$, and there are no other free occurrences of variables in the term. ⌐

In attempting to formulate a definition of substitution for predicate logic that would enable us to retain a *substitutivity-of-equivalence* property, we observed that the universal closure of the sentence

$$\begin{array}{l} if \ \ p(x) \ \equiv \ q(x) \\ then \ \ (\forall x)p(x) \ \equiv \ (\forall x)q(x) \end{array}$$

is not valid. Here the sentence $(\forall x)q(x)$ was formed by replacing the (bound) occurrence of $p(x)$ in $(\forall x)p(x)$ with $q(x)$. In formulating the notion of substitution for predicate logic, we shall require that only free occurrences of subexpressions may be replaced. In this way, we avoid such counterexamples to the *substitutivity-of-equivalence* property.

CAPTURING

Even if we phrase the definition of substitution so that only free occurrences of subexpressions can be replaced, other problems arise.

Example (capturing).   Consider the sentences

$$\mathcal{G} : \ p(x), \quad \mathcal{H} : \ p(y), \quad \text{and} \quad \mathcal{F}\langle \mathcal{G} \rangle : \ (\forall y)p(x).$$

Suppose we define the substitution operation so that $\mathcal{F}\langle \mathcal{H} \rangle$ may denote

$$(\forall y)p(y),$$

that is, the result of replacing the (free) occurrence of $p(x)$ in $(\forall y)p(x)$ with $p(y)$. Then, according to the desired *substitutivity-of-equivalence* property $(*)$ above, the universal closure of the implication

$$\begin{array}{l} if \ \ p(x) \ \equiv \ p(y) \\ then \ \ (\forall y)p(x) \ \equiv \ (\forall y)p(y) \end{array}$$

should be valid; but this is not the case.

To show this, it suffices, by the *universal-closure* proposition, to exhibit a single interpretation under which the implication itself is false.

Consider the interpretation $\mathcal{I}$ over all the integers under which

x is 0

y is 0

p is the nonnegative relation; that is,
for every integer z, $p(z)$ is true if and only if $z \geq 0$.

Under this interpretation, the antecedent,

$$p(x) \equiv p(y),$$

has been given the intuitive meaning

0 is nonnegative if and only if 0 is nonnegative,

which is true. The consequent,

$$(\forall y)p(x) \equiv (\forall y)p(y),$$

has been given the intuitive meaning

For every integer y, 0 is nonnegative
if and only if
for every integer y, y is nonnegative,

that is,

0 is nonnegative
if and only if
every integer is nonnegative,

which is false.

Therefore, the implication

if $p(x) \equiv p(y)$
then $(\forall y)p(x) \equiv (\forall y)p(y)$

is false under $\mathcal{I}$, as we intended to show.

In the example above, although the subsentence $p(x)$ is free in the surrounding sentence $(\forall y)p(x)$, the newly introduced occurrence of $p(y)$ in $(\forall y)p(y)$ is bound. The occurrence of y, which is free in $p(y)$, is bound in $(\forall y)p(y)$; therefore its meaning has been changed by the substitution operation. We shall say that y has been "captured" by the quantifier $(\forall y)$. The definition of substitution for predicate logic will be formulated so that quantified variables are renamed, if necessary, to avoid such capturing.

SAFE SUBSTITUTION

We are now ready to present the notion of "safe" substitution for predicate-logic expressions, which avoids both the above mishaps, i.e., the replacement of bound subexpressions and the capturing of free variables. We distinguish between "total safe substitution," in which all free occurrences of a subexpression are replaced, and "partial safe substitution," in which zero, one, or more, but not necessarily all, free occurrences are replaced.

Definition (total safe substitution)

Suppose $\mathcal{F}$, $\mathcal{G}$, and $\mathcal{H}$ are expressions, where $\mathcal{G}$ and $\mathcal{H}$ are either both terms or both sentences. In preparation for replacing occurrences of $\mathcal{G}$ in $\mathcal{F}$, let us write $\mathcal{F}$ as

$$\mathcal{F}[\mathcal{G}].$$

Then we denote by

$$\mathcal{F}[\mathcal{H}]$$

the expression obtained as follows:
- Replace every free occurrence of $\mathcal{G}$ in $\mathcal{F}[\mathcal{G}]$ with $\mathcal{H}$,

but
- if any free variable y in $\mathcal{H}$ is about to be captured by a quantifier $(\ldots y)$ in $\mathcal{F}[\mathcal{G}]$ as a result of the above replacement, rename the variable y of this quantifier in $\mathcal{F}[\mathcal{G}]$ to a new variable y' before performing the replacement; y' is taken to be a variable that does not already occur in $\mathcal{F}[\mathcal{G}]$ or $\mathcal{H}$.

We shall say that $\mathcal{F}[\mathcal{H}]$ is the result of *safely replacing* every free occurrence of $\mathcal{G}$ in $\mathcal{F}[\mathcal{G}]$ with $\mathcal{H}$. ⌐

Example.   Let $\mathcal{F}[p(x)]$ be the sentence

$$(\forall x)[p(x) \ and \ r(y)]$$
$$and$$
$$if \ p(x) \ then \ (\forall y)[p(x) \ and \ r(y)].$$

Then the result $\mathcal{F}[q(y)]$ of a total safe substitution is the sentence

$$(\forall x)[p(x) \ and \ r(y)]$$
$$and$$
$$if \ q(y) \ then \ (\forall y')[q(y) \ and \ r(y')].$$

Note that the first occurrence of $p(x)$, which is bound, is not replaced by the substitution; the other two occurrences of $p(x)$, which are free, must be replaced. Also note that the variable y of the quantifier $(\forall y)$ has been renamed to the new variable y', to avoid capturing the free variable y in $q(y)$. The first occurrence of y, in the subsentence $r(y)$, is not renamed, because it is not within the scope of the quantifier $(\forall y)$. ⌐

The result $\mathcal{F}[\mathcal{H}]$ of applying the substitution to $\mathcal{F}[\mathcal{G}]$ is not unique, because, to avoid capturing a free variable, we may rename the variable y of the quantifier $(\ldots y)$ to any new variable y'. However, any two results of applying the substitution are equivalent, because either can be obtained from the other by renaming of bound variables.

The corresponding notion of partial safe substitution, described as follows, is analogous to partial substitution in propositional logic.

Definition (partial safe substitution)

Suppose $\mathcal{F}$, $\mathcal{G}$, and $\mathcal{H}$ are expressions, where $\mathcal{G}$ and $\mathcal{H}$ are either both terms or both sentences. In preparation for replacing occurrences of $\mathcal{G}$ in $\mathcal{F}$, let us write $\mathcal{F}$ as

$$\mathcal{F}\langle \mathcal{G}\rangle.$$

Then we denote by

$$\mathcal{F}\langle \mathcal{H}\rangle$$

any of the expressions obtained as follows:

- Replace zero, one, or more free occurrences of $\mathcal{G}$ in $\mathcal{F}$ with $\mathcal{H}$,

but

- if any free variable y in $\mathcal{H}$ is about to be captured by a quantifier $(\ldots y)$ in $\mathcal{F}$ as a result of the above replacement, rename the variable y of this quantifier to a new variable y' before performing the replacement.

We shall say that $\mathcal{F}\langle \mathcal{H}\rangle$ is the result of *safely replacing* zero, one, or more free occurrences of $\mathcal{G}$ in $\mathcal{F}\langle \mathcal{G}\rangle$ with $\mathcal{H}$. ◢

As in propositional logic, partial substitution may result in any of several sentences. Moreover, two distinct results of applying partial substitution (as opposed to total substitution) are not necessarily equivalent.

Example.   Let $\mathcal{F}\langle f(x)\rangle$ be

$$(\forall y)p\big(f(x),\, y\big)$$
$$\textit{and}$$
$$(\exists z)r\big(z,\, f(x)\big).$$

Then the result $\mathcal{F}\langle z\rangle$ of a partial safe substitution may be any of the following four sentences:

1.	$(\forall y)p\big(f(x),\, y\big)$ *and* $(\exists z)r\big(z,\, f(x)\big)$		2.	$(\forall y)p(z,\, y)$ *and* $(\exists z)r\big(z,\, f(x)\big)$	

$$3. \quad \begin{array}{c} (\forall y)p\big(f(x), y\big) \\ and \\ (\exists z')r(z', z) \end{array} \qquad\qquad 4. \quad \begin{array}{c} (\forall y)p(z, y) \\ and \\ (\exists z')r(z', z) \end{array}$$

Note that there are two occurrences of $f(x)$ in the original sentence, both free. In the first result, we replaced neither occurrence of $f(x)$. In the second result, we replaced the first occurrence of $f(x)$; in the third result, we replaced the second occurrence of $f(x)$; in the fourth result, we replaced both occurrences of $f(x)$. Also, in the third and fourth results, we were forced to rename the variable z of the quantifier $(\exists z)$ to the new variable z', to avoid capturing the newly introduced free variable z. ◢

The reader should be aware that we may write $\mathcal{F}$ as $\mathcal{F}[\mathcal{G}]$ or $\mathcal{F}\langle\mathcal{G}\rangle$ and apply a total or partial safe substitution even if $\mathcal{G}$ does not occur free in $\mathcal{F}$. In this case $\mathcal{F}[\mathcal{H}]$ and $\mathcal{F}\langle\mathcal{H}\rangle$ will be the same as $\mathcal{F}$.

MULTIPLE SAFE SUBSTITUTION

The above notions may be extended to allow simultaneous multiple replacements in predicate-logic expressions as follows:

Definition (multiple safe substitution)

Suppose $\mathcal{F}, \mathcal{G}_1, \ldots, \mathcal{G}_n$, and $\mathcal{H}_1, \ldots, \mathcal{H}_n$ are expressions, where $\mathcal{G}_1, \ldots, \mathcal{G}_n$ are distinct and, for each i, $\mathcal{G}_i$ and $\mathcal{H}_i$ are either both terms or both sentences.

- *Total safe substitution*

   In preparation for replacing occurrences of $\mathcal{G}_i$ in $\mathcal{F}$, let us write $\mathcal{F}$ as

   $$\mathcal{F}[\mathcal{G}_1, \ldots, \mathcal{G}_n].$$

   Then we denote by

   $$\mathcal{F}[\mathcal{H}_1, \ldots, \mathcal{H}_n]$$

   the expression obtained as follows:

   - Replace simultaneously every free occurrence of each subexpression $\mathcal{G}_i$ in $\mathcal{F}[\mathcal{G}_1, \ldots, \mathcal{G}_n]$ with the corresponding expression $\mathcal{H}_i$,

   but

   - if any free variable y in $\mathcal{H}_1, \ldots,$ or $\mathcal{H}_n$ is about to be captured by a quantifier $(\ldots y)$ in $\mathcal{F}[\mathcal{G}_1, \ldots, \mathcal{G}_n]$ as a result of one of the above replacements, rename the variable y of this quantifier to a new variable y' before performing the replacement.

We shall say that $\mathcal{F}[\mathcal{H}_1, \ldots, \mathcal{H}_n]$ is the result of *safely replacing* every free occurrence of each of the $\mathcal{G}_i$ in $\mathcal{F}[\mathcal{G}_1, \ldots, \mathcal{G}_n]$ with the corresponding $\mathcal{H}_i$.

- *Partial safe substitution*

  In preparation for replacing occurrences of $\mathcal{G}_i$ in $\mathcal{F}$, let us write $\mathcal{F}$ as

  $$\mathcal{F}\langle \mathcal{G}_1, \ldots, \mathcal{G}_n \rangle.$$

  Then we denote by

  $$\mathcal{F}\langle \mathcal{H}_1, \ldots, \mathcal{H}_n \rangle$$

  any one of the expressions obtained as follows:

    - Replace simultaneously zero, one, or more free occurrences of some of the subexpressions $\mathcal{G}_i$ in $\mathcal{F}\langle \mathcal{G}_1, \ldots, \mathcal{G}_n \rangle$ with the corresponding expression $\mathcal{H}_i$,

  but

    - if any free variable y in $\mathcal{H}_1, \ldots,$ or $\mathcal{H}_n$ is about to be captured by a quantifier $(\ldots y)$ in $\mathcal{F}\langle \mathcal{G}_1, \ldots, \mathcal{G}_n \rangle$ as a result of one of the above replacements, rename the variable y of this quantifier to a new variable y' before performing the replacement.

  We shall say that $\mathcal{F}\langle \mathcal{H}_1, \ldots, \mathcal{H}_n \rangle$ is the result of *safely replacing* zero, one, or more free occurrences of some of the $\mathcal{G}_i$ in $\mathcal{F}\langle \mathcal{G}_1, \ldots, \mathcal{G}_n \rangle$ with the corresponding $\mathcal{H}_i$. ◢

Example.   Let $\mathcal{F}[p(x), f(y), p(f(y))]$ be

> *if* $(\forall z)[p(x)$ *and* $q(y, z)]$
> *then* $p(f(y))$
> *else* $(\exists z)(\forall x)[q(f(y), z)$ *or* $p(x)].$

Then the result $\mathcal{F}[q(a, f(y)), z, false]$ of a multiple total safe substitution is the sentence

> *if* $(\forall z)[q(a, f(y))$ *and* $q(y, z)]$
> *then false*
> *else* $(\exists z')(\forall x)[q(z, z')$ *or* $p(x)].$

Note that, as in propositional logic, multiple substitutions are applied simultaneously in a single stage. Thus, though the first occurrence of $p(x)$ was replaced by $q(a, f(y))$, the newly introduced occurrence of $f(y)$ was not subsequently replaced by z.

Again, in case of a conflict between two expressions, the outermost subexpression is always the one to be replaced. Thus, the first occurrence of $f(y)$ in the given sentence is not replaced by z, because it occurs in a subsentence $p(f(y))$, which is replaced by *false* as a result of the substitution.

As is also the case in a single substitution, we do not replace the second occurrence of $p(x)$, since it is bound. Also, we are forced to rename the variable z of the quantifier $(\exists z)$ to z', to avoid capturing the free occurrence of z introduced by the replacement of the occurrence of $f(y)$ in $q\big(f(y),\, z\big)$ with z. ◢

The next example illustrates the multiple partial safe substitution.

Example.   Let $\mathcal{F}\langle f(x),\, p\big(f(x)\big)\rangle$ be

$(\forall y)\big[\textit{if}\ \ p\big(f(x)\big)\ \ \textit{then}\ \ q(y)\big]$
     and
if $\big(not\ p\big(f(x)\big)\big)$ *then* $r\big(y,\, f(y)\big).$

Then the result $\mathcal{F}\langle g(y),\, \textit{false}\rangle$ of a multiple partial safe substitution may be any of several sentences, including

$(\forall y)\big[\textit{if}\ \ \textit{false}\ \ \textit{then}\ \ q(y)\big]$
     and
if $\big(not\ p\big(f(x)\big)\big)$ *then* $r\big(y, f(y)\big),$

obtained by replacing the first occurrence of $p\big(f(x)\big)$ with *false*;

$(\forall y')\big[\textit{if}\ \ p\big(g(y)\big)\ \ \textit{then}\ \ q(y')\big]$
     and
if $(not\ false)$ *then* $r\big(y,\, f(y)\big),$

obtained by replacing the first occurrence of $f(x)$ with $g(y)$ and the second occurrence of $p\big(f(x)\big)$ with *false*; and

$(\forall y')\big[\textit{if}\ \ p\big(g(y)\big)\ \ \textit{then}\ \ q(y')\big]$
     and
if $\big(not\ p\big(g(y)\big)\big)$ *then* $r\big(y,\, f(y)\big),$

obtained by replacing both occurrences of $f(x)$ with $g(y)$.

Recall that we are not required to apply all the replacements in a multiple partial substitution; thus in the first result we replace no occurrences of $f(x)$; in the last result we replace no occurrences of $p\big(f(x)\big)$. Note that, in the last two cases, we were forced to rename the variable y of the quantifier $(\forall y)$ to y', to avoid capturing the newly introduced free occurrence of y in $g(y)$.

Some further examples of the safe substitution operation are requested in **Problem 3.9**.

3.10   VALID SCHEMATA WITH SUBSTITUTION

Now that we have introduced safe substitution, we can present the substitutivity of equivalence and the general renaming of bound variables and augment our catalog of valid sentence schemata.

SUBSTITUTIVITY OF EQUIVALENCE

Safe substitution has been defined carefully so that certain properties, including an analog of the substitutivity of equivalence from propositional logic, will be true in predicate logic.

Proposition (substitutivity of equivalence)

For any sentences $\mathcal{G}$, $\mathcal{H}$, and $\mathcal{F}\langle\mathcal{G}\rangle$, the universal closure of

$$\textit{if } \mathcal{G} \equiv \mathcal{H}$$
$$\textit{then } \mathcal{F}\langle\mathcal{G}\rangle \equiv \mathcal{F}\langle\mathcal{H}\rangle$$

is valid. ◢

Example. Consider the sentence

$$\mathcal{F}\langle p(x)\rangle : \quad (\forall y)\begin{bmatrix} \textit{if } p(x) \\ \textit{then } r(x,y) \end{bmatrix}.$$

The result of replacing the free occurrence of $p(x)$ in $\mathcal{F}\langle p(x)\rangle$ with $q(y)$ is the sentence

$$\mathcal{F}\langle q(y)\rangle : \quad (\forall y')\begin{bmatrix} \textit{if } q(y) \\ \textit{then } r(x,y') \end{bmatrix}.$$

Then, by the *substitutivity-of-equivalence* proposition, we may conclude that the universal closure of

$$\textit{if } p(x) \equiv q(y)$$

$$\textit{then } \left[(\forall y)\begin{bmatrix} \textit{if } p(x) \\ \textit{then } r(x,y) \end{bmatrix} \equiv (\forall y')\begin{bmatrix} \textit{if } q(y) \\ \textit{then } r(x,y') \end{bmatrix} \right]$$

is valid. ◢

As an important special case of the proposition, we have that the universal closure of

$$\textit{if } \mathcal{G} \equiv \mathcal{H}$$
$$\textit{then } \mathcal{F}[\mathcal{G}] \equiv \mathcal{F}[\mathcal{H}]$$

is valid. This is because the result of a total substitution is one of the possible results of a partial substitution.

We also have the following result:

Corollary (substitutivity of equivalence)

For any sentences $\mathcal{G}$, $\mathcal{H}$, and $\mathcal{F}\langle\mathcal{G}\rangle$,

if $\mathcal{G}$ and $\mathcal{H}$ are equivalent,

then $\mathcal{F}\langle\mathcal{G}\rangle$ and $\mathcal{F}\langle\mathcal{H}\rangle$ are equivalent. ◢

This corollary is similar to the *replacement-of-equivalence* proposition that we introduced in Section 3.8. That proposition, however, performs a simple replacement rather than a safe substitution. In the corollary we replace only free subsentences and we rename bound variables to avoid capturing; in the *replacement-of-equivalence* proposition we may replace bound subsentences and we allow capturing to occur. Subsequently, we shall use the blanket phrase *substitutivity of equivalence* to include the *replacement-of-equivalence* proposition, and the *substitutivity-of-equivalence* proposition and its corollary.

QUANTIFIER INSTANTIATION

The following classes of valid sentence schemata are described in terms of the total safe substitution.

Proposition (quantifier instantiation)
For any variable x, sentence $\mathcal{F}[x]$, and term t, the universal closures of the sentences:

$$\begin{aligned} &if \ \ (\forall x)\mathcal{F}[x] \\ &then \ \ \mathcal{F}[t] \end{aligned}$$ (*universal*)

$$\begin{aligned} &if \ \ \mathcal{F}[t] \\ &then \ \ (\exists x)\mathcal{F}[x] \end{aligned}$$ (*existential*)

are valid. ⌐

We illustrate this important proposition with an example.

Example. Consider the sentence

$$\mathcal{F}[x]: \ \ p(x, a).$$

The result of replacing the free occurrence of x in $\mathcal{F}[x]$ with the term a is the sentence

$$\mathcal{F}[a]: \ \ p(a, a).$$

According to the *universal* part of the proposition, taking t to be a, the sentence

$$\begin{aligned} &if \ \ (\forall x)\mathcal{F}[x] \\ &then \ \ \mathcal{F}[a] \end{aligned} \ : \ \begin{aligned} &if \ \ (\forall x)p(x, a) \\ &then \ \ p(a, a) \end{aligned}$$

is valid.

On the other hand, according to the *existential* part of the proposition, the sentence

$$\begin{aligned} &if \ \ \mathcal{F}[a] \\ &then \ \ (\exists x)\mathcal{F}[x] \end{aligned} \ : \ \begin{aligned} &if \ \ p(a, a) \\ &then \ \ (\exists x)p(x, a) \end{aligned}$$

is also valid. ⌐

Let us illustrate the proposition with an example that requires renaming in applying safe substitution.

Example.   Consider the sentence

$$\mathcal{F}[x]: \quad \begin{array}{l} (\forall\, y)p(x,\, y) \\ \textit{and} \\ p(y,\, x). \end{array}$$

The result of safely replacing the two free occurrences of x in $\mathcal{F}[x]$ with the term $g(y)$ is the sentence

$$\mathcal{F}[g(y)]: \quad \begin{array}{l} (\forall\, y')p\big(g(y),\, y'\big) \\ \textit{and} \\ p\big(y,\, g(y)\big). \end{array}$$

Note that the variable y of the quantifier $(\forall\, y)$ was renamed y' to avoid capturing the free variable y in a newly introduced occurrence of $g(y)$. The free occurrence of y, in $p(y,\, x)$, was not renamed.

According to the *universal* part of the proposition, the universal closure of the sentence

$$\begin{array}{l} \textit{if } (\forall\, x)\mathcal{F}[x] \\ \textit{then } \mathcal{F}[g(y)] \end{array} : \quad \textit{if } (\forall\, x) \begin{bmatrix} (\forall\, y)p(x,\, y) \\ \textit{and} \\ p(y,\, x) \end{bmatrix} \quad \textit{then} \quad \begin{bmatrix} (\forall\, y')p\big(g(y),\, y'\big) \\ \textit{and} \\ p\big(y,\, g(y)\big) \end{bmatrix}$$

is valid.

The renaming required for safe substitution is essential to ensure the truth of the proposition; this is illustrated by the following example.

Example (necessity for renaming).   Consider the sentence

$$\mathcal{F}[x]: \quad (\exists\, y)p(x,\, y).$$

The result of safely replacing the (free) occurrence of x in $\mathcal{F}[x]$ with the term y is the sentence

$$\mathcal{F}[y]: \quad (\exists\, y')p(y,\, y'),$$

where the variable y of the quantifier $(\exists\, y)$ was renamed y'.

According to the *universal* part of the proposition, the universal closure of the sentence

$$\begin{array}{l} \textit{if } (\forall\, x)\mathcal{F}[x] \\ \textit{then } \mathcal{F}[y] \end{array} : \quad \begin{array}{l} \textit{if } (\forall\, x)(\exists\, y)p(x,\, y) \\ \textit{then } (\exists\, y')p(y,\, y') \end{array}$$

is valid.

However, if we had neglected to rename the variable y during the substitution, we would have obtained the sentence

$$\begin{array}{l} \textit{if } (\forall\, x)(\exists\, y)p(x,\, y) \\ \textit{then } (\exists\, y)p(y,\, y), \end{array}$$

which is not valid. In particular, consider the interpretation over the integers under which

p is the less-than relation $<$.

Under this interpretation the sentence has the intuitive meaning

if, for every integer x,
    there exists an integer y such that $x < y$,
then there exists an integer y such that $y < y$,

which is false because its antecedent is true and its consequent is false. ⏌

Let us discuss one point that can be confusing in applying the *existential* part of the proposition.

Remark (existential quantifier instantiation). In a previous example we considered the sentence

$\mathcal{F}[x]:$ $p(x, a)$

and its instance

$\mathcal{F}[a]:$ $p(a, a)$

and concluded, by the *existential* part of the proposition, that the sentence

if $p(a, a)$
then $(\exists x)p(x, a)$

is valid.

Suppose instead we consider the sentence

$\mathcal{F}[x]:$ $p(a, x)$.

The corresponding instance is again the sentence

$\mathcal{F}[a]:$ $p(a, a)$.

According to the *existential* part of the proposition, we can conclude that the sentence

if $p(a, a)$
then $(\exists x)p(a, x)$

is also valid.

Finally, if we consider instead the sentence

$\mathcal{F}[x]:$ $p(x, x)$,

the corresponding instance is again the sentence

$\mathcal{F}[a]:$ $p(a, a)$,

and we may conclude, by the *existential* part of the proposition, that the sentence

if $p(a, a)$
then $(\exists x)p(x, x)$

is also valid.

In short, the *existential* part of the proposition allows us to conclude that all of the following sentences are valid:

$$\begin{array}{lll} if \ p(a, \ a) & if \ p(a, \ a) & if \ p(a, \ a) \\ then \ (\exists x)p(x, \ a) & then \ (\exists x)p(a, \ x) & then \ (\exists x)p(x, \ x). \end{array}$$

In other words, the sentence $p(a, \ a)$ implies each of the three sentences

$$(\exists x)p(x, \ a), \quad (\exists x)p(a, \ x), \quad and \quad (\exists x)p(x, \ x). \quad \lrcorner$$

The *quantifier-instantiation* proposition is stated in terms of total substitution; in fact, the corresponding result for partial substitution does not hold, as the reader is requested to show in **Problem 3.10(a)**.

The *quantifier-instantiation* proposition can be generalized to apply to more than one variable. More precisely, we have the following result.

Proposition (quantifier instantiation, multiple)
For any distinct variables $x_1, \ x_2, \ \ldots, x_n$, sentence $\mathcal{F}[x_1, x_2, \ \ldots, x_n]$, and terms $t_1, \ t_2, \ \ldots, t_n$, the universal closures of the sentences

$$\begin{array}{ll} if \ (\forall x_1, x_2, \ \ldots, x_n)\mathcal{F}[x_1, x_2, \ \ldots, x_n] & \\ then \ \mathcal{F}[t_1, t_2, \ \ldots, t_n] & (universal) \end{array}$$

$$\begin{array}{ll} if \ \mathcal{F}[t_1, t_2, \ \ldots, t_n] & \\ then \ (\exists x_1, x_2, \ \ldots, x_n)\mathcal{F}[x_1, x_2, \ \ldots, x_n] & (existential) \end{array}$$

are valid. $\quad \lrcorner$

Note that we do not require that the variables $x_1, \ x_2, \ \ldots, x_n$ actually occur in $\mathcal{F}[x_1, x_2, \ \ldots, x_n]$, nor that they include all the free variables in $\mathcal{F}[x_1, x_2, \ \ldots, x_n]$.

The proof, which we omit, is by repeated application of the *quantifier-instantiation* proposition for one variable.

CLOSURE INSTANTIATION

Another version of the *quantifier-instantiation* proposition applies to the universal and existential closures of a given sentence.

Proposition (closure instantiation)
For any distinct variables $x_1, \ x_2, \ \ldots, x_n$, sentence $\mathcal{F}[x_1, x_2, \ \ldots, x_n]$, and terms $t_1, t_2, \ \ldots, t_n$, the sentences

$$\begin{array}{ll} if \ (\forall *)\mathcal{F}[x_1, x_2, \ \ldots, x_n] & (universal) \\ then \ (\forall *)\mathcal{F}[t_1, t_2, \ \ldots, t_n] & \end{array}$$

$$\begin{array}{ll} if \ (\exists *)\mathcal{F}[t_1, t_2, \ \ldots, t_n] & (existential) \\ then \ (\exists *)\mathcal{F}[x_1, x_2, \ \ldots, x_n] & \end{array}$$

are valid. $\quad \lrcorner$

Note that, in contrast with the previous proposition, we do not need to refer to the universal closures of the two sentences, because they are already closed.

We illustrate the proposition with one example.

Example.   Consider the sentence

$$\mathcal{F}[x_1,\ x_2]:\quad \begin{aligned} &(\forall\,y)p(x_1,\ y)\\ &and\\ &p(x_2,\ z). \end{aligned}$$

Then the result of safely replacing the free occurrences of x_1 and x_2 with the terms $g(y)$ and z, respectively, in $\mathcal{F}[x_1,\ x_2]$ is the sentence

$$\mathcal{F}\big[g(y),\ z\big]:\quad \begin{aligned} &(\forall\,y')p\big(g(y),\ y'\big)\\ &and\\ &p(z,\ z). \end{aligned}$$

According to the *universal* part of the proposition, the sentence

$$\begin{array}{l} if\ (\forall\,*)\mathcal{F}[x_1,\ x_2]\\ then\ (\forall\,*)\mathcal{F}\big[g(y),\ z\big] \end{array}:\quad \begin{array}{l} if\ (\forall\,x_1,\ x_2,\ z)\left[\begin{array}{l}(\forall\,y)p(x_1,\ y)\\ and\\ p(x_2,\ z)\end{array}\right]\\[2em] then\ (\forall\,y,\ z)\left[\begin{array}{l}(\forall\,y')p\big(g(y),\ y'\big)\\ and\\ p(z,\ z)\end{array}\right] \end{array}$$

is valid.   ⌟

The *closure-instantiation* proposition is stated in terms of total substitution. In fact, the corresponding result for partial substitution does not hold, as the reader is requested to show in **Problem 3.10(b)**.

Problem 3.11 touches on several concepts from this chapter.

PROBLEMS

Problem 3.1 (interpretations)   page 142

Consider the sentences

(a) $p(x, a)$

(b) $p(a, x)\ and\ p\big(x, f(x)\big)$

(c) $(\exists\,y)p(y, x)$

(d) $(\exists\,y)\big[p(y, a)\ or\ p\big(f(y), y\big)\big]$

(e) $(\forall x)(\exists y)p(x,y)$

(f) $(\exists y)(\forall x)p(x,y)$.

Let $\mathcal{I}$ be the interpretation over the nonnegative integers under which a is 0, x is 1, f is the successor function (that is, $f_{\mathcal{I}}(d)$ is $d+1$), and p is the less-than relation (that is, $p_{\mathcal{I}}(d_1, d_2)$ is $d_1 < d_2$). Let $\mathcal{J}$ be the interpretation over all the integers (nonnegative and negative) under which a is 0, x is -1, y is 0, f is the successor function, and p is the less-than relation.

Determine the truth-values of each of the above sentences under the interpretation $\mathcal{I}$ and under the interpretation $\mathcal{J}$.

Problem 3.2 (validity)   page 151

Some of the following sentences are valid; others are not. For each sentence, use the semantic rules to establish either its validity or nonvalidity. If the sentence is not valid, give an interpretation under which its truth-value is false.

(a) $(\exists x)\big[if\ \ p(x)\ \ then\ \ r(x)\big]$
$$\equiv$$
$if\ \ (\forall x)p(x)\ \ then\ \ (\exists x)r(x)$

(b) $if\ \ (\forall x)[p(x)\ \ or\ \ r(x)]$
$then\ \ \big[(\forall x)p(x)\ \ or\ \ (\forall x)r(x)\big]$

(c) $if\ \ \big[(\forall x)p(x)\ \ or\ \ (\forall x)r(x)\big]$
$then\ \ (\forall x)[p(x)\ \ or\ \ r(x)]$

(d) $(\exists x)\big[p(x)\ \equiv\ r(x)\big]$
$$\equiv$$
$[(\exists x)p(x)]\ \equiv\ [(\exists x)r(x)]$

(e) $(\exists y)(\forall x)[if\ \ p(y)\ \ then\ \ p(x)]$

(f) $if\ \ (\forall x,\ y)p(x,\ y)$
$then\ \ (\forall x)p\big(x,\ f(x)\big)$

(g) $(\exists x)\begin{bmatrix}if\ \ p(x)\ \ then\ \ p(a)\\ and\\ if\ \ p(x)\ \ then\ \ p(b)\end{bmatrix}$

(h) $(\exists x)\big[p(x)\ \ and\ \ q(x)\big]$
or
$(\forall x)\big[if\ \ p(x)\ \ then\ \ not\ q(x)\big]$

(i) $(\exists x)(\forall y)\begin{bmatrix}if\ \ \big(q(x,y)\ \ and\ \ not\ q(y,x)\big)\\ then\ \ \big(q(x,x)\ \equiv\ q(y,y)\big)\end{bmatrix}$

(j) $if\ \ (\forall y)(\exists z,\ x)p(x,\ y,\ z)$
$then\ \ (\exists x)(\forall y,\ z)p(x,\ y,\ z)$

(k) $(\forall x)\begin{bmatrix}p\big(if\ \ r(x)\ \ then\ \ a\ \ else\ \ b\big)\\ \equiv\\ if\ \ r(x)\ \ then\ \ p(a)\ \ else\ \ p(b)\end{bmatrix}$.

Problem 3.3 (domains of one and two elements)   page 151

(a) Consider the sentence

$$(\forall x)(\exists y)p(x, y) \quad and \quad (\forall x)[not \; p(x, x)].$$

Can it be true under an interpretation whose domain has exactly one element?

(b) Consider the sentence

$$(\forall x)\big[if \; p(x) \; then \; (p(a) \; or \; p(b))\big].$$

Is it true under every interpretation whose domain has exactly two elements?

In each case justify your answer informally.

Problem 3.4 (domains of n elements)   page 151

(a) Find a sentence that is true under any interpretation whose domain has precisely two elements, but false under some interpretation whose domain has three elements.

(b) Find a sentence that is true under any interpretation whose domain has precisely three elements, but false under some interpretation whose domain has four elements.

*(c) Find a sentence that is true under some interpretation whose domain has infinitely many elements, but false under any interpretation whose domain is finite.

Give an informal justification for your answers.

Problem 3.5 (validity of sentence schemata)   page 157, 158

Show that the universal closures of the following sentence schemata are valid for any sentences $\mathcal{F}$ and $\mathcal{G}$. For those sentences that are implications, show that the universal closures of their converses are not valid for some sentences $\mathcal{F}$ and $\mathcal{G}$.

(a) $(\exists x)[if \; \mathcal{F} \; then \; \mathcal{G}]$
$\equiv$
$if \; (\forall x)\mathcal{F} \; then \; (\exists x)\mathcal{G}$

(b) $if \; [(\forall x)\mathcal{F} \; or \; (\forall x)\mathcal{G}]$
$then \; (\forall x)[\mathcal{F} \; or \; \mathcal{G}]$

(c) $if \; [if \; (\exists x)\mathcal{F} \; then \; (\forall x)\mathcal{G}]$
$then \; (\forall x)[if \; \mathcal{F} \; then \; \mathcal{G}]$

(d) $if \; (\forall x)[\mathcal{F} \equiv \mathcal{G}]$
$then \; (\forall x)\mathcal{F} \equiv (\forall x)\mathcal{G}.$

Problem 3.6 (validity under side conditions)   page 162

Show that the universal closures of the following sentences are valid for any sentences $\mathcal{F}$ and $\mathcal{G}$ such that x is not free in $\mathcal{G}$. Show that the universal closures of these sentences are not valid for some sentences $\mathcal{F}$ and $\mathcal{G}$ such that x does occur free in $\mathcal{G}$.

(a) $(\forall x)[\mathcal{F} \ or \ \mathcal{G}]$

$\equiv$

$(\forall x)\mathcal{F} \ or \ \mathcal{G}$

(b) $(\exists x)[if \ \mathcal{F} \ then \ \mathcal{G}]$

$\equiv$

$if \ (\forall x)\mathcal{F} \ then \ \mathcal{G}$

(c) $(\forall x)[if \ \mathcal{G} \ then \ \mathcal{F}]$

$\equiv$

$if \ \mathcal{G} \ then \ (\forall x)\mathcal{F}$

Problem 3.7 (equivalences of closures)   page 163

Establish the validity of the sentences

(a) $not \ (\exists *)\mathcal{F}$

$\equiv$

$(\forall *)[not \ \mathcal{F}]$

(b) $(\forall *)[\mathcal{F} \ and \ \mathcal{G}]$

$\equiv$

$(\forall *)\mathcal{F} \ and \ (\forall *)\mathcal{G}$

(c) $(\exists *)[\mathcal{F} \ or \ \mathcal{G}]$

$\equiv$

$(\exists *)\mathcal{F} \ or \ (\exists *)\mathcal{G}$

(d) $(\exists *)[if \ \mathcal{F} \ then \ \mathcal{G}]$

$\equiv$

$if \ (\forall *)\mathcal{F} \ then \ (\exists *)\mathcal{G}.$

Problem 3.8 (implication, equivalence, and validity)   page 166

(a) Prove the *implication-and-validity* proposition.

(b) Prove the *equivalence-and-validity* proposition.

Problem 3.9 (safe substitution)   page 179

(a) Suppose $\mathcal{F}[x]$ is

$p(x) \ and \ (\forall y)q(x,y) \ and \ (\exists x)q(x,y) \ and$
$(\forall y)[p(x) \ and \ (\exists y)q(x,y)] \ and \ (\forall z)q(x,z).$

Then what is $\mathcal{F}[y]$?

(b) Suppose $\mathcal{F}[p(f(x)), \ f(x)]$ is

$p(f(x)) \ and \ (\forall y)[p(f(x)) \ and \ q(y)] \ and$
$q(f(x)) \ and \ (\exists x)q(f(x)) \ and \ p(f(y)).$

Then what is $\mathcal{F}[q(y), \ g(x, \ y)]$?

(c) Suppose $\mathcal{F}\langle p(f(x)), \ f(x)\rangle$ is

$p(f(x)) \ and \ (\forall y)[p(f(x)) \ and \ q(y)] \ and$
$q(f(x)) \ and \ (\exists x)q(f(x)) \ and \ p(f(y)).$

Then give three possible results $\mathcal{F}\langle q(y), \ g(x, \ y)\rangle$ of the partial substitution.

Problem 3.10 (instantiation and partial substitution)   pages 184, 185

If we replace total substitution with partial substitution, the corresponding *quantifier-instantiation* and *closure-instantiation* propositions do not necessarily hold.

(a) For each of the following sentences, find a subsentence $\mathcal{F}\langle x\rangle$, a term t, and an interpretation under which the sentence is false.

$$\begin{array}{ll} if \ (\forall x)\mathcal{F}\langle x\rangle & if \ \mathcal{F}\langle t\rangle \\ then \ \mathcal{F}\langle t\rangle & then \ (\exists x)\mathcal{F}\langle x\rangle. \end{array}$$

(b) For each of the following sentences, find a subsentence $\mathcal{F}\langle x_1, x_2, \ldots, x_n\rangle$, terms $t_1, t_2, \ldots, t_n$, and an interpretation under which the sentence is false.

$$\begin{array}{ll} if \ (\forall *)\mathcal{F}\langle x_1, x_2, \ldots, x_n\rangle & if \ (\exists *)\mathcal{F}\langle t_1, t_2, \ldots, t_n\rangle \\ then \ (\forall *)\mathcal{F}\langle t_1, t_2, \ldots, t_n\rangle & then \ (\exists *)\mathcal{F}\langle x_1, x_2, \ldots, x_n\rangle. \end{array}$$

Problem 3.11 (summary)   page 185

Let $\mathcal{F}$ denote

$$if \ (\forall \ x)p(x, \ y) \ or \ (\exists \ y)p(x, \ y)$$

$$then \ (\forall \ x) \left[\begin{array}{l} if \ q(a) \ and \ (\exists \ x)p(a, \ x) \\ then \ \left(\begin{array}{l} if \ not \ (\exists \ x)p(a, \ x) \\ then \ q(b) \end{array} \right) \end{array} \right]$$

$$else \ \left[\begin{array}{c} (\exists \ z) \ [not \ p(z, \ y)] \\ and \\ not \ (\exists \ z)p(x, \ y) \end{array} \right]$$

(a) Circle all bound occurrences of variables. For each bound occurrence of a variable, draw a line to the quantifier that it is bound by.

(b) Find all (eight) closed subsentences of $\mathcal{F}$.

(c) Which (two) closed subsentences of $\mathcal{F}$ are valid? Find interpretations under which each nonvalid closed subsentence of $\mathcal{F}$ is false.

(d) One of the valid closed subsentences of $\mathcal{F}$ is an instance of a valid sentence schema of propositional logic. Use the deductive-tableau system to prove that this valid sentence schema is indeed valid.

(e) Argue (informally) that the universal closure of $\mathcal{F}$ is valid.

4

Apparatus

In this chapter, we present technical notions from predicate logic that are required for developing a predicate-logic deductive system.

A principal result of this chapter will be a method for removing quantifiers from a predicate-logic sentence without affecting its validity, allowing us to treat predicate logic using methods from propositional logic.

4.1 POLARITY

We have already introduced the notion of the polarity of an occurrence of a subsentence of a propositional-logic sentence. We now extend this notion to the subsentences of a sentence in predicate logic.

POLARITY OF OCCURRENCES

We define the polarity of each individual occurrence of a subsentence of a given sentence using the same rules as the propositional-logic definition, plus some new rules for conditional terms and quantified subsentences. We do not assign polarities to the subterms of the sentence.

Definition (polarity of occurrences)

If $\mathcal{S}$ is a sentence, we assign a *polarity*, positive $(+)$, negative $(-)$, or both $(\pm)$, to every occurrence of a subsentence of $\mathcal{S}$ according to the following *polarity-assignment rules*:

- *top rule*

  The sentence S itself is positive in S; that is,

  S^+.

- *propositional-connective rules*

  The rules for the propositional connectives are the same for predicate logic as for propositional logic.

- *conditional-term rule*

  If a subterm of S is of the form

  if $\mathcal{F}$ then r else s,

  then its *if*-clause $\mathcal{F}$ has both positive and negative polarity in S; that is,

  $$\left[if\ \mathcal{F}\ then\ r\ else\ s\right]^{\pi} \Rightarrow if\ \mathcal{F}^{\pm}\ then\ r\ else\ s.$$

  Note that we do not assign polarities to subterms, such as r and s.

- *quantifier rules*

  If a subsentence $\mathcal{E}$ of S is of the form

  $$(\forall x)\mathcal{F} \quad or \quad (\exists x)\mathcal{F},$$

  then its component $\mathcal{F}$ has the same polarity as $\mathcal{E}$ in S; that is,

  $$\left[(\forall x)\mathcal{F}\right]^{\pi} \Rightarrow (\forall x)\mathcal{F}^{\pi}$$

  $$\left[(\exists x)\mathcal{F}\right]^{\pi} \Rightarrow (\exists x)\mathcal{F}^{\pi}.$$

The definition of strict polarity is analogous to the corresponding propositional-logic definition.

Definition (strict polarity of occurrences)

An occurrence of a subsentence $\mathcal{E}$ in a sentence S has *strictly positive polarity* if $\mathcal{E}$ has positive but not negative polarity in S.

Similarly, an occurrence of $\mathcal{E}$ has *strictly negative polarity* in S if $\mathcal{E}$ has negative but not positive polarity in S.

Example.   Let us gradually annotate the sentence

$$S: \quad \begin{array}{l} if\ (\forall x)q(x) \\ then\ (\exists y)p(y)\ \equiv\ r(a) \end{array}$$

with the polarities of each of its subsentences, using the preceding polarity-assignment rules to obtain each row from the previous row (as in propositional logic, the boxes indicate the subsentences being considered at each stage):

$$\boxed{\begin{aligned} &\textit{if}\ \ (\forall x)q(x) \\ &\textit{then}\ \ (\exists y)p(y) \equiv r(a) \end{aligned}}^{+}$$

$$\begin{aligned} &\textit{if}\ \ \boxed{(\forall x)q(x)}^{\ -} \\ &\textit{then}\ \ \boxed{(\exists y)p(y) \equiv r(a)}^{\ +} \end{aligned}$$

$$\begin{aligned} &\textit{if}\ \ (\forall x)\boxed{q(x)}^{\ -} \\ &\textit{then}\ \ \boxed{(\exists y)p(y)}^{\pm} \equiv \boxed{r(a)}^{\pm} \end{aligned}$$

$$\begin{aligned} &\textit{if}\ \ (\forall x)q(x) \\ &\textit{then}\ \ (\exists y)\boxed{p(y)}^{\pm} \equiv r(a). \end{aligned}$$

Thus, as a result of this annotation process, we obtain the full polarity annotation

$$\left[\begin{aligned} &\textit{if}\ \ \Big[(\forall x)\big[q(x)\big]^{-}\Big]^{-} \\ &\textit{then}\ \ \Big[\big[(\exists y)[p(y)]^{\pm}\big]^{\pm} \equiv [r(a)]^{\pm}\big]^{+} \end{aligned}\right]^{+}.$$

The reader is requested in **Problem 4.1** to annotate all the subsentences of several sentences according to their polarity.

THE POLARITY PROPOSITION

The *polarity* proposition for predicate logic is similar to the corresponding proposition for propositional logic.

Proposition (polarity)

Suppose that $\mathcal{E}$, $\mathcal{F}$, and $\mathcal{S}\langle\mathcal{E}^{+}\rangle$ are sentences. Then the universal closure of the sentence

$$\begin{aligned} &\textit{if}\ \ (\textit{if}\ \ \mathcal{E}\ \ \textit{then}\ \ \mathcal{F}) \\ &\textit{then}\ \ \big(\textit{if}\ \ \mathcal{S}\langle\mathcal{E}^{+}\rangle\ \ \textit{then}\ \ \mathcal{S}\langle\mathcal{F}^{+}\rangle\big) \end{aligned}$$ (*positive*)

is valid.

Suppose that $\mathcal{E}$, $\mathcal{F}$, and $\mathcal{S}\langle\mathcal{E}^{-}\rangle$ are sentences. Then the universal closure of the sentence

$$\begin{aligned} &\textit{if}\ \ (\textit{if}\ \ \mathcal{E}\ \ \textit{then}\ \ \mathcal{F}) \\ &\textit{then}\ \ \big(\textit{if}\ \ \mathcal{S}\langle\mathcal{F}^{-}\rangle\ \ \textit{then}\ \ \mathcal{S}\langle\mathcal{E}^{-}\rangle\big) \end{aligned}$$ (*negative*)

is valid.

Here again, we write $\mathcal{S}$ as $\mathcal{S}\langle \mathcal{E}^+ \rangle$ so that later, when we refer to $\mathcal{S}\langle \mathcal{F}^+ \rangle$, it is clear we are safely replacing zero, one, or more strictly positive free occurrences of $\mathcal{E}$ with $\mathcal{F}$. Similarly, we write $\mathcal{S}$ as $\mathcal{S}\langle \mathcal{E}^- \rangle$ so that later, when we refer to $\mathcal{S}\langle \mathcal{F}^- \rangle$, it is clear we are safely replacing zero, one, or more strictly negative free occurrences of $\mathcal{E}$ with $\mathcal{F}$.

The proposition, like its propositional-logic counterpart, says that the truth of a sentence is directly related to the truth of its strictly positive subsentences, but inversely related to the truth of its strictly negative subsentences.

4.2   FORCE OF QUANTIFIERS

The role a quantifier plays in a sentence depends upon the polarity of the subsentence in which it occurs. For example, the existential quantifier in the sentence

$$not\ (\exists x)\mathcal{F}$$

plays the same role as the universal quantifier in the equivalent sentence

$$(\forall x)\big[not\ \mathcal{F}\big]$$

because the surrounding *not* connective of the former sentence gives the existential quantifier a universal "force."

In our deductive system, we assign a force, universal or existential, to each occurrence of a quantifier in a given sentence $\mathcal{S}$. Intuitively, an occurrence of a quantifier is of *universal force* in $\mathcal{S}$ if it is a universal [existential] quantifier in the scope of an even [odd] number of *not*'s. Similarly, an occurrence of a quantifier is of *existential force* in $\mathcal{S}$ if it is an existential [universal] quantifier in the scope of an even [odd] number of *not*'s. When we count *not*'s, we consider implicit as well as explicit negations. The force will give a syntactic indication as to how the quantifier affects the sentence as a whole.

DEFINITIONS

Let us make this rough observation more precise by defining the force (universal, existential, or both) of an occurrence of a quantifier in a sentence.

Definition (force of quantifiers)

Consider an occurrence of a subsentence $(\dots x)\mathcal{F}$ in a sentence $\mathcal{S}$, where $(\dots x)$ is a quantifier, either $(\forall x)$ or $(\exists x)$. We determine the force of this occurrence of the quantifier as follows:

- The occurrence of the quantifier has *universal force* in $\mathcal{S}$, annotated by the superscript $(\dots x)^{\forall}$, if

- it is a universal quantifier and $(\ldots x)\mathcal{F}$ is of positive polarity in $\mathcal{S}$, that is,

$$\left[(\forall x)\mathcal{F}\right]^{+} \;\Rightarrow\; (\forall x)^{\forall}\mathcal{F},$$

or

- it is an existential quantifier and $(\ldots x)\mathcal{F}$ is of negative polarity in $\mathcal{S}$, that is,

$$\left[(\exists x)\mathcal{F}\right]^{-} \;\Rightarrow\; (\exists x)^{\forall}\mathcal{F}.$$

- The occurrence of the quantifier has *existential force* in $\mathcal{S}$, annotated by the superscript $(\ldots x)^{\exists}$, if

  - it is an existential quantifier and $(\ldots x)\mathcal{F}$ is of positive polarity in $\mathcal{S}$, that is,

$$\left[(\exists x)\mathcal{F}\right]^{+} \;\Rightarrow\; (\exists x)^{\exists}\mathcal{F},$$

or

  - it is a universal quantifier and $(\ldots x)\mathcal{F}$ is of negative polarity in $\mathcal{S}$, that is,

$$\left[(\forall x)\mathcal{F}\right]^{-} \;\Rightarrow\; (\forall x)^{\exists}\mathcal{F}.$$

- The occurrence of the quantifier has *both forces* in $\mathcal{S}$, annotated by the superscript $(\ldots x)^{\forall\exists}$, if

  - $(\ldots x)\mathcal{F}$ is of both polarities in $\mathcal{S}$, that is,

$$\left[(\ldots x)\mathcal{F}\right]^{\pm} \;\Rightarrow\; (\ldots x)^{\forall\exists}\mathcal{F}.$$

Intuitively, a quantifier of universal force plays the role of a universal quantifier even though it may be literally of the existential form $(\exists x)$; similarly, a quantifier of existential force plays the role of an existential quantifier even though it may be literally of the universal form $(\forall x)$.

Example. Consider the following sentence, annotated with the polarity of the relevant subsentences and with the forces of all the quantifiers:

$$if \;\; \left[(\forall x)^{\exists}\Big(not \; [(\exists y)^{\exists}q(x,y)]^{+}\Big)\right]^{-}$$
$$then \;\; not \; \left[(\exists x)^{\forall}r(x)\right]^{-}.$$

- Because the subsentence

$$(\exists y)q(x,y)$$

has positive polarity, its quantifier $(\exists y)$ has existential force.

- Because the subsentence

$$(\exists x)r(x)$$

has negative polarity, its quantifier $(\exists x)$ has universal force.

- Because the subsentence

$$(\forall x)\big(not \;\; (\exists y)q(x,y)\big)$$

has negative polarity, its quantifier $(\forall x)$ has existential force.

In **Problem 4.2** the reader is requested to annotate several sentences with the forces of their quantifiers.

Definition (strict force of quantifiers)

We say that an occurrence of a quantifier has

- *strict universal force* if it has universal force but not existential force,
- *strict existential force* if it has existential force but not universal force. ◢

Thus a quantifier has strict force if it does not have both forces.

Note that a quantifier of strict force cannot occur within the scope of a quantifier of both forces. This is because a quantifier of both forces must occur in a subsentence of both polarities, and any subsentence of a subsentence of both polarities also has both polarities.

Example. Consider the following sentence, annotated with the forces of its quantifiers:

$$(\exists x)^{\exists} q(x) \;\; and \;\; \left[\begin{array}{l} (\forall y)^{\forall \exists} \Big(p(y) \;\; or \;\; (\exists z)^{\forall \exists} r(y,z) \Big) \\ \equiv \\ r(z) \end{array} \right].$$

Note that all the quantifiers within the scope of the $\equiv$ connective have both forces. ◢

THE FORCE-MANIPULATION PROPOSITION

Let us consider the following equivalent sentences, obtained by gradually pulling the quantifier $(\forall x)$ outside by equivalences of predicate logic and the substitutivity of equivalence:

$$not \left(\begin{array}{l} if \;\; not \left(\Big[(\forall x)^{\exists} p(x) \Big]^{-} \;\; or \;\; q(y) \right) \\ then \;\; r(y) \end{array} \right)$$

$$not \left(\begin{array}{l} if \;\; not \Big[(\forall x)^{\exists} \big(p(x) \;\; or \;\; q(y) \big) \Big]^{-} \\ then \;\; r(y) \end{array} \right)$$

$$not \left(\begin{array}{l} if \;\; \Big[(\exists x)^{\exists} \big(not \; (p(x) \;\; or \;\; q(y)) \big) \Big]^{+} \\ then \;\; r(y) \end{array} \right)$$

$$not \ \left[(\forall x)^{\exists} \begin{pmatrix} if \ \ not \ (p(x) \ \ or \ \ q(y)) \\ then \ \ r(y) \end{pmatrix} \right]^{-}$$

$$\left[(\exists x)^{\exists} \ not \ \begin{pmatrix} if \ \ not \ (p(x) \ \ or \ \ q(y)) \\ then \ \ r(y) \end{pmatrix} \right]^{+}.$$

Note the interesting phenomenon that the quantifier of each of these sentences is of existential force, although it changes from universal to existential form and back again as it passes across an explicit or implicit negation.

The following proposition makes precise some of our observations about the force of quantifiers.

In the discussion in the rest of this chapter, we often use the abbreviated notation $(\ldots x)$ to stand for either $(\forall x)$ or $(\exists x)$. Then $(\ldots x)^{\forall}$ indicates a quantifier over x of universal force (not necessarily strict), where it is irrelevant if it is itself a universal or existential quantifier; similarly for $(\ldots x)^{\exists}$ and $(\ldots x)^{\forall \exists}$.

We use an informal pictorial notation to make the reading easier. In this notation we write only the part of the sentence in which we are interested; the rest is indicated by a line ___ .

Proposition (force manipulation)

Consider a particular occurrence of the subsentence $(\ldots x)\mathcal{P}$ in the sentence $\mathcal{F}$, denoted by

$$\mathcal{F}: \quad \underline{\quad}(\ldots x)\mathcal{P}\underline{\quad}.$$

We assume that the following restrictions are satisfied:

- The variable x has no free occurrences in $\mathcal{F}$.
- The occurrence of $(\ldots x)\mathcal{P}$ in $\mathcal{F}$ is not within the scope of any quantifier.

Then, if $(\ldots x)^{\forall}$ is of strict universal force in $\mathcal{F}$,

$$\underline{\quad}(\ldots x)^{\forall}\mathcal{P}\underline{\quad}$$

is equivalent to   (*universal*)

$$(\forall x)[\underline{\quad}\mathcal{P}\underline{\quad}]$$

and, if $(\ldots x)^{\exists}$ is of strict existential force in $\mathcal{F}$,

$$\underline{\quad}(\ldots x)^{\exists}\mathcal{P}\underline{\quad}$$

is equivalent to   (*existential*)

$$(\exists x)[\underline{\quad}\mathcal{P}\underline{\quad}],$$

where $\underline{\quad}\mathcal{P}\underline{\quad}$ is the result of removing the occurrence of the quantifier $(\ldots x)$ under consideration from $\mathcal{F}$. ∎

Example.   As we remarked in a previous example, the sentence

$$not \left(\begin{matrix} if \ \ not \ \left(\boxed{(\forall x)^\exists p(x)} \ \ or \ \ q(y) \right) \\ then \ \ r(y) \end{matrix} \right)$$

is equivalent to the sentence

$$(\exists x) \ \ not \ \left(\begin{matrix} if \ \ not \ \left(\boxed{p(x)} \ \ or \ \ q(y) \right) \\ then \ \ r(y) \end{matrix} \right),$$

obtained by "pulling out" the quantifier. The boxes indicate the subsentence
occurrences under consideration.

This example illustrates the *existential* part of the *force-manipulation* proposition; the given sentence is of form

$$\underline{\qquad} (\forall x)^\exists p(x) \underline{\qquad}$$

and the equivalent resulting sentence is of form

$$(\exists x) [\underline{\qquad} p(x) \underline{\qquad}]. \ \blacksquare$$

Note that, by repeated application of the *force-manipulation* proposition, we
could pull all the quantifiers of strict force in a given sentence to the outermost
level, obtaining an equivalent sentence. To ensure that the restrictions of the
proposition are satisfied, we pull out quantifiers in left-to-right order, rename
their bound variables, and use the substitutivity of equivalence as required. This
is illustrated by the following example.

Example.   Suppose we would like to pull to the outermost level the quantifiers
in the sentence

$$\mathcal{F}_1: \quad \begin{matrix} if \ \ \boxed{(\forall x)^\exists p(x)} \ \ and \ \ q(x) \\ then \ \ (\forall y) r(y). \end{matrix}$$

We can start with the leftmost quantifier $(\forall x)$. One restriction of the proposition is not satisfied, because x occurs free in $\mathcal{F}_1$. However, we can rename the
bound variable x to x', to obtain the equivalent sentence

$$\mathcal{F}_2: \quad \begin{matrix} if \ \ \boxed{(\forall x')^\exists p(x')} \ \ and \ \ q(x) \\ then \ \ (\forall y) r(y). \end{matrix}$$

Now the restrictions of the proposition are satisfied, so we can pull out the quantifier $(\forall x')$, to obtain the equivalent sentence

$$\mathcal{F}_3: \quad (\exists x') \begin{bmatrix} if \ \ p(x') \ \ and \ \ q(x) \\ then \ \ \boxed{(\forall y)^\forall r(y)} \end{bmatrix}.$$

Next we would like to pull out the second quantifier $(\forall y)$. This time the other
restriction of the proposition is not satisfied, because the occurrence of $(\forall y) r(y)$

is now within the scope of a quantifier. However, let us consider the subsentence of $\mathcal{F}_3$

$$\mathcal{G}_1: \quad \begin{array}{l} \textit{if } p(x') \textit{ and } q(x) \\ \textit{then } \boxed{(\forall y)^\forall r(y)} \,. \end{array}$$

Here the restrictions of the proposition are satisfied, so we can pull out the quantifier $(\forall y)$, to obtain the equivalent sentence

$$\mathcal{G}_2: \quad (\forall y) \begin{bmatrix} \textit{if } p(x') \textit{ and } q(x) \\ \textit{then } r(y) \end{bmatrix}.$$

Suppose we replace $\mathcal{G}_1$ with $\mathcal{G}_2$ in $\mathcal{F}_3$, to obtain

$$\mathcal{F}_4: \quad (\exists x')(\forall y) \begin{bmatrix} \textit{if } p(x') \textit{ and } q(x) \\ \textit{then } r(y) \end{bmatrix}.$$

By the *substitutivity-of-equivalence* proposition, this sentence is equivalent to $\mathcal{F}_3$, and hence to the original sentence $\mathcal{F}_1$.

Thus we have used repeated application of the *force-manipulation* proposition to pull all the quantifiers of $\mathcal{F}_1$ to the outermost level, obtaining an equivalent sentence $\mathcal{F}_4$. ◢

THE FORCE-INSTANTIATION PROPOSITION

Recall the *quantifier-instantiation* proposition that was presented in Section 3.10:

For any variable x, sentence $\mathcal{F}[x]$, and term t, the universal closures of the sentences

$$\textit{if } (\forall x)\mathcal{F}[x] \textit{ then } \mathcal{F}[t] \qquad\qquad (\textit{universal})$$

$$\textit{if } \mathcal{F}[t] \textit{ then } (\exists x)\mathcal{F}[x] \qquad\qquad (\textit{existential})$$

are valid.

The following *force-instantiation* proposition resembles this proposition, but applies to quantifiers that are not necessarily at the top level of the given sentence.

Proposition (force instantiation)

Consider a particular occurrence of the subsentence $(\dots x)\mathcal{P}[x]$ in the sentence $\mathcal{F}$, denoted by

$$\mathcal{F}: \quad \underline{\quad}(\dots x)\mathcal{P}[x]\underline{\quad}.$$

For any term t,

If the occurrence of the quantifier $(\dots\ x)$ is of strict universal force in $\mathcal{F}$, $\underline{\quad}(\dots\ x)^{\vee}\mathcal{P}[x]\underline{\quad}$, then the universal closure of the sentence

$$if\ \underline{\quad}(\dots\ x)\mathcal{P}[x]\underline{\quad} \qquad\qquad (universal)$$

$$then\ \underline{\quad}\mathcal{P}[t]\underline{\quad}$$

is valid.

If the occurrence of the quantifier $(\dots\ x)$ is of strict existential force in $\mathcal{F}$, $\underline{\quad}(\dots\ x)^{\exists}\mathcal{P}[x]\underline{\quad}$, then the universal closure of the sentence

$$if\ \underline{\quad}\mathcal{P}[t]\underline{\quad} \qquad\qquad (existential)$$

$$then\ \underline{\quad}(\dots\ x)\mathcal{P}[x]\underline{\quad}$$

is valid.

Here $\mathcal{P}[t]$ is the result of dropping the quantifier $(\dots\ x)$ in the occurrence of the subsentence $(\dots\ x)\mathcal{P}[x]$, and replacing the free occurrences of x in $\mathcal{P}[x]$ with t. ◢

We illustrate the proposition with two examples.

Example. In the sentence

$$not\ (\forall y)\boxed{(\exists x)^{\vee}p(x,\ y)},$$

the quantifier $(\exists x)$ is of strict universal force. Therefore, by the *universal* part of the *force-instantiation* proposition, taking $\mathcal{P}[x]$ to be the subsentence $p(x, y)$ and t to be the constant a, the sentence

$$if\ \ not\ (\forall y)\boxed{(\exists x)p(x,\ y)}$$

$$then\ \ not\ (\forall y)p(a,\ y)$$

is valid. ◢

Note that the proposition holds with few restrictions. The next example illustrates this.

Example. In the sentence

$$(\forall y)\boxed{(\exists x)^{\exists}(\forall z)\,q(w,\ x,\ y,\ z)}$$

the quantifier $(\exists x)$ is of strict existential force. Therefore, by the *existential* part of the *force-instantiation* proposition, taking $\mathcal{P}[x]$ to be the subsentence $(\forall z)q(w, x, y, z)$ and t to be the term $f(x, y, z)$, the sentence

$$(\forall w)(\forall x)(\forall z)\left[\begin{array}{l} if\ \ (\forall y)(\forall z')q\big(w,\ f(x,y,z),\ y,\ z'\big) \\ then\ \ (\forall y)(\exists x)(\forall z)q(w,\ x,\ y,\ z) \end{array}\right]$$

is valid. Here the quantifiers $(\forall w)$, $(\forall x)$, and $(\forall z)$ appeared in taking the universal closure. The variable z of the quantifier $(\forall z)$ was renamed z' in performing the safe substitution. Note that the proposition does not require us to rename the variable y of the quantifier $(\forall y)$. ◢

4.3   QUANTIFIER REMOVAL: INTUITIVE PREVIEW

In developing formal methods for predicate logic, it is of great help to eliminate quantifiers from sentences, allowing techniques for proving theorems of propositional logic to be readily extended to predicate logic. In the following sections, we introduce a way to remove quantifiers from closed predicate-logic sentences while preserving their validity. In other words, the sentence we obtain as a result of removing quantifiers will be valid if and only if the given sentence is valid. The process, known as *skolemization*, does not necessarily preserve equivalence; that is, the two sentences may not be equivalent.

Because the skolemization process is somewhat mysterious, we give this intuitive preview before presenting the full details.

We shall remove quantifiers when we are attempting to prove the validity of a given closed sentence. Thus we would be quite concerned if the given sentence were valid but the resulting sentence were not. We would be equally disturbed if the given sentence were not valid but the resulting sentence were. We do not worry, however, if the sentences are not equivalent, that is, if they happen to have different truth-values for some particular interpretation.

The term "quantifier removal" is a bit misleading. While quantifiers of strict universal force are actually eliminated, quantifiers of strict existential force are merely brought to the top level. If we "remove" all the quantifiers from a given closed sentence $\mathcal{F}$, we actually obtain a closed sentence $\mathcal{G}$ of the form $(\exists y_1) \ldots (\exists y_n)\mathcal{G}'$, where $\mathcal{G}'$ has no quantifiers. Later we shall see that, in the deductive tableaux for proving the validity of predicate-logic sentences, we can also drop the outermost quantifiers $(\exists y_1) \ldots (\exists y_n)$.

Often we want to remove all the quantifiers from the given closed sentence, but the skolemization process is more general: it allows us to remove any number of quantifiers from the sentence. This will be of particular importance when we extend skolemization to theories with induction; there we must leave some quantifiers in place to employ the induction principle. On the other hand, repeated application of the process will allow us to remove all the quantifiers if necessary.

In the basic skolemization process, we eliminate a particular quantifier from a given sentence $\mathcal{F}$, obtaining a new, somewhat different sentence $\mathcal{G}$. The way the quantifier is removed will depend on its force in $\mathcal{F}$. If the quantifier is of both forces, we repeatedly apply equivalence-preserving rewritings, until the quantifier is "split" into multiple occurrences of quantifiers of strict force, which may then be removed separately. This will be explained in the more general treatment of skolemization. Henceforth, in this preview, we may consider removing only quantifiers of strict force.

In removing a quantifier of strict force from a closed sentence $\mathcal{F}$, we do not always obtain an equivalent sentence $\mathcal{G}$, but we must be sure that $\mathcal{G}$ is valid if and only if $\mathcal{F}$ is valid. To show this, it is useful to associate with each closed sentence a *validity game*. This will be an infinite game we may imagine we are playing against a malevolent universe. If we win, the sentence is valid; if the universe wins, the sentence is not valid. Thus, to show that skolemization preserves validity, we need show only that the winner of the game for $\mathcal{F}$ is the same as the winner of the game for $\mathcal{G}$.

THE VALIDITY GAME

The game for a closed sentence $\mathcal{F}$ may be regarded as a contest to determine whether or not $\mathcal{F}$ is valid. To establish its validity, we must show that $\mathcal{F}$ is true under all interpretations. In the game, we may expect that the malevolent universe will propose an interpretation under which $\mathcal{F}$ is false, if such an interpretation exists.

In choosing an interpretation, the universe initially selects a domain and assigns values to all the constant, function, and predicate symbols in $\mathcal{F}$, attempting to falsify $\mathcal{F}$ if possible; these values will be domain elements, functions, and relations, respectively.

In the balance of the game, one player or the other chooses values for the quantified variables in $\mathcal{F}$. The universe selects domain elements for variables whose quantifiers have strict universal force in $\mathcal{F}$, while we ourselves select domain elements for variables whose quantifiers have strict existential force in $\mathcal{F}$. In choosing its values, the universe makes things as difficult for us as possible; it selects domain elements that make $\mathcal{F}$ false, if such a selection exists. We, on the other hand, naturally select values making $\mathcal{F}$ true, if possible.

The order in which the values for the variables are selected depends on the order in which the quantifiers occur in the sentence. If one quantifier surrounds another, a value for its variable must be selected first. In making a choice, each player has knowledge of the previous choices of the opposing player, but is ignorant of the subsequent choices.

In this intuitive preview, we do not give all the details of the game, nor do we treat the general skolemization process. We do, however, consider several representative cases.

UNIVERSAL FORCE

For a quantifier of universal force, the universe chooses a value for its variable. In particular, suppose $\mathcal{F}$ is of the form

$$\mathcal{F}: \quad (\forall x)^\forall \mathcal{P}[x].$$

In the validity game for $\mathcal{F}$, the universe first chooses an interpretation $\mathcal{I}$, attempting to falsify $\mathcal{F}$ if possible. The outermost quantifier $(\forall x)$ of $\mathcal{F}$ is of universal force in $\mathcal{F}$; therefore the universe subsequently selects a domain element d to serve as a value for x. The universe will choose d so that the subsentence $\mathcal{P}[x]$ will be false under the modified interpretation $\langle x \leftarrow d \rangle \circ \mathcal{I}$, if such a domain element d exists; otherwise, the universe will choose an arbitrary element.

If we apply the skolemization process (to be described) to eliminate the quantifier $(\forall x)$ from the sentence $\mathcal{F}$, we obtain the sentence

$$\mathcal{G}: \quad \mathcal{P}[a],$$

where a is a "new" constant, i.e., one that does not already occur in $\mathcal{F}$. In the validity game for $\mathcal{G}$, the universe first chooses an interpretation $\mathcal{J}$, attempting to falsify $\mathcal{G}$ if possible.

Suppose the universe was able to win the validity game for $\mathcal{F}$ by choosing an interpretation $\mathcal{I}$ and assigning to x the domain element d, so that $\mathcal{P}[x]$ was indeed false under the modified interpretation $\langle x \leftarrow d \rangle \circ \mathcal{I}$. Then, in playing the game for $\mathcal{G}$, it can choose to assign d to the new constant a, leaving the assignments to the other symbols the same as under $\mathcal{I}$. That is, in the validity game for $\mathcal{G}$, the universe may choose the interpretation $\mathcal{J}$ to be $\langle a \leftarrow d \rangle \circ \mathcal{I}$. The value of the constant a in the game for $\mathcal{G}$, that is, d, will be the same as the value the universe chose for x in the game for $\mathcal{F}$. Thus the universe will be able to make $\mathcal{P}[a]$ false by choosing $\mathcal{J}$. In short, if the universe is able to win the game for $\mathcal{F}$, it will also be able to win the game for $\mathcal{G}$.

On the other hand, suppose the universe can win the validity game for $\mathcal{G}$. That is, it can choose an interpretation $\mathcal{J}$ under which $\mathcal{P}[a]$ is false. Then $\mathcal{J}$ must assign some domain element, say d, to the constant a. In the game for $\mathcal{F}: (\forall x)^{\forall}\mathcal{P}[x]$, the universe can choose the same interpretation $\mathcal{J}$. It can then assign the domain element d to the variable x. The value of x in the game for $\mathcal{F}$ will thus be the same as the value of a in the game for $\mathcal{G}$. If the universe was able to win the game for $\mathcal{G}$, it will also be able to win the game for $\mathcal{F}$.

To summarize, the winner of the validity game for $\mathcal{F}$ is the same as the winner of the validity game for $\mathcal{G}$. That is, $\mathcal{F}$ is valid if and only if $\mathcal{G}$ is valid.

Note that $\mathcal{F}$ and $\mathcal{G}$ are not necessarily equivalent; that is, for individual interpretations, they may have different truth-values. In particular, we may have an interpretation under which $\mathcal{G}: p(a)$ is true but $p(b)$, for instance, is false and hence $\mathcal{F}: (\forall x)p(x)$ is false. There must then be another interpretation, however, under which $\mathcal{G}: p(a)$ is false, and hence neither sentence is valid. In short, validity has been preserved even though equivalence has not.

EXISTENTIAL FORCE

For a quantifier of existential force, we ourselves choose a value for its variable. In particular, suppose $\mathcal{F}$ is of the form

$$\mathcal{F}: \quad (\exists y)^{\exists} \mathcal{P}[y].$$

In the validity game for $\mathcal{F}$, the universe again chooses an interpretation $\mathcal{I}$, attempting to make $\mathcal{F}$ false if possible. This time, the outermost quantifier $(\exists y)$ is of existential force in $\mathcal{F}$; therefore we ourselves get to choose a value d for the variable y. We shall choose the domain element d so that the subsentence $\mathcal{P}[y]$ will be true under the modified interpretation $\langle y \leftarrow d \rangle \circ \mathcal{I}$, if possible.

The quantifier $(\exists y)$ is already in the desired outermost position in $\mathcal{F}$, and therefore will not be changed by the skolemization process. The sentence we obtain,

$$\mathcal{G}: \quad (\exists y)\mathcal{P}[y],$$

is the same as $\mathcal{F}$. Since $\mathcal{F}$ and $\mathcal{G}$ are the same, validity has clearly been preserved.

UNIVERSAL-EXISTENTIAL FORCE

The order in which values for variables are chosen depends on the relative position of their quantifiers in the sentence. In particular, suppose $\mathcal{F}$ is of the form

$$\mathcal{F}: \quad (\forall x)^{\forall}(\exists y)^{\exists} \mathcal{Q}[x, y].$$

This is an instance of the universal-force case in which $\mathcal{P}[x]$ is taken to be $(\exists y)\mathcal{Q}[x, y]$.

In the validity game for $\mathcal{F}$, the universe first selects an interpretation $\mathcal{I}$. Since the outermost quantifier $(\forall x)^{\forall}$ is of universal force in $\mathcal{F}$, the universe gets to choose a value d for x. It will choose d so that the subsentence $(\exists y)\mathcal{Q}[x, y]$ will be false under the modified interpretation $\langle x \leftarrow d \rangle \circ \mathcal{I}$, if possible. Because the next quantifier $(\exists y)^{\exists}$ is of existential force, we then get to choose a value e for y. We attempt to remedy the situation by choosing e so that the subsentence $\mathcal{Q}[x, y]$ will be true under the modified interpretation $\langle y \leftarrow e \rangle \circ \langle x \leftarrow d \rangle \circ \mathcal{I}$, if possible. The universe must make its choice for x blindly, in ignorance of our subsequent choice for y; we, on the other hand, may take the universe's choice for x into account in making our choice for y.

The skolemization process to be described will not allow us to remove a quantifier of existential force, such as $(\exists y)^{\exists}$, if it is surrounded by a quantifier of universal force, such as $(\forall x)^{\forall}$. If we want to remove the quantifier $(\forall x)^{\forall}$ from $\mathcal{F}$, we can apply the process to obtain the sentence

$$\mathcal{G}: \quad (\exists y)^{\exists} \mathcal{Q}[a, y],$$

where a is a new constant. The existential quantifier $(\exists y)$ is already in the desired outermost position in $\mathcal{G}$; it need not be removed by any subsequent skolemization step.

We have seen, in discussing the *universal-force* case, that the winner of the validity game for $\mathcal{F}$ is the same as that for $\mathcal{G}$. In the validity game for $\mathcal{G}$, the universe must choose its value for a blindly, but our choice of a value for y may depend on previous choices the universe has made, including its choice of a value for a.

EXISTENTIAL-UNIVERSAL FORCE

We now consider the most complex aspect of the skolemization process. We suppose the sentence is of form

$$\mathcal{F}: \quad (\exists y)^{\exists}(\forall z)^{\forall}\mathcal{Q}[y,\, z].$$

This is an instance of the existential-force case in which $\mathcal{P}[y]$ is taken to be $(\forall z)\mathcal{Q}[y,\, z]$.

In the validity game for $\mathcal{F}$, the universe first selects an interpretation $\mathcal{I}$, attempting to falsify $\mathcal{F}$ if possible. Since the outermost quantifier $(\exists y)$ is of existential force in $\mathcal{F}$, we ourselves get to choose a value d to assign to the variable y, so that the subsentence $(\forall z)\mathcal{Q}[y,\, z]$ is true under the modified interpretation $\langle y \leftarrow d \rangle \circ \mathcal{I}$, if possible.

The next quantifier $(\forall z)$ is of universal force in $\mathcal{F}$; therefore the universe gets to choose a value e to assign to the variable z, so that the subsentence $\mathcal{Q}[y,\, z]$ is false under the modified interpretation $\langle z \leftarrow e \rangle \circ \langle y \leftarrow d \rangle \circ \mathcal{I}$, if possible.

Although we must choose d blindly, the universe may take our choice of d into account in selecting e.

Suppose the universe can win the validity game for $\mathcal{F}$. Then, whatever domain element d we choose, the universe can choose a domain element e such that $\mathcal{Q}[y,\, z]$ is false under the appropriate modified interpretation. Let $k(d)$ be a function that, for whatever domain element d we choose, yields the corresponding domain element e selected by the universe. We shall call k the *winning function* (for $\mathcal{Q}$).

The existential quantifier $(\exists y)$ is already in the desired outermost position in $\mathcal{F}$; there is no need to do anything to it. If we want to remove the quantifier $(\forall z)$, we may apply the skolemization process to be described to obtain the sentence

$$\mathcal{G}: \quad (\exists y)\mathcal{Q}[y,\, f(y)],$$

where f is a "new" function symbol, i.e., one that does not already occur in $\mathcal{F}$.

In the validity game for $\mathcal{G}$, the universe first chooses an interpretation $\mathcal{J}$, attempting to falsify $\mathcal{G}$ if possible. This must include an assignment of a function to the function symbol f. This choice of a value for f must be made blindly, in ignorance of our subsequent choice of a value for y. Because y is an argument of f in the term $f(y)$, however, the value of $f(y)$ itself may certainly depend on our choice of a value for y.

We now show that the winner of the validity game for $\mathcal{F}$ is the same as that for $\mathcal{G}$. Suppose that the universe was able to win the validity game for $\mathcal{F}$ by choosing an interpretation $\mathcal{I}$ and using the winning function k for $\mathcal{Q}$. Then, in playing the game for $\mathcal{G}$, it can choose to assign k to f, leaving the assignments to the other symbols the same as under $\mathcal{I}$. That is, in the game for $\mathcal{G}$ the universe may choose the interpretation $\mathcal{J}$ to be $\langle f \leftarrow k \rangle \circ \mathcal{I}$, the interpretation that assigns k to f but agrees with $\mathcal{I}$ on all other symbols.

Since the outermost quantifier $(\exists y)$ is of existential force in $\mathcal{G}$, we ourselves get to choose a value d for y. Whatever value we choose, however, the value of the term $f(y)$ in $\mathcal{G}$, that is, $k(d)$, will be the same as the domain element e the universe would have chosen for z in the game for $\mathcal{F}$. Thus, if the universe was able to win the game for $\mathcal{F}$, it will also be able to win the game for $\mathcal{G}$.

On the other hand, suppose that the universe can win the validity game for $\mathcal{G}$. That is, it can choose an interpretation $\mathcal{J}$ under which

$$\mathcal{G}: \quad (\exists y)^{\exists} \mathcal{Q}[y, f(y)]$$

is false. Then $\mathcal{J}$ must assign some function, say k, to the function symbol f. Whatever value d we choose subsequently for y, the value of $\mathcal{Q}[y, f(y)]$ will be false under the appropriate modified interpretation.

In the validity game for

$$\mathcal{F}: \quad (\exists y)^{\exists} (\forall z)^{\forall} \mathcal{Q}[y, z],$$

the universe can choose the same interpretation $\mathcal{J}$. Whatever value d we choose for y, the universe may then assign the domain element $k(d)$ to z. The value of the variable z in the game for $\mathcal{F}$ will thus be the same as the value of $f(y)$ in the game for $\mathcal{G}$. If the universe was able to win the game for $\mathcal{G}$, it will also be able to win the game for $\mathcal{F}$.

To summarize, if the universe can win either game, it will be able to win the other; the winners of the two games will be the same. That is, $\mathcal{F}$ is valid if and only if $\mathcal{G}$ is valid.

In this case, it can be shown that $\mathcal{F}$ and $\mathcal{G}$ are not necessarily equivalent. In particular, it is possible to find an interpretation under which $\mathcal{F}$ is false but $\mathcal{G}$ is true.

NEGATED SENTENCES

Up to now, we have mentioned quantifiers only at the outermost level. In the validity game, quantifiers are treated according to their forces, which are reversed by surrounding negation connectives. For instance, suppose our sentence is of form

$$\mathcal{F}: \quad not\ (\forall y)^\exists (\exists z)^\forall \mathcal{Q}[y, z].$$

The argument here will mirror the argument in the previous case.

In the validity game for $\mathcal{F}$, the universe first selects an interpretation $\mathcal{I}$, attempting to falsify $\mathcal{F}$, if possible. This means that the universe will attempt to make the subsentence $(\forall y)(\exists z)\mathcal{Q}[y, z]$ true. Since the quantifier $(\forall y)^\exists$ is of existential force in $\mathcal{F}$, we ourselves get to choose a value d to assign to the variable y, attempting to force the subsentence $(\exists z)\mathcal{Q}[y, z]$ to be false (under the appropriate modified interpretation), so that $\mathcal{F}$ will be true.

The next quantifier $(\exists z)^\forall$ is of universal force in $\mathcal{F}$; therefore the universe gets to choose a domain element e to assign to z, attempting to force the subsentence $\mathcal{Q}[y, z]$ to be true, so that $\mathcal{F}$ will be false.

Suppose that the universe can win the validity game for $\mathcal{F}$. Then, whatever domain element d we choose, the universe can select a domain element e that forces $\mathcal{Q}[y, z]$ to be true, so that $\mathcal{F}$ will be false. Let $k(d)$ be the function that, for whatever domain element d we choose, yields the corresponding domain element e selected by the universe. We again call k the *winning function*.

We may apply the skolemization process to either quantifier in $\mathcal{F}$. If we want to first remove the quantifier $(\exists z)^\forall$, we obtain the sentence

$$\mathcal{G}: \quad not\ (\forall y)^\exists \mathcal{Q}[y, f(y)],$$

where f is a new function symbol.

In the validity game for $\mathcal{G}$, the universe first chooses an interpretation $\mathcal{J}$ for $\mathcal{G}$. If the universe was able to win the game for $\mathcal{F}$, it may take $\mathcal{J}$ to be $\langle f \leftarrow k \rangle \circ \mathcal{I}$, where k is the winning function.

Since the quantifier $(\forall y)^\exists$ is of existential force in $\mathcal{G}$, we ourselves get to choose a value d for y. Whatever value we choose, however, the value of the term $f(y)$ in $\mathcal{G}$, that is, $k(d)$, will be the same as the domain element e the universe would have chosen for z in the game for $\mathcal{F}$. Thus, if the universe was able to win the game for $\mathcal{F}$, it will also be able to win the game for $\mathcal{G}$.

By an argument similar to that for the previous case, we can also show that if the universe can win the validity game for $\mathcal{G}$, it can win the validity game for $\mathcal{F}$. That is, $\mathcal{F}$ is valid if and only if $\mathcal{G}$ is valid.

If we want to remove the remaining quantifier $(\forall y)^\exists$ from $\mathcal{G}$, we may apply the skolemization process once more, to obtain the sentence

$$\mathcal{G}': \quad (\exists y)\Big[not\ \mathcal{Q}[y, f(y)]\Big].$$

Here the quantifier has not literally been removed, but rather moved to the desired outermost position. Note that (by the *force-manipulation* proposition) this stage of the process has actually preserved equivalence as well as validity.

Quantifiers (of strict force) at deeper levels are treated in the same way, in accordance with their force.

We are now ready to begin the more general treatment of the quantifier-elimination process.

4.4 REMOVING BOTH FORCES

A quantifier of both forces must be within the scope of an $\equiv$ connective or within the *if*-clause of an *if-then-else* conditional connective or conditional constructor. (Recall that we distinguish between the two forms of the conditional operator: the *if-then-else* connective, which yields a sentence, and the *if-then-else* constructor, which yields a term.) The offending constructs, however, can be paraphrased in terms of other constructs, by repeated invocation of the following equivalences:

- For the $\equiv$ connective,

$$\mathcal{F} \equiv \mathcal{G}$$
$$\equiv$$
$$\begin{bmatrix} if\ \mathcal{F}\ then\ \mathcal{G} \\ and \\ if\ \mathcal{G}\ then\ \mathcal{F} \end{bmatrix} \quad \text{or} \quad \begin{bmatrix} \mathcal{F}\ and\ \mathcal{G} \\ or \\ (not\ \mathcal{F})\ and\ (not\ \mathcal{G}) \end{bmatrix}$$

$$\mathcal{F} \equiv \mathcal{G}$$
$$\equiv$$

- For the *if-then-else* connective,

$$if\ \mathcal{F}\ then\ \mathcal{G}\ else\ \mathcal{H}$$
$$\equiv$$
$$\begin{bmatrix} if\ \mathcal{F}\ then\ \mathcal{G} \\ and \\ if\ (not\ \mathcal{F})\ then\ \mathcal{H} \end{bmatrix} \quad \text{or} \quad \begin{bmatrix} \mathcal{F}\ and\ \mathcal{G} \\ or \\ (not\ \mathcal{F})\ and\ \mathcal{H} \end{bmatrix}$$

$$if\ \mathcal{F}\ then\ \mathcal{G}\ else\ \mathcal{H}$$
$$\equiv$$

- For the *if-then-else* constructor,

$$\underline{\quad}(if\ \mathcal{F}\ then\ s\ else\ t)\underline{\quad}$$
$$\equiv$$
$$\begin{bmatrix} if\ \mathcal{F} \\ then\ \underline{\quad}s\underline{\quad} \\ else\ \underline{\quad}t\underline{\quad} \end{bmatrix}$$

Here $\mathcal{E}$: $\underline{\quad}(if\ \mathcal{F}\ then\ s\ else\ t)\underline{\quad}$ refers to any sentence containing an occurrence of the conditional term $(if\ \mathcal{F}\ then\ s\ else\ t)$, and $\underline{\quad}s\underline{\quad}$ and $\underline{\quad}t\underline{\quad}$ refer to the results of replacing that occurrence with s and t, respectively. We choose $\mathcal{E}$ to be small enough so that the conditional term is not within the scope of any quantifier in $\mathcal{E}$. Note that the *if-then-else* on the left side is the conditional constructor, while the *if-then-else* on the right side is the conditional connective.

By the substitutivity of equivalence, we can invoke these equivalences to replace any subsentence of the given sentence, obtaining an equivalent sentence.

We have provided two equivalences for each of the two connectives; we may apply whichever equivalence is found more convenient. The repeated application of any of these equivalences can make the resulting sentence more complex, but once all the $\equiv$ connectives and *if-then-else* connectives and constructors have been removed, we can be certain that no quantifiers of both forces remain.

Example. Consider the sentence

$$(\forall y)(\exists z)\left[\begin{array}{l} (\exists x_1)^{\vee\exists}p(x_1) \\ \equiv \\ q\left(\begin{array}{l} \textit{if } (\forall x_2)^{\vee\exists}p(x_2) \\ \textit{then } f(y) \\ \textit{else } z \end{array}\right) \end{array}\right].$$

Note that the sentence has two quantifier occurrences of both forces. These occurrences are within the scope of the $\equiv$ connective; one of them is also within the *if*-clause of the *if-then-else* constructor.

Invoking the equivalence

$$\underline{\hspace{1em}}(\textit{if } \mathcal{F} \textit{ then } s \textit{ else } t)\underline{\hspace{1em}}$$
$$\equiv$$
$$\left[\begin{array}{l} \textit{if } \mathcal{F} \\ \textit{then } \underline{\hspace{1em}} s \underline{\hspace{1em}} \\ \textit{else } \underline{\hspace{1em}} t \underline{\hspace{1em}} \end{array}\right]$$

we obtain the equivalent sentence

$$(\forall y)(\exists z)\left[\begin{array}{l} (\exists x_1)^{\vee\exists}p(x_1) \\ \equiv \\ \left[\begin{array}{l} \textit{if } (\forall x_2)^{\vee\exists}p(x_2) \\ \textit{then } q\big(f(y)\big) \\ \textit{else } q(z) \end{array}\right] \end{array}\right].$$

Invoking the equivalence

$$\mathcal{F} \equiv \mathcal{G}$$
$$\equiv$$
$$(\textit{if } \mathcal{F} \textit{ then } \mathcal{G}) \textit{ and } (\textit{if } \mathcal{G} \textit{ then } \mathcal{F}),$$

we obtain the equivalent sentence

$$(\forall y)(\exists z)\left[\begin{array}{l} \left[\begin{array}{l} \textit{if } (\exists x_1)^{\vee}p(x_1) \\ \textit{then } \left[\begin{array}{l} \textit{if } (\forall x_2)^{\vee\exists}p(x_2) \\ \textit{then } q\big(f(y)\big) \\ \textit{else } q(z) \end{array}\right] \end{array}\right] \textit{ and } \left[\textit{if } \left[\begin{array}{l} \textit{if } (\forall x_2)^{\vee\exists}p(x_2) \\ \textit{then } q\big(f(y)\big) \\ \textit{else } q(z) \end{array}\right] \\ \textit{then } (\exists x_1)^{\exists}p(x_1) \right] \end{array}\right].$$

Twice invoking the equivalence

> *if $\mathcal{F}$ then $\mathcal{G}$ else $\mathcal{H}$*
>
> $\equiv$
>
> *(if $\mathcal{F}$ then $\mathcal{G}$) and (if (not $\mathcal{F}$) then $\mathcal{H}$)*,

we obtain the equivalent sentence

$$(\forall y)(\exists z)\left[\begin{array}{l} \left[\begin{array}{l} if\ (\exists x_1)^{\forall}p(x_1) \\ then\ \left[\begin{array}{l} \left[\begin{array}{l} if\ (\forall x_2)^{\exists}p(x_2)\ then\ q\big(f(y)\big) \\ and \\ if\ not\ (\forall x_2)^{\forall}p(x_2)\ then\ q(z) \end{array}\right] \end{array}\right] \end{array}\right] \\ and \\ \left[\begin{array}{l} if\ \left[\begin{array}{l} if\ (\forall x_2)^{\forall}p(x_2)\ then\ q\big(f(y)\big) \\ and \\ if\ not\ (\forall x_2)^{\exists}p(x_2)\ then\ q(z) \end{array}\right] \\ then\ (\exists x_1)^{\exists}p(x_1) \end{array}\right] \end{array}\right].$$

Thus, by repeatedly invoking the preceding equivalences, we can remove quantifiers of both forces from a sentence. The resulting sentence may have many "copies" of the original quantifiers, but all will have strict force. In the next two sections, we describe techniques for removing quantifiers of strict universal and existential force.

4.5 REMOVING STRICT UNIVERSAL FORCE

Removing quantifiers of strict universal force is more complicated than the other stages of quantifier removal. Also, it is the only stage of the process that does not necessarily preserve equivalence.

In the procedure for eliminating quantifiers from a given closed sentence $\mathcal{F}$, a quantifier $(\ldots z)^{\forall}$ of strict universal force is dropped; every occurrence of the variable z bound by this quantifier is replaced by a term $f(y_1, \ldots, y_n)$. Here, f is a "new" function symbol, in the sense that it does not already occur in $\mathcal{F}$. We shall refer to f as a "skolem" function symbol. Also, $y_1, \ldots, y_n$ are the variables of all the quantifiers $(\ldots y_1)^{\exists}, \ldots, (\ldots y_n)^{\exists}$ of existential force that surround the eliminated quantifier $(\ldots z)^{\forall}$, that is, that contain $(\ldots z)^{\forall}$ within their scopes. (These quantifiers all have strict force since the force of $(\ldots z)^{\forall}$ is strict.)

Henceforth we abbreviate $y_1, \ldots, y_n$ as $\bar{y}$ and $(\ldots y_1)^{\exists}, \ldots, (\ldots y_n)^{\exists}$ as $(\overline{\ldots y})^{\exists}$. In the special case in which $n = 0$, that is, there are no quantifiers $(\overline{\ldots y})^{\exists}$ surrounding the eliminated quantifier $(\ldots z)^{\forall}$, the occurrences of z are replaced by a new "skolem" constant a.

We now describe the general procedure for removing quantifiers of strict universal force.

Proposition (universal elimination)

Let $\mathcal{F}$ be a closed sentence that satisfies the following restrictions:

- $\mathcal{F}$ contains an occurrence of a subsentence $(\ldots z)^\forall \mathcal{P}[z]$, where $(\ldots z)^\forall$ is a quantifier of strict universal force in $\mathcal{F}$.

- We allow the occurrence $(\ldots z)^\forall \mathcal{P}[z]$ to be within the scope of other quantifiers. The quantifiers of existential force that surround the occurrence are $(\overline{\ldots y})^\exists$, that is, $(\ldots y_1)^\exists, \ldots, (\ldots y_n)^\exists$.

- The variables $\overline{y}$ are all distinct.

In our pictorial notation, we can write $\mathcal{F}$ as

$$\mathcal{F}: \quad \underline{\ \ }(\ldots y_1)^\exists \Big[\ldots \underline{\ \ }(\ldots y_n)^\exists \Big[\underline{\ \ }(\ldots z)^\forall \mathcal{P}[z] \underline{\ \ } \Big] \underline{\ \ } \ldots \Big] \underline{\ \ }.$$

Let $\mathcal{G}$ be the sentence obtained by replacing the subsentence occurrence $(\ldots z)^\forall \mathcal{P}[z]$ with the sentence $\mathcal{P}\big[f(\overline{y})\big]$, where f is a new function symbol, i.e., one that does not occur in $\mathcal{F}$. That is, the resulting sentence is

$$\mathcal{G}: \quad \underline{\ \ }(\ldots y_1)^\exists \Big[\ldots \underline{\ \ }(\ldots y_n)^\exists \Big[\underline{\ \ } \mathcal{P}[f(\overline{y})] \underline{\ \ } \Big] \underline{\ \ } \ldots \Big] \underline{\ \ }.$$

In the special case in which $n = 0$, that is, there are no surrounding quantifiers $(\ldots y_i)^\exists$, we use a new constant a in place of the term $f(\overline{y})$. This agrees with the common convention of identifying constants with function symbols of arity 0. Thus $\mathcal{G}$ is obtained from $\mathcal{F}$ by replacing the subsentence occurrence $(\ldots z)^\forall \mathcal{P}[z]$ with the sentence $\mathcal{P}[a]$, where a is a new constant, i.e., one that does not occur in $\mathcal{F}$.

Then

(a) For every interpretation $\mathcal{I}$,
   if $\mathcal{F}$ is false under $\mathcal{I}$,
   then there is an interpretation $\mathcal{I}'$ such that
       $\mathcal{G}$ is false under $\mathcal{I}'$,
       and $\mathcal{I}$ and $\mathcal{I}'$ agree except perhaps on new symbols.

(b) For every interpretation $\mathcal{J}$,
   if $\mathcal{G}$ is false under $\mathcal{J}$,
   then $\mathcal{F}$ is also false under $\mathcal{J}$.

Therefore

(c) $\mathcal{F}$ is valid
       if and only if
       $\mathcal{G}$ is valid. ◢

We shall refer to f as a *skolem function symbol*, a as a *skolem constant*, and both $f(\bar{y})$ and a as *skolem terms*.

In removing a quantifier of universal force, we may need to rename the variables of some of the quantifiers of existential force, to ensure that they are distinct, as the proposition requires.

Example.   Suppose that $\mathcal{F}$ is the closed sentence

$$\mathcal{F}: \quad (\exists y_1)^\exists \left[q(y_1) \; and \; (\exists y_1)^\exists \boxed{(\forall z)^\forall p(y_1, z)} \right] ,$$

where we have indicated the force of each of the quantifiers. We would like to eliminate the quantifier $(\forall z)$, which is of strict universal force.

The boxed subsentence $(\forall z)p(y_1, z)$ is surrounded by two identical quantifiers $(\exists y_1)^\exists$ of existential force. Thus the requirement that the variables of these quantifiers be distinct is not satisfied. To apply the proposition, let us rename the variable of the second quantifier $(\exists y_1)$ to be y_1'. The resulting sentence $\mathcal{F}'$ is then

$$\mathcal{F}': \quad (\exists y_1)^\exists \left[q(y_1) \; and \; (\exists y_1')^\exists \boxed{(\forall z)^\forall p(y_1', z)} \right] .$$

By the *renaming-of-bound-variables* proposition, $\mathcal{F}'$ is equivalent to $\mathcal{F}$.

Now the conditions of the proposition are satisfied. The boxed subsentence $(\forall z)p(y_1', z)$ is within the scope of two distinct quantifiers of existential force, $(\exists y_1)^\exists$ and $(\exists y_1')^\exists$. Therefore the quantifier $(\forall z)$ can be dropped and the occurrence of z replaced by the skolem term $f(y_1, y_1')$. The resulting sentence is then

$$\mathcal{G}: \quad (\exists y_1)^\exists \left[q(y_1) \; and \; (\exists y_1')^\exists p\big(y_1', f(y_1, y_1')\big) \right] .$$

By the *universal-elimination* proposition, $\mathcal{G}$ is valid if and only if $\mathcal{F}$ is valid. ⌙

By repeated application of the *universal-elimination* proposition, we can remove all the quantifiers of strict universal force from a given sentence, preserving its validity.

Example.   Suppose that $\mathcal{A}$ is the closed sentence

$$\mathcal{A}: \quad \begin{array}{l} if \; (\forall y_1)^\exists (\exists z_1)^\forall p(y_1, z_1) \\ then \; (\forall z_2)^\forall (\exists y_2)^\exists p(y_2, z_2), \end{array}$$

where we have indicated the force of each of the quantifiers. There are two quantifiers of (strict) universal force in this sentence: $(\exists z_1)^\forall$ and $(\forall z_2)^\forall$.

First let us eliminate the quantifier $(\exists z_1)^\forall$. This quantifier is within the scope of the quantifier $(\forall y_1)^\exists$ of (strict) existential force. Therefore the quantifier $(\exists z_1)^\forall$ can be dropped and the occurrence of z_1 replaced by the skolem term $f(y_1)$. The resulting sentence is

$$\mathcal{B}: \quad \begin{array}{l} if \; (\forall y_1)^\exists p\big(y_1, f(y_1)\big) \\ then \; (\forall z_2)^\forall (\exists y_2)^\exists p(y_2, z_2). \end{array}$$

By the *universal elimination* proposition, $\mathcal{B}$ is valid if and only if $\mathcal{A}$ is valid.

This sentence still contains a quantifier $(\forall z_2)^\forall$ of universal force. This quantifier is not within the scope of any quantifier of existential force. Therefore we may drop the quantifier $(\forall z_2)^\forall$ and replace the occurrence of z_2 with a skolem constant a. The resulting sentence is

$$\mathcal{C}: \quad \begin{array}{l} \textit{if } \ (\forall y_1)^\exists p(y_1, \, f(y_1)) \\ \textit{then } \ (\exists y_2)^\exists p(y_2, \, a). \end{array}$$

By the *universal-elimination* proposition, $\mathcal{C}$ is valid if and only if $\mathcal{B}$ is valid, and hence if and only if $\mathcal{A}$ is valid.

In fact, by two applications of the proposition, we can show that, for every interpretation $\mathcal{I}$, if $\mathcal{A}$ is false under $\mathcal{I}$, then $\mathcal{C}$ is false under some interpretation $\mathcal{I}''$, where $\mathcal{I}$ and $\mathcal{I}''$ agree on all symbols except perhaps new symbols. Furthermore, for every interpretation $\mathcal{J}$, if $\mathcal{C}$ is false under $\mathcal{J}$, $\mathcal{A}$ is also false under $\mathcal{J}$.

In **Problem 4.3**, the reader is asked to show that we have not preserved equivalence in passing from sentence $\mathcal{A}$ to sentence $\mathcal{C}$. ◢

In **Problem 4.4**, the reader is asked to use the result of this section to establish the validity of a sentence.

The quantifiers of the sentence $\mathcal{C}$ obtained in the preceding example all have strict existential force. This brings us to the next phase of the skolemization process.

4.6   REMOVING STRICT EXISTENTIAL FORCE

So far, we have discussed only two stages of the quantifier-removal process: the elimination of quantifiers of both forces and of strict universal force. We now consider the final stage: the elimination of quantifiers of strict existential force. As the reader will recall, such quantifiers are not actually removed, but merely moved to the outermost level. We first illustrate the basis for the technique with an example.

Example.   Consider the sentence $\mathcal{C}$ that we obtained in the previous example (by removing both quantifiers of strict universal force from the given sentence $\mathcal{A}$):

$$\mathcal{C}: \quad \begin{array}{l} \textit{if } \ (\forall y_1)^\exists p(y_1, \, f(y_1)) \\ \textit{then } \ (\exists y_2)^\exists p(y_2, \, a). \end{array}$$

Both quantifiers in this sentence have strict existential force. We can eliminate them in either order. We first remove the quantifier $(\forall y_1)^\exists$.

The sentence is equivalent (by the *force-manipulation* proposition) to the sentence

$$\mathcal{D}: \quad (\exists\, y_1) \begin{bmatrix} \textit{if} \;\; p(y_1, f(y_1)) \\ \textit{then} \;\; (\exists\, y_2)^{\exists} p(y_2, a) \end{bmatrix}.$$

Now let us consider a subsentence of $\mathcal{D}$,

$$\mathcal{D}_0: \quad \begin{matrix} \textit{if} \;\; p(y_1, f(y_1)) \\ \textit{then} \;\; (\exists\, y_2)^{\exists} p(y_2, a). \end{matrix}$$

This subsentence is equivalent (by the *force-manipulation* proposition, again) to the sentence

$$\mathcal{E}_0: \quad (\exists\, y_2) \begin{bmatrix} \textit{if} \;\; p(y_1, f(y_1)) \\ \textit{then} \;\; p(y_2, a) \end{bmatrix},$$

obtained by pulling out the quantifier $(\exists\, y_2)^{\exists}$.

Therefore (by the substitutivity of equivalence) the entire sentence $\mathcal{D}$ is equivalent to the sentence

$$\mathcal{E}: \quad (\exists\, y_1)(\exists\, y_2) \begin{bmatrix} \textit{if} \;\; p(y_1, f(y_1)) \\ \textit{then} \;\; p(y_2, a) \end{bmatrix}.$$

From our sentence $\mathcal{C}$ we have obtained an equivalent sentence $\mathcal{E}$ by pulling out its quantifiers of (strict) existential force to the outermost level. (Note that the order of these quantifiers is not significant.) The resulting sentence $\mathcal{E}$ is not equivalent to the original sentence $\mathcal{A}$; we lost equivalence when we dropped the quantifiers of strict universal force. Nevertheless, we know that we have preserved validity; that is, $\mathcal{A}$ is valid if and only if $\mathcal{E}$ is valid. In fact, neither sentence is valid. ⏌

Now let us state the general proposition that justifies removing quantifiers of strict existential force.

Proposition (existential elimination)

Let $\mathcal{F}$ be a closed sentence satisfying the following conditions:

- $\mathcal{F}$ contains an occurrence of a subsentence $(\ldots y)^{\exists}\mathcal{P}$, where $(\ldots y)^{\exists}$ is of strict existential force in $\mathcal{F}$. In our pictorial notation,

$$\mathcal{F}: \quad \text{---} (\ldots y)^{\exists}\mathcal{P} \text{---} .$$

- The occurrence of $(\ldots y)^{\exists}\mathcal{P}$ is surrounded by no quantifier of universal force.
- The occurrence of $(\ldots y)^{\exists}\mathcal{P}$ is surrounded by no other quantifier $(\ldots y)$ with the same variable y.

Let $\mathcal{G}$ be the sentence $(\exists y)\mathcal{G}_0$, where $\mathcal{G}_0$ is obtained from $\mathcal{F}$ by dropping the quantifier $(\ldots y)^{\exists}$ from the occurrence of $(\ldots y)^{\exists}\mathcal{P}$, leaving only $\mathcal{P}$. That is,

$$\mathcal{G}: \quad (\exists y)\Big[\underline{\quad}\mathcal{P}\underline{\quad}\Big].$$

Then

$\mathcal{F}$ is equivalent to $\mathcal{G}$. ◢

The restriction of the *existential-elimination* proposition that $(\ldots y)^{\exists}\mathcal{P}$ be surrounded by no other quantifier $(\ldots y)$ with the same variable can be satisfied by renaming the variables of some of the quantifiers, as in the *universal-elimination* proposition.

The restriction that $(\ldots y)^{\exists}\mathcal{P}$ be surrounded by no quantifier of universal force can be satisfied by invoking the *universal-elimination* proposition to first remove the offending quantifiers.

The *existential-elimination* proposition is a generalization of the *existential* part of the *force-manipulation* proposition. It allows us to move to the outermost level quantifiers of existential force that are within the scope of other quantifiers of existential force.

In the following we shall refer to the *universal-elimination* and the *existential-elimination* propositions collectively as the *quantifier-elimination* proposition.

4.7 SUMMARY OF THE SKOLEMIZATION PROCESS

In some circumstances we may wish to remove only a particular occurrence of a single quantifier, while in other cases we may wish to remove all the quantifiers in a given sentence. Let us describe each process separately.

REMOVAL OF A PARTICULAR OCCURRENCE

Suppose we would like to remove an occurrence of a quantifier from a given closed sentence. Then

- If the occurrence is of both forces, it must be within the scope of one or more $\equiv$ connectives or within the *if*-clause of one or more *if-then-else* connectives or constructors. The offending operators are paraphrased by repeated invocation of predicate-logic equivalences. This will cause multiple occurrences of the quantifier to appear. Each of these occurrences, however, will be of strict force and can be removed separately by the succeeding stages of the process.

- Rename the bound variables of the sentence, if necessary, to ensure they are distinct from one another.

- If the quantifier to be removed is of strict universal force, it is removed by the *universal-elimination* proposition, introducing a skolem constant or skolem function.

- If the quantifier to be removed is of strict existential force, ensure that it is not within the scope of any quantifier of universal force, removing any offending quantifiers by application of the preceding stage of the process. Then, by the *existential-elimination* proposition, pull out the quantifier of strict existential force.

We say that the quantifier we have removed has been *skolemized*; the process is called *skolemization*.

Each of the stages just described preserves the equivalence (and hence validity) of the sentence, except for the removal of a quantifier of strict universal force, which preserves validity but not necessarily equivalence. As a whole, therefore, the entire process preserves the validity of the sentence. In other words, the sentence $\mathcal{G}$ we obtain is valid if and only if the given sentence $\mathcal{F}$ is valid. In fact, if $\mathcal{G}$ is false under some interpretation $\mathcal{I}$, then $\mathcal{F}$ is false under the same interpretation $\mathcal{I}$. And, if $\mathcal{F}$ is false under some interpretation $\mathcal{I}$, then $\mathcal{G}$ is false under an interpretation $\mathcal{I}'$ such that $\mathcal{I}$ and $\mathcal{I}'$ agree on all symbols except perhaps on skolem constant and function symbols.

REMOVAL OF ALL QUANTIFIERS

Suppose we would like to remove all the quantifiers from a given closed sentence. Then

- Remove all occurrences of $\equiv$ connectives that contain quantifiers in their scopes, and all occurrences of *if-then-else* connectives and constructors that contain quantifiers in their *if*-clauses, by invocation of the appropriate equivalences. This ensures that no quantifiers have both forces.

- Rename the bound variables of the sentence to ensure that they are distinct from one another.

- Remove all quantifiers of strict universal force, by repeated application of the *universal-elimination* proposition.

- Remove (pull out) all quantifiers of strict existential force, by repeated application of the *existential-elimination* proposition.

As before, each of these stages preserves the validity of the sentence. Only the removal of the quantifiers of universal force sometimes fails to preserve equivalence. As a result of applying this process to a given closed sentence $\mathcal{F}$, we obtain a sentence $\mathcal{G}$ of form $(\exists *)\mathcal{G}_0$, where $\mathcal{G}_0$ is quantifier-free, such that $\mathcal{F}$ is valid if and only if $\mathcal{G}$ is valid. Again, interpretations that falsify the two sentences, if any, agree on all symbols other than, perhaps, skolem constant and function symbols. We will say that $\mathcal{G}$ is obtained from $\mathcal{F}$ by (*full*) *skolemization*.

The reader is requested in **Problem 4.5** to eliminate the quantifiers of several sentences.

In **Problem 4.6**, the reader is asked to consider cases in which skolemization preserves equivalence.

4.8   UNIFICATION

In proving the validity of predicate-logic sentences, we shall carry over all of our propositional-logic deductive-tableau methods. Many of the rules, however, will require adaptation. The propositional *resolution* rule, for instance, applies to two rows, assertions or goals, with identical subsentences $\mathcal{P}$. The corresponding rule for predicate logic also applies to two rows, but requires subsentences that are not necessarily identical but that instead are "unifiable": they can be made identical by replacing some of their variables with terms. The purpose of this section is to make precise this notion of unification. We introduce a computational method, called the *unification algorithm*, for determining whether given subsentences are unifiable and, if so, for finding a "unifier," a substitution that makes them identical. Both the *resolution* and *equivalence* rules for predicate logic will require this *unification* algorithm.

EXPRESSIONS

The *unification* algorithm will apply to either sentences or terms. We shall talk about unifying quantifier-free expressions, but to simplify the discussion we first restrict our attention to terms, and exclude the conditional term constructor *if-then-else*. In this section, we shall allow 0-ary function symbols $a, b, c, \ldots$ and identify the terms $a(\,), b(\,), c(\,), \ldots$ with the constants $a, b, c, \ldots$. This will enable us to avoid treating constants as a special case.

For two expressions d and e, we shall say that $d = e$ if d and e stand for identical expressions. Thus, if d is $f(x)$ and e is y, we know that $d \neq e$. We say that d *occurs in* e if d is a subexpression of e. We regard an expression as a subexpression of itself; we say that d *occurs properly in* e if d occurs in e and $d \neq e$.

SUBSTITUTIONS

We introduce the notion of a *substitution*, a (finite) set

$$\{x_1 \leftarrow e_1, \ x_2 \leftarrow e_2, \ \ldots, \ x_n \leftarrow e_n\}$$

of *replacement pairs* $x_i \leftarrow e_i$, where the x_i are variables, the e_i are terms, and each x_i is distinct from the corresponding expression e_i and from all the other variables x_j. For example,

$$\{x \leftarrow f(y), y \leftarrow a\}$$

is a substitution, but $\{a \leftarrow x\}$, $\{x \leftarrow x\}$, and $\{x \leftarrow a, x \leftarrow b\}$ are not.

The order of the replacement pairs in a substitution is not significant; two substitutions are regarded as *equal* if they have the same replacement pairs, regardless of the order in which they are written. The *empty substitution* { } has no replacement pairs at all.

For any expression e and substitution $\theta : \{x_1 \leftarrow e_1, x_2 \leftarrow e_2, \ldots, x_n \leftarrow e_n\}$, the result $e \blacktriangleleft \theta$ of *applying* θ to e is obtained by simultaneously replacing every occurrence of a variable x_i in e with the corresponding expression e_i. For example,

$$g(x, y) \blacktriangleleft \{x \leftarrow f(y), y \leftarrow a\} = g\big(f(y), a\big).$$

Note that we do not replace the newly introduced occurrence of y with a, even though the substitution contains a replacement pair $y \leftarrow a$. That is, substitutions are applied in a single stage. For now, since we are only considering quantifier-free expressions, we do not have to worry about bound variables or capturing.

Applying the empty substitution { } to any expression e has no effect; that is,

$$e \blacktriangleleft \{\ \} = e.$$

It can be established that two substitutions θ and λ are equal if, for every variable x, $x \blacktriangleleft \theta = x \blacktriangleleft \lambda$, that is, $x \blacktriangleleft \theta$ and $x \blacktriangleleft \lambda$ stand for the same term. For example, $\{x \leftarrow y\}$ and $\{y \leftarrow x\}$ are not equal, because $x \blacktriangleleft \{x \leftarrow y\} = y$ but $x \blacktriangleleft \{y \leftarrow x\} = x$.

This notion of a substitution application $\blacktriangleleft$ is similar to the total substitution operation of predicate logic, except that here we allow replacements only for variables, not constants or other expressions, and we allow replacement only by terms, not sentences. When we need to distinguish between the two notions of substitution, we shall refer to the original total substitution operation as an *expression substitution*, and the new notion as a *variable substitution*.

Substitution application has an important *monotonicity* property, namely, if d is a proper subexpression of e then $d \blacktriangleleft \theta$ is a proper subexpression of $e \blacktriangleleft \theta$. In other words, if one expression occurs properly in another before application of a substitution, it also does so afterwards.

COMPOSITION

Applying the *composition* $\theta \square \lambda$ of two substitutions θ and λ has the same effect as applying first θ and then λ; that is, for all expressions e,

$$e \blacktriangleleft (\theta \square \lambda) = (e \blacktriangleleft \theta) \blacktriangleleft \lambda.$$

We can compute the composition of two given substitutions by considering their combined effect on all the variables. For example,

$$\{x \leftarrow f(z), y \leftarrow z\} \,\square\, \{x \leftarrow a, z \leftarrow y\} \;=\; \{x \leftarrow f(y), z \leftarrow y\}.$$

Since the first substitution replaces x with $f(z)$ and the second replaces z with y, their composition replaces x with $f(y)$. The replacement $x \leftarrow a$ from the second substitution does not have any effect on the composition, because x is first replaced by $f(z)$. Since the first substitution replaces y with z and the second replaces z with y again, their composition makes no replacement for y. Since the first substitution makes no replacement for z and the second replaces z with y, their composition replaces z with y, too.

The empty substitution $\{\ \}$ is both a left- and right-identity under composition, that is,

$$\{\ \} \,\square\, \theta \;=\; \theta \,\square\, \{\ \} \;=\; \theta,$$

and composition is associative, that is,

$$\theta \,\square\, (\phi \,\square\, \psi) \;=\; (\theta \,\square\, \phi) \,\square\, \psi.$$

Composition is not commutative. For example,

$$\{x \leftarrow y\} \,\square\, \{y \leftarrow x\} \;=\; \{y \leftarrow x\},$$

but

$$\{y \leftarrow x\} \,\square\, \{x \leftarrow y\} \;=\; \{x \leftarrow y\}.$$

The reader is asked to compute the composition of some substitutions in **Problem 4.7**.

PERMUTATIONS

A *permutation* substitution is one that only rearranges its variables. For example, the substitution

$$\pi_0 : \;\; \{x \leftarrow y, y \leftarrow z, z \leftarrow x\}$$

is a permutation because it only replaces its variables x, y, and z with y, z, and x, respectively. On the other hand, $\{x \leftarrow y\}$ is not a permutation, because it replaces its variable x with a new variable y.

Formally, we define a permutation to be a substitution π that has an inverse under composition, that is, a substitution π^{-1} such that

$$\pi \,\square\, \pi^{-1} \;=\; \{\ \}.$$

If π is a permutation, so is its inverse, and

$$\pi^{-1} \,\square\, \pi \;=\; \{\ \}.$$

For example, if π_0 is the preceding permutation, we have

$$\pi_0^{-1} \;=\; \{x \leftarrow z, y \leftarrow x, z \leftarrow y\}$$

because

$$\pi_0 \,\square\, \pi_0^{-1} = \{x \leftarrow y,\, y \leftarrow z,\, z \leftarrow x\} \,\square\, \{x \leftarrow z,\, y \leftarrow x,\, z \leftarrow y\}$$

$$= \{\,\}.$$

Also,

$$\pi_0^{-1} \,\square\, \pi_0 = \{x \leftarrow z,\, y \leftarrow x,\, z \leftarrow y\} \,\square\, \{x \leftarrow y,\, y \leftarrow z,\, z \leftarrow x\}$$

$$= \{\,\}.$$

GENERALITY

A substitution θ is said to be *more general* than another substitution ϕ, written $\theta \succeq_{gen} \phi$, if ϕ can be obtained from θ by composition with some other substitution λ, that is, if

$$\theta \,\square\, \lambda = \phi.$$

Roughly, more general substitutions make smaller changes to an expression. For example,

$$\{x \leftarrow y\} \succeq_{gen} \{x \leftarrow a,\, y \leftarrow a\}$$

because

$$\{x \leftarrow y\} \,\square\, \{y \leftarrow a\} = \{x \leftarrow a,\, y \leftarrow a\}.$$

Any substitution θ is more general than itself, that is,

$$\theta \succeq_{gen} \theta,$$

because $\theta \,\square\, \{\,\} = \theta$. (It would therefore be more accurate to use the phrase "at least as general as" for $\succeq_{gen}$.) Also, the empty substitution is more general than any substitution θ, that is,

$$\{\,\} \succeq_{gen} \theta,$$

because $\{\,\} \,\square\, \theta = \theta$. The generality relation $\succeq_{gen}$ is transitive, that is, for any substitutions, θ, λ, and ϕ,

> *if* $\theta \succeq_{gen} \lambda$ *and* $\lambda \succeq_{gen} \phi$
> *then* $\theta \succeq_{gen} \phi$.

It is possible for two distinct substitutions each to be more general than the other. For example,

$$\{x \leftarrow y\} \succeq_{gen} \{y \leftarrow x\} \qquad \text{and} \qquad \{y \leftarrow x\} \succeq_{gen} \{x \leftarrow y\}$$

because

$$\{x \leftarrow y\} \,\square\, \{y \leftarrow x\} = \{y \leftarrow x\} \qquad \text{and} \qquad \{y \leftarrow x\} \,\square\, \{x \leftarrow y\} = \{x \leftarrow y\}.$$

If two substitutions θ and ϕ are more general than each other, we shall say that they are *equally general*, written $\theta \approx_{gen} \phi$. Thus, because $\{x \leftarrow y\}$ and $\{y \leftarrow x\}$ are each more general than the other, we have that

$$\{x \leftarrow y\} \approx_{gen} \{y \leftarrow x\}.$$

If $\theta \approx_{gen} \phi$, the two substitutions are related by composition with a permutation; in other words, there is a permutation π such that

$$\theta \,\square\, \pi \;=\; \phi \quad \text{and (hence)} \quad \phi \,\square\, \pi^{-1} = \theta.$$

For example,

$$\{x \leftarrow y\} \approx_{gen} \{y \leftarrow x\},$$

and hence we would expect them to be related by composition with a permutation. In fact, $\{x \leftarrow y, y \leftarrow x\}$ is a permutation that is its own inverse, and

$$\{x \leftarrow y\} \,\square\, \{x \leftarrow y, y \leftarrow x\} \;=\; \{y \leftarrow x\}$$

and

$$\{y \leftarrow x\} \,\square\, \{x \leftarrow y, y \leftarrow x\} \;=\; \{x \leftarrow y\}.$$

A substitution θ is a permutation if and only if

$$\theta \approx_{gen} \{\,\}.$$

A proof is requested in **Problem 4.8**.

UNIFIERS

Two expressions are said to be *unifiable* if they can be made identical by application of some substitution θ. We shall say that θ is a *unifier* of the expressions. Let us state this in a definition.

Definition (unifier)

A substitution θ is a *unifier* of two expressions d and e if

$$d \blacktriangleleft \theta \;=\; e \blacktriangleleft \theta.$$

In this case, we also say that θ *unifies* d and e.

Two expressions are *unifiable* if there is a substitution θ that unifies them. ⏺

For example, the expressions

$$f(x,\, b) \quad \text{and} \quad f(a,\, y)$$

are unifiable, and

$$\{x \leftarrow a,\, y \leftarrow b\}$$

is a unifier. On the other hand, the expressions

$$f(x, x) \quad \text{and} \quad f(a, b)$$

are not unifiable.

If d is a proper subexpression of e, then d and e are not unifiable; for example,

$$x \quad \text{and} \quad f(x)$$

are not unifiable. This is so because, if d is a proper subexpression of e, then by monotonicity, for any substitution θ, $d \triangleleft \theta$ is a proper subexpression of $e \triangleleft \theta$; therefore $d \triangleleft \theta$ and $e \triangleleft \theta$ cannot be equal.

Unifiers are not unique; for example,

$$\{x \leftarrow a\}, \qquad \{x \leftarrow a, \, y \leftarrow a\}, \quad \text{and} \quad \{x \leftarrow a, \, y \leftarrow b, \, z \leftarrow c\}$$

are all unifiers of the expressions

$$f(x, y) \quad \text{and} \quad f(a, y).$$

If d and e are equal, then any substitution θ is a unifier of d and e.

In **Problem 4.9**, the reader is requested to identify unifiers for given pairs of expressions.

MOST-GENERAL UNIFIERS

A unifier is said to be *most-general* if it is more general than any other unifier. Let us state this in a definition.

Definition (most-general unifier)

A substitution θ is a *most-general unifier* of two expressions d and e if

θ is a unifier of d and e and

θ is more general than any unifier of d and e. ◢

For example, $\{x \leftarrow a\}$ turns out to be a most-general unifier of $f(x, y)$ and $f(a, y)$. The unifier $\{x \leftarrow a, y \leftarrow a\}$ is not most-general. In fact,

$$\{x \leftarrow a\} \succeq_{gen} \{x \leftarrow a, \, y \leftarrow a\}$$

because $\{x \leftarrow a, \, y \leftarrow a\}$ can be obtained from $\{x \leftarrow a\}$ by composition with some other substitution, namely $\{y \leftarrow a\}$, but there is no substitution λ such that

$$\{x \leftarrow a, \, y \leftarrow a\} \square \lambda \; = \; \{x \leftarrow a\}.$$

Roughly, a most-general unifier makes the two expressions identical without doing any unnecessary work, except perhaps for permuting variables.

If d and e are identical, then the empty substitution $\{\ \}$ is a most-general unifier of d and e. If the variable x does not occur in the expression e, then $\{x \leftarrow e\}$ is a most-general unifier of x and e.

Most-general unifiers are not unique. For example,

$$\{x \leftarrow y\} \quad \text{and} \quad \{y \leftarrow x\}$$

are both most-general unifiers of x and y. If two substitutions θ and ϕ are both most-general unifiers of the same two expressions, then each must be more general than the other. In other words, they must be equally general, that is, $\theta \approx_{gen} \phi$, and either may be obtained from the other by composition with a permutation.

On the other hand, if θ is a most-general unifier for two expressions, and ϕ and θ are equally general, that is, $\theta \approx_{gen} \phi$, then it can easily be shown that ϕ is also a most-general unifier of the two expressions. In short, if θ is a most-general unifier, the set of all most-general unifiers is precisely the set of substitutions equally general to θ, which are the substitutions $\theta \square \pi$, where π is a permutation substitution. In particular, we can show that, if d and e are identical expressions, any permutation substitution is a most-general unifier of d and e.

For example, we know that $\{x \leftarrow f(y)\}$ is a most-general unifier of x and $f(y)$, and that $\{x \leftarrow y, y \leftarrow x\}$ is a permutation substitution. Since

$$\{x \leftarrow f(y)\} \square \{x \leftarrow y, \ y \leftarrow x\} \ = \ \{x \leftarrow f(x), \ y \leftarrow x\},$$

it follows that $\{x \leftarrow f(x), y \leftarrow x\}$ is also a most-general unifier of x and $f(y)$.

Perhaps surprisingly,

$$\phi: \ \{x \leftarrow z, \ y \leftarrow z\}$$

is not a most-general unifier of x and y. In particular, ϕ is not more general than the unifier $\{x \leftarrow y\}$. Intuitively, ϕ has done some unnecessary work by making x and y identical to z.

In adapting our propositional-logic deductive-tableau rules to predicate logic, we shall always want to find a most-general unifier. Finding a less general unifier will cause our rules to derive a conclusion less general than possible. This may cause the procedure to fail to find a proof of a valid predicate-logic sentence.

The reader is asked to compare different unifiers for the same two expressions in **Problem 4.10**.

UNIFICATION

The aim of this section is to produce a *unification algorithm*, a systematic method for testing whether two expressions are unifiable and, if so, producing a most-general unifier. If the two expressions are not unifiable, the algorithm is to indicate failure. The method may be described roughly as follows:

- Given two expressions d and e, we attempt to find a *difference pair* σ, that is, a substitution $\{x \leftarrow s\}$ where the variable x and the term s occupy corresponding positions in d and e (or vice versa), and where x does not occur in s.

For example, a difference pair for $f(x, b)$ and $f(a, y)$ could be either $\{x \leftarrow a\}$ or $\{y \leftarrow b\}$. Our algorithm searches from left to right, so it would find $\{x \leftarrow a\}$. When searching for a difference pair:

- If we discover that the two expressions are actually identical, we yield the most-general unifier $\theta = \{\ \}$.

- If we discover two corresponding subexpressions $f(d_1, \ldots, d_m)$ and $g(e_1, \ldots, e_n)$, where f and g are distinct function symbols, we indicate failure: the given expressions are not unifiable. This includes the case in which f, g, or both are actually constants (0-ary function symbols).

For example, in searching for a difference pair for $f(a, c)$ and $f(b, c)$, we would discover the corresponding subexpressions a and b, that is, $a(\ )$ and $b(\ )$, whose function symbols a and b are distinct. Therefore we would fail to find a difference pair.

- If we discover two corresponding subexpressions x and s, where x occurs properly in s, we also indicate failure.

For example, we would fail in attempting to find a difference pair for $g(x)$ and $g\big(f(x)\big)$ because x occurs properly in the corresponding subexpression $f(x)$. In such a case, we say that the *occurs-check* of the *unification* algorithm has failed.

- If we succeed in finding a nonempty difference pair σ, we apply σ to our expressions, and recursively attempt to unify the resulting expressions $d \blacktriangleleft \sigma$ and $e \blacktriangleleft \sigma$. In attempting the unification:

  - If we fail, then we also indicate failure to unify d and e.

  - If, on the other hand, we succeed in unifying $d \blacktriangleleft \sigma$ and $e \blacktriangleleft \sigma$, obtaining a most-general unifier θ, we yield the composition $\sigma \,\square\, \theta$ as a most-general unifier for the given expressions d and e.

In our examples, the depth of recursion is indicated by the level of indentation.

Example.

Suppose we want to unify the following expressions:

$$d_1 : \ f(x, \ b) \quad \text{and} \quad e_1 : \ f(a, \ y).$$

We discover the difference pair $\sigma_1 : \{x \leftarrow a\}$. We apply σ_1 to d_1 and to e_1 and attempt (recursively) to unify the resulting expressions $d_1 \blacktriangleleft \sigma_1 = d_2$ and $e_1 \blacktriangleleft \sigma_1 = e_2$.

We now must unify the expressions

$$d_2 : \ f(a, \ b) \quad \text{and} \quad e_2 : \ f(a, \ y).$$

We discover the difference pair $\sigma_2 : \{y \leftarrow b\}$. We apply σ_2 to d_2 and e_2 and attempt to unify the resulting expressions $d_2 \blacktriangleleft \sigma_2 = d_3$ and $e_2 \blacktriangleleft \sigma_2 = e_3$.

We now must unify the expressions

$$d_3 : f(a, b) \quad \text{and} \quad e_3 : f(a, b).$$

We discover no difference between d_3 and e_3. Therefore we yield as a most-general unifier for d_3 and e_3 the substitution

$$\theta_3 : \{\ \}.$$

We yield as a most-general unifier for d_2 and e_2 the substitution

$$\theta_2 = \sigma_2 \square \theta_3 : \quad \{y \leftarrow b\} \square \{\ \} = \{y \leftarrow b\}.$$

We yield as a most-general unifier for d_1 and e_1 the substitution

$$\theta_1 = \sigma_1 \square \theta_2 : \quad \{x \leftarrow a\} \square \{y \leftarrow b\} = \{x \leftarrow a, y \leftarrow b\}. \quad \blacksquare$$

Example.   Suppose we want to unify the following expressions:

$$d_1 : f\big(x, g(x)\big) \quad \text{and} \quad e_1 : f(y, y).$$

We discover the difference pair $\sigma_1 : \{x \leftarrow y\}$. We apply σ_1 to d_1 and to e_1 and attempt to unify the resulting expressions $d_1 \blacktriangleleft \sigma_1 = d_2$ and $e_1 \blacktriangleleft \sigma_1 = e_2$.

We now must unify the expressions

$$d_2 : f\big(y, g(y)\big) \quad \text{and} \quad e_2 : f(y, y).$$

We discover corresponding subexpressions y and $g(y)$ where y is a proper subexpression of $g(y)$. Therefore we fail to unify d_2 and e_2.

Because we fail to unify d_2 and e_2, we also fail to unify d_1 and e_1. $\quad \blacksquare$

The *unification* algorithm finds a most-general unifier for the two expressions d and e if a unifier exists, and indicates failure otherwise. This is expressed by the following result.

Proposition (unification)

If the expressions d and e are unifiable, the *unification* algorithm will yield a most-general unifier of d and e; otherwise, the unification algorithm will indicate failure. $\quad \blacksquare$

This proposition expresses the correctness of the *unification* algorithm.

In **Problems 4.11, 4.12,** and **4.13** the reader is requested to unify certain pairs of expressions.

A substitution θ is said to be *idempotent* if

$$\theta \square \theta = \theta.$$

For example, $\{x \leftarrow f(y)\}$ is idempotent, because

$$\{x \leftarrow f(y)\} \,\square\, \{x \leftarrow f(y)\} \ = \ \{x \leftarrow f(y)\}.$$

On the other hand, $\{x \leftarrow f(x)\}$ is not idempotent, because

$$\{x \leftarrow f(x)\} \,\square\, \{x \leftarrow f(x)\} \ = \ \{x \leftarrow f(f(x))\} \ \neq \ \{x \leftarrow f(x)\}.$$

The *unification* algorithm actually produces idempotent most-general unifiers. **Problem 4.14** is concerned with idempotent substitutions and unifiers.

UNIFYING TUPLES

The preceding algorithm applies to two expressions. In formulating the *resolution* rule and other rules for predicate logic, we must often unify more than two expressions. Once we can unify pairs of expressions, however, we can easily extend the algorithm to unify an arbitrary tuple of expressions $\langle e_1, e_2, \ldots, e_n \rangle$.

We define a *unifier* for a tuple of expressions $\langle e_1, e_2, \ldots, e_n \rangle$ as a substitution θ that makes all the elements of the tuple identical, that is,

$$e_1 \blacktriangleleft \theta \ = \ e_2 \blacktriangleleft \theta \ = \ \ldots \ = \ e_n \blacktriangleleft \theta.$$

(We regard any substitution as a unifier for the empty tuple $\langle\ \rangle$ or a singleton tuple of one expression $\langle e \rangle$.) If a tuple of expressions has a unifier, we shall say that it is *unifiable*. A *most-general unifier* for a tuple of expressions must be more general than any other unifier. The *tuple-unification algorithm* is stated as follows:

- To unify an empty tuple $\langle\ \rangle$ or a singleton $\langle e \rangle$, we simply yield the empty substitution $\{\ \}$.

- To unify a tuple t of two or more expressions, we first attempt to unify the first two elements, e_1 and e_2, of the tuple, using the preceding algorithm.

  - If we fail to unify e_1 and e_2, we also fail to unify the tuple t.

  - Otherwise, we obtain a most-general unifier ϕ for e_1 and e_2. We then apply ϕ to $tail(t)$, that is, the tuple $\langle e_2, \ldots, e_n \rangle$ of expressions other than e_1. We attempt (recursively) to unify the resulting tuple $tail(t) \blacktriangleleft \phi$, that is, $\langle e_2 \blacktriangleleft \phi, \ldots, e_n \blacktriangleleft \phi \rangle$. In this unification attempt,

    - If we fail to unify $tail(t) \blacktriangleleft \phi$, we also fail to unify the given tuple t.

    - Otherwise, we obtain a most-general unifier θ for $tail(t) \blacktriangleleft \phi$, and we yield the composition $\phi \,\square\, \theta$ as a most-general unifier of t.

The following proposition expresses the correctness of the algorithm.

Proposition (tuple unification)

If the tuple t of expressions is unifiable, the *tuple-unification* algorithm will yield a most-general unifier of t; otherwise, the algorithm will indicate failure. ◢

Example.   Suppose we want to unify the tuple

$$t_1 : \quad \langle f(a, y, z), \; f(x, b, z), \; f(x, y, c) \rangle.$$

To unify t_1, we first unify the first two expressions $f(a, y, z)$ and $f(x, b, z)$. We obtain the most-general unifier $\phi_1 : \{x \leftarrow a, y \leftarrow b\}$. We attempt (recursively) to unify $t_2 = tail(t_1) \triangleleft \phi_1 : \langle f(x, b, z), \; f(x, y, c) \rangle \triangleleft \phi_1$.

We now must unify the tuple

$$t_2 : \quad \langle f(a, b, z), \; f(a, b, c) \rangle.$$

To unify t_2, we first unify the first two expressions $f(a, b, z)$ and $f(a, b, c)$. We obtain the most-general unifier $\phi_2 : \{z \leftarrow c\}$. We attempt to unify $t_3 = tail(t_2) \triangleleft \phi_2 : \langle f(a, b, c) \rangle \triangleleft \phi_2$.

We now must unify the tuple

$$t_3 : \quad \langle f(a, b, c) \rangle.$$

Because t_3 is a singleton, we immediately yield the empty substitution

$$\theta_3 : \quad \{ \; \}.$$

We yield as a most-general unifier for t_2 the substitution

$$\theta_2 = \phi_2 \square \theta_3 : \quad \{z \leftarrow c\} \square \{ \; \} = \{z \leftarrow c\}.$$

We yield as a most-general unifier for t_1 the substitution

$$\theta_1 = \phi_1 \square \theta_2 : \quad \{x_a, \, y_b\} \square \{z_c\}$$
$$= \{x_a, \, y_b, \, z_c\}. \quad ◢$$

In **Problem 4.15** the reader is requested to unify certain tuples of expressions.

SEPARATELY UNIFYING TUPLES

The preceding algorithm unifies a tuple of expressions. For the *equivalence* and other rules of predicate logic, we shall require an algorithm for *separately unifying* two tuples of expressions.

We say that a substitution θ is a *separate-unifier* of the tuples $t : \langle e_1, \ldots, e_m \rangle$ and $t' : \langle e'_1, \ldots, e'_n \rangle$ if θ unifies t and θ unifies t', that is, if $e_1 \triangleleft \theta = \cdots = e_m \triangleleft \theta$ and $e'_1 \triangleleft \theta = \cdots = e'_n \triangleleft \theta$. Note that the $e_i \triangleleft \theta$ and $e'_j \triangleleft \theta$ may still be distinct. If t and t' have a separate-unifier, we shall say that they are *separately unifiable*.

We say that θ is a *most-general separate-unifier* of the tuples t and t' if θ is itself a separate-unifier of t and t' and θ is more general than any separate-unifier of t and t'.

Example.   For the tuples

$$t : \langle f(x), f(a) \rangle \quad \text{and} \quad t' : \langle g(x, h(x)), g(x, y) \rangle,$$

the substitution

$$\theta : \{x \leftarrow a, y \leftarrow h(a)\}$$

is a most-general separate-unifier. ◢

The *separate-tuple-unification* algorithm can now be described as follows:
Given two tuples of expressions t and t', we first attempt to unify the tuple t,
using the original *tuple-unification* algorithm.

- If we fail to unify t, we also fail to separately unify the two tuples t
  and t'.

- Otherwise, we obtain a most-general tuple unifier ϕ for t. We then
  apply ϕ to t' and use the *tuple-unification* algorithm to attempt to unify
  the resulting tuple $t' \triangleleft \phi$. In this unification attempt,

  - If we fail to unify $t' \triangleleft \phi$, we also fail to separately unify the two
    tuples t and t'.

  - Otherwise, we obtain a most-general tuple unifier λ for $t' \triangleleft \phi$,
    and we yield the composition $\phi \square \lambda$ as a most-general separate-
    unifier of t and t'.

It can be established that if the tuples t and t' are separately unifiable, the
separate-tuple-unification algorithm will yield a most-general separate-unifier for t
and t'; otherwise, it will indicate failure.

Example.   Suppose we want to separately unify the tuples

$$t : \langle f(x), f(a) \rangle \quad \text{and} \quad t' : \langle g(x, h(x)), g(x, y) \rangle$$

of the previous example.

We first use the original *tuple-unification* algorithm to unify t, obtaining the
most-general tuple unifier

$$\phi : \{x \leftarrow a\}.$$

We then apply ϕ to t' and use the *tuple-unification* algorithm to unify the resulting
tuple

$$t' \triangleleft \phi : \langle g(a, h(a)), g(a, y) \rangle.$$

We obtain the *most-general tuple* unifier

$$\lambda : \{y \leftarrow h(a)\}.$$

Finally, we yield the composition

$$\theta = \phi \square \lambda : \{x \leftarrow a, y \leftarrow h(a)\}$$

as the most-general separate-unifier of t and t'. ◢

EXTENDED UNIFICATION

We now extend the notion of substitution introduced in this section to apply to quantifier-free expressions, including sentences as well as terms, of predicate logic. We can then employ the *unification* algorithm to unify predicate-logic expressions.

To achieve this extension, we treat a predicate symbol such as p, a connective such as *if-then*, or the term constructor *if-then-else* just as we would treat a function symbol such as f. Therefore all the results of this section can be applied to quantifier-free predicate-logic expressions.

For example, we can apply the *unification* algorithm to the two sentences

$$if \ p(x) \ then \ q(b) \qquad \text{and} \qquad if \ p(a) \ then \ q(y),$$

to obtain the most-general unifier $\{x \leftarrow a, \ y \leftarrow b\}$. Here we have treated the *if-then* connective and the predicate symbols p and q just as we would treat function symbols. We apply the *unification* algorithm only to quantifier-free expressions. We shall apply substitutions, however, to expressions with quantifiers.

We always apply substitutions safely; that is, we only replace free variables and we rename bound variables as necessary to avoid capturing. For example, if $\mathcal{F}$ is the sentence

$$\mathcal{F}: \ (\forall y)p(x, y)$$

and θ is the substitution $\{y \leftarrow x\}$, then $\mathcal{F} \triangleleft \theta$ is $\mathcal{F}$ itself, that is, $(\forall y)p(x, y)$; the bound variable y is not replaced by a safe substitution. Also, if ϕ is the substitution $\{x \leftarrow y\}$, then $\mathcal{F} \triangleleft \phi$ is the sentence $(\forall y')p(y, y')$; the variable y of the quantifier $(\forall y)$ has been renamed y' to avoid capturing.

If $\mathcal{F}$ is an expression (which may contain quantifiers) and θ a substitution, we henceforth write $\mathcal{F}\theta$, instead of $\mathcal{F} \triangleleft \theta$, to stand for the result of applying θ to $\mathcal{F}$. Similarly, if θ and ϕ are both substitutions, we henceforth write $\theta\phi$, instead of $\theta \square \phi$, to stand for the composition of θ and ϕ.

COMBINED SUBSTITUTION

We now combine the notion of a variable substitution from this section with the expression substitution operation of Section 3.9.

Definition (combined substitution)

Suppose that $\mathcal{G}$ and $\mathcal{H}$ are expressions, either both sentences or both terms, that $\mathcal{F}[\mathcal{G}]$ is an expression, and that θ is a variable substitution. Then

$$\mathcal{F}\theta[\mathcal{H}]$$

denotes the result of

- safely applying θ to $\mathcal{F}[\mathcal{G}]$, obtaining $(\mathcal{F}[\mathcal{G}])\theta$, and then
- safely replacing all free occurrences of $\mathcal{G}\theta$ in $(\mathcal{F}[\mathcal{G}])\theta$ with $\mathcal{H}$. ■

In other words, we first safely apply the variable substitution, then perform the indicated safe expression substitution.

Example.   Suppose

$$\mathcal{F}[p(x)] \quad \text{is} \quad (\forall y)[p(x) \; and \; q(x, y)]$$

$$\theta \qquad\qquad \text{is} \quad \{x \leftarrow a\}.$$

Then (safely applying the variable substitution)

$$(\mathcal{F}[p(x)])\theta \quad \text{is} \quad (\forall y)[p(a) \; and \; q(a, y)]$$

and therefore (safely replacing the expression $p(x)\theta$, that is, $p(a)$, with $p(y)$)

$$\mathcal{F}\theta[p(y)] \qquad \text{is} \quad (\forall y')[p(y) \; and \; q(a, y')].\quad \lrcorner$$

Note that some of the free occurrences of $\mathcal{G}\theta$ in $(\mathcal{F}[\mathcal{G}])\theta$, which must be replaced, may not actually correspond to occurrences of $\mathcal{G}$ in $\mathcal{F}[\mathcal{G}]$.

Example.   Suppose

$$\mathcal{F}[p(x)] \quad \text{is} \quad (p(x) \; and \; p(a))$$

$$\theta \qquad\qquad \text{is} \quad \{x \leftarrow a\}.$$

Then (safely applying the variable substitution)

$$(\mathcal{F}[p(x)])\theta \quad \text{is} \quad (p(a) \; and \; p(a))$$

and therefore (safely replacing the expression $p(x)\theta$, that is, $p(a)$, with $q(a)$)

$$\mathcal{F}\theta[q(a)] \qquad \text{is} \quad (q(a) \; and \; q(a)).$$

Here the second occurrence of $p(x)\theta$, that is, $p(a)$, in $(\mathcal{F}[p(x)])\theta$ does not correspond to an occurrence of $p(x)$ in $\mathcal{F}[p(x)]$. $\lrcorner$

We may define a partial combined substitution analogous to the preceding total substitution. If $\mathcal{F}\langle\mathcal{G}\rangle$ is an expression, in forming

$$\mathcal{F}\theta\langle\mathcal{H}\rangle$$

we safely replace zero, one, or more free occurrences of $\mathcal{G}\theta$ in $(\mathcal{F}\langle\mathcal{G}\rangle)\theta$ with $\mathcal{H}$.

Both the total and partial combined substitution operations may be extended to allow multiple replacements.

Example.   Suppose

$$\mathcal{F}\langle p(x), q(y)\rangle \quad \text{is} \quad p(x) \; and \; p(y) \; and \; q(y)$$

$$\theta \qquad\qquad\qquad \text{is} \quad \{x \leftarrow a, \; y \leftarrow a\}.$$

Then (safely applying the variable substitution)

$$\big(\mathcal{F}\langle p(x),\, q(y)\rangle\big)\theta \quad \text{is} \quad p(a) \ \textit{and}\ p(a)\ \textit{and}\ q(a)$$

and therefore (safely replacing zero, one, or more occurrences of the expressions $p(a)$ and $q(a)$ with $q(b)$ and $p(b)$, respectively),

$$\mathcal{F}\theta\langle q(b),\, p(b)\rangle \quad \text{is} \quad q(b)\ \textit{and}\ p(a)\ \textit{and}\ p(b)$$

$$\text{or} \quad p(a)\ \textit{and}\ q(b)\ \textit{and}\ q(a)$$

or any of several other sentences. ◢

Remark (multiple replacements). Suppose that, in the expression $\mathcal{F}[\mathcal{G}_1, \mathcal{G}_2]$, the variable substitution θ unifies $\mathcal{G}_1$ and $\mathcal{G}_2$, that is, $\mathcal{G}_1\theta$ and $\mathcal{G}_2\theta$ are identical. Then, if we form the new expression $\mathcal{F}\theta[\mathcal{H}_1, \mathcal{H}_2]$, we require that $\mathcal{H}_1$ and $\mathcal{H}_2$ be identical too. Otherwise, the instruction to safely replace all occurrences of $\mathcal{G}_1\theta$ with $\mathcal{H}_1$ and $\mathcal{G}_2\theta$ with $\mathcal{H}_2$ may be inconsistent.

For example, if

$$\mathcal{F}\big[p(x),\, p(y)\big] \quad \text{is} \quad p(x)\ \textit{and}\ p(y)$$

$$\theta \qquad\qquad \text{is} \quad \{x \leftarrow a,\ y \leftarrow a\}$$

then

$$\big(\mathcal{F}\big[p(x),\, p(y)\big]\big)\theta \quad \text{is} \quad p(a)\ \textit{and}\ p(a).$$

Therefore

$$\mathcal{F}\theta\big[q(b),\, q(b)\big] \quad \text{is} \quad q(b)\ \textit{and}\ q(b),$$

but $\mathcal{F}\theta\big[q(b),\, q(c)\big]$ has no meaning.

A similar requirement is imposed if more than two separate replacements are indicated. ◢

PROBLEMS

Problem 4.1 (polarity annotation)   page 193

Annotate all the subsentences of the following sentences according to their polarity:

(a) *if not* $p(x)$
     then $(\exists y)q(y)$

(b) *not* $(q(x)\ \textit{or}\ r(x,y))$
     and
     $(\forall x)q(x)$

(c) *if* $\begin{bmatrix} \textit{if}\ (p(x)\ \textit{and}\ p(y)) \\ \textit{then}\ q(y,z) \\ \textit{else}\ q(y,w) \end{bmatrix}$ *then* $(\exists u)q(y,u).$

Problem 4.2 (force of quantifiers)   page 196

Annotate the following sentences with the forces of their quantifiers:

(a) $(\forall x)\big[not\ (\exists y)q(x,\ y)\big]$

(b)   *if* $(\forall x)p(x)$ *then* $(\forall y)r(y)$

(c) $(\forall x)p(x)\ \equiv\ r(y)$.

Problem 4.3 (universal-quantifier elimination)   page 213

(a) Show that the sentence of our extended example,

$$\mathcal{A}: \quad \begin{aligned} &if\ (\forall y_1)^{\exists}(\exists z_1)^{\forall}p(y_1, z_1) \\ &then\ (\forall z_2)^{\forall}(\exists y_2)^{\exists}p(y_2, z_2), \end{aligned}$$

is not equivalent to the sentence obtained by dropping its quantifiers of universal force,

$$\mathcal{C}: \quad \begin{aligned} &if\ (\forall y_1)^{\exists}p\big(y_1, f(y_1)\big) \\ &then\ (\exists y_2)^{\exists}p(y_2, a). \end{aligned}$$

To do this, construct an interpretation under which one of the sentences is true and the other false.

(b) Construct interpretations $\mathcal{I}$ and $\mathcal{I}''$ such that $\mathcal{A}$ is false under $\mathcal{I}$, $\mathcal{C}$ is false under $\mathcal{I}''$, and $\mathcal{I}$ and $\mathcal{I}''$ assign the same values to all symbols except f and a.

Problem 4.4 (reordering quantifiers)   page 213

Consider the sentences

$$\mathcal{G}: \quad (\forall *)(\exists y)\big[if\ \big[p\big(f(y)\big)\ or\ q(y)\big]\ then\ \mathcal{F}\big]$$

$$\mathcal{H}: \quad (\forall *)(\exists y)\big[if\ \big[p(a)\ or\ q(y)\big]\ then\ \mathcal{F}\big].$$

Assume that $\mathcal{G}$ is valid, that y does not occur free in $\mathcal{F}$, and that a and f do not occur in $\mathcal{F}$. Show informally that then $\mathcal{H}$ is valid.

Hint: $\mathcal{G}$ and $\mathcal{H}$ result from the skolemization of equivalent sentences.

Problem 4.5 (skolemization)   page 217

• Remove the quantifier $(\ldots\ z)$ in each of the following sentences, preserving validity in each case. Remove other quantifiers only if necessary.

• In each case, decide whether the resulting sentence is equivalent to the given sentence. If not, give an interpretation under which they have different truth-values.

• Then remove any remaining quantifiers from each sentence, still preserving validity.

(a) $(\forall z)q(a, z)$

(b) $(\exists y)[r(y) \ \ or \ \ (\exists z)q(y, z)]$

(c) $if \ \ (\forall x)p(x)$
    $then \ \ (\forall z)p(z)$

(d) $(\forall x)\begin{bmatrix} if \ p(x) \\ then \ \ (\forall x, z)q(x, z) \end{bmatrix}$

(e) $(\forall y)(\exists z)q(y, z)$

(f) $(\exists z)r(z) \ \equiv \ p(a).$

(g) $(\exists y)[(\forall z)q(y, z) \ \ and \ \ (\forall x)r(x, y)]$

(h) $if \ (\exists z)(\forall y)p(z, y)$
    $then \ (\exists z)(\forall y)p(y, z)$

(i) $(\exists x)(\forall z)\begin{bmatrix} if \ (\forall x)(\exists y)(\forall z)p(x, y, z) \\ then \ q(a, x) \end{bmatrix}$

(j) $(\exists y)\begin{bmatrix} not \ (\forall z)\begin{bmatrix} if \ p(z, y) \\ then \ (\exists y)p(z, y) \end{bmatrix} \end{bmatrix}$

(k) $(\forall z)\begin{bmatrix} if \ (\forall y)p(z, y) \\ then \ (\forall x)q(z, x) \\ else \ (\exists z)r(z) \end{bmatrix}.$

Problem 4.6 (skolemization and equivalence)   page 217

(a) Use skolemization to find a quantifier-free sentence $\mathcal{F}'$ whose existential closure $(\exists *)\mathcal{F}'$ is valid precisely when the following sentence $\mathcal{F}$ is valid:
$$\mathcal{F}: \quad \begin{array}{l} if \ [not \ (\forall x)(\exists y) \, p(x, y)] \\ then \ (\exists x)(\forall y)[not \ p(x, y)]. \end{array}$$

(b) Is $\mathcal{F}$ equivalent to $(\exists *)\mathcal{F}'$? If so, why? If not, provide an interpretation
under which $\mathcal{F}$ and $(\exists *)\mathcal{F}'$ have different truth-values.

Hint: Is $\mathcal{F}$ valid?

Problem 4.7 (composition)   page 219

Compute the composition of the following substitutions:

(a) $\{x \leftarrow y\} \square \{y \leftarrow a\}$

(b) $\{x \leftarrow y, \ y \leftarrow z\} \square \{y \leftarrow x\}$

(c) $\{x \leftarrow f(z), \ y \leftarrow f(z), \ z \leftarrow x\} \square \{z \leftarrow f(z)\}.$

Problem 4.8 (generality and permutation)   page 221

Show that a substitution θ is a permutation if and only if $\theta \approx_{gen} \{\,\}$.

Problem 4.9 (unifiers)   page 222

Consider the two terms
$$d_1 : \; g(x, z) \quad \text{and} \quad e_1 : \; g\big(y,\, f(y)\big).$$
Which of the following substitutions unify d_1 and e_1?

(a) $\{x \leftarrow y, \; z \leftarrow f(y)\}$

(b) $\{x \leftarrow a, \; y \leftarrow a, \; z \leftarrow f(a)\}$

(c) $\{y \leftarrow x, \; z \leftarrow f(y)\}$

(d) $\{x \leftarrow z, \; y \leftarrow z, \; z \leftarrow f(z)\}$.

Consider the two terms
$$d_1 : \; g\big(x, y, f(x), z, u\big) \quad \text{and} \quad e_2 : \; g\big(a, x, z, f(x), h(v, z)\big).$$
Which of the following substitutions unify d_2 and e_2?

(e) $\{x \leftarrow a, \; y \leftarrow x, \; z \leftarrow f(x), \; u \leftarrow h(v, z)\}$.

(f) $\{x \leftarrow a, \; y \leftarrow a, \; z \leftarrow f(a), \; u \leftarrow h\big(v, f(a)\big)\}$.

(g) $\{x \leftarrow a, \; y \leftarrow a, \; z \leftarrow f(a), \; u \leftarrow h\big(f(a), f(a)\big), \; v \leftarrow z\}$.

(h) $\{x \leftarrow a, \; y \leftarrow a, \; z \leftarrow f(a), \; u \leftarrow h\big(b, f(a)\big), \; v \leftarrow b\}$.

Problem 4.10 (comparing unifiers)   page 223

(a) Find three different unifiers θ_1, θ_2, and θ_3 of
$$f\big(g(x, y), z\big) \quad \text{and} \quad f\big(g(z, a), x\big).$$

(b) Show that θ_1, θ_2, and θ_3 are distinct by exhibiting an expression e such that $e \blacktriangleleft \theta_1$, $e \blacktriangleleft \theta_2$ and $e \blacktriangleleft \theta_3$ are all different expressions.

(c) For each pair of distinct unifiers θ_i and θ_j, state whether $\theta_i \succeq_{gen} \theta_j$ and, if so, find a substitution λ such that $\theta_i \,\square\, \lambda = \theta_j$.

Problem 4.11 (most-general unifiers)   page 225

Consider the two terms
$$d: \; f\big(x, g(y), h(z, a)\big) \quad \text{and} \quad e: \; f\big(y, z, h(g(x), w)\big).$$

(a) Apply the *unification* algorithm to find a most-general unifier θ of d and e. Display the intermediate steps.

(b) Consider the substitutions

$$\phi_1: \quad \{y \leftarrow x, \ z \leftarrow g(y), \ w \leftarrow a\}$$

$$\phi_2: \quad \{x \leftarrow w, \ y \leftarrow w, \ z \leftarrow g(w), \ w \leftarrow a\}$$

$$\phi_3: \quad \{x \leftarrow b, \ y \leftarrow b, \ z \leftarrow g(b), \ w \leftarrow a\}.$$

For each of these substitutions, determine whether

        (i) it is a unifier of d and e

       (ii) it is a most-general unifier of d and e.

Justify your answers.

Problem 4.12 (more most-general unifiers)   page 225

Consider the two terms

$$d: \quad f\big(f(x, \ f(a, z)), \ x\big) \quad\quad \text{and} \quad\quad e: \quad f\big(f(y, \ f(a, u)), \ f(u, z)\big).$$

(a) Apply the *unification* algorithm to find a most-general unifier θ of d and e.

(b) Find another most-general unifier θ' of d and e and show that θ and θ' are indeed equally general.

Problem 4.13 (unification examples)   page 225

Apply the *unification* algorithm to produce a most-general unifier of the following expressions if they are unifiable, and indicate failure otherwise:

(a) $f(x, b)$ and $f(f(y, y), y)$

(b) $f(x, g(x))$ and $f(g(y), y)$

(c) $h(x, f(y, a), g(g(u)))$ and $h(z, f(z, u), y)$

(d) $h(x, f(y, a), g(g(x)))$ and $h(z, f(z, u), y)$

(e) $h(x, f(y, a), y)$ and $h(f(f(b, z), z), x, f(z, a))$.

Display the intermediate steps.

Problem 4.14 (idempotent substitutions and unifiers)   page 226

(a) Show that the empty substitution is the only idempotent permutation.

(b) Find three nonidempotent most-general unifiers of the terms x and $f(y)$.

(c) Show that, for any terms d and e, if θ is a unifier of d and e then

    θ is most-general and idempotent

       if and only if

    for every unifier ϕ of d and e, $\theta \,\square\, \phi = \phi$.

Problem 4.15 (tuple unification)   page 227

Apply the *tuple-unification* algorithm to attempt to unify the following tuples of expressions:

(a) $\qquad \langle f(x, u, a), \; f(g(y), y, v), \; f(w, h(z), z)\rangle$

(b) $\qquad \langle f(x), \; f(g(y)), \; f(y)\rangle.$

You should give intermediate steps of the *tuple-unification* algorithm, but you may omit intermediate steps whenever you unify a pair of expressions.

(c) Find a tuple of three expressions that is not unifiable such that any two of those expressions are unifiable.

5

Deductive
Tableaux

We have already seen, in Chapter 2, the deductive-tableau system for propositional logic; in this chapter we extend the same system to prove the validity of sentences in predicate logic.

5.1 TABLEAUX: NOTATION AND MEANING

As was the case for propositional logic, our basic structure is a tableau of assertions and goals. In this system, however, each assertion and goal is a sentence in predicate logic, not in propositional logic. For example, the tableau $\mathcal{T}_1$ is a predicate-logic deductive tableau.

assertions	goals
A1. $p(a)$	
	G2. $(\forall z)q(y,\, z)$ *and* $p(x)$
A3. $(\exists y)q(x,\, y)$	
	G4. $q(z,\, a)$

Tableau $\mathcal{T}_1$

Note that sentences may contain quantifiers, such as $(\forall z)$ in goal G2 and

$(\exists y)$ in assertion A3, and may contain free variables, such as x and y in goal G2, x in assertion A3, and z in goal G4.

MEANING OF A TABLEAU

As in propositional logic, we may discuss the truth of a tableau only under a given (predicate-logic) interpretation. A tableau will be either true or false according to the following semantic rule for tableaux.

Definition (semantic rule for tableaux)

A tableau with the assertions $\mathcal{A}_1, \mathcal{A}_2, \ldots, \mathcal{A}_m$ and the goals $\mathcal{G}_1, \mathcal{G}_2, \ldots, \mathcal{G}_n$ is *true under* an interpretation $\mathcal{I}$ if the following condition holds:

> if the universal closures $(\forall *)\mathcal{A}_i$ of all the assertions $\mathcal{A}_i$ are true under $\mathcal{I}$,
>
> then the existential closure $(\exists *)\mathcal{G}_j$ of at least one of the goals $\mathcal{G}_j$ is true under $\mathcal{I}$.

On the other hand, the tableau is *false under* $\mathcal{I}$ if the following condition holds:

> the universal closures $(\forall *)\mathcal{A}_i$ of all the assertions $\mathcal{A}_i$ are true under $\mathcal{I}$ and
>
> the existential closures $(\exists *)\mathcal{G}_j$ of all the goals $\mathcal{G}_j$ are false under $\mathcal{I}$. ⌟

Example. In the preceding tableau $\mathcal{T}_1$, the universal closures of the assertions A1 and A3 are

$$p(a) \qquad \text{and} \qquad (\forall x)(\exists y)q(x, y),$$

and the existential closures of the goals G2 and G4 are

$$(\exists y)(\exists x)\big[(\forall z)q(y, z) \text{ and } p(x)\big] \qquad \text{and} \qquad (\exists z)q(z, a).$$

The tableau $\mathcal{T}_1$ is false under an interpretation $\mathcal{I}$ such that:

- The domain of $\mathcal{I}$ is the nonnegative integers.
- The predicate p is assigned the "equals zero" relation, that is, $p_{\mathcal{I}}(d)$ is true if and only if $d = 0$.
- The predicate q is assigned the "less than" relation, that is, $q_{\mathcal{I}}(d, e)$ is true if and only if $d < e$.
- The constant a is assigned 0.

For then the intuitive meanings of the universal closures of the two assertions are

$$0 = 0$$

and

> for every nonnegative integer d_x
>> there exists a nonnegative integer d_y such that
>>> $d_x < d_y,$

respectively, which are both true for the nonnegative integers. On the other hand, the intuitive meanings of the existential closures of the two goals are

> there exist nonnegative integers d_y and d_x such that
>> for every nonnegative integer d_z, $d_y < d_z$ and $d_x = 0,$

and

> there exists a nonnegative integer d_z such that
>> $d_z < 0,$

which are both false for the nonnegative integers. ⌐

Remark (semantic rule). By the semantic rule for tableaux, we may conclude that a tableau $\mathcal{T}$ is true under an interpretation $\mathcal{I}$ if and only if

> the universal closure $(\forall *)\mathcal{A}_i$ of at least one of the assertions $\mathcal{A}_i$ is false under $\mathcal{I}$
>> or
>
> the existential closure $(\exists *)\mathcal{G}_j$ of at least one of the goals $\mathcal{G}_j$ is true under $\mathcal{I}.$

We shall regard this as an alternative form of the semantic rule. ⌐

THE ASSOCIATED SENTENCE

As in propositional logic, the meaning of a tableau can be characterized in terms of a single predicate-logic sentence.

Definition (associated sentence)

> If a tableau contains the assertions
>
> > $\mathcal{A}_1, \mathcal{A}_2, \ldots, \mathcal{A}_m$
>
> and the goals
>
> > $\mathcal{G}_1, \mathcal{G}_2, \ldots, \mathcal{G}_n,$
>
> its *associated sentence* is
>
> > *if* $\left[(\forall *)\mathcal{A}_1 \ \textit{and} \ (\forall *)\mathcal{A}_2 \ \textit{and} \ \ldots \ \textit{and} \ (\forall *)\mathcal{A}_m\right]$
> >
> > *then* $\left[(\exists *)\mathcal{G}_1 \ \textit{or} \ (\exists *)\mathcal{G}_2 \ \textit{or} \ \ldots \ \textit{or} \ (\exists *)\mathcal{G}_n\right].$ ⌐

Example. The associated sentence of the preceding tableau $\mathcal{T}_1$ is

$$if \begin{bmatrix} p(a) \\ and \\ (\forall x)(\exists y)q(x,\,y) \end{bmatrix} then \begin{bmatrix} (\exists y)(\exists x)\Big[(\forall z)q(y,\,z) \ \ and \ \ p(x)\Big] \\ or \\ (\exists z)q(z,\,a) \end{bmatrix}$$

In **Problem 5.1**, the reader is asked to show that the associated sentence of a tableau is equivalent to the sentence

$$(\exists *) \begin{bmatrix} if \ (\mathcal{A}_1 \ and \ \mathcal{A}_2 \ and \ \dots \ and \ \mathcal{A}_m) \\ then \ (\mathcal{G}_1 \ or \ \mathcal{G}_2 \ or \ \dots \ or \ \mathcal{G}_n) \end{bmatrix}.$$

The importance of the associated sentence is apparent from the following proposition.

Proposition (truth of a tableau)

> A tableau is true under an interpretation $\mathcal{I}$
>   if and only if
> its associated sentence is true under $\mathcal{I}$.

Proof. We have

> a tableau is true under an interpretation $\mathcal{I}$

if and only if (by the semantic rule for tableaux)

> if the universal closures $(\forall *)\mathcal{A}_i$ of all the assertions $\mathcal{A}_i$
>   are true under $\mathcal{I}$,
> then the existential closure $(\exists *)\mathcal{G}_j$ of at least one of the goals $\mathcal{G}_j$
>   is true under $\mathcal{I}$

if and only if (by the semantic rules for *and* and *or*)

> if $\Big[(\forall *)\mathcal{A}_1 \ and \ (\forall *)\mathcal{A}_2 \ and \ \dots \ and \ (\forall *)\mathcal{A}_m\Big]$ is true under $\mathcal{I}$,
>
> then $\Big[(\exists *)\mathcal{G}_1 \ or \ (\exists *)\mathcal{G}_2 \ or \ \dots \ or \ (\exists *)\mathcal{G}_n\Big]$ is true under $\mathcal{I}$

if and only if (by the semantic rule for *if-then*)

> the associated sentence is true under $\mathcal{I}$.

VALIDITY AND EQUIVALENCE

The notions of validity and equivalence for tableaux are analogous to the same notions for sentences.

Definition (validity of a tableau)

A tableau $\mathcal{T}$ is *valid* if, for every interpretation $\mathcal{I}$,

$\mathcal{T}$ is true under $\mathcal{I}$.

Alternatively, a tableau is *valid* if and only if its associated sentence is valid. ⏌

As in propositional logic, a tableau is automatically valid if one of its assertions is the truth symbol *false* or if one of its goals is the truth symbol *true*.

Definition (equivalence of tableaux)

Two tableaux $\mathcal{T}$ and $\mathcal{T}'$ are *equivalent* if, for every interpretation $\mathcal{I}$,

$\mathcal{T}$ is true under $\mathcal{I}$
if and only if
$\mathcal{T}'$ is true under $\mathcal{I}$.

Alternatively, two tableaux are *equivalent* if and only if their associated sentences are equivalent. ⏌

Example. The preceding tableau $\mathcal{T}_1$ is not valid; we have already exhibited an interpretation under which it is false.

As we shall see later in this section, the tableau $\mathcal{T}_1$ and the following tableau $\mathcal{T}_2$ are equivalent.

assertions	goals
	G1. *not* $p(a)$
	G2. $(\forall z')q(y, z')$ *and* $p(x)$
A3. $(\exists y)q(z, y)$	
	G4. $q(z, a)$
	G5. $q(b, a)$

Tableau $\mathcal{T}_2$

⏌

For predicate-logic tableaux, the notion of equivalence is sometimes too strong for our purposes. We introduce a weaker notion, that of two tableaux having the "same meaning."

Definition (same meaning of tableaux)

Two tableaux T and T' are said to have the *same meaning* if

T is valid
if and only if
T' is valid. ◢

It is clear that if two tableaux are equivalent, they have the same meaning. It is possible, however, for two tableaux to have the same meaning even though they are not equivalent. In particular, if the two are both not valid, they automatically have the same meaning. They are not equivalent if there is some interpretation under which one is true and the other false.

SUBTABLEAUX

We may introduce notions of a subtableau and of the union of two tableaux for predicate logic just as we did for propositional logic. The corresponding properties are the same.

Definition (subtableau)

A tableau T' is a *subtableau* of a tableau T, written $T' \subseteq T$, if every row of T' is also a row of T. ◢

Proposition (subtableau)

For any tableaux T and T',

if $T' \subseteq T$
then, for any interpretation $\mathcal{I}$,
if T' is true under $\mathcal{I}$
then T is true under $\mathcal{I}$. ◢

Definition (union of tableaux)

The *union* $T_1 \cup T_2$ of two tableaux T_1 and T_2 is the tableau whose rows are all the rows of T_1 and all the rows of T_2. ◢

Proposition (union tableau)

For any tableaux T_1 and T_2 and any interpretation $\mathcal{I}$,

$T_1 \cup T_2$ is true under $\mathcal{I}$
if and only if
T_1 is true under $\mathcal{I}$ or
T_2 is true under $\mathcal{I}$. ◢

Proposition (intermediate tableau)

For any tableaux T_1, T_2, and T_3,

if $T_1 \subseteq T_2 \subseteq T_3$

then, if T_1 is equivalent to T_3,

then T_1 is equivalent to T_2 and T_2 is equivalent to T_3. ⌐

We omit the proofs, which are similar to their propositional-logic counterparts.

As a consequence of the *intermediate-tableau* property, we observe that if we can add a certain number of rows to a tableau while preserving its equivalence, we can add only a portion of those rows and still preserve its equivalence.

We extend the notion of agreement to tableaux.

Definition (agreement)

We say that two interpretations $\mathcal{I}$ and $\mathcal{J}$ *agree* on a tableau T if

T is true under $\mathcal{I}$

if and only if

T is true under $\mathcal{J}$.

In other words, T has the same truth-value under $\mathcal{I}$ and under $\mathcal{J}$. ⌐

The following proposition relates the notions of agreement for symbols and tableaux.

Proposition (agreement for tableaux)

If two interpretations $\mathcal{I}$ and $\mathcal{J}$ agree on all the constant, function, and predicate symbols of a tableau T, then they agree on T itself. ⌐

Note that it is possible for two interpretations $\mathcal{I}$ and $\mathcal{J}$ to agree on a tableau T even if they do not agree on all the constant, function, and predicate symbols of T.

5.2   BASIC PROPERTIES

The properties we have established for propositional-logic tableaux carry over to predicate-logic tableaux. In particular, the *implied-row* and *duality* properties of propositional-logic tableaux have their counterparts in predicate logic. In addition, we have special properties for predicate logic such as the *renaming* and *instantiation* properties. We do not include the properties as deduction rules in our deductive system, but rather use them to justify deduction rules.

IMPLIED-ROW PROPERTY

The *implied-row* property for predicate logic reflects the corresponding property of propositional-logic tableaux.

Proposition (implied row)

Assertion part

Suppose the universal closure of a sentence $\mathcal{A}$ is implied by the universal closures of all the assertions $\mathcal{A}_1, \ldots, \mathcal{A}_m$ of a tableau $\mathcal{T}$; that is,

(†)
$$if \quad (\forall *)\mathcal{A}_1 \quad and \quad \ldots \quad and \quad (\forall *)\mathcal{A}_m$$
$$then \quad (\forall *)\mathcal{A}$$

is valid. Then $\mathcal{T}$ is equivalent to the tableau $\mathcal{T}_\mathcal{A}$ obtained from $\mathcal{T}$ by introducing the new assertion

$\mathcal{A}$	

Goal part

Similarly, suppose the existential closure of a sentence $\mathcal{G}$ implies the existential closures of some of the goals $\mathcal{G}_1, \ldots, \mathcal{G}_n$ of the tableau $\mathcal{T}$; that is,

(‡)
$$if \quad (\exists *)\mathcal{G}$$
$$then \quad (\exists *)\mathcal{G}_1 \quad or \quad \ldots \quad or \quad (\exists *)\mathcal{G}_n$$

is valid. Then $\mathcal{T}$ is equivalent to the tableau $\mathcal{T}_\mathcal{G}$ obtained from $\mathcal{T}$ by introducing the new goal

	$\mathcal{G}$

Remark (valid assertions and contradictory goals).   As in propositional logic, the *implied-row* property tells us that we may add to the tableau as an assertion any sentence whose universal closure is valid; similarly, we may add to the tableau as a goal any sentence whose existential closure is contradictory (i.e., never true). In particular, we may add, or remove, the *trivial* assertion

true	

or the trivial goal

	false

Equivalence of the tableau is preserved in each case.

Proof (implied row).   We prove only the *assertion* part. Under a given interpretation,

the tableau $\mathcal{T}$ is false

if and only if (by the semantic rule for tableaux)

> the universal closures $(\forall *)\mathcal{A}_1, \ldots, (\forall *)\mathcal{A}_m$ of the assertions of $\mathcal{T}$ are true
>> and
>
> the existential closures $(\exists *)\mathcal{G}_1, \ldots, (\exists *)\mathcal{G}_n$ of the goals of $\mathcal{T}$ are false

if and only if (by (†))

> the universal closures $(\forall *)\mathcal{A}_1, \ldots, (\forall *)\mathcal{A}_m$, and $(\forall *)\mathcal{A}$ of the assertions of $\mathcal{T}_\mathcal{A}$ are true
>> and
>
> the existential closures $(\exists *)\mathcal{G}_1, \ldots, (\exists *)\mathcal{G}_n$ of the goals of $\mathcal{T}_\mathcal{A}$ are false

if and only if (by the semantic rule for tableaux, again)

> the tableau $\mathcal{T}_\mathcal{A}$ is false.

In short, under any interpretation, $\mathcal{T}$ is false if and only if $\mathcal{T}_\mathcal{A}$ is false. Hence the two tableaux are equivalent.

The *goal* part is proved similarly. ◢

DUALITY PROPERTY

Predicate-logic tableaux exhibit the same *duality* property as propositional-logic tableaux.

Proposition (duality)

> A tableau containing an assertion $\mathcal{A}$
>> is equivalent to
>
> the tableau containing instead the goal (*not* $\mathcal{A}$).
>> > (*assertion-to-goal*)
>
> A tableau containing a goal $\mathcal{G}$
>> is equivalent to
>
> the tableau containing instead the assertion (*not* $\mathcal{G}$).
>> > (*goal-to-assertion*) ◢

Proof.   We prove only the *assertion-to-goal* part. Observe that, under a given interpretation,

> the original tableau (containing $\mathcal{A}$ as an assertion) is false

if and only if (by the semantic rule for tableaux)

> $(\forall *)\mathcal{A}$ is true,
> the universal closures of all the other assertions are true,
> and the existential closures of all the goals are false

if and only if (by the *duality* part of the *equivalences-of-closures* proposition in Section 3.7)

> the universal closures of all the other assertions are true,
> $(\exists *)(not\ \mathcal{A})$ is false,
> and the existential closures of all the goals are false

if and only if (by the semantic rule for tableaux)

> the new tableau (containing $(not\ \mathcal{A})$ as a goal) is false.

Thus the original tableau (containing $\mathcal{A}$ as an assertion) is false under a given interpretation $\mathcal{I}$ if and only if the new tableau (containing $(not\ \mathcal{A})$ as a goal) is false under $\mathcal{I}$; that is, the two tableaux are equivalent.

The *goal-to-assertion* part is proved similarly. ⌐

Remark (replacing versus adding rows).   Note that the *duality* property allows us to replace one row with another, preserving the equivalence of the tableau. In fact, as in propositional logic, the property also allows us to add the new row without replacing the original one. To see this, we observe that, by the *implied-row* property, we may make an additional copy of the original row, preserving equivalence. We may then (by the *duality* property) replace only one of the two copies. A similar remark applies to any other property that allows us to replace rows. ⌐

RENAMING PROPERTY

The free variables of an assertion or goal of a tableau are "dummies." The *renaming* property states that we may systematically rename the free variables of any row, obtaining an equivalent tableau.

To express this property, we define the notion of a renaming substitution.

Definition (renaming substitution)

> A substitution ρ is a *renaming* on a sentence $\mathcal{F}$ if
>
> > for every variable x, $x\rho$ is also a variable
> > and
> > for all free variables x, y of $\mathcal{F}$, if x and y are
> > distinct then so are $x\rho$ and $y\rho$. ⌐

Example.   The substitution $\{x \leftarrow y\}$ is a renaming on the sentence $p(x)$ but not on the sentence $q(x, y)$. In the latter case, there are two free variables of $q(x, y)$, that is, x and y, such that x and y are distinct but $x\{x \leftarrow y\}$ and $y\{x \leftarrow y\}$ are the same variable y. ⌐

Proposition (renaming)

For any renaming substitution ρ on a sentence $\mathcal{A}$ [or $\mathcal{G}$],

a tableau containing an assertion $\mathcal{A}$ [or goal $\mathcal{G}$]
is equivalent to
the tableau containing instead the assertion $\mathcal{A}\rho$ [or goal $\mathcal{G}\rho$]. ◢

Recall that $\mathcal{A}\rho$ and $\mathcal{G}\rho$ stand for the result of a total safe substitution; therefore, we may have to rename bound variables in $\mathcal{A}$ and $\mathcal{G}$ to avoid capturing during the substitution process.

Example. Suppose a tableau contains the goal

assertions	goals
	$\mathcal{G}: \quad p(x) \quad and \quad (\forall y)q(x, y)$

and suppose we would like to rename x to y in $\mathcal{G}$. We thus take ρ to be

$\{x \leftarrow y\}$.

This is a renaming on $\mathcal{G}$.

The given tableau is equivalent to the altered tableau that contains, instead of $\mathcal{G}$, the goal

	$\mathcal{G}\rho: \quad p(y) \quad and \quad (\forall y')q(y, y')$

Here the variable y of the quantifier $(\forall y)$ has been renamed y' to avoid capturing. ◢

INSTANTIATION PROPERTY

The *instantiation* property states that we may add to the tableau any instance of any of its rows, obtaining an equivalent tableau. That is, we may replace all free occurrences of a variable in any row with an arbitrary term and add the new row to the tableau.

Proposition (instantiation)

For a substitution

$$\theta = \{x_1 \leftarrow t_1, \ x_2 \leftarrow t_2, \ \ldots, \ x_k \leftarrow t_k\}$$

that replaces distinct variables with terms,

> a tableau containing an assertion $\mathcal{A}$ [or goal $\mathcal{G}$]
>> is equivalent to
> the tableau containing in addition the assertion $\mathcal{A}\theta$ [or goal $\mathcal{G}\theta$]. ⌐

Recall that $\mathcal{A}\theta$ and $\mathcal{G}\theta$ stand for the result of a total safe substitution. In other words, all free occurrences of x_i are safely replaced by t_i in $\mathcal{A}$ [or in $\mathcal{G}$], and we may have to rename variables in $\mathcal{A}$ [or in $\mathcal{G}$] to avoid capturing during the substitution process.

Note that this property, in contrast to the *duality* and *renaming* properties, allows us to add a new row but not to replace an old one.

First let us illustrate the property with some examples; afterwards we justify the property.

Example.   If a tableau contains an assertion

assertions	goals
$\mathcal{A}:$ $\Big(p(x)\ \ and\ \ q(x,\,y,\,a)\Big)\ \ or\ \ r(u)$	

and θ is the substitution

$$\{x \leftarrow f(z),\ y \leftarrow b\},$$

then we may add the new assertion

$\mathcal{A}\theta:$ $\Big(p(f(z))\ \ and\ \ q(f(z),\,b,\,a)\Big)\ \ or\ \ r(u)$	

to the tableau; the new tableau is equivalent to the given tableau. ⌐

Example.   If a tableau contains a goal

assertions	goals
	$\mathcal{G}:$ $(\exists z)\big[q(x,\,z)\ \ and\ \ r(z,\,y)\big]$

and θ is the substitution

$$\{x \leftarrow f(x,\,y,\,z)\},$$

then we may add the new goal

	$\mathcal{G}\theta:\quad (\exists z')\big[q(f(x,\, y,\, z),\, z')\ \ and\ \ r(z',\, y)\big]$

to the tableau; the new tableau is equivalent to the given tableau. Note that we have renamed the variable z of the quantifier $(\exists z)$ as z' to avoid capturing the variable z in the substitution. ◢

Now let us justify the property.

Proof (instantiation).   We first justify the assertion case. The *universal* part of the *closure-instantiation* proposition (Section 3.10) states that, for any distinct variables $x_1, x_2, \ldots, x_k$, sentence $\mathcal{A}[x_1, x_2, \ldots, x_k]$, and terms $t_1, t_2, \ldots, t_k$, the sentence

$$if\ \ (\forall *)\mathcal{A}[x_1,\, x_2,\, \ldots,\, x_k]$$
$$then\ \ (\forall *)\mathcal{A}[t_1,\, t_2,\, \ldots,\, t_k]$$

is valid. That is, for the substitution

$$\theta\ =\ \{x_1 \leftarrow t_1,\, x_2 \leftarrow t_2,\, \ldots,\, x_k \leftarrow t_k\},$$

the sentence

$$if\ \ (\forall *)\mathcal{A}$$
$$then\ \ (\forall *)(\mathcal{A}\theta)$$

is valid. Therefore (by the *implied-row* property), the assertion $\mathcal{A}\theta$ may be added to the tableau, preserving equivalence.

The goal case may be proved in a similar way. We use the *existential* part of the *closure-instantiation* proposition to show that

$$if\ \ (\exists *)(\mathcal{G}\theta)$$
$$then\ \ (\exists *)\mathcal{G}$$

is a valid sentence. We then use the *implied-row* property to justify introducing the new goal $\mathcal{G}\theta$.

Alternatively, we may use the assertion case and the *duality* property to justify the goal case. ◢

Remark (**adding versus replacing rows**).   We have remarked that the *instantiation* property does not allow us to replace any row, but only to add a new one. In fact, if we were to delete the assertion $\mathcal{A}$ [or goal $\mathcal{G}$], we might not preserve equivalence.

For example, suppose a tableau consists of the single goal

assertions	goals
	$p(x)$.

The sentence associated with this tableau is

$$\mathcal{S}_1 : \quad (\exists x)p(x).$$

Now suppose we applied the *instantiation* property incorrectly and deleted the goal $p(x)$, introducing in its place the instance $p(a)$. The tableau we obtain consists of the single goal

assertions	goals
	$p(a)$

The sentence associated with this tableau is

$$\mathcal{S}_2 : \quad p(a).$$

Because the sentences associated with these tableaux are not equivalent, the two tableaux are not equivalent either. ◢

JUSTIFICATION CONDITION

In the following sections, we introduce deduction rules for predicate-logic tableaux analogous to the propositional-logic deduction rules. In propositional logic, we required that our rules preserve the equivalence of the tableau. In predicate logic, on the other hand, we say that a rule is *sound* if it merely preserves the validity of the tableau to which it is applied. Of course, if a rule preserves equivalence it also preserves validity, but in predicate logic we shall require a rule to preserve validity but not necessarily equivalence.

In this section, we develop the justification condition for determining whether a predicate-logic deduction rule is sound.

Recall that the *required rows* (assertions and goals) are those rows that must be present in the *old tableau* for a deduction rule to be applied, and the *generated rows* (assertions and goals) are those that are added to the tableau by the rule, to form the *new tableau*. In applying a deduction rule, we always add rows, never delete them.

In the tableau notation, we write a rule in the form

	assertions	goals
$\mathcal{T}_r$:		
$\mathcal{T}_g$:		

where the required rows are those that appear above the double line, and the generated rows are those that appear below the double line. The required rows form the *required subtableau*, denoted by T_r, and the generated rows form the *generated subtableau*, denoted by T_g.

The deduction rule is applied only if the required subtableau T_r occurs as part of the old tableau T_o, that is, $T_r \subseteq T_o$. The new tableau T_n is obtained by adding the generated subtableau to the old tableau, that is, $T_n = T_o \cup T_g$.

The following *justification* proposition will be used to establish the *soundness* of a deduction rule. In other words, it allows us to prove that, by applying a deduction rule, validity is preserved, i.e., the new tableau is valid if and only if the old tableau is valid.

Proposition (general justification)

A deduction rule is sound (i.e., preserves validity) if the following (*general*) *justification condition* holds:

For every interpretation $\mathcal{I}$ and tableau T_o,

if the required subtableau T_r is false under $\mathcal{I}$,

then the generated subtableau T_g is false under some interpretation $\mathcal{I}'$,
where $\mathcal{I}$ and $\mathcal{I}'$ agree on the tableau T_o. ◢

In other words, if the *justification* condition holds, the rule preserves the validity of the tableau to which it is applied.

Proof. We want to show that the new tableau T_n, formed by adding the generated rows, is valid if and only if the old tableau T_o is valid. We actually show that T_n is not valid, i.e., is false under some interpretation if and only if T_o is not valid, i.e., is false under some (perhaps different) interpretation. We prove each direction separately.

One direction is true whether or not the *justification* condition is satisfied. We suppose that $T_n = T_o \cup T_g$ is false under some interpretation $\mathcal{I}$ and show that then T_o is false under the same interpretation $\mathcal{I}$. Since T_o is a subtableau of T_n, that follows from the *subtableau* property.

The other direction makes use of the *justification* condition. We assume that the *justification* condition is satisfied, suppose that T_o is false under some interpretation $\mathcal{I}$, and show that then T_n is false under some interpretation $\mathcal{I}'$. Since T_o is false, its required subtableau T_r is false under $\mathcal{I}$ (by the *subtableau* property). Therefore, by the *justification* condition, there exists some interpretation $\mathcal{I}'$ such that the generated subtableau T_g is false under $\mathcal{I}'$, where $\mathcal{I}$ and $\mathcal{I}'$ agree on T_o.

Because, by our supposition, T_o is false under $\mathcal{I}$, it follows that T_o is false under $\mathcal{I}'$.

Therefore (by the *union* property of tableaux), the new tableau T_n, that is, $T_o \cup T_g$, is false under $\mathcal{I}'$. ◢

In order to justify a deduction rule, it suffices to take $\mathcal{I}'$ to be $\mathcal{I}$ itself and show the following special case.

Proposition (special justification)

A deduction rule preserves the equivalence of any tableau to which it is applied if the following *special justification condition* holds:

For every interpretation $\mathcal{I}$,

if the required subtableau $\mathcal{T}_r$ is false under $\mathcal{I}$,
then the generated subtableau $\mathcal{T}_g$ is false under $\mathcal{I}$. ∎

Note that the *general justification* condition guarantees only the weak property of preserving validity, i.e., the new tableau is valid if and only if the old tableau is valid. On the other hand, the *special justification* condition guarantees the stronger property of preserving equivalence, i.e., the new tableau is equivalent to the old tableau.

In predicate logic, all the deduction rules, with one exception (the ∀-*elimination* rule) have the property of preserving equivalence. This will be shown in the following sections, using the preceding *special justification* condition. The ∀-*elimination* rule does not necessarily preserve equivalence, but it has the weaker property of preserving validity. To justify this rule, we will use the *general justification* condition.

5.3 THE DEDUCTIVE PROCESS

We now give an overview of the deductive-tableau system for predicate logic.

OUTLINE OF THE DEDUCTIVE SYSTEM

The deductive system for predicate logic is modeled on the propositional-logic system. As before, to *prove* the validity of a given (closed) sentence $\mathcal{S}$,

- We form the *initial tableau* whose sole goal is the (simplified) sentence $\mathcal{S}$. We may include as assertions any sentences that have previously been proven valid.
- The tableau is developed by applying *deduction rules* successively; each rule adds one or more rows to the tableau, in such a way that validity is preserved.
- The process continues until the final assertion *false* or the final goal *true* appears in the tableau.

Because the final tableau is valid and the deduction rules preserve validity, we have thus established the validity of the initial tableau and, therefore, of the given sentence S. We shall say that the final tableau is a *proof* of both the initial tableau and of the sentence S. Any sentence that has a proof will be called a *theorem* of predicate logic.

We may add the theorem S as an assertion in all initial tableaux of subsequent predicate-logic proofs.

THE DEDUCTION RULES

The deduction rules for predicate logic are divided into five groups:

- The *rewriting* rule, which replaces a subsentence with an equivalent sentence.
- The *splitting* rules, which break a row down into its logical components.
- The *resolution* rule, which performs a case analysis on the truth of a subsentence.
- The *equivalence* rule, which facilitates our handling of the equivalence connective $\equiv$.
- The *quantifier-elimination* (*skolemization*) rules, which remove quantifiers from the assertions and goals. There are two such rules, $\forall$-*elimination* and $\exists$-*elimination*, for removing quantifiers of universal force and existential force, respectively.

The *splitting* rules are identical to the propositional-logic *splitting* rules. The *rewriting*, *resolution*, and *equivalence* rules are adapted from their propositional counterparts. The *skolemization* rules are entirely new.

Note that, unlike our propositional-logic deductive system, in predicate logic the new generated tableau is not necessarily equivalent to the old tableau. As we have remarked, the *rewriting*, *splitting*, *resolution*, *equivalence*, and $\exists$-*elimination* rules do preserve equivalence; the $\forall$-*elimination* rule does not preserve equivalence in general, but does preserve validity. Thus the deduction rules all preserve validity, which suffices to establish the correctness of our deductive process.

As in propositional logic, recall that duality is a property and not a rule. Therefore we may use duality to justify a rule but may not apply it as a rule. Similarly, the *implied-row*, *renaming*, and *instantiation* properties are not rules. We could have introduced these properties as rules without compromising the soundness of the system, but they are not necessary.

SIMPLIFICATION

Any assertion or goal introduced into a tableau is subject to an automatic simplification process, in which certain subsentences are replaced by equivalent but simpler subsentences. As in propositional logic, simplification is not regarded as a separate rule. Whenever we add a new row to a tableau, it is simplified as much as possible.

Examples of simplifications we had in propositional logic are the *not-not* simplification

$$not\ (not\ \mathcal{F})\ \Rightarrow\ \mathcal{F}$$

and the *and-false* simplification

$$\mathcal{F}\ and\ false\ \Rightarrow\ false.$$

We shall carry over all the simplifications of propositional logic (Section 1.9) into predicate logic. Also, we add the following simplifications for quantifiers and conditional terms:

- Redundant quantifier

$$(\forall x)\mathcal{F}\ \Rightarrow\ \mathcal{F} \qquad \text{if } x \text{ is not free in } \mathcal{F} \qquad\qquad (all)$$

$$(\exists x)\mathcal{F}\ \Rightarrow\ \mathcal{F} \qquad \text{if } x \text{ is not free in } \mathcal{F} \qquad\qquad (some)$$

- Conditional term

$$if\ true\ then\ s\ else\ t\ \Rightarrow\ s \qquad\qquad (cond\text{-}term\ true)$$

$$if\ false\ then\ s\ else\ t\ \Rightarrow\ t \qquad\qquad (cond\text{-}term\ false)$$

$$if\ \mathcal{F}\ then\ s\ else\ s\ \Rightarrow\ s \qquad\qquad (cond\text{-}term\ two)$$

Note that, in the redundant-quantifier simplifications, x is intended to stand for any variable. Thus we can simplify $(\exists y)p(a)$ to $p(a)$. Also, in the conditional-term simplifications, both sides of each simplification are terms. In applying these simplifications, we are replacing a subterm with another term, not a subsentence with another sentence. By the semantic rule for the conditional term constructor, these terms will have the same value under any interpretation; hence the assertion or goal we obtain will be equivalent to the original assertion or goal.

Example. Suppose we are about to introduce into a tableau the assertion

$$\boxed{(\forall z)\,q(a,\,y)}\ \ and\ \ q(a,y).$$

We must first apply the *all* redundant-quantifier simplification to obtain the new sentence

$$\boxed{q(a,\,y)\ \ and\ \ q(a,\,y)}$$

We must then apply the *and-two* propositional simplification to obtain the new sentence

$$q(a,\,y),$$

which is added to the tableau as the assertion

$q(a, y)$	

Note that, according to the redundant-quantifier simplifications, we can perform such operations as replacing $(\forall x)true$ with *true* and $(\exists x)false$ with *false*. Also, any sentence of form $(\forall x)(\forall x)\mathcal{F}$ or $(\exists x)(\forall x)\mathcal{F}$ can be replaced by $(\forall x)\mathcal{F}$.

We now describe each of the deduction rules in turn.

5.4   REWRITING RULE

As in propositional logic, we introduce a *rewriting* rule that allows us to replace certain subsentences of a tableau with equivalent sentences. Each application of the rule replaces only a single subexpression occurrence. In contrast to simplification, rewriting does not always give us a sentence that is simpler and easier to prove. It is not applied automatically, but is considered to be a deduction rule, and is used only at our discretion. Also, we add the rewritten row to the tableau without deleting the original row.

Justification of the *rewriting* rule is straightforward because, by the substitutivity of equivalence, the new row is always equivalent to one of the existing rows. All the propositional-logic rewritings of Section 2.3 are permitted in predicate-logic tableaux. In addition, we include the following rewritings, which apply only to predicate-logic tableaux:

- Quantifier reversal

$$(\forall x)(\forall y)\mathcal{F} \quad \Leftrightarrow \quad (\forall y)(\forall x)\mathcal{F} \qquad\qquad (all)$$

$$(\exists x)(\exists y)\mathcal{F} \quad \Leftrightarrow \quad (\exists y)(\exists x)\mathcal{F} \qquad\qquad (some)$$

- Quantifier duality

$$not\ (\forall x)\mathcal{F} \quad \Leftrightarrow \quad (\exists x)(not\ \mathcal{F}) \qquad\qquad (not\ all)$$

$$not\ (\exists x)\mathcal{F} \quad \Leftrightarrow \quad (\forall x)(not\ \mathcal{F}) \qquad\qquad (not\ some)$$

- Quantifier manipulation

$$(\forall x)\big[\mathcal{F}\ and\ \mathcal{G}\big] \quad \Leftrightarrow \quad (\forall x)\mathcal{F}\ and\ (\forall x)\mathcal{G} \qquad\qquad (all\ and)$$

$$(\exists x)\big[\mathcal{F}\ or\ \mathcal{G}\big] \quad \Leftrightarrow \quad (\exists x)\mathcal{F}\ or\ (\exists x)\mathcal{G} \qquad\qquad (some\ or)$$

$$(\exists x)\big[if\ \mathcal{F}\ then\ \mathcal{G}\big] \quad \Leftrightarrow \quad if\ (\forall x)\mathcal{F}\ then\ (\exists x)\mathcal{G} \qquad\qquad (some\ if)$$

• Conditional manipulation

$p(\bar{r}, \text{ if } \mathcal{F} \text{ then } t_1 \text{ else } t_2, \bar{s}) \quad \Leftrightarrow \quad \text{if } \mathcal{F} \text{ then } p(\bar{r}, t_1, \bar{s}) \text{ else } p(\bar{r}, t_2, \bar{s})$

$$(predicate)$$

$f(\bar{r}, \text{ if } \mathcal{F} \text{ then } t_1 \text{ else } t_2, \bar{s}) \quad \Leftrightarrow \quad \text{if } \mathcal{F} \text{ then } f(\bar{r}, t_1, \bar{s}) \text{ else } f(\bar{r}, t_2, \bar{s})$

$$(function)$$

In the conditional-manipulation rewritings, p is a predicate symbol and f is a function symbol, and $\bar{r}$ and $\bar{s}$ stand for terms $r_1, \ldots, r_m$ and $s_1, \ldots, s_n$, respectively. Note that both sides of the *function* rewriting are terms. In applying this rewriting, we are replacing a subterm with another term. Also note that in the *predicate* rewriting, the left-hand *if-then-else* is the conditional (term) constructor, while the right-hand *if-then-else* is the conditional (sentence) connective.

5.5   SPLITTING RULES

Although the predicate-logic and propositional-logic *splitting* rules are identical, the predicate-logic rules require special justification because of the possible occurrence of free variables in the assertions and goals to which they are applied.

AND-SPLIT RULE

assertions	goals
$\mathcal{A}_1$ and $\mathcal{A}_2$	
$\mathcal{A}_1$	
$\mathcal{A}_2$	

OR-SPLIT RULE

assertions	goals
	$\mathcal{G}_1$ or $\mathcal{G}_2$
	$\mathcal{G}_1$
	$\mathcal{G}_2$

IF-SPLIT-RULE

assertions	goals
	if $\mathcal{A}$ *then* $\mathcal{G}$
$\mathcal{A}$	
	$\mathcal{G}$

Let us justify that the *if-split* rule indeed preserves equivalence, that is, that the new tableau is equivalent to the old tableau. The justifications of the other *splitting* rules are similar.

Justification (if-split).   By the *special justification* proposition, the special case of the *general justification* proposition, it suffices to show that, for any interpretation $\mathcal{I}$ under which the required tableau is false, that is, its associated sentence

$(\exists *)[if \ \mathcal{A} \ then \ \mathcal{G}]$

is false, the generated tableau is false, that is, its associated sentence

$if \ (\forall *)\mathcal{A} \ then \ (\exists *)\mathcal{G}$

is false, under $\mathcal{I}$. This follows from properties of closures (the *equivalences-of-closures* proposition, Section 3.7). ◢

5.6   RESOLUTION RULE

For propositional logic, the *resolution* rule allows us to derive from two assertions

$\mathcal{A}_1[\mathcal{P}]$ and $\mathcal{A}_2[\mathcal{P}]$,

with identical subsentences $\mathcal{P}$, a new assertion

$\mathcal{A}_1[true]$ *or* $\mathcal{A}_2[false]$.

Intuitively, a case analysis is performed on the truth of the common subsentence $\mathcal{P}$ of the two assertions. The extension of this rule to predicate logic allows us to draw a similar conclusion from two assertions with subsentences that are not necessarily identical but that are unifiable.

THE BASIC FORM

We first illustrate the rule.

Example.   Suppose our tableau contains the two assertions

assertions	goals
$\mathcal{A}_1$: $\boxed{p(a,\,y)}^{\,-}$ *or* $r(y)$	
$\mathcal{A}_2$: *if* $\boxed{p(x,\,b)}^{\,+}$ *then* $q(x)$	

The propositional-logic *resolution* rule could not be applied directly to these two assertions because they have no identical subsentences in common. If, however, we apply the substitution

$$\theta : \{x \leftarrow a,\ y \leftarrow b\}$$

to both rows, we obtain the two intermediate assertions

$$\mathcal{A}_1\theta : \quad \boxed{p(a,\,b)}^{\,-} \quad or \quad r(b)$$

and

$$\mathcal{A}_2\theta : \quad if \quad \boxed{p(a,\,b)}^{\,+} \quad then \quad q(a).$$

These assertions can be added to the tableau, by the *instantiation* property, without altering its validity. They have the common subsentence $p(a, b)$; therefore, now we can apply the propositional version of the *resolution* rule directly, obtaining the intermediate sentence

$$false \quad or \quad r(b)$$
$$or$$
$$if \quad true \quad then \quad q(a),$$

which reduces (under *true-false* simplification) to the new assertion

$r(b)$ *or* $q(a)$	

The predicate-logic *resolution* rule allows us to apply the substitution θ and the propositional version of the rule in a single step, without adding the intermediate assertions. The rule also allows us to replace several distinct subsentences $\mathcal{P}_1,\ \ldots,\ \mathcal{P}_k,\ k \geq 1$, of the given rows $\mathcal{A}_1$ and $\mathcal{A}_2$, if these subsentences become identical on application of θ.

The basic form of the *resolution* rule is expressed as follows.

Rule (AA-resolution)

assertions	goals
$\mathcal{A}_1[\mathcal{P}_1, \ldots, \mathcal{P}_k]$	
$\mathcal{A}_2[\mathcal{P}'_1, \ldots, \mathcal{P}'_\ell]$	
$\mathcal{A}_1\theta[false, \ldots, false]$ *or* $\mathcal{A}_2\theta[true, \ldots, true]$	

where

- $\mathcal{P}_1, \ldots, \mathcal{P}_k$ ($k \geq 1$) are free, quantifier-free subsentences that occur in $\mathcal{A}_1$.

- $\mathcal{P}'_1, \ldots, \mathcal{P}'_\ell$ ($\ell \geq 1$) are free, quantifier-free subsentences that occur in $\mathcal{A}_2$.

- The free variables of $\mathcal{A}_1$ and $\mathcal{A}_2$ are renamed so that the rows have no free variables in common.

- θ is a most-general unifier for the tuple of subsentences $\langle \mathcal{P}_1, \ldots, \mathcal{P}_k, \mathcal{P}'_1, \ldots, \mathcal{P}'_\ell \rangle$. ◢

More precisely, to apply the *AA-resolution* rule to two assertions $\mathcal{A}_1$ and $\mathcal{A}_2$ of a tableau:

- Rename the variables of $\mathcal{A}_1$ and $\mathcal{A}_2$ if necessary to ensure that they have no free variables in common.

- Choose some free, quantifier-free subsentences $\mathcal{P}_1, \ldots, \mathcal{P}_k$ ($k \geq 1$) of $\mathcal{A}_1$ and free, quantifier-free subsentences $\mathcal{P}'_1 \ldots, \mathcal{P}'_\ell$ ($\ell \geq 1$) of $\mathcal{A}_2$ such that they are all unifiable by a most-general unifier θ; that is,

$$\mathcal{P}_1\theta, \ldots, \mathcal{P}_k\theta \quad \text{and} \quad \mathcal{P}'_1\theta, \ldots, \mathcal{P}'_\ell\theta$$

  are all the same sentence, which we shall call $\mathcal{P}\theta$. (Note that we invoke the *tuple-unification* algorithm of Section 4.8.)

- Apply θ safely to the two assertions $\mathcal{A}_1$ and $\mathcal{A}_2$; then replace all free occurrences of $\mathcal{P}\theta$ in $\mathcal{A}_1\theta$ with the truth symbol *false* and all free occurrences of $\mathcal{P}\theta$ in $\mathcal{A}_2\theta$ with the truth symbol *true*, obtaining the disjuncts $\mathcal{A}_1\theta[false, \ldots, false]$ and $\mathcal{A}_2\theta[true, \ldots, true]$, respectively. (Note that we use the combined substitution notation of Section 4.8.)

- Simplify the disjunction

$$\mathcal{A}_1\theta[false, \ldots, false] \quad or \quad \mathcal{A}_2\theta[true, \ldots, true].$$

- Add the simplified disjunction to the tableau as a new assertion.

We may find it convenient to write the *resolution* rule in the following abbreviated notation.

assertions	goals
$\mathcal{A}_1[\overline{\mathcal{P}}]$	
$\mathcal{A}_2[\overline{\mathcal{P}'}]$	
$\mathcal{A}_1\theta[\overline{\mathit{false}}]$ *or* $\mathcal{A}_2\theta[\overline{\mathit{true}}]$	

Here

- $\overline{\mathcal{P}}$ stands for $\mathcal{P}_1, \ldots, \mathcal{P}_k$.
- $\overline{\mathcal{P}}'$ stands for $\mathcal{P}'_1, \ldots, \mathcal{P}'_\ell$.
- $\overline{\mathit{false}}$ stands for $\mathit{false}, \ldots, \mathit{false}$ (k times).
- $\overline{\mathit{true}}$ stands for $\mathit{true}, \ldots, \mathit{true}$ (ℓ times).

Henceforth we shall use this abbreviated notation in presenting other rules.

We will say that the new assertion is a *resolvent*, obtained by *applying the resolution rule to* the assertions $\mathcal{A}_1[\overline{\mathcal{P}}]$ and $\mathcal{A}_2[\overline{\mathcal{P}'}]$, *matching* $\overline{\mathcal{P}}$ *and* $\overline{\mathcal{P}'}$, *with* θ.

Although the total substitution notation does not imply that the subsentences $\overline{\mathcal{P}}$ occur in $\mathcal{A}_1[\overline{\mathcal{P}}]$ or that the subsentences $\overline{\mathcal{P}'}$ occur in $\mathcal{A}_2[\overline{\mathcal{P}'}]$, we require here that each subsentence occur at least once.

Reasons for the rule's various restrictions will be presented shortly.

DUAL FORMS

The dual forms of the rule are as follows.

Rule (GG-resolution)

assertions	goals
	$\mathcal{G}_1[\overline{\mathcal{P}}]$
	$\mathcal{G}_2[\overline{\mathcal{P}'}]$
	$\mathcal{G}_1\theta[\overline{\mathit{false}}]$ *and* $\mathcal{G}_2\theta[\overline{\mathit{true}}]$

where $\mathcal{G}_1$ and $\mathcal{G}_2$ satisfy the same conditions as $\mathcal{A}_1$ and $\mathcal{A}_2$, respectively, in the *AA-resolution* rule. ◢

Rule (AG-resolution)

assertions	goals
$\mathcal{A}[\overline{\mathcal{P}}]$	
	$\mathcal{G}[\overline{\mathcal{P}'}]$
	$not\ (\mathcal{A}\theta[\overline{false}])$ *and* $\mathcal{G}\theta[\overline{true}]$

where $\mathcal{A}$ and $\mathcal{G}$ satisfy the same conditions as $\mathcal{A}_1$ and $\mathcal{A}_2$, respectively, in the *AA-resolution* rule. ◢

Rule (GA-resolution)

assertions	goals
	$\mathcal{G}[\overline{\mathcal{P}}]$
$\mathcal{A}[\overline{\mathcal{P}'}]$	
	$\mathcal{G}\theta[\overline{false}]$ *and* $not\ (\mathcal{A}\theta[\overline{true}])$

where $\mathcal{G}$ and $\mathcal{A}$ satisfy the same conditions as $\mathcal{A}_1$ and $\mathcal{A}_2$, respectively, in the *AA-resolution* rule. ◢

POLARITY STRATEGY

The *polarity* strategy we introduced for the propositional-logic *resolution* rule can be applied also to the predicate-logic rule.

Strategy (polarity)

Suppose that $\mathcal{F}_1[\overline{\mathcal{P}}]$ and $\mathcal{F}_2[\overline{\mathcal{P}'}]$ are two assertions or goals in a tableau with free, quantifier-free subsentences, respectively,

$$\overline{\mathcal{P}} = \mathcal{P}_1,\ \ldots,\mathcal{P}_k \quad \text{and} \quad \overline{\mathcal{P}'} = \mathcal{P}'_1,\ \ldots,\mathcal{P}'_\ell.$$

Assume that the *resolution* rule has been applied to $\mathcal{F}_1[\overline{\mathcal{P}}]$ and $\mathcal{F}_2[\overline{\mathcal{P}'}]$, replacing every occurrence of $\mathcal{P}\theta$ in $\mathcal{F}_1\theta$ with *false* and replacing every occurrence of $\mathcal{P}\theta$ in $\mathcal{F}_2\theta$ with *true*.

Then we will say that the rule has been applied in accordance with the *polarity strategy* if

> at least one of the subsentences $\mathcal{P}_1, \ldots, \mathcal{P}_k$ of $\mathcal{F}_1$ (whose instances are replaced by *false* in applying the rule) is of negative polarity in the tableau

and

> at least one of the subsentences $\mathcal{P}'_1, \ldots, \mathcal{P}'_\ell$ of $\mathcal{F}_2$ (whose instances are replaced by *true* in applying the rule) is of positive polarity in the tableau.

These polarities need not be strict. ⌐

EXAMPLES

Before we justify the *resolution* rule, let us illustrate it with some more examples. We start with a simple example applying *AA-resolution* to two assertions $\mathcal{A}_1[\overline{\mathcal{P}}]$ and $\mathcal{A}_2[\overline{\mathcal{P}'}]$, where $\overline{\mathcal{P}}$ and $\overline{\mathcal{P}'}$ are each a single subsentence.

Example.   Suppose that our tableau contains the two assertions

assertions	goals
$\mathcal{A}_1[\mathcal{P}]:$ *if* $q(x,z)$ *then* $\boxed{p(a) \ \ and \ \ q(y,x)}$ $^-$	
$\mathcal{A}_2[\mathcal{P}']:$ $\left(not \ \boxed{p(x) \ \ and \ \ q(x,f(x))} \ ^+ \right)$ *or* $r(x)$	

Here we annotate with boxes and polarities the subsentences $\mathcal{P}$ and $\mathcal{P}'$ to be matched when the *resolution* rule is applied.

These assertions have the free variable x in common. We can escape this coincidence, however, by renaming the variable x as $\widehat{x}$ in the first assertion $\mathcal{A}_1[\mathcal{P}]$, obtaining

$$\widehat{\mathcal{A}_1}[\widehat{\mathcal{P}}]: \quad if \ \ q(\widehat{x},z) \ \ then \ \ \boxed{p(a) \ \ and \ \ q(y,\widehat{x})} \ ^-$$

Consider the boxed subsentences

$$\widehat{\mathcal{P}}: \quad p(a) \ \ and \ \ q(y, \widehat{x})$$

of $\widehat{\mathcal{A}_1}$ and

$$\mathcal{P}': \quad p(x) \ \ and \ \ q(x, f(x))$$

of $\mathcal{A}_2$; these quantifier-free subsentences are free in $\widehat{\mathcal{A}}_1$ and $\mathcal{A}_2$, respectively. Also, they are unifiable, with most-general unifier

$$\theta : \{x \leftarrow a, \ y \leftarrow a, \ \widehat{x} \leftarrow f(a)\}.$$

(Note that, had we not renamed the free variable x as $\widehat{x}$ in $\mathcal{A}_1$, the two subsentences would not have been unifiable.) The resulting common instance is

$$\mathcal{P}\theta : \quad p(a) \ \ and \ \ q\big(a, f(a)\big).$$

To apply the *AA-resolution* rule, we first obtain the intermediate sentences

$$\widehat{\mathcal{A}}_1\theta : \quad if \ \ q\big(f(a), z\big) \ \ then \ \ \boxed{p(a) \ \ and \ \ q(a, f(a))}^{\,-}$$

$$\mathcal{A}_2\theta : \quad \Big(not \ \boxed{p(a) \ \ and \ \ q(a, f(a))}^{\,+}\Big) \ \ or \ \ r(a).$$

We then apply the propositional version of the rule, matching

$$p(a) \ \ and \ \ q(a, f(a)),$$

to obtain the new assertion

$$if \ \ q(f(a), z) \ \ then \ \ false$$
$$\quad or$$
$$(not \ true) \ \ or \ \ r(a),$$

which reduces (by *true-false* simplification) to

$not \ q\big(f(a), \ z\big)$	
$\quad or$	
$r(a)$	

Note that we do not add the renamed assertion $\widehat{\mathcal{A}}_1$, the intermediate assertions $\widehat{\mathcal{A}}_1\theta$ and $\mathcal{A}_2\theta$, and the unsimplified resolvent to the tableau; we regard the (simplified) resolvent

$$not \ q\big(f(a), z\big)$$
$$\quad or$$
$$r(a)$$

as having been obtained directly by an application of the predicate-logic *resolution* rule to the assertions $\mathcal{A}_1$ and $\mathcal{A}_2$.

Note also that the preceding application of the *resolution* rule has been in accordance with the *polarity* strategy. ⌟

In the following example, we apply *GG-resolution* to two goals $\mathcal{G}_1$ and $\mathcal{G}_2$, emphasizing the possible need to rename variables to avoid capturing in applying the substitution θ to $\mathcal{G}_1$ and $\mathcal{G}_2$.

Example.　Suppose our tableau contains the two goals

assertions	goals
	$\mathcal{G}_1[\mathcal{P}]:$　not $\boxed{p(y)}$ $^-$
	$\mathcal{G}_2[\mathcal{P}']:$　$\boxed{p(x)}$ $^+$　and　$(\forall y)q(x,\,y)$

These goals have no free variables in common. The boxed quantifier-free subsentences

$$\mathcal{P}:\ p(y)\qquad\text{and}\qquad\mathcal{P}':\ p(x)$$

are free in $\mathcal{G}_1$ and $\mathcal{G}_2$, respectively. They are unifiable with most-general unifier

$$\theta:\ \{x \leftarrow y\}.$$

To apply the *GG-resolution* rule to $\mathcal{G}_1$ and $\mathcal{G}_2$, we first obtain the intermediate sentences

$$\mathcal{G}_1\theta:\quad not\ \boxed{p(y)}\ ^-$$

$$\mathcal{G}_2\theta:\quad \boxed{p(y)}\ ^+\ \text{and}\ (\forall y')q(y,\,y').$$

(Note that, in applying substitution θ safely to $\mathcal{G}_2$, we have renamed the variable of the quantifier $(\forall y)$ as y', to avoid capturing.) Then we form the goal

> *not false*
> *and*
> *true* and $(\forall y')q(y,\,y')$,

which reduces (by *true-false* simplification) to the resolvent

	$(\forall y')q(y,\,y')$

Note that this application of the *resolution* rule is in accordance with the *polarity* strategy.　◢

In the following example, we apply *AG-resolution* to an assertion $\mathcal{A}[\overline{\mathcal{P}}]$ and a goal $\mathcal{G}[\overline{\mathcal{P}'}]$, where $\overline{\mathcal{P}} = \mathcal{P}_1, \mathcal{P}_2$ in $\mathcal{A}$ and $\overline{\mathcal{P}'} = \mathcal{P}'_1, \mathcal{P}'_2$ in $\mathcal{G}$. This will illustrate the possibility of unifying more than one subsentence of each row.

Example.　Suppose our tableau contains the assertion and the goal

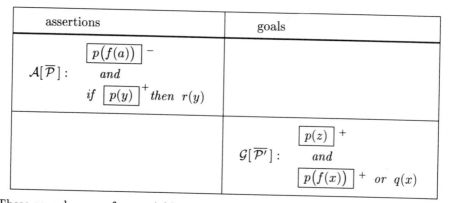

These rows have no free variables in common.

Consider the boxed quantifier-free subsentences

$$\mathcal{P}_1 : \ p\big(f(a)\big) \quad \text{and} \quad \mathcal{P}_2 : \ p(y),$$

which are free in $\mathcal{A}[\overline{\mathcal{P}}]$, and the boxed quantifier-free subsentences

$$\mathcal{P}'_1 : \ p(z) \quad \text{and} \quad \mathcal{P}'_2 : \ p\big(f(x)\big),$$

which are free in $\mathcal{G}[\overline{\mathcal{P}'}]$.

These four subsentences are unifiable, with most-general unifier

$$\theta : \ \{x \leftarrow a, \ y \leftarrow f(a), \ z \leftarrow f(a)\}.$$

Then, to apply AG-*resolution* to $\mathcal{A}$ and $\mathcal{G}$, we first obtain the intermediate assertion

$$\mathcal{A}\theta : \quad \boxed{p\big(f(a)\big)} \\ \text{and} \\ \textit{if} \ \boxed{p\big(f(a)\big)} \ \textit{then} \ r\big(f(a)\big)$$

and goal

$$\mathcal{G}\theta : \quad \boxed{p\big(f(a)\big)} \\ \text{and} \\ \boxed{p\big(f(a)\big)} \ \textit{or} \ q(a).$$

The conjunction

$$\textit{not} \ \mathcal{A}\theta[\overline{\textit{false}}] \\ \textit{and} \\ \mathcal{G}\theta[\overline{\textit{true}}]$$

is the goal

$$\textit{not} \ \Big(\textit{false} \ \textit{and} \ \big(\textit{if false then} \ r\big(f(a)\big)\big)\Big) \\ \textit{and} \\ \textit{true} \ \textit{and} \ \big(\textit{true or} \ q(a)\big),$$

which reduces (by *true-false* simplification) to the final goal

	true

Note that this application of the rule has been in accordance with the *polarity strategy*. Even though the occurrence of $p(y)$ in $\mathcal{A}$, whose instance is replaced by *false* in forming the resolvent, is positive in the tableau, the occurrence of $p(f(a))$ in $\mathcal{A}$, which is also replaced by *false*, is negative in the tableau. ⌙

The following example illustrates that the choice of subsentences to be unified makes a difference.

Example. In the previous example, suppose we had not selected the subsentence $p(f(x))$ to be unified. The annotated rows would then appear as follows:

assertions	goals
$\mathcal{A}:$ $\boxed{p(f(a))}^{\,-}$ and $if \; \boxed{p(y)}^{\,+} \; then \; r(y)$	
	$\mathcal{G}:$ $\boxed{p(z)}^{\,+}$ and $p(f(x)) \; or \; q(x)$

The most-general unifier for the three remaining annotated subsentences is

$$\theta: \; \{y \leftarrow f(a), \; z \leftarrow f(a)\}.$$

No replacement is made for x. Then, by application of the *AG-resolution* rule to $\mathcal{A}$ and $\mathcal{G}$, we obtain the intermediate sentence

$$not \begin{bmatrix} false \\ and \\ if \; false \; then \; r(f(a)) \end{bmatrix} \quad and \quad \begin{bmatrix} true \\ and \\ p(f(x)) \; or \; q(x) \end{bmatrix},$$

which reduces (under *true-false* simplification) to the goal

	$p(f(x)) \; or \; q(x)$

Thus, by neglecting to choose the subsentence $p(f(x))$, we failed to obtain the final goal *true* as before. ⌙

Remark (replace all occurrences).   Suppose our tableau contains the assertions

assertions	goals
$\mathcal{A}_1 :$ $\boxed{p(a)}^{\,-}$	
$\mathcal{A}_2 :$ *if* $\boxed{p(x)}^{\,+}$ *then* $p(a)$	

The boxed subsentences are unifiable under the most-general unifier

$$\theta : \ \{x \leftarrow a\}.$$

The unified subsentence is $p(a)$. In applying the rule, we must therefore replace all occurrences of $p(a)$ in $\mathcal{A}_1\theta$ and $\mathcal{A}_2\theta$ with a truth symbol.

As it turns out, $\mathcal{A}_2\theta$ contains an occurrence of $p(a)$ that does not correspond to a boxed subsentence in $\mathcal{A}_2$. This occurrence must be replaced with *true* in applying the rule, even though it was not selected initially to be replaced.   ◢

JUSTIFICATION

The *AA-resolution* rule actually preserves equivalence, not just validity. To justify it, we show that the new tableau (which includes the resolvent of $\mathcal{A}_1$ and $\mathcal{A}_2$) is equivalent to the old tableau (before the application of the rule). For this purpose, we may use the *special justification* proposition, rather than the *general justification* proposition. The justification of the other forms follows from the *duality* property.

Justification (AA-resolution).   Suppose $\mathcal{A}_1$ and $\mathcal{A}_2$ are two assertions in a tableau. If $\mathcal{A}_1$ and $\mathcal{A}_2$ have free variables in common, let ρ be a renaming of $\mathcal{A}_1$ such that $\mathcal{A}_1\rho$ and $\mathcal{A}_2$ no longer have free variables in common. By the *renaming* property, we may replace $\mathcal{A}_1$ with $\mathcal{A}_1\rho$ in the tableau, obtaining an equivalent tableau. So henceforth we may assume that our two assertions $\mathcal{A}_1$ and $\mathcal{A}_2$ have no free variables in common.

We now suppose that $\mathcal{A}_1$ and $\mathcal{A}_2$ satisfy all the restrictions for applying the *AA-resolution* rule. Consider an interpretation $\mathcal{I}$ under which the required tableau $\mathcal{T}_r$ is false, i.e., the universal closures of the required assertions $\mathcal{A}_1$ and $\mathcal{A}_2$ are both true under $\mathcal{I}$.

By the *special justification* proposition, it suffices to show that the generated tableau $\mathcal{T}_g$ is false under $\mathcal{I}$; that is, the universal closure of the generated resolvent, the disjunction

$$\mathcal{A}_1\theta[\,\overline{false}\,]$$
$$or$$
$$\mathcal{A}_2\theta[\,\overline{true}\,],$$

is true under $\mathcal{I}$.

Because the universal closures of $\mathcal{A}_1$ and $\mathcal{A}_2$ are assumed to be true, the universal closures of $\mathcal{A}_1\theta$ and $\mathcal{A}_2\theta$ are also true under $\mathcal{I}$, by the *universal closure-instantiation* proposition (Section 3.10). Therefore, by the *semantic-rule-for-universal-closure* proposition (Section 3.6), $\mathcal{A}_1\theta$ and $\mathcal{A}_2\theta$ are themselves true under any interpretation that agrees with $\mathcal{I}$ on the constant, function, and predicate symbols of $\mathcal{A}_1\theta$ and $\mathcal{A}_2\theta$. Let $\mathcal{I}'$ be any such interpretation.

The proof now distinguishes between two cases, depending on the truth-value of the unified subsentence $\mathcal{P}\theta$ under $\mathcal{I}'$.

Case: $\mathcal{P}\theta$ is true under $\mathcal{I}'$

Then, because $\mathcal{A}_2\theta$ is true under $\mathcal{I}'$ and because $\mathcal{P}\theta$ and the truth symbol *true* have the same truth-value under $\mathcal{I}'$,

$$\mathcal{A}_2\theta[\,\overline{true}\,]$$

is also true under $\mathcal{I}'$. It follows (by the semantic rule for the *or* connective) that the disjunction

$$\mathcal{A}_1\theta[\,\overline{false}\,]$$
$$or$$
$$\mathcal{A}_2\theta[\,\overline{true}\,]$$

is true under $\mathcal{I}'$.

Case: $\mathcal{P}\theta$ is false under $\mathcal{I}'$

Then, because $\mathcal{A}_1\theta$ is true under $\mathcal{I}'$ and because $\mathcal{P}\theta$ and the truth symbol *false* have the same truth-value under $\mathcal{I}'$,

$$\mathcal{A}_1\theta[\,\overline{false}\,]$$

is also true under $\mathcal{I}'$. It follows (by the semantic rule for the *or* connective) that the disjunction

$$\mathcal{A}_1\theta[\,\overline{false}\,]$$
$$or$$
$$\mathcal{A}_2\theta[\,\overline{true}\,]$$

is true under $\mathcal{I}'$.

In each case, we have concluded that the generated resolvent, i.e., the disjunction

$$\mathcal{A}_1\theta[\,\overline{false}\,]$$
$$or$$
$$\mathcal{A}_2\theta[\,\overline{true}\,],$$

is true under $\mathcal{I}'$, for any interpretation $\mathcal{I}'$ that agrees with $\mathcal{I}$ on the constant, function, and predicate symbols of $\mathcal{A}_1\theta$ and $\mathcal{A}_2\theta$, and hence of the resolvent.

Therefore (by the *semantic-rule-for-universal-closure* proposition) the universal closure of the resolvent is true under $\mathcal{I}$, as we wanted to show.

The generated resolvent is simplified before being introduced into the tableau, but, as usual, the resolvent before simplification is equivalent to the resolvent afterwards.

This concludes the justification of the *AA-resolution* rule. ⌐

WHY DO WE NEED THE CONDITIONS?

The side conditions required by the *resolution* rule, that the rows have no free variables in common, that the subsentences are free and quantifier-free, and that the unifier is most general, are necessary. Let us consider the consequences if not all of these conditions are satisfied.

Suppose that the assertions $\mathcal{A}_1$ and $\mathcal{A}_2$ have free variables in common. In this case, a failure to rename the common free variables will never allow us to draw an unjustifiable conclusion. It may prevent us, however, from finding sets of unifiable subsentences $\mathcal{P}$ and $\mathcal{P}'$ and deriving useful resolvents. A simple example is as follows.

Example (common free variables).   Suppose that our tableau contains the assertion and the goal

assertions	goals
$\mathcal{A}:$ $\boxed{p\big(f(x)\big)}$ $^-$	
	$\mathcal{G}:$ $\boxed{p(x)}$ $^+$

We cannot apply the *resolution* rule at once because $p(f(x))$ and $p(x)$ are not unifiable. It is only an unfortunate accident, however, that the free variable x is used in both of these rows. If we rename the free variable of $\mathcal{A}$ as $\widehat{x}$, we obtain the new assertion

$\widehat{\mathcal{A}}:$ $\boxed{p\big(f(\widehat{x})\big)}$ $^-$

We can then unify the subexpressions $p(f(\widehat{x}))$ and $p(x)$, taking the most-general unifier θ to be $\{x \leftarrow f(\widehat{x})\}$. Therefore we can apply *AG-resolution* to $\mathcal{A}$ and $\mathcal{G}$, obtaining the new goal

not false
   and
true,

which reduces (by *true-false* simplification) to the final goal

	true

⌐

Even if common free variables do not block the *resolution* rule altogether, they may cause us to obtain a resolvent that is less general than we could have reached otherwise. We illustrate this with another example.

Example (common free variables).   Suppose that our tableau contains the assertions

assertions	goals
$\mathcal{A}_1:$ $\boxed{p(a)}^-$ *or* $q(x)$	
$\mathcal{A}_2:$ $\left(not\,\boxed{p(a)}^+\right)$ *or* $r(x)$	

Note that the assertions have the free variable x in common. The boxed subsentences $p(a)$ of $\mathcal{A}_1$ and of $\mathcal{A}_2$ are unifiable, taking the most-general unifier θ to be the empty substitution $\{\ \}$.

If we fail to rename x in these assertions, we obtain (by *AA-resolution*) the assertion

false or $q(x)$
    or
(*not true*) *or* $r(x)$,

which reduces (by *true-false* simplification) to the assertion

$\boxed{q(x)\ or\ r(x)}^-$	

which is certainly a valid conclusion to draw.

If we rename the free variable x as $\widehat{x}$ in $\mathcal{A}_1$, however, yielding the assertion

$\widehat{\mathcal{A}_1}:$ $\boxed{p(a)}^-$ *or* $q(\widehat{x})$

then we can obtain the more general (and hence more useful) resolvent

$\boxed{q(\widehat{x})\ or\ r(x)}^-$	

Such a failure to draw the most general possible conclusion can lead to a failure to complete a proof. For instance, if our tableau also happens to contain the goal

	$\boxed{q(a) \ \ or \ \ r(b)}$ +

then we can apply *AG-resolution* to the more general resolvent

$\quad q(\widehat{x}) \ \ or \ \ r(x),$

and the goal

$\quad q(a) \ \ or \ \ r(b),$

taking the most-general unifier θ to be $\{\widehat{x} \leftarrow a, \ x \leftarrow b\}$, to obtain the final goal

	true

If, however, we have obtained only the less general resolvent

$\quad\quad q(x) \ \ or \ \ r(x),$

we cannot unify this assertion with the goal. ∎

Suppose one or more of the unifiable subsentences $\overline{\mathcal{P}} = \mathcal{P}_1, \ldots, \mathcal{P}_k$ and $\overline{\mathcal{P}'} = \mathcal{P}'_1, \ldots, \mathcal{P}'_\ell$ is not free. If we applied the rule in this case, the rule would not be sound; i.e., it might alter the validity of the tableau.

Example (free subsentences). Suppose that our tableau is simply

assertions	goals
$\mathcal{A}: \quad (\exists x)\boxed{p(x)}$ −	
	$\mathcal{G}: \quad (\forall x)\boxed{p(x)}$ +

Then the identical subsentences $p(x)$ and $p(x)$ are clearly unifiable with the empty substitution { }. However, both subsentences $p(x)$ of $\mathcal{A}$ and $\mathcal{G}$ are not free; they are within the scope of the quantifiers $(\exists x)$ and $(\forall x)$, respectively.

If we disregard the restriction and apply the *AG-resolution* rule, we obtain the new goal

$\quad not \ (\exists x) \ false$
$\quad\quad and$
$\quad (\forall x) \ true$

which reduces (by *true-false* simplification) to the final goal

	true

This is not a justifiable conclusion; the original tableau is not valid. For consider the interpretation, whose domain is the nonnegative integers, that assigns to $p(x)$ the relation "$x = 0$." Then the assertion $\mathcal{A}$ is assigned the intuitive meaning "there exists an integer 0," which is true, but the goal $\mathcal{G}$ is assigned the intuitive meaning "every integer is 0," which is false. Thus the tableau is false under this interpretation and hence is not valid.

The final tableau, on the other hand, is valid because it contains the final goal *true*. Thus, by applying the rule incorrectly, we have altered the validity of the tableau. We have taken a tableau that is not valid and produced one that is. ◢

Suppose the unifier θ of $\overline{\mathcal{P}}$ and $\overline{\mathcal{P}'}$ is not most-general. In this case, the resolvent we obtain is indeed a justifiable conclusion of the required sentences, but it is less general, and hence less useful, than if we had used a most-general unifier.

Example (most-general unifier).   Suppose that our entire tableau is

assertions	goals
A1 : $\boxed{p(y)}$ $^-$	
A2 : *if* $\boxed{p(x)}$ $^+$ *then* $r(x)$	
	G3 : $\boxed{r(b)}$ $^+$

Then the subsentence $p(y)$ of A1 and the subsentence $p(x)$ of A2 are unifiable under the most-general unifier

$$\theta : \ \{x \leftarrow y\}.$$

By applying the *AA-resolution* rule, we obtain the new assertion

> *false*
>
>   *or*
>
> *if   true   then   r(y),*

which reduces (by *true-false* simplification) to

A4 : $\boxed{r(y)}$ $^-$	

The proof may then be concluded by applying *AG-resolution* to the assertion A4 and the goal G3, taking θ to be $\{y \leftarrow b\}$, to obtain the final goal

	G5 : *true*

Suppose, however, that in applying the *resolution* rule to assertions A1 and A2 we use the substitution

$$\theta' : \{x \leftarrow a, \ y \leftarrow a\};$$

this is a unifier of $p(y)$ and $p(x)$ but is not most-general. The resolvent we obtain is then

A4' : $r(a)$	

The assertion A4' is not unifiable with the goal G3. Thus we cannot conclude the proof by applying *AG-resolution* to the new assertion A4' and goal G3, as we did before to A4 and G3. ◢

5.7   EQUIVALENCE RULE

The *equivalence* rule enables us to replace subsentences of the tableau with equivalent sentences, treating the $\equiv$ connective in an especially efficient way.

The predicate-logic version of the *equivalence* rule is an adaptation of the propositional-logic version that allows us to apply a most-general unifier θ to two sentences if that will enable us to match subsentences.

THE BASIC FORM

We first illustrate the rule.

Example.   Suppose our tableau contains the two assertions

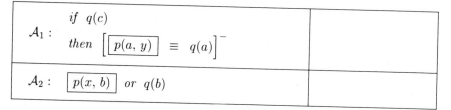

If we were to transport the propositional *equivalence* rule directly into predicate logic, we could not apply it here because the boxed subsentences are not identical. If, however, we apply the unifying substitution

$$\theta : \{x \leftarrow a, \ y \leftarrow b\},$$

we obtain the two instances

$$\mathcal{A}_1\theta : \quad \begin{array}{l} if \quad q(c) \\ then \quad \Big[\boxed{p(a, \ b)} \equiv q(a)\Big] \end{array}$$

and

$$\mathcal{A}_2\theta : \quad \boxed{p(a, \ b)} \ or \ q(b).$$

The boxed subsentences are now identical; we can apply the propositional version of the *equivalence* rule to obtain the intermediate sentence

$$\begin{bmatrix} if \quad q(c) \\ then \ false \end{bmatrix}$$
$$or$$
$$q(a) \ or \ q(b),$$

which reduces (by *true-false* simplification) to

$\big(not \ q(c)\big) \ or \ q(a) \ or \ q(b)$	

     The predicate-logic *equivalence* rule enables us to obtain this row in a single step from the two given assertions, without introducing their instances into the tableau. ◣

     Now let us state the rule. The statement relies on the notion of a most-general separate-unifier for tuples (Section 4.8).

Rule (AA-equivalence, left-to-right)

assertions	goals
$\mathcal{A}_1\big[\mathcal{P} \equiv \mathcal{Q}\big]$	
$\mathcal{A}_2\langle\overline{\mathcal{P}'}\rangle$	
$\mathcal{A}_1\theta\big[\mathit{false}\big]$ or $\mathcal{A}_2\theta\langle\overline{\mathcal{Q}\theta}\rangle$	

where
- $\overline{\mathcal{P} \equiv \mathcal{Q}}$ stands for the free, quantifier-free equivalences $\mathcal{P}_1 \equiv \mathcal{Q}_1$, $\ldots, \mathcal{P}_k \equiv \mathcal{Q}_k$ $(k \geq 1)$, which occur in $\mathcal{A}_1$.

- $\overline{\mathcal{P}'}$ stands for the free, quantifier-free subsentences $\mathcal{P}'_1, \ldots, \mathcal{P}'_\ell$ ($\ell \geq 1$), which occur in $\mathcal{A}_2$.
- The free variables of $\mathcal{A}_1[\overline{\mathcal{P} \equiv \mathcal{Q}}]$ and $\mathcal{A}_2\langle \overline{\mathcal{P}'} \rangle$ are renamed so that the rows have no free variables in common.
- $\overline{\mathcal{Q}\theta}$ stands for $\mathcal{Q}_1\theta, \ldots, \mathcal{Q}_k\theta$.
- θ is a most-general separate-unifier for the tuple of subsentences $\langle \overline{\mathcal{P}}, \overline{\mathcal{P}'} \rangle$ and the tuple of subsentences $\langle \overline{\mathcal{Q}} \rangle$; that is, $\mathcal{P}_1\theta, \ldots, \mathcal{P}_k\theta$ and $\mathcal{P}'_1\theta, \ldots, \mathcal{P}'_\ell\theta$ are all identical sentences and $\mathcal{Q}_1\theta, \ldots, \mathcal{Q}_k\theta$ are all identical sentences. The sentences $\mathcal{P}_1\theta, \ldots, \mathcal{P}_k\theta, \mathcal{P}'_1\theta, \ldots, \mathcal{P}'_\ell\theta$ must be distinct from the sentences $\mathcal{Q}_1\theta, \ldots, \mathcal{Q}_k\theta$.
- $\overline{false}$ stands for $false, \ldots, false$ (k times). ◢

More precisely, to apply the *AA-equivalence* rule to two assertions $\mathcal{A}_1$ and $\mathcal{A}_2$ of a tableau,

- Rename the free variables of $\mathcal{A}_1$ and $\mathcal{A}_2$ if necessary to ensure that they have no free variables in common.
- Select free, quantifier-free subsentences of $\mathcal{A}_1$,

$$\overline{\mathcal{P} \equiv \mathcal{Q}}: \quad \mathcal{P}_1 \equiv \mathcal{Q}_1, \quad \ldots, \quad \mathcal{P}_k \equiv \mathcal{Q}_k \quad (k \geq 1),$$

and free, quantifier-free subsentences of $\mathcal{A}_2$,

$$\overline{\mathcal{P}'}: \quad \mathcal{P}'_1, \ldots, \mathcal{P}'_\ell \quad (\ell \geq 1),$$

such that θ is a most-general separate-unifier of the tuples $\langle \mathcal{P}_1, \ldots, \mathcal{P}_k, \mathcal{P}'_1, \ldots, \mathcal{P}'_\ell \rangle$ and $\langle \mathcal{Q}_1, \ldots, \mathcal{Q}_k \rangle$; that is,

- $\mathcal{P}_1\theta, \ldots, \mathcal{P}_k\theta$ and $\mathcal{P}'_1\theta, \ldots, \mathcal{P}'_\ell\theta$ are all the same sentence, which we shall call $\mathcal{P}\theta$.
- $\mathcal{Q}_1\theta, \ldots, \mathcal{Q}_k\theta$ are all the same sentence, which we shall call $\mathcal{Q}\theta$. We require that $\mathcal{P}\theta$ and $\mathcal{Q}\theta$ be distinct. (Note that we invoke the *separate-tuple-unification* algorithm of Section 4.8.)

- Apply θ safely to the assertion $\mathcal{A}_1$ and replace all free occurrences of $\mathcal{P}\theta \equiv \mathcal{Q}\theta$ in $\mathcal{A}_1\theta$ with *false*, obtaining the disjunct

$$\mathcal{A}_1\theta[\overline{false}].$$

- Apply θ safely to the assertion $\mathcal{A}_2$ and replace safely one or more occurrences of $\mathcal{P}\theta$ in $\mathcal{A}_2\theta$ with $\mathcal{Q}\theta$, obtaining the disjunct

$$\mathcal{A}_2\theta\langle \overline{\mathcal{Q}\theta} \rangle.$$

- Simplify the disjunction

$$\mathcal{A}_1\theta[\overline{false}] \quad or \quad \mathcal{A}_2\theta\langle \overline{\mathcal{Q}\theta} \rangle.$$

- Add the simplified disjunction to the tableau as a new assertion.

In the preceding *left-to-right* version of the rule, we replace instances of the left-hand side $\mathcal{P}_i$ of the equivalence with corresponding instances of the right-hand side $\mathcal{Q}_i$. By the symmetry of the $\equiv$ connective, we can apply the rule *right-to-left* to replace instances of the right-hand side $\mathcal{Q}_i$ with instances of the left-hand side $\mathcal{P}_i$.

Rule (AA-equivalence, right-to-left)

assertions	goals
$\mathcal{A}_1\big[\,\overline{\mathcal{P} \equiv \mathcal{Q}}\,\big]$	
$\mathcal{A}_2\langle\,\overline{\mathcal{Q}'}\,\rangle$	
$\mathcal{A}_1\theta[\,\overline{false}\,]$ or $\mathcal{A}_2\theta\langle\,\overline{\mathcal{P}\theta}\,\rangle$	

where $\mathcal{A}_1$ and $\mathcal{A}_2$ satisfy the conditions analogous to those of the *left-to-right* version of the rule. ◢

POLARITY

The *polarity* strategy we applied in the propositional-logic rule can also be applied to the predicate-logic *equivalence* rule.

Strategy (polarity)

An application of the *AA-equivalence* rule is in accordance with the *polarity strategy* if

at least one of the occurrences of

$$\mathcal{P}_1 \equiv \mathcal{Q}_1, \quad \ldots, \quad \mathcal{P}_k \equiv \mathcal{Q}_k,$$

in $\mathcal{A}_1$, whose instances are replaced by *false* in applying the rule, is of negative polarity in the tableau. ◢

Note that the *polarity* strategy places no restriction on the polarity of the subsentences $\mathcal{P}'_1, \ldots, \mathcal{P}'_\ell$ [or, in the *right-to-left* version, $\mathcal{Q}'_1, \ldots, \mathcal{Q}'_\ell$] of $\mathcal{A}_2$. The negative polarity required by the strategy need not be strict; the equivalence may have both polarities.

Example. Suppose our tableau contains the two assertions

assertions	goals
$\mathcal{A}_1: \quad \Big[\,\big[\,p(x, a)\,\big] \equiv\, q(x)\Big]^{-}$	
$\mathcal{A}_2: \quad \big[\,p(b, y)\,\big]$ and $r(y, x)$	

Let us apply the *AA-equivalence* rule left-to-right to these assertions. The subsentences $\mathcal{P}$ and $\mathcal{P}'$ to be matched are indicated by boxes. Noting that $\mathcal{A}_1$ and $\mathcal{A}_2$ have the free variable x in common, we rename this variable in $\mathcal{A}_2$ to $\hat{x}$, obtaining

$$\widehat{\mathcal{A}_2}: \quad \boxed{p(b,\, y)} \quad \text{and} \quad r(y,\, \hat{x}).$$

Here $\mathcal{A}_1$ contains the free subsentence

$$\mathcal{P}: \quad p(x,\, a)$$

and $\widehat{\mathcal{A}_2}$ contains the free subsentence

$$\mathcal{P}': \quad p(b,\, y).$$

These subsentences are unifiable under the most-general unifier

$$\theta: \quad \{x \leftarrow b,\ y \leftarrow a\}.$$

The unified sentence is

$$\mathcal{P}\theta: \quad p(b,\, a).$$

Applying θ to $\mathcal{A}_1$, we obtain

$$\mathcal{A}_1\theta: \quad \boxed{p(b,\, a)} \ \equiv\ q(b);$$

applying θ to $\widehat{\mathcal{A}_2}$, we obtain

$$\widehat{\mathcal{A}_2}\theta: \quad \boxed{p(b,\, a)} \quad \text{and} \quad r(a,\, \hat{x}).$$

Replacing $(\mathcal{P} \equiv \mathcal{Q})\theta: p(b,a) \equiv q(b)$ with *false* in $\mathcal{A}_1\theta$, we obtain simply

false;

replacing $\mathcal{P}\theta : p(b,a)$ with $\mathcal{Q}\theta : q(b)$ in $\widehat{\mathcal{A}_2}\theta$, we obtain

$$q(b) \quad \text{and} \quad r(a,\, \hat{x}).$$

Taking the disjunction, we obtain the new assertion

false

or

$$q(b) \quad \text{and} \quad r(a,\, \hat{x}),$$

which reduces (by *true-false* simplification) to

$q(b)$ and $r(a,\, \hat{x})$	

This assertion may be added to our tableau.

Note again that the intermediate sentences $\widehat{\mathcal{A}_2}$, $\mathcal{A}_1\theta$, $\widehat{\mathcal{A}_2}\theta$, and the unsimplified disjunction are not added to the tableau; these are only aids in finding the simplified disjunction, which is added to the tableau as a new assertion.

This application of the *equivalence* rule is in accordance with the *polarity* strategy because the equivalence $\mathcal{A}_1$ is of negative polarity in the tableau. ◢

JUSTIFICATION

Let us justify the *AA-equivalence* rule, showing that the old (given) tableau is equivalent to the new tableau. We justify the left-to-right version of the rule. (The justification of the right-to-left version depends on the symmetry of the $\equiv$ connective.) The rule actually preserves equivalence; therefore we may use the *special justification* proposition in proving its soundness. The justification resembles that of the *AA-resolution* rule.

Justification (AA-equivalence).   Suppose that $\mathcal{A}_1$ and $\mathcal{A}_2$ are two assertions that satisfy the restrictions for applying the *AA-equivalence* rule. As in the justification for the *AA-resolution* rule, we may assume that the free variables of $\mathcal{A}_1$ have been renamed as necessary to ensure that the assertions have no free variables in common.

Let $\mathcal{I}$ be an interpretation for $\mathcal{A}_1$ and $\mathcal{A}_2$ under which the required tableau $\mathcal{T}_r$ is false; i.e., the universal closures of the required assertions $\mathcal{A}_1$ and $\mathcal{A}_2$ are both true under $\mathcal{I}$. By the *special justification* proposition, it suffices to establish that the generated tableau $\mathcal{T}_g$ is false under $\mathcal{I}$, that is, that the universal closure of the generated assertion, the disjunction

$$\mathcal{A}_1\theta\left[\,\overline{false}\,\right]$$
$$or$$
$$\mathcal{A}_2\theta\langle\,\overline{\mathcal{Q}\theta}\,\rangle,$$

is also true under $\mathcal{I}$.

Because the universal closures of $\mathcal{A}_1$ and $\mathcal{A}_2$ are assumed to be true under $\mathcal{I}$, the universal closures of $\mathcal{A}_1\theta$ and $\mathcal{A}_2\theta$ are also true under $\mathcal{I}$, by the *universal closure-instantiation* proposition (Section 3.10). Therefore, by the *semantic-rule-for-universal-closure* proposition (Section 3.6), $\mathcal{A}_1\theta$ and $\mathcal{A}_2\theta$ are themselves true under any interpretation that agrees with $\mathcal{I}$ on the constant, function, and predicate symbols of $\mathcal{A}_1\theta$ and $\mathcal{A}_2\theta$. Let $\mathcal{I}'$ be any such interpretation.

The proof now distinguishes between two cases.

Case: $(\mathcal{P} \equiv \mathcal{Q})\theta$ is false under $\mathcal{I}'$

Then, because $\mathcal{A}_1\theta$ is true under $\mathcal{I}'$, and because $(\mathcal{P}\equiv\mathcal{Q})\theta$ and the propositional constant *false* have the same truth-value under $\mathcal{I}'$,

$$\mathcal{A}_1\theta\left[\,\overline{false}\,\right]$$

is also true under $\mathcal{I}'$. It follows (by the semantic rule for the *or* connective) that the disjunction

$$\mathcal{A}_1\theta\left[\,\overline{false}\,\right]$$
$$or$$
$$\mathcal{A}_2\theta\langle\,\overline{\mathcal{Q}\theta}\,\rangle$$

is also true under $\mathcal{I}'$.

Case: $(\mathcal{P} \equiv \mathcal{Q})\theta$ is true under $\mathcal{I}'$

That is, $\mathcal{P}\theta \equiv \mathcal{Q}\theta$ is true under $\mathcal{I}'$. Hence (by the substitutivity of equivalence), because $\mathcal{A}_2\theta$ is true under $\mathcal{I}'$,

$$\mathcal{A}_2\theta\langle \overline{\mathcal{Q}\theta} \rangle$$

is also true under $\mathcal{I}'$. It follows (by the semantic rule for the *or* connective) that the disjunction

$$\mathcal{A}_1\theta\left[\overline{false}\,\right]$$
$$or$$
$$\mathcal{A}_2\theta\langle \overline{\mathcal{Q}\theta} \rangle$$

is true under $\mathcal{I}'$.

In each case, we have concluded that the generated assertion, the disjunction

$$\mathcal{A}_1\theta\left[\overline{false}\,\right]$$
$$or$$
$$\mathcal{A}_2\theta\langle \overline{\mathcal{Q}\theta} \rangle,$$

is true under $\mathcal{I}'$, for any interpretation $\mathcal{I}'$ that agrees with $\mathcal{I}$ on the constant, function, and predicate symbols of $\mathcal{A}_1\theta$ and $\mathcal{A}_2\theta$, and hence of the new assertion.

Therefore (by the *semantic-rule-for-universal-closure* proposition), the universal closure of the generated assertion is true under $\mathcal{I}$, as we wanted to prove. The final simplification step preserves equivalence. ◢

DUAL FORMS

We have given the *AA-equivalence* rule. The corresponding dual forms of the rule are as follows.

Rule (GG-equivalence, left-to-right)

assertions	goals
	$\mathcal{G}_1\left[\, \mathcal{P} \equiv \mathcal{Q}\,\right]$
	$\mathcal{G}_2\langle \overline{\mathcal{P}'} \rangle$
	$\mathcal{G}_1\theta\left[\,\overline{false}\,\right]$ *and* $\mathcal{G}_2\theta\langle \overline{\mathcal{Q}\theta} \rangle$

where $\mathcal{G}_1$ and $\mathcal{G}_2$ satisfy the same conditions as $\mathcal{A}_1$ and $\mathcal{A}_2$, respectively, in the *AA-equivalence* rule. ⌐

Rule (AG-equivalence, left-to-right)

assertions	goals
$\mathcal{A}\big[\,\overline{\mathcal{P} \equiv \mathcal{Q}}\,\big]$	
	$\mathcal{G}\langle\,\overline{\mathcal{P}'}\,\rangle$
	$not\ \big(\mathcal{A}\theta\big[\,\overline{false}\,\big]\big)$ *and* $\mathcal{G}\theta\langle\,\overline{\mathcal{Q}\theta}\,\rangle$

where $\mathcal{A}$ and $\mathcal{G}$ satisfy the same conditions as $\mathcal{A}_1$ and $\mathcal{A}_2$, respectively, in the *AA-equivalence* rule. ⌐

Rule (GA-equivalence, left-to-right)

assertions	goals
	$\mathcal{G}\big[\,\overline{\mathcal{P} \equiv \mathcal{Q}}\,\big]$
$\mathcal{A}\langle\,\overline{\mathcal{P}'}\,\rangle$	
	$\mathcal{G}\theta\big[\,\overline{false}\,\big]$ *and* $not\ \big(\mathcal{A}\theta\langle\,\overline{\mathcal{Q}\theta}\,\rangle\big)$

where $\mathcal{G}$ and $\mathcal{A}$ satisfy the same conditions as $\mathcal{A}_1$ and $\mathcal{A}_2$, respectively, in the *AA-equivalence* rule. ⌐

There are analogous right-to-left forms. The justification of the dual forms follows by duality.

The *polarity* strategy for the dual forms of the rule is analogous to the one for the *AA-equivalence* rule: at least one of the occurrences of $\mathcal{P}_1 \equiv \mathcal{Q}_1, \ldots,$ $\mathcal{P}_k \equiv \mathcal{Q}_k$, whose instances are replaced by *false* in applying the rules, is of negative polarity in the tableau.

Example. Suppose our tableau contains the assertion and the goal

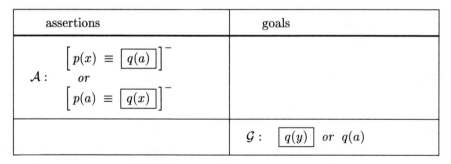

Let us apply the *AG-equivalence* rule right-to-left to $\mathcal{A}$ and $\mathcal{G}$.

We consider the subsentences

$$\mathcal{P}_1 \equiv \mathcal{Q}_1 : p(x) \equiv q(a) \qquad \text{and} \qquad \mathcal{P}_2 \equiv \mathcal{Q}_2 : p(a) \equiv q(x)$$

of $\mathcal{A}$ and the subsentence $\mathcal{Q}' : q(y)$ of $\mathcal{G}$.

The substitution

$$\theta : \{x \leftarrow a, \ y \leftarrow a\}$$

is a most-general substitution that unifies

$$p(x) \quad \text{and} \quad p(a)$$

and also unifies

$$q(a), \quad q(x), \quad \text{and} \quad q(y).$$

The unified subsentences are

$$\mathcal{P}\theta : p(a) \qquad \text{and} \qquad \mathcal{Q}\theta : q(a).$$

Applying θ to $\mathcal{A}$, we obtain

$$\mathcal{A}\theta : \quad \begin{array}{c} p(a) \equiv \boxed{q(a)} \\ or \\ p(a) \equiv \boxed{q(a)} \end{array}.$$

Applying θ to $\mathcal{G}$, we obtain

$$\mathcal{G}\theta : \quad \boxed{q(a)} \ \ or \ \ q(a).$$

Replacing every occurrence of the equivalence $p(a) \equiv q(a)$ with *false* in $\mathcal{A}\theta$, we obtain

$$false \ \ or \ \ false;$$

replacing the selected occurrence of the right-hand side $q(a)$ of the equivalence with the left-hand side $p(a)$ in $\mathcal{G}\theta$, we obtain

$$p(a) \ \ or \ \ q(a).$$

Therefore the new goal is

> *not (false or false)*
>   *and*
> *p(a) or q(a)*,

which reduces (by *true-false* simplification) to the goal

	$p(a)$ or $q(a)$

Note that two equivalence occurrences in $\mathcal{A}\theta$ were replaced by *false*, that only the selected occurrence of $q(a)$ in $\mathcal{G}\theta$ was replaced by $p(a)$, and that the rule was applied in the right-to-left direction. ⏌

5.8   QUANTIFIER-ELIMINATION RULES

The *quantifier-elimination (skolemization)* rules allow us to remove certain quantifiers from the assertions and goals of our tableau. These rules are valuable because they pave the way for other rules, such as *resolution* and *equivalence* rules, that apply only to free, quantifier-free subsentences.

For example, suppose that we have a tableau with the assertion and the goal

assertions	goals
$\mathcal{A}:$ $(\forall x)p(x)$	
	$\mathcal{G}:$ $(\exists y)p(y)$

Intuitively, this tableau is valid, because we can take y in the goal to be any domain element at all. We might expect to be able to apply the *AG-resolution* rule in this case, matching the subsentence $p(y)$ of the goal against the subsentence $p(x)$ of the assertion; this application, however, is forbidden because these subsentences are not free. By applying the *skolemization* rules of this section, we will be able to drop these quantifiers and then apply the *resolution* rule.

FORCE OF A QUANTIFIER

Before we describe the *skolemization* rules, let us extend the notion of the force of a quantifier, which we have defined for predicate logic, to apply to the quantifiers in a tableau.

Definition (force of quantifiers)

In a tableau $\mathcal{T}$,

- An occurrence of a quantifier $(\ldots\, x)$ of a subsentence of the form $\mathcal{E} : (\ldots\, x)\mathcal{F}$ has *universal force* in $\mathcal{T}$, annotated by the superscript $(\ldots\, x)^\forall$, if

   - it is a universal quantifier and $\mathcal{E}$ is of positive polarity in $\mathcal{T}$, that is,

   $$[(\forall x)\mathcal{F}]^+ \;\Rightarrow\; (\forall x)^\forall \mathcal{F},$$

   or

   - it is an existential quantifier and $\mathcal{E}$ is of negative polarity in $\mathcal{T}$, that is,

   $$[(\exists x)\mathcal{F}]^- \;\Rightarrow\; (\exists x)^\forall \mathcal{F}.$$

- An occurrence of a quantifier $(\ldots\, x)$ of a subsentence of the form $\mathcal{E} : (\ldots\, x)\mathcal{F}$ has *existential force* in $\mathcal{T}$, annotated by the superscript $(\ldots\, x)^\exists$, if

   - it is an existential quantifier and $\mathcal{E}$ is of positive polarity in $\mathcal{T}$, that is,

   $$[(\exists x)\mathcal{F}]^+ \;\Rightarrow\; (\exists x)^\exists \mathcal{F},$$

   or

   - it is a universal quantifier and $\mathcal{E}$ is of negative polarity in $\mathcal{T}$, that is,

   $$[(\forall x)\mathcal{F}]^- \;\Rightarrow\; (\forall x)^\exists \mathcal{F}.$$

- An occurrence of a quantifier $(\ldots\, x)$ is of *strict* (*universal* or *existential*) *force* in $\mathcal{T}$ if it does not have both universal and existential force. ∎

As before, if we wish to indicate that an occurrence of a quantifier has universal or existential force in a tableau, we annotate it with the superscript $(\ldots\, x)^\forall$ or $(\ldots\, x)^\exists$, respectively. If an occurrence of a quantifier $(\ldots\, x)$ has both forces, we annotate it with the combined superscript $(\ldots\, x)^{\forall\exists}$. Thus, in the assertion

$if \; \left[(\exists x)^\exists (\forall y)^\forall q(x, y)\right]^+$ $then \; \left[(\forall x)^\exists (\exists y)^\forall q(x, y)\right]^-$	

the quantifiers have been annotated according to their forces in the tableau.

Recall that assertions always have negative polarity in a tableau. Therefore outermost universal quantifiers in an assertion always have existential force, and outermost existential quantifiers always have universal force.

BOTH FORCES

There is no rule for directly eliminating quantifiers of both forces, $(\ldots x)^{\forall\exists}$. Such quantifiers must always occur within the scope of an equivalence connective $\equiv$, or within the *if*-clause of a conditional connective or constructor. Without these symbols, we can have no quantifiers of both forces.

We can eliminate any equivalence or conditional operator by repeated application (left-to-right) of the following rewritings from Sections 2.3 and 5.4:

- Equivalence elimination

$$\mathcal{F} \equiv \mathcal{G} \quad \Leftrightarrow \quad (if \ \mathcal{F} \ then \ \mathcal{G}) \ and \ (if \ \mathcal{G} \ then \ \mathcal{F})$$

$$\mathcal{F} \equiv \mathcal{G} \quad \Leftrightarrow \quad (\mathcal{F} \ and \ \mathcal{G}) \ or \ \big((not \ \mathcal{F}) \ and \ (not \ \mathcal{G})\big)$$

- Conditional (connective) elimination

$$if \ \mathcal{F} \ then \ \mathcal{G} \ else \ \mathcal{H} \quad \Leftrightarrow \quad \begin{aligned}&(if \ \mathcal{F} \ then \ \mathcal{G}) \ and \\ &\big(if \ (not \ \mathcal{F}) \ then \ \mathcal{H}\big)\end{aligned}$$

$$if \ \mathcal{F} \ then \ \mathcal{G} \ else \ \mathcal{H} \quad \Leftrightarrow \quad (\mathcal{F} \ and \ \mathcal{G}) \ or \ \big((not \ \mathcal{F}) \ and \ \mathcal{H}\big)$$

- Conditional (constructor) manipulation

$$p(\overline{r}, \ if \ \mathcal{F} \ then \ t_1 \ else \ t_2, \ \overline{s}) \quad \Leftrightarrow \quad if \ \mathcal{F} \ then \ p(\overline{r}, t_1, \overline{s}) \ else \ p(\overline{r}, t_2, \overline{s})$$

$$f(\overline{r}, \ if \ \mathcal{F} \ then \ t_1 \ else \ t_2, \ \overline{s}) \quad \Leftrightarrow \quad if \ \mathcal{F} \ then \ f(\overline{r}, t_1, \overline{s}) \ else \ f(\overline{r}, t_2, \overline{s})$$

(Note that we have a choice of two rules each for eliminating the conditional and equivalence operators.)

Thus, to eliminate a quantifier of both forces, we can repeatedly apply the preceding rewritings, as appropriate, to all of the surrounding equivalence and conditional operators. The quantifier of both forces in the original sentence is replaced by many quantifiers of strict force in the resulting sentence. These quantifiers can subsequently be removed by the *skolemization* rules.

Example.   Suppose a tableau contains the following goal:

assertions	goals
	$(\exists y) \left[\left(p \left(f \left(\begin{aligned} &if \ (\forall x)^{\forall\exists} q(x) \ \equiv \ r(a) \\ &then \ g(y) \\ &else \ h(y) \end{aligned} \right) \right) \right) \right]$

The annotated quantifier $(\forall x)^{\forall\exists}$ has both forces in the tableau: it is surrounded by both a conditional constructor and an equivalence connective. If we wish to eliminate this quantifier, we must first remove these operators.

We first remove the conditional constructor. By the *conditional-manipulation* rewriting for function symbols, we may obtain

$$(\exists y)\left[p\left(\begin{array}{l} if\ (\forall x)^{\forall\exists}q(x)\ \equiv\ r(a)\\ then\ f(g(y))\\ else\ f(h(y)) \end{array}\right)\right]$$

By the *conditional-manipulation* rewriting for predicate symbols, we may obtain

$$(\exists y)\left[\begin{array}{l} if\ (\forall x)^{\forall\exists}q(x)\ \equiv\ r(a)\\ then\ p(f(g(y)))\\ else\ p(f(h(y))) \end{array}\right]$$

By one of the *conditional-elimination* rewritings, we may obtain

$$(\exists y)\left[\begin{array}{l} if\ ((\forall x)^{\forall\exists}q(x) \equiv r(a))\ \ then\ \ p(f(g(y)))\\ and\\ if\ \ not\ ((\forall x)^{\forall\exists}q(x) \equiv r(a))\ \ then\ \ p(f(h(y))) \end{array}\right]$$

We have succeeded in removing the conditional constructor. Each of the resulting $(\forall x)$ quantifiers, however, is still surrounded by an equivalence connective, and still has both forces. To remove these quantifiers, we (twice) apply an *equivalence-elimination* rewriting, to obtain

$$(\exists y)\left[\begin{array}{l} \left[\begin{array}{l} if\ \left[\begin{array}{l}(\forall x)^{\exists}q(x)\ \ and\ \ r(a)\\ or\\ (not\ (\forall x)^{\forall}q(x))\ \ and\ \ (not\ r(a))\end{array}\right]\\ then\ p(f(q(y)))\end{array}\right]\\ and\\ \left[\begin{array}{l} if\ \ not\ \left[\begin{array}{l}(\forall x)^{\forall}q(x)\ \ and\ \ r(a)\\ or\\ (not\ (\forall x)^{\exists}q(x))\ \ and\ \ (not\ (r(a)))\end{array}\right]\\ then\ p(f(h(y)))\end{array}\right] \end{array}\right]$$

In the resulting goal, we have four occurrences of the quantifier $(\forall x)$, two of strict universal force and two of strict existential force. These quantifiers may be removed by application of the forthcoming *skolemization* rules. ◢

There are two *skolemization* rules: one for eliminating quantifiers of strict universal force, the other for eliminating quantifiers of strict existential force.

∀-ELIMINATION RULE

The following ∀-*elimination* rule, expressed in tableau notation, allows us to remove a quantifier of strict universal force. We first give the rule for removing a quantifier from an assertion.

Rule (∀-elimination, A-form)

assertions	goals
$\mathcal{A}$	
$\mathcal{A}'$	

where
- The required assertion $\mathcal{A}$ contains at least one occurrence of a subsentence

  $$(\dots z)^\forall \mathcal{P}[z],$$

  where $(\dots z)^\forall$ is of strict universal force in the tableau; we designate a particular occurrence of this subsentence.
- The only free variables in $\mathcal{A}$ are $\overline{x}$, that is, $x_1, \dots, x_m$, where $m \geq 0$.
- The only quantifiers of existential force that surround the occurrence $(\dots z)^\forall \mathcal{P}[z]$ are $(\overline{\dots y})^\exists$, that is, $(\dots y_1)^\exists, \dots, (\dots y_n)^\exists$, where $n \geq 0$.
- We rename the bound and free variables of $\mathcal{A}$, as necessary, to ensure that $\overline{x}$ and $\overline{y}$ are all distinct.
- The generated assertion $\mathcal{A}'$ is obtained from $\mathcal{A}$ by replacing the designated occurrence $(\dots z)^\forall \mathcal{P}[z]$ with

  $$\mathcal{P}[f(\overline{x}, \overline{y})],$$

  where f is a new skolem function symbol, i.e., one that has not occurred in the tableau so far.

In the special case in which there are no such free variables $\overline{x}$ and no surrounding quantifiers $(\overline{\dots y})^\exists$, that is, $m = n = 0$, $\mathcal{A}'$ is obtained from $\mathcal{A}$ by replacing the occurrence $(\dots z)^\forall \mathcal{P}[z]$ with

$$\mathcal{P}[a],$$

where a is a new skolem constant symbol, i.e., one that has not occurred in the tableau so far. ⌐

The dual form of the rule, for removing a quantifier of universal force from a goal, is as follows.

Rule (∀-elimination, G-form)

assertions	goals
	$\mathcal{G}$
	$\mathcal{G}'$

Here $\mathcal{G}'$ is obtained from $\mathcal{G}$ in the same way that $\mathcal{A}'$ is obtained from $\mathcal{A}$. The restrictions for applying the G-form are the same as those for the A-form of the ∀-*elimination* rule. ◢

Example. Suppose that our tableau contains the assertion

assertions	goals
$\mathcal{A}:$ $\begin{array}{l} r(x) \;\; or \\ (\forall y)^{\exists}\Big[q(x,\, y) \;\; and \;\; \boxed{(\exists z)^{\forall}p(x,\, y,\, z)}\Big] \end{array}$	

We would like to remove the quantifier $(\exists z)^{\forall}$, annotated with a box. Note that

- The occurrence of the quantifier $(\exists z)^{\forall}$ to be removed is of strict universal force in the tableau.
- The only free variable in $\mathcal{A}$ is x.
- The only quantifier of existential force that contains the occurrence of the subsentence $(\exists z)^{\forall}p(x, y, z)$ within its scope is $(\forall y)^{\exists}$.

Let f be a new binary skolem function symbol. Then we may add to our tableau the new assertion

$\mathcal{A}':$ $\begin{array}{l} r(x) \;\; or \\ (\forall y)\big[q(x,y) \;\; and \;\; p(x,\, y,\, f(x,y))\big] \end{array}$	

obtained from $\mathcal{A}$ by dropping the quantifier $(\exists z)^{\forall}$ and replacing the occurrence of z in $p(x, y, z)$ with the skolem term $f(x, y)$. ◢

Example. Suppose our tableau contains the goal

assertions	goals
	$\mathcal{G}:$ $(\forall y)^{\forall}\Big[q(y) \;\; or \;\; \boxed{(\forall z)^{\forall}p(y,\, z)}\Big]$

We would like to remove the quantifier $(\forall z)^{\forall}$, annotated with a box. Note that

- The occurrence of $(\forall z)^{\forall}$ to be removed is of strict universal force in the tableau.
- There are no free variables in $\mathcal{G}$.
- There are no quantifiers of existential force that contain the occurrence of $(\forall z)^{\forall} p(y, z)$ within their scope.

Let a be a new skolem constant. Then we may add to our tableau the new goal

	$\mathcal{G}' :$ $(\forall y)\big[q(y) \;\; or \;\; p(y, a)\big]$

obtained from $\mathcal{G}$ by dropping the quantifier $(\forall z)^{\forall}$ and replacing the occurrence of z in $p(y, z)$ with the skolem constant a. ⌐

Remark (informal proof).   Suppose we apply the $\forall$-*elimination* rule to a goal

	$(\forall y)^{\forall} q(y)$

obtaining a goal

	$q(a)$

where a is a skolem constant. This corresponds to a step in an informal proof in which, in trying to show a sentence $(\forall y)q(y)$, we consider an arbitrary element a and attempt to show $q(a)$. ⌐

Let us justify the G-form of the $\forall$-*elimination* rule, showing that the old (given) tableau is valid if and only if the new tableau, after adding the generated goal, is valid. The justification of the dual A-form of the rule follows by duality. This is an exceptional rule in the sense that the stronger equivalence result does not hold: the old tableau is not necessarily equivalent to the new tableau. Therefore we cannot use the *special justification* proposition to prove the soundness of the rule, and must instead use the *general justification* proposition.

Justification ($\forall$-elimination, G-form).

By the *general justification* proposition, it suffices to show that, if the required row $\mathcal{T}_r$, that is, the existential closure of the sentence $\mathcal{G}$, is false under some interpretation $\mathcal{I}$, then there exists some interpretation $\mathcal{I}'$ such that the generated row $\mathcal{T}_g$, that is, the existential closure of the sentence $\mathcal{G}'$, is false under $\mathcal{I}'$, where $\mathcal{I}$ and $\mathcal{I}'$ agree on the old tableau. If the existential closure of $\mathcal{G}$ is false under $\mathcal{I}$, then, by the *universal-elimination* proposition (Section 4.5), there exists an interpretation $\mathcal{I}'$ that agrees with $\mathcal{I}$ except perhaps on new symbols, such that the existential closure of $\mathcal{G}'$ is false under $\mathcal{I}'$. Since we know that no new symbols occur in any of the given assertions and goals, $\mathcal{I}$ and $\mathcal{I}'$ agree on the old tableau.

The justification of the special case, in which a skolem constant is introduced instead of a skolem function symbol, is similar. ◢

Remark (why new skolem function?). Let us see why it is important to choose new skolem constant and function symbols.

We "prove" the sentence

$$if \ (\exists x)p(x) \ then \ p(a).$$

This sentence is actually not valid; it is false under any interpretation for which $p(a)$ is false but $p(x)$ is true for some other domain element.

The initial tableau is

assertions	goals
	G1. *if* $(\exists x)^\forall p(x)$ *then* $p(a)$

Then, by the $\forall$-*elimination* rule (erroneously applied), we obtain the goal

$$if \ p(a) \ then \ p(a),$$

which is simplified to the final goal

	G2. *true*

In other words, we proved a nonvalid sentence.

The problem is that, in applying the rule, x was replaced by the constant symbol a, which is not a new constant, since it already occurs in the sentence.

A correct application of the $\forall$-*elimination* rule will yield the goal

	G2′. *if* $p(b)$ *then* $p(a)$

Here x has been replaced by the new constant symbol b. This goal cannot be simplified to the final goal *true*. ◢

The following example illustrates the fact that the $\forall$-*elimination* rule may not preserve equivalence.

Example (equivalence not preserved).   Suppose our tableau consists of the single goal

assertions	goals
	$(\forall\,y)^{\forall}p(y)$

The quantifier has strict universal force in the tableau. By the $\forall$-*elimination* rule, we may drop this quantifier from the goal, replacing the variable y with the skolem constant a. We introduce the new goal

	$p(a)$

Equivalence has not been preserved: there are interpretations under which the old tableau is false but the new tableau is true, that is, the two do not have the same truth-value. For any interpretation under which $p(a)$ is true but $(\forall\,y)p(y)$ is false, the old tableau is false but the new tableau is true.

On the other hand, validity has been preserved, as the preceding justification guarantees. In fact, neither the old tableau nor the new tableau is valid. ◢

∃-ELIMINATION RULE

The $\forall$-*elimination* rule allows us to remove quantifiers of strict universal force; the following $\exists$-*elimination* rule allows us to remove quantifiers of strict existential force. We first give the rule for removing quantifiers from an assertion.

Rule (∃-elimination, A-form)

assertions	goals
$\mathcal{A}$	
$\mathcal{A}'$	

where
- The required assertion $\mathcal{A}$ contains at least one occurrence of a subsentence

  $(\ldots\ y)^{\exists}\mathcal{P}[y],$

  where $(\ldots\ y)^{\exists}$ is of strict existential force in the tableau; we consider a particular occurrence of this subsentence.
- The occurrence of $(\ldots\ y)^{\exists}\mathcal{P}[y]$ is not within the scope of any quantifier of universal force; this can be achieved by prior application of the $\forall$-*elimination* rule if necessary.

- We rename the bound variables of $\mathcal{A}$, as necessary, to ensure that the occurrence of $(\ldots\ y)^\exists\mathcal{P}[y]$ is not within the scope of any other quantifier $(\forall\,y)$ or $(\exists\,y)$ with the same variable.
- We rename the bound variable y or the free variables of $\mathcal{A}$, as necessary, to ensure that the variable y is distinct from any of the free variables of $\mathcal{A}$.

The generated assertion $\mathcal{A}'$ is obtained from $\mathcal{A}$ by dropping the occurrence of the quantifier $(\ldots\ y)^\exists$, that is, by replacing the occurrence of $(\ldots\ y)^\exists\mathcal{P}[y]$ with $\mathcal{P}[y]$. ◢

The dual form of the rule, for removing the quantifier from a goal, is as follows.

Rule ($\exists$-elimination, G-form)

assertions	goals
	$\mathcal{G}$
	$\mathcal{G}'$

Here $\mathcal{G}'$ is obtained from $\mathcal{G}$ in the same way that $\mathcal{A}'$ is obtained from $\mathcal{A}$ in the A-form of the rule. The restrictions for applying the G-form are the same as those for applying the A-form. ◢

Example.   Suppose our tableau contains the goal

assertions	goals
	$\mathcal{G}:\quad (\exists\,y_1)^\exists\Big[p(y_1)\ \ and\ \ \boxed{(\exists\,y_2)^\exists q(y_1,\,y_2)}\Big]$

We would like to remove the inner quantifier $(\exists\,y_2)^\exists$. Note that
- The occurrence of $(\exists\,y_2)^\exists$ to be removed is of strict existential force in the tableau.
- No quantifier of universal force contains the quantifier $(\exists\,y_2)^\exists$ within its scope.
- The occurrence of $(\exists\,y_2)^\exists$ is not within the scope of any other occurrence of a quantifier $(\ldots\ y_2)$.
- The variable y_2 is distinct from any of the free variables of the goal. Then we may add to our tableau the new goal

	$\mathcal{G}':\quad (\exists\,y_1)^\exists\big[p(y_1)\ \ and\ \ q(y_1,y_2)\big]$

obtained from $\mathcal{G}$ by dropping the quantifier $(\exists\,y_2)^\exists$. ◢

We justify the G-form of the rule. The justification of the A-form follows by appeal to the *duality* property.

Justification (∃-elimination, G-form).   By the *special justification* proposition, it suffices to show that, if the existential closure of the required goal $\mathcal{G}$ is false under some interpretation $\mathcal{I}$, then the existential closure of the generated goal $\mathcal{G}'$ is also false under $\mathcal{I}$. But this holds by the *existential-elimination* proposition (Section 4.6). ⌐

Although the ∃-*elimination* rule, like all deduction rules, retains the required row, in this case equivalence would have been preserved even if the required row were dropped.

Remark (conventional treatment of skolemization).   Let us relate our discussion of skolemization to the way the subject is usually treated.

Typically, skolemization is performed in the context of a "refutation" system, which deals only with assertions, not goals. In such a system, the theorem to be proved is negated and treated as an assertion, by duality.

In a refutation system, if a quantifier that occurs with *existential* force in an assertion is removed, a corresponding skolem constant or function symbol is introduced. In the tableau system, if the removed quantifier has *universal* force in the tableau, a corresponding skolem constant or function symbol is introduced. These two conventions actually agree, for the following reason. Because each assertion has negative polarity in the tableau, a quantifier that has existential force in an assertion will have universal force in the tableau. Thus a quantifier will be treated the same way in a refutation system and in the tableau system. ⌐

5.9   EXAMPLES OF COMPLETE PROOFS

In this section we examine proofs of the validity of predicate-logic sentences. These proofs use many deduction rules together. Some of these examples were used earlier in Section 3.5.

Example.   Suppose we would like to prove the validity of the sentence

$$if \ (\exists y)(\forall x)q(x, y)$$
$$then \ (\forall x)(\exists y)q(x, y).$$

We begin with the initial goal

assertions	goals
	G1. *if* $(\exists y)(\forall x)q(x, y)$ *then* $(\forall x)(\exists y)q(x, y)$

By the *if-split* rule, we obtain the new assertion and goal

A2. $(\exists y)^{\forall}(\forall x)q(x, y)$	
	G3. $(\forall x)^{\forall}(\exists y)q(x, y)$

By the $\forall$-*elimination* rule applied to the outermost quantifier $(\exists y)^{\forall}$ of assertion A2, we obtain

A4. $(\forall x)^{\exists}q(x, a)$	

Here we have replaced the variable y with the new skolem constant a.

By the same rule applied to the outermost quantifier $(\forall x)^{\forall}$ of goal G3, we obtain

	G5. $(\exists y)^{\exists}q(b, y)$

Here we have replaced the variable x with the new skolem constant b.

Now that the quantifier $(\forall x)^{\exists}$ of assertion A4 is no longer within the scope of any quantifier of universal force, we can apply the $\exists$-*elimination* rule to drop the quantifier, obtaining

A6. $\boxed{q(x, a)}$ $^-$	

Applying the same rule to goal G5 to drop the quantifier $(\exists y)^{\exists}$, we obtain

	G7. $\boxed{q(b, y)}$ $^+$

We can then apply the *AG-resolution* rule to assertion A6 and goal G7, taking the most-general unifier to be

$$\{x \leftarrow b, y \leftarrow a\},$$

to obtain the final goal

	G8. *true*

Example (attempting to prove a nonvalid sentence). The converse

$$if \ (\forall x)(\exists y)q(x, y)$$
$$then \ (\exists y)(\forall x)q(x, y)$$

of the sentence from the previous example is not valid. Let us attempt to imitate the proof of that example, to show where it breaks down.

We begin with the initial goal

assertions	goals
	G1. *if* $(\forall x)(\exists y)q(x, y)$ *then* $(\exists y)(\forall x)q(x, y)$

By the *if-split* rule, we obtain the new assertion and goal

A2. $(\forall x)^{\exists}(\exists y)q(x, y)$	
	G3. $(\exists y)^{\exists}(\forall x)q(x, y)$

Applying the $\exists$-*elimination* rule twice to drop the outermost quantifiers of assertion A2 and goal G3, we obtain the new assertion and goal

A4. $(\exists y)^{\forall}q(x, y)$	
	G5. $(\forall x)^{\forall}q(x, y)$

respectively.

Applying the $\forall$-*elimination* rule twice to the outermost quantifiers of assertion A4 and goal G5, we obtain the new assertion and goal

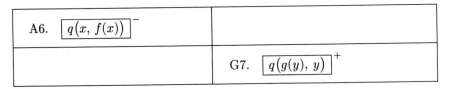

A6. $\boxed{q(x, f(x))}^{\ -}$	
	G7. $\boxed{q(g(y), y)}^{\ +}$

respectively. Here we have replaced the variable y of assertion A4 with the skolem term $f(x)$, where f is a new function symbol; the variable x is free in assertion A4. Similarly, we have replaced the variable x of goal G5 with the skolem term $g(y)$, where g is a new function symbol; the variable y is free in goal G5.

At the analogous point in the previous example, we applied the *AG-resolution* rule to assertion A6 and goal G7. We cannot do this here, however, because these sentences are not unifiable; the occurs-check of the unification algorithm fails.

We cannot conclude from the failure of a single proof attempt that a sentence is not valid. In fact, however, this sentence is not valid. Thus, by the soundness of our deduction rules, no proof of this sentence is possible. ⌐

Example. Suppose we would like to prove the validity of the sentence

$$if \begin{bmatrix} (\forall x)\big[p(x) \equiv q(x)\big] \\ and \\ (\exists x)\big[q(x) \equiv r(x)\big] \end{bmatrix}$$
$$then \ (\exists x)\big[p(x) \equiv r(x)\big].$$

We begin with the initial goal

assertions	goals
	G1. $if \begin{bmatrix} (\forall x)\big[p(x) \equiv q(x)\big] \\ and \\ (\exists x)\big[q(x) \equiv r(x)\big] \end{bmatrix}$ $then \ (\exists x)[p(x) \equiv r(x)]$

By the *if-split* and *and-split* rules, we obtain

assertions	goals
A2. $(\forall x)^{\exists}\big[p(x) \equiv q(x)\big]$	
A3. $(\exists x)^{\forall}\big[q(x) \equiv r(x)\big]$	
	G4. $(\exists x)^{\exists}\big[p(x) \equiv r(x)\big]$

The quantifier $(\forall x)^{\exists}$ in assertion A2 and the quantifier $(\exists x)^{\exists}$ in goal G4 both have strict existential force in the tableau; by the $\exists$-*elimination* rule, we can drop these quantifiers. The quantifier $(\exists x)^{\forall}$ in assertion A3 has strict universal force in the tableau; by the $\forall$-*elimination* rule, we can drop this quantifier, replacing the variable x with a new constant a. We obtain

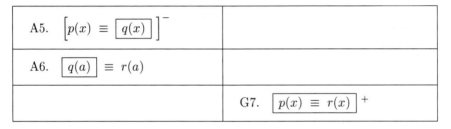

assertions	goals
A5. $\Big[p(x) \equiv \boxed{q(x)}\Big]^{-}$	
A6. $\boxed{q(a)} \equiv r(a)$	
	G7. $\boxed{p(x) \equiv r(x)}^{+}$

Applying the *AA-equivalence* rule (right-to-left) to assertions A5 and A6, with most-general unifier $\{x \leftarrow a\}$, we can replace $q(a)$ with $p(a)$ in assertion A6, obtaining

A8. $\boxed{p(a) \; \equiv \; r(a)}$ $^-$	

Finally, by the *AG-resolution* rule, applied to assertion A8 and goal G7, with most-general unifier $\{x \leftarrow a\}$, we obtain the goal

	G9. *true*

We conclude the chapter with a remark about skolemization.

Remark (outermost skolemization).   If an assertion is universally quantified, i.e., if it is of form

$(\forall \; x_1, \; \ldots, x_m)^{\exists}\mathcal{A}$	

then the outermost universal quantifiers are of strict existential force. Therefore we can drop them by repeatedly applying the ∃-*elimination* rule, obtaining the assertion

$\mathcal{A}$	

Similarly, we can drop the outermost existential quantifiers of an existentially quantified goal

	$(\exists \; x_1, \; \ldots, x_m)^{\exists}\mathcal{G}$

to obtain

	$\mathcal{G}$

To simplify the exposition, we shall often drop such quantifiers without mentioning the application of the rule or the intermediate steps. For example, instead of writing the assertion

$(\forall \; x)(\exists \; y)p(x, \; y)$	

we shall immediately write

$(\exists\, y)p(x,\, y)$	

The reader is requested in **Problem 5.2** to prove the validity of several sentences. **Problems 5.3, 5.4**, and **5.5** are also concerned with deductive tableaux.

PROBLEMS

Problem 5.1 (associated sentence)   page 240

Show that the associated sentence of the tableau with assertions $\mathcal{A}_1, \mathcal{A}_2, \ldots, \mathcal{A}_m$ and goals $\mathcal{G}_1, \mathcal{G}_2, \ldots, \mathcal{G}_n$ is equivalent to the sentence

$$(\exists *) \quad \begin{bmatrix} if \ (\mathcal{A}_1 \ and \ \mathcal{A}_2 \ and \ \ldots \ and \ \mathcal{A}_m) \\ then \ (\mathcal{G}_1 \ or \ \mathcal{G}_2 \ or \ \ldots \ or \ \mathcal{G}_n) \end{bmatrix}.$$

Problem 5.2 (tableau proofs of valid sentences)   page 297

Use the deductive-tableau technique to prove the validity of the following sentences:

(a) $if \ (\forall x)p(x) \ or \ (\forall x)r(x)$
      $then \ (\forall x)[p(x) \ or \ r(x)]$

(b) $if \ (\forall x)\,p(x)$
      $then \ p(a)$

(c) $if \ (\forall x)[p(x) \ \equiv \ not \, q(x)]$
      $then \ ((\exists x)\,p(x)) \ \equiv \ (not \, (\forall x)\, q(x))$

(d) $if \ \begin{bmatrix} (\forall x,\, y,\, z) \begin{bmatrix} if \ p(x,\, y) \ and \ p(y,\, z) \\ then \ p(x,\, z) \end{bmatrix} \\ and \\ (\forall x) \, [not \, p(x,\, x)] \end{bmatrix} \ then \ (\forall x,\, y) \begin{bmatrix} if \ p(x,\, y) \\ then \ not \, p(y,\, x) \end{bmatrix}$

(e) $if \ \begin{bmatrix} (\exists x)\,p(f(x)) \\ and \\ (\forall x)[if \ p(x) \ then \ p(f(x))] \end{bmatrix} \ then \ (\exists x)\,p(f(f(f(x))))$

(f) $if \ \begin{bmatrix} (\forall x)[p(x,\, f(x)) \ or \ p(f(x),\, x)] \\ and \\ (\forall x,\, y)[if \ p(x,\, y) \ then \ p(f(x),\, f(y))] \end{bmatrix} \ then \ (\forall x)(\exists y)p(f(x),\, y)$

(g)   *if* $\left[\begin{array}{l} (\forall\, x)(\exists\, y)\big[if\ p\big(x,\ f(y)\big)\ then\ q(x)\big] \\ and \\ (\exists\, x)\big[not\ q(x)\big]\ \equiv\ (\forall\, x,\ y)p(x,\ y) \end{array}\right]$ *then* $(\forall\, z)q(z)$.

Problem 5.3 (skolemization)   page 297

Suppose that a closed sentence

$$\mathcal{G}:\quad (\exists\, x)(\forall\, y)\mathcal{F}[x,\ y]$$

is the initial goal of a tableau. A student does not remember how to skolemize and, in an attempt to eliminate the quantifiers, adds to the tableau one of the following goals:

$$\mathcal{G}_1:\quad \mathcal{F}[x,\ y] \qquad\qquad \mathcal{G}_2:\quad \mathcal{F}[x,\ a]$$
$$\mathcal{G}_3:\quad \mathcal{F}[x,\ f(x)] \qquad\quad \mathcal{G}_4:\quad \mathcal{F}[x,\ g(x,\ z)].$$

Here a is a new constant symbol, and f and g are new function symbols.

The hapless student goes on to derive successfully the final goal *true*. In which of the four cases, if any, can you conclude that the initial goal $\mathcal{G}$ is valid? Justify your answers.

Hint: For each of the "skolemized" sentences $\mathcal{G}_i$, find a sentence $\mathcal{H}_i$ that actually produces $\mathcal{G}_i$ when correctly skolemized.

Problem 5.4 (uninstantiated variables)   page 297

Suppose we have a deductive-tableau proof of an initial tableau consisting of the goal $\mathcal{F}[x]$, whose only free variable is x. In this proof, assume that the variable x is never replaced by any other variable or term by application of a substitution.

Which of the following sentences are valid? Justify your answers.

$\mathcal{G}_1:\quad (\exists\, x)\mathcal{F}[x]$
$\mathcal{G}_2:\quad \mathcal{F}[a]$, where a is a new constant (not occurring in the tableau)
$\mathcal{G}_3:\quad \mathcal{F}[b]$, where b is any constant
$\mathcal{G}_4:\quad (\forall\, x)\mathcal{F}[x].$

Hint: For each sentence $\mathcal{G}_i$, can the proof of $\mathcal{F}[x]$ be transformed into a proof of $\mathcal{G}_i$?

Problem 5.5 (skolemization of conditionals)   page 297

Suppose the sentence

$$(\forall\, x,\ y,\ z)\ \left[\,f(y)\ =\ \begin{cases} if\ (\forall\, x)\,p\big(f(y),\ x\big) \\ then\ z \\ else\ g\big(x,\ f(z)\big) \end{cases}\right]$$

occurs in a tableau as both an assertion $\mathcal{A}$ and a goal $\mathcal{G}$.

(a) Apply skolemization to $\mathcal{A}$ and $\mathcal{G}$ in such a way that you obtain a quantifier-free assertion $\mathcal{A}'$ and a quantifier-free goal $\mathcal{G}'$, respectively, that are unifiable; provide a most-general unifier.

*(b) Apply skolemization to $\mathcal{A}$ and $\mathcal{G}$ another way, so that the assertion $\mathcal{A}'$ and the goal $\mathcal{G}'$ that you obtain are not unifiable.

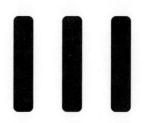

Axiomatic

Theories

6

Foundations

Most of the sentences we will be interested in proving are not valid sentences of predicate logic, i.e., they are not true under every interpretation, but they are true under certain specific interpretations. For example, a sentence such as "For every integer x, $x + 0 = x$," which might be written in predicate logic as $(\forall x)p(f(x,a), x)$, is not valid, but it is certainly true under an interpretation over the integers that assigns

a to be 0

f to be the *addition* function

p to be the *equality* relation.

Our problem is to describe the interpretations under which we intend these sentences to be true. For this purpose, we introduce the general notion of a "theory."

6.1   DEFINITION OF A THEORY

The interpretations we are concerned with are determined by a set of closed sentences, the *axioms* of the theory.

Definition (axioms)

The *axioms* of a theory are a set of closed sentences

$\mathcal{A}_1, \mathcal{A}_2, \mathcal{A}_3, \ldots$.

We will say that the theory is *defined* by its axioms. ⌐

Note that we do not require that the given set of axioms be finite.

Example (family theory).   Suppose we would like to define a theory of family relationships. In the naive "family" interpretation $\mathcal{I}$ we have in mind, the domain is the set of people, and, intuitively speaking,

$f(x)$ means the father of x

$m(x)$ means the mother of x

$p(x, y)$ means y is a parent of x

$gf(x, y)$ means y is a grandfather of x

$gm(x, y)$ means y is a grandmother of x.

(More precisely, $p_{\mathcal{I}}(d, e)$ holds if e is a parent of d, and so forth.) We chose the names of the function symbols, f, m, and predicate symbols, p, gf, gm, to give them mnemonic associations. We may understand unconventional symbols, such as m, gf, and gm, to be informal notations for ordinary symbols of predicate logic, such as g, q, and r.

The axioms of the theory are the following set of closed sentences:

$$\boxed{\mathcal{F}_1 : \quad (\forall x)p\big(x,\, f(x)\big) \hspace{4cm} \textit{(father)}}$$

That is, everyone's father is his or her parent.

$$\boxed{\mathcal{F}_2 : \quad (\forall x)p\big(x,\, m(x)\big) \hspace{4cm} \textit{(mother)}}$$

That is, everyone's mother is his or her parent.

$$\boxed{\mathcal{F}_3 : \quad (\forall x, y)\left[\begin{matrix} \textit{if } \ p(x, y) \\ \textit{then } \ gf\big(x,\, f(y)\big) \end{matrix}\right] \hspace{2cm} \textit{(grandfather)}}$$

That is, the father of one's parent is his or her grandfather.

$$\boxed{\mathcal{F}_4 : \quad (\forall x, y)\left[\begin{matrix} \textit{if } \ p(x, y) \\ \textit{then } \ gm\big(x,\, m(y)\big) \end{matrix}\right] \hspace{2cm} \textit{(grandmother)}}$$

That is, the mother of one's parent is his or her grandmother.

We surround these sentences with a box to indicate that they are axioms. ◢

Let us consider the relationship between the axioms of a theory and the specific interpretation we have in mind.

Definition (model, validity, implication, equivalence, consistency)

Let $\mathcal{A}_i$ be the axioms of a theory T.

An interpretation $\mathcal{I}$ is a *model* for T if each axiom $\mathcal{A}_i$ of the theory is true under $\mathcal{I}$.

A closed sentence $\mathcal{F}$ is *valid* in T if $\mathcal{F}$ is true under every model for T.

A sentence $\mathcal{F}$ *implies* a sentence $\mathcal{G}$ in T if, whenever $\mathcal{F}$ is true under a model $\mathcal{I}$ for T, $\mathcal{G}$ is also true under $\mathcal{I}$.

Two sentences $\mathcal{F}$ and $\mathcal{G}$ are *equivalent* in T if $\mathcal{F}$ and $\mathcal{G}$ have the same truth-value under every model for T.

The theory T is *consistent* if there is at least one model for T.

When we speak of a *theory*, we mean its axioms, its models, and its valid sentences.

As an immediate consequence of the definition, we have that every axiom for a theory is valid in the theory. Also, if a theory is inconsistent, it has no models, and therefore every sentence is "vacuously" valid in the theory. ⟦In the two-volume version of this book, we introduce a restricted vocabulary for each theory. Here each theory employs the entire vocabulary of predicate logic.⟧

In defining a theory, we make sure that the interpretation we have in mind is a model for the theory. In general, however, there are many models for a theory.

Example (models).   The "family" interpretation we had in mind is a model for the family theory defined by the axioms $\mathcal{F}_1, \mathcal{F}_2, \mathcal{F}_3$, and $\mathcal{F}_4$ in the example above because each of the axioms is true under the family interpretation. This is the *intended model* for the theory; however, there are many other models.

Consider the "number" interpretation $\mathcal{I}$ over the domain of the nonnegative integers under which, intuitively speaking,

$$f(x) \qquad \text{is} \quad 2x$$

$$m(x) \qquad \text{is} \quad 3x$$

$$p(x, y) \qquad \text{is} \quad y = 2x \quad \text{or} \quad y = 3x$$

$$gf(x, y) \qquad \text{is} \quad y = 4x \quad \text{or} \quad y = 6x$$

$$gm(x, y) \quad \text{is} \quad y = 6x \quad \text{or} \quad y = 9x.$$

(More precisely, $f_{\mathcal{I}}(d)$ is $2d$, and so forth.) Each of the above axioms $\mathcal{F}_1, \mathcal{F}_2, \mathcal{F}_3$, and $\mathcal{F}_4$ is true under the interpretation $\mathcal{I}$. For instance, the intuitive meaning of the *mother* axiom $\mathcal{F}_2$,

$$(\forall x)p\big(x, m(x)\big),$$

is

for every integer x,
$$3x = 2x \quad \text{or} \quad 3x = 3x,$$

and the intuitive meaning of the *grandfather* axiom $\mathcal{F}_3$,

$$(\forall x, y) \begin{bmatrix} if & p(x, y) \\ then & gf\big(x, f(y)\big) \end{bmatrix},$$

is

> for every integer x and y,
> if $y = 2x$ or $y = 3x$,
> then $2y = 4x$ or $2y = 6x$.

Therefore the "number" interpretation $\mathcal{I}$ is a model for the family theory.   ⌐

For a given closed sentence to be valid in a theory, it must be true under every model for the theory. To establish validity in a theory, we may apply the same techniques we used in predicate logic itself.

Example (validity).   Suppose we would like to establish the validity of the sentence

$$\mathcal{F}: \quad (\forall x)(\exists z)gm(x, z),$$

that is, everyone has a grandmother, in the above "family" theory. Let us give an informal argument based on the semantic rules and our common sense.

Let $\mathcal{I}$ be an arbitrary model for the family theory. Then each of the axioms $\mathcal{F}_1$, $\mathcal{F}_2$, $\mathcal{F}_3$, and $\mathcal{F}_4$ is true under $\mathcal{I}$.

Because the *father* axiom $\mathcal{F}_1$, that is,

$$(\forall x)p\big(x, f(x)\big),$$

is true under $\mathcal{I}$, we know (by the $\forall$ rule) that

> for every domain element d,

$$p\big(x, f(x)\big)$$

is true under the modified interpretation $\langle x \leftarrow d \rangle \circ \mathcal{I}$.

Therefore (by the *application* rule), we know that

> for every domain element d,
>
> (†) $p(x, y)$

is true under $\langle x \leftarrow d \rangle \circ \langle y \leftarrow f_{\mathcal{I}}(d) \rangle \circ \mathcal{I}$,

where $f_{\mathcal{I}}$ is the function assigned to f by $\mathcal{I}$.

Because the *grandmother* axiom $\mathcal{F}_4$, that is,

$$(\forall x, y) \begin{bmatrix} if & p(x, y) \\ then & gm\big(x, m(y)\big) \end{bmatrix},$$

is true under $\mathcal{I}$, we know (by the $\forall$ rule) that, for all domain elements d and e, the subsentence

$$(\ddagger) \quad \begin{array}{l} \textit{if } p(x, y) \\ \textit{then } gm\big(x, m(y)\big) \end{array}$$

is true under $\langle x \leftarrow d \rangle \circ \langle y \leftarrow e \rangle \circ \mathcal{I}$.

Consider an arbitrary domain element d. Taking e to be the domain element $f_{\mathcal{I}}(d)$, we have that

> the implication ($\ddagger$)
> is true under the interpretation $\langle x \leftarrow d \rangle \circ \langle y \leftarrow f_{\mathcal{I}}(d) \rangle \circ \mathcal{I}$.

Because the implication ($\ddagger$) and its antecedent ($\dagger$), that is, $p(x, y)$, are both true under $\langle x \leftarrow d \rangle \circ \langle y \leftarrow f_{\mathcal{I}}(d) \rangle \circ \mathcal{I}$, its consequent

$$gm\big(x, m(y)\big)$$

is also true under $\langle x \leftarrow d \rangle \circ \langle y \leftarrow f_{\mathcal{I}}(d) \rangle \circ \mathcal{I}$.

Therefore (by the *application* rule), the sentence

$$gm(x, z)$$

is true under $\langle x \leftarrow d \rangle \circ \langle z \leftarrow m_{\mathcal{I}}\big(f_{\mathcal{I}}(d)\big) \rangle \circ \mathcal{I}$.

Hence (by the $\exists$ rule),

$$(\exists z)gm(x, z)$$

is true under $\langle x \leftarrow d \rangle \circ \mathcal{I}$.

Because d is an arbitrary domain element, we know (by the $\forall$ rule) that the sentence $\mathcal{F}$, that is,

$$(\forall x)(\exists z)gm(x, z),$$

is true under $\mathcal{I}$.

Because $\mathcal{I}$ was taken to be an arbitrary model for the family theory, this means that $\mathcal{F}$ is valid in the family theory. ⌙

When we wish to distinguish ordinary predicate logic from an axiomatic theory, we shall refer to *pure* predicate logic. One may regard pure predicate logic as an axiomatic theory in which the set of axioms is empty.

Up to now we have been very careful to avoid confusing a symbol in a sentence and its value under an interpretation. For example, we never consider hybrid objects such as $f(a, d)$, in which f is a function symbol, a is a constant symbol, and d is a domain element. Such a construct is neither an expression in predicate logic nor an element in the domain of an interpretation. Our pedantry in this respect, unfortunately, has made our proofs of validity more cumbersome than necessary. Informal arguments may be made more concise and given more intuitive content if we agree to confuse symbols and their meanings under an intended interpretation. The argument in the above example, for instance, can be abbreviated if we say that x "is" a person and $f(x)$ "is" x's father, even though we are confusing symbols and their meanings in this way. We shall call such a style of proof an "intuitive argument."

Example (intuitive argument). Suppose we would like to give an intuitive argument to establish again the validity of the sentence

$$\mathcal{F}: \quad (\forall x)(\exists z)gm(x, z),$$

that is, "Everyone has a grandmother," in the family theory.

Consider an arbitrary person x. By the *father* axiom, $\mathcal{F}_1$, we know that the father $f(x)$ of x is a parent of x; that is,

(†) $\quad p\big(x, f(x)\big).$

By the *grandmother* axiom, $\mathcal{F}_4$, we have (taking y to be $f(x)$), that

$$(\ddagger) \quad \begin{array}{l} if \ p\big(x, f(x)\big) \\ then \ gm\big(x, m(f(x))\big) \end{array}.$$

Hence, by (†) and (‡), we know that the mother $m\big(f(x)\big)$ of the father $f(x)$ of x is a grandmother of x; that is,

$$gm\big(x, m(f(x))\big).$$

Therefore, we know by predicate logic that

$$(\exists z)gm(x, z).$$

Because this has been shown to be true for an arbitrary person x, we can conclude

$$(\forall x)(\exists z)gm(x, z)$$

is a valid sentence of the family theory. Usually this step is omitted from intuitive arguments. ◢

Because such intuitive arguments are shorter and easier to follow than arguments with explicit interpretations, we shall use them from now on, except in situations in which it is important to preserve the distinction between an expression and its meaning. Whenever such an intuitive argument is given, a precise proof could be substituted.

Remark (basic predicate-logic properties). Note that in the intuitive argument we have made use of basic properties of predicate logic without mentioning them. For example, from the *grandmother* axiom $\mathcal{F}_4$,

$$(\forall x, y) \begin{bmatrix} if \ p(x, y) \\ then \ gm\big(x, m(y)\big) \end{bmatrix}$$

we deduced (‡), that is,

$$\begin{array}{l} if \ p\big(x, f(x)\big) \\ then \ gm\big(x, m(f(x))\big) \end{array}.$$

For this purpose, we implicitly appealed twice to the *universal* part of the *quantifier-instantiation* proposition, first taking x to be x itself and then taking y to be $f(x)$.

Henceforth, we shall often appeal to such basic properties with no explicit indication. ◢

In **Problem 6.1**, the reader is asked to give an intuitive argument in the family theory.

6.2   AUGMENTING THEORIES

The sentence $\mathcal{F}$,

$$(\forall x)(\exists z)\, gm(x,\, z),$$

which we have established in the preceding example, will be true under any model for the family theory. In particular, it will be true under the "number" interpretation we gave earlier. The sentence $\mathcal{F}$ then has the intuitive meaning

> for every integer x,
>> there exists an integer z such that
>> $z = 6x$ or $z = 9x$.

In showing that the sentence is valid in the theory, we are showing that it is true under all the models of the theory at once.

Our family theory is "incomplete" in the sense that there are many properties of family relationships that are not valid in the theory. For example, we cannot show the validity of

$$\mathcal{G}:\quad (\forall x)[not\ p(x,\, x)],$$

that is, no one is his or her own parent. Even though this sentence is true under the "family" interpretation we have in mind, it is not true under all models of the theory. In particular, it is not true under the "number" interpretation, for which it has the intuitive meaning

> for every integer x,
>> it is not so that
>> $x = 2x$ or $x = 3x$.

In fact, this sentence is false when x is taken to be 0.

If we want to develop a theory in which $\mathcal{G}$ is valid, we can add $\mathcal{G}$ to the axioms, obtaining an augmented theory defined by the axioms

$$\mathcal{F}_1,\ \mathcal{F}_2,\ \mathcal{F}_3,\ \mathcal{F}_4,\ \text{and}\ \mathcal{G}.$$

The "family" interpretation would still be a model for this new theory, but the "number" interpretation would not.

On the other hand, if we have the "number" interpretation in mind, we may consider adding $(not\ \mathcal{G})$, that is,

$$not\ (\forall x)[not\ p(x,\, x)],$$

or, equivalently,

$$\mathcal{G}':\quad (\exists x)p(x,\, x),$$

as an axiom, obtaining an alternative theory defined by

$$\mathcal{F}_1,\ \mathcal{F}_2,\ \mathcal{F}_3,\ \mathcal{F}_4,\ \text{and}\ \mathcal{G}'.$$

The "family" interpretation would not be a model for this theory, since no one is his or her own parent, but the "number" interpretation would be a model.

Note that, in adding new axioms to a theory, we may reduce its collection of models. In particular, if a new axiom is not true under one of the original models, that interpretation will not be a model for the augmented theory. Therefore, if a sentence is valid in the original theory, it is also valid in the augmented theory, but there may be some sentences that are not valid in the original theory but that are valid in the augmented theory.

In forming or augmenting a theory, we should be careful that the axioms are consistent, i.e., that there is at least one model for the theory.

Example (inconsistency). In our original formulation of the "family" theory defined by the axioms

$$\mathcal{F}_1, \ \mathcal{F}_2, \ \mathcal{F}_3, \ \text{and} \ \mathcal{F}_4,$$

we did not account for the possibility of "first" people such as Adam. We might be tempted to add to our theory an axiom

$$\mathcal{A}: \quad (\forall y)[not \ p(a, \ y)],$$

that is, person a has no parents. However, the augmented theory defined by the axioms

$$\mathcal{F}_1, \ \mathcal{F}_2, \ \mathcal{F}_3, \ \mathcal{F}_4, \ \text{and} \ \mathcal{A}$$

is inconsistent; i.e., there is no model for this theory.

To see this, suppose $\mathcal{I}$ is a model for the augmented theory. Then the *father* axiom $\mathcal{F}_1$, that is,

$$(\forall x)p\big(x, \ f(x)\big),$$

is true under $\mathcal{I}$. Therefore (taking x to be a)

$$p\big(a, \ f(a)\big)$$

is true under $\mathcal{I}$. Thus $\big(\text{taking } y \text{ to be } f(a)\big)$

$$(\exists y)p(a, \ y)$$

is also true under $\mathcal{I}$.

Note that this sentence is equivalent (by the duality between the quantifiers) to the sentence

$$not \ (\forall y)\big[not \ p(a, \ y)\big],$$

which is exactly the negation of the new axiom $\mathcal{A}$. Hence this axiom cannot be true under $\mathcal{I}$, contradicting our original supposition that $\mathcal{I}$ is a model for the augmented theory. ◢

If a theory is inconsistent, it has no models, and therefore every closed sentence is (vacuously) valid in the theory. For this reason, inconsistent theories are not very interesting. By demonstrating the existence of a model for a given set of axioms, we can ensure that the theory it defines is consistent.

We introduce now two axiomatic theories that are of importance in their own right.

6.3   THEORY OF STRICT PARTIAL ORDERINGS

For a given binary predicate symbol p, the *theory of the strict partial ordering p* is the theory defined by the axioms

$$
\begin{array}{lll}
\mathcal{S}_1: & (\forall x, y, z) \begin{bmatrix} if \ \ p(x,\, y) \ \ and \ \ p(y,\, z) \\ then \ \ p(x,\, z) \end{bmatrix} & (transitivity) \\[1.5em]
\mathcal{S}_2: & (\forall x) \begin{bmatrix} not \ \ p(x,\, x) \end{bmatrix} & (irreflexivity)
\end{array}
$$

Under any model for the theory defined by $\mathcal{S}_1$ and $\mathcal{S}_2$, we shall say that p denotes a *strict partial ordering.*

In this theory, we shall use the conventional infix notation $x \prec y$ rather than $p(x,\, y)$. We can thus rewrite $\mathcal{S}_1$ and $\mathcal{S}_2$ as

$$
\begin{array}{lll}
\mathcal{S}_1: & (\forall x, y, z) \begin{bmatrix} if \ \ x \prec y \ \ and \ \ y \prec z \\ then \ \ x \prec z \end{bmatrix} & (transitivity) \\[1.5em]
\mathcal{S}_2: & (\forall x)[not \ \ (x \prec x)] & (irreflexivity)
\end{array}
$$

The reader should understand that here $x \prec y$ is merely an informal notation for $p(x,\, y)$.

Let us consider two models for the theory of the strict partial ordering $\prec$.

Examples (strict partial orderings)

• *The less-than relation*

Consider an interpretation $\mathcal{I}$ over the integers that assigns the less-than relation $<$ to the binary predicate symbol $\prec$. Then $\mathcal{I}$ is a model for the theory of the strict partial ordering $\prec$, because the *transitivity* and *irreflexivity* axioms for $\prec$ both hold under $\mathcal{I}$. The intuitive meanings of these axioms under this interpretation are

> for every integer d_1, d_2, and d_3,
>   if $d_1 < d_2$ and $d_2 < d_3$
>   then $d_1 < d_3$

and

> for every integer d,
>   not $d < d$,

which are both true.

• *A finite relation*

Consider an interpretation $\mathcal{I}$ over the finite domain $\{A, B, C, D\}$ that assigns to $\prec$ the binary relation illustrated by the following diagram:

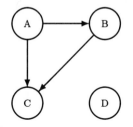

In this representation, an arc leading directly from one element d to another e indicates that the relation holds between these elements; that is, $d \prec_{\mathcal{I}} e$ is true. Thus we have

$$A \prec_{\mathcal{I}} B, \quad B \prec_{\mathcal{I}} C, \quad \text{and} \quad A \prec_{\mathcal{I}} C.$$

The absence of an arc indicates that the relation does not hold between the corresponding elements. Thus

$$\text{not } B \prec_{\mathcal{I}} D, \quad \text{not } B \prec_{\mathcal{I}} B, \quad \text{not } B \prec_{\mathcal{I}} A, \quad \text{and so forth.}$$

The reader may confirm that the *transitivity* and *irreflexivity* axioms for $\prec$ do hold under $\mathcal{I}$; therefore $\mathcal{I}$ is a model for the theory of the strict partial ordering $\prec$. ◢

Now let us consider two interpretations that are not models for the theory of the strict partial ordering $\prec$.

Examples (not strict partial orderings).

• *The inequality relation*

Consider an interpretation $\mathcal{I}$ over the integers that assigns the inequality relation $\neq$ to the binary predicate symbol $\prec$. Then $\mathcal{I}$ is not a model for the theory of the strict partial ordering $\prec$. The *irreflexivity* axiom for $\prec$ does hold under $\mathcal{I}$; its intuitive meaning is

> for every integer d,
>   not $d \neq d$,

which is true. On the other hand, the *transitivity* axiom for $\prec$ does not hold under $\mathcal{I}$; its intuitive meaning is

> for every integer d_1, d_2, and d_3,
>   if $d_1 \neq d_2$ and $d_2 \neq d_3$
>   then $d_1 \neq d_3$,

which is false if d_1 and d_3 are the same integer and d_2 is a different integer.

- *A finite relation*

Consider an interpretation $\mathcal{I}$ over the domain $\{A, B, C\}$ that assigns to $\prec$ the binary relation illustrated by the following diagram:

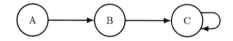

Then $\mathcal{I}$ is not a model for the theory of the strict partial ordering $\prec$. The *transitivity* axiom for $\prec$ does not hold under $\mathcal{I}$, for we have

$$A \prec_{\mathcal{I}} B \quad \text{and} \quad B \prec_{\mathcal{I}} C \quad \text{but not} \quad A \prec_{\mathcal{I}} C.$$

Also, the *irreflexivity* axiom for $\prec$ does not hold, for we have

$$C \prec_{\mathcal{I}} C. \quad \lrcorner$$

In **Problem 6.2**, the reader is asked to construct interpretations for the theory of the strict partial ordering $\prec$ over a finite domain under which one of the axioms is true and the other is not.

ASYMMETRY

Now let us establish the validity of a sentence in the theory.

Proposition (asymmetry of strict partial orderings)

In the theory of the strict partial ordering $\prec$, the sentence

$$S: \quad (\forall x, y) \left[\begin{matrix} if & x \prec y \\ then & not & (y \prec x) \end{matrix} \right] \qquad (asymmetry)$$

is valid. $\quad \lrcorner$

This means that S is true under all models for the theory defined by S_1 and S_2. In other words, for any interpretation under which S_1 and S_2 are true, S is also true. We give an intuitive argument.

Proof.   Suppose that, contrary to the *asymmetry* sentence S, there exist elements x and y such that both $x \prec y$ and $y \prec x$. Then, by the *transitivity* axiom S_1, we have $x \prec x$. But this contradicts the *irreflexivity* axiom S_2. $\quad \lrcorner$

Remark (asymmetry implies irreflexivity).   We have established that, in the theory defined by the *transitivity* axiom S_1 and the *irreflexivity* axiom S_2, the *asymmetry* sentence S is valid.

On the other hand, note that the *asymmetry* sentence $\mathcal{S}$,

$$(\forall x, y) \begin{bmatrix} if & x \prec y \\ then & not & (y \prec x) \end{bmatrix},$$

by itself implies the *irreflexivity* sentence $\mathcal{S}_2$. For, taking y to be x, we obtain

$$(\forall x) \begin{bmatrix} if & x \prec x \\ then & not & (x \prec x) \end{bmatrix}.$$

But (by propositional logic)

$$\begin{array}{l} if \ \ x \prec x \\ then \ \ not \ (x \prec x) \end{array} \quad \text{is equivalent to} \quad not \ (x \prec x).$$

Therefore (by the substitutivity of equivalence)

$$(\forall x) \begin{bmatrix} if & x \prec x \\ then & not & (x \prec x) \end{bmatrix}$$

is equivalent to

$$(\forall x) \big[not \ (x \prec x) \big],$$

which is the *irreflexivity* sentence $\mathcal{S}_2$.   ◢

Up to now we have been discussing a theory whose only axioms are the *transitivity* axiom $\mathcal{S}_1$ and the *irreflexivity* axiom $\mathcal{S}_2$. Consider a theory in which these properties are true for some binary predicate symbol q. In other words, whatever the axioms of the theory are, the sentences

$$(\forall x, y, z) \begin{bmatrix} if & q(x, y) & and & q(y, z) \\ then & q(x, z) & \end{bmatrix}$$

and

$$(\forall x) \big[not \ q(x, x) \big]$$

are valid. We shall say that, in such a theory, q denotes a *strict partial ordering*. Of course, it is possible to have a theory with many binary predicate symbols, each denoting a strict partial ordering.

INVERSE RELATION

In practice, people often use the sentence $x \succ y$ synonymously with $y \prec x$. This can be reflected in our theory by introducing a new axiom. More precisely, we augment the theory of the strict partial ordering $\prec$ by adding an axiom that defines the relation $\succ$, the *inverse* of $\prec$, as follows:

$$\boxed{\ \mathcal{S}_3 : \quad (\forall x, y) \big[x \succ y \ \equiv \ y \prec x \big] \hspace{4cm} (\textit{inverse}) \ }$$

As before, $x \succ y$ is merely an informal notation for an ordinary predicate symbol such as $q_{17}(x, y)$. We shall refer to $\mathcal{S}_3$ as the *definition* of the inverse relation.

Whenever we augment a theory by introducing a new axiom, we run the risk of making our theory inconsistent. If so, the augmented theory will have no model, and therefore any sentence will be valid. We can show that the augmented theory is consistent by exhibiting a model for the enlarged axiom set. In this case, it is clear that there do exist models for the augmented theory obtained by introducing the new axiom $\mathcal{S}_3$ into the strict partial ordering theory.

6.4 THEORY OF EQUIVALENCE RELATIONS

For any binary predicate symbol p, the *theory of the equivalence relation p* is the theory defined by the axioms:

$$\mathcal{Q}_1 : \quad (\forall\, x,\, y,\, z) \begin{bmatrix} if \;\; p(x,\, y) \;\; and \;\; p(y,\, z) \\ then \;\; p(x,\, z) \end{bmatrix} \qquad (transitivity)$$

$$\mathcal{Q}_2 : \quad (\forall\, x,\, y) \begin{bmatrix} if \;\; p(x,\, y) \\ then \;\; p(y,\, x) \end{bmatrix} \qquad (symmetry)$$

$$\mathcal{Q}_3 : \quad (\forall\, x)p(x,\, x) \qquad (reflexivity)$$

Under any model for the theory defined by $\mathcal{Q}_1$, $\mathcal{Q}_2$, and $\mathcal{Q}_3$, we shall say that p denotes an *equivalence relation*.

The convention for an equivalence relation is to write $x \approx y$ rather than $p(x,\, y)$. In other words, we shall use the symbol $\approx$ informally, rather than the predicate symbol p, to denote a relation for which $\mathcal{Q}_1$, $\mathcal{Q}_2$, and $\mathcal{Q}_3$ hold. We shall thus write $\mathcal{Q}_1$, $\mathcal{Q}_2$, and $\mathcal{Q}_3$ as

$$\mathcal{Q}_1 : \quad (\forall\, x,\, y,\, z) \begin{bmatrix} if \;\; x \approx y \;\; and \;\; y \approx z \\ then \;\; x \approx z \end{bmatrix} \qquad (transitivity)$$

$$\mathcal{Q}_2 : \quad (\forall\, x,\, y) \begin{bmatrix} if \;\; x \approx y \\ then \;\; y \approx x \end{bmatrix} \qquad (symmetry)$$

$$\mathcal{Q}_3 : \quad (\forall\, x)\begin{bmatrix} x \approx x \end{bmatrix} \qquad (reflexivity)$$

Let us consider some models for the theory of the equivalence relation $\approx$.

Examples (equivalence relations).

- *The congruence-modulo-2 relation*

Consider an interpretation $\mathcal{I}$ over the integers that assigns to $\approx$ the "congruence modulo 2" relation $\approx_2$, that is, for every integer d_1 and d_2,

$$d_1 \approx_2 d_2$$
if and only if
$$\begin{bmatrix} d_1 \text{ and } d_2 \text{ are both even} \\ \text{or} \\ d_1 \text{ and } d_2 \text{ are both odd} \end{bmatrix}.$$

Thus $2 \approx_2 6$ but not $1 \approx_2 2$.

The reader may confirm that the *transitivity, symmetry,* and *reflexivity* axioms Q_1, Q_2, and Q_3 are true under this interpretation.

● *A finite relation*

Consider an interpretation I over the domain $\{A, B, C, D, E, F, G\}$ that assigns $\approx$ to be the binary relation illustrated by the following diagram:

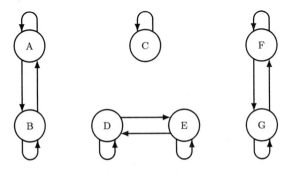

The reader may confirm that the *transitivity, symmetry,* and *reflexivity* axioms Q_1, Q_2, and Q_3 each hold under the interpretation I; therefore I is a model for the theory of the equivalence relation $\approx$. ⌐

Now let us consider some finite interpretations that are not models for the theory of the equivalence relation $\approx$.

Examples (nonequivalence relations).

● *A nontransitive relation*

Over the domain $\{A, B, C\}$, consider the interpretation I that assigns to $\approx$ the binary relation $\approx_I$ illustrated by the following diagram:

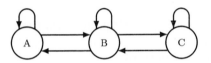

Then I is not a model for the theory of the equivalence relation $\approx$, because the *transitivity* axiom Q_1 does not hold under I. In particular, we have

$$A \approx_I B \quad \text{and} \quad B \approx_I C \quad \text{but not} \quad A \approx_I C.$$

The reader may confirm that the *symmetry* and *reflexivity* axioms do hold under $\mathcal{I}$.

- *A nonsymmetric relation*

Over the domain $\{A, B\}$, consider the interpretation $\mathcal{I}$ that assigns to $\approx$ the binary relation $\approx_\mathcal{I}$ illustrated by the following diagram:

Then $\mathcal{I}$ is not a model for the theory of the equivalence relation $\approx$, because the *symmetry* axiom $\mathcal{Q}_2$ does not hold under $\mathcal{I}$; we have

$$A \approx_\mathcal{I} B \quad \text{but not} \quad B \approx_\mathcal{I} A.$$

The reader may confirm that the *transitivity* and *reflexivity* axioms do hold under $\mathcal{I}$.

- *A nonreflexive relation*

Over the domain $\{A\}$, consider the interpretation $\mathcal{I}$ that assigns to $\approx$ the binary relation $\approx_\mathcal{I}$ illustrated by the following diagram:

In other words, $\approx_\mathcal{I}$ is the empty relation, which holds between no domain elements at all. Then $\mathcal{I}$ is not a model for the theory of the equivalence relation $\approx$, because the *reflexivity* axiom $\mathcal{Q}_3$ does not hold under $\approx_\mathcal{I}$; we have

$$\text{not} \quad A \approx_\mathcal{I} A.$$

The reader may note that the *transitivity* and *symmetry* axioms $\mathcal{Q}_1$ and $\mathcal{Q}_2$ do hold under $\mathcal{I}$, because their antecedents are always false under $\mathcal{I}$. ◢

The above three examples illustrate that the axioms for the equivalence relation $\approx$ are *independent*; in other words, none of them is implied by the other two. For in each example we presented an interpretation under which two of the axioms are true and the third is false. If the two axioms implied the third, all three axioms would be true.

In **Problem 6.3**, the reader is asked to find the bug in a fallacious proof that one of the axioms for the theory of equivalence is implied by the other two.

DOUBLE TRANSITIVITY

From the axioms for the equivalence relation $\approx$, we can show the following result.

Proposition (double transitivity)

The sentence

$$(\forall u, v, x, y) \begin{bmatrix} if & u \approx v & and \\ & u \approx x & and \\ & v \approx y \\ then & x \approx y \end{bmatrix} \qquad (double\ transitivity)$$

is valid in the theory of the equivalence relation $\approx$. ⌙

We give an intuitive justification.

Proof.   Suppose that for arbitrary elements u, v, x, and y,

$$u \approx v, \quad u \approx x, \quad and \quad v \approx y$$

are all true; we attempt to show that then

$$x \approx y$$

is true.

Because $u \approx v$ and $v \approx y$, we have, by the *transitivity* axiom $\mathcal{Q}_1$, that

$$u \approx y.$$

Because $u \approx x$, we have, by the *symmetry* axiom $\mathcal{Q}_2$, that

$$x \approx u.$$

Finally, because $x \approx u$ and $u \approx y$, we have, by the *transitivity* axiom $\mathcal{Q}_1$ again, that

$$x \approx y,$$

which is the desired conclusion. ⌙

6.5   THEORY OF EQUALITY

The equality relation is an important tool that requires special treatment. We want to define a theory of equality under whose intended models a binary predicate symbol p is assigned the equality relation over the domain; i.e., the sentence $p(t_1, t_2)$ is true under a model $\mathcal{I}$ if and only if the terms t_1 and t_2 have the same value under $\mathcal{I}$.

The usual convention is to write $x = y$ rather than $p(x, y)$ to denote the equality relation in the theory of equality. The reader should understand that here $x = y$ is merely an informal notation for $p(x, y)$, where p is a binary predicate symbol. It is not to be confused with our use of the notation $d_1 = d_2$, in giving the intuitive meanings for sentences, to indicate that d_1 and d_2 are the same domain elements.

THE THEORY

Although our previous theories have been defined by finite sets of axioms, the theory of equality requires a possibly infinite axiom set.

- *Basic axioms*

$$\mathcal{E}_1: \quad (\forall\, x,\, y,\, z) \begin{bmatrix} if \ \ x = y \ \ and \ \ y = z \\ then \ \ x = z \end{bmatrix} \qquad (transitivity)$$

$$\mathcal{E}_2: \quad (\forall\, x,\, y) \begin{bmatrix} if \ \ x = y \\ then \ \ y = x \end{bmatrix} \qquad (symmetry)$$

$$\mathcal{E}_3: \quad (\forall\, x)[x = x] \qquad (reflexivity)$$

- *Substitutivity axiom schemata*

For every k-ary function symbol f and for each i from 1 through k,

$$\mathcal{E}_4(f): \quad \begin{matrix} (\forall\, x,\, y) \\ (\forall\, z_1, \ldots, z_{i-1}, z_{i+1}, \ldots, z_k) \end{matrix} \begin{bmatrix} if \ \ x = y \\ then \ \ f(z_1, \ \ldots, z_{i-1}, x, z_{i+1}, \ \ldots, z_k) = \\ f(z_1, \ \ldots, z_{i-1}, y, z_{i+1}, \ \ldots, z_k) \end{bmatrix}$$

$$(functional\ substitutivity\ for\ f)$$

For every ℓ-ary predicate symbol q (other than $=$) and for each j from 1 through ℓ,

$$\mathcal{E}_5(q): \quad \begin{matrix} (\forall\, x,\, y) \\ (\forall\, z_1, \ldots, z_{j-1}, z_{j+1}, \ldots, z_\ell) \end{matrix} \begin{bmatrix} if \ \ x = y \\ then \ \ q(z_1, \ \ldots, z_{j-1}, x, z_{j+1}, \ \ldots, z_\ell) \\ \equiv \\ q(z_1, \ \ldots, z_{j-1} \cdot y, z_{j+1} \cdots, z_\ell) \end{bmatrix}$$

$$(predicate\ substitutivity\ for\ q)$$

Thus both the *functional-substitutivity* axiom schema $\mathcal{E}_4(f)$ and the *predicate-substitutivity* axiom schema $\mathcal{E}_5(q)$ actually represent infinite sets of axioms, one or more for each function symbol f and predicate symbol q. We exclude the instances of the *predicate-substitutivity* axiom for $=$, in which q is the equality symbol $=$, because these instances follow from the other axioms.

Example. For a binary function symbol g, the corresponding instances of the *functional-substitutivity* axiom schema $\mathcal{E}_4(g)$ are

$$(\forall\, x,\, y,\, z_2) \begin{bmatrix} if \ \ x = y \\ then \ \ g(x, z_2) = g(y, z_2) \end{bmatrix}$$

and

$$(\forall x, y, z_1) \begin{bmatrix} if & x = y \\ then & g(z_1, x) = g(z_1, y) \end{bmatrix}.$$

For a unary predicate symbol p, the corresponding instance of the *predicate-substitutivity* axiom schema $\mathcal{E}_5(p)$ is

$$(\forall x, y) \begin{bmatrix} if & x = y \\ then & p(x) \equiv p(y) \end{bmatrix}. \quad \blacksquare$$

Note that the axioms for the theory of equality include the *transitivity, symmetry,* and *reflexivity* axioms from the theory of equivalence relations; in other words, $=$ denotes an equivalence relation. This means that since the *double-transitivity* property,

$$(\forall u, v, x, y) \begin{bmatrix} if & u = v & and \\ & u = x & and \\ & v = y & \\ then & x = y & \end{bmatrix},$$

was proved to be valid in the theory of the equivalence relation $=$, it is also valid in the theory of equality.

The models for the theory of equality exhibit the following property.

Proposition (semantic rule for equality)

Suppose that $\mathcal{I}$ is a model for the theory of equality and t_1 and t_2 are terms.

If

> the value of t_1 under $\mathcal{I}$
> is the same as
> the value of t_2 under $\mathcal{I}$,

then

> $t_1 = t_2$ is true under $\mathcal{I}$. $\quad \blacksquare$

We shall refer to this result as the "$=$ rule."

Proof.   Suppose that the terms t_1 and t_2 each have the same value, the domain element d, under $\mathcal{I}$. We would like to show that the sentence $t_1 = t_2$ is true under $\mathcal{I}$.

Let $=_{\mathcal{I}}$ be the binary relation assigned to the equality predicate symbol $=$ under $\mathcal{I}$. Then (by the *proposition* semantic rule, because the values of t_1 and t_2 under $\mathcal{I}$ are each d)

> the value of $t_1 = t_2$ under $\mathcal{I}$ is $d =_{\mathcal{I}} d$.

We would like to show that

$d =_\mathcal{I} d$ is true.

We have assumed that $\mathcal{I}$ is a model for the theory of equality. In particular, the *reflexivity* axiom $\mathcal{E}_3$,

$(\forall x)[x = x]$,

is true under $\mathcal{I}$. Hence (taking x to be t_1), the sentence

$t_1 = t_1$ is true under $\mathcal{I}$.

We know (according to the *proposition* semantic rule, because the value of t_1 under $\mathcal{I}$ is d) that

the value of $t_1 = t_1$ under $\mathcal{I}$ is $d =_\mathcal{I} d$.

Therefore

$d =_\mathcal{I} d$ is true,

as we wanted to show. ◢

We wanted to formulate a theory of equality under whose models the binary predicate symbol $=$ would be assigned the equality relation over the domain; i.e., under any model $\mathcal{I}$ for the theory, the sentence $t_1 = t_2$ is true under $\mathcal{I}$ if and only if the terms t_1 and t_2 have the same value under $\mathcal{I}$. In fact, this is not the case for the theory of equality we have formulated.

The above semantic rule establishes that the implication holds in one direction; i.e., if the terms t_1 and t_2 have the same value under $\mathcal{I}$, then the sentence $t_1 = t_2$ is true under $\mathcal{I}$.

The converse of the implication, however, is not true: There are some "abnormal" models $\mathcal{I}$ for the theory of equality such that some terms t_1 and t_2 have distinct values under $\mathcal{I}$, but the sentence $t_1 = t_2$ is true under $\mathcal{I}$ nevertheless. This is illustrated by the following example.

Example (abnormal model for equality).   Consider an interpretation $\mathcal{I}$ over the domain $\{\text{A}, \text{B}\}$ of two elements that assigns

a to be A
b to be B

and each predicate symbol (including the equality symbol $=$) to be the relation that is true for all domain elements. (We do not care what functions are assigned to function symbols under $\mathcal{I}$.)

This is a model for the theory of equality; each of the axioms $\mathcal{E}_1$ through $\mathcal{E}_5$ is true under $\mathcal{I}$. For instance, to show that the *symmetry* axiom $\mathcal{E}_2$ is true under $\mathcal{I}$, it suffices to show that, for every domain element d and e, the subsentence

if $x = y$
then $y = x$

is true under the modified interpretation $\langle x \leftarrow d \rangle \circ \langle y \leftarrow e \rangle \circ \mathcal{I}$. But since the equality symbol $=$ is assigned the binary relation that is true for all domain elements, including e and d, the consequent $y = x$ of the implication, and hence the implication itself, is true under the modified interpretation.

The truth under $\mathcal{I}$ of the other axioms for equality may be established similarly. Under $\mathcal{I}$, the terms a and b have distinct values A and B, respectively, but the sentence $a = b$ is true. ⌐

The above example illustrates that the converse of the semantic rule for equality (the $=$ rule) is not true. In other words, there are some models for the theory of equality under which the equality predicate symbol $=$ is not assigned the normal equality relation over the domain. Such "abnormal" models cannot be avoided in predicate logic, but they do not disturb us because the sentences we shall want to prove concerning the equality relation will be true under the abnormal models as well as the normal models.

In **Problem 6.4**, the reader is asked to show that a certain sentence is not valid in the theory of equality.

SUBSTITUTIVITY OF EQUALITY

The most important property of the theory of equality is given in the following proposition.

Proposition (substitutivity of equality)

Suppose s, t, and $r\langle s \rangle$ are terms; then the universal closure of

$$\begin{array}{l} \textit{if } \ s = t \\ \textit{then } \ r\langle s \rangle = r\langle t \rangle \end{array} \qquad\qquad (\textit{term})$$

is valid in the theory of equality.

Suppose s and t are terms and $\mathcal{F}\langle s \rangle$ is a sentence; then the universal closure of

$$\begin{array}{l} \textit{if } \ s = t \\ \textit{then } \ \mathcal{F}\langle s \rangle \ \equiv \ \mathcal{F}\langle t \rangle \end{array} \qquad\qquad (\textit{sentence})$$

is valid in the theory of equality. ⌐

Recall that, for any term $r\langle s \rangle$, the term $r\langle t \rangle$ denotes the result of safely replacing zero, one, or more free occurrences of s in $r\langle s \rangle$ with t. Similarly for sentences $\mathcal{F}\langle s \rangle$ and $\mathcal{F}\langle t \rangle$.

Let us consider an example.

Example.   According to the *term* part of the proposition, the sentence

$$(\forall x, y) \left[\begin{array}{l} if \ \ x = f(y) \\ then \ \ h\big(g(x, \ x)\big) \ = \ h\big(g(f(y), \ x)\big) \end{array} \right]$$

is valid in the theory of equality, because $h\big(g(f(y), \ x)\big)$ is the result of safely replacing one of the free occurrences of x in $h\big(g(x, \ x)\big)$ with $f(y)$.

Also, according to the *sentence* part of the proposition, the sentence

$$(\forall x, y) \left[\begin{array}{l} if \ \ x = f(y) \\ then \ \ \left[\begin{array}{c} (\exists y)p(x, \ y) \\ \equiv \\ (\exists y')p\big(f(y), \ y'\big) \end{array} \right] \end{array} \right]$$

is valid in the theory of equality, because $(\exists y')p\big(f(y), \ y'\big)$ is the result of safely replacing the free occurrence of x in $(\exists y)p(x, \ y)$ with $f(y)$. Note that we have renamed the bound variable y to y'.   ⌐

The truth of the proposition is intuitively clear, but the general proof, which we omit, is rather technical.

REPLACEMENT

Using the *substitutivity-of-equality* proposition one can establish another important property of the theory of equality.

Proposition (replacement)

Suppose x is a variable, t is a term, and $\mathcal{F}[x]$ is a sentence, where x does not occur free in t.

Then

$$(\forall x)\big[if \ \ x = t \ \ then \ \ \mathcal{F}[x]\big] \quad \text{is equivalent to} \quad \mathcal{F}[t] \qquad (universal)$$

and

$$(\exists x)\big[x = t \ \ and \ \ \mathcal{F}[x]\big] \quad \text{is equivalent to} \quad \mathcal{F}[t] \qquad (existential)$$

in the theory of equality.   ⌐

One can also establish a more general version of the proposition, in which n variables $x_1, \ x_2, \ \ldots, \ x_n$ in a sentence $\mathcal{F}[x_1, x_2, \ \ldots, x_n]$ are replaced by n terms $t_1, t_2, \ \ldots, t_n$.

The *replacement* proposition would not hold if we used the partial substitution operation instead of the total substitution operation or if we abolished the

restriction that x does not occur free in t; the reader is requested to show this in
Problem 6.5.

The reader is also requested (in **Problem 6.6**) to show the validity of the
following properties of conditional terms in the theory of equality:

$$(if \ \ true \ \ then \ \ a \ \ else \ \ b) = a \qquad\qquad\qquad (true)$$

$$(if \ \ false \ \ then \ \ a \ \ else \ \ b) = b \qquad\qquad\qquad (false)$$

$$(\forall x) \begin{bmatrix} f\big(if \ \ p(x) \ \ then \ \ a \ \ else \ \ b\big) \\ = \\ if \ \ p(x) \ \ then \ \ f(a) \ \ else \ \ f(b) \end{bmatrix} \qquad\qquad (distributivity)$$

THEORY WITH EQUALITY

Often we wish to define theories whose models assign special meanings to certain
constant, function, and predicate symbols in addition to the equality predicate
symbol $=$. For this purpose we may provide special axioms for the theory, as well
as the equality axioms $\mathcal{E}_1$ through $\mathcal{E}_5$. A theory that is defined by a set of axioms
that includes the equality axioms is called a *theory with equality*.

In general, when we describe a model $\mathcal{I}$ for a theory with equality, we will assume (unless stated otherwise) that the equality symbol $=$ is assigned the normal
equality relation, that is,

$x = y$ is true under $\mathcal{I}$ if and only if $x_\mathcal{I}$ is identical to $y_\mathcal{I}$.

Under such a model all the equality axioms are satisfied.

In any theory with equality there is exactly one equality relation. This is
expressed precisely in the following result. (The proof is requested in **Problem
6.7**.)

Proposition (uniqueness of equality)

In any theory with equality, let $r(x, y)$ be an equality symbol, i.e., a
binary predicate symbol such that the equality axioms $\mathcal{E}_1$ through $\mathcal{E}_5$
are valid for r. (In other words, r satisfies the *transitivity, symmetry,*
and *reflexivity* axioms and the *functional-* and *predicate-substitutivity*
axiom schemata.)

Then r and the equality symbol $=$ denote the same relation; i.e., the
sentence

$$(\forall x, y) [r(x, y) \equiv (x = y)] \qquad\qquad (uniqueness)$$

is valid in the theory. ◢

We have seen that there are abnormal models for the theory of equality, under which an equality symbol is not assigned the normal equality relation over the domain. The above proposition establishes that under any one model for the theory of equality, all the equality symbols must be assigned the same relation, even if that relation is not the normal one.

In the following sections, we give three examples of theories with equality: the theories of weak partial orderings, groups, and pairs.

6.6 THEORY OF WEAK PARTIAL ORDERINGS

Our first example of a theory with equality is the *theory of the weak partial ordering* $\preceq$, where $\preceq$ is any binary predicate symbol, defined by the following special axioms:

$$\mathcal{W}_1: \quad (\forall x, y, z) \begin{bmatrix} if & x \preceq y & and & y \preceq z \\ then & x \preceq z \end{bmatrix} \qquad (transitivity)$$

$$\mathcal{W}_2: \quad (\forall x, y) \begin{bmatrix} if & x \preceq y & and & y \preceq x \\ then & x = y \end{bmatrix} \qquad (antisymmetry)$$

$$\mathcal{W}_3: \quad (\forall x)[x \preceq x] \qquad (reflexivity)$$

As in any theory with equality, we also have the equality axioms $\mathcal{E}_1$ through $\mathcal{E}_5$. In particular, we have two instances $\mathcal{E}_5(\preceq)$ of the *predicate-substitutivity* axiom schema $\mathcal{E}_5(q)$ in which q is taken to be the binary predicate symbol $\preceq$,

$$(\forall x, y, z) \begin{bmatrix} if & x = y \\ then & x \preceq z \equiv y \preceq z \end{bmatrix}$$

$$(left\ predicate\ substitutivity\ for\ \preceq)$$

and

$$(\forall x, y, z) \begin{bmatrix} if & x = y \\ then & z \preceq x \equiv z \preceq y \end{bmatrix}$$

$$(right\ predicate\ substitutivity\ for\ \preceq)$$

In writing these axioms we have dropped the subscripts of z_1 and z_2 that appeared in the general schemata.

The *transitivity* axiom $\mathcal{W}_1$, the *antisymmetry* axiom $\mathcal{W}_2$, and the *reflexivity* axiom $\mathcal{W}_3$ for the weak partial ordering $\preceq$ are independent; i.e., none of them is implied by the other two. The reader is requested to show this (in **Problem 6.8**) by constructing, for each of these axioms, a model for the theory of equality under which the axiom is false but the other two axioms are true.

The following result establishes that the equality relation of this theory can be paraphrased in terms of the weak partial ordering $\preceq$.

Proposition (splitting)

The sentence

$$(\forall x, y) \begin{bmatrix} x = y \\ \equiv \\ x \preceq y \ \text{ and } \ y \preceq x \end{bmatrix} \qquad (\textit{splitting})$$

is valid in the theory of the weak partial ordering $\preceq$. ⌐

We give an intuitive justification.

Proof.   Consider arbitrary elements x and y; it suffices to show that

> *if* $x = y$
> *then* $x \preceq y$ *and* $y \preceq x$

and

> *if* $x \preceq y$ *and* $y \preceq x$
> *then* $x = y$.

The latter sentence follows from the *antisymmetry* axiom $\mathcal{W}_2$.

To show the former sentence, suppose that

> $x = y$;

we would like to show that

> $x \preceq y$ *and* $y \preceq x$.

We know (by the *left predicate-substitutivity* equality axiom for $\preceq$, taking z to be x) that

> *if* $x = y$
> *then* $x \preceq x \ \equiv \ y \preceq x$

and (by the *right predicate-substitutivity equality* axiom for $\preceq$, taking z to be x) that

> *if* $x = y$
> *then* $x \preceq x \ \equiv \ x \preceq y$.

Therefore, because $x = y$ and (by the *reflexivity* axiom $\mathcal{W}_3$) $x \preceq x$, we have (by propositional logic)

> $x \preceq y$ *and* $y \preceq x$,

as we wanted to show. ⌐

We may augment the theory of the weak partial ordering $\preceq$ by introducing a new relation $\prec$, the *irreflexive restriction* of $\preceq$, defined by the axiom

$$\mathcal{W}_4: \quad (\forall x, y) \begin{bmatrix} x \prec y \\ \equiv \\ x \preceq y \ \text{ and } \ not \ (x = y) \end{bmatrix}$$

$$(\textit{irreflexive restriction of } \preceq)$$

Proposition (irreflexive restriction)

The irreflexive restriction $\prec$ of $\preceq$ is a strict partial ordering. ◢

The proof is requested in **Problem 6.9**.

As in the theory of strict partial orderings, we may augment our theory of the weak partial ordering $\preceq$ by introducing a new binary predicate symbol $\succeq$, denoting the *inverse* relation of $\preceq$. It is defined by the new special axiom:

$$\mathcal{W}_5: \quad (\forall\, x,\, y)\,[x \succeq y \;\equiv\; y \preceq x] \hspace{3cm} (inverse)$$

Because the augmented theory is a theory with equality, we also have the corresponding instances $\mathcal{E}_5(\succeq)$ of the *predicate-substitutivity* axiom schema for equality,

$$(\forall\, x,\, y,\, z) \begin{bmatrix} if & x = y \\ then & x \succeq z \;\equiv\; y \succeq z \end{bmatrix}$$

$$(left\ predicate\ substitutivity\ for\ \succeq)$$

$$(\forall\, x,\, y,\, z) \begin{bmatrix} if & x = y \\ then & z \succeq x \;\equiv\; z \succeq y \end{bmatrix}$$

$$(right\ predicate\ substitutivity\ for\ \succeq)$$

We may establish a proposition that resembles the *irreflexive restriction* proposition but that applies in the other direction. Consider a new theory with equality defined by the special axioms for the theory of the strict partial ordering $\prec$.

$$(\forall\, x,\, y,\, z) \begin{bmatrix} if & x \prec y \ \ and \ \ y \prec z \\ then & x \prec z \end{bmatrix} \hspace{2cm} (transitivity)$$

$$(\forall\, x)[not\ \ (x \prec x)] \hspace{2cm} (irreflexivity)$$

Because this is a theory with equality, we also have the equality axioms.

Let us augment this theory by introducing a new *reflexive closure* relation $\preceq$, defined by the axiom

$$(\forall\, x,\, y) \begin{bmatrix} x \preceq y \\ \equiv \\ x \prec y \ or \ x = y \end{bmatrix} \hspace{1.5cm} (reflexive\ closure\ of\ \prec)$$

Proposition (reflexive closure)

The reflexive closure $\preceq$ of $\prec$ is a weak partial ordering. ⌐

In other words, the *transitivity, antisymmetry,* and *reflexivity* axioms for $\preceq$ can be shown to be valid sentences in the new augmented theory. The proof is requested in **Problem 6.10**.

In **Problem 6.11**, the reader is asked to show the consistency and the independence of the axioms of a theory with equality.

6.7   THEORY OF GROUPS

Our second example of a theory with equality is the theory of groups. In this theory we define
- A binary function symbol $x \circ y$, denoting the *group operation*
- A constant symbol e, denoting the *identity* element
- A unary function symbol x^{-1}, denoting the *inverse* function.

Again the reader should understand that the symbols $x \circ y$, e, and x^{-1} are conventional notations for standard symbols of predicate logic, such as $f_{17}(x, y)$, a_3, and $g_{101}(x)$.

The theory of groups is defined by the following special axioms:

$$\mathcal{G}_1: \quad (\forall x)\big[x \circ e = x\big] \qquad \qquad \text{(\textit{right identity})}$$

$$\mathcal{G}_2: \quad (\forall x)\big[x \circ x^{-1} = e\big] \qquad \qquad \text{(\textit{right inverse})}$$

$$\mathcal{G}_3: \quad (\forall x, y, z)\big[(x \circ y) \circ z = x \circ (y \circ z)\big] \qquad \text{(\textit{associativity})}$$

Because the theory of groups is a theory with equality, we also have the *transitivity, symmetry,* and *reflexivity* axioms $\mathcal{E}_1$, $\mathcal{E}_2$, and $\mathcal{E}_3$ for equality, as well as those instances of the *functional-substitutivity* axiom schema $\mathcal{E}_4$ that apply to the function symbols $x \circ y$ and x^{-1} of the theory:

$$(\forall x, y, z) \begin{bmatrix} if \ \ x = y \\ then \ \ x \circ z = y \circ z \end{bmatrix} \quad \text{(\textit{left functional substitutivity for} $\circ$)}$$

$$(\forall x, y, z) \begin{bmatrix} if \ \ x = y \\ then \ \ z \circ x = z \circ y \end{bmatrix}$$
$$\text{(\textit{right functional substitutivity for} $\circ$)}$$

$$(\forall x, y) \begin{bmatrix} if \ \ x = y \\ then \ \ x^{-1} = y^{-1} \end{bmatrix} \quad \text{(\textit{functional substitutivity for inverse})}$$

Because $x \circ y$ is a binary function symbol and x^{-1} is a unary function, we have two instances of the *functional-substitutivity* axiom for $x \circ y$ and one for x^{-1}.

Let us consider some models for this theory.

Examples

- *The plus model*

One model for the theory of groups is the *plus interpretation* $\mathcal{I}$ over the integers, under which

- ▪ The group operation $x \circ y$ is the plus function $x_{\mathcal{I}} + y_{\mathcal{I}}$.
- ▪ The identity symbol e is the integer 0.
- ▪ The inverse function symbol x^{-1} is the unary minus function $-x_{\mathcal{I}}$.

- *The times model*

Another model for the theory of groups is the *times interpretation* $\mathcal{J}$ over the positive real numbers, under which

- ▪ The group operation $x \circ y$ is the times function $x_{\mathcal{J}} \cdot y_{\mathcal{J}}$.
- ▪ The identity symbol e is the number 1.
- ▪ The inverse function x^{-1} is the reciprocal function $1/x_{\mathcal{J}}$.

The reader may confirm that each of these interpretations is a model for the theory of groups. In other words, each of the above axioms is true under both interpretations. For instance, the *right-inverse axiom*

$$(\forall x)[x \circ x^{-1} = e]$$

is true under the times interpretation because, for every positive real number r,

$$r \cdot \left(1/r\right) = 1.$$

Note that there is no model for the theory of groups over all the real numbers under which $x \circ y$ is the times function and e is 1. Whatever unary function $g(r)$ over the reals is assigned to the inverse function symbol x^{-1} under such an interpretation, it cannot be the case that

$$0 \cdot g(0) = 1.$$

Therefore, the *right-inverse* axiom cannot be true under the interpretation.

In the theory of groups, we can prove many properties from very few axioms.

Since the theory of groups is a theory with equality, we know that those sentences in our language that are valid in the theory of equality are also valid in the theory of groups. For instance, we have (by the *substitutivity-of-equality* proposition) that, for all terms s and t and any sentence $\mathcal{F}\langle s \rangle$ in the theory of groups, the universal closure of

> *if* $s = t$
> *then* $\mathcal{F}\langle s \rangle \equiv \mathcal{F}\langle t \rangle$

is valid in the theory of groups.

Let us show the validity of a sentence in the theory of groups.

Proposition (right cancellation)

The sentence

$$(\forall x,\, y,\, z) \begin{bmatrix} \text{if } \ x \circ z = y \circ z \\ \text{then } \ x = y \end{bmatrix} \qquad\qquad (\textit{right cancellation})$$

is valid in the theory of groups. ⌐

Proof.   Suppose that, for arbitrary elements x, y, and z,

(1) $x \circ z = y \circ z$.

We would like to show that $x = y$.

By (1) and the *left functional-substitutivity* equality axiom $\mathcal{E}_4(\circ)$ for the group operation $\circ$,

(2) $(x \circ z) \circ z^{-1} = (y \circ z) \circ z^{-1}$.

By the *associativity* axiom $\mathcal{G}_3$ for $\circ$,

(3) $(x \circ z) \circ z^{-1} = x \circ (z \circ z^{-1})$

and

(4) $(y \circ z) \circ z^{-1} = y \circ (z \circ z^{-1})$.

By the substitutivity of equality applied to (2) and (3), we may replace $(x \circ z) \circ z^{-1}$ with $x \circ (z \circ z^{-1})$ in (2), to obtain

(5) $x \circ (z \circ z^{-1}) = (y \circ z) \circ z^{-1}$.

Similarly, by the substitutivity of equality applied to (4) and (5), we may replace $(y \circ z) \circ z^{-1}$ with $y \circ (z \circ z^{-1})$ in (5), to obtain

(6) $x \circ (z \circ z^{-1}) = y \circ (z \circ z^{-1})$.

By the *right-inverse* axiom $\mathcal{G}_2$, we have

(7) $z \circ z^{-1} = e$.

By the substitutivity of equality applied to (6) and (7), replacing both occurrences of $(z \circ z^{-1})$ with e in (6), we obtain

(8) $x \circ e = y \circ e$.

By the *right-identity* axiom $\mathcal{G}_1$, we have

(9) $x \circ e = x$

and

(10) $y \circ e = y$.

By two applications of the substitutivity of equality applied to (8), (9), and (10), replacing $x \circ e$ with x in (8) and replacing $y \circ e$ with y in the result, we obtain

(11) $x = y$.

This is the desired conclusion. ⌐

Some other valid sentences of the theory of groups are

$$(\forall x)[e \circ x = x] \qquad\qquad (left\ identity)$$

$$(\forall x)[x^{-1} \circ x = e] \qquad\qquad (left\ inverse)$$

$$(\forall x,\ y,\ z) \begin{bmatrix} if & z \circ x = z \circ y \\ then & x = y \end{bmatrix} \qquad\qquad (left\ cancellation)$$

$$(\forall x) \begin{bmatrix} if & x \circ x = x \\ then & x = e \end{bmatrix} \qquad\qquad (nonidempotence)$$

The proofs of the validity of these properties in the theory of groups are left as an exercise (**Problem 6.12**).

Once we have proved these properties for groups, we know that they are true under all models for groups. For example, because the *nonidempotence* property above is valid in the theory of groups and because the *plus* interpretation over the integers is a model for the theory, we can conclude that

> for every integer x,
> if $x + x = x$,
> then $x = 0$.

Similarly, because the *times* interpretation over the positive real numbers is a model for the theory of groups, we can conclude that

> for every positive real number x,
> if $x \cdot x = x$,
> then $x = 1$.

COMMUTATIVITY

Not every property of plus and times is valid in the theory of groups. For example, even though plus is commutative, that is,

$$x + y = y + x$$

is true for all integers x and y, and times is also commutative, that is,

$$x \cdot y = y \cdot x$$

is true for all positive real numbers, the group operation $\circ$ is not necessarily commutative, i.e., the corresponding sentence

$$(\forall x,\ y)[x \circ y = y \circ x]$$

is not valid in the theory of groups. To see this, it suffices to find a single model for the theory under which the commutativity sentence is not true.

Example (permutation model).   Consider the set Π of all permutations on the set of three elements $S = \{A, B, C\}$. These are the unary functions that map distinct elements of S into distinct elements of S; there are precisely six of them:

- The *identity* π_0, which leaves all elements fixed; that is,

$$\pi_0(A) = A \qquad \pi_0(B) = B \qquad \pi_0(C) = C.$$

- The *transpositions* π_A, π_B, and π_C, which leave one element fixed but interchange the other two; that is,

$$\pi_A(A) = A \qquad \pi_A(B) = C \qquad \pi_A(C) = B$$

$$\pi_B(A) = C \qquad \pi_B(B) = B \qquad \pi_B(C) = A$$

$$\pi_C(A) = B \qquad \pi_C(B) = A \qquad \pi_C(C) = C.$$

- The *cycles* π_+ and π_-, which alter all the elements; that is,

$$\pi_+(A) = B \qquad \pi_+(B) = C \qquad \pi_+(C) = A$$

$$\pi_-(A) = C \qquad \pi_-(B) = A \qquad \pi_-(C) = B.$$

For all permutations π and π', let the *composition permutation* $\pi \otimes \pi'$ be the permutation obtained by applying first π and then π'; in other words, for any element s of S,

$$(\pi \otimes \pi')(s) = \pi'\big(\pi(s)\big).$$

The *composition function* maps any two permutations π and π' into their composition permutation $\pi \otimes \pi'$. For example,

$$[\pi_A \otimes \pi_C](A) \;=\; \pi_C\big(\pi_A(A)\big) \;=\; \pi_C(A) \;=\; B$$

$$[\pi_A \otimes \pi_C](B) \;=\; \pi_C\big(\pi_A(B)\big) \;=\; \pi_C(C) \;=\; C$$

$$[\pi_A \otimes \pi_C](C) \;=\; \pi_C\big(\pi_A(C)\big) \;=\; \pi_C(B) \;=\; A.$$

Note that, for each element s of S, $[\pi_A \otimes \pi_C](s) = \pi_+(s)$; thus $\pi_A \otimes \pi_C = \pi_+$.

For any permutation π, let the *inverse permutation* $\widetilde{\pi}$ be defined so that, for any elements s and s' of S,

$$\pi(s) = s' \text{ if and only if } \widetilde{\pi}(s') = s.$$

The *inverse function* maps any permutation π into its inverse permutation $\widetilde{\pi}$. For example,

$$\text{since } \pi_+(A) = B, \text{ we have } \widetilde{\pi}_+(B) = A;$$

$$\text{since } \pi_+(B) = C, \text{ we have } \widetilde{\pi}_+(C) = B;$$

$$\text{since } \pi_+(C) = A, \text{ we have } \widetilde{\pi}_+(A) = C.$$

Note that, for each element s of S, $\widetilde{\pi}_+(s) = \pi_-(s)$; thus $\widetilde{\pi}_+ = \pi_-$.

Now consider the *permutation interpretation* $\mathcal{K}$, whose domain is the set Π of permutations of elements of S, under which

- The function symbol $x \circ y$ is the composition function $x_{\mathcal{K}} \otimes y_{\mathcal{K}}$.
- The constant e is the identity permutation π_0.
- The function symbol x^{-1} is the inverse function $\widetilde{x_{\mathcal{K}}}$.

In **Problem 6.13**, the reader is requested to confirm that $\mathcal{K}$ is a model for the theory of groups, i.e., that the *right-identity* axiom $\mathcal{G}_1$, the *right-inverse* axiom $\mathcal{G}_2$, and the *associativity* axiom $\mathcal{G}_3$ are true under $\mathcal{K}$.

On the other hand, the *commutativity* property

$$(\forall x, y)\big[x \circ y = y \circ x\big]$$

is not true under $\mathcal{K}$. For we have already observed that

$$\pi_A \otimes \pi_C = \pi_+.$$

On the other hand,

$$[\pi_C \otimes \pi_A](A) = \pi_A\big(\pi_C(A)\big) = \pi_A(B) = C$$

$$[\pi_C \otimes \pi_A](B) = \pi_A\big(\pi_C(B)\big) = \pi_A(A) = A$$

$$[\pi_C \otimes \pi_A](C) = \pi_A\big(\pi_C(C)\big) = \pi_A(C) = B.$$

Thus, for each element s of S, $[\pi_C \otimes \pi_A](s) = \pi_-(s)$; that is,

$$\pi_C \otimes \pi_A = \pi_-.$$

Because $\pi_+ \neq \pi_-$, we have

$$\pi_A \otimes \pi_C \neq \pi_C \otimes \pi_A,$$

showing that the composition function on permutations of S is not commutative. ∎

Because we have found a model for the theory of groups under which the *commutativity* property is not true, we have shown that the property is not valid in the theory. If we wish to consider only those models under which the group operation $x \circ y$ is commutative, we can augment the theory of groups by adding the new axiom

$$\mathcal{G}_4: \quad (\forall x, y)\big[x \circ y = y \circ x\big] \qquad\qquad (commutativity)$$

The new theory is called the theory of *commutative* (or *abelian*) *groups*. All the valid sentences of the original theory of groups are also valid in this augmented theory. For the theory of commutative groups, the *plus* and *times* interpretations are still models but the permutation interpretation $\mathcal{K}$ is not.

In **Problem 6.14**, the reader is asked to prove the validity of a sentence in the theory of monoids.

6.8   THEORY OF PAIRS

Another example of a theory with equality is the theory of pairs. Intuitively speaking, in this theory we have certain basic elements, called *atoms*, from which we construct pairs of form $\langle x_1, x_2 \rangle$, where each component x_1 and x_2 is an atom. For example, if the atoms are A, B, and C, then

$$\langle \text{A}, \text{A} \rangle, \quad \langle \text{A}, \text{B} \rangle, \quad \langle \text{B}, \text{A} \rangle, \quad \text{and } \langle \text{C}, \text{A} \rangle$$

are distinct pairs. The intended domain consists of both the atoms and the pairs of atoms.

In the theory of pairs, we define
- A unary predicate symbol $atom(x)$
- A unary predicate symbol $pair(x)$
- A binary function symbol $\langle x_1, x_2 \rangle$, denoting the *pairing* function.

The predicate symbol $atom(x)$ is true if x is an atom and false if x is a pair; $pair(x)$ is true if x is a pair and false if x is an atom. The value of the pairing function $\langle x_1, x_2 \rangle$ is the pair whose first element is the atom x_1 and whose second element is the atom x_2.

Again, do not be confused; we are not adding a new notation $\langle x_1, x_2 \rangle$ to the formal language of predicate logic; we are merely adopting informally the familiar mathematical notation for a pair to represent a standard predicate-logic binary function symbol, such as $f_{101}(x_1, x_2)$.

The theory of pairs is defined by the following special axioms:

$$\mathcal{P}_1: \quad (\forall\, x) \left[\begin{array}{l} pair(x) \\[4pt] \equiv \\[4pt] (\exists\, x_1, x_2) \left[\begin{array}{l} atom(x_1) \ \ and \ \ atom(x_2) \\ and \\ x = \langle x_1,\ x_2 \rangle \end{array} \right] \end{array} \right] \qquad (pair)$$

In other words, every pair is of form $\langle x_1, x_2 \rangle$, where x_1 and x_2 are atoms.

$$\mathcal{P}_2: \quad (\forall\, x)\big[not\ \big(atom(x)\ \ and\ \ pair(x)\big)\big] \qquad (disjoint)$$

In other words, no domain element is both an atom and a pair.

$$\mathcal{P}_3: \quad (\forall\, x_1, x_2, y_1, y_2) \left[\begin{array}{l} if \ \left[\begin{array}{l} atom(x_1) \ \ and \ \ atom(x_2) \\ and \\ atom(y_1) \ \ and \ \ atom(y_2) \end{array} \right] \\[6pt] then \ \ if \ \langle x_1, x_2 \rangle = \langle y_1, y_2 \rangle \\[3pt] \qquad then \ \ x_1 = y_1 \ \ and \ \ x_2 = y_2 \end{array} \right]$$
$$(uniqueness)$$

In other words, a pair can be constructed in only one way from two atoms.

Remark (pairs of nonatoms).   Note that the axioms do not specify the result of applying the pairing function $\langle x_1, x_2 \rangle$ if x_1 or x_2 is itself a pair rather than an atom. Although expressions of this form are legal in the language and although they must have some values under any interpretation, the axioms do not determine these values. Thus if x_1 and x_2 are not both atoms under a given model, the term $\langle x_1, x_2 \rangle$ might have the value A, $\langle A, B \rangle$, $\langle B, C \rangle$, or any other domain element. We simply do not care what the value of the pairing function is in this case. ⌙

Because the theory of pairs is a theory with equality, we also have the equality axioms $\mathcal{E}_1$ through $\mathcal{E}_5$, including the appropriate instances of the *functional-substitutivity* axiom schema $\mathcal{E}_4$:

$$(\forall\ x_1, x_1', x_2) \begin{bmatrix} if\ \ x_1 = x_1' \\ then\ \ \langle x_1, x_2 \rangle = \langle x_1', x_2 \rangle \end{bmatrix}$$

$$\text{(left functional substitutivity for pairing)}$$

$$(\forall\ x_1, x_2, x_2') \begin{bmatrix} if\ \ x_2 = x_2' \\ then\ \ \langle x_1, x_2 \rangle = \langle x_1, x_2' \rangle \end{bmatrix}$$

$$\text{(right functional substitutivity for pairing)}$$

We also have the instances of the *predicate-substitutivity* axiom schema $\mathcal{E}_5$ for equality that apply to the *atom* predicate symbol,

$$(\forall\ x, y) \begin{bmatrix} if\ \ x = y \\ then\ \ atom(x) \ \equiv\ atom(y) \end{bmatrix}$$

$$\text{(predicate substitutivity for atom)}$$

and to the *pair* predicate symbol,

$$(\forall\ x, y) \begin{bmatrix} if\ \ x = y \\ then\ \ pair(x) \ \equiv\ pair(y) \end{bmatrix} \quad \text{(predicate substitutivity for pair)}$$

because these symbols are in our vocabulary.

Example (pairs of integers).   Consider the interpretation $\mathcal{I}$ over the set of integers and pairs of integers under which

- The unary predicate symbol $atom(x)$ is the relation that is true if $x_{\mathcal{I}}$ is an integer and false if $x_{\mathcal{I}}$ is a pair.
- The unary predicate symbol $pair(x)$ is the relation that is true if $x_{\mathcal{I}}$ is a pair and false if $x_{\mathcal{I}}$ is an integer.
- The binary function symbol $\langle x_1, x_2 \rangle$ is any function k such that $k(d_1, d_2)$ is the pair $\langle d_1, d_2 \rangle$, for all integers d_1 and d_2; we do not care what the value of $k(d_1, d_2)$ is if d_1 or d_2 is itself a pair.

The reader may confirm that $\mathcal{I}$ is a model for the theory of pairs. ⌙

THE FIRST AND SECOND FUNCTIONS

Let us now augment our theory of pairs by introducing two unary function symbols *first* and *second*. Intuitively speaking, $first(x)$ and $second(x)$ are the first and second elements, respectively, of the pair x. The axioms that define these functions follow:

$$\mathcal{P}_4: \quad (\forall\, x_1,\, x_2) \begin{bmatrix} if \;\; atom(x_1) \;\; and \;\; atom(x_2) \\ then \;\; first(\langle x_1,\, x_2\rangle) = x_1 \end{bmatrix} \qquad (first)$$

$$\mathcal{P}_5: \quad (\forall\, x_1,\, x_2) \begin{bmatrix} if \;\; atom(x_1) \;\; and \;\; atom(x_2) \\ then \;\; second(\langle x_1,\, x_2\rangle) = x_2 \end{bmatrix} \qquad (second)$$

Note that the axioms do not specify the value of an expression of the form $first(x)$ or $second(x)$ if x is an atom rather than a pair. We do not care what value is assigned to such an expression under a model for the augmented theory.

Because the augmented theory is a theory with equality, we have the appropriate instances of the *functional-substitutivity* axiom schema $\mathcal{E}_4$ for equality,

$$(\forall\, x,\, y) \begin{bmatrix} if \;\; x = y \\ then \;\; first(x) = first(y) \end{bmatrix} \qquad (functional\ substitutivity\ for\ first)$$

$$(\forall\, x,\, y) \begin{bmatrix} if \;\; x = y \\ then \;\; second(x) = second(y) \end{bmatrix}$$
$$(functional\ substitutivity\ for\ second)$$

We can easily establish the validity of the following sentences in the theory of pairs: For the *first* function we have

$$(\forall\, x) \begin{bmatrix} if \;\; pair(x) \\ then \;\; atom\big(first(x)\big) \end{bmatrix} \qquad (sort\ of\ first)$$

For the *second* function we have

$$(\forall\, x) \begin{bmatrix} if \;\; pair(x) \\ then \;\; atom\big(second(x)\big) \end{bmatrix} \qquad (sort\ of\ second)$$

Often we refer to a unary predicate symbol, which characterizes a set of domain elements, as a "sort." The above properties are called the *sort* properties of the *first* and the *second* function, respectively, because they establish that if a given element x is of the sort *pair*, then $first(x)$ and $second(x)$ are elements of the sort *atom*.

THE DECOMPOSITION PROPERTY

In the augmented theory of pairs we can establish the following result.

Proposition (decomposition)

The sentence

$$(\forall\, x) \left[\begin{array}{l} if \ \ pair(x) \\ then \ \ x \ = \ \langle first(x),\ second(x)\rangle \end{array} \right] \qquad (decomposition)$$

is valid in the augmented theory of pairs. ◢

In other words, any pair is the result of pairing its first and second elements.

Proof. For an arbitrary element x, suppose that

$$pair(x).$$

We would like to show that

$$x \ = \ \langle first(x),\ second(x)\rangle.$$

We know (by the *pair* axiom $\mathcal{P}_1$) that

$$(\exists\, x_1,\, x_2) \left[\begin{array}{l} atom(x_1) \ \ and \ \ atom(x_2) \\ \quad and \\ x = \langle x_1,\, x_2\rangle \end{array} \right].$$

Let x_1 and x_2 be elements such that

$$atom(x_1) \ \ and \ \ atom(x_2)$$
$$and$$
$$x = \langle x_1,\, x_2\rangle.$$

Then (by the *symmetry* axiom for equality)

$$\langle x_1,\, x_2\rangle = x.$$

We have (by the definitions of *first* and *second*)

$$if \ \ atom(x_1) \ \ and \ \ atom(x_2)$$
$$then \ \ first(\langle x_1,\, x_2\rangle) = x_1$$

and

$$if \ \ atom(x_1) \ \ and \ \ atom(x_2)$$
$$then \ \ second(\langle x_1,\, x_2\rangle) = x_2.$$

Therefore (by propositional logic, because $atom(x_1)$ and $atom(x_2)$)

$$first(\langle x_1,\, x_2\rangle) = x_1 \qquad and \qquad second(\langle x_1,\, x_2\rangle) = x_2,$$

that is (by the substitutivity of equality, because $\langle x_1,\, x_2\rangle = x$),

$$first(x) = x_1 \qquad and \qquad second(x) = x_2.$$

Therefore (by the *symmetry* axiom for equality)

$$x_1 = first(x) \qquad and \qquad x_2 = second(x).$$

Finally (by two applications of the substitutivity of equality, because $x = \langle x_1,\, x_2\rangle$), we have

$$x \ = \ \langle first(x),\ second(x)\rangle,$$

as we wanted to show. ◢

6.9   RELATIVIZED QUANTIFIERS

We now introduce a notational convention, that of *relativized quantifiers*, to abbreviate sentences in predicate logic. This convention has the effect of allowing quantifiers to range over particular subsets of the domain instead of over the entire domain.

Definition (relativized quantifier)

For any unary predicate symbol p and sentence $\mathcal{F}$,

$$(\forall\, p\, x)\mathcal{F} \quad \text{stands for} \quad (\forall\, x)\begin{bmatrix} if \;\; p(x) \\ then \;\; \mathcal{F} \end{bmatrix}$$

$$(\exists\, p\, x)\mathcal{F} \quad \text{stands for} \quad (\exists\, x)\,[p(x) \;\; and \;\; \mathcal{F}]. \quad \blacksquare$$

Examples.   In the theory of pairs, for a binary predicate symbol q, the sentence

$$(\forall\, atom\, x_1)[not\, q(x_1, x_1)]$$

stands for

$$(\forall\, x_1)\begin{bmatrix} if \;\; atom(x_1) \\ then \;\; not\, q(x_1, x_1) \end{bmatrix}.$$

The sentence

$$(\forall\, pair\, x)(\exists\, atom\, x_1)\big[first(x) = x_1\big]$$

stands for

$$(\forall\, x)\begin{bmatrix} if \;\; pair(x) \\ then \;\; (\exists\, atom\, x_1)\big[first(x) = x_1\big] \end{bmatrix},$$

which stands for

$$(\forall\, x)\begin{bmatrix} if \;\; pair(x) \\ then \;\; (\exists\, x_1)\begin{bmatrix} atom(x_1) \\ and \\ first(x) = x_1 \end{bmatrix} \end{bmatrix}. \quad \blacksquare$$

We can apply the abbreviation to sequences of relativized quantifiers.

Definition (multiple relativized quantifiers)

For any unary predicate symbols $p_1, p_2, \ldots, p_n$ and sentence $\mathcal{F}$,

$$(\forall\, p_1\, x_1)\,(\forall\, p_2\, x_2)\, \ldots\, (\forall\, p_n\, x_n)\, \mathcal{F}$$

stands for

$$(\forall\, x_1, x_2, \ldots, x_n)\begin{bmatrix} if \;\; p_1(x_1) \;\; and \;\; p_2(x_2) \;\; and \;\; \ldots \;\; and \;\; p_n(x_n) \\ then \;\; \mathcal{F} \end{bmatrix},$$

and

$$(\exists \; p_1 \; x_1) \, (\exists \; p_2 \; x_2) \; \ldots \; (\exists \; p_n \; x_n) \; \mathcal{F}$$

stands for

$$(\exists \; x_1, x_2, \ldots, x_n) \begin{bmatrix} p_1(x_1) \;\; and \;\; p_2(x_2) \;\; and \;\; \ldots \;\; and \;\; p_n(x_n) \\ and \\ \mathcal{F} \end{bmatrix}.$$

As a special case,

$$(\forall \; p \; x_1, x_2, \ldots, x_n) \; \mathcal{F}$$

stands for

$$(\forall \; p \; x_1) \, (\forall \; p \; x_2) \; \ldots \; (\forall \; p \; x_n) \; \mathcal{F},$$

which stands for

$$(\forall \; x_1, x_2, \ldots, x_n) \begin{bmatrix} if \;\; p(x_1) \;\; and \;\; p(x_2) \;\; and \;\; \ldots \;\; and \;\; p(x_n) \\ then \;\; \mathcal{F} \end{bmatrix}.$$

Similarly,

$$(\exists \; p \; x_1, x_2, \ldots, x_n) \mathcal{F}$$

stands for

$$(\exists \; x_1, x_2, \ldots, x_n) \begin{bmatrix} p(x_1) \;\; and \;\; p(x_2) \;\; and \;\; \ldots \;\; and \;\; p(x_n) \\ and \\ \mathcal{F} \end{bmatrix}. \quad \lrcorner$$

Examples. In the theory of pairs, the sentence

$$(\forall \; atom \; x_1, x_2) \big[first(\langle x_1, \; x_2 \rangle) = x_1 \big]$$

stands for

$$(\forall \; x_1, x_2) \begin{bmatrix} if \;\; atom(x_1) \;\; and \;\; atom(x_2) \\ then \;\; first(\langle x_1, \; x_2 \rangle) = x_1 \end{bmatrix}.$$

The sentence

$$(\exists \; pair \; x, y) \big[x \preceq y \;\; and \;\; y \preceq x \big]$$

stands for

$$(\exists \; x, y) \begin{bmatrix} pair(x) \;\; and \;\; pair(y) \\ and \\ x \preceq y \;\; and \;\; y \preceq x \end{bmatrix}.$$

The sentence

$$(\forall \; pair \; x) (\exists \; atom \; x_1, x_2) \big[x = \langle x_1, \; x_2 \rangle \big]$$

stands for

$$(\forall\ x)\left[\begin{array}{l}if\ \ pair(x)\\ then\ \ (\exists\ atom\ x_1, x_2)\left[x = \langle x_1,\ x_2 \rangle\right]\end{array}\right],$$

which stands for

$$(\forall\ x)\left[\begin{array}{l}if\ pair(x)\\ then\ \ (\exists\ x_1,\ x_2)\left[\begin{array}{l}atom(x_1)\ \ and\ \ atom(x_2)\\ and\\ x = \langle x_1,\ x_2 \rangle\end{array}\right]\end{array}\right].\ \ \ \blacksquare$$

The relativized quantifier notation can make the sentences in our theory of pairs somewhat clearer. For example, the definition P_1 of the *pair* relation, which was originally written as

$$(\forall\ x)\left[\begin{array}{l}pair(x)\\ \equiv\\ (\exists\ x_1,\ x_2)\left[\begin{array}{l}atom(x_1)\ \ and\ \ atom(x_2)\\ and\\ x = \langle x_1,\ x_2 \rangle\end{array}\right]\end{array}\right],$$

can now be abbreviated as

$$(\forall\ x)\left[\begin{array}{l}pair(x)\\ \equiv\\ (\exists\ atom\ x_1, x_2)\left[x = \langle x_1,\ x_2 \rangle\right]\end{array}\right].$$

The *uniqueness* axiom P_3 for pairs, which was originally written as

$$(\forall\ x_1, x_2, y_1, y_2)\left[\begin{array}{l}if\ \left[\begin{array}{l}atom(x_1)\ \ and\ \ atom(x_2)\\ and\\ atom(y_1)\ \ and\ \ atom(y_2)\end{array}\right]\\ then\ if\ \langle x_1,\ x_2 \rangle\ =\ \langle y_1,\ y_2 \rangle\\ \qquad then\ x_1 = y_1\ \ and\ \ x_2 = y_2\end{array}\right],$$

can now be abbreviated as

$$(\forall\ atom\ x_1, x_2, y_1, y_2)\left[\begin{array}{l}if\ \langle x_1,\ x_2 \rangle\ =\ \langle y_1,\ y_2 \rangle\\ then\ x_1 = y_1\ \ and\ \ x_2 = y_2\end{array}\right].$$

The definitions P_4 and P_5 of the *first* and *second* functions can now be abbreviated as

$$(\forall\ atom\ x_1,\ x_2)\left[\ first(\langle x_1,\ x_2 \rangle) = x_1\right]$$

and

$$(\forall\ atom\ x_1,\ x_2)\left[second(\langle x_1,\ x_2 \rangle) = x_2\right].$$

The *decomposition* proposition may be written as

$$(\forall\ pair\ x)\left[x\ =\ \langle first(x),\ second(x) \rangle\right].\ \ \ \blacksquare$$

When we need to prove a sentence expressed in terms of relativized quantifiers, we can always abandon the abbreviation, rephrase the sentence in terms of ordinary quantifiers, and use ordinary predicate logic arguments. Alternatively, we can identify valid sentence schemata with relativized quantifiers and retain the abbreviation. The relativized-quantifier schemata resemble some of the ordinary valid sentence schemata.

In particular, for all unary predicate symbols p and q, we can establish the validity of the universal closures of the following sentence schemata:

- Reversal of quantifiers

$$(\forall\, p\; x)(\forall\, q\; y)\,\mathcal{F}$$
$$\equiv$$
$$(\forall\, q\; y)(\forall\, p\; x)\,\mathcal{F}$$

$$(\exists\, p\; x)(\exists\, q\; y)\,\mathcal{F}$$
$$\equiv$$
$$(\exists\, q\; y)(\exists\, p\; x)\,\mathcal{F}$$

- Duality of quantifiers

$$(\forall\, p\; x)[not\; \mathcal{F}]$$
$$\equiv$$
$$not\; (\exists\, p\; x)\,\mathcal{F}$$

$$(\exists\, p\; x)[not\; \mathcal{F}]$$
$$\equiv$$
$$not\; (\forall\, p\; x)\,\mathcal{F}.$$

Let us justify the last of these equivalences.

Proposition (duality of relativized quantifiers)

For any unary predicate symbol p,

$$(\exists\, p\; x)[not\; \mathcal{F}] \;\equiv\; not\; (\forall\, p\; x)\,\mathcal{F}. \quad \lrcorner$$

Proof. We have that

$$(\exists\, p\; x)[not\; \mathcal{F}]$$

is an abbreviation of

$$(\exists\, x)\,[p(x)\;\; and\;\; not\; \mathcal{F}],$$

which is equivalent (by propositional logic) to

$$(\exists\, x)\; not\; \begin{bmatrix} if\;\; p(x) \\ then\;\; \mathcal{F} \end{bmatrix},$$

which is equivalent (by the duality property of ordinary quantifiers) to

$$not\; (\forall\, x)\; \begin{bmatrix} if\;\; p(x) \\ then\;\; \mathcal{F} \end{bmatrix},$$

which may be abbreviated as

$$not\; (\forall\, p\; x)\mathcal{F}.$$

This establishes the desired equivalence. $\lrcorner$

The reader is requested (in **Problem 6.15**) to prove two additional equivalences concerning relativized quantifiers.

Remark (pitfall).   We must be careful not to apply properties of ordinary quantifiers blindly to relativized quantifiers. For example, the sentence

> *if* $(\forall\,x)q(x)$
> *then* $(\exists\,x)q(x)$

is valid. However, for any unary predicate symbol p, the analogous sentence with relativized quantifiers,

> *if* $(\forall\,p\,x)q(x)$
> *then* $(\exists\,p\,x)q(x),$

is not valid. This sentence stands for

> *if* $(\forall\,x)\big[if\;\;p(x)\;\;then\;\;q(x)\big]$
> *then* $(\exists\,x)\big[p(x)\;\;and\;\;q(x)\big],$

which is false under any interpretation under which $(\exists\,x)\,p(x)$ is false. Under such an interpretation, the antecedent of this implication is true vacuously, but its consequent is false. On the other hand, the sentence is true under any interpretation under which $(\exists\,x)\,p(x)$ is true.   ⌐

In **Problem 6.16**, the reader is asked to define a theory of triples analogous to the theory of pairs.

PROBLEMS

Problem 6.1 (family theory)   page 308

In the family theory show that

> if Alice is the parent of her own father,
> then Alice's father is his own grandfather.

(First express the sentence in predicate logic, then give an intuitive argument to show it is valid in the family theory. Let the constant a denote Alice.)

Problem 6.2 (strict partial ordering)   page 313

Construct an interpretation over the finite domain $\{A, B, C\}$ under which

(a)   The *transitivity* axiom S_1 is true but the *irreflexivity* axiom S_2 is false.

(b)   The *irreflexivity* axiom S_2 is true but the *transitivity* axiom S_1 is false.

Problem 6.3 (equivalence relation)   page 317

Consider the following "proof" that, in the theory of the equivalence relation $\approx$, the *transitivity* axiom Q_1 and the *symmetry* axiom Q_2 imply the *reflexivity* axiom Q_3.

We would like to show that, for an arbitrary element x, $x \approx x$. Let y be any element such that $x \approx y$. Then (by the *symmetry* axiom Q_2) we have $y \approx x$. Therefore (by the *transitivity* axiom Q_1, because $x \approx y$ and $y \approx x$) we have $x \approx x$, as we wanted to show.

We have already shown, however, that the three axioms for the theory of equivalence are independent, i.e., that no two of them imply the third. Find the fallacious step in the above argument.

*Problem 6.4 (nonvalid equality sentence)   page 322

Show that the following sentence is not valid in the theory of equality:

$$(\exists x)(\forall y)p(x, y)$$

or

$$not \ (\exists x)(\forall y)\big[if \ not \ (x = y) \ then \ p(x, y)\big]$$

or

$$(\forall x, y, z) \left[\begin{array}{l} if \ p(x, y) \ and \ p(y, y) \ and \ p(y, z) \\ then \ p(x, z) \end{array} \right].$$

Hint: Construct an interpretation over a finite domain under which this sentence is false.

Problem 6.5 (replacement)   page 324

Show that the *replacement* proposition would not hold if we had applied a partial substitution rather than a total substitution. More precisely,

(a) *Universal*

Find a term t and a sentence $\mathcal{F}\langle x \rangle$ such that

$$(\forall x)\big[if \ x = t \ then \ \mathcal{F}\langle x \rangle\big]$$

is not equivalent to $\mathcal{F}\langle t \rangle$.

(b) *Existential*

Find a term t and a sentence $\mathcal{F}\langle x \rangle$ such that

$$(\exists x)[x = t \ and \ \mathcal{F}\langle x \rangle]$$

is not equivalent to $\mathcal{F}\langle t \rangle$.

Show that the *replacement* proposition would not hold if x were allowed to occur free in t. More precisely,

(c)   *Universal*

Find a term t and a sentence $\mathcal{F}[x]$ such that x occurs free in t and the sentence

$$(\forall x)\big[if\ x = t\ then\ \mathcal{F}[x]\big]$$

is not equivalent to $\mathcal{F}[t]$.

(d)   *Existential*

Find a term t and a sentence $\mathcal{F}[x]$ such that x occurs free in t and the sentence

$$(\exists x)\big[x = t\ and\ \mathcal{F}[x]\big]$$

is not equivalent to $\mathcal{F}[t]$.

Justify your answer in each case.

Problem 6.6 (conditional terms)   page 324

Establish the validity of the following sentences in the theory of equality:

(a)   *True*

$$(if\ true\ then\ a\ else\ b) = a$$

(b)   *False*

$$(if\ false\ then\ a\ else\ b) = b$$

(c)   *Distributivity*

$$(\forall x)\begin{bmatrix} f(if\ p(x)\ then\ a\ else\ b) \\ = \\ if\ p(x)\ then\ f(a)\ else\ f(b) \end{bmatrix}.$$

Problem 6.7 (uniqueness of equality)   page 324

Prove the *uniqueness-of-equality* proposition.

Problem 6.8 (weak partial ordering)   page 325

Prove that the *transitivity* axiom $\mathcal{W}_1$, the *antisymmetry* axiom $\mathcal{W}_2$, and the *reflexivity* axiom $\mathcal{W}_3$ for the theory of a weak partial ordering $\preceq$ are independent; i.e., for each of these axioms, there is a model for the theory of equality under which the axiom is false but the other two axioms are true.

Problem 6.9 (irreflexive restriction)   page 327

Prove the *irreflexive restriction* proposition.

Problem 6.10 (reflexive closure)   page 328

Prove the *reflexive closure* proposition.

Problem 6.11 (consistency and independence) page 328

Consider the theory with equality defined by the following special axioms:

$$(\forall x)\big[x = f\big(f\big(f(x)\big)\big)\big] \qquad\qquad\qquad (three)$$

$$(\forall x,\, y) \begin{bmatrix} if\ x \neq y \\ then\ x = f(y)\ or\ y = f(x) \end{bmatrix} \qquad\qquad (connected)$$

$$(\forall x)\big[if\ p(x)\ then\ not\ p\big(f(x)\big)\big] \qquad\qquad (skip)$$

$$(\exists x)p(x) \qquad\qquad\qquad (one)$$

(a) Show that the theory is consistent.

Hint: Construct a model with a domain of exactly three elements.

(b) Show that the axioms are independent.

Problem 6.12 (theory of groups) page 331

Prove informally the validity of the following properties in the theory of groups:

(a) *Left identity*

$$(\forall x)[e \circ x = x]$$

[*Hint*: For an arbitrary element x, show that $(e \circ x) \circ x^{-1} = x \circ x^{-1}$.]

(b) *Left inverse*

$$(\forall x)[x^{-1} \circ x = e]$$

[*Hint*: For an arbitrary element x, show that $(x^{-1} \circ x) \circ x^{-1} = e \circ x^{-1}$.]

(c) *Left cancellation*

$$(\forall x,\, y,\, z) \begin{bmatrix} if\ z \circ x = z \circ y \\ then\ x = y \end{bmatrix}$$

[*Hint*: For arbitrary elements x, y, and z such that $z \circ x = z \circ y$, show that $(z^{-1} \circ z) \circ x = (z^{-1} \circ z) \circ y$.]

(d) *Nonidempotence*

$$(\forall x) \begin{bmatrix} if\ x \circ x = x \\ then\ x = e \end{bmatrix}.$$

Note: The order in which these sentences are presented is significant; the proof of each may rely on the validity of the previous sentences.

Problem 6.13 (permutation interpretation)   page 333

Show that the permutation interpretation $\mathcal{K}$ is a model for the theory of groups; i.e., show that

(a)   The *right-identity* axiom $\mathcal{G}_1$

(b)   The *right-inverse* axiom $\mathcal{G}_2$

(c)   The *associativity* axiom $\mathcal{G}_3$

are true under $\mathcal{K}$.

Problem 6.14 (theory of monoids)   page 333

Consider the theory of monoids, a theory with equality defined by the following special axioms:

$$(\forall\, x)[x \circ e \,=\, x] \qquad\qquad\qquad\qquad (right\ identity)$$

$$(\forall\, x)[e \circ x \,=\, x] \qquad\qquad\qquad\qquad (left\ identity)$$

$$(\forall\, x,\, y,\, z)\big[(x \circ y) \circ z \,=\, x \circ (y \circ z)\big] \qquad (associativity)$$

(a) Determine whether the above axioms are independent. Justify your answer.

(b) Prove informally the validity of the following sentence in the theory of monoids:

$$(\forall x,\, y,\, z) \begin{bmatrix} if\ x \circ y = e\ and\ y \circ z = e \\ then\ x = z \end{bmatrix}.$$

Problem 6.15 (relativized quantifiers)   page 342

For all unary predicate symbols p, establish the validity of the universal closures of the following sentence schemata:

(a) *Reversal*

$$(\exists\, p\ x)(\exists\, q\ y)\mathcal{F}$$
$$\equiv$$
$$(\exists\, q\ y)(\exists\, p\ x)\mathcal{F}$$

(b) *Distributivity*

$$(\forall\, p\ x)[\mathcal{F}\ and\ \mathcal{G}]$$
$$\equiv$$
$$(\forall\, p\ x)\mathcal{F}\ and\ (\forall\, p\ x)\mathcal{G}.$$

Problem 6.16 (theory of triples)   page 342

Define a theory of triples, analogous to the theory of pairs, in which, intuitively speaking, $\langle x_1,\ x_2,\ x_3 \rangle$ is a triple of three atoms x_1, x_2, and x_3. Provide the basic axioms for this theory. Use the relativized-quantifier notation.

7

Deductive
Tableaux

We have introduced a deductive-tableau system to prove the validity of sentences in predicate logic. In this chapter, we adapt the system to prove validity in axiomatic theories.

7.1 FINITE THEORIES

In our discussion of axiomatic theories in the previous chapter, we showed how to describe a particular theory by presenting a (possibly infinite) set of closed sentences,

$$\mathcal{A}_1, \mathcal{A}_2, \mathcal{A}_3, \ldots,$$

which are the axioms of the theory. We defined an interpretation to be a *model* of the theory if each axiom $\mathcal{A}_i$ of the theory is true under the interpretation. A closed sentence $\mathcal{S}$ of the theory is *valid* in the theory if $\mathcal{S}$ is true under every model for the theory. Similarly, two sentences are *equivalent* in the theory if they have the same truth-value under every model for the theory.

For instance, we defined the theory of strict partial orderings by the two axioms

$$(\forall x, y, z) \begin{bmatrix} if \ x \prec y \ and \ y \prec z \\ then \ x \prec z \end{bmatrix} \qquad (transitivity)$$

$$(\forall x)[not \ (x \prec x)] \qquad (irreflexivity)$$

Here we take $\prec$ to stand for any binary predicate symbol. This theory has many models, including the less-than ordering $<$ over the integers and the proper-subset relation $\subset$ over the sets. To determine that a closed sentence $\mathcal{S}$ is valid in the strict partial-ordering theory, we must establish that $\mathcal{S}$ is true under all these models.

A tableau is said to be *valid in a theory* if its associated sentence is valid in the theory, and two tableaux are said to be *equivalent in a theory* if their associated sentences are equivalent in the theory.

Suppose we wish to prove that a closed sentence $\mathcal{S}$ is valid in a *finite theory*, that is, one defined by a finite set of axioms. In the deductive-tableau framework, we can do this by proving in predicate logic the initial tableau

assertions	goals
$\mathcal{A}_1$	
$\mathcal{A}_2$	
$\vdots$	
$\mathcal{A}_n$	
	$\mathcal{S}$

where each assertion $\mathcal{A}_i$ is a sentence known to be valid in the theory, either because it is an axiom or because it has been previously proved valid in the theory. A sentence that has been proved valid in a theory is called a *theorem of the theory*.

For example, to establish that a closed sentence $\mathcal{S}$ is valid in the theory of strict partial orderings, defined by the *transitivity* and *irreflexivity* axioms, we prove in predicate logic the initial tableau

assertions	goals
if $x \prec y$ *and* $y \prec z$ (*transitivity*) *then* $x \prec z$	
not $(x \prec x)$ (*irreflexivity*)	
	$\mathcal{S}$

Here, by outermost skolemization (Section 5.9), we have dropped the outermost universal quantifiers from the two assertions.

Once we have proved the validity of a sentence $\mathcal{S}$ in the theory of strict partial orderings, we may add $\mathcal{S}$ as an assertion in any future tableaux.

Example (theory of strict partial orderings).   Suppose we would like to show that the *asymmetry* property is valid in the theory of the strict partial ordering $\prec$; that is,

$$(\forall x,\, y) \begin{bmatrix} if & x \prec y \\ then & not & (y \prec x) \end{bmatrix} \qquad\qquad (asymmetry)$$

is valid. This was established informally in Section 6.3.

For this purpose it suffices to prove in predicate logic the tableau

assertions	goals
if $x \prec y$ *and* $y \prec z$ *then* $x \prec z$ (*transitivity*)	
not $(x \prec x)$ (*irreflexivity*)	
	G1. $(\forall x,\, y)^\forall \begin{bmatrix} if & x \prec y \\ then & not & (y \prec x) \end{bmatrix}$

Note that we did not number the two axioms (as A1 and A2). We shall usually refer to such assertions (axioms or theorems) by name.

Applying the $\forall$-*elimination* rule twice in succession to goal G1, replacing the bound variables x and y with the skolem constants a and b, respectively, we obtain the goal

	G2. *if* $a \prec b$ *then* *not* $(b \prec a)$

By the *if-split* rule, this decomposes into

A3. $\boxed{a \prec b}$ $^-$	
	G4. *not* $\boxed{b \prec a}$ $^-$

By the *resolution* rule, applied to assertion A3 and the *transitivity* axiom

if $\boxed{x \prec y}$ $^+$ *and* $y \prec z$ *then* $x \prec z$	

with $\{x \leftarrow a,\, y \leftarrow b\}$, we obtain

A5. *if* $\boxed{b \prec z}$ +	
then $a \prec z$	

By the *resolution* rule, applied to goal G4 and assertion A5, with $\{z \leftarrow a\}$, we obtain

	G6. $\boxed{not \ (a \prec a)}$ +

By the *resolution* rule, applied to the *irreflexivity* axiom

$\boxed{not \ (x \prec x)}$ −	

and goal G6, with $\{x \leftarrow a\}$, we obtain the final goal

	G7. *true*

Note that henceforth we do not indicate which of the dual forms (AA, AG, and so on) of the *resolution* or *equivalence* rule is being applied; this should be evident.

Because we have proved the validity of the *asymmetry* property, we may add it as an assertion in future proofs within the theory of strict partial orderings.

Example (family theory).   In Section 6.1, we defined a theory of family relationships. In the "family" interpretation $\mathcal{I}$ we have in mind, the domain is the set of people, and, intuitively, for the function symbols f and m,

> $f(x)$ is the father of x
>
> $m(x)$ is the mother of x,

and, for the predicate symbols p, gf, and gm,

> $p(x, y)$ means y is a parent of x
>
> $gf(x, y)$ means y is a grandfather of x
>
> $gm(x, y)$ means y is a grandmother of x.

We define the theory by the following set of axioms:

$$(\forall x)p\big(x,\,f(x)\big) \qquad\qquad\qquad (father)$$

$$(\forall x)p\big(x,\,m(x)\big) \qquad\qquad\qquad (mother)$$

$$(\forall x,\,y)\big[if\ \ p(x,\,y)\ \ then\ \ gf\big(x,\,f(y)\big)\big] \qquad (grandfather)$$

$$(\forall x,\,y)\big[if\ \ p(x,\,y)\ \ then\ \ gm\big(x,\,m(y)\big)\big] \qquad (grandmother)$$

That is, everyone's father or mother is his or her parent, and the father [mother] of one's parent is his or her grandfather [grandmother].

In this *family theory* we gave an informal argument to show the validity of the sentence

$$(\forall x)(\exists z)gm(x,\,z),$$

that is, everyone has a grandmother. We can now prove it as a theorem in the theory using the deductive-tableau system.

We begin with the tableau

assertions	goals
$p\big(x,\,f(x)\big)$ *(father)*	
$p\big(x,\,m(x)\big)$ *(mother)*	
if $p(x,\,y)$ *then* $gf\big(x,\,f(y)\big)$ *(grandfather)*	
if $p(x,\,y)$ *then* $gm\big(x,\,m(y)\big)$ *(grandmother)*	
	G1. $(\forall x)^\forall (\exists z)^\exists gm(x,\,z)$

By the $\forall$-*elimination* and $\exists$-*elimination* rules, we may drop the quantifiers of goal G1, to obtain

	G2. $\boxed{gm(a,\,z)}^{\,+}$

The bound variable x, whose quantifier is of universal force in goal G1, is replaced by the skolem constant a in forming goal G2.

Applying the *resolution* rule to the *grandmother* axiom

if $p(x, y)$ then $\boxed{gm\big(x, m(y)\big)}^{-}$	

and goal G2, with $\{x \leftarrow a, \ z \leftarrow m(y)\}$, we derive the goal

	G3. $\boxed{p(a, y)}^{+}$

By the *resolution* rule, applied to the *father* axiom

$\boxed{p\big(x, f(x)\big)}^{-}$	

and goal G3, with $\{x \leftarrow a, \ y \leftarrow f(a)\}$, we obtain the final goal

	G4. *true*

     The reader may observe that the deductive-tableau proof reflects the informal reasoning given in Section 6.1. In **Problem 7.1**, the reader is requested to carry out another deductive-tableau proof in the family theory. In **Problem 7.2**, a proof in an augmented family theory is requested. In **Problem 7.3**, a deductive-tableau proof in a different axiomatic theory is requested.

     If a theory is defined by an infinite set of axioms, we do not include all the axioms as assertions, because each tableau can have only a finite number of assertions. In the case of a theory with equality, we extend the system instead by introducing a new deduction rule that takes the place of infinitely many axioms.

7.2   EQUALITY RULE

If we want to prove the validity of a sentence $\mathcal{S}$ in a theory with equality, the most straightforward approach would be to add the equality axioms as assertions of our initial tableau. We have three simple axioms and two axiom schemata. The three axioms are

$$(\forall\ x,\ y,\ z) \begin{bmatrix} if\ \ x = y\ \ and\ \ y = z \\ then\ \ x = z \end{bmatrix} \qquad\qquad (transitivity)$$

$$(\forall\ x,\ y) \begin{bmatrix} if\ \ x = y \\ then\ \ y = x \end{bmatrix} \qquad\qquad (symmetry)$$

$$(\forall\ x)[x = x] \qquad\qquad (reflexivity)$$

The two axiom schemata are

For every k-ary function symbol f and for each i from 1 through k,

$$(\forall z_1,\ldots,z_{i-1},z_{i+1},\ldots,z_k) \overset{(\forall\, x,\, y)}{} \begin{bmatrix} if\ \ x = y \\ then\ \ f(z_1,\ \ldots,z_{i-1},x,z_{i+1},\ \ldots,z_k) = \\ f(z_1,\ \ldots,z_{i-1},y,z_{i+1},\ \ldots,z_k) \end{bmatrix}$$

$$(functional\ substitutivity\ for\ f)$$

For every ℓ-ary predicate symbol q (other than $=$) and for each j from 1 through ℓ,

$$(\forall z_1,\ldots,z_{j-1},z_{j+1},\ldots,z_\ell) \overset{(\forall\, x,\, y)}{} \begin{bmatrix} if\ \ x = y \\ then\ \ q(z_1,\ \ldots,z_{j-1},x,z_{j+1},\ \ldots,z_\ell) \\ \equiv \\ q(z_1,\ \ldots,z_{j-1},y,z_{j+1}.\ \ldots,z_\ell) \end{bmatrix}$$

$$(predicate\ substitutivity\ for\ q)$$

The *functional-substitutivity* axiom schema actually represents an infinite set of axioms: one for every k-ary function symbol f and for each i from 1 through k. Similarly, the *predicate-substitutivity* axiom schema represents an infinite set of axioms: one for every ℓ-ary predicate symbol q (other than $=$) and for each j from 1 through ℓ.

This approach fails because we can only have finitely many assertions in a tableau. A more practical approach is to drop the *symmetry, transitivity, functional-substitutivity*, and *predicate-substitutivity* assertions altogether (leaving only the *reflexivity* assertion) and introduce instead an *equality* rule, which resembles the *equivalence* rule for predicate logic and enables us to treat equality in an efficient way.

THE BASIC FORM

The basic form of the equality rule is expressed as follows.

Rule (AA-equality, left-to-right)

assertions	goals
$\mathcal{A}_1\big[\,\overline{s=t}\,\big]$	
$\mathcal{A}_2\big\langle\,\overline{s'}\,\big\rangle$	
$\mathcal{A}_1\theta\big[\,\overline{false}\,\big]$ *or* $\mathcal{A}_2\theta\big\langle\,\overline{t\theta}\,\big\rangle$	

where

- $\overline{s=t}$ stands for the free, quantifier-free equalities $s_1 = t_1, \ldots,$ $s_k = t_k$ $(k \geq 1)$, which occur in $\mathcal{A}_1$.

- $\overline{s'}$ stands for the free, quantifier-free subterms $s'_1, \ldots, s'_\ell$ $(\ell \geq 1)$, which occur in $\mathcal{A}_2$.

- The free variables of $\mathcal{A}_1\big[\,\overline{s=t}\,\big]$ and $\mathcal{A}_2\langle\overline{s'}\rangle$ are renamed so that the rows have no free variables in common.

- $\overline{t\theta}$ stands for $t_1\theta, \ldots, t_k\theta$.

- θ is a most-general separate-unifier for the tuple of subterms $\langle \overline{s}, \overline{s'} \rangle$ and the tuple of subterms $\langle \overline{t} \rangle$; that is, $s_1\theta, \ldots, s_k\theta$ and $s'_1\theta, \ldots, s'_\ell\theta$ are all identical terms and $t_1\theta, \ldots, t_k\theta$ are all identical terms. The terms $s_1\theta, \ldots, s_k\theta, s'_1\theta, \ldots, s'_\ell\theta$ must be distinct from the terms $t_1\theta, \ldots, t_k\theta$.

- $\overline{false}$ stands for *false*, $\ldots,$ *false* (k times). ◾

More precisely, to apply the *AA-equality* rule to two assertions $\mathcal{A}_1$ and $\mathcal{A}_2$ of a tableau:

- Rename the free variables of $\mathcal{A}_1$ and $\mathcal{A}_2$ if necessary to ensure that they have no free variables in common.

- Select free, quantifier-free subsentences of $\mathcal{A}_1$,
$$\overline{s=t}:\ s_1 = t_1,\ \ldots,\ s_k = t_k \qquad (k \geq 1),$$
and free, quantifier-free subterms of $\mathcal{A}_2$,
$$\overline{s'}:\ s'_1,\ \ldots,\ s'_\ell \qquad (\ell \geq 1),$$
such that θ is a most-general separate-unifier of the tuples $\langle s_1, \ldots, s_k,$ $s'_1, \ldots, s'_\ell \rangle$ and $\langle t_1, \ldots, t_k \rangle$; that is,

  - $s_1\theta, \ \ldots, \ s_k\theta$ and $s'_1\theta, \ \ldots, \ s'_\ell\theta$ are all the same term, which we shall call $s\theta$.

- $t_1\theta$, ..., $t_k\theta$ are all the same term, which we shall call $t\theta$. We require that $s\theta$ and $t\theta$ be distinct. (Note that we invoke the *separate-tuple-unification* algorithm of Section 4.8.)
- Apply θ safely to the assertion $\mathcal{A}_1$ and replace all free occurrences of $s\theta = t\theta$ in $\mathcal{A}_1\theta$ with *false*, obtaining the disjunct

  $\mathcal{A}_1\theta\left[\overline{false}\,\right]$.

- Apply θ safely to the assertion $\mathcal{A}_2$ and replace safely one or more occurrences of $s\theta$ in $\mathcal{A}_2\theta$ with $t\theta$, obtaining the disjunct

  $\mathcal{A}_2\theta\langle\,\overline{t\theta}\,\rangle$.

- Simplify the disjunction

  $\mathcal{A}_1\theta\left[\overline{false}\,\right]$ or $\mathcal{A}_2\theta\langle\,\overline{t\theta}\,\rangle$.

- Add the simplified disjunction to the tableau as a new assertion.

Remark (at least one replacement). Although the substitution notation admits the possibility that no equality $\overline{s = t}$ actually occurs in $\mathcal{A}_1$, the wording of the rule requires that some equalities actually do occur. Similarly, we require that at least one subterm of $\mathcal{A}_2\theta$ actually be replaced, even though the notation does not imply this. Otherwise, there would be no point in applying the rule. For the same reason, we do not apply the rule if $s\theta$ and $t\theta$ are identical. ⌐

The *equality* rule allows us to drop the *symmetry*, *transitivity*, *functional-substitutivity*, and *predicate-substitutivity* axioms from our tableau; we must still retain the simple *reflexivity* axiom as an initial assertion

$x = x$	

We also have the following *right-to-left version* of the *equality* rule.

Rule (AA-equality, right-to-left)

assertions	goals
$\mathcal{A}_1\left[\,\overline{s = t}\,\right]$	
$\mathcal{A}_2\langle\,\overline{t'}\,\rangle$	
$\mathcal{A}_1\theta\left[\,\overline{false}\,\right]$ *or* $\mathcal{A}_2\theta\langle\,\overline{s\theta}\,\rangle$	

where $\mathcal{A}_1$ and $\mathcal{A}_2$ satisfy the restrictions analogous to those in the left-to-right version of the rule. ⌐

This rule allows us to replace occurrences of $t\theta$ in $\mathcal{A}_2\theta$ with $s\theta$, rather than the other way around.

POLARITY

The *polarity* strategy for the *AA-equivalence* rule should also be applied to both versions of the *equality* rule.

Strategy (polarity)

An application of the *AA-equality* rule is in accordance with the *polarity strategy* if

at least one of the occurrences of
$$s_1 = t_1, \quad \ldots, \quad s_k = t_k$$
in $\mathcal{A}_1$, whose instances are replaced by *false* in applying the rule, is of negative polarity in the tableau. ◢

In the *polarity* strategy, the negative polarity need not be strict; the occurrence in question may actually have both polarities. Note that the *polarity* strategy places no restriction on the subterms $s'_1, \ldots, s'_\ell$ of $\mathcal{A}_2$.

Example.   Suppose our tableau contains the assertions

assertions	goals
$\mathcal{A}_1:$ *if* $r(x)$ *then* $\left[\,\boxed{f(x,a)} = g(x,y)\,\right]^{-}$	
$\mathcal{A}_2:$ $q\!\left(\boxed{f(b,z)}\,,\, y,\, z\right)$	

Let us apply the *AA-equality* rule, left-to-right, to $\mathcal{A}_1$ and $\mathcal{A}_2$. The subterms to be matched are indicated by boxes.

Note that $\mathcal{A}_1$ and $\mathcal{A}_2$ have the free variable y in common. We therefore rename y as $\widehat{y}$ in $\mathcal{A}_2$, to obtain the assertion
$$\widehat{\mathcal{A}_2}: \quad q\!\left(\boxed{f(b,z)}\,,\, \widehat{y},\, z\right).$$

Consider the free subsentence
$$s = t: \quad f(x,a) = g(x,y)$$
in $\mathcal{A}_1$ and the free subterm
$$s': \quad f(b,z)$$

in $\widehat{\mathcal{A}_2}$. The terms

$$s : \quad f(x, a) \qquad \text{and} \qquad s' : \quad f(b, z)$$

are unifiable under the most-general unifier

$$\theta : \quad \{x \leftarrow b, \, z \leftarrow a\};$$

the unified terms $s\theta$ and $s'\theta$ are identical to $f(b, a)$.

Applying θ to $\mathcal{A}_1$, we obtain

$$\mathcal{A}_1\theta : \quad \text{if } r(b) \text{ then } f(b, a) = g(b, y),$$

where the unified equality is

$$(s = t)\theta : \quad f(b, a) = g(b, y).$$

Replacing the equality $f(b, a) = g(b, y)$ with the truth symbol *false* in $\mathcal{A}_1\theta$, we obtain

$$\mathcal{A}_1^* : \quad \text{if } r(b) \text{ then } false.$$

Applying θ to $\widehat{\mathcal{A}_2}$, we obtain

$$\widehat{\mathcal{A}_2}\theta : \quad q\big(f(b, a), \, \widehat{y}, \, a\big).$$

Replacing the subterm $s\theta : f(b, a)$ with $t\theta : g(b, y)$ in $\widehat{\mathcal{A}_2}\theta$, we obtain

$$\mathcal{A}_2^* : \quad q\big(g(b, y), \, \widehat{y}, \, a\big).$$

Forming the disjunction $(\mathcal{A}_1^* \text{ or } \mathcal{A}_2^*)$, we obtain

$$\text{if } r(b) \text{ then } false$$

$$or$$

$$q\big(g(b, y), \, \widehat{y}, \, a\big).$$

This reduces (under *true-false* simplification) to the new assertion

$not\ r(b)$	
or	
$q\big(g(b, y), \, \widehat{y}, \, a\big)$	

which is added to the tableau.

As usual, we do not add the intermediate sentences $\widehat{\mathcal{A}_2}$, $\mathcal{A}_1\theta$, $\widehat{\mathcal{A}_2}\theta$, $\mathcal{A}_1^*$, $\mathcal{A}_2^*$, or the unsimplified disjunction to the tableau.

This application of the rule is in accordance with the *polarity* strategy because the occurrence of the equality

$$f(x, a) = g(x, y)$$

in $\mathcal{A}_1$ is negative in the tableau. ∎

JUSTIFICATION

To justify the *AA-equality* rule, we show that the old (given) tableau is equivalent to the new tableau. The justification of the *AA-equality* rule is analogous to that of the *AA-equivalence* rule. We justify the left-to-right version of the rule. Because the rule preserves equivalence, we can use the *special justification* proposition (Section 5.2), rather than the *general justification* proposition, in the proof.

Justification (AA-equality).   Suppose that $\mathcal{A}_1$ and $\mathcal{A}_2$ are two assertions that satisfy the restrictions for applying the *AA-equality* rule. As in the justifications for the *AA-resolution* and *AA-equivalence* rules, we may assume that the free variables of $\mathcal{A}_1$ have been renamed as necessary to ensure that the assertions have no free variables in common.

Let $\mathcal{I}$ be an interpretation under which the required tableau $\mathcal{T}_r$ is false; that is, the universal closures of the required assertions $\mathcal{A}_1$ and $\mathcal{A}_2$ are both true under $\mathcal{I}$. By the *special justification* proposition, it suffices to establish that the generated tableau $\mathcal{T}_g$ is false under $\mathcal{I}$, that is, that the universal closure of the generated assertion, the disjunction

$$\mathcal{A}_1\theta\left[\,\overline{false}\,\right]$$
$$or$$
$$\mathcal{A}_2\theta\langle\,\overline{t\theta}\,\rangle,$$

is also true under $\mathcal{I}$.

Because the universal closures of $\mathcal{A}_1$ and $\mathcal{A}_2$ are true under $\mathcal{I}$, the universal closures of $\mathcal{A}_1\theta$ and $\mathcal{A}_2\theta$ are also true under $\mathcal{I}$, by the *universal closure-instantiation* proposition. Therefore, by the *semantic-rule-for-universal-closure* proposition, $\mathcal{A}_1\theta$ and $\mathcal{A}_2\theta$ are themselves true under any interpretation that agrees with $\mathcal{I}$ on the constant, function, and predicate symbols of $\mathcal{A}_1\theta$ and $\mathcal{A}_2\theta$. Let $\mathcal{I}'$ be any such interpretation.

The proof now distinguishes between two cases.

Case: $(s = t)\theta$ is false under $\mathcal{I}'$

That is, the equivalence $(s = t)\theta \equiv false$ is true under $\mathcal{I}'$. Then (by the substitutivity of equivalence), because $\mathcal{A}_1\theta$ is true under $\mathcal{I}'$,

$$\mathcal{A}_1\theta\left[\,\overline{false}\,\right]$$

is also true under $\mathcal{I}'$. It follows (by the semantic rule for the *or* connective) that the disjunction

$$\mathcal{A}_1\theta\left[\,\overline{false}\,\right]$$
$$or$$
$$\mathcal{A}_2\theta\langle\,\overline{t\theta}\,\rangle$$

is also true under $\mathcal{I}'$.

Case: $(s = t)\theta$ is true under $\mathcal{I}'$

That is, $s\theta = t\theta$ is true under $\mathcal{I}'$. Hence, by the *substitutivity-of-equality* proposition (Section 6.5), because $\mathcal{A}_2\theta$ is true under $\mathcal{I}'$,

$$\mathcal{A}_2\theta\langle\,\overline{t\theta}\,\rangle$$

is also true under $\mathcal{I}'$. It follows (by the semantic rule for the *or* connective) that the disjunction

$$\mathcal{A}_1\theta\big[\,\overline{false}\,\big]$$
$$or$$
$$\mathcal{A}_2\theta\langle\,\overline{t\theta}\,\rangle$$

is true under $\mathcal{I}'$.

In each case, we have concluded that the generated assertion, the disjunction

$$\mathcal{A}_1\theta\big[\,\overline{false}\,\big]$$
$$or$$
$$\mathcal{A}_2\theta\langle\,\overline{t\theta}\,\rangle,$$

is true under $\mathcal{I}'$, for any interpretation $\mathcal{I}'$ that agrees with $\mathcal{I}$ on the constant, function, and predicate symbols of $\mathcal{A}_1\theta$ and $\mathcal{A}_2\theta$, and hence of the new assertion. Therefore (by the *semantic-rule-for-universal-closure* proposition), the universal closure of the generated assertion is true under $\mathcal{I}$, as we wanted to prove. The final simplification step preserves equivalence. ◣

The justification of the right-to-left version of the rule can be shown by the symmetry of equality.

DUAL FORMS

We have given the AA-form of the rule, which applies to two assertions. By duality, we can introduce forms of the rule that apply to an assertion and a goal, or to two goals. We present only the AG-form (left-to-right version), which applies to an assertion and a goal. This is the most commonly used form.

Rule (AG-equality, left-to-right)

assertions	goals
$\mathcal{A}\big[\,\overline{s = t}\,\big]$	
	$\mathcal{G}\langle\,\overline{s'}\,\rangle$
	$not\ \big(\mathcal{A}\theta\big[\,\overline{false}\,\big]\big)$ and $\mathcal{G}\theta\langle\overline{t\theta}\rangle$

where $\mathcal{A}$ and $\mathcal{G}$ satisfy the same conditions as $\mathcal{A}_1$ and $\mathcal{A}_2$, respectively, in the *AA-equality* rule. ◢

There are analogous right-to-left forms. The justification of the dual forms of the *equality* rule follows by duality.

The *polarity* strategy for each dual form of the rule is analogous to that for the *AA-equality* rule: at least one of the free occurrences of $s_1 = t_1$, ..., $s_k = t_k$, which are replaced by *false* in applying the rule, should be negative in the tableau.

Example.   Suppose our tableau contains the assertion and goal

assertions	goals
$\mathcal{A}: \ \left[f(x,\, y) \ = \ \boxed{g(x,\, a)} \right]^{-}$	
	$\mathcal{G}: \quad \begin{array}{c} (\forall\, y)\ q\!\left(\boxed{g(b,\, z)}\, ,\ y,\ z \right) \\[4pt] \textit{and} \\[4pt] p\!\left(\boxed{g(u,\, a)} \right) \end{array}$

Let us apply the *AG-equality* rule, right-to-left, to assertion $\mathcal{A}$ and goal $\mathcal{G}$. The subterms to be matched are indicated with boxes. Note that $\mathcal{A}$ and $\mathcal{G}$ have no free variables in common.

Consider the free subsentence

$$s = t: \quad f(x,\, y) \ = \ g(x,\, a)$$

in $\mathcal{A}$, which has negative polarity in the tableau, and consider the free subterms

$$t': \ g(b,\, z) \qquad \text{and} \qquad t'': \ g(u,\, a)$$

in $\mathcal{G}$.

The terms

$$t: \ g(x,\, a), \quad t': \ g(b,\, z), \quad \text{and} \quad t'': \ g(u,\, a)$$

are unifiable, with a most-general unifier

$$\theta: \ \{x \leftarrow b,\ z \leftarrow a,\ u \leftarrow b\};$$

the unified term is $g(b,\, a)$.

We apply θ to the assertion $\mathcal{A}$ and the goal $\mathcal{G}$, obtaining

$$\mathcal{A}\theta: \ f(b,\, y) \ = \ g(b,\, a)$$

and

$$\mathcal{G}\theta : \quad \begin{array}{c} (\forall y) q\big(g(b,\,a),\, y,\, a\big) \\ \text{and} \\ p\big(g(b,\,a)\big), \end{array}$$

respectively. Replacing the equality

$$(s = t)\theta : \quad f(b,\, y) = g(b,\, a)$$

in $\mathcal{A}\theta$ with *false*, and (safely) replacing the two subterms

$$t\theta : \quad g(b,\, a)$$

in $\mathcal{G}\theta$ with

$$s\theta : \quad f(b,\, y),$$

we obtain the new goal

> *not false*
>   *and*
> $(\forall y') \, q\big(f(b,\, y),\, y',\, a\big).$
>   *and*
> $p\big(f(b,\, y)\big).$

Note that we have used the rule to replace two occurrences of $t\theta$ with $s\theta$. Also, we have renamed the variable y of the quantifier $(\forall y)$ as y' to avoid capturing the free occurrence of y in $f(b,\, y)$.

The new goal reduces (by *true-false* simplification) to

	$(\forall y') \, q\big(f(b,\, y),\, y',\, a\big)$ *and* $p\big(f(b,\, y)\big)$

Remark (skolemization in axiomatic theories). The skolemization process has been described and justified for pure predicate logic. We have been applying the process, however, to remove quantifiers in axiomatic theories. Removing a quantifier of both forces or a quantifier of strict existential force presents no problem because these phases of the process preserve equivalence; if two sentences are equivalent in predicate logic, they are equivalent in any axiomatic theory.

The trouble arises when we attempt to remove quantifiers of strict universal force, because this phase does not preserve equivalence, but only validity; a process that preserves validity in predicate logic may not preserve validity in an axiomatic theory. In predicate logic, to be valid a sentence must be true under all interpretations; in a theory, to be valid a sentence must be true only under the models of the theory. Therefore the removal of quantifiers of universal force requires special justification for each theory we consider. We shall not do this here, but only indicate why it must be done.

For a finite theory, the justification of this phase of the skolemization process is straightforward. We choose as our skolem function (or skolem constant) a symbol that does not occur in any of the axioms.

This approach does not suffice if our theory is infinite and defined by one or more axiom schemata. In this case, it may happen that every constant and function symbol occurs in some instance of an axiom schema.

For example, in the theory of equality, suppose we remove a quantifier of strict universal force by introducing a new unary skolem function symbol f. In that case, we automatically provide the appropriate instance of the *functional substitutivity* axiom schema,

$$(\forall x, y) \begin{bmatrix} \text{if} \ \ x = y \\ \text{then} \ \ f(x) = f(y) \end{bmatrix} \qquad (\textit{functional substitutivity for } f)$$

In an infinite theory, the danger we face is that, in removing a quantifier of strict universal force from a sentence that is not valid, we introduce a skolem function symbol f and obtain a sentence that is valid in the theory, because it is a consequence of some instances of our axiom schemata that refer to f. This turns out to be impossible in the theory of equality or any of the other theories we shall consider. Therefore we shall use the skolemization process freely in these theories. ◢

In **Problem 7.4**, the reader is requested to show that the *transitivity, symmetry*, and *substitutivity* properties of equality can actually be proved in a tableau with the *equality* rule. In **Problem 7.5**, the reader is asked to prove the validity of one sentence in the theory of equality and to show the nonvalidity of another sentence.

7.3 FINITE THEORIES WITH EQUALITY

A tableau that includes among its initial assertions the *reflexivity* axiom and to which we may apply the *equality* rule, as well as any of the predicate-logic rules, will be called a *tableau with equality*.

We have seen that we can prove a sentence S within a particular finite theory by adding the axioms for the theory as the initial assertions in a predicate-logic tableau, and adding S as the initial goal. In the same way, if we want to prove a sentence S in a finite theory with equality (that is, one defined by the equality axioms plus a finite set of special axioms), we may add the special axioms as the initial assertions of a tableau with equality that has S as its initial goal.

In the following sections, we apply the deductive-tableau framework to prove the validity of sentences in two finite theories with equality. We start with the theory of weak partial orderings.

THEORY OF WEAK PARTIAL ORDERINGS

We have defined earlier (Section 6.6) the theory of a weak partial ordering $\preceq$ as the theory with equality whose special axioms are

$$(\forall x, y, z) \begin{bmatrix} if \ x \preceq y \ and \ y \preceq z \\ then \ x \preceq z \end{bmatrix} \qquad (transitivity)$$

$$(\forall x, y) \begin{bmatrix} if \ x \preceq y \ and \ y \preceq x \\ then \ x = y \end{bmatrix} \qquad (antisymmetry)$$

$$(\forall x)[x \preceq x] \qquad (reflexivity)$$

To prove the validity of a sentence $\mathcal{S}$ in the theory of the weak partial ordering $\preceq$ within the tableau framework, we need only prove the following tableau with equality:

assertions		goals
if $x \preceq y$ and $y \preceq z$ then $x \preceq z$	(transitivity)	
if $x \preceq y$ and $y \preceq x$ then $x = y$	(antisymmetry)	
$x \preceq x$	(reflexivity)	
		$\mathcal{S}$

Here again, by outermost skolemization, we have dropped the outermost universal quantifiers from the initial assertions.

Recall that, because this is a tableau with equality, we also include the *reflexivity* axiom $(x = x)$ among our initial assertions, and during the proof we may apply the *equality* rule (both the left-to-right and right-to-left versions) as well as the other predicate-logic rules. We need not include the axioms for equality (other than *reflexivity*) as assertions in the tableau.

Example (irreflexive restriction). Consider the augmented theory formed by adding to the theory of the weak partial ordering $\preceq$ the following axiom, which defines the *irreflexive restriction* $\prec$ associated with $\preceq$:

$$(\forall x, y) \begin{bmatrix} x \prec y \\ \equiv \\ x \preceq y \ \ and \ \ not \ (x = y) \end{bmatrix} \qquad \text{(irreflexive restriction)}$$

It can then be shown that $\prec$ is indeed a strict partial ordering, i.e., that $\prec$ is transitive and irreflexive. This is stated in the *irreflexive-restriction* proposition of the theory of the weak partial ordering $\preceq$ (Section 6.6). We show the irreflexivity of $\prec$ here; its transitivity is left as an exercise (**Problem 7.6**).

Suppose we would like to show the validity of the *irreflexivity* property

$$(\forall x)\big[not \ (x \prec \ x)\big] \qquad \qquad \text{(irreflexivity)}$$

in this theory.

We begin with a tableau over the theory of weak partial orderings that contains, in addition to the *reflexivity* axiom for equality and the axioms for a weak partial ordering, the definition of the irreflexive-restriction relation

assertions	goals
$\begin{bmatrix} \boxed{x \prec y} \\ \equiv \\ x \preceq y \ \ and \ \ not \ (x = y) \end{bmatrix}^{-}$ *(irreflexive restriction)*	

as an initial assertion and the desired *irreflexivity* property,

	G1. $(\forall x)^{\forall}[not \ (x \prec \ x)]$

as its initial goal.

By the $\forall$-*elimination* rule, we may drop the quantifier $(\forall x)^{\forall}$ from the initial goal G1, replacing the bound variable x with the skolem constant a, to obtain

	G2. $not \ \boxed{a \prec \ a}$

Applying the *equivalence* rule to the *irreflexive restriction* axiom and goal G2, with $\{x \leftarrow a, \ y \leftarrow a\}$, we obtain the goal

	G3. $not \ \Big(a \preceq a \ \ and \ \ not \ \boxed{a = a}^{+}\Big)$

Applying the *resolution* rule to the *reflexivity* axiom for equality,

$\boxed{x = x}$ $^{-}$	

and goal G3, we obtain the final goal

	G4. *true*

In **Problem 7.7** the reader is requested to provide a tableau proof of the *reflexive-closure* proposition, i.e., that in a theory with equality defined by the axioms for a strict partial ordering, the reflexive closure $\preceq$ of $\prec$ is a weak partial ordering (Section 6.8).

Remark (reflexivity of equality).   In the final step of the previous example, we applied the *resolution* rule to goal G3 and the *reflexivity* axiom $(x = x)$, to obtain the goal G4. Resolution with the *reflexivity* axiom is a frequent step in proofs in theories with equality. It will be convenient for us to apply this step automatically whenever a positive subsentence of the form $(t = t)$ appears in an assertion or a goal. For brevity we may then say that goal G4 is obtained from goal G3 "by the reflexivity of equality," without giving the assertion or mentioning the resolution step. We shall still annotate the subsentence $(a = a)$ in G3 with a box indicating its positive polarity.

If a positive subsentence of form $(t = t')$ appears, where t and t' are unifiable but not identical, we shall not apply the resolution step automatically. Also, we shall mention the rule, the assertion, and the most-general unifier explicitly in this case. ◢

THEORY OF GROUPS

We have defined the theory of groups (Section 6.7) as the theory with equality whose special axioms are

$(\forall x)\big[x \circ e \;=\; x\big]$	(*right identity*)
$(\forall x)\big[x \circ x^{-1} \;=\; e\big]$	(*right inverse*)
$(\forall x,\, y,\, z)\Big[(x \circ y) \circ z \;=\; x \circ (y \circ z)\Big]$	(*associativity*)

To prove the validity of a sentence $\mathcal{S}$ in this theory, we must prove the following tableau with equality:

assertions		goals
$x \circ e = x$	*(right identity)*	
$x \circ x^{-1} = e$	*(right inverse)*	
$(x \circ y) \circ z = x \circ (y \circ z)$	*(associativity)*	
		$\mathcal{S}$

Again, because this is a tableau with equality, it includes implicitly the *reflexivity* axiom $(x = x)$ among its assertions, and during the proof we may apply the *equality* rule, as well as the other predicate-logic deduction rules.

Example (right cancellation).   Suppose we would like to prove the validity of the property

$$(\forall x,\, y,\, z) \begin{bmatrix} if & x \circ z = y \circ z \\ then & x = y \end{bmatrix} \qquad\qquad (right\ cancellation)$$

in the theory of groups. Our deductive-tableau proof resembles the informal proof of the same proposition in Section 6.7.

We consider the initial goal

assertions	goals
	G1. $(\forall x,\, y,\, z)^{\vee} \begin{bmatrix} if & x \circ z = y \circ z \\ then & x = y \end{bmatrix}$

By the $\forall$-*elimination* rule, we may drop the quantifiers from goal G1, replacing the bound variables x, y, and z with skolem constants a, b, and c, respectively, to obtain

	G2. *if* $\ a \circ c = b \circ c$ *then* $\ a = b$

By the *if-split* rule, we decompose goal G2 into the assertion and goal

A3. $\left[\boxed{a \circ c} = b \circ c \right]^{-}$	
	G4. $\boxed{a} = b$

Applying the *equality* rule (right-to-left) to the *right-identity* axiom,

$$\left[x \circ e \;=\; \boxed{x}\right]^{-}$$

and goal G4, with $\{x \leftarrow a\}$, we replace a with $a \circ e$ in the goal, to obtain

G5. $a \circ e \;=\; \boxed{b}$

Applying the *equality* rule (right-to-left) once more to the *right-identity* axiom and goal G5, with $\{x \leftarrow b\}$, we replace b with $b \circ e$ in the goal, to obtain

G6. $a \circ \boxed{e} \;=\; b \circ e$

Applying the *equality* rule (right-to-left) to the *right-inverse* axiom,

$$\left[x \circ x^{-1} \;=\; \boxed{e}\right]^{-}$$

with $\{\,\}$, we replace the annotated occurrence of e in goal G6 with $x \circ x^{-1}$, to obtain

G7. $a \circ (x \circ x^{-1}) \;=\; b \circ \boxed{e}$

We would like to apply the *equality* rule again to the *right-inverse* axiom and goal G7; these rows, however, have the free variable x in common. We rename the variables in these rows to avoid this coincidence, to obtain

$$\left[x_1 \circ x_1^{-1} \;=\; \boxed{e}\right]^{-}$$

G7′. $a \circ (x_2 \circ x_2^{-1}) \;=\; b \circ \boxed{e}$

(To avoid future renaming, we have actually renamed x in both rows.)

Now we may apply the *equality* rule (right-to-left) to replace e with $x_1 \circ x_1^{-1}$ in goal G7′, obtaining

| | G8. | $\boxed{a \circ (x_2 \circ x_2^{-1})}$ | $=$ | $\boxed{b \circ (x_1 \circ x_1^{-1})}$ |

By two applications of the *equality* rule (right-to-left) to the *associativity* axiom,

$$\left[\, (x \circ y) \circ z \;=\; \boxed{x \circ (y \circ z)} \,\right]^{-}$$

and goal G8, with $\{x \leftarrow a,\ y \leftarrow x_2,\ z \leftarrow x_2^{-1}\}$ and then with $\{x \leftarrow b,\ y \leftarrow x_1,\ z \leftarrow x_1^{-1}\}$, we may rewrite the goal as

| | G9. | $\left(\boxed{a \circ x_2}\right) \circ x_2^{-1} \;=\; (b \circ x_1) \circ x_1^{-1}$ |

By the *equality* rule, applied to assertion A3 and goal G9, with $\{x_2 \leftarrow c\}$, we replace $a \circ x_2$ with $b \circ c$ in the goal, to obtain

| | G10. | $\boxed{(b \circ c) \circ c^{-1} \;=\; (b \circ x_1) \circ x_1^{-1}}^{+}$ |

At last, applying the *resolution* rule to the *reflexivity* axiom $(x = x)$ and goal G10, with $\{x_1 \leftarrow c,\ x \leftarrow (b \circ c) \circ c^{-1}\}$, we obtain the final goal

| | G11. | *true* |

Now that we have proved the *right-cancellation* property, we can add it as an assertion to the tableau of any subsequent proof in the theory of groups. ⌐

In **Problem 7.8** the reader is requested to use the deductive-tableau technique to prove the following properties of the theory of groups:

$$(\forall x)\big[e \circ x \;=\; x\big] \qquad\qquad\qquad\qquad \textit{(left identity)}$$

$$(\forall x)\big[x^{-1} \circ x \;=\; e\big] \qquad\qquad\qquad\qquad \textit{(left inverse)}$$

$$(\forall x, y, z)\left[\begin{array}{l} \textit{if}\ \ z \circ x \;=\; z \circ y \\ \textit{then}\ \ x \;=\; y \end{array}\right] \qquad\qquad \textit{(left cancellation)}$$

$$(\forall x)\left[\begin{array}{l} \textit{if}\ \ x \circ x \;=\; x \\ \textit{then}\ \ x \;=\; e \end{array}\right] \qquad\qquad\qquad \textit{(nonidempotence)}$$

The following example illustrates how, within an axiomatic theory, we may define new functions by providing additional axioms.

Example (quotient).   Suppose we define the quotient x/y of two elements x and y of a group by the following axiom:

$$(\forall x, y)\big[x/y \;=\; x \circ y^{-1}\big] \qquad\qquad (quotient)$$

We would like to prove that the *cancellation* property holds, that is,

$$(\forall\, x, y)\big[(x/y) \circ y \;=\; x\big] \qquad\qquad (cancellation)$$

We attempt to prove the initial tableau over the theory of groups,

assertions	goals
$\Big[\boxed{x/y} \;=\; x \circ y^{-1}\Big]^{-}$ (*quotient*)	
	G1. $(\forall\, x, y)^{\forall}\big[(x/y) \circ y \;=\; x\big]$

The *quotient* axiom for the quotient function is included among the assertions; because the tableau is over the theory of groups, the group axioms and previously proved group theorems are also present.

By the $\forall$-*elimination* rule, we may drop the quantifiers of goal G1, to obtain

	G2. $\boxed{a/b} \circ b \;=\; a$

By the *equality* rule, applied to the *quotient* axiom and the goal G2, with $\{x \leftarrow a, y \leftarrow b\}$, we obtain

	G3. $\boxed{(a \circ b^{-1}) \circ b} \;=\; a$

By the *equality* rule, applied to the *associativity* axiom

$\Big[\boxed{(x \circ y) \circ z} \;=\; x \circ (y \circ z)\Big]^{-}$	

and goal G3, with $\{x \leftarrow a, y \leftarrow b^{-1}, z \leftarrow b\}$, we obtain

	G4. $\quad a \circ \left(\boxed{b^{-1} \circ b} \right) = a$

By the *equality* rule, applied to the *left-inverse* property

$\left[\boxed{x^{-1} \circ x} = e \right]^{-}$	

and goal G4, with $\{x \leftarrow b\}$, we obtain

	G5. $\quad \boxed{a \circ e = a}^{+}$

Applying the *resolution* rule to the *right-identity* axiom

$\boxed{x \circ e = x}^{-}$	

and goal G5, with $\{x \leftarrow a\}$, we obtain the final goal

	G6. *true*

Note that the proof of the *cancellation* property depends on the proof of the *left-inverse* property, which was requested as an exercise. Had we attempted to prove the *cancellation* theorem without having proved the other theorem first, the proof, of course, would have been more cumbersome.

In **Problem 7.9** we interchange the roles of the *quotient* axiom and *cancellation* property. We assume that the quotient function x/y is defined alternatively by the axiom

$$(\forall \, x, y)\left[(x/y) \circ y = x\right] \qquad\qquad\qquad \textit{(cancellation)}$$

and ask the reader to prove that the quotient x/y is then the same as $x \circ y^{-1}$, that is,

$$(\forall \, x, y)\left[x/y = x \circ y^{-1}\right] \qquad\qquad\qquad \textit{(quotient)}$$

PROBLEMS

Use the deductive-tableau technique to carry out the following proofs.

Problem 7.1 (family theory)   page 352

In the family theory, prove that

> if Alice is the parent of her own father,
> then Alice's father is his own grandfather.

An informal argument to show this was requested in Problem 6.1.

Problem 7.2 (augmented family theory)   page 352

Suppose we augment the family theory with the following axiom:

$$(\forall x,\, y,\, z) \begin{bmatrix} \textit{if } p(x,\, z) \textit{ and } p(y,\, z) \\ \textit{then } s(x,\, y) \end{bmatrix} \qquad (\textit{sibling})$$

where $s(x,\, y)$ is intended to mean that x and y are siblings.

In this augmented theory, show that

> If the mother of Bob is a parent of Alice
> then Alice and Bob are siblings.

More precisely:

(a) Find a sentence $\mathcal{F}$ whose intuitive meaning is given by the English sentence above. Let the constants a and b denote Alice and Bob, respectively.

(b) Give a deductive-tableau proof of $\mathcal{F}$ in the family theory augmented by the *sibling* axiom.

Problem 7.3 (redhead)   page 352

Suppose the *grandparent theory* is defined by the single axiom

$$(\forall\ x,\, z) \Big[gp(x,\, z)\ \equiv\ (\exists y)[p(x,\, y)\ \textit{and}\ p(y,\, z)] \Big] \qquad (\textit{grandparent})$$

Intuitively, this means that z is a grandparent of x if and only if, for some person y, y is a parent of x and z is a parent of y. Within this theory, give a proof of the following sentence:

$$\textit{if }\ (\exists\ x,\, z) \begin{bmatrix} gp(x,\, z)\ \textit{and} \\ red(x)\ \textit{and}\ \textit{not } red(z) \end{bmatrix}$$

$$\textit{then }\ (\exists\ x,\, z) \begin{bmatrix} p(x,\, z)\ \textit{and} \\ red(x)\ \textit{and}\ \textit{not } red(z) \end{bmatrix} \qquad (\textit{redhead})$$

Intuitively, if $red(x)$ stands for "x is a redhead," this means that if some redhead has a nonredheaded grandparent, then some redhead has a nonredheaded parent.

Problem 7.4 (properties of equality)   page 362

In a tableau with equality, show the following properties of equality:

(a) *Transitivity*

$$(\forall\, x,\, y,\, z) \begin{bmatrix} if & x = y \ \ and \ \ y = z \\ then & x = z \end{bmatrix}$$

(b) *Symmetry*

$$(\forall\, x,\, y) \begin{bmatrix} if & x = y \\ then & y = x \end{bmatrix}$$

(c) *Functional Substitutivity*

$$(\forall\, x,\, y,\, z) \begin{bmatrix} if & x = y \\ then & f(x,\, z) = f(y,\, z) \end{bmatrix}$$

(d) *Predicate Substitutivity*

$$(\forall\, x,\, y,\, z) \begin{bmatrix} if & x = y \\ then & q(z,\, x) \equiv q(z,\, y) \end{bmatrix}.$$

Problem 7.5 (**valid equality**)   page 362

Let $\mathcal{F}[x]$ stand for the sentence

$$\mathcal{F}[x]: \quad (\forall\, y,\, z) \begin{bmatrix} if \ f(g(x)) = x \\ then \ if \ g(y) = g(z) \\ \qquad then \ h(g(y),\, z) = h(g(z),\, y) \end{bmatrix}.$$

(a) In a deductive tableau with equality, prove the validity of $(\exists\, x)\mathcal{F}[x]$.

(b) Show that $(\forall\, x)\mathcal{F}[x]$ is not valid in the theory of equality.

Problem 7.6 (**irreflexive restriction**)   page 364

In the theory of a weak partial ordering $\preceq$, prove that the irreflexive restriction $\prec$ associated with $\preceq$ is transitive, that is,

$$(\forall\, x,\, y,\, z) \begin{bmatrix} if & x \prec y \ \ and \ \ y \prec z \\ then & x \prec z \end{bmatrix} \qquad (transitivity)$$

Problem 7.7 (**reflexive closure**)   page 365

Consider a theory with equality defined by the axioms of the theory of a strict partial ordering $\prec$. Prove that the corresponding *reflexive-closure* relation, defined by

$$(\forall\, x,\, y) \begin{bmatrix} x \preceq y \\ \equiv \\ x \prec y \ \ or \ \ x = y \end{bmatrix} \qquad (reflexive \ closure)$$

is a weak partial ordering, i.e., that the following properties hold:

(a) *Transitivity*

$$(\forall x,\ y,\ z) \begin{bmatrix} if\ \ x \preceq y\ \ and\ \ y \preceq z \\ then\ \ x \preceq z \end{bmatrix}$$

(b) *Antisymmetry*

$$(\forall x,\ y) \begin{bmatrix} if\ \ x \preceq y\ \ and\ \ y \preceq x \\ then\ \ x = y \end{bmatrix}$$

(c) *Reflexivity*

$$(\forall x)[x \preceq x].$$

Problem 7.8 (theory of groups)   page 368

Prove the following properties of the theory of groups:

(a) *Left identity*

$$(\forall x)\big[e \circ x = x\big]$$

(b) *Left inverse*

$$(\forall x)\big[x^{-1} \circ x\ =\ e\big]$$

(c) *Left cancellation*

$$(\forall x,\ y,\ z) \begin{bmatrix} if\ \ z \circ x\ =\ z \circ y \\ then\ \ x\ =\ y \end{bmatrix}$$

(d) *Nonidempotence*

$$(\forall x) \begin{bmatrix} if\ \ x \circ x\ =\ x \\ then\ \ x\ =\ e \end{bmatrix}.$$

Problem 7.9 (quotient versus inverse)   page 370

Suppose we define the quotient x/y of two elements x and y of a group by the following axiom:

$$(\forall\ x,\ y)\big[(x/y) \circ y\ =\ x\big] \hspace{3cm} (cancellation)$$

Prove that the quotient x/y is then the same as $x \circ y^{-1}$, that is,

$$(\forall\ x,\ y)\big[x/y\ =\ x \circ y^{-1}\big] \hspace{3cm} (quotient)$$

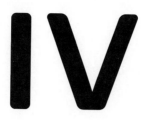

IV

Theories

With

Induction

8

Nonnegative Integers

The most important axiomatic theories for us will be those defined by the *principle of mathematical induction*. This principle is represented here as an axiom schema, an infinite set of axioms, like the functional- and predicate-substitutivity axioms for equality. Theories with induction include those of the nonnegative integers, tuples, trees, and other fundamental structures. We begin with the nonnegative integers, which are the most familiar and the most important.

8.1 BASIC PROPERTIES

In the theory of the nonnegative integers, we define

- A constant symbol 0, denoting the integer *zero*
- A unary function symbol x^+, denoting the *successor* function
- A unary predicate symbol $integer(x)$.

The reader should understand that 0 is an informal notation for a constant symbol (such as a or b) and is not to be confused with the actual integer zero, which is a domain element. Under the intended model for the theory, the symbol 0 will be assigned the integer zero as its value.

Also the symbol x^+ is an informal notation for a unary function symbol (such as $f(x)$ or $g(x)$). Under the intended model for the theory, the function symbol x^+ will be assigned the successor function, i.e., the function that maps the integer d into the integer $d + 1$.

The terms of the theory include

$$0, \quad 0^+, \quad (0^+)^+, \quad ((0^+)^+)^+, \quad \ldots .$$

Conventionally, 0^+ is abbreviated as 1, $(0^+)^+$ as 2, $((0^+)^+)^+$ as 3, and so forth. The symbols 1, 2, 3, ... are merely informal abbreviations for these terms; they are not notations for constant symbols. Under the intended model they denote the actual domain elements one, two, three, ...

The predicate symbol $integer(x)$ is intended to be true if x is assigned a nonnegative integer, and false otherwise. In the simplest models for the theory, all the domain elements will be nonnegative integers, and hence $integer(x)$ will always be true. Later, however, we shall introduce elements into our domain that are not nonnegative integers; the predicate symbol $integer(x)$ will then be used to distinguish between the nonnegative integers and the other domain elements.

The theory of the nonnegative integers is a theory with equality defined by the following axioms:

- The *generation* axioms

$integer(0)$	*(zero)*
$(\forall\ integer\ x)\big[integer(x^+)\big]$	*(successor)*

- The *uniqueness* axioms

$(\forall\ integer\ x)\big[not\ (x^+ = 0)\big]$	*(zero)*
$(\forall\ integer\ x, y)\begin{bmatrix} if\ \ x^+ = y^+ \\ then\ \ x = y \end{bmatrix}$	*(successor)*

- The *induction* principle

> For each sentence $\mathcal{F}[x]$ in the theory, the universal closure of the sentence
> $$if\ \begin{bmatrix} \mathcal{F}[0] \\ and \\ (\forall\ integer\ x)\begin{bmatrix} if\ \ \mathcal{F}[x] \\ then\ \ \mathcal{F}[x^+] \end{bmatrix} \end{bmatrix} \qquad (induction)$$
> $$then\ (\forall\ integer\ x)\mathcal{F}[x]$$
> is an axiom.

The two generation axioms have the intuitive meaning that any element that can be constructed from the zero element 0 and the successor function x^+ is a nonnegative integer. Thus 0, 0^+, $(0^+)^+$, ... all denote nonnegative integers.

The two uniqueness axioms have the intuitive meaning that each nonnegative integer can be constructed in at most one way from the zero element 0 and the successor function x^+. Thus 0, 0^+, $(0^+)^+$, ... denote distinct nonnegative integers.

Note that the axioms for the theory include two *zero* axioms and two *successor* axioms. In referring to them later we shall always discriminate between them by speaking of the *zero* generation axiom or the *zero* uniqueness axiom and of the *successor* generation axiom or the *successor* uniqueness axiom.

The *induction* principle is actually an axiom schema, because it represents an infinite set of axioms, one for each sentence $\mathcal{F}[x]$ in the theory. The sentence $\mathcal{F}[x]$ is called the *inductive sentence*. The subsentence

$$\mathcal{F}[0]$$

is called the *base case* of the induction. The subsentence

$$(\forall \ integer \ x) \begin{bmatrix} if & \mathcal{F}[x] \\ then & \mathcal{F}[x^+] \end{bmatrix}$$

is called the *inductive step*; the subsentences $\mathcal{F}[x]$ and $\mathcal{F}[x^+]$ of the inductive step are called the *induction hypothesis* and the *desired conclusion*, respectively. The variable x is called the *inductive variable*.

The inductive sentence $\mathcal{F}[x]$ may have free variables other than x. The *induction* principle asserts that the universal closure of the implication is valid, i.e., true under every model of the theory. This implies that the implication itself is true under every model.

The *induction* principle may be paraphrased intuitively as follows:

> To show that a sentence $\mathcal{F}[x]$ is true for every nonnegative integer x (under a given interpretation), it suffices to show the base case
>
> $\mathcal{F}[0]$ is true
>
> and the inductive step
>
> for an arbitrary nonnegative integer x,
>> if $\mathcal{F}[x]$ is true,
>> then $\mathcal{F}[x + 1]$ is also true.

The *induction* principle states that, to show that a sentence is true for all the nonnegative integers, it suffices to show that the sentence is true for 0 and that, whenever it is true for a nonnegative integer x, it is also true for the successor x^+. Therefore it is true for 0^+ (by one application of the inductive step), for $(0^+)^+$ (by another application of the inductive step), and so forth.

In **Problem 8.13**, the reader is requested to show that a schema obtained by renaming a bound variable in the *induction* principle, which is therefore apparently equivalent to the *induction* principle, is actually not valid. (This exercise is included as one of the last problems in this chapter because of its theoretical nature.)

Since the theory of the nonnegative integers is a theory with equality, we include the equality axioms. In particular, we have the appropriate instances of the *substitutivity* axiom schemata,

$$(\forall x, y) \begin{bmatrix} if & x = y \\ then & x^+ = y^+ \end{bmatrix} \qquad (functional\ substitutivity\ for\ x^+)$$

$$(\forall x, y) \begin{bmatrix} if & x = y \\ then & integer(x) \equiv integer(y) \end{bmatrix}$$
$$(predicate\ substitutivity\ for\ integer)$$

In the intended model for the theory, the domain consists of the ordinary nonnegative integers $0, 1, 2, \ldots$ and the function symbol x^+ is assigned the successor function over the nonnegative integers. The reader will see (in Chapter 14) that there are actually some quite different "nonstandard" models for this theory.

In this chapter, when we speak about the validity of a sentence, we shall always mean validity in the theory of the nonnegative integers. Let us show the validity of a sentence in this theory.

Proposition (decomposition)
The sentence

$$(\forall\ integer\ x) \begin{bmatrix} if & not\ (x = 0) \\ then & (\exists\ integer\ y)\,[x = y^+] \end{bmatrix} \qquad (decomposition)$$

is valid (in the theory of the nonnegative integers).

Proof.   The proof employs the instance of the *induction* principle in which the inductive sentence is taken to be

$$\mathcal{F}[x]: \quad \begin{array}{l} if\ not\ (x = 0) \\ then\ (\exists\ integer\ y)\,[x = y^+] \end{array}$$

To show

$$(\forall\ integer\ x)\mathcal{F}[x]$$

(under an interpretation), it suffices, by the *induction* principle and propositional logic, to establish the base case,

$$\mathcal{F}[0],$$

and the inductive step,

$$(\forall\ integer\ x) \begin{bmatrix} if & \mathcal{F}[x] \\ then & \mathcal{F}[x^+] \end{bmatrix}$$

We show the base case and the inductive step separately.

Base Case

We want to show
$$\mathcal{F}[0]: \quad \begin{array}{l} \textit{if } \; not \; (0 = 0) \\ \textit{then } \; (\exists \; integer \; y)\big[0 = y^+\big] \end{array}$$
Because (by the *reflexivity* axiom for equality) $0 = 0$, the antecedent
$$not \; (0 = 0)$$
of this implication is false and therefore the entire sentence is true.

Inductive Step

We want to show
$$(\forall \; integer \; x) \begin{bmatrix} \textit{if } \; \mathcal{F}[x] \\ \textit{then } \; \mathcal{F}[x^+] \end{bmatrix},$$
that is,
$$(\forall \; integer \; x) \begin{bmatrix} \textit{if } & \begin{bmatrix} \textit{if } \; not \; (x = 0) \\ \textit{then } \; (\exists \; integer \; y)[x = y^+] \end{bmatrix} \\ \textit{then } & \begin{bmatrix} \textit{if } \; not \; (x^+ = 0) \\ \textit{then } \; (\exists \; integer \; y)[x^+ = y^+] \end{bmatrix} \end{bmatrix}.$$

Consider an arbitrary nonnegative integer x, that is, an element x such that
$$integer(x).$$
We assume the induction hypothesis
$$\mathcal{F}[x]: \quad \begin{array}{l} \textit{if } \; not \; (x = 0) \\ \textit{then } \; (\exists \; integer \; y)\big[x = y^+\big] \end{array}$$
and would like to show the desired conclusion
$$\mathcal{F}[x^+]: \quad \begin{array}{l} \textit{if } \; not \; (x^+ = 0) \\ \textit{then } \; (\exists \; integer \; y)\big[x^+ = y^+\big]. \end{array}$$
It suffices to show the consequent,
$$(\exists \; integer \; y)\big[x^+ = y^+\big],$$
of the desired conclusion $\mathcal{F}[x^+]$.

Because we have supposed $integer(x)$ and we know (by the *reflexivity* axiom for equality) that $x^+ = x^+$, we have
$$\begin{array}{l} integer(x) \\ \quad and \\ x^+ = x^+. \end{array}$$
Therefore (by the *existential quantifier-instantiation* proposition, taking y to be x) we have
$$(\exists y) \begin{bmatrix} integer(y) \\ \quad and \\ x^+ = y^+ \end{bmatrix}$$

or, in terms of our relative quantifier notation,

$$(\exists \ integer \ y)\big[x^+ = y^+\big],$$

as we wanted to show.

Since we have established both the base case and the inductive step, the proof is complete. ⏝

The above proof has the unusual feature that it requires the *induction* principle but makes no use of the induction hypothesis in the inductive step. Nevertheless, the principle is essential in this proof. If the principle were deleted from the theory of the nonnegative integers, there would be models for the resulting theory under which the *decomposition* property would not be true. The reader is requested to show this in **Problem 8.14**. (This problem, like Problem 8.13, is placed late in the list because of its theoretical nature.)

8.2   THE ADDITION FUNCTION

Suppose we augment our theory of the nonnegative integers by formulating two axioms that define a binary function symbol $x + y$, denoting, under the intended model, the *addition* (*plus*) function over the nonnegative integers. As usual, $x + y$ is merely a conventional notation for a standard binary function symbol of predicate logic, such as $f_{97}(x, y)$.

The axioms for addition are as follows:

$$(\forall \ integer \ x)\big[x + 0 = x\big] \qquad\qquad\qquad (right \ zero)$$

$$(\forall \ integer \ x, y)\big[x + y^+ \ = \ (x + y)^+\big] \qquad (right \ successor)$$

As usual, when we introduce a new function symbol into a theory with equality, we automatically provide the corresponding instances of the *functional-substitutivity* axiom schema for addition, that is,

$$(\forall x, y, z)\begin{bmatrix} if \ \ x = y \\ then \ \ x + z = y + z \end{bmatrix} \qquad (left \ functional \ substitutivity)$$

and

$$(\forall x, y, z)\begin{bmatrix} if \ \ x = y \\ then \ \ z + x = z + y \end{bmatrix} \qquad (right \ functional \ substitutivity)$$

We also provide those instances of the *induction* principle for which the inductive sentence $\mathcal{F}[x]$ contains occurrences of the new symbol $x + y$.

The *right-zero* and *right-successor* axioms for addition are in the form of a typical "recursive" definition for the function. The *right-zero* axiom defines the function for the case in which its second argument is 0. The *right-successor* axiom defines the function for the case in which its second argument is of form y^+; the value of $x + y^+$ is defined in terms of the value of $x + y$. Because (by the *decomposition* proposition) the second argument must either be 0 or of the form y^+, the two axioms cover all possibilities. These axioms suggest a method for computing the addition function, as we shall see in a subsequent remark.

As before, whenever we add new axioms to a theory, we run the risk of making it inconsistent. Usually we disregard this issue and assume that the axioms we provide do not introduce inconsistencies. One can show that the axioms for addition, and in general other sets of axioms of the same (recursive) form, preserve the consistency of the theory.

It may not be obvious that the *right-zero* and *right-successor* axioms actually define the addition function we are familiar with in everyday life. We cannot state or prove this within the theory, but we can try to convince ourselves that it is so by showing that the function defined by the axioms satisfies the properties we expect the addition function to have.

In our augmented theory we can establish the validity of the following properties of addition:

$$(\forall \ integer \ x, \ y)\big[integer(x + y)\big] \qquad\qquad (sort)$$

$$(\forall \ integer \ x)\big[x + 1 \ = \ x^+\big] \qquad\qquad (right \ one)$$

$$(\forall \ integer \ x)\big[0 + x \ = \ x\big] \qquad\qquad (left \ zero)$$

$$(\forall \ integer \ x, \ y)\big[(x + 1) + y = (x + y) + 1\big] \qquad (left \ successor)$$

$$(\forall \ integer \ x, \ y)\big[x + y = y + x\big] \qquad\qquad (commutativity)$$

The *sort* property establishes that the result $x+y$ of adding two nonnegative integers is also a nonnegative integer.

Recall that, in the *right-one* property, 1 is merely an abbreviation for 0^+, the binary function symbol $+$ in the term $x+1$ denotes the addition function, and the unary function symbol $^+$ in the term x^+ denotes the successor function. Once we have established the *right-one* property, we can use the more conventional expression $t + 1$, rather than t^+, to denote the successor of t, for any term t that denotes a nonnegative integer. For example, in the *left-successor* property, we write $x+1$ and $(x+y)+1$, in terms of the addition function, rather than x^+ and $(x+y)^+$, in terms of the successor function.

The order in which the properties are presented is significant; some of their proofs make use of earlier properties on the list. We will give proofs for the last four of these properties, illustrating various features of mathematical proofs; the proof for the first one is routine and is left as an exercise (**Problem 8.1(a)**).

PROOF WITHOUT INDUCTION

We begin with the *right-one* property; its proof does not require the *induction principle*.

Proposition (right one)
   The sentence
$$(\forall\ integer\ x)\big[x + 1\ =\ x^+\big]$$
   is valid. ⌙

Proof.   Consider an arbitrary nonnegative integer x, that is, an element x such that
$$integer(x).$$
We would like to prove that
$$x + 1\ =\ x^+.$$
Because 1 is an abbreviation for 0^+, we actually want to show
$$x + 0^+\ =\ x^+.$$

Because $integer(x)$ and (by the *zero* generation axiom) $integer(0)$, we have (by the *right-successor* axiom for addition)
$$(\dagger) \qquad x + 0^+\ =\ (x + 0)^+.$$

Because $integer(x)$, we have (by the *right-zero* axiom for addition)
$$x + 0\ =\ x.$$
Therefore, by the *functional-substitutivity* equality axiom for the successor function,
$$(\ddagger) \qquad (x + 0)^+\ =\ x^+.$$

Finally, by ($\dagger$), ($\ddagger$), and the *transitivity* axiom for equality, we obtain
$$x + 0^+\ =\ x^+,$$
as we wanted to show. ⌙

As usual, in the above proof we have invoked basic properties of predicate logic without mentioning them. For example, when we applied the *functional-substitutivity* axiom to derive ($\ddagger$), we appealed implicitly to the *universal* part of the *quantifier-instantiation* proposition. Let us now discuss some other features of the above proof.

Remark (sort conditions).   In the above proof, before we could apply the *right-successor* axiom for addition to conclude (†), that

$$x + 0^+ = (x + 0)^+,$$

it was necessary to establish the "sort conditions" that x and 0 are both nonnegative integers, that is,

$$integer(x) \quad \text{and} \quad integer(0).$$

This is because the axiom reads (after renaming the bound variables to avoid confusion)

$$(\forall \ integer \ u, v)\left[u + v^+ = (u + v)^+\right]$$

or, abandoning the relative quantifier notation,

$$(\forall u, v) \begin{bmatrix} if \ \ integer(u) \ \ and \ \ integer(v) \\ then \ \ u + v^+ = (u + v)^+ \end{bmatrix}.$$

In other words, the axiom applies only if u and v are nonnegative integers. In particular, taking u to be x and v to be 0, we have

$$if \ \ integer(x) \ \ and \ \ integer(0)$$
$$then \ \ x + 0^+ = (x + 0)^+.$$

Then, because $integer(x)$ and $integer(0)$, we can conclude that

$$x + 0^+ = (x + 0)^+,$$

as we did in the proof.

For the same reason, before we could apply the *right-zero* axiom for addition, to conclude that

$$x + 0 = x,$$

it was necessary to establish that x is a nonnegative integer, that is,

$$integer(x).$$

In future proofs we shall not always bother to establish such sort conditions, i.e., that the terms we construct denote nonnegative integers, since these aspects of a proof tend to be repetitive and straightforward. Sort conditions may be assumed without proof in all the exercises, unless otherwise requested. ⌟

Remark (equality).   We shall assume henceforth that the reader is so familiar with the theory of equality that we do not need to mention its properties explicitly during a proof.

Thus we may abbreviate the above argument, showing that $x + 0^+ = x^+$, as follows:

for an arbitrary nonnegative integer x,

$$x + 0^+ = (x + 0)^+$$
$$\text{(by the } \textit{right-successor} \text{ axiom for addition)}$$

$$= x^+$$
(by the *right-zero* axiom for addition).

Here we have not mentioned the *functional-substitutivity* and *transitivity* axioms for equality. ◢

We have established the *right-one* property, i.e., that

$$(\forall \ integer \ x)\big[x + 1 = x^+\big].$$

In particular, for any term t, we may conclude (by the *universal quantifier-instantiation* proposition) that

if integer(t)
then $t + 1 = t^+$.

Hence (by the substitutivity of equality) if t stands for a nonnegative integer, any sentence $\mathcal{F}\langle t^+ \rangle$ containing the term t^+ is equivalent to the corresponding sentence $\mathcal{F}\langle t+1 \rangle$ containing instead the term $t+1$. Therefore as we have remarked earlier, we may now use the conventional notation $t + 1$ freely in place of our original notation t^+, to denote the successor of t.

Remark (computation of addition).   The axioms for the addition function can be used to prove properties of the function, such as the above *right-one* property. Furthermore, the axioms actually suggest a way to compute the function, in terms of the constant 0 and the successor function x^+. In other words, the axioms can be regarded as a "program" for performing addition. This is illustrated by the following example.

Suppose we would like to compute $3+2$, that is, $((0^+)^+)^+ + (0^+)^+$. In other words, we would like to find a term equal to $((0^+)^+)^+ + (0^+)^+$ expressed solely in terms of the constant 0 and the successor function x^+, not the addition function $x + y$. We have

$$((0^+)^+)^+ + (0^+)^+ \ = \ (((0^+)^+)^+ + 0^+)^+$$
(by the *right-successor* axiom for addition)

$$= \ ((((0^+)^+)^+ + 0)^+)^+$$
(by the *right-successor* axiom for addition)

$$= \ ((((0^+)^+)^+)^+)^+$$
(by the *right-zero* axiom for addition).

In short,

$$((0^+)^+)^+ + (0^+)^+ \ = \ ((((0^+)^+)^+)^+)^+,$$

that is,

$$3 + 2 = 5.$$

In the computation we have applied properties of equality without mentioning them explicitly. We have also disregarded the *sort* conditions, e.g., that *integer*(0) and *integer*(0^+) are true. ◢

A SIMPLE INDUCTION PROOF

The proof of the *right-one* property did not require induction. The proof of the *decomposition* property did use induction, but the inductive step did not use the induction hypothesis. Now let us consider a proof that makes use of the *induction* principle in a more conventional way.

Proposition (left zero)

The sentence

$$(\forall \ integer \ x)\big[0 + x \ = \ x\big]$$

is valid. ⌐

Proof.   The proof employs the instance of the *induction* principle in which the inductive sentence is taken to be

$$\mathcal{F}[x]: \quad 0 + x \ = \ x.$$

To prove

$$(\forall \ integer \ x)\mathcal{F}[x],$$

it suffices, by the *induction* principle, to establish the base case,

$$\mathcal{F}[0],$$

and the inductive step,

$$(\forall \ integer \ x) \begin{bmatrix} if & \mathcal{F}[x] \\ then & \mathcal{F}[x+1] \end{bmatrix}.$$

(Note that here we use the more familiar notation $x + 1$ rather than x^+.)

We establish the base case and the inductive step separately.

Base Case

We want to prove

$$\mathcal{F}[0]: \quad 0 + 0 \ = \ 0.$$

But this is an instance of the *right-zero* axiom for addition,

$$(\forall \ integer \ x)[x + 0 \ = \ x].$$

Inductive Step

We want to prove

$$(\forall \ integer \ x) \begin{bmatrix} if & \mathcal{F}[x] \\ then & \mathcal{F}[x+1] \end{bmatrix}.$$

For an arbitrary nonnegative integer x, we assume the induction hypothesis

$$\mathcal{F}[x]: \quad 0 + x \ = \ x$$

and attempt to establish the desired conclusion

$$\mathcal{F}[x+1]: \quad 0 + (x+1) = x+1.$$

But we have

$$0 + (x+1) = (0+x)+1$$
$$\text{(by the } \textit{right-successor} \text{ axiom for addition)}$$

$$= x+1$$
$$\text{(by our induction hypothesis).} \quad \lrcorner$$

CHOICE OF VARIABLES

The principle of mathematical induction states that

for all sentences $\mathcal{F}[x]$ in the theory of the nonnegative integers, the universal closure of

$$if \quad \begin{bmatrix} \mathcal{F}[0] \\ \quad and \\ (\forall \ integer \ x) \begin{bmatrix} if \ \ \mathcal{F}[x] \\ then \ \ \mathcal{F}[x+1] \end{bmatrix} \end{bmatrix}$$

$$then \ (\forall \ integer \ x)\mathcal{F}[x]$$

is an axiom.

Note that x can be taken to be any variable; thus we can apply the principle to prove sentences $(\forall \ integer \ x)\mathcal{F}[x]$ by "induction on x," $(\forall \ integer \ y)\mathcal{F}[y]$ by "induction on y," or $(\forall \ integer \ z)\mathcal{F}[z]$ by "induction on z," and so forth.

The following proposition illustrates a proof by induction on y.

Proposition (left successor)

The sentence

$$(\forall \ integer \ x, \ y)\big[(x+1) + y = (x+y) + 1\big]$$

is valid. $\quad \lrcorner$

Proof.   Consider an arbitrary nonnegative integer x; we attempt to prove

$$(\forall \ integer \ y)\big[(x+1) + y = (x+y) + 1\big].$$

The proof is by induction on y; we take the inductive sentence to be

$$\mathcal{F}[y]: \quad (x+1) + y = (x+y) + 1.$$

To prove

$$(\forall \ integer \ y)\mathcal{F}[y],$$

it suffices, by the *induction* principle, to establish the base case,

$$\mathcal{F}[0],$$

and the inductive step,

$$(\forall \ integer \ y) \begin{bmatrix} if \ \mathcal{F}[y] \\ then \ \mathcal{F}[y+1] \end{bmatrix}.$$

We establish the base case and the inductive step separately.

Base Case

We would like to prove

$$\mathcal{F}[0]: \quad (x+1)+0 \ = \ (x+0)+1.$$

But we have

$$(x+1)+0 \ = \ x+1$$
$$\text{(by the } right\text{-}zero \text{ axiom for addition)}$$

$$= \ (x+0)+1$$
$$\text{(by the } right\text{-}zero \text{ axiom for addition again).}$$

Inductive Step

For an arbitrary nonnegative integer y, we assume the induction hypothesis

$$\mathcal{F}[y]: \quad (x+1)+y \ = \ (x+y)+1$$

and attempt to prove the desired conclusion

$$\mathcal{F}[y+1]: \quad (x+1)+(y+1) \ = \ \big(x+(y+1)\big)+1.$$

But we have

$$(x+1)+(y+1) \ = \ \big((x+1)+y\big)+1$$
$$\text{(by the } right\text{-}successor \text{ axiom for addition)}$$

$$= \ \big((x+y)+1\big)+1$$
$$\text{(by our induction hypothesis)}$$

$$= \ \big(x+(y+1)\big)+1$$
$$\text{(by the } right\text{-}successor \text{ axiom for}$$
$$\text{addition again).} \quad \lrcorner$$

Note that in the above proof the inductive sentence $\mathcal{F}[y]$, that is,

$$(x+1)+y \ = \ (x+y)+1,$$

contained free occurrences of x as well as y.

Remark (choice of variables). The proof illustrates some of the strategic aspects of the use of the *induction* principle. It might seem more straightforward to attempt the proof by induction on x, taking the inductive sentence to be

$$\mathcal{F}[x]: \quad (\forall \ integer \ y)\big[(x+1)+y \ = \ (x+y)+1\big].$$

In such a proof, we would first attempt to establish the base case

$$\mathcal{F}[0]: \quad (\forall\ integer\ y)\big[(0+1)+y\ =\ (0+y)+1\big].$$

Considering an arbitrary nonnegative integer y, we would try to prove

$$(0+1)+y\ =\ (0+y)+1$$

or, equivalently (by two applications of the *left-zero* property of addition),

$$1+y\ =\ y+1.$$

For this purpose, we would have to prove that

$$(\forall\ integer\ y)[1+y\ =\ y+1],$$

requiring an additional application of the *induction* principle, on y. An attempt to establish the inductive step of such a proof would lead to similar obstructions.

In other words, a decision to use induction on x, rather than on y, in proving the *left-successor* property of addition would lead to a needlessly complicated proof. In general, part of the strategic aspect of using the *induction* principle is deciding on which variable to do induction. This decision depends on the axioms and properties we have available. Sometimes an unsuccessful proof attempt will suggest a variable on which to do induction. ⌐

USE OF EARLIER RESULTS

Once we have established the validity of a sentence in the theory of the nonnegative integers, we can use it in the proofs of other sentences, just as we would use an axiom. The proof of the following *commutativity* property relies on the validity of the *left-zero* property,

$$(\forall\ integer\ x)\big[0+x\ =\ x\big],$$

and the *left-successor* property,

$$(\forall\ integer\ x,\ y)\big[(x+1)+y\ =\ (x+y)+1\big],$$

which we established in the preceding sections.

Proposition (commutativity)

The sentence

$$(\forall\ integer\ x,\ y)\big[x+y\ =\ y+x\big]$$

is valid. ⌐

Proof.   Consider an arbitrary nonnegative integer x; we would like to prove

$$(\forall\ integer\ y)\big[x+y\ =\ y+x\big].$$

The proof is by induction on y; we take the inductive sentence to be

$$\mathcal{F}[y]: \quad x + y = y + x.$$

To prove

$$(\forall \text{ integer } y)\mathcal{F}[y],$$

it suffices, by the *induction* principle, to establish the base case,

$$\mathcal{F}[0],$$

and the inductive step,

$$(\forall \text{ integer } y) \begin{bmatrix} if \ \mathcal{F}[y] \\ then \ \mathcal{F}[y+1] \end{bmatrix}.$$

Base Case

We would like to prove

$$\mathcal{F}[0]: \quad x + 0 = 0 + x.$$

But we have

$$x + 0 = x$$

$$(\text{by the } right\text{-}zero \text{ axiom for addition})$$

$$= 0 + x$$

$$(\text{by the } left\text{-}zero \text{ property of addition}).$$

Inductive Step

For an arbitrary nonnegative integer y, we assume the induction hypothesis

$$\mathcal{F}[y]: \quad x + y = y + x$$

and attempt to establish the desired conclusion

$$\mathcal{F}[y+1]: \quad x + (y+1) = (y+1) + x.$$

But we have

$$x + (y+1) = (x+y) + 1$$

$$(\text{by the } right\text{-}successor \text{ axiom for addition})$$

$$= (y+x) + 1$$

$$(\text{by our induction hypothesis})$$

$$= (y+1) + x$$

$$(\text{by the } left\text{-}successor \text{ property of addition}). \quad \lrcorner$$

The proof of the *commutativity* proposition for addition above made use of the *left-zero* and the *left-successor* properties of addition, whose validity we established earlier. Had we attempted to prove the *commutativity* proposition without having proved the other two properties first, we would have had to include the proof of the two required properties within the proof of the proposition, making the combined proof rather unwieldy.

We can also establish the validity of the following properties of the addition function:

$$(\forall \ integer \ x, y, z)\big[(x + y) + z = x + (y + z)\big] \qquad (associativity)$$

$$(\forall \ integer \ x, y, z) \begin{bmatrix} if \ \ z + x = z + y \\ then \ \ x = y \end{bmatrix} \qquad (left \ cancellation)$$

$$(\forall \ integer \ x, y, z) \begin{bmatrix} if \ \ x + z = y + z \\ then \ \ x = y \end{bmatrix} \qquad (right \ cancellation)$$

$$(\forall \ integer \ x, y) \begin{bmatrix} if \ \ x + y = 0 \\ then \ \ x = 0 \ \ and \ \ y = 0 \end{bmatrix} \qquad (annihilation)$$

The proofs are left as an exercise (**Problem 8.1(b)-(e)**).

Note that once we have established the *associativity* property of addition we can freely use the conventional notation $r + s + t$, rather than $(r + s) + t$ or $r + (s + t)$, because both terms have the same value under every model.

8.3   MULTIPLICATION AND EXPONENTIATION

In this section we extend the theory by defining two new functions. We shall also illustrate some of the strategic aspects of using the *induction* principle.

MULTIPLICATION

Let us further augment our theory of the nonnegative integers by introducing axioms that define a binary function symbol $x \cdot y$, denoting, under the intended model, the *multiplication* (*times*) function over the nonnegative integers.

The axioms for multiplication are as follows:

$$(\forall \ integer \ x)\big[x \cdot 0 \ = \ 0\big] \qquad\qquad (right \ zero)$$

$$(\forall \ integer \ x, y)\big[x \cdot (y + 1) \ = \ x \cdot y + x\big] \qquad (right \ successor)$$

We write $x \cdot y + x$ as an abbreviation of $(x \cdot y) + x$.

As before, we introduce the corresponding instances of the *functional-substitutivity* equality axiom schema for multiplication automatically:

$$(\forall x,\, y,\, z) \begin{bmatrix} if & x = y \\ then & x \cdot z = y \cdot z \end{bmatrix} \qquad (left\ functional\ substitutivity)$$

$$(\forall x,\, y,\, z) \begin{bmatrix} if & x = y \\ then & z \cdot x = z \cdot y \end{bmatrix} \qquad (right\ functional\ substitutivity)$$

We also introduce automatically those instances of the *induction* principle for which the inductive sentence contains occurrences of the new function symbol $x \cdot y$. Henceforth we shall not mention these additional axioms.

Note also that we retain the axioms that define the addition function.

In our augmented theory we can establish the validity of the following properties of multiplication:

$$(\forall\ integer\ x,\, y)\big[integer(x \cdot y)\big] \qquad (sort)$$

$$(\forall\ integer\ x)\big[x \cdot 1 \ = \ x\big] \qquad (right\ one)$$

$$(\forall\ integer\ x)\big[0 \cdot x \ = \ 0\big] \qquad (left\ zero)$$

$$(\forall\ integer\ x,\, y)\big[(x + 1) \cdot y \ = \ x \cdot y + y\big] \qquad (left\ successor)$$

$$(\forall\ integer\ x)\big[1 \cdot x \ = \ x\big] \qquad (left\ one)$$

From these properties we can establish the associativity, commutativity, and distributivity of multiplication:

$$(\forall\ integer\ x,\, y,\, z)\big[x \cdot (y + z) \ = \ x \cdot y + x \cdot z\big] \quad (right\ distributivity)$$

$$(\forall\ integer\ x,\, y,\, z)\big[(x \cdot y) \cdot z \ = \ x \cdot (y \cdot z)\big] \qquad (associativity)$$

$$(\forall\ integer\ x,\, y)\big[x \cdot y \ = \ y \cdot x\big] \qquad (commutativity)$$

$$(\forall\ integer\ x,\, y,\, z)\big[(x + y) \cdot z \ = \ x \cdot z + y \cdot z\big] \quad (left\ distributivity)$$

The proofs of all these properties are left as an exercise (**Problem 8.2**). As usual, the order in which the properties are presented is significant; some of their proofs make use of earlier properties on the list.

EXPONENTIATION

Let us augment our theory of the nonnegative integers further by introducing two axioms that define a binary function symbol x^y, denoting, under the intended model, the *exponentiation* function over the nonnegative integers.

The axioms for exponentiation are as follows:

$$(\forall \ integer \ x)\left[x^0 \ = \ 1\right] \qquad\qquad (exp \ zero)$$

$$(\forall \ integer \ x, \ y)\left[x^{y+1} \ = \ x^y \cdot x\right] \qquad (successor)$$

(Note that, under these axioms, 0^0 is taken to be 1, not 0.)

From these axioms we can establish the validity of the following properties of exponentiation:

$$(\forall \ integer \ x, \ y)\left[integer(x^y)\right] \qquad\qquad (sort)$$

$$(\forall \ integer \ x)\left[x^1 \ = \ x\right] \qquad\qquad (exp \ one)$$

$$(\forall \ integer \ y)\left[\begin{matrix} if \ \ not \ (y = 0) \\ then \ \ 0^y = 0 \end{matrix}\right] \qquad\qquad (zero \ exp)$$

$$(\forall \ integer \ y)\left[1^y \ = \ 1\right] \qquad\qquad (one \ exp)$$

$$(\forall \ integer \ x, \ y, \ z)\left[x^{y+z} \ = \ (x^y) \cdot (x^z)\right] \qquad\qquad (exp \ plus)$$

$$(\forall \ integer \ x, \ y, \ z)\left[x^{y \cdot z} \ = \ (x^y)^z\right] \qquad\qquad (exp \ times)$$

The proofs of these properties are left as an exercise (**Problem 8.3**).

THE NEED FOR GENERALIZATION

In proving a property by mathematical induction, it is frequently necessary to prove a stronger, more general property instead. This phenomenon is illustrated in the proof of the following proposition.

Proposition (alternative exponentiation)

Suppose we define a new ternary function, denoted by *exp3*, by the following two axioms:

$$(\forall \; integer \; x, \; z)\big[exp3(x, \; 0, \; z) \; = \; z\big] \qquad\qquad (zero)$$

$$(\forall \; integer \; x, \; y, \; z)\big[exp3(x, \; y+1, \; z) \; = \; exp3(x, \; y, \; x \cdot z)\big] \; (successor)$$

Then the sentence

$$(\forall \; integer \; x, \; y)\big[exp3(x, \; y, \; 1) \; = \; x^y\big] \qquad\qquad (special \; exp3)$$

is valid. ◢

Before we prove the proposition, let us explain the *exp3* function. For any nonnegative integers x, y, and z, the function is defined in such a way that

$$exp3(x, \; y, \; z) \; = \; x^y \cdot z.$$

Following the axioms, to compute $exp3(x, \; y, \; z)$ we multiply z by x precisely y times.

Example (computation of exp3). We have

$$exp3(3, \; 2, \; 4) \; = \; exp3\big(3, \; (0+1)+1, \; 4\big)$$
$$\text{(because 2 is an abbreviation for } (0+1)+1)$$

$$= \; exp3(3, \; 0+1, \; 3 \cdot 4)$$
$$\text{(by the } successor \text{ axiom for } exp3)$$

$$= \; exp3(3, \; 0, \; 3 \cdot 3 \cdot 4)$$
$$\text{(by the } successor \text{ axiom for } exp3 \text{ again)}$$

$$= \; 3 \cdot 3 \cdot 4$$
$$\text{(by the } zero \text{ axiom for } exp3).$$

In other words

$$exp3(3, \; 2, \; 4) \; = \; 3 \cdot 3 \cdot 4 \; = \; 3^2 \cdot 4.$$ ◢

The proposition suggests that we can use the axioms for $exp3(x, \; y, \; z)$ as an alternative method for computing x^y, simply by taking z to be 1 and computing $exp3(x, \; y, \; 1)$.

Let us prove the proposition.

Proof (alternative exponentiation). Rather than proving the original *special exp3* property,

$$(\forall \; integer \; x, \; y)\big[exp3(x, \; y, \; 1) \; = \; x^y\big],$$

we prove instead the stronger, more general property

$$(\forall \; integer \; x, \; y, \; z)\big[exp3(x, \; y, \; z) \; = \; x^y \cdot z\big] \qquad\qquad (general \; exp3)$$

which fully characterizes the *exp3* function.

Once we have proved the *general exp3* property, we can infer the desired *special exp3* property easily. For consider arbitrary nonnegative integers x and y; we have

$$exp3(x,\ y,\ 1)\ =\ x^y \cdot 1$$

(by the more general sentence)

$$=\ x^y$$

(by the *right-one* property of multiplication).

To prove the *general exp3* property, consider an arbitrary nonnegative integer x; we would like to show

$$(\forall\ integer\ y, z)\big[exp3(x,\ y,\ z)\ =\ x^y \cdot z\big].$$

The proof is by induction on y, taking the inductive sentence to be

$$\mathcal{F}[y]:\quad (\forall\ integer\ z)\big[exp3(x,\ y,\ z)\ =\ x^y \cdot z\big].$$

Base Case

We would like to prove

$$\mathcal{F}[0]:\quad (\forall\ integer\ z)\big[exp3(x,\ 0,\ z)\ =\ x^0 \cdot z\big].$$

For an arbitrary nonnegative integer z, we have

$$exp3(x,\ 0,\ z)\ =\ z$$

(by the *zero* axiom for *exp3*).

But on the other hand, we have

$$x^0 \cdot z\ =\ 1 \cdot z$$

(by the *exp-zero* axiom for exponentiation)

$$=\ z$$

(by the *left-one* property of multiplication).

Inductive Step

For an arbitrary nonnegative integer y, we assume the induction hypothesis

$$\mathcal{F}[y]:\quad (\forall\ integer\ z)\big[exp3(x,\ y,\ z)\ =\ x^y \cdot z\big]$$

and attempt to show the desired conclusion

$$\mathcal{F}[y+1]:\quad (\forall\ integer\ z')\big[exp3(x,\ y+1,\ z')\ =\ (x^{y+1}) \cdot z'\big].$$

(Here we have renamed the bound variable z of the desired conclusion to z', to avoid confusion with the variable z in the induction hypothesis.)

For an arbitrary nonnegative integer z', we have

$$exp3(x,\ y+1,\ z')\ =\ exp3(x,\ y,\ x \cdot z')$$

(by the *successor* axiom for *exp3*).

But on the other hand, we have

$$(x^{y+1}) \cdot z'\ =\ (x^y \cdot x) \cdot z'$$

(by the *successor* axiom for exponentiation)

$$= x^y \cdot (x \cdot z')$$
$$\text{(by the } associativity \text{ property of multiplication)}$$
$$= exp3(x, \, y, \, x \cdot z')$$
$$\text{(by the induction hypothesis, taking } z \text{ to be } x \cdot z').$$

In short, we have established that

$$exp3(x, \, y+1, \, z') \;=\; (x^{y+1}) \cdot z',$$

as we wanted to show. ◢

The proof of the above proposition illustrates some of the strategic aspects of discovering a proof by induction.

Remark (generalization). We proved the original *special exp3* property

$$(\forall \; integer \; x, \, y)\big[exp3(x, \, y, \, 1) \;=\; x^y\big]$$

by establishing the *general exp3* property

$$(\forall \; integer \; x, \, y, \, z)\big[exp3(x, \, y, \, z) \;=\; x^y \cdot z\big].$$

Had we attempted to prove the *special exp3* property without first generalizing, the above proof would not have worked. It would be difficult to establish the original property directly, because in establishing the inductive step in the proof, we would assume the induction hypothesis,

$$\mathcal{F}'[y]: \quad exp3(x, \, y, \, 1) \;=\; x^y,$$

and attempt to prove the desired conclusion,

$$\mathcal{F}'[y+1]: \quad exp3(x, \, y+1, \, 1) \;=\; x^{y+1}.$$

It suffices to show (by the *successor* axioms for *exp3* and exponentiation) that

$$exp3(x, \, y, \, x \cdot 1) \;=\; x^y \cdot x.$$

The desired conclusion is concerned with $exp3(x, \, y, \, x \cdot 1)$, that is, $exp3(x, \, y, \, x)$, while the induction hypothesis gives us information only about $exp3(x, \, y, \, 1)$.

Thus in attempting to prove the original weaker property, we have a correspondingly weaker induction hypothesis, one that is no longer strong enough to prove the desired conclusion. By proving the more general property, we have the advantage of the correspondingly more general induction hypothesis. For the *alternative-exponentiation* proposition, it is paradoxically easier to prove the more general, stronger property than it is to prove the weaker special case.

In proving a property by induction, it often requires ingenuity to discover a generalization that enables the proof to go through. Sometimes an unsuccessful attempt to prove the original property will suggest an appropriate generalization. ◢

Generalization is also required to solve **Problem 8.4**, which is concerned with the *factorial* function $x!$.

Remark (treatment of quantifiers).   In proving the property

$$(\forall\ integer\ x,\ y,\ z)\big[exp3(x,\ y,\ z)\ =\ x^y \cdot z\big],$$

we treated each of the quantifiers differently:

- To dispose of the quantifier $(\forall\ integer\ x)$, we considered an arbitrary nonnegative integer at the beginning of the proof.
- To dispose of $(\forall\ integer\ y)$, we performed induction on y.
- To dispose of $(\forall\ integer\ z)$, we allowed the quantifier to remain in the inductive sentence $\mathcal{F}[y]$ and considered arbitrary nonnegative integers z both in the base case and in the inductive step.

The success of a proof may depend on how we treat quantifiers. To see this, the reader may attempt to prove the property differently, e.g., by induction on x, taking the inductive sentence to be

$$(\forall\ integer\ y,\ z)\big[exp3(x,\ y,\ z) = x^y \cdot z\big].$$

The proof will be considerably more complex.

Had we originally been given the quantifiers in a different order, say,

$$(\forall\ integer\ z,\ x,\ y)\big[exp3(x,\ y,\ z)\ =\ x^y \cdot z\big],$$

we would have needed to reorder them. If we had chosen arbitrary nonnegative integers x and z before performing induction on y, the inductive sentence would have had no quantifiers and both the induction hypothesis and the desired conclusion would contain the same variable z. The step in the above proof in which we took z to be $x \cdot z'$, where z and z' are the bound variables of the induction hypothesis and the desired conclusion, respectively, would have been impossible.

The decision about how to treat each quantifier depends on the form of the axioms and properties we have for our function and predicate symbols.   ⌐

8.4   PREDECESSOR AND SUBTRACTION

Before we define the predecessor and subtraction functions, let us introduce a useful unary predicate symbol.

POSITIVE

We augment our theory by defining a unary predicate symbol $positive(x)$, denoting, under the intended model, the relation that is true for positive integers and false for zero. It is defined by the axiom

$$(\forall x) \begin{bmatrix} positive(x) \\ \equiv \\ integer(x) \ \ and \ \ not \ (x = 0) \end{bmatrix} \qquad\qquad (positive)$$

Using this predicate symbol in relativized quantifiers enables us to abbreviate many properties. For example, we can express the *decomposition* property for the nonnegative integers, that is,

$$(\forall \ integer \ x) \begin{bmatrix} if \ \ not \ (x = 0) \\ then \ \ (\exists \ integer \ y)[x = y + 1] \end{bmatrix},$$

as

$$(\forall \ positive \ x)(\exists \ integer \ y)\big[x = y + 1\big].$$

From the *zero* uniqueness axiom, it follows that

$$(\forall \ integer \ x)\big[positive(x + 1)\big] \qquad\qquad (sort)$$

PREDECESSOR

Suppose we augment our theory by introducing axioms to define a unary function symbol x^-, denoting, under the intended model, the *predecessor* function over the nonnegative integers, i.e., the function that maps the positive integer d into the integer $d - 1$. The axiom for the predecessor function is

$$(\forall \ integer \ x)\big[(x + 1)^- = x\big] \qquad\qquad (predecessor)$$

Remark (the value of 0^-).   Note that the above axiom does not specify the value of the term 0^-. Although this term is legal in the language, the axioms do not force it to have any particular value.

For example, we might have many different models for the augmented theory over the nonnegative integers, each assigning a different value to the term 0^-. This vagueness is intentional; we do not care what the value of 0^- is under a model for the augmented theory.   ◢

In the augmented theory, we can prove the following properties of the predecessor function:

$$(\forall \ positive \ x)\big[integer(x^-)\big] \qquad\qquad (sort)$$

$$(\forall \ positive \ x)\big[x \ = \ x^- + 1\big] \qquad\qquad (decomposition)$$

The proof of the *sort* property is omitted; the proof of the *decomposition* property is left as an exercise (**Problem 8.5(a)**). Our earlier *decomposition* property

$$(\forall \ positive \ x)(\exists \ integer \ y)\big[x = y + 1\big]$$

follows immediately from this one by the *existential quantifier-instantiation* proposition.

SUBTRACTION

Suppose we augment our theory further by formulating axioms that define a binary function symbol $x - y$, denoting the *subtraction* (*minus*) function under the intended model for the nonnegative integers.

The axioms for the subtraction function are as follows:

$$(\forall\ integer\ x)\big[x - 0\ =\ x\big] \qquad\qquad\qquad (right\ zero)$$

$$(\forall\ integer\ x,\ y)\big[(x + 1) - (y + 1)\ =\ x - y\big] \qquad (successor)$$

Example (computation of minus).   To illustrate the axioms, we show the computation of the value of $3 - 2$. We have

$$3 - 2\ =\ \big(((0 + 1) + 1) + 1\big)\ -\ \big((0 + 1) + 1\big)$$

$$=\ \big((0 + 1) + 1\big)\ -\ (0 + 1)$$
$$\text{(by the } successor \text{ axiom)}$$

$$=\ (0 + 1) - 0$$
$$\text{(by the } successor \text{ axiom again)}$$

$$=\ 0 + 1$$
$$\text{(by the } right\text{-}zero \text{ axiom)}$$

$$=\ 1.$$

In short,

$$3 - 2\ =\ 1. \quad \lrcorner$$

Remark (unspecified values).   Note that these axioms do not specify the value of terms of the form $s - t$, where the value of s is less than the value of t. Although such terms are legal in the language, the axioms do not force them to have any particular value.

For example, we might have many different models for the extended theory, each assigning a different domain element to the term $2 - 3$, that is,

$$\big((0 + 1) + 1\big) - \big(((0 + 1) + 1) + 1\big).$$

However, according to the *successor* axiom, the value assigned to the term

$$\big((0 + 1) + 1\big) - \big(((0 + 1) + 1) + 1\big)$$

must be the same as the value assigned to

$$(0 + 1) - \big((0 + 1) + 1\big),$$

whatever that is. $\lrcorner$

In the augmented theory, we can prove the following properties of subtraction:

$$(\forall \; positive \; x)[x - 1 \; = \; x^-] \qquad\qquad (right \; one)$$

$$(\forall \; integer \; x, y)\big[(x + y) - y \; = \; x\big] \qquad\qquad (addition)$$

The proofs of these properties, and an additional one, are left as an exercise (**Problem 8.5(b)-(d)**).

Note that in the *right-one* property the function symbol $-$ in $x - 1$ denotes the binary subtraction function, while the function symbol $^-$ in the term x^- denotes the unary predecessor function. Once we have established this property, we may use the more conventional notation $t - 1$, in place of t^-, to denote the predecessor of t, if we know that t is positive.

Problem 8.6 introduces a new axiom for the subtraction function.

DECOMPOSITION INDUCTION

Using the definition of the predecessor function, we can prove an alternative version of the *induction* principle.

Proposition (decomposition induction)

For each sentence $\mathcal{F}[x]$, the universal closure of the sentence

$$if \; \begin{bmatrix} \mathcal{F}[0] \\ and \\ (\forall \; positive \; x) \begin{bmatrix} if \; \; \mathcal{F}[x - 1] \\ then \; \; \mathcal{F}[x] \end{bmatrix} \end{bmatrix}$$

$$then \; (\forall \; integer \; x)\mathcal{F}[x] \qquad\qquad (decomposition \; induction)$$

is valid. ∎

The decomposition version of the *induction* principle may be paraphrased informally as follows:

> To show that a sentence $\mathcal{F}[x]$ is true for every nonnegative integer x (under a given interpretation), it suffices to show the base case
>
> $\mathcal{F}[0]$ is true
>
> and the inductive step
>
> for an arbitrary positive integer x,
> if $\mathcal{F}[x - 1]$ is true
> then $\mathcal{F}[x]$ is also true.

The only difference between the decomposition version of the *induction* principle and the original version is that in the decomposition version we infer $\mathcal{F}[x]$

from $\mathcal{F}[x-1]$, where x is positive, while in the original version we infer $\mathcal{F}[x+1]$ from $\mathcal{F}[x]$, where x is nonnegative.

The proof of the *decomposition-induction* proposition is requested in **Problem 8.15**. (This problem, like Problem 8.13 and 8.14, is placed at the end because of its theoretical nature.)

Because the *decomposition induction* principle is valid in the theory of the nonnegative integers, we can use either the original or the decomposition version of the *induction* principle in establishing the validity of a sentence in the theory. Which version is more convenient to use in a proof depends on how we choose to formulate our axioms and properties. If these tend to refer to the successor $x+1$, the original version will be more convenient; if they refer to the predecessor $x-1$, the decomposition version will be more convenient. In this book we typically use the successor function; therefore the original version is usually easier to use.

8.5   THE LESS-THAN RELATION

In this section, we introduce two versions of the less-than relation, which turn out to be weak and strict partial relations, respectively.

THE WEAK LESS-THAN RELATION

Suppose we augment our theory further by formulating two axioms that define a binary predicate symbol $x \leq y$, denoting the *weak less-than relation* under the intended model for the nonnegative integers.

The axioms for the weak less-than relation are as follows:

$$
(\forall \ integer \ x)
\begin{bmatrix}
x \leq 0 \\
\equiv \\
x = 0
\end{bmatrix}
\qquad\qquad (right \ zero)
$$

$$
(\forall \ integer \ x, y)
\begin{bmatrix}
x \leq y + 1 \\
\equiv \\
x = y + 1 \ \ or \ \ x \leq y
\end{bmatrix}
\qquad (right \ successor)
$$

Example (computation of $\leq$).   Let us use the axioms to compute the truth-value of $0 \leq 1$, that is, $0 \leq 0 + 1$. We have

$$0 \leq 0 + 1$$

if and only if (by the *right-successor* axiom)

$$0 = 0 + 1 \quad or \quad 0 \leq 0$$

if and only if (because, by the *zero* uniqueness axiom, *not* $(0 = 0 + 1)$)

$$0 \leq 0$$

if and only if (by the *right-zero* axiom)

$$0 = 0,$$

which is true. ⌐

In **Problem 8.7**, we request the reader to prove the following basic property of the weak less-than relation:

$$(\forall \; integer \; x, \; y) \begin{bmatrix} x \leq y \\ \equiv \\ (\exists \; integer \; z)[x + z = y] \end{bmatrix} \qquad (left \; addition)$$

The weak less-than relation we have defined can be shown to be a weak partial ordering; in other words, we can establish the validity in the theory of the nonnegative integers of the three weak partial-ordering axioms for $\leq$:

$$(\forall \; integer \; x, \; y, \; z) \begin{bmatrix} if \;\; x \leq y \;\; and \;\; y \leq z \\ then \;\; x \leq z \end{bmatrix} \qquad (transitivity)$$

$$(\forall \; integer \; x, \; y) \begin{bmatrix} if \;\; x \leq y \;\; and \;\; y \leq x \\ then \;\; x = y \end{bmatrix} \qquad (antisymmetry)$$

$$(\forall \; integer \; x)[x \leq x] \qquad (reflexivity)$$

We can also establish the following properties of the weak less-than relation:

$$(\forall \; integer \; x)\big[0 \leq x\big] \qquad (left \; zero)$$

$$(\forall \; integer \; x, \; y)\big[x \leq x + y\big] \qquad (right \; addition)$$

$$(\forall \; integer \; x, \; y)\big[x \leq y \;\; or \;\; y \leq x\big] \qquad (totality)$$

The predicate symbol $\geq$ denotes the *weak greater-than relation*, which is the inverse of the weak less-than relation $\leq$. It is defined by the following axiom:

$$\boxed{(\forall \; integer \; x, \; y) \, [x \geq y \equiv y \leq x] \qquad (weak \; greater\text{-}than)}$$

EXPRESSING PROPERTIES OF FUNCTIONS

We can now express the properties of several other functions in terms of the weak less-than relation. For the subtraction function, we can establish the following properties:

$$(\forall \ integer \ x, y) \begin{bmatrix} if & x \le y \\ then & integer(y - x) \end{bmatrix} \qquad (sort)$$

$$(\forall \ integer \ x, y) \begin{bmatrix} if & x \le y \\ then & x + (y - x) = y \end{bmatrix} \qquad (decomposition)$$

$$(\forall \ integer \ x, y, z) \begin{bmatrix} if & x \le y \\ then & \begin{bmatrix} x + z = y \\ \equiv \\ z = y - x \end{bmatrix} \end{bmatrix} \qquad (cancellation)$$

We can augment our theory further by introducing two binary function symbols $max(x, y)$ and $min(x, y)$, denoting the *maximum* and *minimum*, respectively, of the nonnegative integers x and y. The axioms that define these functions are as follows:

$$(\forall \ integer \ x, y) \begin{bmatrix} max(x, y) = \begin{cases} if & x \le y \\ then & y \\ else & x \end{cases} \end{bmatrix} \qquad (maximum)$$

$$(\forall \ integer \ x, y) \begin{bmatrix} min(x, y) = \begin{cases} if & x \le y \\ then & x \\ else & y \end{cases} \end{bmatrix} \qquad (minimum)$$

From these axioms we can establish the following properties of the maximum and minimum functions:

$$(\forall \ integer \ x, y) \begin{bmatrix} max(x, y) \ge x \\ and \\ max(x, y) \ge y \end{bmatrix} \qquad (greater\text{-}than)$$

$$(\forall \ integer \ x, y) \begin{bmatrix} min(x, y) \le x \\ and \\ min(x, y) \le y \end{bmatrix} \qquad (less\text{-}than)$$

$$(\forall \ integer \ x, y, z) \begin{bmatrix} min\big(x, \ max(y, z)\big) \\ = \\ max\big(min(x, y), \ min(x, z)\big) \end{bmatrix} \qquad (minimax)$$

$$(\forall \ integer \ x, y, z) \begin{bmatrix} max\big(x, \ min(y, z)\big) \\ = \\ min\big(max(x, y), \ max(x, z)\big) \end{bmatrix} \qquad (maximin)$$

The reader is requested to establish the *greater-than* and *minimax* properties in **Problem 8.8**.

THE STRICT LESS-THAN RELATION

We have already remarked that the weak less-than relation $\leq$ is a weak partial ordering. Let us augment the theory further to define a new binary predicate symbol $<$, denoting the (*strict*) *less-than relation,* by the following axiom:

$$(\forall\ integer\ x,\ y)\ \begin{bmatrix} x < y \\ \equiv \\ x \leq y\ \ and\ \ not\ (x = y) \end{bmatrix} \qquad (less\text{-}than)$$

In other words, $<$ denotes the irreflexive restriction of the weak less-than relation $\leq$. Thus we know (by the *irreflexive-restriction* proposition of the theory of the weak partial ordering $\leq$) that $<$ is a strict partial ordering in the augmented theory of the nonnegative integers; i.e., the sentences

$$(\forall\ integer\ x,\ y,\ z)\ \begin{bmatrix} if\ \ x < y\ \ and\ \ y < z \\ then\ \ x < z \end{bmatrix} \qquad (transitivity)$$

$$(\forall\ integer\ x)\big[not\ (x < x)\big] \qquad (irreflexivity)$$

are valid. Therefore any property we can prove in the theory of the strict partial ordering $<$ is valid in our augmented theory of the nonnegative integers. For example, the *asymmetry* property

$$(\forall\ integer\ x,\ y)\ \begin{bmatrix} if\ \ x < y \\ then\ \ not\ (y < x) \end{bmatrix} \qquad (asymmetry)$$

is valid.

We have defined the strict less-than predicate symbol $<$ to denote the irreflexive restriction of the weak less-than relation $\leq$. We can also show that the weak less-than predicate symbol $\leq$ denotes the reflexive closure of $<$, that is,

$$(\forall\ integer\ x,\ y)\ \begin{bmatrix} x \leq y \\ \equiv \\ x < y\ \ or\ \ x = y \end{bmatrix} \qquad (reflexive\ closure)$$

The less-than relation $<$ can be shown to be total, that is,

$$(\forall\ integer\ x,\ y)\big[x < y\ \ or\ \ y < x\ \ or\ \ x = y\big] \qquad (totality)$$

It follows (because $<$ is asymmetric and $\leq$ is its reflexive closure) that

$$(\forall\ integer\ x,\ y)\ \begin{bmatrix} not\ (x < y) \\ \equiv \\ y \leq x \end{bmatrix} \qquad (total\ asymmetry)$$

The predicate symbol $>$, denoting the corresponding *(strict) greater-than relation*, is defined by the axiom

$$(\forall \; integer \; x, y) \, [x > y \; \equiv \; y < x] \qquad\qquad (greater\text{-}than)$$

We can also establish the following properties of the strict less-than relation:

$$(\forall \; integer \; x, y) \begin{bmatrix} x < y \\ \equiv \\ (\exists \; positive \; z)[x + z = y] \end{bmatrix} \qquad (left \; addition)$$

$$(\forall \; positive \; x) \, [0 < x] \qquad\qquad (left \; zero)$$

$$(\forall \; integer \; x) \, [not \; (x < 0)] \qquad\qquad (right \; zero)$$

$$(\forall \; integer \; x) \, [x < x + 1] \qquad\qquad (adjacent)$$

$$(\forall \; integer \; x)(\forall \; positive \; y) \, [x < x + y] \qquad (right \; addition)$$

$$(\forall \; integer \; x, y) \begin{bmatrix} x < y + 1 \\ \equiv \\ x \le y \end{bmatrix} \qquad\qquad (right \; successor)$$

$$(\forall \; integer \; x, y) \begin{bmatrix} x < y \\ \equiv \\ x + 1 \le y \end{bmatrix} \qquad\qquad (left \; successor)$$

In **Problem 8.16**, the reader is asked to consider a version of the theory of the nonnegative integers without the induction principle. (Again, this problem is placed at the end of the list because of its theoretical nature.)

8.6   THE COMPLETE INDUCTION PRINCIPLE

Using the less-than relation $<$, we can state and prove an alternative version of the *induction* principle, which is often much more convenient to use.

Proposition (complete induction)

For each sentence $\mathcal{F}[x]$, the universal closure of the sentence

$$if \ (\forall \ integer \ x) \begin{bmatrix} if \ (\forall \ integer \ x') \begin{bmatrix} if \ x' < x \\ then \ \mathcal{F}[x'] \end{bmatrix} \\ then \ \mathcal{F}[x] \end{bmatrix}$$
$$then \ (\forall \ integer \ x)\mathcal{F}[x]$$

(*complete induction*)

where x' does not occur free in $\mathcal{F}[x]$, is valid. ◢

As usual, the sentence $\mathcal{F}[x]$ is called the *inductive sentence* and the variable x is called the *inductive variable*. The antecedent of the principle,

$$(\forall \ integer \ x) \begin{bmatrix} if \ (\forall \ integer \ x') \begin{bmatrix} if \ x' < x \\ then \ \mathcal{F}[x'] \end{bmatrix} \\ then \ \mathcal{F}[x] \end{bmatrix},$$

is called the *inductive step*; the subsentences

$$(\forall \ integer \ x') \begin{bmatrix} if \ x' < x \\ then \ \mathcal{F}[x'] \end{bmatrix} \quad \text{and} \quad \mathcal{F}[x]$$

of the inductive step are called the *induction hypothesis* and the *desired conclusion*, respectively.

The *complete induction* principle may be paraphrased informally as follows:

To show that a sentence $\mathcal{F}[x]$ is true for every nonnegative integer x (under a given interpretation), it suffices to show the inductive step

for an arbitrary nonnegative integer x,
if $\mathcal{F}[x']$ is true for every nonnegative integer x'
such that $x' < x$,
then $\mathcal{F}[x]$ is also true.

In other words, to show that a sentence $\mathcal{F}[x]$ is true for every nonnegative integer x, it suffices to show that, for an arbitrary nonnegative integer x, if

$$\mathcal{F}[0], \quad \mathcal{F}[1], \quad \mathcal{F}[2], \quad \ldots, \quad \text{and} \quad \mathcal{F}[x-1]$$

are all true, then

$$\mathcal{F}[x]$$

is also true.

The reader may have wondered why we include in the *complete induction* principle the constraint that x' does not occur free in $\mathcal{F}[x]$. In fact, if this constraint is violated, the sentence may not be valid.

Counterexample (constraint is essential). In the theory of the nonnegative integers, take

$$\mathcal{F}[x] : \ x < x'.$$

Note that, contrary to the constraint, x' occurs free in $\mathcal{F}[x]$.

The *complete induction* principle in this case is

$$(\forall \ integer \ x') \left[if \ (\forall \ integer \ x) \left[if \ (\forall \ integer \ x') \left[\begin{matrix} if \ x' < x \\ then \ x' < x' \end{matrix} \right] \\ then \ x < x' \right] \\ then \ (\forall \ integer \ x)[x < x'] \right].$$

(The outermost quantifier ($\forall \ integer \ x'$) was introduced in taking the universal closure.)

The subsentence

> *if* $x' < x$
> *then* $x' < x'$

is equivalent (by properties of the nonnegative integers and propositional logic) to

> *not* $(x' < x)$.

Let us make this replacement in the principle. The resulting subsentence

$$(\forall \ integer \ x')\left[not \ (x' < x) \right]$$

is equivalent (by properties of the nonnegative integers) to

> $x = 0.$

Let us make this replacement. The resulting subsentence

$$(\forall \ integer \ x) \left[\begin{matrix} if \ x = 0 \\ then \ x < x' \end{matrix} \right]$$

is equivalent (by predicate logic) to

> $0 < x'.$

Let us make this replacement. The resulting sentence is

$$(\forall \ integer \ x') \left[\begin{matrix} if \ 0 < x' \\ then \ (\forall \ integer \ x)[x < x'] \end{matrix} \right].$$

If we take x' to be 1 and x to be 2, we have

> *if* $0 < 1$
> *then* $2 < 1,$

which is false. ◢

To distinguish between the induction principles, we refer to the earlier induction, including *decomposition induction*, as *stepwise induction*.

Let us postpone the proof of the *complete induction* principle until we have had a chance to illustrate its application.

8.7   QUOTIENT AND REMAINDER

Suppose we augment our theory by defining two binary function symbols, $quot(x, y)$ and $rem(x, y)$. Under the intended model for the nonnegative integers, these symbols denote the *quotient* and *remainder*, respectively, of dividing a nonnegative integer x by a positive integer y. The axioms for the quotient of dividing x by y are

$$(\forall\ integer\ x)\ \left[\begin{matrix} if\ x < y \\ then\ \ quot(x,\ y) = 0 \end{matrix}\right] \qquad (less\text{-}than)$$
$$(\forall\ positive\ y)$$

$$(\forall\ integer\ x) \atop (\forall\ positive\ y) \left[quot(x+y,\ y)\ =\ quot(x,\ y)+1\right] \qquad (addition)$$

The axioms for the remainder of dividing x by y are

$$(\forall\ integer\ x)\ \left[\begin{matrix} if\ x < y \\ then\ \ rem(x,\ y) = x \end{matrix}\right] \qquad (less\text{-}than)$$
$$(\forall\ positive\ y)$$

$$(\forall\ integer\ x) \atop (\forall\ positive\ y) \left[rem(x+y,\ y)\ =\ rem(x,\ y)\right] \qquad (addition)$$

Note that the axioms for the quotient and remainder do not specify the values of terms of form $quot(s,\ 0)$ or $rem(s,\ 0)$, although such terms are legal in the language.

From these axioms, we can establish the usual *sort* properties for the quotient function,

$$(\forall\ integer\ x) \atop (\forall\ positive\ y) \left[integer\left(quot(x,\ y)\right)\right] \qquad (sort)$$

and for the remainder function,

$$(\forall\ integer\ x) \atop (\forall\ positive\ y) \left[integer\left(rem(x,\ y)\right)\right] \qquad (sort)$$

The reader is requested to prove these properties in **Problem 8.9(a)(b).**

The following proposition expresses a relationship between the quotient and remainder functions.

Proposition (quotient-remainder)

The sentence

$$(\forall \ integer \ x) \atop (\forall \ positive \ y) \left[{x \ = \ y \cdot quot(x, \ y) + rem(x, \ y) \atop and \atop rem(x, \ y) < y} \right]$$

(*quotient-remainder*)

is valid. ⏌

The proof illustrates the use of the *complete induction* principle.

Proof.   We actually prove the equivalent sentence

$$(\forall \ positive \ y) \atop (\forall \ integer \ x) \left[{x \ = \ y \cdot quot(x, \ y) + rem(x, \ y) \atop and \atop rem(x, \ y) < y} \right]$$

(obtained by reversing the quantifiers).

Consider an arbitrary positive integer y. We would like to show that

$$(\forall \ integer \ x) \left[{x \ = \ y \cdot quot(x, \ y) + rem(x, \ y) \atop and \atop rem(x, \ y) < y} \right].$$

The proof is by complete induction on x; we take the inductive sentence to be

$$\mathcal{F}[x] : \quad {x \ = \ y \cdot quot(x, \ y) + rem(x, \ y) \atop and \atop rem(x, \ y) < y.}$$

To prove $(\forall \ integer \ x)\mathcal{F}[x]$, it suffices to establish the inductive step.

Inductive Step

We would like to show

$$(\forall \ integer \ x) \left[{if \ (\forall \ integer \ x') \left[{if \ x' < x \atop then \ \mathcal{F}[x']} \right] \atop then \ \mathcal{F}[x]} \right].$$

For an arbitrary nonnegative integer x, we assume the induction hypothesis

$$(\forall \ integer \ x') \left[{if \ x' < x \atop then \ \mathcal{F}[x']} \right]$$

and attempt to show the desired conclusion

$$\mathcal{F}[x],$$

that is,

$$x \ = \ y \cdot quot(x, \ y) + rem(x, \ y) \atop and \atop rem(x, \ y) < y.$$

Following the way the quotient and remainder are defined, we distinguish between two subcases, depending on whether or not $x < y$.

Case: $x < y$

Then (by the *less-than* axioms for the quotient and remainder, because y is positive) we have

$$quot(x, y) = 0 \quad and \quad rem(x, y) = x.$$

The desired conclusion $\mathcal{F}[x]$ then reduces to

$$x = y \cdot 0 + x$$
$$and$$
$$x < y.$$

The first conjunct follows from the *right-zero* axiom for multiplication and the *left-zero* property of addition; the second conjunct is the assumption for this subcase.

Case: $not\ (x < y)$

Then (by the *total-asymmetry* property of the less-than relation $<$)

$$y \leq x$$

and hence (by the *decomposition* property of the weak less-than relation $\leq$)

$$y + (x - y) = x,$$

that is (by the *commutativity* property of addition),

$$x = (x - y) + y.$$

Hence (by the *addition* axioms for the quotient and remainder, because y is positive) we have

$$quot(x, y) = quot\big((x - y) + y, \ y\big) = quot(x - y, \ y) + 1$$

and

$$rem(x, y) = rem\big((x - y) + y, \ y\big) = rem(x - y, \ y).$$

We would like to show $\mathcal{F}[x]$, that is,

$$x = y \cdot quot(x, y) + rem(x, y)$$
$$and$$
$$rem(x, y) < y,$$

which expands (in this case) to

$$x = y \cdot \big(quot(x - y, \ y) + 1\big) + rem(x - y, \ y)$$
$$and$$
$$rem(x - y, \ y) < y.$$

This can be transformed (by the *right-successor* axiom for multiplication) into

$$x = \big(y \cdot quot(x - y, \ y) + y\big) + rem(x - y, \ y)$$
$$and$$
$$rem(x - y, \ y) < y.$$

This can be transformed further (by the *commutativity* and *associativity* properties of addition) into

$$x = \big(y \cdot quot(x - y,\ y) + rem(x - y,\ y)\big) + y$$
$$and$$
$$rem(x - y,\ y) < y.$$

Therefore (by the *cancellation* property of subtraction, because, in this case, $y \le x$) it suffices to establish

$$x - y = y \cdot quot(x - y,\ y) + rem(x - y,\ y)$$
$$and$$
$$rem(x - y,\ y) < y,$$

which is precisely $\mathcal{F}[x - y]$.

We have assumed as our induction hypothesis that

$$(\forall\ integer\ x')\ \begin{bmatrix} if & x' < x \\ then & \mathcal{F}[x'] \end{bmatrix}.$$

In particular, taking x' to be $x - y$, we have

$$if\ \ x - y < x$$
$$then\ \ \mathcal{F}[x - y].$$

Because $(x - y) + y = x$ and y is positive, it follows (by the *left-addition* property of the less-than relation $<$) that

$$x - y < x,$$

and thus we have the desired result $\mathcal{F}[x - y]$.

Because we have completed the proof of the inductive step, we have established the *quotient-remainder* proposition. ⌟

Remark (why not stepwise induction?).   Note that the above proposition would be awkward to prove by stepwise induction rather than complete induction. In the inductive step we showed that, to prove our desired conclusion $\mathcal{F}[x]$, it suffices (in the case in which *not* $(x < y)$) to establish the condition

$$\mathcal{F}[x - y].$$

This turned out to be implied by our induction hypothesis

$$(\forall\ integer\ x')\ \begin{bmatrix} if & x' < x \\ then & \mathcal{F}[x'] \end{bmatrix},$$

taking x' to be $x - y$, since in this case $x - y < x$.

Had we attempted the proof by the (*decomposition* version of) stepwise induction, our induction hypothesis would have been simply

$$\mathcal{F}[x - 1].$$

This does not necessarily imply $\mathcal{F}[x-y]$, because we do not know that $y = 1$. The induction hypothesis of the complete-induction proof tells us not only $\mathcal{F}[x - 1]$ but the entire conjunction of

$$\mathcal{F}[0], \quad \mathcal{F}[1], \quad \ldots, \quad \mathcal{F}[x - 2], \quad \text{and} \quad \mathcal{F}[x - 1].$$

(A similar obstacle would have been encountered had we attempted the proof by the original version of stepwise induction.) ⌡

Remark (where is the base case?).   The reader may be puzzled to note that, although the earlier *stepwise induction* principle requires us to prove a base case and an inductive step, the *complete induction* principle requires only an inductive step. At first glance, it may seem as if we are getting something for nothing in using complete induction.

This appearance is misleading: In proving the inductive step for complete induction,

$$(\forall \ integer \ x) \ \begin{bmatrix} if \ (\forall \ integer \ x') \ \begin{bmatrix} if \ x' < x \\ then \ \mathcal{F}[x'] \end{bmatrix} \\ then \ \mathcal{F}[x] \end{bmatrix},$$

we must actually consider the possibility that the arbitrary nonnegative integer x is 0. In this case our induction hypothesis is

$$(\forall \ integer \ x') \ \begin{bmatrix} if \ x' < 0 \\ then \ \mathcal{F}[x'] \end{bmatrix}.$$

Because (by the *right-zero* property for the less-than relation $<$) there are no nonnegative integers x' such that $x' < 0$, we can never make use of the induction hypothesis in this case. Therefore we must prove the desired conclusion $\mathcal{F}[x]$, that is, $\mathcal{F}[0]$, without the help of the induction hypothesis, just as in the base case of a stepwise induction proof.

In the *quotient-remainder* proposition above, for instance, we treated separately the case in which $x < y$. Because we have taken y to be positive, this case includes the possibility that $x = 0$. The case was handled without appealing to the induction hypothesis. ⌡

The proposition we have just established states that, for any nonnegative integer x and positive integer y, the quotient $quot(x, y)$ and the remainder $rem(x, y)$ exhibit the *quotient-remainder* relationship

$$x = y \cdot quot(x, \ y) + rem(x, \ y)$$
$$and$$
$$rem(x, \ y) < y.$$

It can actually be shown that $quot(x, \ y)$ and $rem(x, \ y)$ are unique, in the sense that, for all nonnegative integers u and v satisfying the *quotient-remainder* relationship

$$x = y \cdot u + v$$
$$and$$
$$v < y,$$

we have

$$u = quot(x, y) \quad and \quad v = rem(x, y).$$

The proof is requested in **Problem 8.9(c)**.

Remark (program correctness).   The axioms for the quotient and remainder functions suggest a method for computing these functions. In other words, these axioms have computational content; we may regard them as a program for computing the quotient and remainder.

It is not immediately obvious that the functions defined by these axioms are actually the quotient and remainder functions we expect. We might have made an error in the axioms and thus defined some other functions.

The *quotient-remainder* property is a description of the intended behavior of the quotient and remainder functions. In this sense, it may be regarded as a specification for the program that computes these functions. In proving the property, we establish the correctness of the program at least with respect to this specification. In other words, we can be more confident that the program computes the functions we expect.   ⌙

8.8   PROOF OF COMPLETE INDUCTION

We are now ready to give the proof of the *complete induction* principle.

Proof (complete induction).   For an arbitrary sentence $\mathcal{F}[x]$, suppose that

$$(*) \qquad (\forall\ integer\ x) \left[\begin{array}{l} if\ (\forall\ integer\ x') \left[\begin{array}{l} if\ x' < x \\ then\ \ \mathcal{F}[x'] \end{array} \right] \\ then\ \ \mathcal{F}[x] \end{array} \right]$$

is true, where x' is not free in $\mathcal{F}[x]$; we would like to show that then

$$(\dagger) \qquad (\forall\ integer\ x)\mathcal{F}[x]$$

is true.

We actually prove an alternative property

$$(\ddagger) \qquad (\forall\ integer\ y)\mathcal{F}'[y],$$

where $\mathcal{F}'[y]$ is

$$\mathcal{F}'[y]: \quad (\forall\ integer\ x') \left[\begin{array}{l} if\ x' < y \\ then\ \ \mathcal{F}[x'] \end{array} \right]$$

and y is a new variable. Intuitively speaking, $\mathcal{F}'[y]$ is the conjunction of

$$\mathcal{F}[0], \quad \mathcal{F}[1], \quad \mathcal{F}[2], \quad \ldots, \quad \text{and} \quad \mathcal{F}[y-1].$$

Proof that (‡) $\Rightarrow$ (†)

To show that the alternative property (‡), that is, ($\forall$ *integer* y)$\mathcal{F}'[y]$, implies the original property (†), that is, ($\forall$ *integer* x)$\mathcal{F}[x]$, suppose that

$$(\forall \text{ integer } y)\mathcal{F}'[y],$$

and consider an arbitrary nonnegative integer x; we attempt to show that

$$\mathcal{F}[x]$$

is true.

From the supposition (taking y to be $x + 1$) we have $\mathcal{F}'[x+1]$, that is,

$$(\forall \text{ integer } x') \begin{bmatrix} if & x' < x+1 \\ then & \mathcal{F}[x'] \end{bmatrix}.$$

In particular, taking x' to be x, we have (because x' is not free in $\mathcal{F}[x]$)

$$\begin{aligned} &if \quad x < x+1 \\ &then \quad \mathcal{F}[x]. \end{aligned}$$

By the *adjacent* property of the less-than relation $<$, we know $x < x+1$. Therefore we conclude

$$\mathcal{F}[x],$$

as we wanted to show.

Proof that (∗) $\Rightarrow$ (‡)

The proof of (‡),

$$(\forall \text{ integer } y)\mathcal{F}'[y],$$

is by the *stepwise induction* principle; we take the inductive sentence to be $\mathcal{F}'[y]$.

Base Case

We would like to show $\mathcal{F}'[0]$, that is,

$$(\forall \text{ integer } x') \begin{bmatrix} if & x' < 0 \\ then & \mathcal{F}[x'] \end{bmatrix}.$$

But, for an arbitrary nonnegative integer x', we have (by the *right-zero* property of the less-than relation $<$)

$$not \ (x' < 0).$$

Therefore the entire implication is true.

Inductive Step

For an arbitrary nonnegative integer y, we assume the induction hypothesis (for the *stepwise induction* principle)

$$\mathcal{F}'[y]: \quad (\forall \; integer \; x') \left[\begin{matrix} if \; x' < y \\ then \; \mathcal{F}[x'] \end{matrix} \right]$$

and establish the desired conclusion (for the *stepwise induction* principle)

$$\mathcal{F}'[y+1]: \quad (\forall \; integer \; x') \left[\begin{matrix} if \; x' < y+1 \\ then \; \mathcal{F}[x'] \end{matrix} \right].$$

Consider an arbitrary nonnegative integer x' such that

$$x' < y+1;$$

we would like to show that

$$\mathcal{F}[x'].$$

Since $x' < y+1$, we have (by the *right-successor* property of the less-than relation $<$) that $x' \leq y$ or, equivalently (because $\leq$ is the reflexive closure of $<$),

$$x' < y \;\; or \;\; x' = y.$$

We treat each subcase separately.

Case: $x' < y$

By our induction hypothesis $\mathcal{F}'[y]$, we have

    if $x' < y$

    then $\mathcal{F}[x']$.

Therefore, because (in this case) $x' < y$, we obtain the desired result

$$\mathcal{F}[x'].$$

Case: $x' = y$

In this case we would like to show $\mathcal{F}[y]$. From our initial supposition $(*)$ (taking x to be y) we have

    if $(\forall \; integer \; x') \left[\begin{matrix} if \; x' < y \\ then \; \mathcal{F}[x'] \end{matrix} \right]$

    then $\mathcal{F}[y]$.

Therefore it suffices to show

$$(\forall \; integer \; x') \left[\begin{matrix} if \; x' < y \\ then \; \mathcal{F}[x'] \end{matrix} \right];$$

but this is precisely our induction hypothesis $\mathcal{F}'[y]$.

Because we have completed the base case and the inductive step of the stepwise induction proof, we have established the validity of the *complete induction* principle. ◢

As the proof of the above proposition illustrates, any sentence we can prove by complete induction we can also prove by stepwise induction, but the stepwise-induction proof may require a more complex inductive sentence.

In **Problem 8.10**, the reader is requested to prove the *quotient-remainder* proposition by stepwise induction, without using complete induction.

Some further applications of the *complete induction* principle are illustrated in the next section.

8.9   THE DIVIDES RELATION

In this section we introduce a new relation over the nonnegative integers and further illustrate the usefulness of the *complete induction* principle.

DIVIDES

Suppose we augment our theory by defining a new predicate symbol $x \preceq_{div} y$, denoting the *divides* relation, which holds when x divides y with no remainder. (The conventional symbol for this relation is $x|y$.)

The axiom for the divides relation is

$$(\forall \ integer \ x, \ y) \begin{bmatrix} x \preceq_{div} y \\ \equiv \\ (\exists \ integer \ z)\big[x \cdot z = y\big] \end{bmatrix} \qquad (divides)$$

Thus,

$$1 \preceq_{div} 6 \qquad 2 \preceq_{div} 6 \qquad 3 \preceq_{div} 6 \qquad 6 \preceq_{div} 6 \qquad 6 \preceq_{div} 0,$$

but not $0 \preceq_{div} 6$.

From this axiom we can establish the validity of the following properties of the divides relation:

$$(\forall \ integer \ x)\big[x \preceq_{div} 0\big] \qquad\qquad (right \ zero)$$

$$(\forall \ positive \ y)\big[not \ (0 \preceq_{div} y)\big] \qquad\qquad (left \ zero)$$

$$(\forall \ integer \ x, \ y, \ z) \begin{bmatrix} x \preceq_{div} y \ \ and \ \ x \preceq_{div} z \\ \equiv \\ x \preceq_{div} y \ \ and \ \ x \preceq_{div} (y + z) \end{bmatrix} \qquad (addition)$$

$$(\forall \ integer \ x, \ y, \ z) \begin{bmatrix} if \ \ x \preceq_{div} y \ \ or \ \ x \preceq_{div} z \\ then \ \ x \preceq_{div} (y \cdot z) \end{bmatrix} \qquad (multiplication)$$

$$\begin{matrix} (\forall \ positive \ x) \\ (\forall \ integer \ y) \end{matrix} \begin{bmatrix} x \preceq_{div} y \\ \equiv \\ rem(y, \ x) = 0 \end{bmatrix} \qquad (remainder)$$

We can also show that the divides relation is a weak partial ordering; in other words, we can establish the validity in the theory of the nonnegative integers of the three weak-partial-ordering axioms for the divides relation, that is,

$$(\forall \ integer \ x, \ y, \ z) \begin{bmatrix} if \ \ x \preceq_{div} y \ \ and \ \ y \preceq_{div} z \\ then \ \ x \preceq_{div} z \end{bmatrix} \qquad (transitivity)$$

$$(\forall \ integer \ x, \ y) \begin{bmatrix} if \ \ x \preceq_{div} y \ \ and \ \ y \preceq_{div} x \\ then \ \ x = y \end{bmatrix} \qquad (antisymmetry)$$

$$(\forall \ integer \ x) \begin{bmatrix} x \preceq_{div} x \end{bmatrix} \qquad (reflexivity)$$

Note that we cannot establish the *totality* property for the divides relation; that is, the sentence

$$(\forall \ integer \ x, \ y) \begin{bmatrix} x \preceq_{div} y \ \ or \ \ y \preceq_{div} x \end{bmatrix}$$

is not valid. For instance, neither $2 \preceq_{div} 3$ nor $3 \preceq_{div} 2$ is true.

Note that the definition of the divides relation does not immediately suggest a method of computing the relation, i.e., of determining whether $s \preceq_{div} t$ for terms s and t denoting particular nonnegative integers. For this purpose it is necessary (according to the definition) to decide whether

$$(\exists \ integer \ z)[s \cdot z = t].$$

But since there are infinitely many nonnegative integers z to be tested, this is impossible.

There are other properties of the divides relation that do suggest methods to compute it. For example, we can establish the validity of the following properties:

$$\begin{matrix} (\forall \ integer \ x) \\ (\forall \ positive \ y) \end{matrix} \begin{bmatrix} if \ \ x > y \\ then \ \ not \ (x \preceq_{div} y) \end{bmatrix} \qquad (greater\text{-}than)$$

$$(\forall \ integer \ x, \ y) \begin{bmatrix} if \ x \le y \\ then \begin{bmatrix} x \preceq_{div} y \\ \equiv \\ x \preceq_{div} (y - x) \end{bmatrix} \end{bmatrix} \qquad (subtraction)$$

These two properties, together with the *right-zero* and *left-zero* properties above, suggest a method for computing the divides relation.

Example (computation of $\preceq_{div}$).   Suppose we would like to determine whether 2 divides 4. We have

$$2 \preceq_{div} 4$$

if and only if (by the *subtraction* property, because $2 \leq 4$)

$$2 \preceq_{div} (4 - 2)$$

if and only if

$$2 \preceq_{div} 2$$

if and only if (by the *subtraction* property, because $2 \leq 2$)

$$2 \preceq_{div} (2 - 2)$$

if and only if

$$2 \preceq_{div} 0,$$

which is true (by the *right-zero* property). Note that we could have used the *reflexivity* property to determine that $2 \preceq_{div} 2$ is true, obtaining a shorter computation.

On the other hand, suppose we would like to determine whether 2 divides 3. We have

$$2 \preceq_{div} 3$$

if and only if (by the *subtraction* property, because $2 \leq 3$)

$$2 \preceq_{div} (3 - 2)$$

if and only if

$$2 \preceq_{div} 1,$$

which is false (by the *greater-than* property, because $2 > 1$ and 1 is positive). ⌐

In **Problem 8.11**, the reader is requested to show the validity of the *right-zero*, *left-zero*, *greater-than*, and *subtraction* properties of the divides relation and to show that these properties in fact constitute an alternative definition for the relation.

The *proper-divides* relation, denoted by $\prec_{div}$, is the irreflexive restriction of $\preceq_{div}$, defined by the axiom

$$(\forall \; integer \; x, y) \begin{bmatrix} x \prec_{div} y \\ \equiv \\ x \preceq_{div} y \;\; and \;\; not \; (x = y) \end{bmatrix} \qquad (proper \; divides)$$

Because we have established that $\preceq_{div}$ is a weak partial ordering, we know immediately (by the *irreflexive-restriction* proposition of the theory of the weak partial ordering $\preceq_{div}$) that its irreflexive restriction $\prec_{div}$ is a strict partial ordering, i.e., it is transitive and irreflexive.

The proper-divides relation $\prec_{div}$ may also be shown to satisfy the following property

$$(\forall \text{ positive } x, y) \begin{bmatrix} x \prec_{div} y \\ \equiv \\ (\exists \text{ integer } z) \begin{bmatrix} x \cdot z = y \text{ and} \\ 1 < z \end{bmatrix} \end{bmatrix} \qquad (multiplication)$$

GREATEST COMMON DIVISOR

Let us further augment our system by defining a binary function symbol $gcd(x, y)$ intended to denote the *greatest common divisor* of x and y. The axioms for the greatest-common-divisor function are

$$(\forall \text{ integer } x)\big[gcd(x, 0) = x\big] \qquad (zero)$$

$$\begin{matrix} (\forall \text{ integer } x) \\ (\forall \text{ positive } y) \end{matrix} \big[gcd(x, y) = gcd\big(y, rem(x, y)\big)\big] \qquad (remainder)$$

We illustrate the use of the axioms to compute the greatest common divisor of two particular nonnegative integers.

Example (computation of gcd).   Suppose we would like to determine the greatest common divisor of 6 and 9, assuming we can compute the remainder function rem. We have

$$
\begin{aligned}
gcd(6, 9) &= gcd\big(9, rem(6,9)\big) \\
&\qquad \text{(by the } remainder \text{ axiom, because 9 is positive)} \\[4pt]
&= gcd(9, 6) \\[4pt]
&= gcd\big(6, rem(9,6)\big) \\
&\qquad \text{(by the } remainder \text{ axiom, because 6 is positive)} \\[4pt]
&= gcd(6, 3) \\[4pt]
&= gcd\big(3, rem(6,3)\big) \\
&\qquad \text{(by the } remainder \text{ axiom, because 3 is positive)} \\[4pt]
&= gcd(3, 0) \\[4pt]
&= 3 \\
&\qquad \text{(by the } zero \text{ axiom).}
\end{aligned}
$$

In short,

$$gcd(6, 9) = 3. \quad \lrcorner$$

Remark (consistency).   As usual when we introduce new axioms, we run the risk of making the theory inconsistent. Here the risk is greater than usual, because these axioms do not fit the same form as our previous recursive definitions. Typically, in defining a function f, we have used a *successor* axiom, which expresses the value of $f(x,\ y + 1)$ in terms of the value of $f(x,\ y)$. Here the *remainder* axiom expresses the value of $gcd(x,\ y)$, for positive y, in terms of the value of $gcd(y,\ rem(x,\ y))$. The augmented theory is in fact consistent, as can be shown by exhibiting the model under which gcd is assigned the greatest common divisor function. ⌐

It may not be clear at this point why the function defined by these axioms is called the "greatest common divisor." The following proposition establishes that $gcd(x,\ y)$ is a "common divisor" of x and y; later we shall observe that it is indeed the "greatest" of the common divisors.

Proposition (common divisor)

The sentence

$$(\forall\ integer\ x,\ y)\ \begin{bmatrix} gcd(x,\ y) \preceq_{div} x \\ and \\ gcd(x,\ y) \preceq_{div} y \end{bmatrix} \qquad (common\ divisor)$$

is valid. ⌐

In other words, $gcd(x,\ y)$ divides both x and y.

Proof.   We actually prove (rearranging the quantifiers) the equivalent sentence

$$(\forall\ integer\ y,\ x)\ \begin{bmatrix} gcd(x,\ y) \preceq_{div} x \\ and \\ gcd(x,\ y) \preceq_{div} y \end{bmatrix}.$$

The proof is by *complete induction* on y, taking the inductive sentence to be

$$\mathcal{F}[y]: \quad (\forall\ integer\ x)\ \begin{bmatrix} gcd(x,\ y) \preceq_{div} x \\ and \\ gcd(x,\ y) \preceq_{div} y \end{bmatrix}.$$

To prove $(\forall\ integer\ y)\mathcal{F}[y]$, it suffices to establish the inductive step.

Inductive Step

We would like to show

$$(\forall\ integer\ y)\ \begin{bmatrix} if\ (\forall\ integer\ y')\ \begin{bmatrix} if\ y' < y \\ then\ \mathcal{F}[y'] \end{bmatrix} \\ then\ \mathcal{F}[y] \end{bmatrix}.$$

For an arbitrary nonnegative integer y, we assume the induction hypothesis

$$(\forall \; integer \; y') \begin{bmatrix} if \;\; y' < y \\ then \;\;\; \mathcal{F}[y'] \end{bmatrix}$$

and attempt to show the desired conclusion

$$\mathcal{F}[y],$$

that is,

$$(\forall \; integer \; x) \begin{bmatrix} gcd(x, \, y) \preceq_{div} x \\ and \\ gcd(x, \, y) \preceq_{div} y \end{bmatrix}.$$

Consider an arbitrary nonnegative integer x; we would like to show that

$$gcd(x, \, y) \preceq_{div} x$$
$$and$$
$$gcd(x, \, y) \preceq_{div} y.$$

Following the axioms for the *gcd* function, we distinguish between two subcases, depending on whether or not $y = 0$.

Case: $y = 0$

Then (by the *zero* axiom for the *gcd*) we have

$$gcd(x, \, y) \;=\; x.$$

The statement we would like to show then reduces to

$$x \preceq_{div} x \;\; and \;\; x \preceq_{div} 0.$$

The first conjunct follows from the *reflexivity* property of the divides relation, and the second from the *right-zero* property.

Case: $not \; (y = 0)$

In other words, y is positive. Then (by the *remainder* axiom for *gcd*)

$$gcd(x, \, y) \;=\; gcd\big(y, \, rem(x, \, y)\big).$$

We would like to show

$$gcd(x, \, y) \preceq_{div} x$$
$$and$$
$$gcd(x, \, y) \preceq_{div} y,$$

which (in this case) may be expanded to

$$gcd\big(y, \, rem(x, y)\big) \preceq_{div} x$$
$$and$$
$$gcd\big(y, \, rem(x, \, y)\big) \preceq_{div} y.$$

We know (by the *quotient-remainder* proposition, because y is positive) that

$$x = y \cdot quot(x, y) + rem(x, y).$$

Therefore the statement we would like to show may be expanded further, to

$$gcd(y, rem(x, y)) \preceq_{div} y \cdot quot(x, y) + rem(x, y)$$
and
$$gcd(y, rem(x, y)) \preceq_{div} y.$$

Thus (by the *addition* property of the divides relation) it suffices to establish

$$gcd(y, rem(x, y)) \preceq_{div} y \cdot quot(x, y)$$
and
$$gcd(y, rem(x, y)) \preceq_{div} rem(x, y)$$
and
$$gcd(y, rem(x, y)) \preceq_{div} y.$$

Hence (by the *multiplication* property of the divides relation) it suffices to establish

$$\left[\begin{array}{l} gcd(y, rem(x, y)) \preceq_{div} y \\ \quad or \\ gcd(y, rem(x, y)) \preceq_{div} quot(x, y) \end{array} \right]$$
and
$$gcd(y, rem(x, y)) \preceq_{div} rem(x, y)$$
and
$$gcd(y, rem(x, y)) \preceq_{div} y,$$

which is equivalent (by propositional logic) to

$$gcd(y, rem(x, y)) \preceq_{div} y$$
(*)   and
$$gcd(y, rem(x, y)) \preceq_{div} rem(x, y).$$

We have assumed as our induction hypothesis that

$$(\forall\ integer\ y') \left[\begin{array}{l} if\ y' < y \\ then\ \mathcal{F}[y'] \end{array} \right].$$

In particular (taking y' to be $rem(x, y)$), we have

$$if\ rem(x, y) < y$$
$$then\ \mathcal{F}\big[rem(x, y)\big].$$

Since (by the *quotient-remainder* proposition, because y is positive in this case)

$$rem(x, y) < y,$$

we have $\mathcal{F}[rem(x, y)]$, that is,

$$(\forall\ integer\ x')\ \begin{bmatrix} gcd(x',\ rem(x,\ y)) \preceq_{div} x' \\ and \\ gcd(x',\ rem(x,\ y)) \preceq_{div} rem(x,\ y) \end{bmatrix}.$$

(Note that we have renamed the bound variable x of the induction hypothesis to x', to avoid capturing the free occurrence of x in $rem(x, y)$.) In particular (taking x' to be y), we obtain

$$gcd(y,\ rem(x,\ y)) \preceq_{div} y$$
$$and$$
$$gcd(y,\ rem(x,\ y)) \preceq_{div} rem(x,\ y),$$

which is the statement $(*)$ we were trying to establish.

Because we have established the desired result in both cases, we have completed the proof.   ◣

Note that the proof of the inductive step for the case in which $y = 0$ was completed without appealing to the induction hypothesis. This corresponds to the base case in a stepwise induction proof.

Remark (why not stepwise induction?).   The above proof would be awkward to carry out by stepwise induction rather than complete induction. In the inductive step we attempted to prove our desired conclusion $\mathcal{F}[y]$, which is of the form

$$(\forall\ integer\ x)\mathcal{G}[x,\ y],$$

where

$$\mathcal{G}[x,\ y]:\ \begin{array}{c} gcd(x,\ y) \preceq_{div} x \\ and \\ gcd(x,\ y) \preceq_{div} y. \end{array}$$

For an arbitrary nonnegative integer x, we found (in the case in which *not* $(y = 0)$) that to establish $\mathcal{G}[x, y]$ it suffices to establish the corresponding condition $(*)$,

$$\mathcal{G}[y,\ rem(x,\ y)].$$

We were then able to apply our induction hypothesis,

$$(\forall\ integer\ y')\ \begin{bmatrix} if\ y' < y \\ then\ (\forall\ integer\ x)\mathcal{G}[x,\ y'] \end{bmatrix},$$

to establish (renaming x to x' and taking y' to be $rem(x, y)$, since $rem(x, y) < y$) that

$$(\forall\ integer\ x')\mathcal{G}[x',\ rem(x,\ y)].$$

This gives the desired condition $(*)$, taking x' to be y.

Had we attempted the proof by the (*decomposition* version of) stepwise induction on y, our induction hypothesis would have been simply

$$(\forall\ integer\ x)\mathcal{G}[x,\ y-1].$$

This does not necessarily give us the condition $(*)$, that is, $\mathcal{G}[y,\ rem(x,\ y)]$, because $rem(x,\ y)$ can be any nonnegative integer less than y. A successful stepwise-induction proof (whether by the *decomposition* version or the original version) requires a more complex inductive sentence.   ◢

The proof of the *common-divisor* proposition illustrates some of the strategic aspects of performing a proof by induction.

Remark (generalization).   The proof of the *common-divisor* proposition did not require us to generalize the sentence to be proved, but it can be used to illustrate the need for generalization. Suppose, instead of being given the sentence

$$(\forall\ integer\ x,\ y)\begin{bmatrix}gcd(x,\ y) \preceq_{div} x \\ and \\ gcd(x,\ y) \preceq_{div} y\end{bmatrix}$$

to prove, we had been given only the left conjunct,

$$(\forall\ integer\ x,\ y)\big[gcd(x,\ y) \preceq_{div} x\big].$$

Although this is a weaker sentence, we would not be able to establish it by imitating the above proof. We can see this as follows:

Suppose we reverse the quantifiers and attempt to prove

$$(\forall\ integer\ y,\ x)\big[gcd(x,\ y) \preceq_{div} x\big]$$

by complete induction on y, taking the inductive sentence to be

$$\mathcal{F}[y]:\quad (\forall\ integer\ x)\big[gcd(x,\ y) \preceq_{div} x\big].$$

The desired conclusion of the inductive step would also be

$$(\forall\ integer\ x)\big[gcd(x,\ y) \preceq_{div} x\big].$$

For an arbitrary nonnegative integer x, we would succeed in showing (in the case in which *not* $(y = 0)$) that, to establish the subsentence

$$gcd(x,\ y) \preceq_{div} x,$$

it suffices to establish the sentence $(*)$,

$$gcd\big(y,\ rem(x,\ y)\big) \preceq_{div} y$$
$$and$$
$$gcd\big(y,\ rem(x,\ y)\big) \preceq_{div} rem(x,\ y),$$

as in our original proof.

However, because we are attempting to show a weaker sentence, our induction hypothesis is the correspondingly weaker sentence

$$(\forall\ integer\ y')\begin{bmatrix}if\ y' < y \\ then\ (\forall\ integer\ x)\big[gcd(x,\ y') \preceq_{div} x\big]\end{bmatrix}.$$

Our weaker induction hypothesis would allow us to show (taking y' to be $rem(x, y)$ and x to be y, because $rem(x, y) < y$) that

$$gcd\big(y,\ rem(x,\ y)\big) \preceq_{div} y,$$

which is the first conjunct of the sentence $(*)$ we need to establish. We could not easily show the second conjunct, that

$$gcd\big(y,\ rem(x,y)\big) \preceq_{div} rem(x,y).$$

In fact, if initially we were only given the single condition

$$(\forall\ integer\ x,\ y)\big[gcd(x,\ y) \preceq_{div} x\big]$$

to prove, we would have had to discover the second condition ourselves and prove the more general, stronger statement consisting of the conjunction of the two conditions together, as we did in the proposition. This generalization process may require some ingenuity.   ⌐

The proposition we have just established states that, for all nonnegative integers x and y, the nonnegative integer $gcd(x, y)$ is indeed a common divisor of x and y, i.e., it exhibits the common-divisor relationship

$$gcd(x,\ y) \preceq_{div} x \quad and \quad gcd(x,\ y) \preceq_{div} y.$$

It can also be shown that $gcd(x, y)$ is the "greatest" common divisor of x and y, where "greatest" means greatest with respect to the divides relation $\preceq_{div}$. In other words, for every nonnegative integer z, if z is a common divisor of x and y, that is, if

$$z \preceq_{div} x \quad and \quad z \preceq_{div} y,$$

then $gcd(x, y)$ is "greater" than z, that is,

$$z \preceq_{div} gcd(x,\ y).$$

In short,

$$(\forall\ integer\ x,\ y,\ z) \begin{bmatrix} if\ \ z \preceq_{div} x\ \ and\ \ z \preceq_{div} y \\ then\ \ z \preceq_{div} gcd(x,\ y) \end{bmatrix} \qquad (greatest)$$

The proof of this property is left as an exercise (**Problem 8.12**).

We have defined the greatest-common-divisor function $gcd(x, y)$ in terms of the rather unnatural looking *zero* and *remainder* axioms; we can then establish that $gcd(x, y)$ is indeed a greatest common divisor of x and y. In an alternative augmentation of the theory, we can define the function by axioms that express the desired property, that $gcd(x, y)$ is a greatest common divisor of x and y. In other words, we take the *common-divisor* and *greatest* properties to be the axioms for *gcd*, and then prove the original *zero* and *remainder* axioms as properties. These alternative axioms, however, do not suggest a method for computing the *gcd* function.

8.10   THE LEAST-NUMBER PRINCIPLE

In this section, we establish a basic property of the nonnegative integers, which turns out to be equivalent to the *complete induction* principle.

Proposition (least-number principle)

For each sentence $\mathcal{G}[x]$, the universal closure of the sentence

$$\begin{aligned} &if \ \ (\exists \ integer \ x)\mathcal{G}[x] \\ &then \ \ (\exists \ integer \ x) \left[\begin{matrix} \mathcal{G}[x] \\ and \\ (\forall \ integer \ x') \left[\begin{matrix} if \ \ x' < x \\ then \ \ not \ \mathcal{G}[x'] \end{matrix} \right] \end{matrix} \right] \end{aligned}$$

$$(least \ number)$$

where x' does not occur free in $\mathcal{G}[x]$, is valid. $\quad\blacksquare$

In other words, if a statement $\mathcal{G}[x]$ is true for some nonnegative integer x, there must be a least nonnegative integer x' for which it is true.

Proof.   Consider an arbitrary sentence $\mathcal{G}[x]$, where x' is not free in $\mathcal{G}[x]$.

Recall that the *complete induction* principle asserted that, for each sentence $\mathcal{F}[x]$, the universal closure of the sentence

$$\begin{aligned} &if \ \ (\forall \ integer \ x) \left[\begin{matrix} if \ \ (\forall \ integer \ x') \left[\begin{matrix} if \ \ x' < x \\ then \ \ \mathcal{F}[x'] \end{matrix} \right] \\ then \ \ \mathcal{F}[x] \end{matrix} \right] \\ &then \ \ (\forall \ integer \ x)\mathcal{F}[x] \end{aligned}$$

is valid, where x' is not free in $\mathcal{F}[x]$. If we take $\mathcal{F}[x]$ to be *not* $\mathcal{G}[x]$, we obtain

$$\begin{aligned} &if \ \ (\forall \ integer \ x) \left[\begin{matrix} if \ \ (\forall \ integer \ x') \left[\begin{matrix} if \ \ x' < x \\ then \ \ not \ \mathcal{G}[x'] \end{matrix} \right] \\ then \ \ not \ \mathcal{G}[x] \end{matrix} \right] \\ &then \ \ (\forall \ integer \ x)\big[not \ \mathcal{G}[x]\big]. \end{aligned}$$

Using the propositional-logic equivalence

$$\left[\begin{matrix} if \ \ \mathcal{H}_1 \\ then \ \ not \ \mathcal{H}_2 \end{matrix} \right] \ \equiv \ not \ \big[\mathcal{H}_1 \ and \ \mathcal{H}_2\big],$$

we obtain the equivalent sentence

$$\begin{aligned} &if \ \ (\forall \ integer \ x) \ not \ \left[\begin{matrix} (\forall \ integer \ x') \left[\begin{matrix} if \ \ x' < x \\ then \ \ not \ \mathcal{G}[x'] \end{matrix} \right] \\ and \\ \mathcal{G}[x] \end{matrix} \right] \\ &then \ \ (\forall \ integer \ x)\big[not \ \mathcal{G}[x]\big]. \end{aligned}$$

By the duality between the universal and existential quantifiers, this is equivalent to

$$if \ \ not \ (\exists \ integer \ x) \begin{bmatrix} (\forall \ integer \ x') \begin{bmatrix} if \ \ x' < x \\ then \ \ not \ \mathcal{G}[x'] \end{bmatrix} \\ and \\ \mathcal{G}[x] \end{bmatrix}$$

$$then \ \ not \ (\exists \ integer \ x)\mathcal{G}[x].$$

Because any sentence is equivalent to its contrapositive, that is,

$$\begin{bmatrix} if \ \ not \ \mathcal{H}_1 \\ then \ \ not \ \mathcal{H}_2 \end{bmatrix} \ \equiv \ \begin{bmatrix} if \ \ \mathcal{H}_2 \\ then \ \ \mathcal{H}_1 \end{bmatrix}$$

is valid in propositional logic, we obtain

$$if \ \ (\exists \ integer \ x)\mathcal{G}[x]$$

$$then \ \ (\exists \ integer \ x) \begin{bmatrix} (\forall \ integer \ x') \begin{bmatrix} if \ \ x' < x \\ then \ \ not \ \mathcal{G}[x'] \end{bmatrix} \\ and \\ \mathcal{G}[x] \end{bmatrix}$$

or equivalently, reversing the conjuncts,

$$if \ \ (\exists \ integer \ x)\mathcal{G}[x]$$

$$then \ \ (\exists \ integer \ x) \begin{bmatrix} \mathcal{G}[x] \\ and \\ (\forall \ integer \ x') \begin{bmatrix} if \ \ x' < x \\ then \ \ not \ \mathcal{G}[x'] \end{bmatrix} \end{bmatrix}.$$

This is precisely the *least-number* principle for the sentence $\mathcal{G}[x]$. ◢

Note that the proof of the validity of the *least-number* principle required only the *complete induction* principle and properties of propositional and predicate logic; it made no mention of other properties of the less-than relation < or of the nonnegative integers. One can actually establish that the *least-number* principle and the *complete induction* principle are equivalent in predicate logic.

PROBLEMS

As usual, you may use in your proofs any property that is stated in the text earlier than the page reference for the problem, even if that property is given without proof; and you may use the results of any previous problem, even if you haven't solved that problem yourself.

Problem 8.1 (addition) page 384, 392

Establish the validity of the following sentences in the theory of the nonnegative integers, augmented by the axioms for addition:

(a) *Sort*

$$(\forall \ integer \ x, \ y)\big[integer(x + y)\big]$$

(b) *Associativity*

$$(\forall \ integer \ x, \ y, \ z)\big[(x + y) + z \ = \ x + (y + z)\big]$$

(c) *Left cancellation*

$$(\forall \ integer \ x, \ y, \ z)\begin{bmatrix} if & z + x = z + y \\ then & x = y \end{bmatrix}$$

(d) *Right cancellation*

$$(\forall \ integer \ x, \ y, \ z)\begin{bmatrix} if & x + z = y + z \\ then & x = y \end{bmatrix}$$

(e) *Annihilation*

$$(\forall \ integer \ x, \ y)\begin{bmatrix} if & x + y = 0 \\ then & x = 0 \ and \ y = 0 \end{bmatrix}.$$

Problem 8.2 (multiplication) page 393

Establish the validity of the following sentences in the theory of the nonnegative integers, augmented by the axioms for addition and multiplication:

(a) *Sort*

$$(\forall \ integer \ x, \ y)\big[integer(x \cdot y)\big]$$

(b) *Right one*

$$(\forall \ integer \ x)\big[x \cdot 1 \ = \ x\big]$$

(c) *Left zero*

$$(\forall \ integer \ x)\big[0 \cdot x \ = \ 0\big]$$

(d) *Left successor*

$$(\forall \ integer \ x, \ y)\big[(x + 1) \cdot y \ = \ x \cdot y + y\big]$$

(e) *Left one*

$$(\forall \ integer \ x)\big[1 \cdot x \ = \ x\big]$$

(f) *Right distributivity*

$$(\forall \ integer \ x, \ y, \ z)\big[x \cdot (y + z) \ = \ x \cdot y + x \cdot z\big]$$

(g) *Associativity*
$$(\forall\ integer\ x,\ y,\ z)\big[(x \cdot y) \cdot z\ =\ x \cdot (y \cdot z)\big]$$

(h) *Commutativity*
$$(\forall\ integer\ x,\ y)\big[x \cdot y\ =\ y \cdot x\big]$$

(i) *Left distributivity*
$$(\forall\ integer\ x,\ y,\ z)\big[(x + y) \cdot z\ =\ x \cdot z + y \cdot z\big].$$

Problem 8.3 (exponentiation)   page 394

(a) Use the axioms for the exponentiation function to determine the value of 3^2.

Establish the validity of the following sentences in the theory of the nonnegative integers, augmented by the axioms for addition, multiplication, and exponentiation:

(b) *Sort*
$$(\forall\ integer\ x,\ y)\big[integer(x^y)\big]$$

(c) *Exp one*
$$(\forall\ integer\ x)\big[x^1\ =\ x\big]$$

(d) *Zero exp*
$$(\forall\ integer\ y)\left[\begin{array}{l} if\ \ not\ (y = 0) \\ then\ \ 0^y = 0 \end{array}\right]$$

(e) *One exp*
$$(\forall\ integer\ y)\big[1^y\ =\ 1\big]$$

(f) *Exp plus*
$$(\forall\ integer\ x,\ y,\ z)\big[x^{y+z}\ =\ (x^y) \cdot (x^z)\big]$$

(g) *Exp times*
$$(\forall\ integer\ x,\ y,\ z)\big[x^{y \cdot z}\ =\ (x^y)^z\big].$$

Problem 8.4 (factorial)   page 398

Suppose we augment our theory of the nonnegative integers by formulating two axioms that define a unary function symbol $x!$, denoting the *factorial* function under the intended model for the nonnegative integers. The axioms are

$$0!\ =\ 1 \qquad\qquad\qquad\qquad (zero)$$

$$(\forall\ integer\ x)\big[(x + 1)!\ =\ (x + 1) \cdot (x!)\big] \qquad\qquad (successor)$$

For example,
$$3! \ = \ 3 \cdot (2!) \ = \ 3 \cdot 2 \cdot (1!) \ = \ 3 \cdot 2 \cdot 1 \cdot (0!) \ = \ 3 \cdot 2 \cdot 1 \cdot 1 \ = \ 6.$$

Let us introduce an alternative definition of the factorial function by formulating two additional axioms that define a binary function symbol $fact2(x, \ y)$, as follows:

$$(\forall \ integer \ y)\big[fact2(0, \ y) \ = \ y\big] \qquad\qquad (zero)$$

$$(\forall \ integer \ x, \ y) \begin{bmatrix} fact2(x + 1, \ y) \\ = \\ fact2\big(x, \ (x + 1) \cdot y\big) \end{bmatrix} \qquad\qquad (successor)$$

Prove that the sentence

$$(\forall \ integer \ x)\big[fact2(x, \ 1) \ = \ x!\big] \qquad\qquad (alternative \ definition)$$

is valid.

Hint: Prove a more general property.

Problem 8.5 (predecessor and subtraction)   page 399, 401

Establish the validity of the following sentences in the theory of the non-negative integers augmented by the axioms for the addition, predecessor, and subtraction functions and the *positive* relation:

(a) *Decomposition*
$$(\forall \ positive \ x)\big[x \ = \ (x^-) + 1\big]$$

(b) *Right one*
$$(\forall \ positive \ x)[x - 1 \ = \ x^-]$$

(c) *Addition*
$$(\forall \ integer \ x, \ y)\big[(x + y) - y \ = \ x\big]$$

(d) *Negative*
$$(\forall \ integer \ x, \ y)\big[x - (y + x) \ = \ 0 - y\big].$$

Problem 8.6 (subtraction axiom)   page 401

(a) Show that the sentence
$$\mathcal{F}: \quad (\forall \ integer \ x, \ y, \ z)\big[(x - y) + z \ = \ (x + z) - y\big]$$
is not valid in the augmented theory of the nonnegative integers.

(b) If we add $\mathcal{F}$ to the theory as a new axiom, is the resulting theory consistent? Justify your answer.

Problem 8.7 (weak less-than)　　page 403

In the augmented theory of the nonnegative integers, establish the validity of the *left-addition* property for the weak less-than relation, that is,

$$(\forall\ integer\ x,\ y) \left[\begin{array}{c} x \leq y \\ \equiv \\ (\exists\ integer\ z)[x + z = y] \end{array} \right].$$

Problem 8.8 (max and min)　　page 405

In the augmented theory of the nonnegative integers, establish the validity of the following properties of the maximum and minimum functions:

(a)　*Greater-than*

$$(\forall\ integer\ x,\ y) \left[\begin{array}{c} max(x,\ y) \geq x \\ and \\ max(x,\ y) \geq y \end{array} \right]$$

(b)　*Minimax*

$$(\forall\ integer\ x,\ y,\ z) \left[\begin{array}{c} min(x,\ max(y,\ z)) \\ = \\ max(min(x,\ y),\ min(x,\ z)) \end{array} \right].$$

Problem 8.9 (quotient-remainder)　　page 409, 414

In the augmented theory of the nonnegative integers, establish the validity of the following properties of the quotient and remainder functions:

(a)　*Sort (for quotient)*

$$\begin{array}{c} (\forall\ integer\ x) \\ (\forall\ positive\ y) \end{array} [integer\,(quot(x,\ y))]$$

(b)　*Sort (for remainder)*

$$\begin{array}{c} (\forall\ integer\ x) \\ (\forall\ positive\ y) \end{array} [integer\,(rem(x,\ y))]$$

(c)　*Uniqueness*

$$(\forall\ integer\ x,\ y,\ u,\ v) \left[if\ \left[\begin{array}{c} x = y \cdot u + v \\ and \\ v < y \end{array} \right]\ then\ \left[\begin{array}{c} u = quot(x,\ y) \\ and \\ v = rem(x,\ y) \end{array} \right] \right].$$

Problem 8.10 (quotient-remainder by stepwise induction) page 417

Prove the *quotient-remainder* proposition by stepwise induction, without using complete induction. More precisely, do the following:

(a) Suggest an inductive sentence $\mathcal{F}$ for the stepwise induction proof.

(b) Give the stepwise induction proof of your inductive sentence.

(c) Use the validity of $\mathcal{F}$ to establish the *quotient-remainder* proposition.

Problem 8.11 (divides relation) page 419

In the theory of the nonnegative integers augmented by the definition of the
divides relation, establish the validity of the following sentences:

(a) *Right zero*
$$(\forall \ integer \ x)[x \preceq_{div} 0]$$

(b) *Left zero*
$$(\forall \ positive \ y)\big[not \ (0 \preceq_{div} y)\big]$$

(c) *Greater than*
$$(\forall \ integer \ x) \begin{bmatrix} if \ \ x > y \\ then \ \ not \ (x \preceq_{div} y) \end{bmatrix}$$
$$(\forall \ positive \ y)$$

(d) *Subtraction*
$$(\forall \ integer \ x, \ y) \begin{bmatrix} if \ \ x \le y \\ \\ then \ \begin{bmatrix} x \preceq_{div} y \\ \equiv \\ x \preceq_{div} (y - x) \end{bmatrix} \end{bmatrix}.$$

Show also that these properties constitute an alternative definition for the
divides relation. In other words, in the theory of the nonnegative integers augmented by the above four properties, establish the validity of the original definition of $\preceq_{div}$:

(e) *Divides*
$$(\forall \ integer \ x, \ y) \begin{bmatrix} x \preceq_{div} y \\ \equiv \\ (\exists \ integer \ z)[x \cdot z = y] \end{bmatrix}.$$

Problem 8.12 (greatest common divisor) page 426

Establish that the greatest common divisor $gcd(x, y)$ is indeed the "greatest"
of the common divisors of x and y, with respect to the divides relation $\preceq_{div}$; in
other words, in the augmented theory of the nonnegative integers, establish the
validity of the sentence

$$(\forall \ integer \ x, \ y, \ z) \begin{bmatrix} if \ \ z \preceq_{div} x \ \ and \ \ z \preceq_{div} y \\ then \ \ z \preceq_{div} gcd(x, y) \end{bmatrix}.$$

Problem 8.13 (fallacious induction principle)   page 379

One would expect that, for each sentence $\mathcal{F}[x]$ in the theory of the nonnegative integers, the universal closure of the following sentence would be valid:

$$if \begin{bmatrix} \mathcal{F}[0] \\ and \\ (\forall \ integer \ y) \begin{bmatrix} if & \mathcal{F}[y] \\ then & \mathcal{F}[y^+] \end{bmatrix} \end{bmatrix}$$
$$then \ (\forall \ integer \ x)\mathcal{F}[x].$$

After all, the above sentence is obtained from the original *induction* principle by "renaming" the bound variable x of the inductive step to y.

In fact, if y occurs free in $\mathcal{F}[x]$, the sentence is not always true. Find a sentence $\mathcal{F}[x]$ in the theory for which the universal closure of the above implication is not valid.

Problem 8.14 (decomposition property)   page 382

Consider a theory defined by the axioms of the unaugmented theory of the nonnegative integers without the *induction* principle. Show that the *decomposition* property is not valid in this theory. That is, present an interpretation under which all the axioms (other than the *induction* principle) are true but the *decomposition* property is false.

Problem 8.15 (decomposition induction principle)   page 402

Establish the *decomposition induction* principle, that is, show that for each sentence $\mathcal{F}[x]$, the universal closure of the sentence

$$if \begin{bmatrix} \mathcal{F}[0] \\ and \\ (\forall \ positive \ x) \begin{bmatrix} if & \mathcal{F}[x-1] \\ then & \mathcal{F}[x] \end{bmatrix} \end{bmatrix}$$
$$then \ (\forall \ integer \ x)\mathcal{F}[x]$$

is valid.

Problem 8.16 (no induction principle)   page 406

Consider a theory defined by the two generation axioms and the two uniqueness axioms for the nonnegative integers and the two axioms for addition. Note that this theory does not have an induction principle.

Show that the valid sentences of this theory are not the same as the valid sentences of the augmented theory of the nonnegative integers, by exhibiting a model $\mathcal{I}$ for the six axioms of this theory such that the sentence

$$(\forall \ integer \ x, \ y)(\exists \ integer \ z)\big[x + z = y \ or \ y + z = x\big]$$

is false. Intuitively speaking, this sentence says that for all integers x and y, either $x \leq y$ or $y \leq x$.

9

Tuples

Induction principles are used to define many theories besides that of the non-negative integers. In this chapter we introduce a very simple and fundamental theory with induction, the theory of tuples. Intuitively speaking, a tuple is a finite collection of elements, called *atoms*, in which we regard both the order of the elements and their multiplicity as significant. Thus we regard

$$\langle A, B \rangle, \quad \langle B, A \rangle, \quad \text{and} \quad \langle A, A, B \rangle$$

as distinct tuples. We include among the tuples those consisting of a single atom, such as $\langle A \rangle$, and the empty tuple, denoted by $\langle \; \rangle$, which has no atoms at all. The set of atoms may be either finite or infinite, but each tuple must be finite, i.e., must contain only finitely many atoms.

9.1 THE THEORY

In the theory of tuples, we define

- A constant symbol $\langle \; \rangle$, denoting the *empty tuple*
- A unary predicate symbol $atom(x)$
- A unary predicate symbol $tuple(x)$
- A binary function symbol $u \diamond x$, denoting the *insertion* function.

As usual these notations are our private pseudonyms for standard constant, predicate, and function symbols such as a_{17}, $p_{22}(x)$, $q_3(x)$, and $f_{101}(u, x)$.

Under the intended models for the theory certain domain elements are atoms and certain elements are tuples. The atom relation $atom(x)$ is true if x denotes an atom, and false otherwise. The tuple relation $tuple(x)$ is true precisely if x

denotes a tuple. Also the value of the insertion function $u \diamond x$ is the tuple obtained by inserting the atom u at the beginning of the tuple x. Thus if u is the atom A and x is the tuple $\langle$A, B$\rangle$, then $u \diamond x$ is the tuple $\langle$A, A, B$\rangle$. The axioms do not specify the result $u \diamond x$ of inserting u into x if u is not an atom or x is not a tuple.

Thus the terms of the theory include $\langle\ \rangle$, $u \diamond \langle\ \rangle$, $u \diamond (v \diamond \langle\ \rangle)$, and so forth. Notations such as A, $\langle$A, B, B, C$\rangle$ and $\langle$A$\rangle$ are informal representations of domain elements and are not part of the language of the theory. Under a particular model for the theory, if u is A, v is B, and w is C, the value of the term $u \diamond (v \diamond (v \diamond (w \diamond \langle\ \rangle)))$ is the tuple $\langle$A, B, B, C$\rangle$ in the domain of the model.

The theory of tuples is a theory with equality defined by the following axioms:

- The *generation* axioms

$tuple(\langle\ \rangle)$	(*empty*)
$\genfrac{}{}{0pt}{}{(\forall\ atom\ u)}{(\forall\ tuple\ x)}[tuple(u \diamond x)]$	(*insertion*)

- The *uniqueness* axioms

$\genfrac{}{}{0pt}{}{(\forall\ atom\ u)}{(\forall\ tuple\ x)}[not\ (u \diamond x = \langle\ \rangle)]$	(*empty*)
$\genfrac{}{}{0pt}{}{(\forall\ atom\ u, v)}{(\forall\ tuple\ x, y)}\begin{bmatrix}if\ \ u \diamond x = v \diamond y\\ then\ \ u = v\ \ and\ \ x = y\end{bmatrix}$	(*insertion*)

- The (stepwise) *induction* principle

For each sentence $\mathcal{F}[x]$ in the theory, the universal closure of the sentence

$$if\ \begin{bmatrix}\mathcal{F}[\langle\ \rangle]\\ and\\ (\forall\ atom\ u)\begin{bmatrix}if\ \ \mathcal{F}[x]\\ (\forall\ tuple\ x)\begin{bmatrix}then\ \ \mathcal{F}[u \diamond x]\end{bmatrix}\end{bmatrix}\end{bmatrix}\quad (induction)$$
$$then\ \ (\forall\ tuple\ x)\mathcal{F}[x],$$

where u does not occur free in $\mathcal{F}[x]$, is an axiom.

The two generation axioms have the intuitive meaning that any element that can be constructed in the appropriate way from the empty tuple $\langle\ \rangle$, the atoms, and the insertion function $u \diamond x$ is a tuple. The two uniqueness axioms have the intuitive meaning that a tuple can be constructed in at most one such way from the empty tuple $\langle\ \rangle$, the atoms, and the insertion function $u \diamond x$.

DISCUSSION OF INDUCTION

In the *induction* principle, the sentence $\mathcal{F}[x]$ is called the *inductive sentence*. The subsentence

$$\mathcal{F}[\langle\ \rangle]$$

is called the *base case* of the induction. The subsentence

$$(\forall\ atom\ u) \begin{bmatrix} if & \mathcal{F}[x] \\ (\forall\ tuple\ x) & then & \mathcal{F}[u \diamond x] \end{bmatrix}$$

is called the *inductive step*; the subsentences $\mathcal{F}[x]$ and $\mathcal{F}[u \diamond x]$ of the inductive step are called the *induction hypothesis* and the *desired conclusion*, respectively. The variable x is called the *inductive variable*.

The *induction* principle may be paraphrased intuitively as follows:

To show that a sentence $\mathcal{F}[x]$ is true for every tuple x (under a given interpretation), it suffices to show the base case

$\mathcal{F}[\langle\ \rangle]$ is true

and the inductive step

for an arbitrary atom u (where u does not occur free in $\mathcal{F}[x]$) and tuple x,
if $\mathcal{F}[x]$ is true,
then $\mathcal{F}[u \diamond x]$ is also true.

The constraint on the *induction* principle that the variable u does not occur free in the sentence $\mathcal{F}[x]$ is essential. In **Problem 9.1**, the reader is requested to show that the *induction* principle is not valid for a sentence $\mathcal{F}[x]$ that violates the constraint. If we want to use the *induction* principle with an inductive sentence $\mathcal{F}[x]$ that violates the constraint, we can simply rename the variable u in the inductive step of the principle to a new variable.

DISCUSSION OF EQUALITY

Since the theory of tuples is a theory with equality, we include the equality axioms. The converse of the *insertion* uniqueness axiom,

$$(\forall\ atom\ u,v) \begin{bmatrix} if & u = v & and & x = y \\ (\forall\ tuple\ x,y) & then & u \diamond x = v \diamond y \end{bmatrix},$$

follows from the equality axioms for the insertion function.

The theory of tuples is deliberately vague about whether the empty tuple is an atom and, more generally, whether tuples and atoms are disjoint. In some models, tuples and atoms are disjoint; in others, they are not. In **Problem 9.2**, the reader is asked to construct a model for a theory in which the atoms and tuples are identical.

DECOMPOSITION

In this chapter, when we refer to the validity of a sentence, we shall always mean validity in the theory of the tuples. Let us show the validity of a sentence in this theory.

Proposition (decomposition)

The sentence

$$(\forall \ tuple \ x) \left[\begin{array}{l} if \ \ not \ (x = \langle \ \rangle) \\ then \ \ \begin{array}{l} (\exists \ atom \ v) \\ (\exists \ tuple \ y) \end{array} [x = v \diamond y] \end{array} \right]$$

is valid (in the theory of tuples). ∎

This proposition is analogous to the *decomposition* proposition for the non-negative integers, which established that

$$(\forall \ integer \ x) \left[\begin{array}{l} if \ \ not \ (x = 0) \\ then \ \ (\exists \ integer \ y)[x = y^+] \end{array} \right].$$

Proof.   The proof is by induction on x, taking the inductive sentence to be

$$\mathcal{F}[x]: \qquad \begin{array}{l} if \ \ not \ (x = \langle \ \rangle) \\ then \ \ \begin{array}{l} (\exists \ atom \ v) \\ (\exists \ tuple \ y) \end{array} [x = v \diamond y]. \end{array}$$

To prove

$$(\forall \ tuple \ x)\mathcal{F}[x],$$

it suffices to establish the base case,

$$\mathcal{F}[\langle \ \rangle],$$

and the inductive step,

$$(\forall \ atom \ u) \left[\begin{array}{l} if \ \ \mathcal{F}[x] \\ then \ \ \mathcal{F}[u \diamond x] \end{array} \right].$$
$$(\forall \ tuple \ x)$$

(Note that u does not occur free in $\mathcal{F}[x]$.)

Base Case

We want to prove

$$\mathcal{F}[\langle\,\rangle]: \quad \begin{array}{l} if \ \ not \ (\langle\,\rangle = \langle\,\rangle) \\[4pt] then \ \ \genfrac{}{}{0pt}{}{(\exists \ atom \ v)}{(\exists \ tuple \ y)}[\langle\,\rangle = v \diamond y] \end{array}$$

Because $\langle\,\rangle = \langle\,\rangle$, the antecedent

$$not \ (\langle\,\rangle = \langle\,\rangle)$$

of this implication is false and the entire sentence is true.

Inductive Step

We want to prove

$$(\forall \ atom \ u) \begin{bmatrix} if \ \ \mathcal{F}[x] \\ then \ \ \mathcal{F}[u \diamond x] \end{bmatrix}$$
$$(\forall \ tuple \ x) \quad .$$

Consider an arbitrary atom u and tuple x, that is, elements u and x such that

$$atom(u) \quad and \quad tuple(x).$$

We assume the induction hypothesis

$$\mathcal{F}[x]: \quad \begin{array}{l} if \ \ not \ (x = \langle\,\rangle) \\[4pt] then \ \ \genfrac{}{}{0pt}{}{(\exists \ atom \ v)}{(\exists \ tuple \ y)}[x = v \diamond y] \end{array}$$

and would like to show the desired conclusion

$$\mathcal{F}[u \diamond x]: \quad \begin{array}{l} if \ \ not \ (u \diamond x = \langle\,\rangle) \\[4pt] then \ \ \genfrac{}{}{0pt}{}{(\exists \ atom \ v)}{(\exists \ tuple \ y)}[u \diamond x = v \diamond y]. \end{array}$$

It suffices to show the consequent,

$$\genfrac{}{}{0pt}{}{(\exists \ atom \ v)}{(\exists \ tuple \ y)}[u \diamond x = v \diamond y],$$

of the desired conclusion.

Because we have supposed $atom(u)$ and $tuple(x)$ and because we know that $u \diamond x = u \diamond x$, we have

$$atom(u) \quad and \quad tuple(x)$$
$$and$$
$$u \diamond x = u \diamond x.$$

The desired result then follows (from the *existential quantifier-instantiation* proposition), taking v to be u and y to be x.

Since we have established both the base case and the inductive step, the proof is complete. ◢

Like the proof of the *decomposition* property in the theory of nonnegative integers, the above proof has the unusual feature that it requires the *induction* principle but makes no use of the induction hypothesis in the inductive step. Nevertheless, the principle is essential in this proof.

9.2   BASIC FUNCTIONS AND RELATIONS

We can augment our theory by introducing additional functions and relations.

THE HEAD AND TAIL FUNCTIONS

We now augment the theory of tuples by defining two unary function symbols, $head(x)$ and $tail(x)$. Under the intended models for the augmented theory, $head(x)$ denotes the first atom of a nonempty tuple x, and $tail(x)$ denotes the tuple of all but the first atom of x; for example, in our informal notation,

$$head(\langle B, A, C, A\rangle) = B \quad \text{and} \quad tail(\langle B, A, C, A\rangle) = \langle A, C, A\rangle.$$

The axioms that define the *head* and *tail* functions are

$$(\forall\ atom\ u) \atop (\forall\ tuple\ x) \left[head(u \diamond x) = u\right] \qquad\qquad (head)$$

$$(\forall\ atom\ u) \atop (\forall\ tuple\ x) \left[tail(u \diamond x) = x\right] \qquad\qquad (tail)$$

Note that these axioms do not specify the values of the terms $head(\langle\ \rangle)$ and $tail(\langle\ \rangle)$. Although these terms are legal in the language of the theory, the axioms do not force them to have any particular values.

From these axioms we can prove the following properties of *head* and *tail*:

$$(\forall\ tuple\ x) \begin{bmatrix} if\ \ not\ (x = \langle\ \rangle) \\ then\ \ atom\big(head(x)\big) \end{bmatrix} \qquad\qquad (sort)$$

$$(\forall\ tuple\ x) \begin{bmatrix} if\ \ not\ (x = \langle\ \rangle) \\ then\ \ tuple\big(tail(x)\big) \end{bmatrix} \qquad\qquad (sort)$$

In other words, the head of a nonempty tuple is an atom, and the tail of a nonempty tuple is also a tuple.

$$(\forall\ tuple\ x) \begin{bmatrix} if\ \ not\ (x = \langle\ \rangle) \\ then\ \ x = head(x) \diamond tail(x) \end{bmatrix} \qquad\qquad (decomposition)$$

In other words, every nonempty tuple is the result of inserting its head into its tail. The proofs of these properties are left as an exercise (**Problem 9.3**).

THE APPEND FUNCTION

Let us further augment our theory by defining a binary function symbol $x \diamondsuit y$. Under the intended models, $x \diamondsuit y$ denotes the *append* function, whose elements are the elements of the tuple x followed by the elements of the tuple y; thus,

$$\langle A, B \rangle \diamondsuit \langle B, C \rangle = \langle A, B, B, C \rangle.$$

The axioms that define the append function are

$$(\forall \ tuple \ y)[\langle \ \rangle \diamondsuit y = y] \qquad\qquad\qquad\qquad (left \ empty)$$

$$\begin{matrix} (\forall \ atom \ u) \\ (\forall \ tuple \ x, y) \end{matrix}[(u \diamondsuit x) \diamondsuit y = u \diamondsuit (x \diamondsuit y)] \qquad (left \ insertion)$$

The axioms suggest a way to compute the append function.

Example (computation of append).   In our informal notation, suppose we would like to compute

$$\langle A \rangle \diamondsuit \langle C, B \rangle, \quad \text{that is,} \quad (A \diamondsuit \langle \ \rangle) \diamondsuit (C \diamondsuit (B \diamondsuit \langle \ \rangle)).$$

Then we have

$$(A \diamondsuit \langle \ \rangle) \diamondsuit (C \diamondsuit (B \diamondsuit \langle \ \rangle)) = A \diamondsuit ((\langle \ \rangle \diamondsuit (C \diamondsuit (B \diamondsuit \langle \ \rangle))))$$
$$\text{(by the } left\text{-}insertion \text{ axiom)}$$

$$= A \diamondsuit (C \diamondsuit (B \diamondsuit \langle \ \rangle))$$
$$\text{(by the } left\text{-}empty \text{ axiom)}.$$

In other words,

$$\langle A \rangle \diamondsuit \langle C, B \rangle = \langle A, C, B \rangle. \quad \rule[-0.3ex]{1.2ex}{1.2ex}$$

From the axioms for append, we can establish the validity of the following basic properties:

$$(\forall \ tuple \ x, y)[tuple(x \diamondsuit y)] \qquad\qquad\qquad\qquad (sort)$$

$$(\forall \ tuple \ x)[x \diamondsuit \langle \ \rangle = x] \qquad\qquad\qquad\qquad (right \ empty)$$

$$(\forall \ tuple \ x, y, z)[(x \diamondsuit y) \diamondsuit z = x \diamondsuit (y \diamondsuit z)] \qquad (associativity)$$

By the *associativity* property, we can omit parentheses from the terms $(r \diamondsuit s) \diamondsuit t$ and $r \diamondsuit (s \diamondsuit t)$ and write $r \diamondsuit s \diamondsuit t$ in each case.

We can also establish the following properties:

$$(\forall \ tuple \ x, y)\begin{bmatrix} if \ x \diamondsuit y = \langle \ \rangle \\ then \ x = \langle \ \rangle \ and \ y = \langle \ \rangle \end{bmatrix} \qquad (annihilation)$$

In other words, if the result of appending two tuples is empty, both tuples must themselves be empty.

$$(\forall \, tuple \; x, y) \left[\begin{array}{l} if \;\; not \; (x = \langle \, \rangle) \\ then \;\; head(x \diamond y) = head(x) \end{array} \right] \qquad (head)$$

$$(\forall \, tuple \; x, y) \left[\begin{array}{l} if \;\; not \; (x = \langle \, \rangle) \\ then \;\; tail(x \diamond y) = tail(x) \diamond y \end{array} \right] \qquad (tail)$$

Let us prove the *annihilation* property; the proofs of the others are left as exercises (**Problem 9.4**).

Proposition (annihilation)

The sentence

$$(\forall \, tuple \; x, y) \left[\begin{array}{l} if \;\; x \diamond y = \langle \, \rangle \\ then \;\; x = \langle \, \rangle \;\; and \;\; y = \langle \, \rangle \end{array} \right]$$

is valid. ◢

The proof does not require induction.

Proof.   The proof is by contradiction. We consider arbitrary tuples x and y and suppose that

$(\dagger)$ $x \diamond y = \langle \, \rangle$

but that, contrary to the proposition,

     $not \; (x = \langle \, \rangle \;\; and \;\; y = \langle \, \rangle)$,

that is,

$(\ddagger)$ $not \; (x = \langle \, \rangle) \;\; or \;\; not \; (y = \langle \, \rangle)$.

We distinguish between two cases, depending on whether or not $x = \langle \, \rangle$, and derive a contradiction in each case.

Case: $x = \langle \, \rangle$

Then we have, by $(\ddagger)$, that

     $not \; (y = \langle \, \rangle)$.

We know

     $x \diamond y \;=\; \langle \, \rangle \diamond y$
               (by our case assumption)

         $=\; y$
               (by the *left-empty* axiom for append).

Therefore, because $not \; (y = \langle \, \rangle)$ and $x \diamond y = y$, we have

     $not \; (x \diamond y = \langle \, \rangle)$,

contradicting our supposition $(\dagger)$.

Case: $not\ (x = \langle\,\rangle)$

Then (by the *decomposition* proposition) there exist an atom u and a tuple x' such that

$$x = u \diamond x'.$$

Thus

$$x \diamond y \;=\; (u \diamond x') \diamond y$$

$$=\; u \diamond (x' \diamond y)$$
$$\text{(by the *left-insertion* axiom for append).}$$

Because (by the *empty* uniqueness axiom for tuples)

$$not\ (u \diamond (x' \diamond y) = \langle\,\rangle)$$

and because $x \diamond y = u \diamond (x' \diamond y)$, it follows that

$$not\ (x \diamond y = \langle\,\rangle),$$

again contradicting our supposition (†). ⌐

THE MEMBER RELATION

Let us further augment our theory by defining a binary predicate symbol $u \in x$. Under the intended model, $u \in x$ denotes the *member* relation, which indicates that the atom u is one of the elements of the tuple x; for example,

$$\text{B} \in \langle \text{A, B, C} \rangle \qquad \text{but not} \qquad \text{B} \in \langle \text{A, A, C} \rangle.$$

The member relation is defined by the axioms

$$(\forall\ atom\ u)\big[not\ (u \in \langle\,\rangle)\big] \tag{empty}$$

$$\begin{array}{l}(\forall\ atom\ u, v)\\ (\forall\ tuple\ x)\end{array} \left[\begin{array}{c} u \in (v \diamond x) \\ \equiv \\ u = v \ \ or \ \ u \in x \end{array}\right] \tag{insertion}$$

The *insertion* axiom for the member relation immediately implies the property

$$\begin{array}{l}(\forall\ atom\ u)\\ (\forall\ tuple\ x)\end{array}\big[u \in u \diamond x\big] \tag{component}$$

We can use the member relation to describe an important property of the append function

$$\begin{array}{l}(\forall\ atom\ u)\\ (\forall\ tuple\ x, y)\end{array} \left[\begin{array}{c} u \in (x \diamond y) \\ \equiv \\ u \in x \ \ or \ \ u \in y \end{array}\right] \tag{member}$$

The reader is requested to prove this property in **Problem 9.5(a)**.

THE SINGLETON FUNCTION AND RELATION

The unary function symbol $\langle u \rangle$ denotes the *singleton* function, which takes an atom u and yields the tuple whose sole element is u. It is defined by the axiom

$$(\forall\ atom\ u)\big[\langle u \rangle\ =\ u \diamond \langle\ \rangle\big] \qquad\qquad (singleton\ function)$$

We can immediately establish the following properties of *head* and *tail*:

$$(\forall\ atom\ u)\big[head(\langle u \rangle) = u\big] \qquad\qquad (singleton)$$

$$(\forall\ atom\ u)\big[tail(\langle u \rangle) = \langle\ \rangle\big] \qquad\qquad (singleton)$$

In other words, the head of a tuple consisting of a single atom is the atom itself, and its tail is the empty tuple.

We can establish the following property of the append function:

$$\begin{matrix}(\forall\ atom\ u) \\ (\forall\ tuple\ x)\end{matrix}\big[\langle u \rangle \diamond x\ =\ u \diamond x\big] \qquad\qquad (singleton)$$

The member relation can be characterized in terms of the append and singleton functions by the property

$$\begin{matrix}(\forall\ atom\ u) \\ (\forall\ tuple\ x)\end{matrix}\left[\begin{matrix}u \in x \\ \equiv \\ (\exists\ tuple\ y_1, y_2)\big[x = y_1 \diamond \langle u \rangle \diamond y_2\big]\end{matrix}\right]$$
$$(append\text{-}singleton)$$

The reader is requested to prove both properties in **Problem 9.5(b)–(e)**.

The following properties concerning the result of "suffixing," i.e., of inserting an atom at the end of a tuple, can be expressed using the singleton function:

$$\begin{matrix}(\forall\ atom\ u) \\ (\forall\ tuple\ x)\end{matrix}\big[not\ (x \diamond \langle u \rangle\ =\ \langle\rangle)\big] \qquad\qquad (suffix\ nonempty)$$

$$(\forall\ tuple\ x)\left[\begin{matrix}if\quad not\ (x = \langle\ \rangle) \\ then\quad \begin{matrix}(\exists\ atom\ u) \\ (\exists\ tuple\ y)\end{matrix}\big[x = y \diamond \langle u \rangle\big]\end{matrix}\right]$$
$$(suffix\ decomposition)$$

$$\begin{matrix}(\forall\ atom\ u, v) \\ (\forall\ tuple\ x, y)\end{matrix}\left[\begin{matrix}if\quad x \diamond \langle u \rangle = y \diamond \langle v \rangle \\ then\quad x = y\ \ and\ \ u = v\end{matrix}\right] \qquad (suffix\ uniqueness)$$

$$(\forall\ tuple\ x)\ \begin{bmatrix} x = \langle\ \rangle \\ or \\ (\exists\ atom\ u)\big[x = \langle u \rangle\big] \\ or \\ \begin{matrix}(\exists\ atom\ u, v) \\ (\exists\ tuple\ y)\end{matrix}\big[x = \langle u \rangle \diamond y \diamond \langle v \rangle\big] \end{bmatrix}$$

$$(prefix\text{-}suffix\ decomposition)$$

The reader is requested to establish their validity in **Problem 9.6**.

The unary predicate symbol $singleton(x)$ denotes the *singleton* relation, which is true if the tuple x contains exactly one atom; it is defined by the axiom

$$(\forall\ tuple\ x)\ \begin{bmatrix} singleton(x) \\ \equiv \\ (\exists\ atom\ u)\big[x = \langle u \rangle\big] \end{bmatrix} \qquad (singleton\ relation)$$

THE SAME RELATION

The unary predicate symbol $same(x)$ denotes the relation that is true if all the elements of the tuple x are identical; thus $same(\langle A,\ A,\ A\rangle)$ is true, but $same(\langle A,\ A,\ B\rangle)$ is false.

The *same* relation is defined by the axioms

$$same(\langle\ \rangle) \qquad\qquad\qquad\qquad\qquad\qquad\qquad\qquad (empty)$$

$$(\forall\ atom\ u)\big[same(\langle u \rangle)\big] \qquad\qquad\qquad\qquad\qquad (singleton)$$

$$\begin{matrix}(\forall\ atom\ u, v) \\ (\forall\ tuple\ x)\end{matrix}\ \begin{bmatrix} same\big(u \diamond (v \diamond x)\big) \\ \equiv \\ u = v\ \ and\ \ same(v \diamond x) \end{bmatrix} \qquad (double\ insertion)$$

The *same* relation is characterized by the property

$$(\forall\ tuple\ x)\ \begin{bmatrix} same(x) \\ \equiv \\ (\forall\ atom\ u, v)\begin{bmatrix} if\ \ u \in x\ \ and\ \ v \in x \\ then\ \ u = v \end{bmatrix} \end{bmatrix} \qquad (equality)$$

The reader is requested (in **Problem 9.7**) to show that this property constitutes an alternative definition of the *same* relation.

THE EQUAL-MULTIPLICITY RELATION

The ternary predicate symbol $eqmult(u,\ x,\ y)$, denoting the *equal-multiplicity* relation for tuples, holds if the atom u has the same multiplicity, i.e., number of occurrences, in each of the tuples x and y.

The multiplicity relation *eqmult* is defined by the following axioms:

$$(\forall\ atom\ u)\left[eqmult(u,\ \langle\ \rangle,\ \langle\ \rangle)\right] \qquad\qquad (empty)$$

$$\begin{array}{l}(\forall\ atom\ u)\\(\forall\ tuple\ y)\end{array}\left[not\ (eqmult(u,\ \langle\ \rangle,\ u \diamond y))\right] \qquad (empty\ insertion)$$

$$\begin{array}{l}(\forall\ atom\ u)\\(\forall\ tuple\ x)\end{array}\left[not\ (eqmult(u,\ u \diamond x,\ \langle\ \rangle))\right] \qquad (insertion\ empty)$$

$$\begin{array}{l}(\forall\ atom\ u,v)\\(\forall\ tuple\ x,y)\end{array}\left[\begin{array}{l}eqmult(u,\ v \diamond x,\ v \diamond y)\\ \equiv\\ eqmult(u,\ x,\ y)\end{array}\right] \qquad (equal\ insertion)$$

$$\begin{array}{l}(\forall\ atom\ u,v)\\(\forall\ tuple\ x,y)\end{array}\left[\begin{array}{l}if\ \ not\ (u = v)\\ then\ \left[\begin{array}{l}eqmult(u,\ v \diamond x,\ y)\\ \equiv\\ eqmult(u,\ x,\ y)\end{array}\right]\end{array}\right] \qquad (left\ insertion)$$

$$\begin{array}{l}(\forall\ atom\ u,v)\\(\forall\ tuple\ x,y)\end{array}\left[\begin{array}{l}if\ \ not\ (u = v)\\ then\ \left[\begin{array}{l}eqmult(u,\ x,\ v \diamond y)\\ \equiv\\ eqmult(u,\ x,\ y)\end{array}\right]\end{array}\right] \qquad (right\ insertion)$$

From these axioms we can establish the following properties:

$$\begin{array}{l}(\forall\ atom\ u)\\(\forall\ tuple\ x,y)\end{array}\left[\begin{array}{l}eqmult(u,\ x,\ y)\\ \equiv\\ eqmult(u,\ y,\ x)\end{array}\right] \qquad (symmetry)$$

$$\begin{array}{l}(\forall\ atom\ u)\\(\forall\ tuple\ x)\end{array}\left[eqmult(u,\ x,\ x)\right] \qquad (reflexivity)$$

$$\begin{array}{l}(\forall\ atom\ u)\\(\forall\ tuple\ x,y)\end{array}\left[\begin{array}{l}if\ eqmult(u,\ x,\ y)\\ then\ \ [u \in x\ \equiv\ u \in y]\end{array}\right] \qquad (member)$$

$$(\forall \ atom \ u,v) \atop (\forall \ tuple \ x_1,x_2,y_1,y_2) \left[{eqmult\bigl(u, \ x_1 \diamond \langle v \rangle \diamond x_2, \ y_1 \diamond \langle v \rangle \diamond y_2\bigr) \atop {\equiv \atop eqmult(u, \ x_1 \diamond x_2, \ y_1 \diamond y_2)}} \right]$$

(*append-singleton*)

The *append-singleton* property says that an atom u has the same multiplicity in two tuples with a common element v if and only if u has the same multiplicity in the tuples obtained by deleting v from each.

9.3   THE REVERSE FUNCTION

We now define a unary function symbol *reverse*(x). Under the intended models, *reverse*(x) denotes the tuple obtained by reversing the order of the atoms of the tuple x; for example,

$$reverse(\langle \text{A, A, B, C} \rangle) = \langle \text{C, B, A, A} \rangle.$$

The axioms that define the *reverse* function are

$reverse(\langle \ \rangle) = \langle \ \rangle$ (*empty*)

$(\forall \ atom \ u) \atop (\forall \ tuple \ x) \bigl[reverse(u \diamond x) \ = \ reverse(x) \diamond \langle u \rangle \bigr]$ (*insertion*)

The axioms suggest a method for computing the *reverse* function.

Example (computation of reverse).   Suppose we would like to reverse the tuple

$$\langle \text{A, B} \rangle, \quad \text{that is,} \quad \text{A} \diamond (\text{B} \diamond \langle \ \rangle).$$

Then we have

$$\begin{aligned}
reverse\bigl(\text{A} \diamond (\text{B} \diamond \langle \ \rangle)\bigr) \ &= \ reverse(\text{B} \diamond \langle \ \rangle) \diamond \langle \text{A} \rangle \\
&\qquad \text{(by the \emph{insertion} axiom for \emph{reverse})} \\[4pt]
&= \ \bigl(reverse(\langle \ \rangle) \diamond \langle \text{B} \rangle\bigr) \diamond \langle \text{A} \rangle \\
&\qquad \text{(by the \emph{insertion} axiom for \emph{reverse} again)} \\[4pt]
&= \ (\langle \ \rangle \diamond \langle \text{B} \rangle) \diamond \langle \text{A} \rangle \\
&\qquad \text{(by the \emph{empty} axiom for \emph{reverse})} \\[4pt]
&= \ \text{B} \diamond (\text{A} \diamond \langle \ \rangle) \\
&\qquad \text{(by properties of tuples).}
\end{aligned}$$

In other words,

$$reverse(\langle \text{A}, \text{B} \rangle) = \langle \text{B}, \text{A} \rangle. \quad \lrcorner$$

From the axioms for *reverse* we can establish the validity of the following properties:

$$(\forall \ tuple \ x) \big[tuple \big(reverse(x) \big) \big] \qquad\qquad (sort)$$

$$(\forall \ atom \ u) \big[reverse(\langle u \rangle) = \langle u \rangle \big] \qquad\qquad (singleton)$$

$$(\forall \ tuple \ x, y) \big[reverse(x \diamondsuit y) = reverse(y) \diamondsuit reverse(x) \big] \quad (append)$$

$$(\forall \ tuple \ x) \big[reverse \big(reverse(x) \big) = x \big] \qquad\qquad (reverse)$$

$$\begin{matrix} (\forall \ atom \ u) \\ (\forall \ tuple \ x) \end{matrix} \big[reverse(x \diamondsuit \langle u \rangle) = u \diamondsuit reverse(x) \big] \qquad (suffix)$$

The *singleton* and *suffix* properties can be established directly without the use of the *induction* principle. We give a proof of the *append* property here. The proof of the *reverse* property is left as an exercise (**Problem 9.8**). The proof of the *sort* property is omitted.

Proposition (append)

The sentence

$$(\forall \ tuple \ x, y) \big[reverse(x \diamondsuit y) = reverse(y) \diamondsuit reverse(x) \big]$$

is valid. $\lrcorner$

Proof.   We reverse the quantifiers and prove

$$(\forall \ tuple \ y, x) \big[reverse(x \diamondsuit y) = reverse(y) \diamondsuit reverse(x) \big].$$

Consider an arbitrary tuple y; we attempt to show

$$(\forall \ tuple \ x) \big[reverse(x \diamondsuit y) = reverse(y) \diamondsuit reverse(x) \big].$$

The proof is by induction on x, taking the inductive sentence to be

$$\mathcal{F}[x]: \quad reverse(x \diamondsuit y) = reverse(y) \diamondsuit reverse(x).$$

Base Case

We would like to prove

$$\mathcal{F}[\langle \ \rangle]: \quad reverse(\langle \ \rangle \diamondsuit y) = reverse(y) \diamondsuit reverse(\langle \ \rangle).$$

We have

$$reverse(\langle \ \rangle \diamondsuit y) = reverse(y)$$
$$\text{(by the } left\text{-}empty \text{ axiom for append)}.$$

But on the other hand,

$$reverse(y) \diamondsuit reverse(\langle\ \rangle)$$

$$= reverse(y) \diamondsuit \langle\ \rangle$$
(by the *empty* axiom for *reverse*)

$$= reverse(y)$$
(by the *right-empty* property of append).

Inductive Step

For an arbitrary atom u and tuple x, we assume the induction hypothesis

$$\mathcal{F}[x]: \quad reverse(x \diamondsuit y) \;=\; reverse(y) \diamondsuit reverse(x)$$

and attempt to show the desired conclusion

$$\mathcal{F}[u \diamondsuit x]: \quad reverse\big((u \diamondsuit x) \diamondsuit y\big) \;=\; reverse(y) \diamondsuit reverse(u \diamondsuit x).$$

Because we have supposed that u is an atom, we have

$$reverse\big((u \diamondsuit x) \diamondsuit y\big) \;=\; reverse\big(u \diamondsuit (x \diamondsuit y)\big)$$
(by the *left-insertion* axiom for append)

$$= reverse(x \diamondsuit y) \diamondsuit \langle u \rangle$$
(by the *insertion* axiom for *reverse*)

$$= \big(reverse(y) \diamondsuit reverse(x)\big) \diamondsuit \langle u \rangle$$
(by our induction hypothesis).

But on the other hand,

$$reverse(y) \diamondsuit reverse(u \diamondsuit x)$$

$$= reverse(y) \diamondsuit \big(reverse(x) \diamondsuit \langle u \rangle\big)$$
(by the *insertion* axiom for *reverse*)

$$= \big(reverse(y) \diamondsuit reverse(x)\big) \diamondsuit \langle u \rangle$$
(by the *associativity* property of append).   ◢

Remark (treatment of quantifiers).   The property we established in the *append* proposition was of the form

$$(\forall\ tuple\ x, y)\ \mathcal{G}[x,\ y].$$

In the above proof we reversed the quantifiers, considered an arbitrary tuple y, and established the subsentence

$$(\forall\ tuple\ x)\ \mathcal{G}[x,\ y]$$

by induction on x, taking the inductive sentence to be

$$\mathcal{F}[x]: \quad \mathcal{G}[x,\ y].$$

Alternatively, we could have proved the original property

$$(\forall \; tuple \; x, y) \; \mathcal{G}[x, \, y]$$

directly by induction on x, taking the inductive sentence to be

$$\mathcal{F}[x] : \quad (\forall \; tuple \; y) \, \mathcal{G}[x, \; y].$$

The resulting proof, however, would have been slightly more complex, because we would have had to dispose of the quantifier $(\forall \; tuple \; y)$ twice, once in the base case and once in the inductive step. In the following *alternative reverse* proposition, we shall see a proof in which we must adopt the more complex approach. ⌐

ALTERNATIVE DEFINITION

Let us give an alternative definition for the *reverse* function. Suppose we define a new binary function symbol $rev2(x, \; y)$ by the following two axioms:

$$(\forall \; tuple \; y) \big[rev2(\langle \; \rangle, \; y) \; = \; y \big] \qquad\qquad\qquad (left \; empty)$$

$$\begin{array}{l}(\forall \; atom \; u) \\ (\forall \; tuple \; x, y)\end{array} \big[rev2(u \diamond x, \; y) \; = \; rev2(x, \; u \diamond y) \big] \qquad (left \; insertion)$$

Intuitively speaking, $rev2(x, \; y)$ is the function that reverses the tuple x and appends the result with the tuple y; for example,

$$rev2(\langle \text{A, A, B} \rangle, \; \langle \text{C, D} \rangle) = \langle \text{B, A, A, C, D} \rangle.$$

That the function $rev2$ gives us an alternative definition of the *reverse* function is expressed more precisely in the following proposition.

Proposition (alternative reverse)

The sentence

$$(\forall \; tuple \; x) \big[reverse(x) \; = \; rev2(x, \; \langle \; \rangle) \big]$$

is valid. ⌐

Before proving the proposition, let us see how it suggests an alternative method for reversing a tuple.

Example (computation of rev2).   Assuming the proposition is true, suppose we would like to reverse the tuple $\langle \text{A, B} \rangle$, that is, $\text{A} \diamond (\text{B} \diamond \langle \; \rangle)$. Then we have

$$reverse\big(\text{A} \diamond (\text{B} \diamond \langle \; \rangle)) \big) \; = \; rev2\big(\text{A} \diamond (\text{B} \diamond \langle \; \rangle), \; \langle \; \rangle \big)$$
$$\text{(by the proposition)}$$

$$= \; rev2(\text{B} \diamond \langle \; \rangle, \; \text{A} \diamond \langle \; \rangle)$$
$$\text{(by the \textit{left-insertion} axiom for rev2)}$$

$$= rev2(\langle\ \rangle,\ \text{B} \diamond (\text{A} \diamond \langle\ \rangle))$$
　　　　(by the *left-insertion* axiom for *rev2*)

$$= \text{B} \diamond (\text{A} \diamond \langle\ \rangle)$$
　　　　(by the *left-empty* axiom for *rev2*).

In other words,

$$reverse(\langle\text{A},\ \text{B}\rangle)\ =\ \langle\text{B},\ \text{A}\rangle.$$

Note that the computation method suggested by the axioms for *rev2* is more "efficient" than that suggested by the axioms for the *reverse* function itself, because we are not required to apply properties of the append function $\diamond$ during the computation. ⌐

Proof (alternative reverse).　We actually prove the more general sentence

$$(\forall\ tuple\ x, y)[rev2(x,\ y)\ =\ reverse(x) \diamond y],$$

which fully describes the behavior of the function *rev2*. Once we have proved this sentence, we can infer the sentence we really want to prove,

$$(\forall\ tuple\ x)[reverse(x)\ =\ rev2(x,\ \langle\ \rangle)].$$

For in the more general sentence, considering an arbitrary tuple x and taking y to be $\langle\ \rangle$, we obtain

$$rev2(x,\ \langle\ \rangle)\ =\ reverse(x) \diamond \langle\ \rangle.$$

It follows (by the *right-empty* property of append) that

$$rev2(x,\ \langle\ \rangle) = reverse(x).$$

　　The proof of the more general sentence

$$(\forall\ tuple\ x, y)[rev2(x,\ y)\ =\ reverse(x) \diamond y]$$

is by induction on x, taking the inductive sentence to be

$$\mathcal{F}[x]:\quad (\forall\ tuple\ y)[rev2(x,\ y)\ =\ reverse(x) \diamond y].$$

Base Case

　　We would like to show

$$\mathcal{F}[\langle\ \rangle]:\quad (\forall\ tuple\ y)[rev2(\langle\ \rangle,\ y)\ =\ reverse(\langle\ \rangle) \diamond y].$$

For an arbitrary tuple y, we have

$$rev2(\langle\ \rangle,\ y)\ =\ y$$
　　　　　　(by the *left-empty* axiom for *rev2*).

But on the other hand,

$$reverse(\langle\ \rangle) \diamond y\ =\ \langle\ \rangle \diamond y$$
　　　　　　(by the *empty* axiom for *reverse*)

$$=\ y$$
　　　　　　(by the *left-empty* axiom for append).

Inductive Step

For arbitrary atom u and tuple x, we assume the induction hypothesis

$$\mathcal{F}[x]: \quad (\forall \ tuple \ y)\big[rev2(x, y) \ = \ reverse(x) \diamond y\big]$$

and would like to show the desired conclusion

$$\mathcal{F}[u \diamond x]: \quad (\forall \ tuple \ y')\big[rev2(u \diamond x, y') \ = \ reverse(u \diamond x) \diamond y'\big].$$

(Here we have renamed the bound variable y of the desired conclusion to y', to avoid confusion with the variable y in the induction hypothesis.)

Recall we have supposed that u is an atom. Then for an arbitrary tuple y', we have

$$rev2(u \diamond x, \ y') \ = \ rev2(x, \ u \diamond y')$$
$$\text{(by the } \textit{left-insertion} \text{ axiom for } rev2).$$

But on the other hand,

$$reverse(u \diamond x) \diamond y'$$

$$= \ \big(reverse(x) \diamond \langle u \rangle\big) \diamond y'$$
$$\text{(by the } \textit{insertion} \text{ axiom for } reverse)$$

$$= \ reverse(x) \diamond \big(\langle u \rangle \diamond y'\big)$$
$$\text{(by the } \textit{associativity} \text{ property of append)}$$

$$= \ reverse(x) \diamond \big(u \diamond y'\big)$$
$$\text{(by the } \textit{singleton} \text{ property of append).}$$

Therefore it suffices to establish that

$$rev2(x, \ u \diamond y') \ = \ reverse(x) \diamond (u \diamond y').$$

But this follows from our induction hypothesis,

$$(\forall \ tuple \ y)\big[rev2(x, \ y) \ = \ reverse(x) \diamond y\big],$$

taking y to be $u \diamond y'$. ◢

Note that we were forced to generalize the original property,

$$(\forall \ tuple \ x)\big[reverse(x) \ = \ rev2(x, \ \langle \ \rangle)\big].$$

The stronger property we used as our inductive sentence was

$$(\forall \ tuple \ x, y)\big[rev2(x, \ y) \ = \ reverse(x) \diamond y\big].$$

Had we taken the inductive sentence to be the original property, without first generalizing, we would not have been able to establish the inductive step.

Some additional functions over the tuples are defined in **Problem 9.9**. In **Problem 9.10**, the reader is asked to provide axioms for another function over the tuples.

An alternative *induction* principle over the tuples, based on suffixing rather than prefixing, is introduced in **Problem 9.11**. Using this *induction* principle, the reader is asked to establish an alternative definition of the append function in **Problem 9.12**.

9.4   THE DECOMPOSITION INDUCTION PRINCIPLE

In the theory of the nonnegative integers, we introduced a *decomposition induction* principle. This principle is expressed in terms of the predecessor function x^-, just as the original *induction* principle is expressed in terms of the successor function x^+.

In the theory of tuples, the original *induction* principle is expressed in terms of the insertion function $u \diamond x$; we now introduce a corresponding *decomposition induction* principle expressed in terms of the tail function $tail(x)$.

Proposition (decomposition induction)

For each sentence $\mathcal{F}[x]$, the universal closure of the sentence

$$if \left[\begin{array}{l} \mathcal{F}[\langle \, \rangle] \\ \quad and \\ (\forall \ tuple \ x) \left[\begin{array}{l} if \ \ not \ (x = \langle \, \rangle) \\ then \ \ if \ \ \mathcal{F}[tail(x)] \\ \qquad then \ \ \mathcal{F}[x] \end{array} \right] \end{array} \right] \qquad (decomposition \\ induction)$$

$$then \ \ (\forall \ tuple \ x)\mathcal{F}[x]$$

is valid. ⌐

The decomposition version of the *induction* principle is more convenient to use when we are dealing with axioms and properties that are expressed in terms of the tail function $tail(x)$ rather than the insertion function $u \diamond x$. In this book, we typically use the insertion function; therefore the original version is usually easier to use. To illustrate the use of the *decomposition induction* principle, however, we define below a new relation in terms of the *tail* function rather than the insertion function, and we prove one of its properties by decomposition induction rather than by the original induction.

THE END RELATION

Let us introduce a binary predicate symbol $x \preceq_{end} y$ to denote the *end* relation; this relation is true if the tuple x is at the end of the tuple y, that is, x can be obtained from y by dropping some (perhaps none) of the initial atoms of y. For instance,

$$\langle A, \ T \rangle \preceq_{end} \langle C, \ A, \ T \rangle, \qquad \langle T \rangle \preceq_{end} \langle C, \ A, \ T \rangle,$$

$$\langle \, \rangle \preceq_{end} \langle C, \ A, \ T \rangle, \qquad \langle C, \ A, \ T \rangle \preceq_{end} \langle C, \ A, \ T \rangle.$$

If $x \preceq_{end} y$, we shall say in words that x is an *end* of y.

We define the end relation formally by the following two axioms:

$$(\forall \ tuple \ x) \quad \begin{bmatrix} x \preceq_{end} \langle \ \rangle \\ \equiv \\ x = \langle \ \rangle \end{bmatrix} \qquad (empty)$$

$$(\forall \ tuple \ x, y) \quad \begin{bmatrix} if \ \ not \ (y = \langle \ \rangle) \\ then \quad \begin{bmatrix} x \preceq_{end} y \\ \equiv \\ x = y \ \ or \ \ x \preceq_{end} tail(y) \end{bmatrix} \end{bmatrix} \qquad (tail)$$

From these axioms we establish the following property of the end relation.

Proposition (end append)

The sentence

$$(\forall \ tuple \ x, y) \quad \begin{bmatrix} x \preceq_{end} y \\ \equiv \\ (\exists \ tuple \ z)[z \diamond x = y] \end{bmatrix} \qquad (append)$$

is valid. ◢

In other words, x is an end of y if and only if y can be obtained by appending some tuple z to x.

To facilitate the use of *decomposition* induction in the proof, we suppose that we have established the validity of the following property of append, which paraphrases the *left-insertion* axiom for append in terms of the *head* and *tail* function:

$$(\forall \ tuple \ x, y) \quad \begin{bmatrix} if \ \ not \ (x = \langle \ \rangle) \\ then \ \ x \diamond y \ = \ head(x) \diamond \big(tail(x) \diamond y\big) \end{bmatrix} \qquad (head\text{-}tail)$$

Let us prove the *end-append* proposition.

Proof.   By predicate logic, it suffices to establish the validity of the two sentences:

$$(\Rightarrow) \qquad (\forall \ tuple \ x, y) \quad \begin{bmatrix} if \ \ x \preceq_{end} y \\ then \ \ (\exists \ tuple \ z)[z \diamond x = y] \end{bmatrix}$$

and

$$(\Leftarrow) \qquad (\forall \ tuple \ x, y) \quad \begin{bmatrix} if \ \ (\exists \ tuple \ z)[z \diamond x = y] \\ then \ \ x \preceq_{end} y \end{bmatrix} .$$

We prove only the ($\Leftarrow$) part here; the proof of the ($\Rightarrow$) part is left as an exercise (**Problem 9.13**). To prove the ($\Leftarrow$) part, consider an arbitrary tuple x; we would like to show

$$(\forall \ tuple \ y) \quad \begin{bmatrix} if \ \ (\exists \ tuple \ z)[z \diamond x = y] \\ then \ \ x \preceq_{end} y \end{bmatrix} .$$

The proof is by decomposition induction on y, taking the inductive sentence to be

$$\mathcal{F}[y]: \quad \begin{array}{l} \textit{if} \ (\exists \textit{ tuple } z)\big[z \diamond x = y\big] \\ \textit{then} \ \ x \preceq_{end} y. \end{array}$$

Base Case

We would like to show

$$\mathcal{F}[\langle\,\rangle]: \quad \begin{array}{l} \textit{if} \ (\exists \textit{ tuple } z)\big[z \diamond x = \langle\,\rangle\big] \\ \textit{then} \ \ x \preceq_{end} \langle\,\rangle. \end{array}$$

Suppose that, for some tuple z,

$$z \diamond x = \langle\,\rangle;$$

then (by the *annihilation* property of append)

$$z = \langle\,\rangle \ \ \textit{and} \ \ x = \langle\,\rangle.$$

Therefore (by the *empty* axiom for the end relation $\preceq_{end}$, because $x = \langle\,\rangle$)

$$x \preceq_{end} \langle\,\rangle,$$

which is the consequent of our base case $\mathcal{F}[\langle\,\rangle]$.

Inductive Step

For an arbitrary tuple y, suppose

$$\textit{not} \ (y = \langle\,\rangle)$$

and assume the induction hypothesis

$$\mathcal{F}[tail(y)]: \quad \begin{array}{l} \textit{if} \ (\exists \textit{ tuple } z)\big[z \diamond x = tail(y)\big] \\ \textit{then} \ \ x \preceq_{end} tail(y). \end{array}$$

We would like to establish the desired conclusion

$$\mathcal{F}[y]: \quad \begin{array}{l} \textit{if} \ (\exists \textit{ tuple } z')\big[z' \diamond x = y\big] \\ \textit{then} \ \ x \preceq_{end} y. \end{array}$$

(Here we have renamed the bound variable z of the desired conclusion to z', to avoid confusion with the bound variable z of the induction hypothesis.)

Suppose that, for some tuple z',

$$z' \diamond x = y;$$

we would like to show that

$$x \preceq_{end} y.$$

The proof distinguishes between two cases, depending on whether or not z' is empty.

Case: $z' = \langle\,\rangle$

Then (by the supposition above)

$$\langle\,\rangle \diamond x = y,$$

and hence (by the *left-empty* axiom for append)

$$x = y.$$

Therefore (by the *tail* axiom for the relation $\preceq_{end}$, because *not* $(y = \langle\,\rangle)$)

$$x \preceq_{end} y,$$

which is the desired result.

Case: *not* $(z' = \langle\,\rangle)$

Then (by the *head-tail* property of append, because *not* $(z' = \langle\,\rangle)$) we can rewrite our supposition $z' \diamond x = y$ as

$$head(z') \diamond (tail(z') \diamond x) \;=\; y.$$

Therefore

$$tail\big(head(z') \diamond (tail(z') \diamond x)\big) \;=\; tail(y)$$

and hence (by the definition of the *tail* function)

$$tail(z') \diamond x \;=\; tail(y).$$

It follows (by the *existential quantifier-instantiation* proposition, taking z to be $tail(z')$) that

$$(\exists\ tuple\ z)\big[z \diamond x \;=\; tail(y)\big].$$

Hence (by our induction hypothesis)

$$x \preceq_{end} tail(y)$$

and (by the *tail* axiom for the relation $\preceq_{end}$, because *not* $(y = \langle\,\rangle)$)

$$x \preceq_{end} y,$$

which is the desired result. ◢

9.5   THE SUBTUPLE RELATION

The binary predicate symbol $x \preceq_{tuple} y$ denotes the *subtuple* relation. We say that a tuple x is a subtuple of a tuple y if, for each occurrence of an element in x, there corresponds a distinct occurrence of the same element in y, and the elements occur in the same order. Thus $x \preceq_{tuple} y$ holds if the elements of x occur in y in the same order but not necessarily consecutively. For example,

$$\langle A,\ C\rangle \preceq_{tuple} \langle A,\ A,\ B,\ C\rangle$$

$$\langle A,\ A,\ B\rangle \preceq_{tuple} \langle C,\ A,\ C,\ A,\ B\rangle$$

but

$$not\quad \langle A,\ B,\ B\rangle \preceq_{tuple} \langle A,\ A,\ B,\ C\rangle$$

$$not\quad \langle B,\ A\rangle \preceq_{tuple} \langle A,\ A,\ B,\ C\rangle.$$

The *subtuple* relation is defined by the following four axioms:

$$(\forall \; tuple \; y)\left[\langle \; \rangle \; \preceq_{tuple} \; y\right] \qquad\qquad (left \; empty)$$

$$\begin{array}{l}(\forall \; atom \; u)\\(\forall \; tuple \; x)\end{array}\left[not \; \left(u \diamond x \; \preceq_{tuple} \; \langle \; \rangle\right)\right] \qquad (right \; empty)$$

$$\begin{array}{l}(\forall \; atom \; u)\\(\forall \; tuple \; x, y)\end{array}\left[\begin{array}{l} u \diamond x \; \preceq_{tuple} \; u \diamond y\\ \qquad\equiv\\ x \; \preceq_{tuple} \; y \end{array}\right] \qquad (equal \; insertion)$$

$$\begin{array}{l}(\forall \; atom \; u, v)\\(\forall \; tuple \; x, y)\end{array}\left[\begin{array}{l} if \;\; not \; (u = v)\\ then \;\; \left[\begin{array}{l} u \diamond x \; \preceq_{tuple} \; v \diamond y\\ \qquad\equiv\\ u \diamond x \; \preceq_{tuple} \; y \end{array}\right] \end{array}\right] \quad (nonequal \; insertion)$$

From these axioms we can establish the properties

$$(\forall \; tuple \; x, y)\left[\begin{array}{l} if \;\; x \preceq_{tuple} y\\ then \;\; (\forall \; atom \; u)\left[\begin{array}{l} if \;\; u \in x\\ then \;\; u \in y\end{array}\right]\end{array}\right] \qquad (member)$$

$$\begin{array}{l}(\forall \; atom \; u)\\(\forall \; tuple \; x, y)\end{array}\left[\begin{array}{l} if \;\; u \diamond x \preceq_{tuple} y\\ then \;\; u \in y \;\; and \;\; x \preceq_{tuple} y\end{array}\right] \qquad (left \; insertion)$$

From the axioms we may establish that the subtuple relation is a weak partial ordering, that is,

$$(\forall \; tuple \; x, y, z)\left[\begin{array}{l} if \;\; x \preceq_{tuple} y \;\; and \;\; y \preceq_{tuple} z\\ then \;\; x \preceq_{tuple} z\end{array}\right] \qquad (transitivity)$$

$$(\forall \; tuple \; x, y)\left[\begin{array}{l} if \;\; x \preceq_{tuple} y \;\; and \;\; y \preceq_{tuple} x\\ then \;\; x = y\end{array}\right] \qquad (antisymmetry)$$

$$(\forall \; tuple \; x)\left[x \preceq_{tuple} x\right] \qquad (reflexivity)$$

We can also establish the following properties:

$$(\forall \; tuple \; x, y)\left[x \preceq_{tuple} x \diamond y\right] \qquad (left \; append)$$

$$(\forall \; tuple \; x, y)\left[y \preceq_{tuple} x \diamond y\right] \qquad (right \; append)$$

The *proper-subtuple* relation, denoted by $x \prec_{tuple} y$, is the irreflexive restriction of the subtuple relation $\preceq_{tuple}$, defined by the axiom

$$(\forall \ tuple \ x, y) \left[\begin{array}{l} x \prec_{tuple} y \\ \equiv \\ x \preceq_{tuple} y \ \ and \ \ not \ (x = y) \end{array}\right] \qquad (proper \ subtuple)$$

Because the subtuple relation $\preceq_{tuple}$ is a weak partial ordering, we know (by the *irreflexive-restriction* proposition of the theory of the weak partial ordering $\preceq_{tuple}$) that the proper-subtuple relation $\prec_{tuple}$ is a strict partial ordering, and hence has the following properties:

$$(\forall \ tuple \ x, y, z) \left[\begin{array}{l} if \ \ x \prec_{tuple} y \ \ and \ \ y \prec_{tuple} z \\ then \ \ x \prec_{tuple} z \end{array}\right] \qquad (transitivity)$$

$$(\forall \ tuple \ x) \left[not \ (x \prec_{tuple} x) \right] \qquad (irreflexivity)$$

$$(\forall \ tuple \ x, y) \left[\begin{array}{l} if \ \ x \prec_{tuple} y \\ then \ \ not \ (y \prec_{tuple} x) \end{array}\right] \qquad (asymmetry)$$

We can also establish the mixed-transitivity properties

$$(\forall \ tuple \ x, y, z) \left[\begin{array}{l} if \ \ x \preceq_{tuple} y \ \ and \ \ y \prec_{tuple} z \\ then \ \ x \prec_{tuple} z \end{array}\right]$$
$$(left \ mixed \ transitivity)$$

$$(\forall \ tuple \ x, y, z) \left[\begin{array}{l} if \ \ x \prec_{tuple} y \ \ and \ \ y \preceq_{tuple} z \\ then \ \ x \prec_{tuple} z \end{array}\right]$$
$$(right \ mixed \ transitivity)$$

Using properties of tuples, we can show the following properties of $\prec_{tuple}$:

$$(\forall \ tuple \ x) \left[not \ (x \prec_{tuple} \langle \, \rangle) \right] \qquad (right \ empty)$$

$$\begin{array}{l} (\forall \ atom \ u) \\ (\forall \ tuple \ x) \end{array} \left[x \prec_{tuple} u \diamond x \right] \qquad (insertion \ adjacent)$$

$$\begin{array}{l}(\forall\ atom\ u) \\ (\forall\ tuple\ x)\end{array}\Big[x \prec_{tuple} x \diamond \langle u\rangle\Big] \qquad\qquad (suffix\ adjacent)$$

$$\begin{array}{l}(\forall\ atom\ u) \\ (\forall\ tuple\ x,\ y)\end{array}\Big[x \diamond y \ \prec_{tuple}\ x \diamond \langle u\rangle \diamond y\Big] \qquad (append\text{-}singleton)$$

$$(\forall\ tuple\ x)\ \begin{bmatrix}if\ \ not\ (x = \langle\ \rangle) \\ then\ \ tail(x) \prec_{tuple} x\end{bmatrix} \qquad\qquad (tail)$$

⟦In the two-volume version of this book, we write $\subseteq$ instead of $\preceq_{tuple}$.⟧

9.6   THE COMPLETE INDUCTION PRINCIPLE

Using the proper-subtuple relation $\prec_{tuple}$, we can state and prove an alternative version of the *induction* principle for tuples. This principle is called the *complete induction principle* for the tuples; it is analogous to the *complete induction* principle for the nonnegative integers.

Proposition (complete induction)

For each sentence $\mathcal{F}[x]$, the universal closure of the sentence

$$if\ (\forall\ tuple\ x)\ \begin{bmatrix}if\ (\forall\ tuple\ x')\begin{bmatrix}if\ x' \prec_{tuple} x \\ then\ \mathcal{F}[x']\end{bmatrix} \\ then\ \mathcal{F}[x]\end{bmatrix}$$
$$then\ (\forall\ tuple\ x)\mathcal{F}[x]$$

$$(complete\ induction)$$

where x' does not occur free in $\mathcal{F}[x]$, is valid. ⌟

To distinguish between the two induction principles, we refer to the original induction, including *decomposition* induction, as *stepwise induction*.

We omit the proof of the proposition. Let us illustrate its application here.

PALINDROMES

We first introduce the notion of a "palindrome," a symmetric tuple, which reads the same left to right as right to left. For example, $\langle$C, A, A, C$\rangle$ and $\langle$C, A, B, A, C$\rangle$ are palindromes; the empty tuple $\langle\ \rangle$ is regarded as a palindrome.

Formally we introduce a unary predicate symbol $palin(x)$ to denote that the tuple x is a palindrome. It is defined by the following axiom:

$$(\forall\ tuple\ x)\ \begin{bmatrix} palin(x) \\ \equiv \\ x = reverse(x) \end{bmatrix} \qquad\qquad (palindrome)$$

From this axiom we establish the following property of palindromes.

Proposition (palindrome)

The sentence

$$(\forall\ tuple\ x)\ \begin{bmatrix} palin(x) \\ \equiv \\ \begin{bmatrix} (\exists\ tuple\ y)\,[x\ =\ y \diamond reverse(y)] \\ or \\ \begin{matrix}(\exists\ atom\ u)\\(\exists\ tuple\ y)\end{matrix}\,[x\ =\ y \diamond \langle u\rangle \diamond reverse(y)] \end{bmatrix} \end{bmatrix}$$

is valid. ⌐

Note that, in stating the proposition, we may write $y \diamond \langle u\rangle \diamond reverse(y)$ without parentheses because the append function $\diamond$ is associative.

Intuitively speaking, the proposition states that a palindrome is built up in one of two ways: Either it has an even number of atoms and is of the form $y \diamond reverse(y)$, or it has an odd number of atoms and is of the form $y\diamond\langle u\rangle\diamond reverse(y)$, for some atom u and tuple y. For example,

$$\langle C,\ A,\ A,\ C\rangle\ =\ \langle C,\ A\rangle \diamond reverse(\langle C,\ A\rangle)$$

$$\langle C,\ A,\ B,\ A,\ C\rangle\ =\ \langle C,\ A\rangle \diamond \langle B\rangle \diamond reverse(\langle C,\ A\rangle).$$

The proof of this proposition, which uses the *complete induction* principle for tuples, is more complex than those we have seen previously. It relies on the following property of the append function:

$$(\forall\ tuple\ x)\ \begin{bmatrix} x = \langle\ \rangle \\ or \\ singleton(x) \\ or \\ \begin{matrix}(\exists\ atom\ v,w)\\(\exists\ tuple\ y)\end{matrix}\,[x = \langle v\rangle \diamond y \diamond \langle w\rangle] \end{bmatrix}$$

$$(prefix\text{-}suffix\ decomposition)$$

In other words, a tuple is either empty or a singleton, or (if it has at least two atoms) it may be obtained by affixing atoms to the beginning and end of some other tuple. The reader was asked to prove this property in Problem 9.6(d).

Proof (palindrome).   By predicate logic it suffices to prove the two sentences

$$(\Rightarrow) \quad (\forall \ tuple \ x) \begin{bmatrix} if \ palin(x) \\ then \begin{bmatrix} (\exists \ tuple \ y)\big[x \ = \ y \diamond reverse(y)\big] \\ or \\ \begin{matrix} (\exists \ atom \ u) \\ (\exists \ tuple \ y) \end{matrix}\big[x \ = \ y \diamond \langle u \rangle \diamond reverse(y)\big] \end{bmatrix} \end{bmatrix}$$

and

$$(\Leftarrow) \quad (\forall \ tuple \ x) \begin{bmatrix} if \begin{bmatrix} (\exists \ tuple \ y)\big[x \ = \ y \diamond reverse(y) \\ or \\ \begin{matrix} (\exists \ atom \ u) \\ (\exists \ tuple \ y) \end{matrix}\big[x \ = \ y \diamond \langle u \rangle \diamond reverse(y)\big] \end{bmatrix} \\ then \ palin(x) \end{bmatrix}$$

We prove only the ($\Rightarrow$) part here; the proof of the ($\Leftarrow$) part is left as an exercise (**Problem 9.14**).

The proof of the ($\Rightarrow$) part is by complete induction on x, taking the inductive sentence to be

$$\mathcal{F}[x]: \quad \begin{matrix} if \ palin(x) \\ then \end{matrix} \begin{bmatrix} (\exists \ tuple \ y)\big[x \ = \ y \diamond reverse(y)\big] \\ or \\ \begin{matrix} (\exists \ atom \ u) \\ (\exists \ tuple \ y) \end{matrix}\big[x \ = \ y \diamond \langle u \rangle \diamond reverse(y)\big] \end{bmatrix}$$

To prove

$$(\forall \ tuple \ x)\mathcal{F}[x],$$

it suffices to establish a single inductive step.

Inductive Step

We would like to show

$$(\forall \ tuple \ x) \begin{bmatrix} if \ (\forall \ tuple \ x') \begin{bmatrix} if \ x' \prec_{tuple} x \\ then \ \mathcal{F}[x'] \end{bmatrix} \\ then \ \mathcal{F}[x] \end{bmatrix}$$

For an arbitrary tuple x, we assume the induction hypothesis

$$(\forall \ tuple \ x') \begin{bmatrix} if \ x' \prec_{tuple} x \\ then \ \mathcal{F}[x'] \end{bmatrix}$$

and attempt to show the desired conclusion

$$\mathcal{F}[x],$$

that is,

$$if \ palin(x)$$
$$then \begin{bmatrix} (\exists \ tuple \ y)[x \ = \ y \diamond reverse(y)] \\ or \\ (\exists \ atom \ u) \\ (\exists \ tuple \ y) \end{bmatrix} [x \ = \ y \diamond \langle u \rangle \diamond reverse(y)] \end{bmatrix}.$$

Suppose that x is a palindrome, that is,

$$palin(x);$$

then we want to show

(†)
$$(\exists \ tuple \ y)[x \ = \ y \diamond reverse(y)]$$
$$or$$
$$\begin{matrix} (\exists \ atom \ u) \\ (\exists \ tuple \ y) \end{matrix} [x \ = \ y \diamond \langle u \rangle \diamond reverse(y)].$$

We distinguish among three cases, according to whether x is empty, a single-ton, or a longer tuple.

Case: $x = \langle \ \rangle$

Then we have

$$x \ = \ \langle \ \rangle \diamond \langle \ \rangle$$
         (by the *left-empty* axiom for append)

$$= \ \langle \ \rangle \diamond reverse(\langle \ \rangle)$$
         (by the *empty* axiom for *reverse*).

Hence (by the *existential quantifier-instantiation* proposition, taking y to be $\langle \ \rangle$),

$$(\exists \ tuple \ y)[x \ = \ y \diamond reverse(y)].$$

This is one disjunct of the desired result (†).

Case: $singleton(x)$

Then we have (by the definition of the *singleton* relation) that there exists an atom u such that

$$x \ = \ \langle u \rangle.$$

Therefore,

$$x \ = \ \langle \ \rangle \diamond \langle u \rangle \diamond \langle \ \rangle$$
         (by the *left-empty* axiom and the *right-empty* property
         of append)

$$= \ \langle \ \rangle \diamond \langle u \rangle \diamond reverse(\langle \ \rangle)$$
         (by the *empty* axiom for *reverse*).

Hence (by the *existential quantifier-instantiation* proposition, taking y to be $\langle\,\rangle$, because u is an atom) we have

$$\begin{matrix}(\exists\ atom\ u)\\(\exists\ tuple\ y)\end{matrix}\left[x\ =\ y \diamond \langle u \rangle \diamond reverse(y)\right].$$

This is one disjunct of the desired result (†).

Case: $not\ (x = \langle\,\rangle)\ and\ not\ \big(singleton(x)\big)$

Then (by the *prefix-suffix decomposition* property of append mentioned above) we have

$$\begin{matrix}(\exists\ atom\ v,w)\\(\exists\ tuple\ x')\end{matrix}\left[x\ =\ \langle v \rangle \diamond x' \diamond \langle w \rangle\right].$$

Let v and w be atoms and x' be a tuple such that

$$x\ =\ \langle v \rangle \diamond x' \diamond \langle w \rangle.$$

We shall first show that x' is a proper subtuple of x, so that we can apply the induction hypothesis to x'.

Proof that $x' \prec_{tuple} x$

We know (by the *left-append* property of $\preceq_{tuple}$) that

$$x'\ \preceq_{tuple}\ x' \diamond \langle w \rangle.$$

Also (by the *insertion-adjacent* property of $\prec_{tuple}$, because v is an atom) we have

$$x' \diamond \langle w \rangle\ \prec_{tuple}\ v \diamond (x' \diamond \langle w \rangle),$$

that is (by the *atom* property for append, because v is an atom),

$$x' \diamond \langle w \rangle\ \prec_{tuple}\ \langle v \rangle \diamond x' \diamond \langle w \rangle.$$

Hence (by the *left mixed-transitivity* property of the subtuple relation)

$$x'\ \prec_{tuple}\ \langle v \rangle \diamond x' \diamond \langle w \rangle,$$

that is (because $x = \langle v \rangle \diamond x' \diamond \langle w \rangle$),

$$x'\ \prec_{tuple}\ x.$$

Thus x' is a proper subtuple of x, and we can apply the induction hypothesis to x'.

The induction hypothesis now tells us that $\mathcal{F}[x']$, that is,

$$(\ddagger)\qquad\begin{matrix}if\ \ palin(x')\\[4pt]then\end{matrix}\quad\begin{bmatrix}(\exists\ tuple\ y')\left[x'\ =\ y' \diamond reverse(y')\right]\\or\\(\exists\ atom\ u')\\(\exists\ tuple\ y')\end{bmatrix}\left[x'\ =\ y' \diamond \langle u' \rangle \diamond reverse(y')\right]\end{bmatrix}$$

Note that we have renamed the bound variables y and u to y' and u', respectively, to avoid future confusion.

Let us now show that x' is a palindrome, so that we may deduce the consequent of (‡).

Proof of palin(x')

We have (recalling that v and w are atoms)

$$v \diamond (x' \diamond \langle w \rangle) \;=\; \langle v \rangle \diamond x' \diamond \langle w \rangle$$
$$\text{(by the } singleton \text{ property of append)}$$

$$=\; x$$

$$=\; reverse(x)$$
$$\text{(by the definition of palindrome}$$
$$\text{and our supposition that } palin(x))$$

$$=\; reverse(\langle v \rangle \diamond x' \diamond \langle w \rangle)$$

$$=\; reverse(x' \diamond \langle w \rangle) \diamond reverse(\langle v \rangle)$$
$$\text{(by the } append \text{ property of } reverse)$$

$$=\; reverse(x' \diamond \langle w \rangle) \diamond \langle v \rangle$$
$$\text{(by the } singleton \text{ property of } reverse)$$

$$=\; \big(w \diamond reverse(x')\big) \diamond \langle v \rangle$$
$$\text{(by the } suffix \text{ property of } reverse)$$

$$=\; w \diamond \big(reverse(x') \diamond \langle v \rangle\big)$$
$$\text{(by the } left\text{-}insertion \text{ axiom for append).}$$

In short,

$$v \diamond (x' \diamond \langle w \rangle) \;=\; w \diamond \big(reverse(x') \diamond \langle v \rangle\big).$$

Hence (by the *insertion* uniqueness axiom for tuples)

$$v \;=\; w \qquad \text{and} \qquad x' \diamond \langle w \rangle \;=\; reverse(x') \diamond \langle v \rangle.$$

Consequently (by the *suffix-uniqueness* property for append, because w and v are atoms),

$$x' \;=\; reverse(x')$$

and hence (by the definition of palindrome)

$$palin(x').$$

We therefore can conclude from (‡) that

$$(\exists \; tuple \; y')\big[x' \;=\; y' \diamond reverse(y')\big]$$
$$or$$
$$(\exists \; atom \; u')\big[x' \;=\; y' \diamond \langle u' \rangle \diamond reverse(y')\big].$$
$$(\exists \; tuple \; y')$$

It remains to show the desired result (†).

Proof of (†)

Let y' be a tuple and u' an atom such that
$$x' = y' \diamond reverse(y')$$
or
$$x' = y' \diamond \langle u' \rangle \diamond reverse(y').$$

Therefore (appending the atom v on the left and right, by the substitutivity of equality)
$$\langle v \rangle \diamond x' \diamond \langle v \rangle = \langle v \rangle \diamond y' \diamond reverse(y') \diamond \langle v \rangle$$
or
$$\langle v \rangle \diamond x' \diamond \langle v \rangle = \langle v \rangle \diamond y' \diamond \langle u' \rangle \diamond reverse(y') \diamond \langle v \rangle.$$

Then, because $\langle v \rangle \diamond x' \diamond \langle w \rangle = x$ and $w = v$, we have
$$x = \langle v \rangle \diamond y' \diamond reverse(y') \diamond \langle v \rangle$$
or
$$x = \langle v \rangle \diamond y' \diamond \langle u' \rangle \diamond reverse(y') \diamond \langle v \rangle.$$

Hence (by the *singleton* property of append applied to $\langle v \rangle \diamond y'$ and the *insertion* axiom for *reverse* applied to $reverse(y') \diamond \langle v \rangle$, because v is an atom) we have
$$x = (v \diamond y') \diamond reverse(v \diamond y')$$
or
$$x = (v \diamond y') \diamond \langle u' \rangle \diamond reverse(v \diamond y').$$

In the case in which
$$x = (v \diamond y') \diamond reverse(v \diamond y'),$$
we have (by the *existential quantifier-instantiation* proposition, taking y to be $v \diamond y'$, because $v \diamond y'$ is a tuple)
$$(\exists \ tuple \ y)\big[x = y \diamond reverse(y)\big]$$
which is one disjunct of our desired result (†).

In the case in which
$$x = (v \diamond y') \diamond \langle u' \rangle \diamond reverse(v \diamond y'),$$
we have (by the *existential quantifier-instantiation* proposition, again, taking u to be u' and y to be $v \diamond y'$, because u' is an atom and $v \diamond y'$ is a tuple)
$$\begin{matrix}(\exists \ atom \ u) \\ (\exists \ tuple \ y)\end{matrix}\big[x = y \diamond \langle u \rangle \diamond reverse(y)\big],$$
which is the other disjunct of our desired result (†). ∎

The *palindrome* proposition would have been less convenient to prove by step-wise induction. In the inductive step of, say, a decomposition induction proof, we consider an arbitrary nonempty tuple x, assume the induction hypothesis $\mathcal{F}[tail(x)]$, and attempt to establish the desired conclusion $\mathcal{F}[x]$. But this induction hypothesis would be of little use in the above proof, because if x is a palindrome, $tail(x)$ generally is not. To find a subtuple x' that is a palindrome, to which the (complete) induction hypothesis could be applied, it was necessary to chop off both the first atom v and the last atom w of x, not just the first atom.

INITIAL- AND CONSECUTIVE-SUBTUPLE RELATIONS

We have introduced an end relation $x \preceq_{end} y$, which holds if the elements of tuple x occur at the end of tuple y. We shall also find it convenient to introduce an *initial-subtuple* relation $x \preceq_{init} y$, which holds if the elements of x occur at the beginning of tuple y. For example,

$$\langle A,\ B \rangle \preceq_{init} \langle A,\ B,\ C \rangle.$$

The new binary predicate symbol $x \preceq_{init} y$ is defined by the following three axioms

$$
\begin{array}{ll}
(\forall\ tuple\ y)\left[\langle\ \rangle\ \preceq_{init}\ y\right] & (\textit{left empty}) \\[2em]
\begin{array}{l}(\forall\ atom\ u) \\ (\forall\ tuple\ x)\end{array}\left[not\ (u \diamond x\ \preceq_{init}\ \langle\ \rangle)\right] & (\textit{right empty}) \\[2em]
\begin{array}{l}(\forall\ atom\ u,\ v) \\ (\forall\ tuple\ x, y)\end{array}\left[\begin{array}{c} u \diamond x\ \preceq_{init}\ v \diamond y \\ \equiv \\ u = v\ and\ x \preceq_{init}\ y\end{array}\right] & (\textit{insertion})
\end{array}
$$

From these axioms, we can establish the property

$$
(\forall\ tuple\ x, y)\left[\begin{array}{c} x \preceq_{init}\ y \\ \equiv \\ (\exists\ tuple\ z)\left[x \diamond z = y\right]\end{array}\right] \qquad (\textit{append})
$$

The proof is requested in **Problem 9.15**.

We have defined the subtuple relation $x \preceq_{tuple} y$ so that it holds if the elements of x occur in y in the same order but not necessarily consecutively. For example,

$$\langle A,\ A,\ B \rangle \preceq_{tuple} \langle C,\ A,\ C,\ A,\ B \rangle.$$

Suppose we define a new binary predicate symbol $x \preceq_{tuple1} y$ by the following four axioms:

$$(\forall \ tuple \ y)\big[\langle\ \rangle \ \preceq_{tuple1} y\big] \qquad\qquad (left \ empty)$$

$$\begin{matrix}(\forall \ atom \ u)\\(\forall \ tuple \ x)\end{matrix}\big[not \ \big(u \diamond x \preceq_{tuple1} \langle\ \rangle\big)\big] \qquad (right \ empty)$$

$$\begin{matrix}(\forall \ atom \ u)\\(\forall \ tuple \ x,y)\end{matrix}\begin{bmatrix}u \diamond x \ \preceq_{tuple1} \ u \diamond y\\ \equiv \\ x \ \preceq_{init} y \ \ or \ \ u \diamond x \ \preceq_{tuple1} \ y\end{bmatrix} \qquad (equal \ insertion)$$

$$\begin{matrix}(\forall \ atom \ u,v)\\(\forall \ tuple \ x,y)\end{matrix}\begin{bmatrix}if \ \ not \ (u=v)\\ \\ then \quad \begin{bmatrix}u \diamond x \ \preceq_{tuple1} \ v \diamond y\\ \equiv \\ u \diamond x \ \preceq_{tuple1} \ y\end{bmatrix}\end{bmatrix} \qquad (nonequal \ insertion)$$

The relation $x \preceq_{tuple1} y$ holds if the elements of x occur consecutively in y in the same order. For example,

$$\langle A, \ A, \ B\rangle \preceq_{tuple1} \langle C, \ A, \ A, \ B, \ C\rangle$$

but

$$not \ \langle A, \ A, \ B\rangle \preceq_{tuple1} \langle A, \ C, \ A, \ B\rangle.$$

In **Problem 9.16**, the reader is asked to prove some properties of the consecutive-subtuple relation. In **Problem 9.17**, an alternative definition of the relation is proposed.

9.7 NONNEGATIVE INTEGERS AND TUPLES

Under the intended models for the theory of the nonnegative integers, every term denotes a nonnegative integer. Under the intended models for the theory of tuples, every term denotes a tuple or an atom. But how do we formulate a theory whose sentences may discuss nonnegative integers, tuples, and atoms? For example, we might wish to define a function $length(x)$, denoting the number of atoms in a given tuple x, and to establish that, for all tuples x and y,

$$length(x \diamond y) = length(x) + length(y).$$

We cannot define the *length* function and establish the above property in either theory alone. In this section we show how to combine the theories of the nonnegative integers and the tuples into a single theory in which we can establish properties that discuss objects from both theories.

The axioms for the combined theory include all the axioms for the constituent theories. In the combined theory we have a single binary equality predicate symbol =, satisfying the usual axioms for equality.

Because the axioms for the combined theory include the axioms for the constituent theories, any sentence we can prove valid in the theory of the nonnegative integers or the theory of tuples is also valid in the combined theory. We also include the axioms that define new functions and relations, such as the addition function and the subtuple relation.

Note that the axioms for the combined theory do not specify the relationship between the nonnegative integers and the tuples. In some augmentations of the combined theory we will assume that the two classes are disjoint; this will be expressed by adding the axiom

$$(\forall\ x)\big[not\ (integer(x)\ and\ tuple(x))\big] \qquad\qquad (disjoint)$$

Under the models for a combined theory that includes this axiom, no domain element can be both a nonnegative integer and a tuple.

But first let us establish some results in a combined theory (without the *disjoint* axiom) in which we know nothing about the relationship between nonnegative integers and tuples.

THE LENGTH FUNCTION

Let us define a unary function symbol $length(x)$ in the combined theory of the nonnegative integers and tuples. Under the intended model for the combined theory, $length(x)$ denotes the number of atoms in the tuple x; for example,

$$length(\langle A,\ A,\ B\rangle)\ =\ 3.$$

As we have remarked, this function can only be defined in the combined theory, because its argument is a tuple and its value is a nonnegative integer.

The *length* function is defined by the axioms

$$length(\langle\ \rangle)\ =\ 0 \qquad\qquad (empty)$$

$$(\forall\ atom\ u) \atop (\forall\ tuple\ x) \big[length(u \diamond x)\ =\ length(x) + 1\big] \qquad (insertion)$$

From these axioms we can establish the validity of the following properties of the *length* function in the combined theory:

$$(\forall \ tuple \ x)\big[integer\,(length(x))\big] \hspace{3cm} (sort)$$

$$(\forall \ tuple \ x)\begin{bmatrix}if \ \ length(x) = 0 \\ then \ \ x = \langle\,\rangle\end{bmatrix} \hspace{3cm} (zero)$$

$$(\forall \ atom \ u)\big[length(\langle u\rangle) = 1\big] \hspace{3cm} (singleton)$$

$$(\forall \ tuple \ x,y)\big[length(x \diamond y) \ = \ length(x) + length(y)\big] \hspace{1cm} (append)$$

$$(\forall \ tuple \ x)\big[length\,(reverse(x)) \ = \ length(x)\big] \hspace{2cm} (reverse)$$

$$(\forall \ tuple \ x,y)\begin{bmatrix}if \ \ x \prec_{tuple} y \\ then \ \ length(x) < length(y)\end{bmatrix} \hspace{1.5cm} (proper \ subtuple)$$

We establish the *append* property here; the proofs of the other properties are left as an exercise (**Problem 9.18**).

Proposition (append)

The sentence

$$(\forall \ tuple \ x,y)\big[length(x \diamond y) \ = \ length(x) + length(y)\big]$$

is valid (in the combined theory). ⌐

Proof.   We actually prove the equivalent sentence

$$(\forall \ tuple \ y,x)\big[length(x \diamond y) \ = \ length(x) + length(y)\big],$$

obtained by reversing the quantifiers. Consider an arbitrary tuple y; we would like to show

$$(\forall \ tuple \ x)\big[length(x \diamond y) \ = \ length(x) + length(y)\big].$$

The proof is by stepwise induction over the tuples, taking the inductive sentence to be

$$\mathcal{F}[x]: \quad length(x \diamond y) \ = \ length(x) + length(y).$$

Base Case

We want to prove

$$\mathcal{F}[\langle\,\rangle]: \quad length(\langle\,\rangle \diamond y) \ = \ length(\langle\,\rangle) + length(y).$$

We have

$$length(\langle\,\rangle) + length(y)$$

$$= \ 0 + length(y)$$
$$\text{(by the } \textit{empty} \text{ axiom for the } \textit{length} \text{ function)}$$

$$= \ length(y)$$
$$\text{(by the } \textit{left-zero} \text{ property of addition)}$$

$$= \ length(\langle \, \rangle \diamond y)$$
$$\text{(by the } \textit{left-empty} \text{ axiom for append).}$$

Inductive Step

For an arbitrary atom u and tuple x, assume the induction hypothesis

$$\mathcal{F}[x]: \quad length(x \diamond y) \ = \ length(x) + length(y).$$

We would like to show the desired conclusion

$$\mathcal{F}[u \diamond x]: \quad length\big((u \diamond x) \diamond y\big) \ = \ length(u \diamond x) + length(y).$$

Because u is an atom, we have

$$length\big((u \diamond x) \diamond y\big) \ = \ length\big(u \diamond (x \diamond y)\big)$$
$$\text{(by the } \textit{left-insertion} \text{ axiom for append)}$$

$$= \ length(x \diamond y) + 1$$
$$\text{(by the } \textit{insertion} \text{ axiom for } \textit{length})$$

$$= \ \big(length(x) + length(y)\big) + 1$$
$$\text{(by our induction hypothesis).}$$

But on the other hand,

$$length(u \diamond x) + length(y)$$

$$= \ \big(length(x) + 1\big) + length(y)$$
$$\text{(by the } \textit{insertion} \text{ axiom for the } \textit{length} \text{ function again)}$$

$$= \ \big(length(x) + length(y)\big) + 1$$
$$\text{(by the } \textit{left-successor} \text{ property of addition).} \quad \lrcorner$$

In **Problem 9.19**, we introduce functions $left(x)$ and $right(x)$, which divide a tuple x into two roughly equal parts, and relate these functions to the *length* function. In **Problem 9.20**, we introduce a periodicity relation on tuples.

THE COUNT FUNCTION

The binary function symbol $count(u, x)$ denotes the number of occurrences of the atom u in the tuple x. It is defined by the following axioms:

$$(\forall\ atom\ u)\left[count(u,\ \langle\ \rangle)\ =\ 0\right] \qquad\qquad (empty)$$

$$\begin{array}{l}(\forall\ atom\ u)\\(\forall\ tuple\ x)\end{array}\left[count(u,\ u \diamond x)\ =\ count(u,\ x) + 1\right]$$

$$(equal\ insertion)$$

$$\begin{array}{l}(\forall\ atom\ u, v)\\(\forall\ tuple\ x)\end{array}\left[\begin{array}{l}if\quad not\ (u = v)\\then\quad count(u,\ v \diamond x)\ =\ count(u,\ x)\end{array}\right]$$

$$(nonequal\ insertion)$$

In terms of the *count* function we can characterize the *member* relation by the property

$$\begin{array}{l}(\forall\ atom\ u)\\(\forall\ tuple\ x)\end{array}\left[\begin{array}{c}u \in x\\\equiv\\not\ (count(u,\ x) = 0)\end{array}\right] \qquad (count\ of\ member)$$

We can also characterize the equal-multiplicity relation *eqmult* by the property

$$\begin{array}{l}(\forall\ atom\ u)\\(\forall\ tuple\ x, y)\end{array}\left[\begin{array}{c}eqmult(u,\ x,\ y)\\\equiv\\count(u,\ x)\ =\ count(u,\ y)\end{array}\right] \qquad (count\ of\ eqmult)$$

THE ELEMENT FUNCTION

The binary function symbol $[x]_z$ denotes the zth element of the tuple x, where z is a nonnegative integer. For example,

$$[\langle A,\ B,\ C\rangle]_0\ =\ A$$

$$[\langle A,\ B,\ C\rangle]_1\ =\ B$$

$$[\langle A,\ B,\ C\rangle]_2\ =\ C.$$

Note that we enumerate the elements of the tuple x beginning with 0, not 1.

The *element* function is defined by the axioms

$$\begin{array}{l}(\forall\ atom\ u)\\(\forall\ tuple\ x)\end{array}\left[[u \diamond x]_0\ =\ u\right] \qquad\qquad (zero)$$

$$\begin{array}{l}(\forall\ atom\ u)\\(\forall\ tuple\ x)\\(\forall\ integer\ z)\end{array}\left[[u \diamond x]_{z+1}\ =\ [x]_z\right] \qquad\qquad (successor)$$

Note that the axioms do not specify the value of $[y]_z$ if y is the empty tuple or, in general, if z is greater than or equal to $length(x)$. For example, they do not specify the value of $\big[\langle A,\ B,\ C\rangle\big]_3$.

The append function is related to the element function by the following two properties:

$$(\forall\ tuple\ x,y)\ \begin{bmatrix} if\ \ z < length(x) \\ then\ \ [x \diamond y]_z\ =\ [x]_z \end{bmatrix} \qquad\qquad (left\ element)$$
$$(\forall\ integer\ z)$$

$$(\forall\ tuple\ x,y)\ \begin{bmatrix} if\ \ z < length(y) \\ then\ \ [x \diamond y]_{length(x)+z}\ =\ [y]_z \end{bmatrix} \qquad\qquad (right\ element)$$
$$(\forall\ integer\ z)$$

The proofs are left as an exercise (**Problem 9.21**).

THE ALTER FUNCTION

The ternary function symbol $alter(x, z, u)$ denotes the tuple obtained by replacing the zth element of the tuple x with the atom u, where z is a nonnegative integer. For example,

$$alter\big(\langle A,\ B,\ B\rangle,\ 2,\ C\big)\ =\ \langle A,\ B,\ C\rangle.$$

Again we begin our enumeration of the elements of the tuple with 0, not 1.

The $alter$ function is defined by the following axioms:

$$(\forall\ atom\ u,v)\ \big[alter(u \diamond x,\ 0,\ v)\ =\ v \diamond x\big] \qquad\qquad (zero)$$
$$(\forall\ tuple\ x)$$

$$(\forall\ atom\ u,v)\ \begin{bmatrix} alter(u \diamond x,\ z+1,\ v) \\ = \\ u \diamond alter(x,\ z,\ v) \end{bmatrix} \qquad\qquad (successor)$$
$$(\forall\ tuple\ x)$$
$$(\forall\ integer\ z)$$

Note that these axioms specify the result $alter(x,\ z,\ v)$ of altering the zth element of a tuple x only if z is less than $length(x)$. For example, the values of $alter\big(\langle\ \rangle,\ 0,\ D\big)$ and of $alter\big(\langle A, B, C\rangle,\ 3,\ D\big)$ are not specified.

From these axioms we can establish the following properties:

$$\begin{array}{l} (\forall \ atom \ v) \\ (\forall \ tuple \ x) \\ (\forall \ integer \ z) \end{array} \left[\begin{array}{l} if \ \ z < length(x) \\ then \ \ tuple\big(alter(x, \ z, \ v)\big) \end{array} \right] \qquad (sort)$$

$$\begin{array}{l} (\forall \ atom \ v) \\ (\forall \ tuple \ x) \\ (\forall \ integer \ z) \end{array} \left[\begin{array}{l} if \ \ z < length(x) \\ then \ \ \big[alter(x, \ z, \ v)\big]_z = v \end{array} \right] \qquad (equal)$$

$$\begin{array}{l} (\forall \ atom \ v) \\ (\forall \ tuple \ x) \\ (\forall \ integer \ z, z') \end{array} \left[\begin{array}{l} if \ \ z < length(x) \ \ and \ \ z' < length(x) \\ then \ \ if \ \ not \ (z = z') \\ \qquad then \ \ \big[alter(x, \ z, \ v)\big]_{z'} = \big[x\big]_{z'} \end{array} \right] \qquad (nonequal)$$

9.8   THE PERMUTATION RELATION

A tuple is said to be a *permutation* of another tuple if each can be obtained from the other simply by rearranging the elements; thus $\langle A, A, B \rangle$ is a permutation of $\langle B, A, A \rangle$ but not of $\langle A, A, C \rangle$, $\langle A, B \rangle$, or $\langle A, B, B \rangle$. Note that, for one tuple to be a permutation of another, any atom must have the same multiplicity in each tuple.

We define the permutation relation $perm(x, y)$, which holds if x is a permutation of y, by the following three axioms:

$$\boxed{ \ perm(\langle \ \rangle, \ \langle \ \rangle) \qquad\qquad\qquad\qquad\qquad\qquad (empty) \ }$$

$$\boxed{ \begin{array}{l} \\ (\forall \ atom \ u) \\ (\forall \ tuple \ x_1, x_2, y_1, y_2) \end{array} \left[\begin{array}{l} perm(x_1 \Diamond \langle u \rangle \Diamond x_2, \ y_1 \Diamond \langle u \rangle \Diamond y_2) \\ \equiv \\ perm(x_1 \Diamond x_2, \ y_1 \Diamond y_2) \\ \qquad\qquad\qquad\qquad (append\text{-}singleton) \end{array} \right] }$$

The *append-singleton* axiom states that two tuples having a common element u are permutations if and only if the tuples obtained by deleting the element u from each of them are also permutations.

$$\boxed{ (\forall \ tuple \ x, y) \left[\begin{array}{l} if \ \ perm(x, y) \\ then \ \ (\forall \ atom \ u) \left[\begin{array}{l} u \in x \\ \equiv \\ u \in y \end{array} \right] \end{array} \right] \qquad (member) }$$

The *member* axiom states that if two tuples are permutations, they have the same elements.

These axioms suggest a method for computing whether two tuples x and y are permutations:

- If x and y are empty, they are indeed permutations (by the *empty* axiom).
- Otherwise, if x and y have a common element u, we delete u from each tuple (by the *append-singleton* axiom) and compute whether the resulting tuples are permutations.
- Otherwise, some element of one of the tuples is not an element of the other; therefore (by the contrapositive of the *member* axiom) the tuples are not permutations.

It is not immediately clear, however, that the relation defined by the above axioms coincides with our intuitive notion of permutation. This is made more plausible by the following result.

Proposition (equal multiplicity)

The sentence

$$(\forall \ tuple \ x, y) \begin{bmatrix} perm(x, \ y) \\ \equiv \\ (\forall \ atom \ u)\big[eqmult(u, \ x, \ y)\big] \end{bmatrix} \qquad (eqmult)$$

is valid. ⌐

In other words, two tuples are permutations if and only if every atom has the same multiplicity in either tuple.

Proof. The proof is by stepwise induction on x, taking the inductive sentence to be

$$\mathcal{F}[x]: \quad (\forall \ tuple \ y) \begin{bmatrix} perm(x, \ y) \\ \equiv \\ (\forall \ atom \ u)\big[eqmult(u, \ x, \ y)\big] \end{bmatrix}.$$

Base Case

We would like to show

$$\mathcal{F}[\langle \ \rangle]: \quad (\forall \ tuple \ y) \begin{bmatrix} perm(\langle \ \rangle, \ y) \\ \equiv \\ (\forall \ atom \ u)\big[eqmult(u, \ \langle \ \rangle, \ y)\big] \end{bmatrix}.$$

Consider an arbitrary tuple y; we must show

$$perm(\langle \ \rangle, \ y)$$
$$\equiv$$
$$(\forall \ atom \ u)\big[eqmult(u, \ \langle \ \rangle, \ y)\big].$$

We distinguish between two cases, according to whether or not y is empty.

Case: $y = \langle\,\rangle$

In this case, the left-hand side

$$perm(\langle\,\rangle,\ \langle\,\rangle)$$

is true (by the *empty* axiom for *perm*) and the right-hand side

$$(\forall\ atom\ u)\big[eqmult(u,\ \langle\,\rangle,\ \langle\,\rangle)\big]$$

is true (by the *empty* axiom for *eqmult*); therefore the entire equivalence is true.

Case: $not\ (y = \langle\,\rangle)$

Then (by the *decomposition* property of tuples) there exist an atom w and a tuple y' such that

$$y\ =\ w \diamond y'.$$

We know (by the *empty* axiom for the member relation $\in$) that

$$not\ (w \in \langle\,\rangle)$$

and (by the *component* property of the member relation $\in$) that

$$w\ \in\ w \diamond y'.$$

Thus (by the *member* axiom for *perm*) the left-hand side

$$perm(\langle\,\rangle,\ w \diamond y')$$

is false. Also (by the *empty-insertion* axiom for *eqmult*, taking u to be w), the right-hand side

$$(\forall\ atom\ u)\big[eqmult(u,\ \langle\,\rangle,\ w \diamond y')\big]$$

is false. Therefore the entire equivalence is true.

Inductive Step

For an arbitrary atom v and tuple x, assume the induction hypothesis

$$\mathcal{F}[x]:\quad (\forall\ tuple\ y)\ \begin{bmatrix} perm(x,\ y) \\ \equiv \\ (\forall\ atom\ u)\big[eqmult(u,\ x,\ y)\big] \end{bmatrix}.$$

We would like to show that then

$$\mathcal{F}[v \diamond x]:\quad (\forall\ tuple\ y')\ \begin{bmatrix} perm(v \diamond x,\ y') \\ \equiv \\ (\forall\ atom\ u)\big[eqmult(u,\ v \diamond x,\ y')\big] \end{bmatrix}.$$

Consider an arbitrary tuple y'; we must show that

$$perm(v \diamond x,\ y')$$
$$\equiv$$
$$(\forall\ atom\ u)\big[eqmult(u,\ v \diamond x,\ y')\big].$$

We distinguish between two cases, depending on whether or not $v \in y'$.

Case: $v \in y'$

Then (by the *append-singleton* property of the member relation $\in$) there exist tuples y_1 and y_2 such that
$$y' \;=\; y_1 \diamond \langle v \rangle \diamond y_2.$$

The left-hand side of the desired equivalence in this case,
$$perm(v \diamond x, \; y_1 \diamond \langle v \rangle \diamond y_2),$$
holds if and only if (by the *singleton* property of append)
$$perm(\langle v \rangle \diamond x, \; y_1 \diamond \langle v \rangle \diamond y_2)$$
if and only if (by the *left-empty* axiom for append)
$$perm(\langle \; \rangle \diamond \langle v \rangle \diamond x, \; y_1 \diamond \langle v \rangle \diamond y_2)$$
if and only if (by the *append-singleton* axiom for *perm*)
$$perm(\langle \; \rangle \diamond x, \; y_1 \diamond y_2)$$
if and only if (by the *left-empty* axiom for append again)
$$perm(x, \; y_1 \diamond y_2).$$

On the other hand, the right-hand side of the desired equivalence in this case,
$$(\forall \; atom \; u)\big[eqmult(u, \; v \diamond x, \; y_1 \diamond \langle v \rangle \diamond y_2)\big],$$
holds if and only if (by the *singleton* property of append)
$$(\forall \; atom \; u)\big[eqmult(u, \; \langle v \rangle \diamond x, \; y_1 \diamond \langle v \rangle \diamond y_2)\big]$$
if and only if (by the *left-empty* axiom for append)
$$(\forall \; atom \; u)\big[eqmult(u, \; \langle \; \rangle \diamond \langle v \rangle \diamond x, \; y_1 \diamond \langle v \rangle \diamond y_2)\big]$$
if and only if (by the *append-singleton* property of *eqmult*)
$$(\forall \; atom \; u)\big[eqmult(u, \; \langle \; \rangle \diamond x, \; y_1 \diamond y_2)\big]$$
if and only if (by the *left-empty* axiom for append again)
$$(\forall \; atom \; u)\big[eqmult(u, \; x, \; y_1 \diamond y_2)\big]$$
if and only if (by our induction hypothesis $\mathcal{F}[x]$, taking y to be $y_1 \diamond y_2$)
$$perm(x, \; y_1 \diamond y_2).$$

Therefore the desired equivalence is true in this case.

Case: *not* $(v \in y')$

We know (by the *component* property of the member relation $\in$) that
$$v \; \in \; v \diamond x.$$

Then the left-hand side of the desired equivalence,
$$perm(v \diamond x, \; y'),$$

is false (by the *member* axiom for *perm*, because $v \in v \diamond x$ and *not* $(v \in y')$).

But the right-hand side of the desired equivalence,

$$(\forall \, atom \, u)[eqmult(u, \, v \diamond x, \, y')],$$

is also false (taking u to be v, by the *member* property of *eqmult*, because we have $v \in v \diamond x$ and *not* $(v \in y')$).

Therefore the desired equivalence is true in this case too. ◢

Actually, the *eqmult* property of the permutation relation provides an alternative definition of the relation. The proof is requested as an exercise (**Problem 9.22**). Another alternative definition of the permutation relation is given in **Problem 9.23**.

It is possible to establish that the permutation relation *perm* is an equivalence relation over the tuples, that is,

$$(\forall \, tuple \, x, y, z) \begin{bmatrix} if \;\; perm(x, \, y) \;\; and \;\; perm(y, \, z) \\ then \;\; perm(x, \, z) \end{bmatrix} \qquad (transitivity)$$

$$(\forall \, tuple \, x, y) \begin{bmatrix} if \;\; perm(x, \, y) \\ then \;\; perm(y, \, x) \end{bmatrix} \qquad (symmetry)$$

$$(\forall \, tuple \, x)[perm(x, \, x)] \qquad (reflexivity)$$

We can also establish the following properties of the permutation relation:

$$\begin{matrix}(\forall \, atom \, u, v) \\ (\forall \, tuple \, x)\end{matrix}[perm(u \diamond (v \diamond x), \; v \diamond (u \diamond x))] \qquad (exchange)$$

$$\begin{matrix}(\forall \, atom \, u) \\ (\forall \, tuple \, x, y)\end{matrix} \begin{bmatrix} perm(u \diamond x, \; u \diamond y) \\ \equiv \\ perm(x, \, y) \end{bmatrix} \qquad (equal \; insertion)$$

$$(\forall \, tuple \, x_1, x_2, y_1, y_2) \begin{bmatrix} if \;\; perm(x_1, \, y_1) \;\; and \\ \quad perm(x_2, \, y_2) \\ then \;\; perm(x_1 \diamond x_2, \; y_1 \diamond y_2) \end{bmatrix} \qquad (append)$$

$$\begin{matrix}(\forall \, atom \, u) \\ (\forall \, tuple \, x_1, x_2, y)\end{matrix} \begin{bmatrix} perm(x_1 \diamond (u \diamond x_2), \; u \diamond y) \\ \equiv \\ perm(x_1 \diamond x_2, \, y) \end{bmatrix} \qquad (append\text{-}insertion)$$

The proof of the *equal-insertion* property is straightforward; the proofs of the other three are left as an exercise (**Problem 9.24**).

9.9 THE ORDERED RELATION

Consider a combined theory of the tuples and the nonnegative integers in which the atoms of the tuples are identified with the nonnegative integers. This is expressed by the axiom

$$(\forall\, x) \begin{bmatrix} atom(x) \\ \equiv \\ integer(x) \end{bmatrix}. \qquad\qquad (atom\text{-}integer)$$

We shall call this the theory of *tuples of nonnegative integers*.

A tuple in this combined theory is said to be *ordered* if its elements are (weakly) increasing; thus $\langle 2,\ 4,\ 4,\ 7 \rangle$ is ordered but $\langle 3,\ 2 \rangle$ is not. Note that an ordered tuple may have multiple occurrences of the same element.

The *ordered* relation is defined by the following axioms:

$$ordered(\langle\ \rangle) \qquad\qquad\qquad\qquad (empty)$$

$$(\forall\ atom\ u)\big[ordered(\langle u\rangle)\big] \qquad\qquad (singleton)$$

$$\begin{array}{l} (\forall\ atom\ u,v) \\ \quad (\forall\ tuple\ x) \end{array} \begin{bmatrix} ordered(u \diamond (v \diamond x)) \\ \equiv \\ u \leq v\ \ and\ \ ordered(v \diamond x) \end{bmatrix} \quad (double\ insertion)$$

Here $\leq$ is the weak less-than relation over the nonnegative integers.

From these axioms we can prove the following result.

Proposition (insertion)

The sentence

$$\begin{array}{l} (\forall\ atom\ u) \\ (\forall\ tuple\ x) \end{array} \begin{bmatrix} ordered(u \diamond x) \\ \equiv \\ \begin{bmatrix} ordered(x) \\ and \\ (\forall\ atom\ v) \begin{bmatrix} if\ \ v \in x \\ then\ \ u \leq v \end{bmatrix} \end{bmatrix} \end{bmatrix} \qquad (insertion)$$

is valid. ◢

In other words, a nonempty tuple is ordered if and only if its tail is ordered and its head is less than or equal to every element of its tail.

Proof.   The proof is by stepwise induction on x, taking our inductive sentence to be

$$\mathcal{F}[x]: \quad (\forall \; atom \; u) \left[\begin{array}{c} ordered(u \diamond x) \\ \equiv \\ \left[\begin{array}{c} ordered(x) \\ and \\ (\forall \; atom \; v) \left[\begin{array}{c} if \;\; v \in x \\ then \;\; u \leq v \end{array}\right] \end{array}\right] \end{array}\right].$$

Base Case

We would like to show

$$\mathcal{F}[\langle \; \rangle]: \quad (\forall \; atom \; u) \left[\begin{array}{c} ordered(u \diamond \langle \; \rangle) \\ \equiv \\ \left[\begin{array}{c} ordered(\langle \; \rangle) \\ and \\ (\forall \; atom \; v) \left[\begin{array}{c} if \;\; v \in \langle \; \rangle \\ then \;\; u \leq v \end{array}\right] \end{array}\right] \end{array}\right].$$

Consider an arbitrary atom u. The left-hand side,

$$ordered(u \diamond \langle \; \rangle),$$

is true (by the *singleton* axiom for the *ordered* relation).

The first conjunct of the right-hand side,

$$ordered(\langle \; \rangle),$$

holds (by the *empty* axiom for the *ordered* relation). The second conjunct,

$$(\forall \; atom \; v) \left[\begin{array}{c} if \;\; v \in \langle \; \rangle \\ then \;\; u \leq v \end{array}\right],$$

is true vacuously, because, for any atom v, the antecedent $v \in \langle \; \rangle$ is false (by the *empty* axiom for the member relation $\in$).

Therefore the entire equivalence is true.

Inductive Step

For an arbitrary atom w and tuple x, assume as our induction hypothesis that

$$\mathcal{F}[x]: \quad (\forall \; atom \; u) \left[\begin{array}{c} ordered(u \diamond x) \\ \equiv \\ \left[\begin{array}{c} ordered(x) \\ and \\ (\forall \; atom \; v) \left[\begin{array}{c} if \;\; v \in x \\ then \;\; u \leq v \end{array}\right] \end{array}\right] \end{array}\right].$$

We would like to show that then

$$\mathcal{F}[w \diamond x]: \quad (\forall\, atom\ u') \left[\begin{array}{c} ordered\big(u' \diamond (w \diamond x)\big) \\ \equiv \\ \left[\begin{array}{c} ordered(w \diamond x) \\ and \\ (\forall\, atom\ v') \left[\begin{array}{c} if\ \ v' \in (w \diamond x) \\ then\ \ u' \le v' \end{array} \right] \end{array} \right] \end{array} \right].$$

    We prove only one direction of the equivalence. Consider an arbitrary atom u' and suppose that

$$ordered\big(u' \diamond (w \diamond x)\big).$$

We show that then

$$(\dagger) \quad ordered(w \diamond x)$$

and

$$(\ddagger) \quad (\forall\, atom\ v') \left[\begin{array}{c} if\ \ v' \in (w \diamond x) \\ then\ \ u' \le v' \end{array} \right].$$

    Because $ordered\big(u' \diamond (w \diamond x)\big)$, we have (by the *double-insertion* axiom for the ordered relation) that

$$u' \le w$$

and

$$ordered(w \diamond x).$$

The latter sentence, $ordered(w \diamond x)$, is one of our desired conditions, ($\dagger$), and it also implies (by our induction hypothesis $\mathcal{F}[x]$, taking u to be w) that

$$ordered(x)$$

and

$$(*) \quad (\forall\, atom\ v) \left[\begin{array}{c} if\ \ v \in x \\ then\ \ w \le v \end{array} \right].$$

    To establish our remaining desired condition ($\ddagger$), consider an arbitrary atom v', and suppose that

$$v' \in (w \diamond x).$$

We must show that then

$$u' \le v'.$$

Because $v' \in (w \diamond x)$, we have (by the *insertion* axiom for the member relation $\in$) that

$$v' = w \ \ or \ \ v' \in x.$$

    In the case in which $v' = w$, our earlier conclusion $u' \le w$ implies the desired result $u' \le v'$.

In the alternate case, in which $v' \in x$, we know (by our earlier conclusion $(*)$, taking v to be v') that

$$w \leq v'.$$

Therefore by our earlier conclusion $u' \leq w$, we have (by the transitivity of the less-than relation $\leq$) the desired result $u' \leq v'$.

This concludes the proof in one direction. The proof in the other direction, which is simpler, is requested in **Problem 9.25**. ⏌

Remark (transitivity). Although we have assumed initially that the elements of our tuples are identified with the nonnegative integers, the only property of the nonnegative integers we require in the proof of the *insertion* proposition is the transitivity of the less-than relation $\leq$. Therefore we could establish the same results in an augmented theory of tuples in which $\leq$ is replaced by an arbitrary transitive relation over the atoms, without mentioning the nonnegative integers at all. ⏌

The *empty* axiom and the *insertion* property actually provide an alternative definition of the *ordered* relation; the proof is left as an exercise (**Problem 9.26**).

A connection between the *ordered* relation and the append function is expressed by the property

$$(\forall\ tuple\ x, y)\ \begin{bmatrix} ordered(x \diamondsuit y) \\[4pt] \equiv \\[4pt] \begin{bmatrix} ordered(x)\ \ and\ \ ordered(y) \\ \quad and \\[4pt] (\forall\ atom\ u, v)\ \begin{bmatrix} if\ \ u \in x\ \ and\ \ v \in y \\ then\ \ u \leq v \end{bmatrix} \end{bmatrix} \end{bmatrix} \qquad (append)$$

In other words, the result of appending two tuples x and y is ordered if and only if the two tuples are themselves ordered and every element of x is less than or equal to every element of y. The proof is left as an exercise (**Problem 9.27**).

9.10   INSERTION SORT

Consider again the theory of tuples of nonnegative integers. We define a unary function symbol $insort(x)$ which, for any tuple x, produces a tuple whose elements are the same as those of x but rearranged into (weakly) increasing order. For example,

$$insort(\langle 4,\ 2,\ 1,\ 2 \rangle)\ =\ \langle 1,\ 2,\ 2,\ 4 \rangle.$$

Note that the multiplicity of each element in $insort(x)$ is the same as its multiplicity in x.

The $insort$ function is defined in terms of an auxiliary binary function symbol $insert(u, y)$. If u is a nonnegative integer and y is a tuple already in increasing order, $insert(u, y)$ is the tuple obtained by inserting u in its place in order among the elements of y. For example,

$$insert\big(3,\ \langle 1,\ 2,\ 4 \rangle\big)\ =\ \langle 1,\ 2,\ 3,\ 4 \rangle$$

$$insert\big(2,\ \langle 1,\ 2,\ 4 \rangle\big)\ =\ \langle 1,\ 2,\ 2,\ 4 \rangle.$$

The $insort$ function is defined by the axioms

$$insort(\langle\,\rangle)\ =\ \langle\,\rangle \qquad\qquad\qquad\qquad\qquad\qquad\qquad (empty)$$

$$\begin{matrix}(\forall\ atom\ u)\\(\forall\ tuple\ x)\end{matrix}\big[insort(u \diamond x)\ =\ insert\big(u,\ insort(x)\big)\big] \qquad (insertion)$$

In other words, if the given tuple is empty, the value of the $insort$ function is also empty. On the other hand, if the given tuple is of form $u \diamond x$, the value of the $insort$ function is obtained by arranging the elements of x in increasing order and inserting u in its place in order among them.

The auxiliary function $insert$ is defined by the axioms

$$(\forall\ atom\ u)\big[insert\big(u,\ \langle\,\rangle\big)\ =\ \langle u \rangle\big] \qquad\qquad\qquad\qquad (empty)$$

$$\begin{matrix}(\forall\ atom\ u, v)\\(\forall\ tuple\ x)\end{matrix}\left[insert(u,\ v \diamond x)\ =\ \begin{cases}if\ \ u \leq v\\then\ \ u \diamond (v \diamond x)\\else\ \ v \diamond insert(u,\ x)\end{cases}\right]$$

$$(insertion)$$

In other words, the result of inserting a nonnegative integer u in its place in the empty tuple $\langle\,\rangle$ is simply the singleton tuple $\langle u \rangle$. The result of inserting u in its place in the nonempty tuple $v \diamond x$ is obtained by putting u at the beginning if $u \leq v$, and inserting u in its place in x otherwise.

The axioms for $insort$ and $insert$ suggest a method for sorting a given tuple, as illustrated in the next example.

Example (sorting).   Suppose we would like to sort the tuple $\langle 4,\ 1,\ 2 \rangle$, that is, $4 \diamond (1 \diamond (2 \diamond \langle\,\rangle))$. Then we have

$$insort\big(4 \diamond (1 \diamond (2 \diamond \langle\,\rangle))\big)$$

$$= \; insert\big(4, \; insert(1 \diamond (2 \diamond \langle \, \rangle))\big)$$
$$\text{(by the } insertion \text{ axiom for } insort)$$

$$= \; insert\big(4, \; insert(1, \; insert(2, \; insort(\langle \, \rangle)))\big)$$
$$\text{(by the } insertion \text{ axiom for } insort, \text{ twice more)}$$

$$= \; insert\big(4, \; insert(1, \; insert(2, \; \langle \, \rangle))\big)$$
$$\text{(by the } empty \text{ axiom for } insort)$$

$$= \; insert\big(4, \; insert(1, \; 2 \diamond \langle \, \rangle)\big)$$
$$\text{(by the } empty \text{ axiom for } insert)$$

$$= \; insert\big(4, \; 1 \diamond (2 \diamond \langle \, \rangle)\big)$$
$$\text{(by the } insertion \text{ axiom for } insert, \text{ because } 1 \leq 2)$$

$$= \; 1 \diamond insert\big(4, \; 2 \diamond \langle \, \rangle\big)$$
$$\text{(by the } insertion \text{ axiom for } insert, \text{ because } not \; (4 \leq 1))$$

$$= \; 1 \diamond \big(2 \diamond insert(4, \; \langle \, \rangle)\big)$$
$$\text{(by the } insertion \text{ axiom for } insert, \text{ because } not \; (4 \leq 2))$$

$$= \; 1 \diamond \big(2 \diamond \big(4 \diamond \langle \, \rangle\big)\big)$$
$$\text{(by the } empty \text{ axiom for } insert).$$

In short,

$$insort(\langle 4, \, 1, \, 2 \rangle) \; = \; \langle 1, \, 2, \, 4 \rangle. \qquad \lrcorner$$

From the axioms, we can prove that the functions $insort$ and $insert$ always yield a tuple, that is,

$$(\forall \; tuple \; x)\big[tuple\,(insort(x))\big] \tag{sort}$$

$$\begin{array}{l} (\forall \; atom \; u) \\ (\forall \; tuple \; x) \end{array} \big[tuple\,(insert(u, \; x))\big] \tag{sort}$$

The proofs are omitted.

We would like to show two properties of the $insort$ function: that the tuple $insort(x)$ is in increasing order, that is,

$$(\forall \; tuple \; x)\big[ordered\,(insort(x))\big] \tag{ordered}$$

and that the elements of the tuple $insort(x)$ are the same as those of the tuple x, that is,

$$(\forall \; tuple \; x)\big[perm\,(x, \; insort(x))\big] \tag{permutation}$$

For this purpose we shall have to establish two corresponding properties of the auxiliary function $insert$.

Proposition (insert)

The sentences

$$(\forall \ atom \ u) \begin{bmatrix} if \ \ ordered(x) \\ then \ \ ordered(insert(u, x)) \end{bmatrix} \qquad (ordered)$$

$$(\forall \ atom \ u) \\ (\forall \ tuple \ x) [perm(u \diamond x, \ insert(u, \ x))] \qquad (permutation)$$

are valid.　　⌙

In other words, if the tuple x is in increasing order, so is the tuple $insert(u, x)$, and the elements of the tuple $insert(u, x)$ are precisely the atom u and the elements of the tuple x.

We establish the *permutation* property of the *insert* proposition first and then use it in the proof of the *ordered* property.

Proof (*permutation* of *insert*).　　Consider an arbitrary atom u; we would like to establish

$$(\forall \ tuple \ x)[perm(u \diamond x, \ insert(u, \ x))].$$

The proof is by stepwise induction on x, taking the inductive sentence to be

$$\mathcal{F}[x]: \quad perm(u \diamond x, \ insert(u, \ x)).$$

Base Case

We would like to show

$$\mathcal{F}[\langle \ \rangle]: \quad perm(u \diamond \langle \ \rangle, \ insert(u, \ \langle \ \rangle))$$

or, equivalently (by the *empty* axiom for *insert*),

$$perm(u \diamond \langle \ \rangle, \ u \diamond \langle \ \rangle).$$

But this is true (by the *reflexivity* property of *perm*).

Inductive Step

We would like to show

$$(\forall \ atom \ v) \begin{bmatrix} if \ \ \mathcal{F}[x] \\ then \ \ \mathcal{F}[v \diamond x] \end{bmatrix}$$

For an arbitrary atom v and tuple x, assume the induction hypothesis

$$\mathcal{F}[x]: \quad perm(u \diamond x, \ insert(u, \ x)).$$

We must establish the desired conclusion

$$\mathcal{F}[v \diamond x]: \quad perm(u \diamond (v \diamond x), \ insert(u, \ v \diamond x)).$$

The proof distinguishes between two cases, depending on whether or not $u \leq v$.

Case: $u \leq v$

Then we have

$$perm\big(u \diamond (v \diamond x), \; insert(u, \; v \diamond x)\big)$$

if and only if (by the *insertion* axiom for *insert*, because $u \leq v$)

$$perm\big(u \diamond (v \diamond x), \; u \diamond (v \diamond x)\big),$$

which is true (by the *reflexivity* property of *perm*).

Case: *not* $(u \leq v)$

Then we have

$$perm\big(u \diamond (v \diamond x), \; insert(u, \; v \diamond x)\big)$$

if and only if (by the *insertion* axiom for *insert*, because *not* $(u \leq v)$)

$$perm\big(u \diamond (v \diamond x), \; v \diamond insert(u, \; x)\big)$$

if and only if (by the *exchange* and the *transitivity* properties of *perm*)

$$perm\big(v \diamond (u \diamond x), \; v \diamond insert(u, \; x)\big)$$

if and only if (by the *equal-insertion* property of *perm*)

$$perm\big(u \diamond x, \; insert(u, \; x)\big),$$

which is true (by our induction hypothesis $\mathcal{F}[x]$). $\quad\lrcorner$

We can now establish the first part of the *insert* proposition, the *ordered* property of *insert*.

Proof (*ordered* of *insert*). ⁀ We would like to show

$$(\forall \; atom \; u) \begin{bmatrix} if \;\; ordered(x) \\ then \;\; ordered(insert(u, \; x)) \end{bmatrix}$$
$$(\forall \; tuple \; x)$$

Consider an arbitrary atom u; we must establish

$$(\forall \; tuple \; x) \begin{bmatrix} if \;\; ordered(x) \\ then \;\; ordered(insert(u, \; x)) \end{bmatrix}$$

The proof is by stepwise induction on x, taking the inductive sentence to be

$$\mathcal{F}[x] : \quad \begin{aligned} &if \;\; ordered(x) \\ &then \;\; ordered(insert(u, \; x)). \end{aligned}$$

Base Case

We would like to show

$$\mathcal{F}[\langle \; \rangle] : \quad \begin{aligned} &if \;\; ordered(\langle \; \rangle) \\ &then \;\; ordered(insert(u, \; \langle \; \rangle)). \end{aligned}$$

But we have

$$ordered\big(insert(u, \; \langle \; \rangle)\big)$$

if and only if (by the *empty* axiom for *insert*)

$$ordered(u \diamond \langle \; \rangle),$$

which is true (by the *singleton* axiom for the *ordered* relation).

Inductive Step

     We would like to show

$$(\forall \; atom \; v) \begin{bmatrix} if & \mathcal{F}[x] \\ then & \mathcal{F}[v \diamond x] \end{bmatrix}.$$
$$(\forall \; tuple \; x)$$

For an arbitrary atom v and tuple x, assume the induction hypothesis

$$\mathcal{F}[x]: \quad \begin{array}{l} if \; ordered(x) \\ then \; ordered(insert(u, \; x)). \end{array}$$

We must establish the desired conclusion

$$\mathcal{F}[v \diamond x]: \quad \begin{array}{l} if \; ordered(v \diamond x) \\ then \; ordered(insert(u, \; v \diamond x)). \end{array}$$

     Suppose that

(∗) $ordered(v \diamond x).$

Then (by the *insertion* property of the *ordered* relation)

(†) $ordered(x)$

and

(‡) $(\forall \; atom \; w) \begin{bmatrix} if & w \in x \\ then & v \leq w \end{bmatrix}.$

     We would like to show that

$$ordered(insert(u, \; v \diamond x)).$$

The proof distinguishes between two cases, depending on whether or not $u \leq v$.

Case: $u \leq v$

     Then we have

$$ordered(insert(u, \; v \diamond x))$$

if and only if (by the *insertion* axiom for *insert*, because $u \leq v$)

$$ordered(u \diamond (v \diamond x))$$

if and only if (by the *double-insertion* axiom for the *ordered* relation)

$$u \leq v \;\; and \;\; ordered(v \diamond x),$$

which is true by our case assumption and our supposition (∗).

Case: *not* $(u \le v)$

Then we have

$$ordered(insert(u, \, v \diamond x))$$

if and only if (by the *insertion* axiom for *insert*, because *not* $(u \le v)$)

$$ordered(v \diamond insert(u, \, x))$$

if and only if (by the *insertion* property of the *ordered* relation)

$$ordered(insert(u, \, x))$$

and

$$(\forall \, atom \, w) \begin{bmatrix} if & w \in insert(u, \, x) \\ then & v \le w \end{bmatrix}.$$

To show the first of these conditions, $ordered(insert(u, \, x))$, it suffices (by our induction hypothesis $\mathcal{F}[x]$) to establish

$$ordered(x),$$

but this is our earlier conclusion (†).

To show the second of the above conditions, consider an arbitrary atom w and suppose that

$$w \in insert(u, \, x).$$

We would like to show that

$$v \le w.$$

We know (by the *permutation* property of *insert*, which is the second part of this proposition) that

$$perm(u \diamond x, \, insert(u, \, x)).$$

Therefore (by the *member* axiom for *perm*, since $w \in insert(u, \, x)$ by our supposition) we have

$$w \in (u \diamond x)$$

and hence (by the *insertion* axiom for the member relation $\in$)

$$w = u \;\; or \;\; w \in x.$$

We distinguish between these two subcases.

Subcase: $w = u$

We would like to show $v \le w$, that is,

$$v \le u.$$

But this follows (by the *totality* of the weak less-than relation $\le$) from our case assumption *not* $(u \le v)$.

Subcase: $w \in x$

Then (by our earlier conclusion (‡)) we have
$$v \leq w,$$
as we wanted to show. ⏌

PROPERTIES OF INSORT

We are now ready to establish the desired properties of the *insort* function.

Proposition (insort)
  The sentences
$$(\forall \; tuple \; x)\big[ordered\big(insort(x)\big)\big] \qquad\qquad (ordered)$$

$$(\forall \; tuple \; x)\big[perm\big(x, \; insort(x)\big)\big] \qquad\qquad (permutation)$$
  are valid. ⏌

We establish the *ordered* property of the *insort* proposition first.

Proof (*ordered* of *insort*).   We would like to show
$$(\forall \; tuple \; x)\big[ordered\big(insort(x)\big)\big].$$
The proof is by stepwise induction on x, taking our inductive sentence to be
$$\mathcal{F}[x]: \quad ordered\big(insort(x)\big).$$
Base Case

We would like to show
$$\mathcal{F}\big[\langle\,\rangle\big]: \quad ordered\big(insort(\langle\,\rangle)\big)$$
or, equivalently (by the *empty* axiom for *insort*),
$$ordered\big(\langle\,\rangle\big).$$
But this is true (by the *empty* axiom for *ordered*).

Inductive Step

For an arbitrary atom v and tuple x, assume the induction hypothesis
$$\mathcal{F}[x]: \quad ordered\big(insort(x)\big).$$
We must establish the desired conclusion
$$\mathcal{F}[v \diamond x]: \quad ordered\big(insort(v \diamond x)\big)$$
or, equivalently (by the *insertion* axiom for *insort*),
$$ordered\big(insert\big(v, \; insort(x)\big)\big).$$
It suffices (by the *ordered* property of *insert*, proved in the *insert* proposition) to show that
$$ordered\big(insort(x)\big),$$
but this is precisely our induction hypothesis $\mathcal{F}[x]$. ⏌

We next establish the second part of the *insort* proposition, the *permutation* property of *insort*.

Proof (*permutation* of *insort*). We would like to show that

$$(\forall\ tuple\ x)\big[perm\big(x,\ insort(x)\big)\big].$$

The proof is by stepwise induction on x, taking the inductive sentence to be

$$\mathcal{F}[x]:\quad perm\big(x,\ insort(x)\big).$$

Base Case

We would like to show

$$\mathcal{F}[\langle\,\rangle]:\quad perm\big(\langle\,\rangle,\ insort(\langle\,\rangle)\big)$$

or, equivalently (by the *empty* axiom for *insort*),

$$perm\big(\langle\,\rangle,\ \langle\,\rangle\big).$$

But this is true (by the *empty* axiom for *perm*).

Inductive Step

For an arbitrary atom v and tuple x, assume the induction hypothesis

$$\mathcal{F}[x]:\quad perm\big(x,\ insort(x)\big).$$

We must establish the desired conclusion

$$\mathcal{F}[v\diamond x]:\quad perm\big(v\diamond x,\ insort(v\diamond x)\big)$$

or, equivalently (by the *insertion* axiom for *insort*).

$$(*)\qquad perm\big(v\diamond x,\ insert\big(v,\ insort(x)\big)\big).$$

We know (by our induction hypothesis $\mathcal{F}[x]$) that

$$perm\big(x,\ insort(x)\big).$$

Therefore (by the *equal-insertion* property of *perm*) we have

$$perm\big(v\diamond x,\ v\diamond insort(x)\big).$$

Also (by the *permutation* property of *insert*, proved in the *insert* proposition) we know

$$perm\big(v\diamond insort(x),\ insert\big(v,\ insort(x)\big)\big).$$

Therefore (by the *transitivity* property of *perm*) we have

$$perm\big(v\diamond x,\ insert(v,\ insort(x))\big),$$

which is our desired result $(*)$.   ◢

Remark (less-than relation is not essential). As in the section on the *ordered* relation, we have assumed initially that the atoms of our tuples are identified with the nonnegative integers; however, the only properties of the nonnegative integers we require for the proof of the *insort* proposition are the totality of the less-than relation $\leq$ (in the proof of the *ordered* property of *insert*) and its transitivity (in the proof of the *insertion* property of *ordered*).

Therefore we could define our function *insort* and establish the same results in an augmented theory of tuples without mentioning the nonnegative integers at all. The symbol $\leq$ would be replaced by an arbitrary predicate symbol $\preceq$, defined by the *transitivity* axiom

$$(\forall\ atom\ x, y, z)\big[if\ (x \preceq y\ and\ y \preceq z)\ then\ x \preceq z\big]$$

and the *totality* axiom

$$(\forall\ atom\ x, y)\big[x \preceq y\ or\ y \preceq x\big]\ \blacksquare$$

The function *insort* can be shown to be the only function that satisfies the *ordered* and *permutation* properties, that is,

$$(\forall\ tuple\ x, y) \begin{bmatrix} if\ \ ordered(y)\ \ and \\ \quad perm(x,\ y) \\ then\ \ y = insort(x) \end{bmatrix} \qquad (uniqueness)$$

Of course there are alternative definitions of the function *insort*.

We can also show that applying the function *insort* twice to a given tuple has the same effect as applying it once, that is,

$$(\forall\ tuple\ x)\big[insort(insort(x))\ =\ insort(x)\big] \qquad (idempotence)$$

The proofs of the *uniqueness* and *idempotence* properties are requested in **Problem 9.28**.

Remark (program correctness).   The axioms for *insort* and *insert* have computational content; in this sense they may be regarded as a program for computing the sorting function.

The *ordered* and *permutation* properties express the intended purpose of the sorting program; in this sense, they may be regarded as a specification for the program. In establishing the properties, we have proved the correctness of the program, with respect to this specification. $\blacksquare$

9.11   QUICKSORT

The reasoning involved in the following example is typical of that found in many proofs of the correctness of programs.

THE QUICKSORT FUNCTION

We provide an alternative definition of the sorting function by introducing a unary function $quicksort(x)$, which sorts the elements of a tuple x of nonnegative integers by a different method. This function is defined in terms of two auxiliary binary functions, *lesseq* and *greater*. If u is a nonnegative integer and y is a tuple, $lesseq(u, y)$ is the subtuple of all elements of y less than or equal to u, and $greater(u, y)$ is the subtuple of all elements of y strictly greater than u. For example,

$$lesseq\big(2, \ \langle 3, \ 2, \ 1, \ 5, \ 2, \ 4 \rangle\big) \ = \ \langle 2, \ 1, \ 2 \rangle$$

$$greater\big(2, \ \langle 3, \ 2, \ 1, \ 5, \ 2, \ 4 \rangle\big) \ = \ \langle 3, \ 5, \ 4 \rangle.$$

The function *quicksort* is defined by the axioms

$$
\begin{array}{ll}
quicksort(\langle\,\rangle) \ = \ \langle\,\rangle & (empty) \\[2em]
(\forall\ atom\ u) \ (\forall\ tuple\ y) \left[\begin{array}{l} quicksort(u \diamond y) \\ = \\ \left[\begin{array}{l} quicksort\big(lesseq(u,\ y)\big) \diamond \\ \langle u \rangle \diamond \\ quicksort\big(greater(u,\ y)\big) \end{array} \right] \end{array} \right] & (insertion)
\end{array}
$$

In other words, if the given tuple is the empty tuple $\langle\ \rangle$, the value of the function *quicksort* is also $\langle\ \rangle$. On the other hand, if the given tuple is of form $u \diamond y$, the value of the function is a tuple consisting of

- Those elements of y less than or equal to u (in increasing order),

- The element u itself, and

- Those elements of y strictly greater than u (in increasing order).

The auxiliary function $lesseq(u, y)$ is defined by the axioms

$$
\begin{array}{ll}
(\forall\ atom\ u)\big[lesseq(u,\ \langle\ \rangle)\ =\ \langle\ \rangle\big] & (empty) \\[2em]
(\forall\ atom\ u,\ v)\ (\forall\ tuple\ x) \left[lesseq(u,\ v \diamond x)\ =\ \left\{ \begin{array}{l} if\ \ v \leq u \\ then\ \ v \diamond lesseq(u,\ x) \\ else\ \ lesseq(u,\ x) \end{array} \right\} \right] & \\
& (insertion)
\end{array}
$$

Similarly, the auxiliary function $greater(u, y)$ is defined by the axioms

$$(\forall \ atom \ u)\big[greater\,(u, \ \langle\ \rangle) \ = \ \langle\ \rangle\big] \hspace{3cm} (empty)$$

$$\begin{array}{l}(\forall \ atom \ u, \ v) \\ \quad (\forall \ tuple \ x)\end{array} \left[greater(u, \ v \diamond x) \ = \ \left\{ \begin{array}{ll} if & not \ (v \leq u) \\ then & v \diamond greater(u, \ x) \\ else & greater(u, \ x) \end{array} \right\} \right]$$

$$\hspace{9cm} (insertion)$$

In the *insertion* axiom for *greater*, we have written *not* $(v \leq u)$ rather than $v > u$ to simplify the discussion.

The axioms for the function $quicksort(x)$ suggest a way to sort a tuple x.

Example (computation of quicksort).   Suppose we want to "quicksort" the tuple $\langle 2, \ 2, \ 4, \ 1, \ 3\rangle$. Then we have

$$quicksort\big(\langle 2, 2, 4, 1, 3\rangle\big)$$

$$= \ quicksort\big(2 \diamond \langle 2, \ 4, \ 1, \ 3\rangle\big)$$

$$= \ quicksort\big(lesseq\big(2, \ \langle 2, \ 4, \ 1, \ 3\rangle\big)\big) \diamond \langle 2\rangle \diamond$$
$$quicksort\big(greater\big(2, \ \langle 2, \ 4, \ 1, \ 3\rangle\big)\big)$$
$$\text{(by the } insertion \text{ axiom for } quicksort)$$

$$= \ quicksort\big(\langle 2, \ 1\rangle\big) \diamond \langle 2\rangle \diamond quicksort\big(\langle 4, \ 3\rangle\big)$$
$$\text{(by repeated application of the axioms}$$
$$\text{for } lesseq \text{ and } greater)$$

$$= \ \langle 1, \ 2\rangle \diamond \langle 2\rangle \diamond \langle 3, \ 4\rangle$$
$$\text{(by repeated application of the axioms)}$$

$$= \ \langle 1, \ 2, \ 2, \ 3, \ 4\rangle.$$

In short,

$$quicksort\big(\langle 2, \ 2, \ 4, \ 1, \ 3\rangle\big) \ = \ \langle 1, \ 2, \ 2, \ 3, \ 4\rangle. \ \ \lrcorner$$

We would like to show that the function *quicksort* provides an alternative definition of *insort*, that is, that

$$(\forall \ tuple \ x)\big[quicksort(x) \ = \ insort(x)\big] \hspace{3cm} (insort)$$

For this purpose, it suffices (by the *uniqueness* property of *insort*) to show that the tuple $quicksort(x)$ is in increasing order, that is,

$$(\forall \ tuple \ x)\big[ordered\,(quicksort(x))\big] \hspace{3cm} (ordered)$$

and that the elements of $quicksort(x)$ are the same as those of x, that is,

$$(\forall \ tuple \ x)\big[perm\,(x, \ quicksort(x))\big] \hspace{2.5cm} (permutation)$$

PROPERTIES USED

We shall use several properties of the auxiliary functions *lesseq* and *greater*.

From the axioms for *lesseq* we can prove the properties

$$\begin{array}{l}(\forall\ atom\ u)\\(\forall\ tuple\ x)\end{array}\left[tuple\left(lesseq(u,\ x)\right)\right] \qquad\qquad (sort)$$

$$\begin{array}{l}(\forall\ atom\ u)\\(\forall\ tuple\ x)\end{array}\left[lesseq(u,x)\ \preceq_{tuple}\ x\right] \qquad\qquad (subtuple)$$

$$\begin{array}{l}(\forall\ atom\ u,\ v)\\(\forall\ tuple\ x)\end{array}\left[\begin{array}{l}if\ \ v\in lesseq(u,\ x)\\then\ \ v\leq u\end{array}\right] \qquad\qquad (bound)$$

From the axioms for *greater* we can prove the properties

$$\begin{array}{l}(\forall\ atom\ u)\\(\forall\ tuple\ x)\end{array}\left[tuple\left(greater(u,\ x)\right)\right] \qquad\qquad (sort)$$

$$\begin{array}{l}(\forall\ atom\ u)\\(\forall\ tuple\ x)\end{array}\left[greater(u,\ x)\ \preceq_{tuple}\ x\right] \qquad\qquad (subtuple)$$

$$\begin{array}{l}(\forall\ atom\ u,\ v)\\(\forall\ tuple\ x)\end{array}\left[\begin{array}{l}if\ \ v\in greater(u,\ x)\\then\ \ not\ (v\leq u)\end{array}\right] \qquad\qquad (bound)$$

We can then prove that the elements of x are the same as the elements of $lesseq(u,\ x)$ and $greater(u,\ x)$ together, that is,

$$\begin{array}{l}(\forall\ atom\ u)\\(\forall\ tuple\ x)\end{array}\left[perm\left(x,\ lesseq(u,\ x)\diamond greater(u,\ x)\right)\right]\quad (permutation)$$

and that the *quicksort* function always yields a tuple, that is,

$$(\forall\ tuple\ x)\left[tuple\left(quicksort(x)\right)\right] \qquad\qquad (sort)$$

Proofs of some of these properties are requested in **Problem 9.29**.

Furthermore, we shall use several properties that were proved or mentioned in previous chapters, including

Properties of the weak less-than relation $\leq$

$$(\forall\ integer\ x,\ y,\ z)\left[\begin{array}{l}if\ \ x\leq y\ \ and\ \ y\leq z\\then\ \ x\leq z\end{array}\right] \qquad\qquad (transitivity)$$

$$(\forall\ integer\ x,\ y)\left[x\leq y\ \ or\ \ y\leq x\right] \qquad\qquad (totality)$$

Property of the append function $\diamond$

$$\begin{array}{l}(\forall\ atom\ u)\\(\forall\ tuple\ x)\end{array}\left[\langle u\rangle\diamond x\ =\ u\diamond x\right] \qquad\qquad (singleton)$$

Properties of the subtuple $\preceq_{tuple}$ and proper-subtuple $\prec_{tuple}$ relations

$$(\forall\ atom\ u) \atop (\forall\ tuple\ x) \left[x \prec_{tuple} (u \diamond x) \right] \qquad\qquad (insertion\ adjacent)$$

$$(\forall\ tuple\ x,\ y,\ z) \left[\begin{array}{l} if\ \ x \preceq_{tuple} y\ \ and\ \ y \prec_{tuple} z \\ then\ \ x \prec_{tuple} z \end{array} \right]$$
$$(left\ mixed\ transitivity)$$

Property of the permutation relation

$$(\forall\ tuple\ x_1,\ x_2,\ y_1,\ y_2) \left[\begin{array}{l} if\ \ perm(x_1,\ y_1)\ \ and \\ \quad perm(x_2,\ y_2) \\ then\ \ perm(x_1 \diamond x_2,\ y_1 \diamond y_2) \end{array} \right] \qquad (append)$$

Properties of the *ordered* relation

$$(\forall\ atom\ u) \atop (\forall\ tuple\ x) \left[\begin{array}{c} ordered(u \diamond x) \\ \equiv \\ \left[\begin{array}{c} ordered(x) \\ and \\ (\forall\ atom\ v) \left[\begin{array}{l} if\ \ v \in x \\ then\ \ u \leq v \end{array} \right] \end{array} \right] \end{array} \right] \qquad (insertion)$$

$$(\forall\ tuple\ x,\ y) \left[\begin{array}{c} ordered(x \diamond y) \\ \equiv \\ \left[\begin{array}{c} ordered(x)\ \ and\ \ ordered(y) \\ and \\ (\forall\ atom\ v,\ w) \left[\begin{array}{l} if\ \ v \in x\ \ and\ \ w \in y \\ then\ \ v \leq w \end{array} \right] \end{array} \right] \end{array} \right] \qquad (append)$$

We shall use other properties of the theory of tuples as well.

CORRECTNESS

Let us establish the desired properties of *quicksort*.

Proposition (quicksort)

The sentences

$$(\forall\ tuple\ x) \left[perm \left(x,\ quicksort(x) \right) \right] \qquad\qquad (permutation)$$

$$(\forall\ tuple\ x) \left[ordered \left(quicksort(x) \right) \right] \qquad\qquad (ordered)$$

$$(\forall\ tuple\ x) \left[quicksort(x)\ =\ insort(x) \right] \qquad\qquad (insort)$$

are valid. ⌟

We have already remarked that (by the *uniqueness* property of the function *insort*) the *ordered* and *permutation* properties imply the *insort* property; thus we need prove only the first two properties. We prove the *permutation* property first, and then use it in the proof of the *ordered* property.

Proof (*permutation* of *quicksort*).   We show

$$(\forall \ tuple \ x)\left[perm\left(x, \ quicksort(x)\right)\right].$$

The proof is by complete induction, taking the inductive sentence to be

$$\mathcal{F}[x]: \quad perm\left(x, \ quicksort(x)\right).$$

Inductive Step

We would like to show

$$(\forall \ tuple \ x)\left[\begin{matrix} if \ (\forall \ tuple \ x') \begin{bmatrix} if \ x' \prec_{tuple} x \\ then \ \ \mathcal{F}[x'] \end{bmatrix} \\ then \ \ \mathcal{F}[x] \end{matrix}\right].$$

Consider an arbitrary tuple x, and assume the induction hypothesis

$$(\dagger) \qquad (\forall \ tuple \ x') \begin{bmatrix} if \ x' \prec_{tuple} x \\ then \ \ \mathcal{F}[x'] \end{bmatrix}.$$

We would like to show that then the desired conclusion $\mathcal{F}[x]$ is true, that is,

$$perm\left(x, \ quicksort(x)\right).$$

The proof distinguishes between two cases.

Case: $x = \langle \ \rangle$

We then would like to show $\mathcal{F}[\langle \ \rangle]$, that is,

$$perm\left(\langle \ \rangle, \ quicksort(\langle \ \rangle)\right),$$

or, equivalently (by the *empty* axiom for *quicksort*),

$$perm\left(\langle \ \rangle, \ \langle \ \rangle\right).$$

But this is true (by the *empty* axiom for the permutation relation).

Case: $not \ \left(x = \langle \ \rangle\right)$

Then (by the *decomposition* property of tuples), for some atom u and tuple y,

$$x \ = \ u \diamond y.$$

We therefore would like to show $\mathcal{F}[u \diamond y]$, that is,

$$perm\left(u \diamond y, \ quicksort(u \diamond y)\right),$$

or, equivalently (by the *insertion* axiom for *quicksort*),

$$perm\left(u \diamond y, \ \left\{\begin{matrix} quicksort\left(lesseq(u, \ y)\right) \diamond \\ \langle u \rangle \diamond \\ quicksort\left(greater(u, \ y)\right) \end{matrix}\right\}\right)$$

or, equivalently (by the *singleton* property of the append function $\diamond$ and the *left-empty* axiom for $\diamond$),

$$perm \left(\langle \, \rangle \diamond \langle u \rangle \diamond y, \; \left\{ \begin{array}{l} quicksort\,(lesseq(u,\,y)) \diamond \\ \langle u \rangle \diamond \\ quicksort\,(greater(u,\,y)) \end{array} \right\} \right)$$

This is equivalent (by the *append-singleton* axiom for the permutation relation) to

$$perm \left(\langle \, \rangle \diamond y, \; \left\{ \begin{array}{l} quicksort\,(lesseq(u,\,y)) \\ \diamond \\ quicksort\,(greater(u,\,y)) \end{array} \right\} \right),$$

which is equivalent (by the *left-empty* axiom for the append function $\diamond$) to

$$(\dagger\dagger) \qquad perm \left(y, \; \left\{ \begin{array}{l} quicksort\,(lesseq(u,\,y)) \\ \diamond \\ quicksort\,(greater(u,\,y)) \end{array} \right\} \right).$$

Proof of $(\dagger\dagger)$

To show $(\dagger\dagger)$, we first want to use the induction hypothesis $(\dagger)$ twice, taking x' to be $lesseq(u,\,y)$ and $greater(u,\,y)$, respectively. To justify this use of the induction hypothesis, we must show that $lesseq(u,\,y)$ and $greater(u,\,y)$ are proper subtuples of x, that is (because $x = u \diamond y$),

$$lesseq(u,\,y) \prec_{tuple} u \diamond y \qquad and \qquad greater(u,\,y) \prec_{tuple} u \diamond y.$$

We know (by the *subtuple* properties of *lesseq* and *greater*) that

$$lesseq(u,\,y) \preceq_{tuple} y \qquad and \qquad greater(u,\,y) \preceq_{tuple} y.$$

Also (by the *insertion adjacent* property of the proper-subtuple relation $\prec_{tuple}$) we have

$$y \prec_{tuple} u \diamond y.$$

Therefore (by the *left mixed-transitivity* property of the subtuple relation $\preceq_{tuple}$)

$$lesseq(u,\,y) \prec_{tuple} u \diamond y \qquad and \qquad greater(u,\,y) \prec_{tuple} u \diamond y.$$

By our induction hypothesis $(\dagger)$ (taking x' to be $lesseq(u,y)$ and $greater(u,y)$, respectively), we know, because $x = u \diamond y$,

$$\begin{array}{ccc} if \;\; lesseq(u,\,y) \prec_{tuple} u \diamond y & & if \;\; greater(u,\,y) \prec_{tuple} u \diamond y \\ & and & \\ then \;\; \mathcal{F}[lesseq(u,\,y)] & & then \;\; \mathcal{F}[greater(u,\,y)]. \end{array}$$

Therefore, we have $\mathcal{F}[lesseq(u,\,y)]$ and $\mathcal{F}[greater(u,\,y)]$, that is,

$$perm \Big(lesseq(u,\,y), \; quicksort\,(lesseq(u,\,y)) \Big)$$

and

$$perm \Big(greater(u,\,y), \; quicksort\,(greater(u,\,y)) \Big).$$

Therefore (by the *append* property of the permutation relation)

$$perm\left(\left\{\begin{array}{l} lesseq(u,\ y) \\ \diamond \\ greater(u,\ y) \end{array}\right\},\ \left\{\begin{array}{l} quicksort\,(lesseq(u,\ y)) \\ \diamond \\ quicksort\,(greater(u,\ y)) \end{array}\right\}\right).$$

We know (by the *permutation* property of *lesseq* and *greater*) that

$$perm\left(y,\ \left\{\begin{array}{l} lesseq(u,\ y) \\ \diamond \\ greater(u,\ y) \end{array}\right\}\right).$$

Therefore (by the *transitivity* property of the permutation relation)

$$perm\left(y,\ \left\{\begin{array}{l} quicksort\,(lesseq(u,\ y)) \\ \diamond \\ quicksort\,(greater(u,\ y)) \end{array}\right\}\right).$$

But this is the condition (††) we wanted to show. ⌟

The proof of the *ordered* property depends on the *permutation* property of *quicksort*, which we have just proved.

Proof (*ordered* of *quicksort*).   We now want to show

$$(\forall\ tuple\ x)\big[ordered\,(quicksort(x))\big].$$

The proof is again by complete induction, taking the inductive sentence to be

$$\mathcal{F}[x]:\quad ordered\,(quicksort(x)).$$

Inductive Step

We would like to show

$$(\forall\ tuple\ x)\left[\begin{array}{l} if\ (\forall\ tuple\ x')\left[\begin{array}{l} if\ x'\ \prec_{tuple}\ x \\ then\ \ \mathcal{F}[x'] \end{array}\right] \\ then\ \ \mathcal{F}[x] \end{array}\right].$$

Consider an arbitrary tuple x, and assume the induction hypothesis

$$(†) \qquad (\forall\ tuple\ x')\left[\begin{array}{l} if\ x'\ \prec_{tuple}\ x \\ then\ \ \mathcal{F}[x'] \end{array}\right].$$

We would like to show that then the desired conclusion $\mathcal{F}[x]$ is true, that is,

$$ordered\,(quicksort(x)).$$

The proof distinguishes between two cases.

Case: $x = \langle\ \rangle$

We therefore would like to show $\mathcal{F}[\langle\ \rangle]$, that is,

$$ordered\,(quicksort(\langle\ \rangle)),$$

or, equivalently (by the *empty* axiom for *quicksort*),

$$ordered(\langle\ \rangle).$$

But this is true (by the *empty* axiom for the *ordered* relation).

Case: not $(x = \langle \, \rangle)$

Then (by the *decomposition* property of tuples), for some atom u and tuple y,

$$x = u \diamond y.$$

We therefore would like to show $\mathcal{F}[u \diamond y]$, that is,

$$ordered\,(quicksort(u \diamond y)),$$

or, equivalently (by the *insertion* axiom for *quicksort*),

$$ordered \begin{pmatrix} quicksort\,(lesseq(u,\, y)) \diamond \\ \langle u \rangle \diamond \\ quicksort\,(greater(u,\, y)) \end{pmatrix},$$

that is (by the *singleton* property of the append function),

$$ordered \begin{pmatrix} quicksort\,(lesseq(u, y)) \\ \diamond \\ (u \diamond quicksort\,(greater(u, y))) \end{pmatrix}.$$

It suffices (by the *append* property of the *ordered* relation) to establish the conjunction of the three conditions

(1) $ordered\,(quicksort\,(lesseq(u,\, y)))$

(2) $ordered\,(u \diamond quicksort\,(greater(u,\, y)))$

(3) $(\forall \ atom \ v, \ w)$ $\left[if \begin{bmatrix} v \ \in \ quicksort\,(lesseq(u,\, y)) \\ and \\ w \ \in \ u \diamond quicksort\,(greater(u,\, y)) \end{bmatrix} \\ then \ \ v \leq w \right].$

Condition (2) expands (by the *insertion* property of the *ordered* relation) to the conjunction of the two conditions

(2A) $ordered\,(quicksort\,(greater(u,\, y)))$

(2B) $(\forall \ atom \ v)$ $\begin{bmatrix} if \ \ v \in quicksort\,(greater(u,\, y)) \\ then \ \ u \leq v \end{bmatrix}.$

We must show each of the conditions (1), (2A), (2B), and (3).

Proof of (1) *and* (2A)

As in the proof of the *permutation* part of this proposition, we can establish that

$$lesseq(u,\, y) \prec_{tuple} u \diamond y \qquad and \qquad greater(u,\, y) \prec_{tuple} u \diamond y.$$

Therefore, by our induction hypothesis (†), taking x' to be $lesseq(u, y)$ and $greater(u, y)$, respectively, we can conclude $\mathcal{F}[lesseq(u,\, y)]$ and $\mathcal{F}[greater(u,\, y)]$, that is,

$$ordered\,(quicksort\,(lesseq(u,\, y)))$$

and
$$ordered\bigl(quicksort\bigl(greater(u,\ y)\bigr)\bigr).$$
These are precisely the first two conditions (1) and (2A) we wanted to show.

Proof of (2B)

To show condition (2B), consider an arbitrary atom v such that

(‡) $v\ \in\ quicksort\bigl(greater(u,\ y)\bigr).$

We would like to show that then

(††) $u \leq v.$

We know (by the *permutation* property of *quicksort*, the first part of this proposition, taking x to be $greater(u,\ y)$) that
$$perm\bigl(greater(u,\ y),\ quicksort\bigl(greater(u,\ y)\bigr)\bigr).$$
Therefore (by the *member* axiom for the permutation relation) we have

$$v\ \in\ greater(u,\ y)$$
$$\equiv$$
$$v\ \in\ quicksort\bigl(greater(u,\ y)\bigr).$$

Consequently, we can reduce our earlier supposition (‡) to

$$v\ \in\ greater(u,\ y).$$

We can therefore conclude (by the *bound* property of *greater*) that

$$not\ (v \leq u).$$

Then (by the *totality* property of the less-than relation $\leq$) we obtain the desired condition (††), that is, $u \leq v.$

Proof of (3)

To show condition (3), consider arbitrary atoms v and w such that

(∗) $v\ \in\ quicksort\bigl(lesseq(u,\ y)\bigr)$

and
$$w\ \in\ u \diamond quicksort\bigl(greater(u,\ y)\bigr),$$
and therefore (by the *insertion* axiom for the member relation $\in$)

(∗∗) $w = u\quad or\quad w \in quicksort\bigl(greater(u,\ y)\bigr).$

We would like to show that then

(‡‡) $v \leq w.$

We know (by the *permutation* property of *quicksort*, the first part of this proposition, taking x to be $lesseq(u,\ y)$ and $greater(u,\ y)$, respectively) that
$$perm\Bigl(lesseq(u,\ y),\ quicksort\bigl(lesseq(u,\ y)\bigr)\Bigr)$$

and

$$perm\Big(greater(u, \ y), \ quicksort\big(greater(u, \ y)\big)\Big).$$

Therefore (by the *member* axiom for the permutation relation, because v and w are atoms) we have

$$v \ \in \ lesseq(u, \ y)$$

$$\equiv$$

$$v \ \in \ quicksort\big(lesseq(u, \ y)\big)$$

and

$$w \ \in \ greater(u, \ y)$$

$$\equiv$$

$$w \ \in \ quicksort\big(greater(u, \ y)\big).$$

Consequently, we can reduce our earlier conditions $(*)$ and $(**)$ to

$$v \ \in \ lesseq(u, \ y)$$

and

$$w = u \quad or \quad w \ \in \ greater(u, \ y).$$

We can therefore conclude (by the *bound* properties of *lesseq* and *greater*) that

$$v \leq u$$

and

$$w = u \quad or \quad not \ (w \leq u).$$

In the case in which $w = u$, the desired condition $(\ddagger\ddagger)$, that is, $v \leq w$, follows (because $v \leq u$).

In the case in which $not \ (w \leq u)$, we have (by the totality of the less-than relation $\leq$) that $u \leq w$. Therefore (by the transitivity of the less-than relation, because $v \leq u$) we have the desired condition $(\ddagger\ddagger)$, that is, $v \leq w$. ◢

Remark (less-than relation is not essential).   In this section we have assumed that the atoms of our tuples are identified with the nonnegative integers. The only properties of the nonnegative integers we require for the proof of the *quicksort* proposition, however, are the transitivity and the totality of the weak less-than relation $\leq$.

Therefore, as we noted in connection with the function *insort*, we could define our sorting function and establish the same results in an augmented theory of tuples, without mentioning the nonnegative integers at all. The symbol $\leq$ would be replaced by an arbitrary predicate symbol $\preceq$, defined by the *transitivity* and *totality* axioms. ◢

Remark (why complete induction?).   The preceding proofs could not have been carried out in the same way by stepwise induction over the tuples. In the complete induction proof, to prove $\mathcal{F}[u \diamond y]$, we used the induction hypothesis

$$(\forall \ tuple \ x') \begin{bmatrix} if \ \ x' \ \prec_{tuple} \ (u \diamond y) \\ then \ \ \mathcal{F}[x'] \end{bmatrix},$$

taking x' to be $lesseq(u, y)$ and $greater(u, y)$, respectively, to establish the two conditions $\mathcal{F}[lesseq(u, y)]$ and $\mathcal{F}[greater(u, y)]$, which then implied the desired conclusion $\mathcal{F}[u \diamond y]$. In a corresponding stepwise induction proof, the induction hypothesis $\mathcal{F}[y]$ is too weak to establish the conditions $\mathcal{F}[lesseq(u, y)]$ and $\mathcal{F}[greater(u, y)]$. A stepwise induction proof would require a more complex inductive sentence. ◢

Complete induction can be used to prove the correctness of another sorting function.

SELECTION SORT

Suppose we define a unary *minimum* function $mintuple(x)$, which is intended to produce the least element of a nonempty tuple x. The minimum function is defined over the tuples of nonnegative integers by the axioms

$$(\forall \ atom \ u)\big[mintuple(\langle u \rangle) = u\big] \qquad\qquad (singleton)$$

$$\begin{matrix}(\forall \ atom \ u) \\ (\forall \ tuple \ x)\end{matrix} \begin{bmatrix} if \ \ not \ (x = \langle \ \rangle) \\ \\ then \ \begin{bmatrix} mintuple(u \diamond x) = \begin{cases} if \ \ u \le mintuple(x) \\ then \ \ u \\ else \ \ mintuple(x) \end{cases} \end{bmatrix} \end{bmatrix}$$

$$(insertion)$$

Note that these axioms do not specify any particular value for the term $mintuple(\langle \ \rangle)$

We can establish that $mintuple(x)$ is indeed the least element of the nonempty tuple x, that is,

$$(\forall \ tuple \ x) \begin{bmatrix} if \ \ not \ (x = \langle \ \rangle) \\ \\ then \ \begin{bmatrix} mintuple(x) \in x \\ and \\ (\forall \ atom \ u) \begin{bmatrix} if \ \ u \in x \\ then \ \ mintuple(x) \le u \end{bmatrix} \end{bmatrix} \end{bmatrix} \qquad (least)$$

The proof is left as an exercise (**Problem 9.30**). The reader is also requested (in **Problem 9.31**) to prove properties of an alternative minimum function.

Using the *mintuple* function, we can define the unary function *selsort*(x) by the axioms

$$selsort(\langle\,\rangle) = \langle\,\rangle \qquad\qquad\qquad (empty)$$

$$(\forall\ atom\ u) \atop (\forall\ tuple\ x,\ y)\ \ \left\lvert\ then\ \begin{bmatrix} if\ \ u = mintuple\,(x \diamond \langle u\rangle \diamond y) \\ \left[selsort\,(x \diamond \langle u\rangle \diamond y) \right] \\ = \\ u \diamond selsort(x \diamond y) \end{bmatrix}\ \right\rvert \qquad (append)$$

In **Problem 9.32** the reader is requested to prove that the *selsort* function provides an alternative definition of the sorting function.

PROBLEMS

Problem 9.1 (constraint on induction principle)   page 437

Show that the constraint on the *induction* principle, that the variable u not occur free in the sentence $\mathcal{F}[x]$, is essential. In other words, show that the *induction* principle is false under some interpretation for a particular inductive sentence that violates this constraint.

Problem 9.2 (atoms and tuples)   page 438

Suppose we augment the theory of tuples with the axiom

$$(\forall x)\big[atom(x)\ \equiv\ tuple(x)\big].$$

Give a model for the augmented theory.

Problem 9.3 (head and tail)   page 440

Without using the *induction* principle, establish the following properties of the *head* and *tail* functions:

(a)   *Sort (of head)*

$$(\forall\ tuple\ x)\ \begin{bmatrix} if\ \ not\ (x = \langle\,\rangle) \\ then\ \ atom\,(head(x)) \end{bmatrix}$$

(b)   *Sort (of tail)*

$$(\forall\ tuple\ x)\ \begin{bmatrix} if\ \ not\ (x = \langle\,\rangle) \\ then\ \ tuple\,(tail(x)) \end{bmatrix}$$

(c) *Decomposition*

$$(\forall\ tuple\ x)\begin{bmatrix}if\ \ not\ (x=\langle\,\rangle)\\then\ \ x\ =\ head(x)\diamond tail(x)\end{bmatrix}.$$

Problem 9.4 (append) page 442

Establish the following properties of append:

(a) *Sort*

$$(\forall\ tuple\ x,y)\big[tuple(x\diamond y)\big]$$

(b) *Right empty*

$$(\forall\ tuple\ x)\big[x\diamond\langle\,\rangle=x\big]$$

(c) *Associativity*

$$(\forall\ tuple\ x,y,z)\big[(x\diamond y)\diamond z\ =\ x\diamond(y\diamond z)\big]$$

(d) *Head*

$$(\forall\ tuple\ x,y)\begin{bmatrix}if\ \ not\ (x=\langle\,\rangle)\\then\ \ head(x\diamond y)=head(x)\end{bmatrix}$$

(e) *Tail*

$$(\forall\ tuple\ x,y)\begin{bmatrix}if\ \ not\ (x=\langle\,\rangle)\\then\ \ tail(x\diamond y)=tail(x)\diamond y\end{bmatrix}.$$

Problem 9.5 (member and singleton) page 444

Establish the following properties:

(a) *Member (of append)*

$$\begin{matrix}(\forall\ atom\ u)\\(\forall\ tuple\ x,y)\end{matrix}\begin{bmatrix}u\in(x\diamond y)\\\equiv\\u\in x\ \ or\ \ u\in y\end{bmatrix}$$

(b) *Singleton (of head)*

$$(\forall\ atom\ u)\big[head(\langle u\rangle)=u\big]$$

(c) *Singleton (of tail)*

$$(\forall\ atom\ u)\big[tail(\langle u\rangle)=\langle\,\rangle\big]$$

(d) *Singleton (of append)*

$$\begin{matrix}(\forall\ atom\ u)\\(\forall\ tuple\ x)\end{matrix}\big[\langle u\rangle\diamond x\ =\ u\diamond x\big]$$

(e) *Append-singleton (of member)*

$$\begin{matrix}(\forall\ atom\ u)\\(\forall\ tuple\ x)\end{matrix}\begin{bmatrix}u\in x\\\equiv\\(\exists\ tuple\ y_1,y_2)\big[x=y_1\diamond\langle u\rangle\diamond y_2\big]\end{bmatrix}.$$

Problem 9.6 (suffix append)   page 445

Establish the following properties of suffixing:

(a)   *Suffix nonempty*
$$\begin{array}{l}(\forall \; atom \; u) \\ (\forall \; tuple \; x)\end{array}\left[not \; (x \diamond \langle u \rangle = \langle \, \rangle)\right]$$

(b)   *Suffix decomposition*
$$(\forall \; tuple \; x)\left[\begin{array}{l} if \;\; not \; (x = \langle \, \rangle) \\ then \quad \begin{array}{l}(\exists \; atom \; u) \\ (\exists \; tuple \; y)\end{array}\left[x = y \diamond \langle u \rangle\right]\end{array}\right]$$

(c)   *Suffix uniqueness*
$$\begin{array}{l}(\forall \; atom \; u, v) \\ (\forall \; tuple \; x, y)\end{array}\left[\begin{array}{l} if \;\; x \diamond \langle u \rangle = y \diamond \langle v \rangle \\ then \;\; x = y \;\; and \;\; u = v\end{array}\right]$$

(d)   *Prefix-suffix decomposition*
$$(\forall \; tuple \; x)\left[\begin{array}{l} x = \langle \, \rangle \\ \\ or \\ \\ (\exists \; atom \; u)\left[x = \langle u \rangle\right] \\ \\ or \\ \\ \begin{array}{l}(\exists \; atom \; u, v) \\ (\exists \; tuple \; y)\end{array}\left[x = \langle u \rangle \diamond y \diamond \langle v \rangle\right]\end{array}\right].$$

Problem 9.7 (the same relation)   page 445

Establish that the following property provides an alternative definition for the *same* relation:
$$(\forall \; tuple \; x)\left[\begin{array}{l} same(x) \\ \equiv \\ (\forall \; atom \; u, v)\left[\begin{array}{l} if \;\; u \in x \;\; and \;\; v \in x \\ then \;\; u = v\end{array}\right]\end{array}\right] \qquad (equality)$$

In other words,

(a) Show that this property follows from the three axioms defining the *same* relation.

(b) Show that, if we replace the original three axioms for the *same* relation with this sentence, we can establish the validity of each of the original three axioms in the altered theory.

Problem 9.8 (reverse)   page 448

Establish the *reverse* property of *reverse*, that is,
$$(\forall \; tuple \; x)\left[reverse\left(reverse(x)\right) = x\right].$$

Problem 9.9 (front and last) page 452

Suppose we augment the theory of tuples by defining two unary function symbols $front(x)$ and $last(x)$. Under the intended model, $last(x)$ is the last atom of a nonempty tuple x, and $front(x)$ is the tuple of all but the last atom of x; for example,

$$front(\langle \text{B, A, A, B, C} \rangle) = \langle \text{B, A, A, B} \rangle \quad \text{and} \quad last(\langle \text{B, A, A, B, C} \rangle) = \text{C}.$$

The axioms are

$$\begin{array}{l} (\forall \ atom \ u) \\ (\forall \ tuple \ x) \end{array} \left[front(x \diamond \langle u \rangle) \ = \ x \right] \qquad\qquad (front)$$

$$\begin{array}{l} (\forall \ atom \ u) \\ (\forall \ tuple \ x) \end{array} \left[last(x \diamond \langle u \rangle) \ = \ u \right] \qquad\qquad (last)$$

Without using the *induction* principle, establish the following properties of *front* and *last*:

(a) *Sort (of front)*

$$(\forall \ tuple \ x) \left[\begin{array}{l} if \ \ not \ (x = \langle \ \rangle) \\ then \ \ tuple\,(front(x)) \end{array} \right]$$

(b) *Sort (of last)*

$$(\forall \ tuple \ x) \left[\begin{array}{l} if \ \ not \ (x = \langle \ \rangle) \\ then \ \ atom\,(last(x)) \end{array} \right]$$

(c) *Decomposition*

$$(\forall \ tuple \ x) \left[\begin{array}{l} if \ \ not \ (x = \langle \ \rangle) \\ then \ \ x \ = \ front(x) \diamond \langle last(x) \rangle \end{array} \right]$$

(d) *Tail-reverse*

$$(\forall \ tuple \ x) \left[\begin{array}{l} if \ \ not \ (x = \langle \ \rangle) \\ then \ \ front(x) \ = \ reverse\,(tail\,(reverse(x))) \end{array} \right]$$

(e) *Head-reverse*

$$(\forall \ tuple \ x) \left[\begin{array}{l} if \ \ not \ (x = \langle \ \rangle) \\ then \ \ last(x) \ = \ head\,(reverse(x)) \end{array} \right].$$

Hint: Use the *suffix-decomposition* property of append.

Problem 9.10 (delete) page 452

Suppose we augment the theory of tuples by defining a binary function symbol $delete(u, x)$. Under the intended model, $delete(u, x)$ is the result of deleting all occurrences of the atom u from the tuple x. For example,

$$delete(\text{A}, \langle \text{A, B, A, C} \rangle) \ = \ \langle \text{B, C} \rangle$$

$$delete(\text{A}, \langle \text{B, B, C} \rangle) \ = \ \langle \text{B, B, C} \rangle.$$

(a) Give axioms that define the function *delete*. The only symbols your axioms
    may contain are *delete* and symbols from the unaugmented theory of tuples;
    e.g., you may not use $\diamond$ or *reverse*. Using your axioms, establish the following
    properties of *delete*.

(b) *nonmember*

$$\begin{matrix}(\forall\ atom\ u)\\(\forall\ tuple\ x)\end{matrix}\left[not\ \left(u \in delete(u,\ x)\right)\right]$$

(c) *member*

$$\begin{matrix}(\forall\ atom\ u,\ v)\\(\forall\ tuple\ x)\end{matrix}\left[\begin{matrix}if\ not\ (u = v)\\then\ v \in delete(u,\ x)\end{matrix}\quad\equiv\quad v \in x\right].$$

Problem 9.11 (suffix induction principle)   page 452

Establish the following *suffix induction principle*:

For each sentence $\mathcal{F}[x]$ in the theory, the universal closure of the sentence

$$if\ \begin{bmatrix}\mathcal{F}[\langle\ \rangle]\\and\\(\forall\ atom\ u)\\(\forall\ tuple\ x)\end{bmatrix}\begin{bmatrix}if\ \mathcal{F}[x]\\then\ \mathcal{F}[x \diamond \langle u\rangle]\end{bmatrix}\end{bmatrix}\qquad(suffix\ induction)$$

$$then\ (\forall\ tuple\ x)\mathcal{F}[x],$$

where u does not occur free in $\mathcal{F}[x]$, is valid.

Hint: Use the *reverse* function.

Problem 9.12 (suffix append)   page 452

Suppose we define a new binary function symbol *append1*(x, y) by the following two axioms:

$$(\forall\ tuple\ y)\left[append1(\langle\ \rangle,\ y)\ =\ y\right]\qquad\qquad(left\ empty)$$

$$\begin{matrix}(\forall\ atom\ u)\\(\forall\ tuple\ x, y)\end{matrix}\left[append1(x \diamond \langle u\rangle,\ y)\ =\ append1(x,\ u \diamond y)\right]$$

$$(left\ suffix)$$

Show that these axioms provide an alternative definition for the append function,
in the sense that the sentence

$$(\forall\ tuple\ x, y)\left[x \diamond y\ =\ append1(x,\ y)\right]$$

is valid.

Hint: Use the above *suffix induction* principle.

Problem 9.13 (end append) page 454

(a) Establish the validity of the ($\Rightarrow$) part of the *end-append* proposition, that is,

$$(\forall\, tuple\ x, y) \begin{bmatrix} if\ x \preceq_{end} y \\ then\ (\exists\, tuple\ z)[z \diamond x\ =\ y] \end{bmatrix}.$$

(b) Provide axioms for the end relation expressed in terms of the insertion function $u \diamond x$ rather than the tail function $tail(x)$; show that your axioms provide an alternative definition for the end relation. In other words, your axioms follow from the original axioms and the original axioms follow from your axioms.

Problem 9.14 (palindrome) page 461

Without the use of any *induction* principle, establish the ($\Leftarrow$) part of the *palindrome* proposition, that is,

$$(\forall\, tuple\ x) \begin{bmatrix} if & \begin{bmatrix} (\exists\, tuple\ y)[x\ =\ y \diamond reverse(y)] \\ or \\ \begin{matrix} (\exists\, atom\ u) \\ (\exists\, tuple\ y) \end{matrix}[x = y \diamond \langle u \rangle \diamond reverse(y)] \end{bmatrix} \\ then\ \ palin(x) \end{bmatrix}.$$

Problem 9.15 (initial-subtuple relation) page 466

Establish the *append* property of the initial-subtuple relation, that is,

$$(\forall\, tuple\ x, y) \begin{bmatrix} x \preceq_{init} y \\ \equiv \\ (\exists\, tuple\ z)[x \diamond z = y] \end{bmatrix}.$$

Problem 9.16 (consecutive-subtuple relation) page 467

Prove that the following two properties of the consecutive-subtuple relation $x \preceq_{tuple1} y$ are valid.

(a) *Subtuple*

$$(\forall\, tuple\ x, y) \begin{bmatrix} if\ x \preceq_{tuple1} y \\ then\ x \preceq_{tuple} y \end{bmatrix}$$

(b) *Append*

$$(\forall\, tuple\ x, y) \begin{bmatrix} x \preceq_{tuple1} y \\ \equiv \\ (\exists\, tuple\ z_1, z_2)[z_1 \diamond x \diamond z_2\ =\ y] \end{bmatrix}.$$

Problem 9.17 (alternative consecutive-subtuple relation)   page 467

Suppose we define a new binary predicate symbol $x \preceq_{tuple2} y$ by the following three axioms:

$$\langle\,\rangle \preceq_{tuple2} \langle\,\rangle \qquad\qquad\qquad (empty\ empty)$$

$$\begin{array}{l}(\forall\ atom\ u) \\ (\forall\ tuple\ x)\end{array} \big[not\ (u \diamond x \preceq_{tuple2} \langle\,\rangle) \big] \qquad\qquad (right\ empty)$$

$$\begin{array}{l}(\forall\ atom\ u) \\ (\forall\ tuple\ x, y)\end{array} \left[\begin{array}{c} x \preceq_{tuple2} u \diamond y \\ \equiv \\ x \preceq_{init} u \diamond y \ \ or \ \ x \preceq_{tuple2} y\end{array}\right] \qquad (right\ insertion)$$

(a) Show that these axioms provide an alternative definition for the consecutive-subtuple relation $\preceq_{tuple1}$, in the sense that

$$(\forall\ tuple\ x, y) \big[x \preceq_{tuple1} y \ \ \equiv \ \ x \preceq_{tuple2} y \big]$$

is valid.

(b) Use the axioms for $\preceq_{tuple2}$ to determine whether $\langle B,\ C\rangle$ is a consecutive subtuple of $\langle A,\ B,\ C,\ A\rangle$ and whether $\langle A\rangle$ is a consecutive subtuple of $\langle B\rangle$.

Problem 9.18 (length)   page 469

In the combined theory of nonnegative integers and tuples, establish the following properties of the *length* function:

(a) *Sort*

$$(\forall\ tuple\ x) \big[integer\,(length(x)) \big]$$

(b) *Zero*

$$(\forall\ tuple\ x) \left[\begin{array}{l} if\ \ length(x) = 0 \\ then\ \ x = \langle\,\rangle\end{array}\right]$$

(c) *Singleton*

$$(\forall\ atom\ u) \big[length(\langle u\rangle) = 1 \big]$$

(d) *Reverse*

$$(\forall\ tuple\ x) \big[length\,(reverse(x)) \ = \ length(x) \big]$$

(e) *Proper subtuple*

$$(\forall\ tuple\ x, y) \left[\begin{array}{l} if\ \ x \prec_{tuple} y \\ then\ \ length(x) < length(y)\end{array}\right].$$

Problem 9.19 (left and right)   page 470

In the theory of tuples, we would like to define two unary function symbols *left(x)* and *right(x)* to denote functions that divide the tuple x into two roughly equal parts. Thus,

$$left(\langle A, B, C, D\rangle) = \langle A, B\rangle \qquad right(\langle A, B, C, D\rangle) = \langle C, D\rangle$$

$$left(\langle A, B, C\rangle) = \langle A, B\rangle \qquad right(\langle A, B, C\rangle) = \langle C\rangle.$$

(a) Give axioms that define these functions in the theory of tuples (not in the combined theory of nonnegative integers and tuples). Make sure that your axioms suggest a method for computing the functions.

(b) Using your axioms, establish the following *append* property of *left* and *right*:

$$(\forall\ tuple\ x)\big[left(x) \diamond right(x) = x\big].$$

(c) In the combined theory of nonnegative integers and tuples, using your axioms, establish the following *length* property of *left* and *right*:

$$(\forall\ tuple\ x) \begin{bmatrix} length\,(left(x)) = length\,(right(x)) \\ or \\ length\,(left(x)) = length\,(right(x)) + 1 \end{bmatrix}.$$

Problem 9.20 (periodicity)   page 470

In the combined theory of nonnegative integers and tuples, suppose we define the relation *periodic(x, y)* to hold if the tuple y can be obtained by appending 0 or more copies of the tuple x. For example,

$$periodic(\langle A, B\rangle, \langle A, B, A, B\rangle)$$

$$periodic(\langle A, B\rangle, \langle A, B\rangle)$$

$$periodic(\langle A, B\rangle, \langle\ \rangle)$$

but not

$$periodic(\langle A, B\rangle, \langle A\rangle)$$

The relation *periodic(x, y)* is defined by the following axioms:

$$(\forall\ tuple\ x)[periodic(x, \langle\ \rangle)] \qquad\qquad (right\ empty)$$

$$(\forall\ tuple\ y) \begin{bmatrix} if\ not\ (y = \langle\ \rangle) \\ then\ not\ periodic(\langle\ \rangle, y) \end{bmatrix} \qquad (left\ empty)$$

$$(\forall\ tuple\ x,\ y) \left[\begin{array}{l} if\ not\ (x = \langle\rangle)\ and\ not\ (y = \langle\rangle) \\ then\ periodic(x,\ y)\ \equiv \\ \qquad (\exists\ tuple\ y') \left[\begin{array}{c} x \Diamond y' = y \\ and \\ periodic(x,\ y') \end{array} \right] \end{array} \right]$$

(right nonempty)

Using complete induction, establish the validity of the sentence

$$(\forall\ tuple\ x,\ y) \left[\begin{array}{l} if\ periodic(x,\ y) \\ then\ length(x) \preceq_{div} length(y) \end{array} \right]$$

in the combined theory of nonnegative integers and tuples.

Hint: First prove the following property of *append*:

$$(\forall\ tuple\ x,\ y) \left[\begin{array}{l} if\ not(x = \langle\rangle) \\ then\ y\ \prec_{tuple}\ x \Diamond y \end{array} \right].$$

Problem 9.21 (element of append)   page 472

In the combined theory of nonnegative integers and tuples, establish the properties that relate the append function and the element function; that is,

(a) *Left element*

$$(\forall\ tuple\ x, y) \atop (\forall\ integer\ z)} \left[\begin{array}{l} if\ \ z < length(x) \\ then\ \ [x \Diamond y]_z\ =\ [x]_z \end{array} \right]$$

(b) *Right element*

$$(\forall\ tuple\ x, y) \atop (\forall\ integer\ z)} \left[\begin{array}{l} if\ \ z < length(y) \\ then\ \ [x \Diamond y]_{length(x)+z}\ =\ [y]_z \end{array} \right].$$

Problem 9.22 (eqmult)   page 477

Show that the *eqmult* property of the permutation relation,

$$(\forall\ tuple\ x, y) \left[\begin{array}{l} perm(x,\ y) \\ \equiv \\ (\forall\ atom\ u) \big[eqmult(u,\ x,\ y) \big] \end{array} \right],$$

provides an alternative definition for the relation. In other words, if we replace the three axioms for *perm*, i.e., the *empty*, *append-singleton*, and *member* axioms, with this sentence, we can establish the validity of each of the original three axioms in the altered theory.

Problem 9.23 (extract)   page 477

Suppose we want to augment the theory of tuples by defining a binary function symbol $extract(u, x)$. Under the intended model, $extract(u, x)$ is the tuple containing all the occurrences of the atom u in the tuple x. For example,

$$extract(\text{A}, \langle \text{A}, \text{B}, \text{A}, \text{A}, \text{C} \rangle) = \langle \text{A}, \text{A}, \text{A} \rangle$$

$$extract(\text{B}, \langle \text{A}, \text{B}, \text{A}, \text{A}, \text{C} \rangle) = \langle \text{B} \rangle$$

$$extract(\text{D}, \langle \text{A}, \text{B}, \text{A}, \text{A}, \text{C} \rangle) = \langle \, \rangle.$$

(a) Give axioms that define the function *extract*. The only symbols your axioms may contain are *extract* and symbols from the unaugmented theory of tuples; e.g., you may not use $\diamond$ or *reverse*.

(b) Using your axioms, establish the following property of *eqmult*:

$$(\forall \, atom \; u) \atop (\forall \, tuple \; x, \; y) \left[eqmult(u, \; x, \; y) \atop \equiv \atop extract(u, \; x) = extract(u, \; y) \right] \qquad (extract)$$

(c) Use the *extract* function to provide an alternative definition of the permutation relation $perm(x, y)$. The only symbols your axioms may contain are *perm*, *extract*, and symbols from the unaugmented theory of tuples.

(d) Prove the alternative definition of *perm* from Part (c).

Problem 9.24 (permutation relation)   page 477

Establish the validity of the following properties of the permutation relation:

(a)   *Exchange*

$$(\forall \; atom \; u, v) \atop (\forall \; tuple \; x) \left[perm \big(u \diamond (v \diamond x), \; v \diamond (u \diamond x) \big) \right]$$

(b)   *Append*

$$(\forall \; tuple \; x_1, x_2, y_1, y_2) \left[\begin{array}{l} if \; perm(x_1, \; y_1) \; and \\ \quad perm(x_2, \; y_2) \\ then \; perm(x_1 \diamond x_2, \; y_1 \diamond y_2) \end{array} \right]$$

(c)   *Append-insertion*

$$(\forall \; atom \; u) \atop (\forall \; tuple \; x_1, \; x_2, \; y) \left[perm \big(x_1 \diamond (u \diamond x_2), \; u \diamond y \big) \atop \equiv \atop perm(x_1 \diamond x_2, \; y) \right].$$

Problem 9.25 (insertion of ordered)   page 481

The inductive step of the *insertion* proposition was proved in the text in only one direction. Complete the proof in the other direction.

Problem 9.26 (alternative definition of ordered)   page 481

Show that the *empty* axiom for *ordered*,

$$ordered(\langle\,\rangle),$$

and the *insertion* property of *ordered*,

$$(\forall\ atom\ u)\ (\forall\ tuple\ x)\ \left[\begin{array}{l} ordered(u \diamond x) \\[4pt] \equiv \\[4pt] \left[\begin{array}{l} ordered(x) \\ and \\ (\forall\ atom\ v)\ \left[\begin{array}{l} if\ \ v \in x \\ then\ \ u \le v \end{array}\right] \end{array}\right] \end{array}\right],$$

provide an alternative definition of the *ordered* relation. In other words, if we replace the *singleton* and *double-insertion* axioms for *ordered* with the *insertion* property, we can establish the validity of the *singleton* and *double-insertion* axioms in the altered theory.

Problem 9.27 (ordered relation)   page 481

In the theory of tuples of nonnegative integers, establish the *append* property of the *ordered* relation, that is,

$$(\forall\ tuple\ x, y)\ \left[\begin{array}{l} ordered(x \diamond y) \\[4pt] \equiv \\[4pt] \left[\begin{array}{l} ordered(x)\ \ and\ \ ordered(y) \\ and \\ (\forall\ atom\ u, v)\ \left[\begin{array}{l} if\ \ u \in x\ \ and\ \ v \in y \\ then\ \ u \le v \end{array}\right] \end{array}\right] \end{array}\right].$$

Problem 9.28 (insertion sort function)   page 490

In the theory of tuples of nonnegative integers, establish the validity of the following sentences:

(a) *Ordered permutation*

$$(\forall\ tuple\ x, y)\ \left[\begin{array}{l} if\ \ perm(x,\ y)\ \ and \\ \quad ordered(x)\ \ and \\ \quad ordered(y) \\ then\ \ x = y \end{array}\right]$$

(b) *Uniqueness (of insort)*

$$(\forall\ tuple\ x, y)\ \left[\begin{array}{l} if\ \ ordered(y)\ \ and \\ \quad perm(x,\ y) \\ then\ \ y = insort(x) \end{array}\right]$$

(c)   *Idempotence* (*of insort*)

$$(\forall \ tuple \ x)\big[insort(insort(x)) = insort(x)\big].$$

List all the new properties of the nonnegative integers you use; you need not prove them. As usual, you may use without proof any appropriate *sort* properties.

Problem 9.29 (quicksort function)   page 493

In the theory of tuples of nonnegative integers, establish the validity of the following properties of the auxiliary functions for *quicksort*:

(a)   *Sort* (*of lesseq*)

$$\begin{matrix} (\forall \ atom \ u) \\ (\forall \ tuple \ x) \end{matrix} \big[tuple\,(lesseq(u, \ x))\big]$$

(b)   *Subtuple* (*of lesseq*)

$$\begin{matrix} (\forall \ atom \ u) \\ (\forall \ tuple \ x) \end{matrix} \big[lesseq(u, x) \preceq_{tuple} x\big]$$

(c)   *Bound* (*of lesseq*)

$$\begin{matrix} (\forall \ atom \ u, \ v) \\ (\forall \ tuple \ x) \end{matrix} \begin{bmatrix} if \ \ v \in lesseq(u, \ x) \\ then \ \ v \le u \end{bmatrix}$$

(d)   *Permutation* (*of lesseq and greater*)

$$\begin{matrix} (\forall \ atom \ u) \\ (\forall \ tuple \ x) \end{matrix} \big[perm\,(x, \ lesseq(u, \ x) \diamond greater(u, \ x))\big].$$

Problem 9.30 (minimum function)   page 502

In the theory of tuples of nonnegative integers, establish the *least* property of the minimum function, that is,

$$(\forall \ tuple \ x) \begin{bmatrix} if \ \ not \ (x = \langle \ \rangle) \\ \\ then \quad \begin{bmatrix} mintuple(x) \in x \\ and \\ (\forall \ atom \ u) \begin{bmatrix} if \ \ u \in x \\ then \ \ mintuple(x) \le u \end{bmatrix} \end{bmatrix} \end{bmatrix}.$$

In other words, $mintuple(x)$ is the least element of a nonempty tuple x.

Problem 9.31 (cumulative minimum)   page 502

In the theory of tuples of nonnegative integers, consider the minimum function $mintuplec(x)$ defined by the axioms

$$(\forall \ integer \ u)\big[mintuplec(\langle u \rangle) \ = \ u\big] \qquad\qquad (singleton)$$

$$(\forall\ integer\ u,\ v) \atop (\forall\ tuple\ x)} \left[mintuplec\big(u \diamond (v \diamond x)\big) \ = \ \left\{ \begin{array}{l} if\ \ u \le v \\ then\ \ mintuplec(u \diamond x) \\ else\ \ mintuplec(v \diamond x) \end{array} \right\} \right]$$

(*double insertion*)

Show that the function $mintuplec(x)$ computes the minimum element of a given (nonempty) tuple x, in the sense that

(a) *Member*

$$(\forall\ tuple\ x) \left[\begin{array}{l} if\ \ not\ \big(x = \langle\ \rangle\big) \\ then\ \ mintuplec(x) \in x \end{array} \right]$$

(b) *Least*

$$(\forall\ tuple\ x) \atop (\forall\ integer\ u)} \left[\begin{array}{l} if\ \ u \in x \\ then\ \ mintuplec(x) \le u \end{array} \right].$$

Hint: Use complete induction for both parts.

Problem 9.32 (selection sort function)   page 502

Consider the theory of tuples of nonnegative integers. Show that the function *selsort* provides an alternative definition of the sorting function by showing the following properties:

(a) *Permutation*

The tuple $selsort(x)$ is a permutation of the tuple x, that is,

$$(\forall\ tuple\ x) \big[perm\big(x,\ selsort(x)\big) \big].$$

(b) *Ordered*

The tuple $selsort(x)$ is in (weakly) increasing order, that is,

$$(\forall\ tuple\ x) \big[ordered\big(selsort(x)\big) \big].$$

(c) *Insort*

The function *selsort* is identical to the function *insort*, that is,

$$(\forall\ tuple\ x) \big[selsort(x)\ =\ insort(x) \big].$$

Indicate clearly all the properties of tuples used in your proofs; you need not prove them.

Hint: Use complete induction for parts (a) and (b).

10

Trees

In this section we present another theory with induction, the theory of trees. The development of the theory is analogous to that of the theory of tuples. Intuitively speaking, we are given a set of elements (called the *atoms*) and consider binary trees whose leaves are atoms. For example, if the set of atoms is {A, B, C}, then

are all trees.

The set of atoms may be either finite or infinite, but each tree must be finite, i.e., must contain only finitely many nodes and leaves. Our trees are binary; in other words, each node ● has precisely two arcs descending from it.

10.1   BASIC PROPERTIES

In the theory of trees, we define

- A unary predicate symbol $atom(x)$
- A unary predicate symbol $tree(x)$
- A binary function symbol $x \bullet y$, denoting the *construction* function.

Under the intended models for the theory, the relation $atom(x)$ is true if x is an atom and false otherwise. Also, if x and y denote two trees, $x \bullet y$ denotes the tree

Thus if under a particular interpretation x denotes the atom A and y denotes the atom B, then $x \bullet (x \bullet y)$ denotes the tree

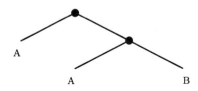

We shall also use A $\bullet$ (A $\bullet$ B) as an informal notation for the above tree.

The theory of trees is a theory with equality defined by the following axioms:

- The *generation* axioms

$$(\forall\ atom\ x)[tree(x)] \hspace{5cm} (atom)$$

$$(\forall\ tree\ x, y)\big[tree(x \bullet y)\big] \hspace{3.5cm} (construction)$$

- The *uniqueness* axioms

$$(\forall\ tree\ x, y)\big[not\ (atom(x \bullet y))\big] \hspace{3cm} (atom)$$

$$(\forall\ tree\ x_1, x_2, y_1, y_2)\begin{bmatrix} if\ \ x_1 \bullet x_2 = y_1 \bullet y_2 \\ then\ \ x_1 = y_1\ \ and\ \ x_2 = y_2 \end{bmatrix}$$
$$(construction)$$

- The *(stepwise) induction* principle

> For each sentence $\mathcal{F}[x]$ in the theory, the universal closure of
> the sentence
> $$if\ \begin{bmatrix} (\forall\ atom\ u)\mathcal{F}[u] \\ and \\ (\forall\ tree\ x_1, x_2)\begin{bmatrix} if\ \mathcal{F}[x_1]\ and\ \mathcal{F}[x_2] \\ then\ \ \mathcal{F}[x_1 \bullet x_2] \end{bmatrix} \end{bmatrix}$$
> $$(induction)$$
> then $(\forall\ tree\ x)\mathcal{F}[x]$,
>
> where u, x_1, and x_2 do not occur free in $\mathcal{F}[x]$, is an axiom.

The two generation axioms have the intuitive meaning that every atom is a tree and the result of applying the construction function to two trees is also a tree. The two uniqueness axioms have the intuitive meaning that a tree can be constructed in at most one way from the atoms and the construction function $x \bullet y$.

For the induction principle, the sentence $\mathcal{F}[x]$ is called the *inductive* sentence. The subsentence

$$(\forall \ atom \ u)\mathcal{F}[u]$$

is called the *base case*. The subsentence

$$(\forall \ tree \ x_1, x_2) \begin{bmatrix} if \ \mathcal{F}[x_1] \ and \ \mathcal{F}[x_2] \\ then \ \mathcal{F}[x_1 \bullet x_2] \end{bmatrix}$$

is called the *inductive step*; the subsentences $\mathcal{F}[x_1]$ and $\mathcal{F}[x_2]$ of the inductive step are called the *induction hypotheses*, and the subsentence $\mathcal{F}[x_1 \bullet x_2]$ is called the *desired conclusion*.

Since the theory of trees is a theory with equality, we include among our axioms the *transitivity*, *symmetry*, and *reflexivity* axioms for equality, as well as the instances of the *functional-substitutivity* axiom schema for the construction function and the instances of the *predicate-substitutivity* axiom schema for the *atom* and *tree* relations.

In this theory we can establish the following decomposition property:

$$(\forall \ tree \ x) \begin{bmatrix} if \ not \ (atom(x)) \\ then \ (\exists \ tree \ x_1, x_2) [x = x_1 \bullet x_2] \end{bmatrix} \qquad (decomposition)$$

The proof is analogous to that of the *decomposition* properties of earlier theories.

There is some similarity between the theory of tuples and the theory of trees. Roughly speaking, the *atom* predicate for the trees is analogous to the *atom* predicate for the tuples, and the construction function $x \bullet y$ for the trees is analogous to the insertion function $u \diamond x$ for the tuples. This analogy is not precise, however, because the axioms for the insertion function $u \diamond x$ presuppose that the first argument u is an atom, while the axioms for the construction function $x \bullet y$ admit the possibility that the first argument x is any tree, not necessarily an atom. In contrast with the tuples, we include the atoms themselves among the trees. Also there is an empty tuple $\langle \ \rangle$ but no empty tree. These are the basic differences between the two theories.

10.2   THE LEFT AND RIGHT FUNCTIONS

We may augment our theory of trees by defining two unary function symbols $left(x)$ and $right(x)$, denoting the *left subtree* and *right subtree*, respectively, of

x. These functions are analogous to the *head* and *tail* functions over the tuples; they are defined by the following axioms:

$$(\forall\ tree\ x, y)\big[left(x \bullet y)\ =\ x\big] \qquad (left)$$

$$(\forall\ tree\ x, y)\big[right(x \bullet y)\ =\ y\big] \qquad (right)$$

For example, the *left* and *right* functions applied to the tree $(C \bullet A) \bullet ((B \bullet A) \bullet C)$, that is,

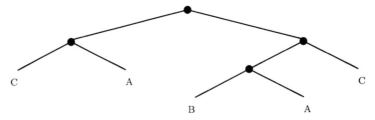

yield the trees $C \bullet A$ and $(B \bullet A) \bullet C$, that is,

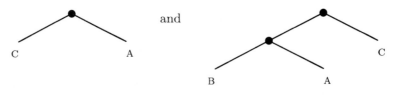

respectively.

Note that these axioms do not specify the values of the terms *left*(u) and *right*(u) if u denotes an atom. Although such terms are legal in the language, our axioms do not force them to have any particular value.

From the axioms for *left* and *right* we can establish the following properties:

$$(\forall\ tree\ x)\begin{bmatrix} if\ \ not\ (atom(x)) \\ then\ \ tree\,(left(x)) \end{bmatrix} \qquad (sort\ of\ left)$$

$$(\forall\ tree\ x)\begin{bmatrix} if\ \ not\ (atom(x)) \\ then\ \ tree\,(right(x)) \end{bmatrix} \qquad (sort\ of\ right)$$

$$(\forall\ tree\ x)\begin{bmatrix} if\ \ not\ (atom(x)) \\ then\ \ x\ =\ left(x) \bullet right(x) \end{bmatrix} \qquad (decomposition)$$

The proofs, which are straightforward, are left as an exercise (**Problem 10.1**).

The *left* and *right* functions may be used to express a *decomposition version* of the induction principle for trees.

Proposition (decomposition induction principle)
For each sentence $\mathcal{F}[x]$, the universal closure of the sentence

$$
if \left[\begin{array}{l} (\forall\ atom\ u)\mathcal{F}[u] \\ \quad and \\ (\forall\ tree\ x) \left[\begin{array}{l} if\ \ not\ (atom(x)) \\ then\ if\ \ \mathcal{F}\big[left(x)\big]\ \ and\ \ \mathcal{F}\big[right(x)\big] \\ \qquad then\ \ \mathcal{F}[x] \end{array} \right] \end{array} \right]
$$

$then\ \ (\forall\ tree\ x)\mathcal{F}[x],$

(*decomposition induction*)

where u does not occur free in $\mathcal{F}[x]$, is valid. ⌐

The proof is left as an exercise (**Problem 10.2**).

The decomposition induction principle is more convenient to use when dealing with axioms and properties expressed in terms of the *left* and *right* functions. Because in this book we typically express our properties in terms of the construction function $x \bullet y$ instead, we find the original version of the induction principle more useful.

10.3   THE SUBTREE RELATION

The *subtrees* of a given tree x are the tree itself, the left and right subtrees of x (if x is not an atom), the left and right subtrees of $left(x)$ and $right(x)$ (if they are not atoms), and so forth. For example, the subtrees of the tree A $\bullet$ (B $\bullet$ C), that is,

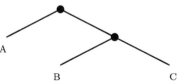

are A $\bullet$ (B $\bullet$ C) itself, the left subtree A, the right subtree B $\bullet$ C, and its subtrees B and C. That is,

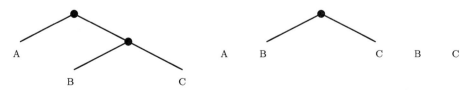

The *proper subtrees* of a given tree x are the subtrees of x other than x itself.

Formally, we augment our theory by simultaneously defining two binary predicate symbols, $x \preceq_{tree} y$ and $x \prec_{tree} y$, denoting that x is a *subtree* and a *proper subtree*, respectively, of y. The two relations are defined by the following three axioms:

$$(\forall\ tree\ x, y) \begin{bmatrix} x \preceq_{tree} y \\ \equiv \\ x \prec_{tree} y \ \ or \ \ x = y \end{bmatrix} \qquad (subtree)$$

$$\begin{matrix}(\forall\ atom\ u) \\ (\forall\ tree\ x)\end{matrix} \big[not\ (x \prec_{tree} u)\big] \qquad (atom)$$

$$(\forall\ tree\ x, y, z) \begin{bmatrix} x \prec_{tree} y \bullet z \\ \equiv \\ x \preceq_{tree} y \ \ or \ \ x \preceq_{tree} z \end{bmatrix} \qquad (construction)$$

Note that these definitions depend on each other: The definition of the subtree relation $\preceq_{tree}$ refers to the proper-subtree relation $\prec_{tree}$, and the definition of the proper-subtree relation $\prec_{tree}$ refers to the subtree relation $\preceq_{tree}$. Such definitions are said to be "mutually recursive."

We can establish the following properties of the two relations:

$$\begin{matrix}(\forall\ atom\ u) \\ (\forall\ tree\ x)\end{matrix} \begin{bmatrix} if\ \ x \preceq_{tree} u \\ then\ \ x = u \end{bmatrix} \qquad (atom)$$

$$(\forall\ tree\ x, y) \big[x \prec_{tree} x \bullet y\big] \qquad (left\ construction)$$

$$(\forall\ tree\ x, y) \big[y \prec_{tree} x \bullet y\big] \qquad (right\ construction)$$

$$(\forall\ tree\ x) \begin{bmatrix} if\ \ not\ (atom(x)) \\ then\ \ left(x) \prec_{tree} x \end{bmatrix} \qquad (left)$$

$$(\forall\ tree\ x) \begin{bmatrix} if\ \ not\ (atom(x)) \\ then\ \ right(x) \prec_{tree} x \end{bmatrix} \qquad (right)$$

The proofs are straightforward.

We would like to establish that the proper-subtree relation $\prec_{tree}$ is a strict partial ordering, i.e., that it is transitive and irreflexive. It is convenient to establish first the right mixed transitivity of $\preceq_{tree}$.

Proposition (right mixed transitivity)

The sentence

$$(\forall \ tree \ x, y, z) \begin{bmatrix} if \ x \prec_{tree} y \ and \ y \preceq_{tree} z \\ then \ x \prec_{tree} z \end{bmatrix}$$

(right mixed transitivity)

is valid. ⌐

Proof. We shall actually show the equivalent sentence

$$(\forall \ tree \ x, y) \begin{bmatrix} if \ x \prec_{tree} y \\ then \ (\forall \ tree \ z) \begin{bmatrix} if \ y \preceq_{tree} z \\ then \ x \prec_{tree} z \end{bmatrix} \end{bmatrix}.$$

Consider arbitrary trees x and y such that

(*) $x \prec_{tree} y$.

It suffices to show that

$$(\forall \ tree \ z) \begin{bmatrix} if \ y \preceq_{tree} z \\ then \ x \prec_{tree} z \end{bmatrix}.$$

The proof is by induction on z, taking the inductive sentence to be

$$\mathcal{F}[z]: \quad \begin{array}{l} if \ y \preceq_{tree} z \\ then \ x \prec_{tree} z. \end{array}$$

Base Case

We would like to show

$$(\forall \ atom \ u)\mathcal{F}[u],$$

that is,

$$(\forall \ atom \ u) \begin{bmatrix} if \ y \preceq_{tree} u \\ then \ x \prec_{tree} u \end{bmatrix}.$$

For an arbitrary atom u, suppose that

$$y \preceq_{tree} u;$$

then (by the *atom* property of the subtree relation $\preceq_{tree}$)

$$y = u$$

and hence (by our initial assumption (*) that $x \prec_{tree} y$)

$$x \prec_{tree} u,$$

which is our desired result.

Note that the result $x \prec_{tree} u$ actually contradicts the *atom* property of the proper-subtree relation $\prec_{tree}$. In other words, our supposition that $y \preceq_{tree} u$, cannot be true, and the base case holds vacuously.

Inductive Step

We would like to show

$$(\forall \; tree \; z_1, z_2) \begin{bmatrix} if \;\; \mathcal{F}[z_1] \;\; and \;\; \mathcal{F}[z_2] \\ then \;\; \mathcal{F}[z_1 \bullet z_2] \end{bmatrix}.$$

For arbitrary trees z_1 and z_2, assume the two induction hypotheses

$$\mathcal{F}[z_1]: \quad \begin{array}{l} if \;\; y \preceq_{tree} z_1 \\ then \;\; x \prec_{tree} z_1 \end{array}$$

and

$$\mathcal{F}[z_2]: \quad \begin{array}{l} if \;\; y \preceq_{tree} z_2 \\ then \;\; x \prec_{tree} z_2. \end{array}$$

We would like to establish the desired conclusion

$$\mathcal{F}[z_1 \bullet z_2]: \quad \begin{array}{l} if . \; y \preceq_{tree} z_1 \bullet z_2 \\ then \;\; x \prec_{tree} z_1 \bullet z_2. \end{array}$$

Suppose that

$$y \preceq_{tree} z_1 \bullet z_2;$$

we would like to show that

$$x \prec_{tree} z_1 \bullet z_2.$$

Because $y \preceq_{tree} z_1 \bullet z_2$, we have (by the definition of the subtree relation $\preceq_{tree}$)
that

$$y \prec_{tree} z_1 \bullet z_2 \quad or \quad y = z_1 \bullet z_2.$$

We treat each case separately.

Case: $y = z_1 \bullet z_2$

By our initial assumption $(*)$ that $x \prec_{tree} y$, we have

$$x \prec_{tree} z_1 \bullet z_2.$$

Case: $y \prec_{tree} z_1 \bullet z_2$

Then (by the *construction* axiom for the proper-subtree relation $\prec_{tree}$) we
have

$$y \preceq_{tree} z_1 \quad or \quad y \preceq_{tree} z_2.$$

By our two induction hypotheses $\mathcal{F}[z_1]$ and $\mathcal{F}[z_2]$, therefore, we have

$$x \prec_{tree} z_1 \quad or \quad x \prec_{tree} z_2$$

and hence (by the definition of the subtree relation $\preceq_{tree}$)

$$x \preceq_{tree} z_1 \quad or \quad x \preceq_{tree} z_2.$$

It follows (by the *construction* axiom for the proper-subtree relation $\prec_{tree}$ again)
that

$$x \prec_{tree} z_1 \bullet z_2,$$

as we wanted to show. ⌐

PARTIAL ORDERING

We have established the *right mixed-transitivity* property of $\preceq_{tree}$. Using this property one can establish that $\prec_{tree}$ is a strict partial ordering, that is,

$$(\forall \ tree \ x, y, z) \begin{bmatrix} if \ \ x \prec_{tree} y \ \ and \ \ y \prec_{tree} z \\ then \ \ x \prec_{tree} z \end{bmatrix}. \qquad (transitivity)$$

$$(\forall \ tree \ x) \big[not \ (x \prec_{tree} x) \big] \qquad\qquad (irreflexivity)$$

The reader is requested in **Problem 10.3** to prove the transitivity of $\prec_{tree}$. Let us establish the irreflexivity of $\prec_{tree}$.

Proposition (irreflexivity)

The sentence

$$(\forall \ tree \ x) \big[not \ (x \prec_{tree} x) \big] \qquad\qquad (irreflexivity)$$

is valid. ⌐

Proof.   The proof is by induction on x, taking the inductive sentence to be

$$\mathcal{F}[x]: \quad not \ (x \prec_{tree} x).$$

Base Case

We would like to show

$$(\forall \ atom \ u) \big[not \ (u \prec_{tree} u) \big],$$

but this follows from the *atom* axiom for $\prec_{tree}$, taking x to be u.

Inductive Step

For arbitrary trees x_1 and x_2, assume the two induction hypotheses

$$\mathcal{F}[x_1]: \quad not \ (x_1 \prec_{tree} x_1)$$

and

$$\mathcal{F}[x_2]: \quad not \ (x_2 \prec_{tree} x_2);$$

we would like to establish the desired conclusion

$$\mathcal{F}[x_1 \bullet x_2]: \quad not \ (x_1 \bullet x_2 \prec_{tree} x_1 \bullet x_2).$$

Suppose, contrary to our desired conclusion,

$$x_1 \bullet x_2 \prec_{tree} x_1 \bullet x_2.$$

Then (by the *construction* axiom for the proper-subtree relation $\prec_{tree}$)

$$x_1 \bullet x_2 \preceq_{tree} x_1 \quad or \quad x_1 \bullet x_2 \preceq_{tree} x_2.$$

We know (by the *left-* and *right-construction* properties of the proper subtree relation $\prec_{tree}$) that

$$x_1 \prec_{tree} x_1 \bullet x_2 \quad and \quad x_2 \prec_{tree} x_1 \bullet x_2.$$

Therefore (by the *right mixed-transitivity* property of the subtree relation $\preceq_{tree}$)

$$x_1 \prec_{tree} x_1 \quad or \quad x_2 \prec_{tree} x_2.$$

But each of these conditions contradicts one of our induction hypotheses $\mathcal{F}[x_1]$ and $\mathcal{F}[x_2]$. ⏹

We have established that $\prec_{tree}$ is transitive and irreflexive; in other words, it is a strict partial ordering. It follows from the *reflexive-closure* proposition (Section 6.6) that $\preceq_{tree}$ is a weak partial ordering, that is,

$$(\forall\ tree\ x, y, z) \left[\begin{array}{l} if\ \ x \preceq_{tree} y\ \ and\ \ y \preceq_{tree} z \\ then\ \ x \preceq_{tree} z \end{array} \right] \qquad (transitivity)$$

$$(\forall\ tree\ x, y) \left[\begin{array}{l} if\ \ x \preceq_{tree} y\ \ and\ \ y \preceq_{tree} x \\ then\ \ x = y \end{array} \right] \qquad (antisymmetry)$$

$$(\forall\ tree\ x) \left[x \preceq_{tree} x \right] \qquad (reflexivity)$$

THE COMPLETE INDUCTION PRINCIPLE

Using the proper-subtree relation $\prec_{tree}$, we can state and prove another induction principle. This principle is the *complete induction principle* for the trees; it is analogous to the *complete induction* principles for the nonnegative integers and tuples.

Proposition (complete induction)

For each sentence $\mathcal{F}[x]$, the universal closure of the sentence

$$if\ (\forall\ tree\ x) \left[if\ (\forall\ tree\ x') \left[\begin{array}{l} if\ \ x' \prec_{tree} x \\ then\ \ \mathcal{F}[x'] \end{array} \right] \right]$$
$$then\ \ \mathcal{F}[x]$$
$$then\ (\forall\ tree\ x)\mathcal{F}[x]$$

$$(complete\ induction)$$

where x' does not occur free in $\mathcal{F}[x]$, is valid. ⏹

10.4   TUPLES AND TREES

We have seen in the previous chapter that the theory of the tuples can be combined with the theory of the nonnegative integers. We now introduce a theory that combines the theories of the tuples and the trees.

In the combined theory we shall identify the atoms of the tuples with the atoms of the trees; this is expressed by using a single predicate symbol $atom(x)$ to characterize the atoms of both theories. (If we did not want to identify the atoms of the two theories, we would have had to replace the symbol $atom$ with some other symbol in all the axioms of one of the theories.)

Let us augment our combined theory by defining a unary function symbol $flattree(x)$. Under the intended models, for any tree x the value of $flattree(x)$ is the tuple whose elements are the leaves of x, in left-to-right order. For example, if x is the tree $\text{A} \bullet \big((\text{D} \bullet \text{C}) \bullet \text{B}\big)$, that is,

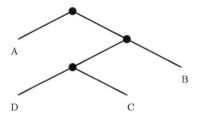

then $flattree(x)$ is the tuple $\langle \text{A, D, C, B} \rangle$.

The function is defined by the axioms

$$(\forall\ atom\ u)\big[flattree(u) = \langle u \rangle\big] \qquad\qquad (atom)$$

$$(\forall\ tree\ x, y)\left[\begin{matrix} flattree(x \bullet y) = \\ flattree(x) \diamond flattree(y) \end{matrix}\right] \qquad (construction)$$

Here $\diamond$ is the append function for tuples.

From these axioms we can establish the appropriate *sort* property of *flattree*, namely,

$$(\forall\ tree\ x)\big[tuple\big(flattree(x)\big)\big] \qquad\qquad (sort)$$

Now let us introduce an alternative method of flattening a tree. We define a new binary function symbol $flattree2(x, z)$; intuitively speaking, for a given tree x and tuple z, $flattree2(x, z)$ flattens x and appends the resulting tuple with the tuple z. For example, if x is the tree $\text{A} \bullet \big((\text{D} \bullet \text{C}) \bullet \text{B}\big)$ and z is the tuple $\langle \text{B, A} \rangle$ then $flattree2(x, z)$ is the tuple $\langle \text{A, D, C, B, B, A} \rangle$.

The *flattree2* function is defined by the following axioms:

$$\begin{matrix} (\forall \; atom \; u) \\ (\forall \; tuple \; z) \end{matrix} \left[flattree2(u, \; z) \; = \; u \diamond z \right] \hspace{2cm} (atom)$$

$$\begin{matrix} (\forall \; tree \; x, y) \\ (\forall \; tuple \; z) \end{matrix} \left[\begin{matrix} flattree2(x \bullet y, \; z) \; = \\ flattree2\big(x, \; flattree2(y, \; z)\big) \end{matrix} \right] \hspace{1cm} (construction)$$

Note that, in the above *atom* axiom, $u \diamond z$ is the tuple insertion function applied to the atom u and tuple z; in the *construction* axiom, $x \bullet y$ is the tree construction function applied to the trees x and y.

As before, we can establish the appropriate *sort* property,

$$\begin{matrix} (\forall \; tree \; x) \\ (\forall \; tuple \; z) \end{matrix} \left[tuple\big(flattree2(x, \; z)\big) \right] \hspace{2cm} (sort)$$

That *flattree2* provides an alternative definition for the *flattree* function is expressed in the following proposition.

Proposition (alternative flattree)

The sentence

$$(\forall \; tree \; x) \left[flattree(x) \; = \; flattree2(x, \; \langle \; \rangle) \right] \hspace{1cm} (special \; flattree2)$$

is valid.   ◢

The proof provides another example of the need for generalization.

Proof.   We actually establish the more general sentence

$$\begin{matrix} (\forall \; tree \; x) \\ (\forall \; tuple \; z) \end{matrix} \left[flattree2(x, \; z) \; = \; flattree(x) \diamond z \right] \hspace{1cm} (general \; flatree2)$$

which expresses the relationship between the two functions. This implies the original sentence, taking z to be $\langle \; \rangle$ (by the *right-empty* property of the append function $\diamond$).

The proof of the *general flattree2* property is by stepwise induction on the tree x, taking the inductive sentence to be

$$\mathcal{F}[x] : \hspace{0.5cm} (\forall \; tuple \; z) \left[flattree2(x, \; z) \; = \; flattree(x) \diamond z \right].$$

Base Case

We would like to show

$$(\forall \; atom \; u) \mathcal{F}[u],$$

that is,

$$\begin{matrix} (\forall \; atom \; u) \\ (\forall \; tuple \; z) \end{matrix} \left[flattree2(u, \; z) \; = \; flattree(u) \diamond z \right].$$

Consider an arbitrary atom u and tuple z; then we have

$$flattree2(u,\ z) \ =\ u \diamond z$$
$$\text{(by the } atom \text{ axiom for } flattree2\text{)}.$$

But, on the other hand,

$$flattree(u) \diamond z \ =\ \langle u \rangle \diamond z$$
$$\text{(by the } atom \text{ axiom for } flattree\text{)}$$

$$=\ u \diamond z$$
$$\text{(by the } singleton \text{ property of append)}.$$

Inductive Step

We would like to show

$$(\forall\ tree\ x_1, x_2)\ \begin{bmatrix} if\ \ \mathcal{F}[x_1]\ \ and\ \ \mathcal{F}[x_2] \\ then\ \ \mathcal{F}[x_1 \bullet x_2] \end{bmatrix}.$$

For arbitrary trees x_1 and x_2, assume the two induction hypotheses,

$$\mathcal{F}[x_1]: \quad (\forall\ tuple\ z_1)\big[flattree2(x_1,\ z_1) \ =\ flattree(x_1) \diamond z_1\big]$$

and

$$\mathcal{F}[x_2]: \quad (\forall\ tuple\ z_2)\big[flattree2(x_2,\ z_2) \ =\ flattree(x_2) \diamond z_2\big].$$

(Note that to avoid confusion we have renamed the bound variables of the two induction hypotheses.)

We would like to establish the desired conclusion

$$\mathcal{F}[x_1 \bullet x_2]: \quad (\forall\ tuple\ z)\big[flattree2(x_1 \bullet x_2,\ z) \ =\ flattree(x_1 \bullet x_2) \diamond z\big].$$

For an arbitrary tuple z, we have

$$flattree2(x_1 \bullet x_2,\ z) \ =\ flattree2\big(x_1,\ flattree2(x_2,\ z)\big)$$
$$\text{(by the } construction \text{ axiom for } flattree2\text{)}$$

$$=\ flattree(x_1) \diamond flattree2(x_2,\ z)$$
$$\text{(by our first induction hypothesis } \mathcal{F}[x_1],$$
$$\text{taking } z_1 \text{ to be } flattree2(x_2, z)\text{)}$$

$$=\ flattree(x_1) \diamond \big(flattree(x_2) \diamond z\big)$$
$$\text{(by our second induction hypothesis } \mathcal{F}[x_2],$$
$$\text{taking } z_2 \text{ to be } z\text{)}.$$

But on the other hand,

$$flattree(x_1 \bullet x_2) \diamond z \ =\ \big(flattree(x_1) \diamond flattree(x_2)\big) \diamond z$$
$$\text{(by the } construction \text{ axiom for } flattree\text{)}$$

$$=\ flattree(x_1) \diamond \big(flattree(x_2) \diamond z\big)$$
$$\text{(by the associativity of append)}. \ \blacksquare$$

Another alternative definition for *flattree* is given in **Problem 10.4**. In **Problem 10.5**, some relationships between the number of nodes, the number of leaves, and the depth of a tree are formulated in a combined theory of trees and nonnegative integers. In **Problem 10.6**, we establish an alternative method for counting the leaves of a tree. In **Problem 10.7**, we introduce a function for reversing a tree and ask the reader to establish one of its properties. In **Problem 10.8**, the reader is requested to consider whether certain variations on the induction principles of the theories of nonnegative integers, tuples, and trees are valid.

In **Problem 10.9**, we ask the reader to design an original theory of integers that includes negative as well as nonnegative integers. This problem is placed here not because it requires particular results from the theory of trees, but because it demands the sophistication the reader has acquired by being exposed to a variety of theories.

PROBLEMS

Problem 10.1 (left and right)   page 518

Establish the following properties:

(a) *Sort of left*

$$(\forall \ tree \ x) \begin{bmatrix} if \ \ not \ (atom(x)) \\ then \ \ tree\,(left(x)) \end{bmatrix}$$

(b) *Sort of right*

$$(\forall \ tree \ x) \begin{bmatrix} if \ \ not \ (atom(x)) \\ then \ \ tree\,(right(x)) \end{bmatrix}$$

(c) *Decomposition*

$$(\forall \ tree \ x) \begin{bmatrix} if \ \ not \ (atom(x)) \\ then \ \ x \ = \ left(x) \ \bullet \ right(x) \end{bmatrix}.$$

Problem 10.2 (decomposition induction principle)   page 519

Establish the decomposition induction principle, that is,
for each sentence $\mathcal{F}[x]$, the universal closure of the sentence

$$if \begin{bmatrix} (\forall \ atom \ u)\mathcal{F}[u] \\ and \\ (\forall \ tree \ x) \begin{bmatrix} if \ \ not \ (atom(x)) \\ then \ if \ \mathcal{F}\big[left(x)\big] \ \ and \ \ \mathcal{F}\big[right(x)\big] \\ then \ \mathcal{F}[x] \end{bmatrix} \end{bmatrix}$$

   then $(\forall \ tree \ x)\mathcal{F}[x]$,

where u does not occur free in $\mathcal{F}[x]$, is valid.

Problem 10.3 (proper-subtree relation)   page 523

Establish the following transitivity property of the proper-subtree relation:

$$(\forall\ tree\ x, y, z) \begin{bmatrix} if\ \ x \prec_{tree} y\ \ and\ \ y \prec_{tree} z \\ then\ \ x \prec_{tree} z \end{bmatrix}.$$

Problem 10.4 (another alternative definition for flattree)   page 527

In the combined theory of tuples and trees, suppose we define a new unary function symbol $flattree1(x)$ by the following axioms:

$$(\forall\ atom\ u) \big[flattree1(u) = \langle u \rangle \big] \qquad\qquad (atom)$$

$$\begin{matrix} (\forall\ atom\ u) \\ (\forall\ tree\ y) \end{matrix} \big[flattree1(u \bullet y) = u \diamond flattree1(y) \big]$$

$$(atom\ construction)$$

$$(\forall\ tree\ x_1, x_2, y) \big[flattree1\big((x_1 \bullet x_2) \bullet y \big) = flattree1\big(x_1 \bullet (x_2 \bullet y) \big) \big]$$

$$(construction)$$

(a) Establish that

$$(\forall\ tree\ x) \big[tuple\big(flattree1(x) \big) \big].$$

Hint: First show that

$$(\forall\ tree\ x, y) \begin{bmatrix} if\ \ tuple\big(flattree1(y) \big) \\ then\ \ tuple\big(flattree1(x \bullet y) \big) \end{bmatrix}.$$

(b) Establish that

$$(\forall\ tree\ x, y) \big[flattree1(x \bullet y) = flattree1(x) \diamondsuit flattree1(y) \big].$$

(c) Show that $flattree1$ provides an alternative definition for the $flattree$ function, in the sense that

$$(\forall\ tree\ x) \big[flattree(x) = flattree1(x) \big].$$

Problem 10.5 (size, tips, and depth)   page 527

In a combined theory of trees and nonnegative integers, we define three unary functions:

- $size(x)$, the number of nodes and leaves in a tree x, by the axioms

$$(\forall\ atom\ u) \big[size(u) = 1 \big] \qquad\qquad (atom)$$

$$(\forall\ tree\ x, y) \big[size(x \bullet y) = size(x) + size(y) + 1 \big] \qquad (construction)$$

- $tips(x)$, the number of leaves in a tree x, by the axioms

$$(\forall\ atom\ u) \big[tips(u) = 1 \big] \qquad\qquad (atom)$$

$$(\forall\ tree\ x, y)\big[tips(x \bullet y) \ = \ tips(x) + tips(y)\big] \qquad (construction)$$

- $depth(x)$, the number of nodes and leaves in the longest path of a tree x, by the axioms

$$(\forall\ atom\ u)\big[depth(u) = 1\big] \qquad\qquad (atom)$$

$$(\forall\ tree\ x, y) \begin{bmatrix} depth(x \bullet y) \\ = \\ max\big(depth(x),\ depth(y)\big) + 1 \end{bmatrix} \qquad (construction)$$

For example, if x is the tree

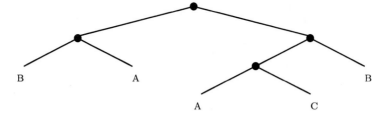

then $size(x) = 9$, $tips(x) = 5$, and $depth(x) = 4$.

     Establish the validity of the following properties:

(a) $(\forall\ tree\ x)\big[size(x) \ = \ 2 \cdot tips(x) - 1\big]$

(b) $(\forall\ tree\ x)\big[size(x) \ \leq \ 2^{depth(x)} - 1\big].$

You may use whatever properties of the nonnegative integers you wish without proof, but provide a list of the properties you use.

Problem 10.6 (alternative definition for tips)   page 528

     In the previous problem, the function $tips(x)$ was defined to count the number of leaves in a tree x. In the same theory, suppose the function $tips1(x)$ is defined by the following axioms:

$$(\forall\ atom\ u)[tips1(u) \ = \ 1] \qquad\qquad (atom)$$

$$\begin{matrix}(\forall\ atom\ u) \\ (\forall\ tree\ y)\end{matrix}[tips1(u \bullet y) \ = \ 1 + tips1(y)] \qquad (atom\ construction)$$

$$(\forall\ tree\ x_1,\ x_2,\ x_3)\big[tips1\big((x_1 \bullet x_2) \bullet y\big) \ = \ tips1\big(x_1 \bullet (x_2 \bullet y)\big)\big]$$
$$(construction)$$

     Show that $tips1$ provides an alternative definition for the $tips$ function, in the sense that

$$(\forall\ tree\ x)\big[tips(x) \ = \ tips1(x)\big].$$

Hint: Establish a sequence of valid sentences analogous to those in Problem 10.4.

Problem 10.7 (reversing a tree)   page 528

Suppose we define a new unary function symbol $revtree(x)$ by the following axioms:

$$(\forall\ atom\ u)\big[revtree(u)\ =\ u\big] \tag{atom}$$

$$(\forall\ tree\ x,y)\big[revtree(x \bullet y)\ =\ revtree(y) \bullet revtree(x)\big]$$
$$\text{(construction)}$$

Thus $revtree(x)$ is the mirror image of the tree x, that is, the tree obtained by interchanging the left and right subtrees at every level of x.

For example, if x is the tree $A \bullet \big((D \bullet C) \bullet B\big)$, that is,

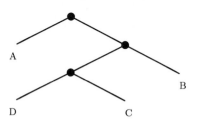

then $revtree(x)$ is the tree

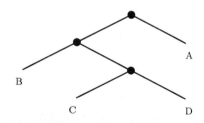

Establish the validity of the following property:

$$(\forall\ tree\ x)\big[revtree(revtree(x))\ =\ x\big] \tag{revtree-revtree}$$

Problem 10.8 (variations on the induction principles)   page 528

Each of the following schemata alters an induction principle in some way. State whether, for every sentence $\mathcal{F}[x]$, its universal closure is valid in the corresponding theory. If so, give a brief justification; if not, give a sentence $\mathcal{F}[x]$ for which the universal closure is not valid, and explain briefly why not.

(a) In the theory of the nonnegative integers,

$$if\ (\forall\ integer\ x)\left[\begin{array}{l} if\ (\forall\ integer\ x')\left[\begin{array}{l} if\ x' \leq x \\ then\ \mathcal{F}[x'] \end{array}\right] \\ then\ \mathcal{F}[x] \end{array}\right]$$
$$then\ (\forall\ integer\ x)\mathcal{F}[x]$$

where x' does not occur free in $\mathcal{F}[x]$.

(b) In the theory of the nonnegative integers,

$$
if \left[(\forall\ integer\ x) \begin{bmatrix} if\ \mathcal{F}[x] \\ then\ \mathcal{F}[x^+] \end{bmatrix} \right]
$$

$then\ (\forall\ integer\ x)\mathcal{F}[x].$

(c) In the theory of tuples,

$$
if \begin{bmatrix} \mathcal{F}[\langle\ \rangle] \\ and \\ (\forall\ tuple\ x,\ y) \begin{bmatrix} if\ \mathcal{F}[x]\ and\ \mathcal{F}[y] \\ then\ \mathcal{F}[x \Diamond y] \end{bmatrix} \end{bmatrix}
$$

$then\ (\forall\ tuple\ x)\mathcal{F}[x]$

where y does not occur free in $\mathcal{F}[x]$.

(d) In the theory of trees,

$$
if \begin{bmatrix} (\forall\ atom\ u)\mathcal{F}[u] \\ and \\ (\forall\ atom\ u,\ v)\mathcal{F}[u \bullet v] \\ and \\ (\forall\ tree\ x,\ y) \begin{bmatrix} if\ \mathcal{F}[x]\ and\ \mathcal{F}[y] \\ then\ \mathcal{F}[x \bullet y] \end{bmatrix} \end{bmatrix}
$$

$then\ (\forall\ tree\ z)\mathcal{F}[z]$

where u, v, x, and y do not occur free in $\mathcal{F}[z]$.

*Problem 10.9 (theory of the integers — comprehensive problem)

page 528

Design a theory of the integers. In other words, write a set of axioms for all the integers, including the negative integers. Try to make your axiom system concise and elegant (as well as correct and consistent).

In addition to some of the original symbols and the usual predicate and function symbols for the nonnegative integers, you may wish to define the following predicate and function symbols:

- $positive(x)$: x is a (strictly) positive integer (i.e., $x > 0$)
- $negative(x)$: x is a (strictly) negative integer (i.e., $x < 0$)
- $whole(x)$: x is any integer, positive, negative, or zero
- $-x$: minus x.

Note that the minus function $-x$ is unary and is distinct from the subtraction function $x - y$, which is binary. Whereas in the theory of the nonnegative integers, the axioms did not specify the value of the subtraction function $x - y$ for $x < y$, the axioms for this theory should specify the value of $x - y$ for all integers x and y. Similarly, the value of the predecessor x^- should be specified for all integers x.

Remember that you will need some form of induction axiom.

Within your theory prove the following properties (unless they are already axioms):

(a) *Successor predecessor*
$$(\forall\ whole\ x)\left[-(x^+)\ =\ (-x)^-\right]$$

(b) *Predecessor zero*
$$(\forall\ negative\ x)\left[not\ (x^- = 0)\right]$$

(c) *Cancellation*
$$(\forall\ whole\ x, y, z)\left[\begin{matrix} x + y = z \\ \equiv \\ x = z - y \end{matrix}\right]$$

(d) *Subtraction addition*
$$(\forall\ whole\ x, y)\left[(x - y) + y\ =\ x\right]$$

(e) *Two*
$$not\ (2 = -2),$$
where 2 is $(0^+)^+$

(f) *Positive negative*
$$(\forall\ whole\ x)\left[if\ \begin{bmatrix} positive(x) \\ \equiv \\ negative(x) \end{bmatrix} \atop then\ x = 0\right].$$

11

Deductive Tableaux

We have introduced a deductive-tableau system to prove the validity of sentences in predicate logic and in finite theories, with or without equality. In this chapter, we adapt the system to prove validity in more complex theories, theories with induction.

We have seen how we can add axioms as assertions into tableaux in predicate logic (with or without equality) to establish the validity of sentences in particular finite theories. The various forms of the principle of mathematical induction, however, are all axiom schemata, each corresponding to an infinite set of axioms. We have devised no method for dealing with axiom schemata within the tableau framework. We cannot introduce an infinite set of assertions into a tableau. Instead, for each theory, we represent the induction principle as a new deduction rule.

11.1 NONNEGATIVE INTEGERS

We begin by reviewing a typical theory with stepwise induction, that of the nonnegative integers. In this theory, we shall use k, ℓ, and m, with or without subscripts, as additional constant symbols.

AXIOMS

The nonnegative integers have been defined by a set of generation and uniqueness axioms and by the induction principle. Let us consider first the axioms.

In the theory of nonnegative integers we have the generation axioms

$integer(0)$	*(zero)*
$(\forall \, integer \; x)\big[integer(x+1)\big]$	*(successor)*

and the uniqueness axioms

$(\forall \, integer \; x)\big[not \; (x+1 \; = \; 0)\big]$	*(zero)*
$(\forall \, integer \; x, \, y) \begin{bmatrix} if \;\; x+1 \; = \; y+1 \\ then \;\; x \; = \; y \end{bmatrix}$	*(successor)*

A tableau over the nonnegative integers is a tableau with equality with the *zero* and *successor* generation axioms and the *zero* and *successor* uniqueness axioms as initial assertions.

The relativized-quantifier notation ($\forall \, integer \; \ldots$) requires special attention here. Without using this notation, the *successor* generation axiom, for example, is actually

$$(\forall \, x) \begin{bmatrix} if \;\; integer(x) \\ then \;\; integer(x+1) \end{bmatrix}.$$

Thus the corresponding assertion should be (applying outermost skolemization)

assertions		goals
$if \;\; integer(x)$ $then \;\; integer(x+1)$ *(successor)*		

Similarly for the uniqueness axioms:

$if \;\; integer(x)$ $then \;\; not \; (x+1=0)$ *(zero)*		
$if \;\; integer(x) \;\; and \;\; integer(y)$ $then \;\; if \;\; x+1=y+1$ $then \;\; x=y$ *(successor)*		

The axioms that define new functions (e.g., multiplication) or new relations (e.g., less than) are included as assertions, as before. Once we have proved a property over the nonnegative integers, we may add it as an assertion to all subsequent tableaux over the nonnegative integers.

Because the tableau is with equality, we include the *reflexivity* axiom $(x = x)$ among our assertions, and we may also use the *equality* rule.

INDUCTION RULE

In addition to the generation and uniqueness axioms, the nonnegative integers were also defined in terms of the (stepwise) induction principle:

$$
\text{if} \quad
\begin{bmatrix}
\mathcal{F}[0] \\
\text{and} \\
(\forall \, integer \; x)
\begin{bmatrix}
if \;\; \mathcal{F}[x] \\
then \;\; \mathcal{F}[x + 1]
\end{bmatrix}
\end{bmatrix}
\qquad (induction)
$$

$$
\text{then} \quad (\forall \, integer \; x)\mathcal{F}[x]
$$

For each sentence $\mathcal{F}[x]$ in the theory, the universal closure of the sentence

is an axiom.

We would like to incorporate this axiom schema, which was used for informal proofs, into our deductive-tableau framework as a deduction rule. We therefore include in a tableau over the nonnegative integers a new deduction rule for mathematical induction. This induction rule allows us to establish a goal of form

$$(\forall \, integer \; x)\mathcal{F}[x]$$

by proving the conjunction of a base case and an inductive step.

Rule (stepwise induction)

For a closed sentence

$$(\forall \, integer \; x)\mathcal{F}[x],$$

we have

assertions	goals
	$(\forall \, integer \; x)\mathcal{F}[x]$
	$\mathcal{F}[0]$ $\quad$ and $\quad$ $\begin{bmatrix} if \;\; integer(m) \\ then \;\; if \;\; \mathcal{F}[m] \\ \qquad\qquad then \;\; \mathcal{F}[m+1] \end{bmatrix}$

where m is a new constant.

Here the conjunct

$$\mathcal{F}[0]$$

corresponds to the base case, and the conjunct

$$
\begin{aligned}
&if\ \ integer(m)\\
&\quad then\ \ if\ \ \mathcal{F}[m]\\
&\qquad\qquad then\ \ \mathcal{F}[m+1]
\end{aligned}
$$

corresponds to the inductive step of an informal stepwise-induction proof.

Remark (closed sentence).   We are permitted to apply the *stepwise induction* rule only if the goal is a closed sentence. Otherwise, if the goal

$$(\forall\ integer\ x)\mathcal{F}[x]$$

contains a free variable y, it actually stands for the existentially quantified goal

$$(\exists\ y)(\forall\ integer\ x)\mathcal{F}[x].$$

We cannot apply the *induction* principle to prove an existentially quantified sentence. ◣

We give an informal justification of the rule.

Justification (stepwise induction).   The induction rule preserves validity, not equivalence. Let us show that, if the required goal

assertions	goals
	$(\forall\ integer\ x)\mathcal{F}[x]$

appears in the tableau, then we may add the generated rows without affecting the validity of the tableau.

By the *stepwise induction* principle, we know that, to show the truth of a closed sentence

$$(\forall integer\ x)\mathcal{F}[x],$$

it suffices to establish the conjunction

$$\mathcal{F}[0]$$
$$and$$
$$(\forall\ integer\ x)\left[\begin{array}{l}if\ \ \mathcal{F}[x]\\ then\ \ \mathcal{F}[x+1]\end{array}\right].$$

(We need not consider the universal closure of the sentence since by our assumption it contains no free variables.)

Thus (by the *implied-row* property) we may add to our tableau the new goal

$$
\begin{array}{|c|c|}
\hline
& \begin{array}{l} \mathcal{F}[0] \\ \quad and \\ (\forall\ integer\ x) \left[\begin{array}{l} if\ \ \mathcal{F}[x] \\ then\ \ \mathcal{F}[x+1] \end{array}\right] \end{array} \\
\hline
\end{array}
$$

that is,

$$
\begin{array}{|c|c|}
\hline
& \begin{array}{l} \mathcal{F}[0] \\ \quad and \\ (\forall\,x)^{\forall} \left[\begin{array}{l} if\ \ integer(x) \\ then\ if\ \ \mathcal{F}[x] \\ \qquad then\ \ \mathcal{F}[x+1] \end{array}\right] \end{array} \\
\hline
\end{array}
$$

Because the quantifier $(\forall x)$ of this goal is of universal force, we may drop the quantifier (by the $\forall$-*elimination* rule), replacing the variable x with the new skolem constant m (because the goal has no free variables), to obtain

$$
\begin{array}{|c|c|}
\hline
& \begin{array}{l} \mathcal{F}[0] \\ \quad and \\ \left[\begin{array}{l} if\ \ integer(m) \\ then\ if\ \ \mathcal{F}[m] \\ \qquad then\ \ \mathcal{F}[m+1] \end{array}\right] \end{array} \\
\hline
\end{array}
$$

This is precisely the goal derived by the rule. By the *intermediate-tableau* property (Section 5.1), we do not need to include the intermediate goal. ◢

EXAMPLES

We illustrate the proof of some properties in the theory of nonnegative integers. The reader may observe that there is a close correspondence between these deductive-tableau proofs and informal proofs of the same properties in Section 8.2.

Example (left-zero).   The addition function $+$ is defined by the two axioms

$$
\begin{array}{|ll|}
\hline
& \\
(\forall\ integer\ x)\big[x+0\ =\ x\big] & \qquad\qquad\ (right\ zero) \\
& \\
(\forall\ integer\ x,\,y)\big[x+(y+1)\ =\ (x+y)+1\big] & \quad (right\ successor) \\
& \\
\hline
\end{array}
$$

We would like to show that 0 is a left identity for addition, that is,

$$(\forall \, integer \; x)\big[0 + x \; = \; x\big] \qquad\qquad (left \; zero)$$

We begin with the goal

assertions	goals
	G1. $(\forall \, integer \; x)\big[0 + x \; = \; x\big]$

in a tableau over the nonnegative integers.

The tableau contains among its assertions the generation and uniqueness axioms for the nonnegative integers, the *reflexivity* axiom for equality, and the two axioms for addition,

if integer(x) *then* $x + 0 \; = \; x$ *(right zero)*	
if integer(x) *and integer*(y) *then* $x + (y + 1) \; = \; (x + y) + 1$ *(right successor)*	

Applying the *stepwise induction* rule to goal G1, we obtain the goal

	G2. $\boxed{0 + 0 \; = \; 0}^{+}$ *and* $\begin{bmatrix} if \; integer(m) \\ then \; if \; 0 + m \; = \; m \\ \qquad then \; 0 + (m + 1) \; = \; m + 1 \end{bmatrix}$

The first conjunct corresponds to the base case and the second to the inductive step of an informal stepwise-induction proof.

Recall the *right-zero* axiom for addition,

if integer(x) *then* $\boxed{x + 0 \; = \; x}^{-}$	

By the *resolution* rule, applied to the axiom and goal G2, with $\{x \leftarrow 0\}$, the first conjunct of goal G2 may be dropped, leaving

<table>
<tr><td></td><td>

G3. $\boxed{integer(0)}^{+}$

and

$$\left[\begin{array}{l} if\ integer(m) \\ then\ if\ 0+m\ =\ m \\ \qquad then\ 0+(m+1)\ =\ m+1 \end{array}\right]$$

</td></tr>
</table>

Recall the *zero* generation axiom

<table>
<tr><td>$\boxed{integer(0)}^{-}$</td><td></td></tr>
</table>

By the *resolution* rule, applied to the axiom and goal G3, the first conjunct of the goal may be dropped, leaving

<table>
<tr><td></td><td>

G4.   *if* $integer(m)$
     then if $0+m\ =\ m$
         then $0+(m+1)\ =\ m+1$

</td></tr>
</table>

We have thus proved the base case of the induction; it remains to show the inductive step, i.e., goal G4.

By two applications of the *if-split* rule, we may break down goal G4 into

<table>
<tr><td>A5. $integer(m)$</td><td></td></tr>
<tr><td>A6. $0+m\ =\ m$</td><td></td></tr>
<tr><td></td><td>G7. $\boxed{0+(m+1)}\ =\ m+1$</td></tr>
</table>

Assertion A6 corresponds to the induction hypothesis, and goal G7 to the desired conclusion, of the inductive step of an informal induction proof. Assertion A5 corresponds to the phrase "Consider an arbitrary nonnegative integer m. ..."

Recall the *right-successor* axiom for addition,

<table>
<tr><td>

if $integer(x)$ *and* $integer(y)$
then $\left[\boxed{x+(y+1)}\ =\ (x+y)+1\right]^{-}$

</td><td></td></tr>
</table>

By the *equality* rule, with $\{x \leftarrow 0,\ y \leftarrow m\}$, we obtain

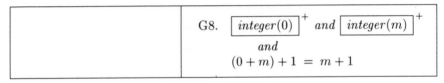

	G8. $\boxed{integer(0)}^{+}$ and $\boxed{integer(m)}^{+}$ *and* $(0+m)+1 = m+1$

Recall the *zero* generation axiom,

$\boxed{integer(0)}^{-}$	

and the assertion A5,

$\boxed{integer(m)}^{-}$	

By two applications of the *resolution* rule, to these assertions and the goal G8, we obtain

	G9. $\boxed{0+m}+1 = m+1$

By the *equality* rule again, using the induction hypothesis (assertion A6),

$\left[\boxed{0+m} = m\right]^{-}$	

we may reduce goal G9 to

	G10. $\boxed{m+1 = m+1}^{+}$

Finally, by the reflexivity of equality, we obtain the goal

	G11. *true*

This completes the proof of the *left-zero* property

$$(\forall\, integer\ x)\left[0+x = x\right].$$

We may now include this property as an assertion in future tableaux over the nonnegative integers. ⌐

Note that the base case and the inductive step of an informal proof by induction correspond to a single proof in the deductive-tableau system.

Remark (beware of hasty skolemization). In a pure predicate-logic tableau proof, there is little harm in applying the skolemization rules to eliminate all quantifiers, at least those of strict force. On the other hand, in a tableau proof over the nonnegative integers, we must exercise some discretion in removing quantifiers. If we remove the outermost universal quantifier ($\forall$ *integer* x) of a goal, we cannot apply induction on x to the resulting goal. ◢

Remark (removal of sort conditions). Many of the steps in the above proof had the effect of removing sort conditions, such as *integer*(0) or *integer*(m), by resolution with an assertion. Removal of sort conditions is often a routine and monotonous part of a proof; in such cases, we shall omit the details and justify the step with the annotation "removal of sort conditions."

Sometimes it is necessary to apply more than one resolution step to remove a sort condition. For instance, to remove a sort condition *integer*$(m + 1)$ in a goal, we may apply the *resolution* rule to the *successor* generation axiom and the goal, obtaining the new condition *integer*(m). The new condition can then be removed by resolution with an assertion. In the following proof, one such step will be spelled out in detail; subsequent steps of this kind will be omitted and justified by the annotation "removal of sort conditions." ◢

Example (left successor). Suppose we would like to show the *left-successor* property of addition, that is,

$$(\forall\, integer\ x, y)\, \big[(x + 1) + y\ =\ (x + y) + 1\big] \qquad (left\ successor)$$

In the theory of the nonnegative integers, we begin with the goal

assertions	goals
	G1. $(\forall\, integer\ x, y)\big[(x + 1) + y\ =\ (x + y) + 1\big]$

We have several options in applying skolemization and induction on x and y. Following the informal proof (Section 8.2), we prefer to skolemize x first and then to apply induction on y.

Abandoning the relativized-quantifier notation in ($\forall$ *integer* x), we can express goal G1 as

	G1'. $(\forall x)^{\forall} \begin{bmatrix} if & integer(x) \\ then & (\forall\ integer\ y) \begin{bmatrix}(x + 1) + y\ = \\ (x + y) + 1 \end{bmatrix} \end{bmatrix}$

By application of the $\forall$-*elimination* rule, we may drop the outermost quantifier of goal G1', replacing the variable x with the skolem constant k, to obtain

	G2. *if integer*(k) *then* $(\forall\ integer\ y)\big[(k+1)+y=(k+y)+1\big]$

Henceforth we shall abandon the relativized-quantifier notation implicitly as part of the process of eliminating a relativized quantifier, without mentioning it as a separate step.

By the *if-split* rule, goal G2 may be decomposed into

A3. *integer*(k)	
	G4. $(\forall\ integer\ y)\big[(k+1)+y=(k+y)+1\big]$

By the *stepwise induction* rule applied to goal G4, we obtain

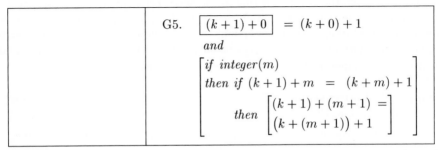

	G5. $\boxed{(k+1)+0}\ =\ (k+0)+1$ *and* $\begin{bmatrix} if\ integer(m) \\ then\ if\ (k+1)+m\ =\ (k+m)+1 \\ \qquad then\ \begin{bmatrix}(k+1)+(m+1)\ = \\ \big(k+(m+1)\big)+1\end{bmatrix} \end{bmatrix}$

Here the first conjunct corresponds to the base case and the second to the inductive step of an informal proof. We first establish the base case.

Base Case

Recall the *right-zero* axiom for addition,

if integer(x) *then* $\Big[\boxed{x+0}\ =\ x\Big]^{-}$	

By the *equality* rule, applied to the axiom and goal G5, with $\{x \leftarrow k+1\}$, the goal is transformed to

	G6. $\boxed{integer(k+1)}^{+}$
	        and
	$k+1\ =\ (k+0)+1$
	        and
	$[\ \cdots\ ]$

We do not write the last conjunct, the inductive step, because it plays no role in this portion of the proof.

For this step, we spell out the details of how to remove the sort condition $integer(k + 1)$. Recall the *successor* generation axiom

if $integer(x)$ *then* $\boxed{integer(x + 1)}^{-}$	

By the *resolution* rule, applied to the axiom and goal G6, with $\{x \leftarrow k\}$, we obtain

	G7. $\boxed{integer(k)}^{+}$ *and* $k + 1 \;=\; (k + 0) + 1$ *and* $[\;\;\cdots\;\;]$

Recall the assertion A3

$\boxed{integer(k)}^{-}$	

By the *resolution* rule, applied to assertion A3 and goal G7, we drop the remaining sort condition, leaving

	G8. $k + 1 \;=\; \boxed{k + 0} + 1$ *and* $[\;\;\cdots\;\;]$

Subsequently, all such patterns of reasoning will be justified by the phrase "removal of sort conditions."

By the *equality* rule, applied once more to the *right-zero* axiom and goal G8, with $\{x \leftarrow k\}$, the goal is transformed further (removing a sort condition) to

	G9. $\boxed{k + 1 = k + 1}^{+}$ *and* $[\;\;\cdots\;\;]$

By the reflexivity of equality, the first conjunct of goal G9 may now be dropped altogether, leaving the goal

	G10. *if integer*(m)
	then if $(k+1)+m = (k+m)+1$
	then $(k+1)+(m+1) = \big(k+(m+1)\big)+1$

The remaining goal corresponds to the inductive step of an informal stepwise-induction proof.

Inductive Step

By two applications of the *if-split* rule, we may break down goal G10 into

A11. *integer*(m)	
A12. $\left[\dfrac{\boxed{(k+1)+m}}{(k+m)+1} \right]^{-}$	
	G13. $\dfrac{\boxed{(k+1)+(m+1)}}{\boxed{k+(m+1)}+1}$

Assertion A12 corresponds to the induction hypothesis and goal G13 to the desired conclusion of the inductive step. Assertion A11 corresponds to the phrase "Consider an arbitrary nonnegative integer m ... ."

Recall the *right-successor* axiom for addition,

if integer(x) *and integer*(y)	
then $\Big[\boxed{x+(y+1)} = (x+y)+1\Big]^{-}$	

By the *equality* rule, applied twice to the axiom and goal G13, first with the most-general unifier $\{x \leftarrow k+1,\ y \leftarrow m\}$ and then with $\{x \leftarrow k,\ y \leftarrow m\}$, we may transform the goal (removing sort conditions) into

	G14. $\dfrac{\boxed{(k+1)+m}+1}{((k+m)+1)+1}$

Applying the *equality* rule to the induction hypothesis (assertion A12) and goal G14, we may transform the goal into

	G15. $\begin{array}{c} \boxed{\begin{array}{c}\left((k+m)+1\right)+1 \\ = \\ \left((k+m)+1\right)+1\end{array}}^{+} \end{array}$

Finally, by the reflexivity of equality, we obtain the final goal

	G16. *true*

The proof in the following example uses each of the previous two properties as assertions. It shows that it may be necessary to prove some properties before proving others.

Example (commutativity).   Suppose we would like to show that addition is commutative, i.e., that

$$(\forall \; integer \; x, \; y)\big[x+y \; = \; y+x\big] \qquad\qquad (commutativity)$$

It turns out to be convenient to first prove the slightly different property

$$(\forall \; integer \; x)\Big[(\forall \; integer \; y)[x+y=y+x]\Big] \qquad\qquad (alternative)$$

The two properties are equivalent but not identical because of the way the relativized quantifier is defined (Section 6.9). The *commutativity* property is an abbreviation of

$$(\forall \; x, \; y) \begin{bmatrix} if \; integer(x) \;\; and \;\; integer(y) \\ then \; x+y=y+x \end{bmatrix} .$$

The *alternative* property, on the other hand, is an abbreviation of

$$(\forall \; x) \begin{bmatrix} if \; integer(x) \\ then \; (\forall \; y) \begin{bmatrix} if \; integer(y) \\ then \; x+y=y+x \end{bmatrix} \end{bmatrix} .$$

The latter will be easier to prove. Then we will be able to use it as an assertion in a simple proof of the original *commutativity* property.

- *Proof of the Alternative Property*

To prove the *alternative* property, we begin with the initial goal

assertions	goals
	G1. $(\forall \; integer \; x)\Big[(\forall \; integer \; y)[x+y=y+x]\Big]$

Again, we have some freedom in applying skolemization and induction on x and y. In this proof, we prefer to skolemize x first and to apply induction on y later.

By application of the $\forall$-*elimination* rule, we may drop the quantifier $(\forall x)$ of goal G1, replacing the variable x with the skolem constant ℓ, and then apply the *if-split* rule, to obtain

A2. $integer(\ell)$	
	G3. $(\forall \ integer \ y)[\ell + y \ = \ y + \ell]$

Applying stepwise induction on y to goal G3, we obtain

	G4. $\ell + 0 \ = \ \boxed{0 + \ell}$ *and* $\begin{bmatrix} if \ integer(m) \\ then \ if \ \ell + m \ = \ m + \ell \\ \qquad then \ \ell + (m+1) \ = \ (m+1) + \ell \end{bmatrix}$

Base Case

In an earlier example, we proved the *left-zero* property for addition, which we may therefore include in our tableau as an assertion,

$if \ integer(x)$ $then \ \left[\ \boxed{0 + x} \ = \ x\ \right]^{-}$	

By the *equality* rule, applied to the property and goal G4, with $\{x \leftarrow \ell\}$, removing a sort condition, the goal is reduced to

	G5. $\boxed{\ell + 0 \ = \ \ell}^{+}$ *and* $\begin{bmatrix} if \ integer(m) \\ then \ if \ \ell + m \ = \ m + \ell \\ \qquad then \ \ell + (m+1) \ = \ (m+1) + \ell \end{bmatrix}$

Recall the *right-zero* axiom for addition,

if integer(x) *then* $\boxed{x + 0 \; = \; x}$ $^{-}$	

By the *resolution* rule, applied to the axiom and goal G5, with $\{x \leftarrow \ell\}$, removing a sort condition, the first conjunct of the goal may now be dropped, leaving

	G6. *if integer*(m) *then if* $\ell + m \; = \; m + \ell$ *then* $\ell + (m + 1) \; = \; (m + 1) + \ell$

We have thus disposed of the base case; it remains to complete the inductive step.

Inductive Step

By two applications of the *if-split* rule, we may break down goal G6 into the assertions

A7. *integer*(m)	
A8. $\left[\ell + m \; = \; \boxed{m + \ell}\right]^{-}$	

and the goal

	G9. $\ell + (m + 1) \; = \; \boxed{(m + 1) + \ell}$

Assertion A8 corresponds to the induction hypothesis, and goal G9 to the desired conclusion, of the inductive step. Assertion A7 corresponds to the phrase "Consider an arbitrary nonnegative integer m. ..."

Recall the *left-successor* property for addition (which we proved in the preceding example),

if integer(x) *and integer*(y) *then* $\left[\boxed{(x + 1) + y} \; = \; (x + y) + 1\right]^{-}$	

By the *equality* rule, applied to the property and goal G9, with $\{x \leftarrow m, \; y \leftarrow \ell\}$, removing sort conditions, we may transform the goal into

	G10. $\ell + (m + 1) \; = \; \boxed{m + \ell} + 1$

By the *equality* rule (right-to-left), applied to the induction hypothesis (assertion A8) and goal G10, we may transform the goal into

	G11. $\boxed{\ell + (m + 1) \;=\; (\ell + m) + 1}^{+}$

Recall the *right-successor* axiom for addition,

if integer(x) *and integer*(y) *then* $\boxed{x + (y + 1) \;=\; (x + y) + 1}^{-}$	

By the *resolution* rule, applied to the axiom and goal G11, with $\{x \leftarrow \ell, \, y \leftarrow m\}$, removing sort conditions, we obtain the final goal

	G12. *true*

                                                                ■

We have remarked that the preceding proof of the *alternative* property used both the *left-zero* and *left-successor* properties as assertions. Had we attempted to prove the *alternative* property without having proved the other two properties first, it would have been difficult to complete the proof.

Now that we have completed the proof of the *alternative* property

$$(\forall \; integer \; x)\Big[(\forall \; integer \; y)[x + y = y + x]\Big],$$

we may use it as an assertion in the proof of the original *commutativity* property

$$(\forall \; integer \; x, \, y)[x + y = y + x].$$

- *Proof of the Commutativity Property*

We begin with a tableau in which the (unabbreviated) *alternative* property is given as an assertion

assertions	goals

if integer(x)
   then if integer(y)
      then $\boxed{x + y = y + x}^{-}$	

and the initial goal is the *commutativity* property

	G1. $(\forall \; integer \; x, \, y)[x + y = y + x]$

By the ∀-elimination rule, we may drop the quantifiers of goal G1, and apply the *if-split* and *and-split* rules, leaving

A2. $integer(\ell)$	
A3. $integer(m)$	
	G4. $\boxed{\ell + m = m + \ell}^{+}$

Here the bound variables x and y of the goal G1 have been replaced by the skolem constants ℓ and m, respectively.

By the *resolution* rule, applied to the *alternative* property and the goal G4, with $\{x \leftarrow \ell, y \leftarrow m\}$, removing sort conditions, we obtain the final goal

	G5. *true*

This concludes the proof of the original *commutativity* property

$$(\forall \ integer \ x, \ y)[x + y = y + x]. \quad \rule[0pt]{6pt}{6pt}$$

In the above sequence, we had the foresight to prove the *alternative* property before attempting to prove the original *commutativity* property. In practice, if in the course of a proof we discover we need an instance of some other property, we may interrupt the main proof and attempt to prove the required property as a subsidiary proposition, or *lemma*, in a separate tableau. Once we have completed the proof of the lemma, we can add it as an assertion in the tableau of the interrupted main proof, and continue the main proof.

The proofs of some properties of the multiplication, exponentiation, and factorial functions are requested in **Problems 11.1**, **11.2**, and **11.3**, respectively. The *fibonacci* function is introduced in **Problem 11.4**. A relation that distinguishes between even and odd nonnegative integers is presented in **Problem 11.5**.

A-FORM OF INDUCTION RULE

The *stepwise induction* rule applies to goals. There is a dual assertion version that applies to assertions.

Rule (stepwise induction, A-form)

For a closed sentence

$$(\exists \ integer \ x)\mathcal{F}[x],$$

we have

assertions	goals
$(\exists\ integer\ x)\mathcal{F}[x]$	
$\mathcal{F}[0]$ or $\begin{bmatrix} integer(m) \ \ and \\ \left(not\ \mathcal{F}[m]\right)\ \ and \\ \mathcal{F}[m+1] \end{bmatrix}$	

where m is a new constant. ⌐

We seldom use this version. Roughly, it says that if $\mathcal{F}[x]$ is true for some integer x, either it is true for 0 or there is some point at which it becomes true. Its justification is requested in **Problem 11.6**.

We do not introduce a tableau form of the *complete induction* principle described in Section 8.6. Complete induction will be seen to be a special case of well-founded induction, which is discussed in the following two chapters.

11.2   TUPLES

In the same way that we introduced the *stepwise induction* rule over the nonnegative integers as a new deduction rule, we can incorporate the *stepwise induction* rules for other theories with induction, including tuples and trees. We consider first the theory of tuples. In this theory, we shall use r, s, and t, with or without subscripts, as additional constant symbols.

AXIOMS AND INDUCTION RULE

A tableau over the tuples is a tableau with equality with the generation axioms

assertions		goals
$tuple(\langle\ \rangle)$	$(empty)$	
$if\ \ atom(u)\ \ and\ \ tuple(x)$ $then\ \ tuple(u \diamond x)$	$(insertion)$	

and the uniqueness axioms

if atom(u) and tuple(x) *then not (u ⬦ x = ⟨ ⟩)* (*empty*)	

if atom(u) and atom(v) and
   tuple(x) and tuple(y)
 then if u ⬦ x = v ⬦ y (*insertion*)
   then u = v and x = y	

The axioms that define any new constructs (e.g., append of tuples) are also included as assertions. As usual, any previously proved properties may be incorporated as assertions.

Because the tableau is with equality, we also include the *reflexivity* axiom $(x = x)$ among our assertions, and we may use the *equality* rule in conducting any proof.

In addition, we include in a tableau over the tuples a new deduction rule for stepwise induction. The *stepwise induction* rule for tuples allows us to establish a goal of form $(\forall \, tuple \, x)\mathcal{F}[x]$ by proving the conjunction of a base case and an inductive step.

Rule (stepwise induction)

For a closed sentence

$$(\forall \, tuple \, x)\mathcal{F}[x],$$

we have

assertions	goals
	$(\forall \, tuple \, x)\mathcal{F}[x]$
	$\mathcal{F}[\langle \, \rangle]$ *and* $\begin{bmatrix} if \ atom(a) \ and \ tuple(r) \\ then \ if \ \mathcal{F}[r] \\ \qquad then \ \mathcal{F}[a \diamond r] \end{bmatrix}$

where a and r are new constants. ⌟

Here the conjunct

$$\mathcal{F}[\langle \, \rangle]$$

corresponds to the base case, and the conjunct

> *if atom(a) and tuple(r)*
> *then if $\mathcal{F}[r]$*
> *then $\mathcal{F}[a \diamond r]$*

corresponds to the inductive step of an informal induction proof. Note that, as in the theory of the nonnegative integers, we are permitted to apply the *stepwise induction* rule only if the goal is a closed sentence.

The justification for the rule is analogous to that for the *stepwise induction* rule over the nonnegative integers (**Problem 11.7(a)**). The reader is requested to formulate and justify an A-form of this rule, which applies to assertions (**Problem 11.7(b)**).

EXAMPLE

In the following example, we illustrate the proof of a property in the theory of tuples. Again, the reader can observe the close similarity between this proof and the corresponding informal proof in Section 9.3.

The example illustrates some of the strategic aspects of the use of the induction principle: the treatment of generalization in a tableau setting and the importance of the order in which skolemization and induction are applied.

Example (alternative reverse).   The *reverse* function, which reverses the elements in a tuple, is defined by the following two axioms:

$$reverse(\langle\,\rangle) = \langle\,\rangle \qquad\qquad\qquad\qquad (empty)$$

$$(\forall\,atom\ u)\,(\forall\,tuple\ x)\Big[reverse(u \diamond x) = reverse(x) \diamond \langle u\rangle\Big] \qquad (insertion)$$

The append function $\diamond$, used in the *insertion* axiom for *reverse*, is defined by the following two axioms:

$$(\forall\,tuple\ y)\big[\langle\,\rangle \diamond y = y\big] \qquad\qquad\qquad\qquad (left\ empty)$$

$$(\forall\,atom\ u)\,(\forall\,tuple\ x,\ y)\Big[(u \diamond x) \diamond y = u \diamond (x \diamond y)\Big] \qquad (left\ insertion)$$

From these axioms, let us assume that we have previously proved within the deductive-tableau system the following properties of append:

$$(\forall\ atom\ u) \atop (\forall\ tuple\ y) \left[\langle u \rangle \diamond y \;=\; u \diamond y \right] \hspace{3cm} (singleton)$$

$$(\forall\ tuple\ x) \left[x \diamond \langle\ \rangle \;=\; x \right] \hspace{3cm} (right\ empty)$$

$$(\forall\ tuple\ x,\ y,\ z) \left[(x \diamond y) \diamond z \;=\; x \diamond (y \diamond z) \right] \hspace{1.5cm} (associativity)$$

Therefore we are permitted to include these properties as assertions in subsequent initial tableaux.

Suppose we define a function $rev2(x,\ y)$, which reverses the tuple x and appends the result with the tuple y, by the following two axioms:

$$(\forall\ tuple\ y)[rev2(\langle\ \rangle,\ y) \;=\; y] \hspace{3cm} (left\ empty)$$

$$(\forall\ atom\ u) \atop (\forall\ tuple\ x,\ y) \left[rev2(u \diamond x,\ y) \;=\; rev2(x,\ u \diamond y) \right] \hspace{1cm} (left\ insertion)$$

The property we would like to show in this example is that the function $rev2$ gives us an alternative definition of the *reverse* function, that is,

$$(\forall\ tuple\ x) \left[reverse(x) \;=\; rev2(x,\ \langle\ \rangle) \right] \hspace{2cm} (special)$$

We must first prove the more general property

$$(\forall\ tuple\ x,\ y) \left[rev2(x,\ y) \;=\; reverse(x) \diamond y \right] \hspace{2cm} (general)$$

Then we will be able to use the *general* property as an assertion in the proof of the desired *special* property.

- *Proof of the General Property*

To prove the *general* property, we begin with the goal

assertions	goals
	G1. $(\forall\ tuple\ x, y) \left[rev2(x,\ y) \;=\; reverse(x) \diamond y \right]$

As in the informal proof (Section 9.3) we have a choice among applying skolemization and induction on x and y. In this case we prefer to apply induction on x first, eliminating the quantifier for y later. This order is essential, as we shall explain afterwards.

By the *stepwise induction* rule applied to goal G1, it suffices to prove the conjunction of a base case and an inductive step,

	G2. $(\forall\, tuple\ y)^{\vee}\big[rev2(\langle\ \rangle,\ y)\ =\ reverse(\langle\ \rangle)\diamond y\big]$ *and* $\begin{bmatrix} if\ \ atom(a)\ and\ tuple(r) \\[4pt] then\ \ if\ (\forall\, tuple\ y')\begin{bmatrix} rev2(r,\ y')\ = \\ reverse(r)\diamond y' \end{bmatrix} \\[12pt] \qquad then\ \ (\forall\, tuple\ y'')\begin{bmatrix} rev2(a\diamond r,\ y'')\ = \\ reverse(a\diamond r)\diamond y'' \end{bmatrix} \end{bmatrix}$

The quantified variable y was renamed to clarify the exposition in the following steps.

By the $\forall$-*elimination* rule, we may drop the $(\forall\, tuple\ y)$ quantifier of goal G2, leaving

	G3. $\begin{bmatrix} if\ tuple(t) \\[4pt] then\ \boxed{rev2(\langle\ \rangle,\ t)}\ =\ \boxed{reverse(\langle\ \rangle)}\diamond t \end{bmatrix}$ *and* $\begin{bmatrix} if\ \ atom(a)\ and\ tuple(r) \\[4pt] then\ \ if\ (\forall\, tuple\ y')\begin{bmatrix} rev2(r,\ y')\ = \\ reverse(r)\diamond y' \end{bmatrix} \\[12pt] \qquad then\ \ (\forall\, tuple\ y'')\begin{bmatrix} rev2(a\diamond r,\ y'')\ = \\ reverse(a\diamond r)\diamond y'' \end{bmatrix} \end{bmatrix}$

Note that the bound variable y of goal G2 has been replaced in goal G3 by the skolem constant t.

Base Case

Recall the *left-empty* axiom for *rev2* and the *empty* axiom for *reverse*,

$\begin{bmatrix} if\ tuple(y) \\[4pt] then\ \Big[\boxed{rev2(\langle\ \rangle,\ y)}\ =\ y\Big]^{-} \end{bmatrix}$	
$\Big[\boxed{reverse(\langle\ \rangle)}\ =\ \langle\ \rangle\Big]^{-}$	

By the *equality* rule, applied twice in succession to the two axioms and goal G3, with $\{y \leftarrow t\}$, we obtain

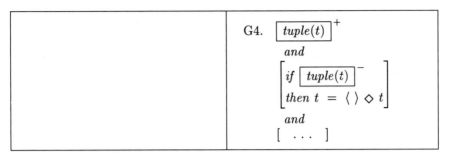

G4. $\boxed{tuple(t)}^{+}$

and

$$\begin{bmatrix} if\ \boxed{tuple(t)}^{-} \\ then\ t\ =\ \langle\,\rangle \diamond t \end{bmatrix}$$

and

$[\ \ \ldots\ \ ]$

We do not write the last conjunct because it plays no part in this portion of the proof.

The next step illustrates a different way to remove sort conditions, in which we apply the *resolution* rule to an earlier goal rather than an assertion, so we spell out the details here. By the *resolution* rule applied to our earlier goal G3,

$$\begin{bmatrix} if\ \boxed{tuple(t)}^{-} \\ then\ rev2(\langle\,\rangle, t)\ =\ reverse(\langle\,\rangle) \diamond t \end{bmatrix}$$

and

$[\ \ \ldots\ \ ]$

and to goal G4, we may reduce the goal to

G5. $\quad t\ =\ \boxed{\langle\,\rangle \diamond t}$

and

$[\ \ \ldots\ \ ]$

Recall the *left-empty* axiom for append,

if $tuple(y)$

then $\left[\boxed{\langle\,\rangle \diamond y}\ =\ y\right]^{-}$

By the *equality* rule, applied to the axiom and goal G5, with $\{y \leftarrow t\}$, we may reduce the base case of G5 further, to

G6. $\boxed{t\ =\ t}^{+}$

and

$[\ \ \ldots\ \ ]$

(The sort condition *tuple(t)* was again removed by applying the *resolution* rule to the earlier goal G3.)

By the reflexivity of equality, we may now drop the first conjunct of goal G6, leaving only the last conjunct, the inductive step

	G7. *if atom(a) and tuple(r)* *then if* ($\forall$ *tuple* y') $\begin{bmatrix} rev2(r,\ y') & = \\ reverse(r) \diamond y' \end{bmatrix}$ *then* ($\forall$ *tuple* y'') $\begin{bmatrix} rev2(a \diamond r,\ y'') & = \\ reverse(a \diamond r) \diamond y'' \end{bmatrix}$

Inductive Step

By two applications of the *if-split* rule, and one application of the *and-split* rule, we have

A8. *atom(a)*	
A9. *tuple(r)*	
A10. ($\forall$ *tuple* y')$^{\exists}$ $\begin{bmatrix} rev2(r,\ y') & = \\ reverse(r) \diamond y' \end{bmatrix}$	

and

	G11. ($\forall$ *tuple* y'')$^{\forall}$ $\begin{bmatrix} rev2(a \diamond r,\ y'') & = \\ reverse(a \diamond r) & \diamond y'' \end{bmatrix}$

By the $\forall$- and $\exists$-*elimination* rules, we may drop the remaining quantifiers of assertion A10 and goal G11, and then apply the *if-split* rule to the goal, leaving

A12.   *if tuple(y')*
      then rev2(r, y') =
          reverse(r) $\diamond$ y'	

A13. *tuple(s)*	
	G14. $\boxed{rev2(a \diamond r,\ s)}$ = *reverse(a $\diamond$ r) $\diamond$ s*

Note that the bound variable y'' of goal G11 was replaced by the skolem constant s in goal G14. Here assertion A12 corresponds to the induction hypothesis, and goal G14 to the desired conclusion of the inductive step.

Recall the *left-insertion* axiom for *rev2*,

$$\textit{if } atom(u) \textit{ and } tuple(x) \textit{ and } tuple(y)$$
$$\textit{then } \left[\boxed{rev2(u \diamond x, \, y)} \; = \; rev2(x, \, u \diamond y) \right]^{-}$$

By the *equality* rule, applied to the axiom and goal G14, with $\{u \leftarrow a, \, x \leftarrow r, \, y \leftarrow s\}$, and removal of sort conditions, we obtain

$$\text{G15.} \quad rev2(r, \, a \diamond s) \; = \; \boxed{reverse(a \diamond r)} \diamond s$$

Recall the *insertion* axiom for *reverse*,

$$\textit{if } atom(u) \textit{ and } tuple(x)$$
$$\textit{then } \left[\boxed{reverse(u \diamond x)} \; = \; reverse(x) \diamond \langle u \rangle \right]^{-}$$

By the *equality* rule, applied to the axiom and goal G15, with $\{u \leftarrow a, \, x \leftarrow r\}$, and removal of sort conditions, we obtain

$$\text{G16.} \quad rev2(r, \, a \diamond s) \; = \; \boxed{(reverse(r) \diamond \langle a \rangle) \diamond s}$$

Recall the *associativity* property of append,

$$\textit{if } tuple(x) \textit{ and } tuple(y) \textit{ and } tuple(z)$$
$$\textit{then } \left[\boxed{(x \diamond y) \diamond z} \; = \; x \diamond (y \diamond z) \right]^{-}$$

By the *equality* rule, applied to the property and goal G16, with $\{x \leftarrow reverse(r), \, y \leftarrow \langle a \rangle, \, z \leftarrow s\}$, and removal of sort conditions, we obtain

	G17. $rev2(r,\ a \diamond s) \ = $ $reverse(r) \diamond \boxed{\langle a \rangle \diamond s}$

Recall the *singleton* property of append,

if atom(u) and tuple(y) *then* $\left[\boxed{\langle u \rangle \diamond y} \ = u \diamond y\right]^{-}$	

By the *equality* rule, applied to the axiom and goal G17, with $\{u \leftarrow a,\ y \leftarrow s\}$, and removal of sort conditions, we obtain

	G18.	$\boxed{\begin{array}{l} rev2(r,\ a \diamond s) \ = \\ reverse(r) \diamond (a \diamond s) \end{array}}^{+}$

Recall our induction hypothesis (assertion A12),

if tuple(y′) *then* $\boxed{\begin{array}{l} rev2(r,\ y') \ = \\ reverse(r) \diamond y' \end{array}}^{-}$	

By the *resolution* rule, applied to the induction hypothesis and goal G18, with $\{y' \leftarrow a \diamond s\}$, we obtain the final goal

	G19. *true*

Now that we have completed the proof of the *general* property of *rev2*,

$$(\forall\ tuple\ x,\ y)\big[rev2(x,\ y) \ = \ reverse(x) \diamond y\big],$$

we may use it as an assertion in the proof of the *special* property of *rev2*,

$$(\forall\ tuple\ x)\big[reverse(x) \ = \ rev2(x,\ \langle\ \rangle)\big].$$

- *Proof of the Special Property*

We begin with the tableau in which the *general* property of *rev2* is given as an assertion

assertions	goals
if tuple(x) *and tuple*(y) *then* $\left[\boxed{rev2(x,\,y)} \;=\; reverse(x)\diamond y\right]^{-}$	

and the initial goal is the *special* property

	G1. $(\forall \ tuple \ x)^{\forall} \left[\begin{array}{l} reverse(x) \;= \\ rev2(x,\,\langle\,\rangle) \end{array}\right]$

By the $\forall$-*elimination* rule, we may drop the quantifier of goal G1 and apply the *if-split* rule, leaving

A2. $tuple(s)$	
	G3. $reverse(s) \;=\; \boxed{rev2(s,\,\langle\,\rangle)}$

Here the bound variable x of the goal G1 has been replaced by the skolem constant s.

By the *equality* rule, applied to the *general* property of *rev2* and goal G3, with $\{x \leftarrow s,\ y \leftarrow \langle\,\rangle\}$, and removal of sort conditions, we obtain

	G4. $reverse(s) \;=\; \boxed{reverse(s)\diamond\langle\,\rangle}$

Recall the *right-empty* property of append,

if tuple(x) *then* $\left[\boxed{x\diamond\langle\,\rangle} \;=\; x\right]^{-}$	

By the *equality* rule, applied to the property and goal G4, with $\{x \leftarrow reverse(s)\}$, and removal of sort conditions, we obtain

	G5. $\boxed{reverse(s) \;=\; reverse(s)}^{+}$

By the reflexivity of equality, we obtain the final goal

	G6. *true*

This concludes the proof of the desired *special* property

$$(\forall\ tuple\ x)\left[reverse(x)\ =\ rev2(x, \langle\ \rangle)\right]. \quad \lrcorner$$

Note that, in the proof of the *general* property, we did not apply the ∀-*elimination* rule to remove the second quantifier (∀ *tuple y*) in goal G1 until after we had applied the induction principle. This was crucial: had we removed this quantifier too early, the proof would not have succeeded. As it turned out, the induction hypothesis, assertion A12, contained the variable y'. The variable y' was then replaced by the term $a \diamond s$ in resolution with goal G18. Had we removed the quantifier first, the induction hypothesis would have contained a skolem constant instead of the variable y', and this step would have been impossible.

In this example, we mentioned all the properties used in the proof at the beginning. Henceforth, we shall usually not mention such properties until they are used. We shall assume, nevertheless, that they are present in the initial tableau.

Remark (associativity and commutativity).   In the example, we obtained goal G17 by applying the *equality* rule to the *associativity* property of append and goal G16. Henceforth we shall not include *associativity* properties explicitly as assertions in our tableaux; rather, we shall say that the new row has been obtained "by associativity" of the operator in question. For instance, we shall say that goal G17 has been obtained from goal G15 by application of the *equality* rule and "the associativity of append," without mentioning the intermediate goal G16 at all.

Similarly, when we use the *commutativity* property of an operator, we shall omit the property and say that the new row has been obtained "by commutativity" of the operator in question.   ⌐

Proofs of some properties of the append function are requested in **Problem 11.8**. Another property of tuples, that the *reverse* function "distributes" over the append function $\diamond$, is proposed in **Problem 11.9**. A property of a relation over tuples is set forth in **Problem 11.10**.

11.3 TREES

A tableau over the trees is a tableau with equality with the generation axioms

assertions		goals
if $atom(x)$ *then* $tree(x)$	(*atom*)	
if $tree(x)$ *and* $tree(y)$ *then* $tree(x \bullet y)$	(*construction*)	

and the uniqueness axioms

if $tree(x)$ *and* $tree(y)$ *then* *not* $\left(atom(x \bullet y)\right)$	(*atom*)	
if $tree(x_1)$ *and* $tree(x_2)$ *and* $\quad tree(y_1)$ *and* $tree(y_2)$ *then* *if* $x_1 \bullet x_2 = y_1 \bullet y_2$ $\qquad$ *then* $x_1 = y_1$ *and* $x_2 = y_2$	(*construction*)	

In this theory, we shall use r, s, and t, with or without subscripts, as additional constant symbols.

Because the tableau is with equality, we also include the *reflexivity* axiom $(x = x)$ among our assertions, and we may use the *equality* rule in conducting any proof.

In addition, we include in a tableau over the trees a new deduction rule for stepwise induction. The *stepwise induction* rule for trees allows us to establish a goal of form $(\forall\, tree\ x)\mathcal{F}[x]$ by proving the conjunction of a base case and an inductive step.

Rule (stepwise induction)

For a closed sentence

$$(\forall\, tree\ x)\mathcal{F}[x],$$

we have

assertions	goals
	$(\forall\ tree\ x)\mathcal{F}[x]$
	$if\ atom(a)\ then\ \mathcal{F}[a]$ $\quad and$ $\begin{bmatrix} if\ tree(r_1)\ and\ tree(r_2) \\ then\ if\ \mathcal{F}[r_1]\ and\ \mathcal{F}[r_2] \\ then\ \mathcal{F}[r_1 \bullet r_2] \end{bmatrix}$

where a, r_1, and r_2 are new constants. ◢

Here the conjunct

$$if\ atom(a)\ then\ \mathcal{F}[a]$$

corresponds to the base case, and the conjunct

$$if\ tree(r_1)\ and\ tree(r_2)$$
$$then\ if\ \mathcal{F}[r_1]\ and\ \mathcal{F}[r_2]$$
$$then\ \mathcal{F}[r_1 \bullet r_2]$$

corresponds to the inductive step of an informal induction proof. Note that, as in the other theories, we are permitted to apply the *stepwise induction* rule only if the goal is a closed sentence.

In **Problem 11.11**, the reader is asked to conduct a proof in a combined theory of nonnegative integers, tuples, and trees.

PROBLEMS

Proofs for the problems in this chapter should use the deductive-tableau technique. You may remove sort conditions without spelling out the details.

Many of the problems request tableau proofs of properties that appear in earlier chapters. For these proofs, you may not use properties that appear after the requested property in the earlier chapter. For example, Problem 11.1(c) requests a tableau proof of the *left-successor* property of multiplication, which appears in Chapter 8. In this proof, you may use the *right-successor* axiom for multiplication, which appears before the requested property, but not the *left-distributivity* property of multiplication, which appears afterwards.

Problem 11.1 (multiplication) page 551

Prove the following properties of multiplication in the theory of the nonnegative integers:

(a) *Right one*

$$(\forall\, integer\ x)[x \cdot 1 \ = \ x]$$

Hint: Recall that 1 is a notation for $(0 + 1)$.

(b) *Left zero*

$$(\forall\, integer\ x)[0 \cdot x \ = \ 0]$$

(c) *Left successor*

$$(\forall\, integer\ x,\ y)\big[(x + 1) \cdot y \ = \ x \cdot y + y\big]$$

(d) *Right distributivity*

$$(\forall\, integer\ x,\ y,\ z)\big[x \cdot (y + z) \ = \ x \cdot y + x \cdot z\big].$$

Problem 11.2 (exponentiation) page 551

Prove, in the theory of the nonnegative integers, that the function *exp3* provides an alternative definition for the exponentiation function x^y, in the sense that

$$(\forall\, integer\ x,\ y)\big[x^y \ = \ exp3(x,\ y,\ 1)\big].$$

Hint: In a separate tableau, first prove a more general property. See the informal proof in Section 8.3.

Problem 11.3 (factorial) page 551

Prove, in the theory of the nonnegative integers, that the function *fact2* does indeed provide an alternative definition for the factorial function $x!$, in the sense that

$$(\forall\, integer\ x)\big[x! \ = \ fact2(x,\ 1)\big]$$

Hint: Prove a more general property.

Problem 11.4 (fibonacci function) page 551

Suppose the *fibonacci function* $fib(x)$ is defined by the following axioms:

$$fib(0) \ = \ 0 \qquad\qquad\qquad\qquad (zero)$$

$$fib(1) \ = \ 1 \qquad\qquad\qquad\qquad (one)$$

$$(\forall\, integer\ x)\big[fib\big((x + 1) + 1\big) \ = \ fib(x + 1) + fib(x)\big] \qquad (plus\ two)$$

The sequence of successive values $fib(0)$, $fib(1)$, $fib(2)$, ..., that is, 0, 1, 1, 2, 3, 5, 8, ... is known as the *fibonacci sequence*.

Suppose the function $fib3(x, y, z)$ is defined by the following axioms:

$$(\forall\ integer\ y,\ z)\big[fib3(0,\ y,\ z)\ =\ y\big] \qquad\qquad (zero)$$

$$(\forall\ integer\ x,\ y,\ z)\big[fib3(x + 1,\ y,\ z)\ =\ fib3(x,\ z,\ y + z)\big]$$
$$(successor)$$

(a) Prove, in the theory of the nonnegative integers, that

$$(\forall\ integer\ x,\ y,\ z)\big[fib3(x + 1,\ y,\ z)\ =\ y \cdot fib(x)\ +\ z \cdot fib(x + 1)\big].$$

(b) Prove, in the theory of the nonnegative integers, that the function $fib3$ provides an alternative definition for the fibonacci function, in the sense that

$$(\forall\ integer\ x)\big[fib(x)\ =\ fib3(x,\ 0,\ 1)\big].$$

Problem 11.5 (even)   page 551

In the theory of the nonnegative integers, suppose the relation $even(x)$ is defined by the axioms

$$even(0) \qquad\qquad (zero)$$

$$not\ even(1) \qquad\qquad (one)$$

$$(\forall\ integer\ x)\big[even\big((x + 1) + 1\big)\ \equiv\ even(x)\big] \qquad\qquad (plus\ two)$$

Prove that

$$(\forall\ integer\ x)[even(x)\ or\ even(x + 1)].$$

Problem 11.6 (A-form)   page 552

Justify the A-form of the *stepwise induction* rule for the nonnegative integers.

Problem 11.7 (tuples)   page 554

(a) Justify the *stepwise induction* rule for tuples.

(b) Formulate and justify an A-form of the *stepwise induction* rule for tuples.

Problem 11.8 (append)   page 562

In the theory of tuples, prove the following properties of the append function:

(a) *Right empty*

$$(\forall\ tuple\ x)[x \diamond \langle\,\rangle\ =\ x]$$

(b) *Associativity*

$$(\forall\ tuple\ x,\ y,\ z)\big[(x \diamond y) \diamond z\ =\ x \diamond (y \diamond z)\big].$$

Problem 11.9 (reverse)   page 562

In the theory of tuples, prove that the *reverse* function distributes over the append function $\diamond$, that is,

$$(\forall \ tuple \ x, \ y)\left[reverse(x \diamond y) \ = \ reverse(y) \diamond reverse(x)\right] \quad (append)$$

Hint: Use the results of Problem 11.8.

Problem 11.10 (initial subtuple)   page 562

In the theory of tuples, show that the initial-subtuple relation $x \preceq_{init} y$ does indeed hold if and only if x is an initial subtuple of y, that is, the sentence

$$(\forall \ tuple \ x, \ y) \left[\begin{array}{c} x \preceq_{init} y \\ \equiv \\ (\exists \ tuple \ z)[x \diamond z \ = \ y] \end{array} \right] \quad (append)$$

is valid.

Hint: Prove each direction separately.

Problem 11.11 (length of flattree)   page 564

Consider a combined theory of the nonnegative integers, tuples, and trees. In this theory, suppose that the function $tips(x)$, which counts the number of leaves in a tree x, is defined as in Problem 10.5. Prove that

$$(\forall \ tree \ x)\left[length\left(flattree(x)\right) \ = \ tips(x)\right].$$

Well-founded
Induction

12

Foundations

In previous chapters, we presented a number of theories, each with a separate *complete induction* principle. In this part, we introduce a single new principle, called the *well-founded induction* principle. All the *complete induction* principles we saw before will turn out to be instances of the *well-founded induction* principle. In fact, even the various *stepwise induction* principles may be regarded as instances of well-founded induction. Furthermore, for many proofs, it is easier to use well-founded induction than any of the earlier induction principles.

12.1   WELL-FOUNDED RELATIONS

The *well-founded induction* principle resembles the *complete induction* principle for the nonnegative integers, except that we introduce an abstract class of "objects" in place of the nonnegative integers, and an abstract "well-founded" relation in place of the less-than relation $<$. The *well-founded induction* principle also resembles the *complete induction* principles for tuples and trees; here, the well-founded relation takes the place of the proper-subtuple and proper-subtree relations, respectively.

Intuitively, a binary relation $\prec$ is *well-founded* over a class of objects if it satisfies the *no-decreasing* condition, that there is no infinite sequence of objects decreasing with respect to that relation. In other words, there are no sequences $\langle x_0, x_1, x_2, \ldots \rangle$ of objects x_i such that

$$x_0 \succ x_1 \succ x_2 \succ \ldots,$$

where $\succ$ is the inverse of $\prec$.

For example, the less-than relation $<$ is well-founded over the class of nonnegative integers because there are no infinite sequences of nonnegative integers decreasing with respect to $<$. In other words, there is no sequence $\langle x_0, x_1, x_2, \ \ldots \rangle$ of nonnegative integers x_i such that

$$x_0 > x_1 > x_2 > \ \ldots \ .$$

Similarly, the proper-subtuple relation $\prec_{tuple}$ is well-founded over the class of tuples.

On the other hand, the less-than relation $<$ is not well-founded over the class of all the integers, including the negative integers, or over the class of nonnegative rational numbers. For example,

$$\langle 1, 0, -1, -2, \ \ldots \rangle$$

is an infinite sequence of integers decreasing with respect to $<$, and

$$\langle 1, 1/2, 1/4, 1/8, \ \ldots \rangle$$

is an infinite sequence of nonnegative rationals decreasing with respect to $<$.

Also, the greater-than relation $>$ is not well-founded over the class of non-negative integers. For example,

$$\langle 0, 1, 2, 3, \ \ldots \rangle$$

is an infinite sequence of nonnegative integers "decreasing" with respect to $>$. Thus we must be careful to specify the class of objects when we say that a relation is well-founded.

As a convention, we shall suppose that the class of objects is characterized (in a given theory) by a unary predicate symbol obj. In other words, $obj(x)$ holds if and only if x belongs to the class of objects. We shall say that $\prec$ is well-founded over obj. We use obj schematically to state general results in place of some particular unary predicate symbol of the theory, such as $integer$, $tuple$, or $tree$. For example, we shall say that $<$ is well-founded over $integer$, that $\prec_{tuple}$ is well-founded over $tuple$, and that $\prec_{tree}$ is well-founded over $tree$.

In the definition of well-foundedness, we shall restrict our attention to infinite sequences that can be described by terms. Each term $t[u]$ describes an infinite sequence

$$\langle \ t[0], \ t[1], \ t[2], \ t[3], \ \ldots \rangle.$$

For example, the term 2^u describes the infinite sequence

$$\langle \ 1, \ 2, \ 4, \ 8, \ldots \rangle.$$

Definition (well-founded relation)

In a given theory, a binary relation $\prec$ is said to be *well-founded* over a unary predicate symbol obj if

There are no infinite sequences $\langle t[0], \ t[1], \ t[2], \ \ldots \rangle$ of objects $t[u]$ such that,

$$(\forall \ integer \ u)\big[\ obj(t[u]) \ \big]$$

$$and \hspace{3cm} (no\text{-}decreasing \ condition)$$

$$(\forall \ integer \ u)\big[\ t[u] \succ t[u + 1] \ \big] \quad \lrcorner$$

In the rest of this chapter, when we refer to sequences x_0, x_1, x_2, ... , we shall have in mind only sequences $t[0]$, $t[1]$, $t[2]$, ... that can be described by a term $t[u]$.

Well-founded relations are useful to us because of the role they play in well-founded induction. It is worthwhile to spend some time establishing a catalog of well-founded relations, allowing us to use them as the basis for future proofs by well-founded induction.

CATALOG OF WELL-FOUNDED RELATIONS

Because we consider only infinite sequences here, we shall use the word "sequence" to mean "infinite sequence."

Empty relation

For any theory and any unary predicate symbol obj, the $empty$ relation

$$x \prec_{empty} y,$$

which is false for all objects x and y, is defined by the axiom

$$\boxed{(\forall\ obj\ x, y)\left[not\ (x \prec_{empty} y)\right]} \qquad (empty)$$

We have

the empty relation $\prec_{empty}$ is well-founded over any unary predicate symbol obj.

Because there are no objects x_i and x_{i+1} such that

$$x_i \succ_{empty} x_{i+1},$$

there are certainly no sequences of objects decreasing with respect to the empty relation.

Less-than relation over integer

As we mentioned above,

the less-than relation $<$ is well-founded over $integer$ in the theory of the nonnegative integers.

Less-than relation over positive

In the theory of the nonnegative integers, since the positive integers form a subclass of the nonnegative integers, and because the less-than relation $<$ is well-founded over $integer$, it follows that

the less-than relation $<$ is well-founded over $positive$ in the theory of the nonnegative integers.

This is because any sequence of positive integers decreasing with respect to $<$ would also be a sequence of nonnegative integers decreasing with respect to $<$, which is impossible.

Predecessor relation

In the theory of nonnegative integers, let the *predecessor* relation $\prec_{pred}$ be defined by the axiom

$$(\forall\ integer\ x, y) \begin{bmatrix} x \prec_{pred} y \\ \equiv \\ x + 1 = y \end{bmatrix} \qquad (predecessor\ relation)$$

That is, $x \prec_{pred} y$ is true if and only if x is the predecessor of y. We have

the predecessor relation $\prec_{pred}$ is well-founded over *integer* in the theory of the nonnegative integers.

This is because, if $x \prec_{prec} y$, it follows that $x < y$. Therefore, any sequence of nonnegative integers decreasing with respect to $\prec_{pred}$ would also be decreasing with respect to $<$, which is impossible.

Proper-divides relation over positive

In the theory of the nonnegative integers, suppose the proper-divides relation $x \prec_{div} y$, which holds when x divides y, with no remainder, and x and y are distinct, is defined (Section 8.9) by the axiom

$$(\forall\ integer\ x, y) \begin{bmatrix} x \prec_{div} y \\ \equiv \\ x \preceq_{div} y\ and\ not\ (x = y) \end{bmatrix} \qquad (proper\ divides)$$

That is, $\prec_{div}$ is the irreflexive restriction of the divides relation $\preceq_{div}$. Thus

$$1 \prec_{div} 6, \quad 2 \prec_{div} 6, \quad 3 \prec_{div} 6, \quad \text{but not} \quad 6 \prec_{div} 6.$$

Also

$$6 \prec_{div} 0, \quad \text{but not} \quad 0 \prec_{div} 6.$$

We have

the proper-divides relation $\prec_{div}$ is well-founded over *positive* in the theory of the nonnegative integers.

This is because any sequence of positive integers decreasing with respect to $\prec_{div}$ is also decreasing with respect to $<$, which is impossible.

Proper-divides relation over integer

We have

the proper-divides relation $\prec_{div}$ is well-founded over *integer* in the theory of the nonnegative integers.

This is because any sequence of nonnegative integers decreasing with respect to $\prec_{div}$ can contain 0 only as its first element, because 0 does not properly divide any nonnegative integer. Deleting the first element yields a sequence of positive integers decreasing with respect to $\prec_{div}$, which is impossible.

Bounded-increase relation over integer

For each nonnegative integer n, consider the relation $\prec_{bd(n)}$, defined by the axiom

$$(\forall\ integer\ x, y)\ \left[\begin{array}{l} x \prec_{bd(n)} y \\ \equiv \\ x > y\ and\ y \leq n \end{array}\right] \qquad (bounded\ increase)$$

We have that

> for any nonnegative integer n, the relation $\prec_{bd(n)}$ is well-founded over *integer* in the theory of the nonnegative integers.

This is because if there were a sequence of nonnegative integers $\langle x_0, x_1, x_2, \ldots \rangle$ decreasing with respect to $\prec_{bd(n)}$, the corresponding sequence

$$\langle\ n - x_0,\ n - x_1,\ n - x_2,\ \ldots \rangle$$

of nonnegative integers would be decreasing with respect to $<$, which is impossible.

Proper-subtuple relation over tuple

We have

> the proper-subtuple relation $\prec_{tuple}$ is well-founded over *tuple* in the theory of tuples.

This is because if there were a sequence of tuples $\langle x_0, x_1, x_2, \ldots \rangle$ decreasing with respect to $\prec_{tuple}$, the corresponding sequence

$$\langle\ length(x_0),\ length(x_1),\ length(x_2),\ \ldots \rangle$$

of nonnegative integers would be decreasing with respect to $<$, which is impossible.

Proper consecutive-subtuple relation over tuple

Suppose we define the proper consecutive-subtuple relation $\prec_{tuple1}$ to be the irreflexive restriction of the ordinary consecutive-subtuple relation (Section 9.6), that is,

$$(\forall\ tuple\ x, y)\ \left[\begin{array}{l} x \prec_{tuple1} y \\ \equiv \\ x \preceq_{tuple1} y\ and\ not\ (x = y) \end{array}\right] \qquad (proper\ consecutive\ subtuple)$$

In other words, $x \prec_{tuple1} y$ holds if the elements of x occur consecutively and in the same order in y, and x and y are distinct.

> For example,
>
> $\langle A, A, B \rangle \prec_{tuple1} \langle C, A, A, B, C \rangle$, but not $\langle A, A, B \rangle \prec_{tuple1} \langle A, C, A, B \rangle$.

Then we have

> the proper consecutive-subtuple relation $\prec_{tuple1}$ is well-founded over *tuple* in the theory of tuples.

This is because any sequence of tuples decreasing with respect to $\prec_{tuple1}$ is also decreasing with respect to $\prec_{tuple}$, which is impossible.

Proper-end relation over tuples

In the theory of tuples, we defined (Section 9.4) the end relation $x \preceq_{end} y$, which is true if the tuple x is at the end of the tuple y, that is, if x can be obtained from y by dropping some (perhaps none) of the initial atoms of y.

Its irreflexive restriction, the proper-end relation $x \prec_{end} y$, is defined by the axiom

$$(\forall \ tuple \ x, \ y) \begin{bmatrix} x \prec_{end} y \\ \equiv \\ x \preceq_{end} \quad and \quad not(x = y) \end{bmatrix} \qquad (proper \ end)$$

For example,

$$\langle B, \ C \rangle \prec_{end} \langle A, \ B, \ C \rangle, \qquad \langle C \rangle \prec_{end} \langle A, \ B, \ C \rangle, \qquad \langle \ \rangle \prec_{end} \langle A, \ B, \ C \rangle.$$

The following properties can be proved from the axioms:

$$(\forall \ tuple \ x, y) \begin{bmatrix} x \prec_{end} y \\ \equiv \\ (\exists \ tuple \ z) [z \diamond x = y \ and \ not \ (z = \langle \ \rangle)] \end{bmatrix}$$

$$(append)$$

$$(\forall \ tuple \ x, y) \begin{bmatrix} if \ x \prec_{end} y \\ then \ x \prec_{tuple} y \end{bmatrix} \qquad (subtuple)$$

We have that

> the proper-end relation $\prec_{end}$ is well-founded over *tuple* in the theory of tuples.

This is because any sequence of tuples decreasing with respect to $\prec_{end}$ is also decreasing with respect to $\prec_{tuple}$, which is impossible.

Length relation over tuple

In a combined theory of nonnegative integers and tuples, the *length* relation is defined by the axiom

$$(\forall \ tuple \ x, y) \begin{bmatrix} x \prec_{length} y \\ \equiv \\ length(x) < length(y) \end{bmatrix} \qquad (length \ relation)$$

Note that this relation over the tuples is distinct from the proper-subtuple relation $\prec_{tuple}$; for instance,

$$\langle A, \ B \rangle \prec_{length} \langle C, \ D, \ E \rangle, \qquad but \ not \quad \langle A, \ B \rangle \prec_{tuple} \langle C, \ D, \ E \rangle.$$

We have

the length relation $\prec_{length}$ is well-founded over *tuple* in the combined theory of nonnegative integers and tuples.

This is because if there were a sequence of tuples $\langle x_0, x_1, x_2, \ldots \rangle$ decreasing with respect to the length relation, the corresponding sequence

$$\langle \ length(x_0), \ length(x_1), \ length(x_2), \ \ldots \ \rangle$$

of nonnegative integers would be decreasing with respect to $<$, which is impossible.

Proper-subtree relation over tree

We have

the proper-subtree relation $\prec_{tree}$ is well-founded over *tree* in the theory of trees.

This is because if there were a sequence of trees $\langle x_0, x_1, x_2, \ldots \rangle$ decreasing with respect to the proper-subtree relation, the corresponding sequence of sizes of those trees (i.e., the number of nodes and leaves in the tree) would be decreasing with respect to $<$, which is impossible.

In **Problem 12.1**, the reader is asked to decide which of several given relations are well-founded.

PROPERTIES OF WELL-FOUNDED RELATIONS

What properties follow from the well-foundedness of a relation?

Irreflexive

We can easily see that a relation that is well-founded over *obj* must also be irreflexive over *obj*; that is,

$$(\forall \ obj \ x)\big[not \ (x \prec x)\big]$$

must be valid (in the theory). For if there were an object x such that $x \prec x$, the "constant" sequence $\langle x, x, x, \ldots \rangle$ would be decreasing with respect to $\prec$; that is,

$$x \succ x \succ x \succ \ \ldots \ .$$

Asymmetric

Furthermore, a relation that is well-founded over *obj* must also be asymmetric over *obj*; that is,

$$(\forall \ obj \ x, y) \begin{bmatrix} if \ x \prec y \\ then \ not \ (y \prec x) \end{bmatrix}$$

must be valid. For if there were two objects x and y such that $x \prec y$ and $y \prec x$, the "alternating" sequence $\langle x, y, x, y, \ldots \rangle$ would be decreasing; that is,

$$x \succ y \succ x \succ y \succ \ \ldots \ .$$

Not necessarily transitive

A well-founded relation need not be transitive over the class of objects. In particular, consider the predecessor relation $\prec_{pred}$ over the nonnegative integers. This relation is well-founded over the nonnegative integers, but it is not transitive. For example,

$$1 \prec_{pred} 2 \quad \text{and} \quad 2 \prec_{pred} 3,$$

but not $1 \prec_{pred} 3$.

THE UNION RELATION

We have seen a catalog of particular relations that are well-founded; we may use them in subsequent proofs by well-founded induction. If we know that some relations are well-founded, we can sometimes combine them to form additional well-founded relations. One way of combining well-founded relations is given here.

In a given theory, suppose that obj_1 and obj_2 are unary predicate symbols, which characterize two classes of objects, and that $\prec_1$ and $\prec_2$ are binary relations. Let the unary predicate symbol obj characterize the union of the two classes, that is,

$$(\forall\, x) \begin{bmatrix} obj(x) \\ \equiv \\ obj_1(x) \quad or \quad obj_2(x) \end{bmatrix},$$

is valid in the theory.

Then the *union* relation $\prec_{union}$ (over obj) of $\prec_1$ (over obj_1) and $\prec_2$ (over obj_2) is defined by the axiom

$$(\forall\, obj\ x, y) \begin{bmatrix} x \prec_{union} y \\ \equiv \\ \begin{bmatrix} obj_1(x) \quad and \quad obj_2(y) \\ or \\ obj_1(x) \quad and \quad obj_1(y) \quad and \quad x \prec_1 y \\ or \\ obj_2(x) \quad and \quad obj_2(y) \quad and \quad x \prec_2 y \end{bmatrix} \end{bmatrix} \qquad (union\ relation)$$

In other words, with respect to $\prec_{union}$, each of the object$_1$'s is regarded as less than any of the object$_2$'s; and $\prec_{union}$ agrees with $\prec_1$ on object$_1$'s and with $\prec_2$ on object$_2$'s. Note that the definition of $\prec_{union}$ depends on the choice of $\prec_1$, $\prec_2$, obj_1, and obj_2.

For example, suppose $\prec_1$ is the proper-subtuple relation $\prec_{tuple}$ over the tuples, and $\prec_2$ is the less-than relation $<$ over the nonnegative integers. Let obj

characterize the union of the tuples and the nonnegative integers. Then, for any two objects (tuples or nonnegative integers) x and y, the union relation $x \prec_{union} y$ (of $\prec_{tuple}$ and $<$) is true if x is a tuple and y is a nonnegative integer, or x and y are both tuples and $x \prec_{tuple} y$, or x and y are both nonnegative integers and $x < y$. Thus

$$\langle A, B \rangle \prec_{union} 2, \qquad \langle A, B \rangle \prec_{union} \langle D, A, B, C \rangle, \qquad 2 \prec_{union} 3.$$

In **Problem 12.2**, the reader is requested to show that, under certain circumstances, if two relations are well-founded, their union is also well-founded.

Problem 12.3 pertains to other ways of combining well-founded relations. The reader is asked in **Problem 12.4** to establish the well-foundedness of an additional relation.

12.2   THE WELL-FOUNDED INDUCTION PRINCIPLE

In the theory of the nonnegative integers, we introduced (Section 8.6) the *complete induction* proposition

For each sentence $\mathcal{F}[x]$ without free occurrences of x',
the universal closure of the sentence

$$if \ (\forall \ integer \ x) \begin{bmatrix} if \ (\forall \ integer \ x') \begin{bmatrix} if \ x' < x \\ then \ \mathcal{F}[x'] \end{bmatrix} \\ then \ \mathcal{F}[x] \end{bmatrix}$$

$$then \ (\forall \ integer \ x)\mathcal{F}[x]$$

is valid.

The proposition was proved in Section 8.8.

Similarly, in the theory of the tuples, we introduced (Section 9.6) the *complete induction* proposition

For each sentence $\mathcal{F}[x]$ with no free occurrences of x',
the universal closure of the sentence

$$if \ (\forall \ tuple \ x) \begin{bmatrix} if \ (\forall \ tuple \ x') \begin{bmatrix} if \ x' \prec_{tuple} x \\ then \ \mathcal{F}[x'] \end{bmatrix} \\ then \ \mathcal{F}[x] \end{bmatrix}$$

$$then \ (\forall \ tuple \ x)\mathcal{F}[x]$$

is valid.

Also, in the theory of the trees, we introduced (Section 10.3) the *complete induction* proposition

For each sentence $\mathcal{F}[x]$ with no free occurrences of x', the universal closure of the sentence

$$
if \ (\forall \ tree \ x) \ \left[\begin{array}{l} if \ (\forall \ tree \ x') \ \left[\begin{array}{l} if \ x' \prec_{tree} x \\ then \ \mathcal{F}[x'] \end{array} \right] \\ then \ \mathcal{F}[x] \end{array} \right]
$$

$$
then \ (\forall \ tree \ x)\mathcal{F}[x]
$$

is valid.

The *well-founded induction* principle generalizes these three *complete induction* principles to an arbitrary well-founded relation.

In the following discussion, we take *obj* to stand for a unary predicate symbol, such as *integer*, *tuple*, or *tree*, and $\prec$ to stand for a binary predicate symbol, such as $<$, $\prec_{tuple}$, or $\prec_{tree}$.

Proposition (well-founded induction)

In a given theory,

A binary relation $\prec$ is well-founded over *obj*

if and only if

For each sentence $\mathcal{F}[x]$ without free occurrences of x', the universal closure of the sentence

$$
if \ (\forall \ obj \ x) \ \left[\begin{array}{l} if \ (\forall \ obj \ x') \ \left[\begin{array}{l} if \ x' \prec x \\ then \ \mathcal{F}[x'] \end{array} \right] \\ then \ \mathcal{F}[x] \end{array} \right]
$$

$$
then \ (\forall \ obj \ x)\mathcal{F}[x]
$$

                                  (*well-founded induction principle*)

is valid (in the given theory).   ◢

In the case in which *obj* is *integer* and $\prec$ is the less-than relation $<$, this reduces to the *complete induction* principle for the nonnegative integers. In the case in which *obj* is *tuple* and $\prec$ is the proper-subtuple relation $\prec_{tuple}$, the *well-founded induction* principle reduces to the *complete induction* principle for the tuples. Also, in the case in which *obj* is *tree* and $\prec$ is the proper-subtree relation $\prec_{tree}$, the *well-founded induction* principle reduces to the *complete induction* principle for the trees.

In the *well-founded induction* principle, the sentence $\mathcal{F}[x]$ is called the *inductive sentence* and the variable x is called the *inductive variable*. The antecedent of the principle,

$$
(\forall \ obj \ x) \ \left[\begin{array}{l} if \ (\forall \ obj \ x') \ \left[\begin{array}{l} if \ x' \prec x \\ then \ \mathcal{F}[x'] \end{array} \right] \\ then \ \mathcal{F}[x] \end{array} \right],
$$

is called the *inductive step*; the subsentences

$$(\forall\ obj\ x') \begin{bmatrix} if\ x' \prec x \\ then\ \mathcal{F}[x'] \end{bmatrix} \qquad \text{and} \qquad \mathcal{F}[x]$$

of the inductive step are called the *induction hypothesis* and the *desired conclusion*, respectively.

The *well-founded induction* principle may be paraphrased informally as follows:

> To show that a sentence $\mathcal{F}[x]$ is true for every object x (under a given interpretation), it suffices to show the inductive step
>
>> for an arbitrary object x,
>> if $\mathcal{F}[x']$ is true for every object x' such that $x' \prec x$,
>> then $\mathcal{F}[x]$ is also true.

In Section 8.6, we give a counterexample that provides the reason for the constraint in the *complete induction* principle that x' does not occur free in $\mathcal{F}[x]$. The same counterexample applies here.

MINIMAL-ELEMENT PRINCIPLE

In the theory of the nonnegative integers, the *complete induction* principle was found to be equivalent to a *least-number* principle (Section 8.10). By the same token, the *well-founded induction* principle is equivalent to a so-called *minimal-element* principle. With respect to a given relation $\prec$, an element x is said to be *minimal* in a given class (not necessarily finite) if there exists no element y of the class such that $y \prec x$. For instance, with respect to the subtuple relation $\prec_{tuple}$, the two tuples $\langle A \rangle$ and $\langle C \rangle$ are both minimal elements of the class $\{\langle A \rangle, \langle C \rangle, \langle A,\ B \rangle\}$, but $\langle A,\ B \rangle$ is not minimal because $\langle A \rangle \prec_{tuple} \langle A,\ B \rangle$.

A relation $\prec$ satisfies the *minimal-element* condition over a class of objects if every nonempty subclass of the class has a minimal element with respect to $\prec$.

The *no-decreasing* condition and the *minimal-element* condition are equivalent. Let us show the equivalence.

Minimal-element condition $\Rightarrow$ *no-decreasing condition*

Suppose that $\prec$ satisfies the *minimal-element* condition over obj, but that, contrary to the *no-decreasing* condition, there exists an infinite sequence $\langle x_0, x_1, x_2, \ldots \rangle$ decreasing with respect to $\prec$. We claim that then the class of elements $C : \{x_0, x_1, x_2, \ldots\}$ is a nonempty class with no minimal element, contradicting the *minimal-element* condition. No element x_j of C can be minimal for, since the sequence is decreasing with respect to $\prec$, we know $x_{j+1} \prec x_j$.

No-decreasing condition ⇒ *minimal-element condition*

Suppose that $\prec$ satisfies the *no-decreasing* condition over *obj* but that, contrary to the *minimal-element* condition, there exists a nonempty class C with no minimal element. We construct a sequence decreasing with respect to $\prec$, contradicting the *no-decreasing* condition.

Because C is nonempty, it has some element, call it x_0. Because C has no minimal elements, it must have some element, call it x_1, such that $x_1 \prec x_0$. Because x_1 cannot be minimal either, there must be some element of C, call it x_2, such that $x_2 \prec x_1$. Continuing in this way, we construct the sequence $\langle x_0, x_1, x_2, \ldots \rangle$ of objects in C that is decreasing with respect to $\prec$.

To express the *minimal-element* condition in predicate logic, we consider the subclass characterized by a sentence $\mathcal{G}[x]$; that is, the subclass of all objects x such that $\mathcal{G}[x]$ is true.

Proposition (minimal-element)

In a given theory,

> A binary relation $\prec$ is well-founded over a unary predicate symbol *obj*

if and only if

> For each sentence $\mathcal{G}[x]$ with no free occurrences of x',
> the universal closure of the sentence

$$\textit{if} \ \ (\exists \ obj \ x)\mathcal{G}[x]$$

$$\textit{then} \ \ (\exists \ obj \ x) \begin{bmatrix} \mathcal{G}[x] \\ \quad and \\ (\forall \ obj \ x') \begin{bmatrix} \textit{if} \ \ x' \prec x \\ \textit{then} \ \ not \ \mathcal{G}[x'] \end{bmatrix} \end{bmatrix}$$

(*minimal-element condition*)

is valid (in the given theory). ◢

The *minimal-element* condition states that, if a sentence $\mathcal{G}[x]$ is true for some object x, it must be true for some "minimal" object x, that is, one such that $\mathcal{G}[x]$ is true and $\mathcal{G}[x']$ is not true for any "smaller" object x'.

The proof of the *minimal-element* proposition is the same as that of the *least-number* proposition in the theory of the nonnegative integers (Section 8.10). Generally speaking, to show that the above *minimal-element* principle implies the *well-founded induction* principle, we consider any sentence $\mathcal{F}[x]$, and take $\mathcal{G}[x]$ in the preceding schema to be its negation $(not \ \mathcal{F}[x])$. Applying equivalences of propositional and predicate logic, we obtain precisely the *well-founded induction* principle. Similarly, to show that the *well-founded induction* principle implies the *minimal-element* principle, we consider any sentence $\mathcal{G}[x]$, and take $\mathcal{F}[x]$ in the *well-founded induction* principle to be its negation $(not \ \mathcal{G}[x])$, obtaining by logical manipulations precisely the *minimal-element* principle.

Example (least-number principle). In the theory of the nonnegative integers, take *obj* in the *minimal-element* condition to be the unary predicate symbol *integer*, and ≺ to be the less-than relation <, which is well-founded over *integer*. We obtain

> For each sentence $\mathcal{G}[x]$ without free occurrences of x',
> the universal closure of the sentence
>
> *if* $(\exists\ integer\ x)\mathcal{G}[x]$
>
> *then* $(\exists\ integer\ x)$
> $$\begin{bmatrix} \mathcal{G}[x] \\ and \\ (\forall\ integer\ x')\begin{bmatrix} if\ \ x' < x \\ then\ \ not\ \mathcal{G}[x'] \end{bmatrix} \end{bmatrix}$$
>
> (*least-number principle*)
>
> is valid.

This is the *least-number* principle over the nonnegative integers (Section 8.10). Thus the *least-number* principle is an instance of the *minimal-element* condition. ◢

The *minimal-element* principle enables us to give a proof (requested in **Problem 12.5**) of the *asymmetry* property, that any well-founded relation ≺ (over *obj*) is asymmetric (over *obj*).

12.3 USE OF WELL-FOUNDED INDUCTION

Typically, we define a theory using *stepwise induction* principles, establish the well-foundedness of various relations in that theory, and then use well-founded induction with respect to those relations in proofs. For example, in Chapter 8 we defined the theory of the nonnegative integers using the *stepwise induction* principle. By proving the *complete induction* principle, we then actually established the well-foundedness of the less-than relation <. We subsequently used well-founded induction, i.e., complete induction, for proofs that would have been awkward with stepwise induction.

The choice of a well-founded relation ≺ can influence the difficulty of a well-founded induction proof. A proof that is straightforward by induction with respect to one relation may be clumsy with respect to another.

Now that we have established that several relations are well-founded, we know that the *well-founded induction* principle holds for these relations. Let us see how to use the *well-founded induction* principle in proofs.

EXAMPLE: PRIME DECOMPOSITION

We shall use the *well-founded induction* principle to prove the following property of the nonnegative integers:

Every integer x greater than 1 can be expressed as a product

$$x_1 \cdot x_2 \cdot \cdots \cdot x_n$$

of (one or more) primes $x_1, x_2, \ldots, x_n$.

A prime is an integer greater than 1 that cannot be expressed as a product of positive integers other than itself and 1; thus 2, 3, 5, and 7 are primes, but 6 is not because $6 = 2 \cdot 3$. The primes are characterized by the predicate $prime(x)$, defined by the axiom

$$(\forall \, integer \; x) \left[\begin{array}{l} prime(x) \\[4pt] \equiv \\[4pt] \left[\begin{array}{l} 1 < x \;\; and \\[6pt] not \;\; (\exists \, integer \; y, z) \left[\begin{array}{l} x = y \cdot z \\ and \;\; 1 < y \\ and \;\; 1 < z \end{array} \right] \end{array} \right] \end{array} \right] \qquad (prime)$$

To express the property we want, we first define the *decomposition* relation $decomp(x)$, which is true if x can be decomposed into a product of (one or more) primes, by the axiom

$$(\forall \, integer \; x) \left[\begin{array}{l} decomp(x) \\[4pt] \equiv \\[4pt] \left[\begin{array}{l} prime(x) \\[4pt] or \\[4pt] (\exists \, integer \; y, \, z) \left[\begin{array}{l} decomp(y) \;\; and \\ decomp(z) \;\; and \\ x = y \cdot z \end{array} \right] \end{array} \right] \end{array} \right] \qquad (decomp)$$

This axiom immediately implies the two properties

$$(\forall \, integer \; x) \left[\begin{array}{l} if \;\; prime(x) \\ then \;\; decomp(x) \end{array} \right] \qquad\qquad (prime)$$

$$(\forall \, integer \; x, \, y) \left[\begin{array}{l} if \;\; decomp(x) \;\; and \;\; decomp(y) \\ then \;\; decomp(x \cdot y) \end{array} \right] \quad (multiplication)$$

In other words, each prime is decomposable into a product of primes (namely, itself) and, if two nonnegative integers are decomposable, so is their product.

The property we would like to establish is then expressed as follows:

Proposition (prime decomposition)
 The sentence
$$(\forall \, integer \; x) \begin{bmatrix} if \;\; 1 < x \\ then \;\; decomp(x) \end{bmatrix} \qquad (prime \; decomposition)$$
 is valid. ⌐

In our proof, we shall use simple properties of the nonnegative integers without mentioning them.

Proof.   It suffices to establish the sentence
$$(\forall \, positive \; x) \begin{bmatrix} if \;\; 1 < x \\ then \;\; decomp(x) \end{bmatrix}.$$

The proof is by well-founded induction over *positive* with respect to the proper-divides relation $\prec_{div}$; this relation is well-founded over *positive*.

 We shall use the following property of the proper-divides relation $\prec_{div}$:
$$(\forall \, positive \; x, \, y) \begin{bmatrix} x \prec_{div} y \\ \equiv \\ (\exists \, integer \; z) \begin{bmatrix} x \cdot z = y \\ and \;\; 1 < z \end{bmatrix} \end{bmatrix} \qquad (multiplication)$$

 We take the inductive sentence to be
$$\mathcal{F}[x] : \quad \begin{array}{l} if \;\; 1 < x \\ then \;\; decomp(x) \end{array}$$
and prove
$$(\forall \, positive \; x)\mathcal{F}[x].$$

Inductive Step
 We would like to show
$$(\forall \, positive \; x) \begin{bmatrix} if \;\; (\forall \, positive \; x') \begin{bmatrix} if \;\; x' \prec_{div} x \\ then \;\; \mathcal{F}[x'] \end{bmatrix} \\ then \;\; \mathcal{F}[x] \end{bmatrix}.$$
Consider an arbitrary positive integer x, and assume the induction hypothesis

(†) $(\forall \, positive \; x') \begin{bmatrix} if \;\; x' \prec_{div} x \\ then \;\; \mathcal{F}[x'] \end{bmatrix}.$

We would like to show that then the desired conclusion $\mathcal{F}[x]$ is true, that is,
$$\begin{array}{l} if \;\; 1 < x \\ then \;\; decomp(x). \end{array}$$

 Suppose that
$$1 < x;$$
we must show that

(††) $decomp(x).$

The proof distinguishes between two cases.

Case: *prime*(*x*)

Then (by the *prime* property of *decomp*)

$$decomp(x),$$

as we wanted to show.

Case: *not prime*(*x*)

Then (by the *prime* axiom, because $1 < x$) there exist nonnegative integers y and z such that

$$x = y \cdot z \ \text{ and } \ 1 < y \ \text{ and } \ 1 < z.$$

Since (by the *commutativity* property of multiplication)

$$\begin{array}{ccc} y \cdot z = x & & z \cdot y = x \\ \text{and } 1 < z & \text{and} & \text{and } 1 < y, \end{array}$$

we have (by the preceding *multiplication* property of the proper-divides relation $\prec_{div}$) that

$$y \prec_{div} x \qquad \text{and} \qquad z \prec_{div} x.$$

By our induction hypothesis (†), taking x' to be y (because y is positive) and taking x' to be z (because z is positive), we have

$$\begin{array}{ccc} \text{if } \ y \prec_{div} x & & \text{if } \ z \prec_{div} x \\ \text{then } \ \mathcal{F}[y] & \text{and} & \text{then } \ \mathcal{F}[z]. \end{array}$$

Therefore (because $y \prec_{div} x$ and $z \prec_{div} x$), we have $\mathcal{F}[y]$ and $\mathcal{F}[z]$, that is,

$$\begin{array}{ccc} \text{if } \ 1 < y & & \text{if } \ 1 < z \\ \text{then } \ decomp(y) & \text{and} & \text{then } \ decomp(z). \end{array}$$

But we know that $1 < y$ and $1 < z$; therefore

$$decomp(y) \ \text{ and } \ decomp(z).$$

It follows (by the *multiplication* property of *decomp*) that

$$decomp(y \cdot z),$$

that is (since $x = y \cdot z$),

$$decomp(x),$$

as we wanted to show (††). ⌐

Remark (why well-founded induction?).   The preceding proof is much more convenient to carry out by well-founded induction than by stepwise induction. If we attempted to use the decomposition version, say, of the *stepwise induction* principle, we would not have been able to use the induction hypothesis $\mathcal{F}[x - 1]$ to establish $\mathcal{F}[y]$ and $\mathcal{F}[z]$; we know that y and z are proper divisors of x, but it may not be the case that $y = x - 1$ or that $z = x - 1$. To establish the same result by stepwise induction would require a more complex inductive sentence. ⌐

EXAMPLE: ALTERNATIVE REVERSE

Recall that, in the theory of tuples, we defined (Section 9.3) the function $reverse(x)$, which reverses the atoms of the tuple x, by the following axioms:

$$reverse(\langle\,\rangle) = \langle\,\rangle \qquad\qquad\qquad\qquad\qquad (empty)$$

$$\begin{matrix}(\forall\ atom\ u)\\(\forall\ tuple\ y)\end{matrix}\left[reverse(u \diamond y) \;=\; reverse(y) \diamond \langle u\rangle\right] \qquad (insertion)$$

Some properties of the *reverse* function that we established are

$$(\forall\ atom\ u)\left[reverse(\langle u\rangle) \;=\; \langle u\rangle\right] \qquad\qquad\qquad (singleton)$$
$$(\forall\ tuple\ x)\left[reverse\left(reverse(x)\right) \;=\; x\right] \qquad\qquad\qquad (reverse)$$

We have already seen an alternative definition of the *reverse* function in terms of an auxiliary binary function symbol $rev2(x, y)$.

Now consider the unary function $rev1$, defined by the following axioms:

$$rev1(\langle\,\rangle) \;=\; \langle\,\rangle \qquad\qquad\qquad\qquad\qquad (empty)$$

$$(\forall\ atom\ u)\left[rev1(\langle u\rangle) \;=\; \langle u\rangle\right] \qquad\qquad\qquad (singleton)$$

$$\begin{matrix}(\forall\ atom\ u)\\(\forall\ tuple\ y)\end{matrix}\left[\begin{matrix}if\ \ not\ (y = \langle\,\rangle)\\ then\ \ rev1(u \diamond y) \;=\;\\ \qquad\left\{\begin{matrix}head\left(rev1(y)\right)\diamond\\ rev1\left(u \diamond rev1\left(tail\left(rev1(y)\right)\right)\right)\end{matrix}\right\}\end{matrix}\right] \qquad (insertion)$$

This is intended to be another alternative definition for the *reverse* function. It was concocted (by E. Ashcroft) to show that *reverse* could be computed using only the simple functions $u \diamond y$, $head(y)$, and $tail(y)$, and without using an auxiliary function such as $rev2$.

The explanation of the obscure *insertion* axiom is that, if $rev1$ does in fact reverse the atoms of a tuple, $head\left(rev1(y)\right)$ is the last atom of $u \diamond y$, and $u \diamond rev1\left(tail\left(rev1(y)\right)\right)$ is the result of deleting the last atom of $u \diamond y$, where y is nonempty. For example, if u is A and y is $\langle$B, C$\rangle$, $head\left(rev1(y)\right)$ is C and $u \diamond rev1\left(tail\left(rev1(y)\right)\right)$ is $\langle$A, B$\rangle$.

We would like to show that $rev1$ does indeed provide an alternative definition of the *reverse* function.

Proposition (alternative definition of reverse)

The sentence

$$(\forall\, tuple\; x)\big[reverse(x) \;=\; rev1(x)\big]$$

is valid. ◢

In our proof we use the following axioms and properties: The *decomposition* property of tuples

$$(\forall\, tuple\; x) \begin{bmatrix} if \;\; not\,(x\,=\,\langle\,\rangle) \\[4pt] then \;\; \genfrac{}{}{0pt}{}{(\exists\, atom\; u)}{(\exists\, tuple\; y)}[x\,=\,u \diamond y] \end{bmatrix} \qquad\qquad (decomposition)$$

The *left-insertion* axiom for append

$$\genfrac{}{}{0pt}{}{(\forall\, atom\; u)}{(\forall\, tuple\; x,\, y)}\big[(u \diamond x) \diamond y \,=\, u \diamond (x \diamond y)\big] \qquad\qquad (left\; insertion)$$

The decomposition property of *head* and *tail*

$$(\forall\, tuple\; x) \begin{bmatrix} if \;\; not\,(x\,=\,\langle\,\rangle) \\[2pt] then \;\; x\,=\, head(x) \diamond tail(x) \end{bmatrix} \qquad\qquad (decomposition)$$

We shall also use several properties of the *length* function over tuples (Section 9.7), including the axiom

$$\genfrac{}{}{0pt}{}{(\forall\, atom\; u)}{(\forall\, tuple\; x)}\big[length(u \diamond x) \,=\, length(x) + 1\big] \qquad\qquad (insertion)$$

and the properties

$$(\forall\, tuple\; x)\big[length\big(reverse(x)\big) \,=\, length(x)\big] \qquad\qquad (reverse)$$

$$(\forall\, tuple\; x) \begin{bmatrix} if \;\; not\,(x=\langle\,\rangle) \\[2pt] then \;\; length\big(tail(x)\big) < length(x) \end{bmatrix} \qquad\qquad (tail)$$

We shall use properties of the nonnegative integers without explicitly mentioning them.

Proof.   We want to show that

$$(\forall\, tuple\; x)\big[reverse(x) \;=\; rev1(x)\big].$$

The proof is by well-founded induction with respect to the length relation $\prec_{length}$, which was defined by the axiom

$$(\forall\, tuple\; x,\, y) \begin{bmatrix} x \prec_{length} y \\[2pt] \equiv \\[2pt] length(x) < length(y) \end{bmatrix} \qquad\qquad (length\; relation)$$

This relation is well-founded over *tuple*.

We take the inductive sentence to be

$$\mathcal{F}[x]: \quad reverse(x) \;=\; rev1(x)$$

and prove

$$(\forall\, tuple\; x)\mathcal{F}[x].$$

Inductive Step

We would like to show

$$(\forall \ tuple \ x) \left[if \ (\forall \ tuple \ x') \left[\begin{matrix} if \ x' \prec_{length} x \\ then \ \mathcal{F}[x'] \end{matrix} \right] \\ then \ \mathcal{F}[x] \right].$$

Consider an arbitrary tuple x, and assume the induction hypothesis

$(\dagger)$ $\qquad (\forall \ tuple \ x') \left[\begin{matrix} if \ x' \prec_{length} x \\ then \ \mathcal{F}[x'] \end{matrix} \right].$

We show that then the desired conclusion $\mathcal{F}[x]$ is true, that is,

$$reverse(x) \ = \ rev1(x).$$

The proof distinguishes among three cases, corresponding to the three axioms for *rev1*.

Case: $x = \langle \ \rangle$

Then we would like to show $\mathcal{F}[\langle \ \rangle]$, that is,

$$reverse(\langle \ \rangle) \ = \ rev1(\langle \ \rangle).$$

But we have

$$reverse(\langle \ \rangle) \ = \ \langle \ \rangle$$
$$\text{(by the \textit{empty} axiom for \textit{reverse})}$$

$$= \ rev1(\langle \ \rangle)$$
$$\text{(by the \textit{empty} axiom for \textit{rev1}).}$$

Case: $singleton(x)$

Then, in this case (by the *singleton-relation* axiom), there exists an atom u such that

$$x = \langle u \rangle.$$

We would like to show $\mathcal{F}[x]$, that is,

$$reverse(\langle u \rangle) \ = \ rev1(\langle u \rangle).$$

But (because u is an atom) we have

$$reverse(\langle u \rangle) \ = \ \langle u \rangle$$
$$\text{(by the \textit{singleton} property of \textit{reverse})}$$

$$= \ rev1(\langle u \rangle)$$
$$\text{(by the \textit{singleton} axiom for \textit{rev1}).}$$

Case: $not\ (x = \langle\ \rangle)$ *and* $not\ (singleton(x))$

Then (by the *decomposition* property of tuples, because $not\ (x = \langle\ \rangle)$), there exist an atom u and a tuple y such that

$$x\ =\ u \diamond y.$$

We can conclude that

$$not\ (y = \langle\ \rangle)$$

because, otherwise (by the *singleton-function* axiom), $x = u \diamond \langle\ \rangle = \langle u \rangle$, and hence $singleton(x)$, contrary to our case assumption.

Because $x = u \diamond y$, we must show $\mathcal{F}[u \diamond y]$, that is,

$$reverse(u \diamond y)\ =\ rev1(u \diamond y),$$

or, equivalently (by the *insertion* axioms for *reverse* and *rev1*, because we concluded that $not\ (y = \langle\ \rangle)$),

$$(1) \qquad reverse(y) \diamond \langle u \rangle\ =\ \left\{ \begin{array}{l} head\,(rev1(y))\diamond \\ rev1\,(u \diamond rev1\,(tail\,(rev1(y)))) \end{array} \right\}.$$

We use the induction hypothesis three times (steps 1 to 3) to replace the three occurrences of *rev1* in (1) with *reverse* and then (step 4) prove the resulting equality.

Step 1: replacement of first rev1

By our induction hypothesis (†), taking x' to be y, we have

$$if\ \ y \prec_{length} x$$
$$then\ \ \mathcal{F}[y],$$

that is (because $x = u \diamond y$),

$$if\ \ y \prec_{length} u \diamond y$$
$$then\ \ reverse(y)\ =\ rev1(y).$$

But because (by the *insertion* axiom for the *length* function)

$$length(y)\ \ <\ \ length(u \diamond y),$$

it follows (by the definition of $\prec_{length}$) that

$$y\ \prec_{length}\ u \diamond y.$$

Therefore we can conclude that

$$reverse(y)\ =\ rev1(y).$$

Our desired result (1) can thus be transformed to

$$(2) \qquad reverse(y) \diamond \langle u \rangle\ =\ \left\{ \begin{array}{l} head\,(reverse(y))\diamond \\ rev1\,(u \diamond rev1\,(tail\,(reverse(y)))) \end{array} \right\}.$$

Step 2: replacement of second rev1

By our induction hypothesis (†), taking x' to be $tail(reverse(y))$, we have

   if $tail(reverse(y)) \prec_{length} x$
   then $\mathcal{F}[tail(reverse(y))]$;

that is (because $x = u \diamond y$),

   if $tail(reverse(y)) \prec_{length} u \diamond y$
   then $reverse(tail(reverse(y))) = rev1(tail(reverse(y)))$.

But (by properties of the *length* function, because $not\,(y = \langle\,\rangle)$ and therefore $not(reverse(y) = \langle\,\rangle)$) we have

$$length(tail(reverse(y))) < length(reverse(y))$$

$$= length(y)$$

$$< length(u \diamond y),$$

and hence (by the definition of the $\prec_{length}$ relation)

   $tail(reverse(y)) \prec_{length} u \diamond y.$

Therefore we may conclude that

   $reverse(tail(reverse(y))) = rev1(tail(reverse(y))).$

Our desired result (2) can thus be transformed to

 (3) $reverse(y) \diamond \langle u \rangle = \left\{ \begin{array}{l} head(reverse(y)) \diamond \\ rev1(u \diamond reverse(tail(reverse(y)))) \end{array} \right\}.$

Step 3: replacement of third rev1

By our induction hypothesis (†), this time taking x' to be the expression $u \diamond reverse(tail(reverse(y)))$, we have

   if $u \diamond reverse(tail(reverse(y))) \prec_{length} x$
   then $\mathcal{F}[u \diamond reverse(tail(reverse(y)))]$;

that is (because $x = u \diamond y$),

   if $u \diamond reverse(tail(reverse(y))) \prec_{length} u \diamond y$
   then $\left[\begin{array}{l} reverse(u \diamond reverse(tail(reverse(y)))) \\ = \\ rev1(u \diamond reverse(tail(reverse(y)))) \end{array} \right].$

But (by properties of the *length* function, because $not\,(y = \langle\,\rangle)$ and therefore $not\,(reverse(y) = \langle\,\rangle)$), we have

   $length(u \diamond reverse(tail(reverse(y))))$

     $= length(reverse(tail(reverse(y)))) + 1$

$$= \quad length\big(tail\big(reverse(y)\big)\big) + 1$$

$$< \quad length\big(reverse(y)\big) + 1$$

$$= \quad length(y) + 1$$

$$= \quad length(u \diamond y).$$

In short,

$$length\big(u \diamond reverse\big(tail\big(reverse(y)\big)\big)\big) \;<\; length(u \diamond y),$$

and hence (by the definition of the $\prec_{length}$ relation)

$$u \diamond reverse\big(tail\big(reverse(y)\big)\big) \;\prec_{length}\; u \diamond y.$$

Therefore we can conclude that

$$reverse\big(u \diamond reverse\big(tail\big(reverse(y)\big)\big)\big)$$
$$=$$
$$rev1\big(u \diamond reverse\big(tail\big(reverse(y)\big)\big)\big).$$

Our desired result (3) can thus be transformed to

$$(4) \qquad reverse(y) \diamond \langle u \rangle \;=\; \left\{ \begin{array}{l} head\big(reverse(y)\big) \diamond \\ reverse\big(u \diamond reverse\big(tail\big(reverse(y)\big)\big)\big) \end{array} \right\}.$$

Step 4: *proof of the equality*

We have

$$\left\{ \begin{array}{l} head\big(reverse(y)\big) \diamond \\ reverse\big(u \diamond reverse\big(tail\big(reverse(y)\big)\big)\big) \end{array} \right\}$$

$$= \left\{ \begin{array}{l} head\big(reverse(y)\big) \diamond \\ \big(reverse\big(reverse\big(tail\big(reverse(y)\big)\big)\big) \diamond \langle u \rangle\big) \end{array} \right\}$$
$$\text{(by the \emph{insertion} axiom for \emph{reverse})}$$

$$= \quad head\big(reverse(y)\big) \diamond \big(tail\big(reverse(y)\big) \diamond \langle u \rangle\big)$$
$$\text{(by the \emph{reverse} property of \emph{reverse})}$$

$$= \quad \big(head\big(reverse(y)\big) \diamond tail\big(reverse(y)\big)\big) \diamond \langle u \rangle$$
$$\text{(by the \emph{left-insertion} axiom for append)}$$

$$= \quad reverse(y) \diamond \langle u \rangle$$
$$\text{(by the \emph{decomposition} property of \emph{head} and \emph{tail},}$$
$$\text{because } not \; (reverse(y) = \langle \, \rangle)).$$

In short,

$$reverse(y) \diamond u \;=\; \left\{ \begin{array}{l} head\big(reverse(y)\big) \diamond \\ reverse\big(u \diamond reverse\big(tail\big(reverse(y)\big)\big)\big) \end{array} \right\},$$

which is our desired result (4). ∎

Remark (why the length relation?).   The preceding proof uses well-founded induction with respect to the length relation $\prec_{length}$ over the tuples. It would have been difficult to conduct the proof by well-founded induction over the proper-subtuple relation $\prec_{tuple}$, that is, by complete induction over the tuples. In particular, we have

$$tail\big(reverse(y)\big) \prec_{length} u \diamond y,$$

but not that

$$tail\big(reverse(y)\big) \prec_{tuple} u \diamond y,$$

which would have been required to justify the use of the induction hypothesis in a complete induction proof.

The choice of a well-founded relation for a particular proof is often suggested by the form of the axioms or other valid sentences of the theory. ⌟

Problem 12.6 requires the use of the *well-founded induction* principle.

EXAMPLE: SQUARE ROOT

In the theory of the nonnegative integers, let the *integer square root* of a given nonnegative integer x be the largest nonnegative integer z such that $z^2 \le x$. For example, the integer square root of 5 is 2, the integer square root of 8 is also 2, but the integer square root of 9 is 3.

The unary function $binsqrt(x)$, which is intended to compute the integer square root of x using binary search, is defined by the axiom

$$(\forall\, integer\ x)\big[binsqrt(x)\ =\ binsqrt2(x, 1)\big] \qquad (binsqrt)$$

where the auxiliary function $binsqrt2(x, u)$ is defined by the axiom

$$
\begin{array}{l}
(\forall\, integer\ x) \\
(\forall\, positive\ u)
\end{array}
\left[
\begin{array}{l}
binsqrt2(x, u) = \\
\left\{
\begin{array}{l}
if\ \ u \le x \\
then\ \ if\ \ \big[binsqrt2(x, 2 \cdot u) + u\big]^2 \le x \\
\qquad then\ \ binsqrt2(x, 2 \cdot u) + u \\
\qquad else\ \ binsqrt2(x, 2 \cdot u) \\
else\ \ 0
\end{array}
\right.
\end{array}
\right] \qquad (binsqrt2)
$$

Here the auxiliary function $binsqrt2(x, u)$ yields a nonnegative integer that is within a positive tolerance u less than $\sqrt{x}$, the real square root of x. In other words, we can show that

$$binsqrt2(x,\ u)\ \le\ \sqrt{x}\ <\ binsqrt2(x,\ u) + u$$

or, equivalently,

$$(\forall \, integer \,\, x) \atop (\forall \, positive \,\, u) \left[\begin{array}{l} \big(binsqrt2(x,u)\big)^2 \leq x \\ \text{and} \\ not \,\, \big[(binsqrt2(x,u) + u)^2 \leq x\big] \end{array} \right] \qquad (tolerance)$$

and therefore

$$(\forall \, integer \,\, x) \left[\begin{array}{l} \big(binsqrt(x)\big)^2 \leq x \\ \text{and} \\ not \,\, \big[(binsqrt(x) + 1)^2 \leq x\big] \end{array} \right] \qquad (range)$$

We may then conclude

$$(\forall \, integer \,\, x) \left[\begin{array}{l} \big(binsqrt(x)\big)^2 \leq x \\ \text{and} \\ (\forall \, integer \,\, y) \left[\begin{array}{l} if \,\, y^2 \leq x \\ then \,\, y \leq binsqrt(x) \end{array} \right] \end{array} \right] \qquad (square \,\, root)$$

In other words, the $binsqrt(x)$ function indeed computes the integer square root of x.

The intuitive rationale for the curious auxiliary program $binsqrt2(x, u)$ is as follows. If the error tolerance u is sufficiently large (i.e., greater than x), then 0 is a good enough approximation, that is, 0 is within u less than $\sqrt{x}$. Otherwise, the program finds a cruder approximation $b = binsqrt2(x, 2 \cdot u)$, which must be within $2 \cdot u$ less than $\sqrt{x}$. If $(b + u)^2 \leq x$, that is, if $b + u \leq \sqrt{x}$, then $b + u$ is a good enough approximation, that is, $b + u$ is within u less than $\sqrt{x}$. Otherwise, $\sqrt{x} < b + u$, and hence b itself is a good enough approximation, that is, b is within u less than $\sqrt{x}$.

The reader is requested to prove the preceding properties in **Problem 12.7**.

In **Problem 12.8** the reader is requested to devise an analogous set of axioms that define a binary function $binquot(x, y)$ that computes the quotient of dividing x by y.

12.4   LEXICOGRAPHIC RELATIONS

In this section, we introduce a way of combining two well-founded relations, over two classes of objects, into a single well-founded relation over the class of pairs of these objects. If we know that two relations $\prec_1$ and $\prec_2$ are well-founded over $object_1$'s and $object_2$'s, respectively, we can combine them to define a lexicographic relation $\prec_{lex}$ that is well-founded over pairs of $object_1$'s and $object_2$'s.

These are pairs of the form $\langle x_1, x_2 \rangle$, where $obj_1(x_1)$ and $obj_2(x_2)$. They are characterized by the predicate symbol *pair*. In certain proofs, it is convenient to use such a composite relation as the basis for a well-founded induction argument.

THEORY OF PAIRS

The theory of pairs was introduced in Section 6.8; here we use a slightly altered version. In the original theory, the elements of a pair are each from the same class of objects. In the altered theory, the first element is from one class and the second is from another, possibly different, class.

Suppose that, in a given theory, the unary predicate symbols obj_1 and obj_2 characterize two classes of elements, respectively. Then the vocabulary of the theory of pairs (over obj_1 and obj_2) consists of the following additional symbols:

- A unary predicate symbol $pair(x)$.

- A binary function symbol $\langle x_1, x_2 \rangle$, denoting the *pairing* function.

Under the intended model, $pair(x)$ characterizes the pairs $\langle x_1, x_2 \rangle$ of elements x_1 and x_2 satisfying obj_1 and obj_2, respectively. The value of the pairing function $\langle x_1, x_2 \rangle$ is the pair whose first element is the object$_1$ x_1 and whose second element is the object$_2$ x_2. As usual, we write the pairing function as $\langle x_1, x_2 \rangle$, using the familiar mathematical notation, rather than a standard predicate-logic binary function symbol such as $f_{101}(x_1, x_2)$.

The theory of pairs (over obj_1 and obj_2) is a theory with equality and the following axioms:

$$(\forall x) \begin{bmatrix} pair(x) \\ \equiv \\ (\exists\, obj_1\ x_1) \\ (\exists\, obj_2\ x_2) \end{bmatrix} [x = \langle x_1,\, x_2 \rangle] \qquad (pair)$$

$$(\forall\, obj_1\ x_1,\, y_1) \begin{bmatrix} if\ \langle x_1,\, x_2 \rangle = \langle y_1,\, y_2 \rangle \\ then\ \ x_1 = y_1\ \ and\ \ x_2 = y_2 \end{bmatrix} \qquad (uniqueness)$$

In other words, every pair is of form $\langle x_1, x_2 \rangle$, where x_1 is an object$_1$, x_2 is an object$_2$, and the pair can be constructed in only one way. We do not specify whether the object$_1$'s and object$_2$'s may themselves be pairs.

In this theory, we can define unary functions $first(x)$ and $second(x)$, the first and second elements, respectively, of the pair x, by the axioms

$$
\begin{array}{l}
(\forall\, obj_1\ x_1) \\
(\forall\, obj_2\ x_2)
\end{array}
\big[first(\langle x_1,\ x_2\rangle) = x_1\big]
\qquad\qquad (first)
$$

$$
\begin{array}{l}
(\forall\, obj_1\ x_1) \\
(\forall\, obj_2\ x_2)
\end{array}
\big[second(\langle x_1,\ x_2\rangle) = x_2\big]
\qquad\qquad (second)
$$

We can then establish the following property of the *first* and *second* functions:

$$
(\forall\, pair\ x)\big[x = \langle first(x),\ second(x)\rangle\big]
\qquad (decomposition)
$$

THE INDUCTION PRINCIPLE

Up to now, we have been able to apply the *well-founded induction* principle to only a single inductive variable at a time. If a proof involves induction over more than one variable, we have been required to apply the rule several times in succession. The following proposition gives us a way to apply the induction principle to two variables at a time.

Proposition (well-founded induction over pairs)

In the theory of pairs over obj_1 and obj_2, suppose the binary relation $\prec$ is well-founded over *pair*.

Then, for each sentence $\mathcal{F}[x_1,\, x_2]$ without free occurrences of x_1' and x_2', the universal closure of the sentence

$$
if\ \begin{array}{l}(\forall\, obj_1\ x_1)\\(\forall\, obj_2\ x_2)\end{array}
\left[
if\ \begin{array}{l}(\forall\, obj_1\ x_1')\\(\forall\, obj_2\ x_2')\end{array}
\left[
\begin{array}{l}
if\ \langle x_1',\, x_2'\rangle \prec \langle x_1,\, x_2\rangle\\
then\ \ \mathcal{F}[x_1',\, x_2']
\end{array}
\right]
\ \begin{array}{l}\\ then\ \ \mathcal{F}[x_1,\, x_2]\end{array}
\right]
$$

$$
then\ \begin{array}{l}(\forall\, obj_1\ x_1)\\(\forall\, obj_2\ x_2)\end{array}\mathcal{F}[x_1,\, x_2]
$$

$$
(well\text{-}founded\ induction\ over\ pairs)
$$

is valid. ⏚

LEXICOGRAPHIC RELATION

We may now define the lexicographic relation in the altered theory of pairs.

Suppose that obj_1 and obj_2 are unary predicate symbols and that $\prec_1$ and $\prec_2$ are binary relations. Then, in the theory of pairs (over obj_1 and obj_2), the *lexicographic relation* $\prec_{lex}$ (*corresponding to* $\prec_1$ *and* $\prec_2$) is defined by the axiom

$$
\begin{array}{ll}
(\forall\ obj_1\ x_1,\ y_1) & \left[\begin{array}{l}
\langle x_1,\ x_2 \rangle \prec_{lex} \langle y_1,\ y_2 \rangle \\
\equiv \\
\left[\begin{array}{l}
x_1 \prec_1 y_1 \\
or \\
x_1 = y_1\ \ and\ \ x_2 \prec_2 y_2
\end{array}\right]
\end{array}\right] \qquad (lexicographic \\
(\forall\ obj_2\ x_2,\ y_2) & \hspace{7cm} relation)
\end{array}
$$

In other words, the lexicographic relation $\prec_{lex}$ between two pairs initially compares the first components of the pairs; only if these are equal does it compare their second components. Thus the definition of $\prec_{lex}$ depends on the choice of $\prec_1$ and $\prec_2$; in using a single symbol $\prec_{lex}$, we are disguising the fact that the relation actually depends on our choice of component relations. Had we chosen a different $\prec_1$ or $\prec_2$, we would have obtained a different $\prec_{lex}$.

Example. Take

$\prec_1$ to be the proper-subtuple relation $\prec_{tuple}$ over tuples

and

$\prec_2$ to be the less-than relation $<$ over the nonnegative integers.

Consider the theory of pairs over tuples and nonnegative integers; that is, obj_1 is *tuple* and obj_2 is *integer*.

Then, for any tuples x_1, y_1 and any nonnegative integers x_2, y_2, we have

$$
\langle x_1,\ x_2 \rangle \prec_{lex} \langle y_1,\ y_2 \rangle \quad \text{if and only if} \quad \left\{\begin{array}{c}
x_1 \prec_{tuple} y_1 \\
or \\
x_1 = y_1 \text{ and } x_2 < y_2
\end{array}\right\}.
$$

Thus

$$\langle \text{ABC},\ 100 \rangle \prec_{lex} \langle \text{DABCE},\ 2 \rangle \quad \text{because ABC} \prec_{tuple} \text{DABCE},$$

$$\langle \text{ABC},\ 2 \rangle \prec_{lex} \langle \text{ABC},\ 3 \rangle \qquad \text{because ABC} = \text{ABC and } 2 < 3,$$

but

$$\text{not} \quad \langle \text{AB},\ 2 \rangle \prec_{lex} \langle \text{BCE},\ 3 \rangle,$$

$$\text{not} \quad \langle \text{ABC},\ 3 \rangle \prec_{lex} \langle \text{ABC},\ 2 \rangle,$$

$$\text{not} \quad \langle \text{ABC},\ 3 \rangle \prec_{lex} \langle \text{ABC},\ 3 \rangle. \quad \blacksquare$$

We now show that the lexicographic relation $\prec_{lex}$ is well-founded over *pair* if its component relations $\prec_1$ and $\prec_2$ are well-founded over obj_1 and obj_2, respectively.

Proposition (lexicographic relation)

In the theory of pairs over obj_1 and obj_2, let $\prec_1$ and $\prec_2$ be binary relations and $\prec_{lex}$ be the corresponding lexicographic relation.

If $\prec_1$ and $\prec_2$ are well-founded over obj_1 and obj_2, respectively, then $\prec_{lex}$ is well-founded over *pair*. $\quad \blacksquare$

Let us sketch an informal proof of this proposition.

Proof.   It will be convenient in the proof to introduce a change of notation. Let us write obj and $\prec$ instead of obj_1 and $\prec_1$, and $\widetilde{obj}$ and $\widetilde{\prec}$ instead of obj_2 and $\prec_2$. Then we can use subscripted variables to stand for elements of sequences.

We establish that, if $\prec$ and $\widetilde{\prec}$ are well-founded over obj and $\widetilde{obj}$, respectively, then the corresponding lexicographic relation $\prec_{lex}$ is well-founded over the appropriate class of pairs. For suppose, to the contrary, that

$$\langle x_0, \widetilde{x}_0\rangle, \ \langle x_1, \widetilde{x}_1\rangle, \ \ldots, \ \langle x_i, \widetilde{x}_i\rangle, \ \langle x_{i+1}, \widetilde{x}_{i+1}\rangle, \ \ldots$$

is a sequence of pairs decreasing with respect to $\prec_{lex}$, that is,

$$\langle x_0, \widetilde{x}_0\rangle \ \succ_{lex} \ \langle x_1, \widetilde{x}_1\rangle \ \succ_{lex} \ \cdots \ \succ_{lex} \ \langle x_i, \widetilde{x}_i\rangle \ \succ_{lex} \ \langle x_{i+1}, \widetilde{x}_{i+1}\rangle \ \succ_{lex} \ \cdots .$$

By the definition of the lexicographic relation, we know that, for each nonnegative i,

$$x_i \succ x_{i+1}$$

$$or$$

$$x_i = x_{i+1} \ and \ \widetilde{x}_i \widetilde{\succ} \widetilde{x}_{i+1},$$

and hence

(*) $x_i \succ x_{i+1} \ or \ x_i = x_{i+1}.$

Let us consider the sequence of first components $\langle x_0, x_1, \ldots, x_i, x_{i+1}, \ldots \rangle$. By (*) and the *no-decreasing* condition for $\prec$, we know that, after a certain point x_k, all the objects in the sequence must be equal; that is,

$$x_k = x_{k+1} = \cdots = x_{k+j} = x_{k+j+1} = \cdots .$$

Otherwise, for each object in the sequence we could find a subsequent object strictly less with respect to $\prec$. In this way, we could select an infinite subsequence of objects decreasing with respect to $\prec$, contradicting the well-foundedness of $\prec$ over obj.

We know that, for each nonnegative j,

$$\langle x_{k+j}, \widetilde{x}_{k+j}\rangle \ \succ_{lex} \ \langle x_{k+j+1}, \widetilde{x}_{k+j+1}\rangle.$$

Therefore, by the definition of the lexicographic relation,

$$x_{k+j} \succ x_{k+j+1}$$

$$or$$

$$x_{k+j} = x_{k+j+1} \ and \ \widetilde{x}_{k+j} \widetilde{\succ} \widetilde{x}_{k+j+1}.$$

But we also know (by the way x_k was chosen) that $x_{k+j} = x_{k+j+1}$. Hence (by the irreflexivity of $\prec$), we have *not* $(x_{k+j} \succ x_{k+j+1})$. Therefore

$$\widetilde{x}_{k+j} \widetilde{\succ} \widetilde{x}_{k+j+1}.$$

It follows that the subsequence $\langle \widetilde{x}_k, \widetilde{x}_{k+1}, \ldots, \widetilde{x}_{k+j}, \widetilde{x}_{k+j+1}, \ldots \rangle$ of second components is a sequence of objects decreasing with respect to $\widetilde{\prec}$, contradicting the well-foundedness of $\widetilde{\prec}$ over $\widetilde{obj}$. ∎

Combining the results of the earlier *well-founded induction over pairs* proposition and the *lexicographic-relation* proposition, just proved, we obtain the following important result.

Corollary (lexicographic well-founded induction)

In the theory of pairs over obj_1 and obj_2, suppose the binary relations $\prec_1$ and $\prec_2$ are well-founded over obj_1 and obj_2, respectively. Let $\prec_{lex}$ be the corresponding well-founded relation.

Then, for each sentence $\mathcal{F}[x_1, x_2]$ without free occurrences of x_1' and x_2', the universal closure of the sentence

$$if \; \begin{matrix} (\forall \, obj_1 \; x_1) \\ (\forall \, obj_2 \; x_2) \end{matrix} \left[if \; \begin{matrix} (\forall \, obj_1 \; x_1') \\ (\forall \, obj_2 \; x_2') \end{matrix} \begin{bmatrix} if \; \langle x_1', \, x_2' \rangle \prec_{lex} \langle x_1, \, x_2 \rangle \\ then \; \mathcal{F}[x_1', \, x_2'] \end{bmatrix} \right. $$
$$\left. then \; \mathcal{F}[x_1, \, x_2] \right]$$

$$then \; \begin{matrix} (\forall \, obj_1 \; x_1) \\ (\forall \, obj_2 \; x_2) \end{matrix} \mathcal{F}[x_1, \, x_2]$$

(lexicographic well-founded induction)

is valid. ◢

This induction principle can accomplish in a single application what may require two applications of the ordinary *well-founded induction* principle.

Remark (lexicographic relation for triples). The above definition and results can be extended to apply to more than two binary relations. For instance, to extend the definition to three relations, we would use a theory of triples, analogous to the theory of pairs, over three unary predicate symbols obj_1, obj_2, and obj_3. In this theory, for three binary relations $\prec_1$, $\prec_2$, and $\prec_3$, we define the lexicographic relation $\prec_{lex}$ by the axiom

$$\begin{matrix} (\forall \, obj_1 \; x_1, \, y_1) \\ (\forall \, obj_2 \; x_2, \, y_2) \\ (\forall \, obj_3 \; x_3, \, y_3) \end{matrix} \begin{bmatrix} \langle x_1, \, x_2, \, x_3 \rangle \prec_{lex} \langle y_1, \, y_2, \, y_3 \rangle \\ \\ \equiv \\ \begin{bmatrix} x_1 \prec_1 y_1 \\ or \\ x_1 = y_1 \; and \; x_2 \prec_2 y_2 \\ or \\ x_1 = y_1 \; and \; x_2 = y_2 \; and \; x_3 \prec_3 y_3 \end{bmatrix} \end{bmatrix}.$$

In the same way, we could define lexicographic relations over "quadruples," over "quintuples," and so on. For simplicity, however, we shall continue to deal only with pairs.

The lexicographic relation can be generalized to combine n well-founded relations $\prec_1$, $\prec_2$, ..., $\prec_n$ over obj_1, obj_2, ..., obj_n, respectively, into a single well-founded relation $\prec_{lex}$ over n-tuples of form $\langle x_1, x_2, \ldots, x_n \rangle$, where $obj_1(x_1)$, $obj_2(x_2)$, ..., and $obj_n(x_n)$. ◢

In **Problem 12.9**, the reader is asked to show that the $\prec_{lex}$ relation is well-founded over triples if its three component relations are well-founded over their respective classes of objects, but that a plausible lexicographic relation over all tuples is actually not well-founded.

12.5 USE OF LEXICOGRAPHIC INDUCTION

Now let us illustrate the use of lexicographic well-founded induction over pairs.

EXAMPLE: ACKERMANN FUNCTION

The binary Ackermann function $ack(x, y)$ is defined in the theory of the nonnegative integers by the following three axioms:

$$(\forall \, integer \; y)\big[ack(0, \, y) \; = \; y+1\big] \qquad\qquad (left\ zero)$$

$$(\forall \, integer \; x)\big[ack(x+1, \, 0) \; = \; ack(x, \, 1)\big] \qquad\qquad (right\ zero)$$

$$(\forall \, integer \; x, \, y)\big[ack(x+1, \, y+1) \; = \; ack\big(x, \, ack(x+1, \, y)\big)\big]$$
$$(double\ successor)$$

From these axioms, we can establish the following properties of the Ackermann function:

$$(\forall \, integer \; x, \, y)\big[integer\big(ack(x, \, y)\big)\big] \qquad\qquad (sort)$$

$$(\forall \, integer \; x, \, y)\big[ack\big(x, \, y\big) > y\big] \qquad\qquad (greater\ than)$$

$$(\forall \, integer \; x, \, y, \, z)\left[\begin{array}{l} if \;\; x < y \\ then \;\; ack(z, \, x) < ack(z, \, y) \end{array}\right]$$
$$(right\ monotonicity)$$

$$(\forall \, integer \; x, \, y, \, z)\left[\begin{array}{l} if \;\; x < y \\ then \;\; ack(x, \, z) < ack(y, \, z) \end{array}\right]$$
$$(left\ monotonicity)$$

$$(\forall \, integer \; x)\big[ack(x, \, x) \; \geq \; 2^x\big] \qquad\qquad (exponent)$$

The function is interesting because its values grow extremely quickly, as suggested by the last property. For example,

$$ack(0, \, 0) = 1, \quad ack(1, \, 1) = 3, \quad ack(2, \, 2) = 7, \quad ack(3, \, 3) = 61,$$

and

$$ack(4, 4) = 2^{2^{2^{2^{16}}}} - 3.$$

We prove the *greater-than* property here. The proofs of the other properties are left as an exercise (**Problem 12.10**).

Proposition (greater than)

The sentence

$$(\forall \, integer \ x, \ y)\big[ack(x, \ y) > y\big]$$

is valid. ⌐

In our proof, we use simple properties of the nonnegative integers without mentioning them.

Proof. The proof is by lexicographic well-founded induction, taking both $\prec_1$ and $\prec_2$ to be the less-than relation $<$, and both obj_1 and obj_2 to be *integer*.

We show (renaming x to x_1 and y to x_2)

$$(\forall \, integer \ x_1, \ x_2)\big[ack(x_1, \ x_2) > x_2\big],$$

taking the inductive sentence to be

$$\mathcal{F}[x_1, \ x_2] : \quad ack(x_1, \ x_2) > x_2.$$

Inductive Step

For arbitrary nonnegative integers x_1 and x_2, we assume as our induction hypothesis that

(†) $(\forall \, integer \ x_1', \ x_2') \begin{bmatrix} if \ \langle x_1', \ x_2' \rangle \prec_{lex} \langle x_1, \ x_2 \rangle \\ then \ \mathcal{F}[x_1', \ x_2'] \end{bmatrix}.$

We would like to show that then $\mathcal{F}[x_1, \ x_2]$, that is,

(††) $ack(x_1, \ x_2) > x_2.$

The proof distinguishes among several cases, suggested by the axioms for ack.

Case: $x_1 = 0$

Since (by the *left-zero* axiom for ack)

$$ack(0, \ x_2) = x_2 + 1,$$

we have

$$ack(0, \ x_2) > x_2,$$

which is the desired result (††) in this case.

Case: *not* $(x_1 = 0)$

Then (by the *decomposition* property of the nonnegative integers), there exists some nonnegative integer y_1 such that

$$x_1 = y_1 + 1.$$

We distinguish between two subcases.

Subcase: $x_2 = 0$

We would like to establish (††), that is, in this subcase (since $x_1 = y_1 + 1$ and $x_2 = 0$), that

$$ack(y_1 + 1, 0) > 0$$

or, equivalently (by the *right-zero* axiom for *ack*),

$$ack(y_1, 1) > 0.$$

By our induction hypothesis (†), taking x_1' to be y_1 and x_2' to be 1, we have (because $x_1 = y_1 + 1$ and $x_2 = 0$)

> *if* $\langle y_1, 1\rangle \prec_{lex} \langle y_1 + 1, 0\rangle$
> *then* $\mathcal{F}[y_1, 1]$.

But, because $y_1 < y_1 + 1$, we have (by the definition of the lexicographic relation)

$$\langle y_1, 1\rangle \prec_{lex} \langle y_1 + 1, 0\rangle$$

and therefore $\mathcal{F}[y_1, 1]$, that is,

$$ack(y_1, 1) > 1.$$

Hence

$$ack(y_1, 1) > 0,$$

as we wanted to show in this subcase.

Subcase: *not* $(x_2 = 0)$

Then (by the *decomposition* property of the nonnegative integers), there exists some nonnegative integer y_2 such that

$$x_2 = y_2 + 1.$$

We would like to establish (††), that is, in this subcase (since $x_1 = y_1 + 1$ and $x_2 = y_2 + 1$), that

$$ack(y_1 + 1, y_2 + 1) > y_2 + 1$$

or, equivalently (by the *double-successor* axiom for *ack*),

(‡‡) $ack\big(y_1, ack(y_1 + 1, y_2)\big) > y_2 + 1.$

Taking x_1' to be y_1 and x_2' to be $ack(y_1 + 1, y_2)$ in our induction hypothesis (†), we have (because $x_1 = y_1 + 1$ and $x_2 = y_2 + 1$)

> *if* $\langle y_1, ack(y_1 + 1, y_2)\rangle \prec_{lex} \langle y_1 + 1, y_2 + 1\rangle$
> *then* $\mathcal{F}\big[y_1, ack(y_1 + 1, y_2)\big].$

But, since $y_1 < y_1 + 1$, we have (by the definition of the lexicographic relation)
$$\langle y_1,\ ack(y_1 + 1,\ y_2)\rangle \ \prec_{lex}\ \langle y_1 + 1,\ y_2 + 1\rangle$$
and therefore $\mathcal{F}[y_1,\ ack(y_1 + 1,\ y_2)]$, that is,

(1) $\qquad ack(y_1,\ ack(y_1 + 1,\ y_2))\ >\ ack(y_1 + 1,\ y_2).$

By our induction hypothesis (†) again, taking x_1' to be $y_1 + 1$ and x_2' to be y_2, we have (because $x_1 = y_1 + 1$ and $x_2 = y_2 + 1$)

$\qquad$ *if* $\langle y_1 + 1,\ y_2\rangle \ \prec_{lex}\ \langle y_1 + 1,\ y_2 + 1\rangle$

$\qquad$ *then* $\mathcal{F}[y_1 + 1,\ y_2]$.

But, since $y_1 + 1 = y_1 + 1$ and $y_2 < y_2 + 1$, we have (by the definition of the lexicographic relation)
$$\langle y_1 + 1,\ y_2\rangle \ \prec_{lex}\ \langle y_1 + 1,\ y_2 + 1\rangle$$
and therefore $\mathcal{F}[y_1 + 1,\ y_2]$, that is,
$$ack(y_1 + 1,\ y_2)\ >\ y_2.$$

Hence

(2) $\qquad ack(y_1 + 1,\ y_2)\ \geq\ y_2 + 1.$

From (1) and (2) we have
$$ack(y_1,\ ack(y_1 + 1,\ y_2))\ >\ y_2 + 1,$$
which is our desired result (‡‡). ∎

Remark (why lexicographic relation?).   The definition of the Ackermann function suggests that the lexicographic relation will be the basis for the induction in the proofs of its properties. For, in each axiom in which a term $ack(s_1,\ s_2)$ constitutes the left-hand side of an equality and a term $ack(t_1,\ t_2)$ occurs in the corresponding right-hand side, we have
$$\langle s_1,\ s_2\rangle \ \succ_{lex}\ \langle t_1,\ t_2\rangle.$$
In particular, in the *right-zero* axiom we have
$$\langle x + 1,\ 0\rangle \ \succ_{lex}\ \langle x,\ 1\rangle,$$
and in the *double-successor* axiom we have
$$\langle x + 1,\ y + 1\rangle \ \succ_{lex}\ \langle x,\ ack(x + 1,\ y)\rangle$$
$$\langle x + 1,\ y + 1\rangle \ \succ_{lex}\ \langle x + 1,\ y\rangle,$$
for all nonnegative integers x and y. These are the three properties of the lexicographic relation we required for the three applications of the induction hypothesis in the preceding proof. ∎

EXAMPLE: GCDPLUS FUNCTION

Recall that in the theory of the nonnegative integers we defined a binary function $gcd(x, y)$ to be the greatest common divisor of x and y (Section 8.9). The gcd function was defined by the axioms

$$(\forall \, integer \, x)\big[gcd(x, 0) = x\big] \qquad\qquad\qquad (zero)$$

$$\begin{matrix}(\forall \, integer \, x)\\(\forall \, positive \, y)\end{matrix}\big[gcd(x, y) \; = \; gcd\big(y, \, rem(x, \, y)\big)\big] \qquad (remainder)$$

We showed, by complete induction over the nonnegative integers, that $gcd(x, y)$ is indeed a common divisor of x and y, that is,

$$(\forall \, integer \, x, \, y) \begin{bmatrix} gcd(x, \, y) \preceq_{div} x \\ and \\ gcd(x, \, y) \preceq_{div} y \end{bmatrix} \qquad (common \; divisor)$$

We indicated also that $gcd(x, y)$ is the greatest of the common divisors of x and y (with respect to the divides relation $\preceq_{div}$), that is,

$$(\forall \, integer \, x, \, y, \, z) \begin{bmatrix} if \;\; z \preceq_{div} x \;\; and \;\; z \preceq_{div} y \\ then \;\; z \preceq_{div} gcd(x, \, y) \end{bmatrix} \qquad (greatest)$$

In this example, we present an alternative definition for the greatest-common-divisor function.

Let the binary function $gcdplus(x, y)$ be defined by the following axioms:

$$(\forall \, integer \, x)\big[gcdplus(0, \, x) \; = \; x\big] \qquad\qquad (left \; zero)$$

$$(\forall \, integer \, x, \, y)\big[gcdplus(x, \, x + y) \; = \; gcdplus(x, \, y)\big] \qquad (addition)$$

$$(\forall \, integer \, x, \, y)\big[gcdplus(x, \, y) \; = \; gcdplus(y, \, x)\big] \qquad (symmetry)$$

We first illustrate the use of the axioms to compute the greatest common divisor of two particular nonnegative integers.

Example (computation of gcdplus).   Suppose we would like to determine the greatest common divisor of 6 and 3. Then

$$gcdplus(6, \, 3) \; = \; gcdplus(3, \, 6)$$
$$\text{(by the } symmetry \text{ axiom)}$$

$$= \; gcdplus(3, \, 3 + 3)$$

$$= \; gcdplus(3, \, 3)$$
$$\text{(by the } addition \text{ axiom)}$$

$$= \; gcdplus(3, \, 3+0)$$

$$= \; gcdplus(3, \, 0)$$
$$\text{(by the } addition \text{ axiom)}$$

$$= \; gcdplus(0, \, 3)$$
$$\text{(by the } symmetry \text{ axiom)}$$

$$= \; 3$$
$$\text{(by the } left\text{-}zero \text{ axiom).}$$

In short,

$$gcdplus(6, \, 3) = 3. \quad \lrcorner$$

Note that a judicious use of the axioms for *gcdplus* is required to avoid an infinite computation. Otherwise, we could repeatedly apply the *symmetry* axiom without ever reaching a final value.

We would like to show that *gcdplus* provides an alternative definition of the *gcd* function.

Proposition (gcdplus)

The sentences

$$(\forall \, integer \; x, \, y) \begin{bmatrix} gcdplus(x, \, y) \preceq_{div} x \\ and \\ gcdplus(x, \, y) \preceq_{div} y \end{bmatrix} \qquad (common \; divisor)$$

$$(\forall \, integer \; x, \, y, \, z) \begin{bmatrix} if \; z \preceq_{div} x \; and \; z \preceq_{div} y \\ then \; z \preceq_{div} gcdplus(x, \, y) \end{bmatrix} \qquad (greatest)$$

$$(\forall \, integer \; x) \big[gcdplus(x, \, y) \; = \; gcd(x, \, y) \big] \qquad (gcd)$$

are valid in the theory of nonnegative integers. $\quad \lrcorner$

We first show that the *gcd* property is implied by the *common-divisor* and *greatest* properties; this proof does not require induction. We then show the *greatest* property, that *gcdplus*(x, y) is the greatest of the common divisors of x and y (with respect to the divides relation $\preceq_{div}$). The proof of the *common-divisor* property, that *gcdplus*(x, y) is a common divisor of x and y, is left as an exercise (**Problem 12.11**).

Proof (*gcd* property of *gcdplus*).   Assume that we have established the *common-divisor* and *greatest* properties of the *gcdplus* function. We would like to prove the *gcd* property.

Consider arbitrary nonnegative integers x and y. We know (by the *common-divisor* property of the *gcd* function) that

$$gcd(x,\ y) \preceq_{div} x$$
$$and$$
$$gcd(x,\ y) \preceq_{div} y.$$

Also (by the *greatest* property of the *gcdplus* function, taking z to be $gcd(x,\ y)$),

$$if \quad \begin{bmatrix} gcd(x,\ y) \preceq_{div} x \\ and \\ gcd(x,\ y) \preceq_{div} y \end{bmatrix}$$
$$then \quad gcd(x,\ y) \preceq_{div} gcdplus(x,\ y).$$

Therefore we have

(†) $\qquad gcd(x,\ y) \preceq_{div} gcdplus(x,\ y).$

Similarly (by the *common-divisor* property of the *gcdplus* function), we know

$$gcdplus(x,\ y) \preceq_{div} x$$
$$and$$
$$gcdplus(x,\ y) \preceq_{div} y.$$

Also (by the *greatest* property of the *gcd* function, taking z to be $gcdplus(x,\ y)$),

$$if \quad \begin{bmatrix} gcdplus(x,\ y) \preceq_{div} x \\ and \\ gcdplus(x,\ y) \preceq_{div} y \end{bmatrix}$$
$$then \quad gcdplus(x,\ y) \preceq_{div} gcd(x,\ y).$$

Therefore

(‡) $\qquad gcdplus(x,\ y) \preceq_{div} gcd(x,\ y).$

From (†) and (‡) (by the antisymmetry of the divides relation $\preceq_{div}$), we have

$$gcdplus(x,\ y) \ =\ gcd(x,\ y),$$

as we wanted to show. ⌐

Proof (*greatest* property of *gcdplus*).   We would like to show (renaming x to x_1 and y to x_2)

$$(\forall\ integer\ x_1,\ x_2,\ z) \begin{bmatrix} if\ z \preceq_{div} x_1\ and\ z \preceq_{div} x_2 \\ then\ z \preceq_{div} gcdplus(x_1,\ x_2) \end{bmatrix}.$$

Consider an arbitrary nonnegative integer z; we must show

$$(\forall\ integer\ x_1,\ x_2) \begin{bmatrix} if\ z \preceq_{div} x_1\ and\ z \preceq_{div} x_2 \\ then\ z \preceq_{div} gcdplus(x_1,\ x_2) \end{bmatrix}.$$

The proof is by lexicographic well-founded induction, taking both $\prec_1$ and $\prec_2$ to be the less-than relation $<$ and both obj_1 and obj_2 to be *integer*.

We prove
$$(\forall \, integer \; x_1, x_2)\mathcal{F}[x_1, x_2],$$
where the inductive sentence is
$$\mathcal{F}[x_1, \, x_2] : \quad \begin{array}{l} if \;\; z \preceq_{div} x_1 \;\; and \;\; z \preceq_{div} x_2 \\ then \;\; z \preceq_{div} \; gcdplus(x_1, \, x_2) \end{array}.$$

Inductive Step

For arbitrary nonnegative integers x_1 and x_2, we assume as our induction hypothesis that

(†) $\qquad (\forall \, integer \; x_1', \, x_2') \left[\begin{array}{l} if \; \langle x_1', \, x_2' \rangle \prec_{lex} \langle x_1, \, x_2 \rangle \\ then \;\; \mathcal{F}[x_1', \, x_2'] \end{array} \right].$

We would like to show that then $\mathcal{F}[x_1, \, x_2]$, that is,
$$\begin{array}{l} if \;\; z \preceq_{div} x_1 \;\; and \;\; z \preceq_{div} x_2 \\ then \;\; z \preceq_{div} \; gcdplus(x_1, \, x_2). \end{array}$$

Suppose that

(‡) $\qquad z \preceq_{div} x_1 \;\; and \;\; z \preceq_{div} x_2.$

We show that then

(‡‡) $\qquad z \preceq_{div} \; gcdplus(x_1, \, x_2).$

The proof distinguishes among three cases.

Case: $x_1 = 0$

We would like to show (‡‡), that is (in this case),
$$z \;\; \preceq_{div} \;\; gcdplus(0, \, x_2)$$
or, equivalently (by the *left-zero* axiom for *gcdplus*),
$$z \;\; \preceq_{div} \;\; x_2.$$
But this follows from our initial supposition (‡).

Case: *not* $(x_1 = 0)$ *and* $x_2 < x_1$

We would like to show (‡‡), that is (by the *symmetry* axiom for *gcdplus*),
$$z \;\; \preceq_{div} \;\; gcdplus(x_2, \, x_1).$$

Because, in this case, $x_2 < x_1$, we have (by the definition of the lexicographic relation)
$$\langle x_2, \, x_1 \rangle \prec_{lex} \langle x_1, \, x_2 \rangle.$$

By our induction hypothesis (†), taking x_1' to be x_2 and x_2' to be x_1, we have

> *if* $\langle x_2, x_1 \rangle \prec_{lex} \langle x_1, x_2 \rangle$
> *then* $\mathcal{F}[x_2, x_1]$.

Hence we have $\mathcal{F}[x_2, x_1]$, that is,

> *if* $z \preceq_{div} x_2$ *and* $z \preceq_{div} x_1$
> *then* $z \preceq_{div} gcdplus(x_2, x_1)$.

But by our initial supposition (‡)

> $z \preceq_{div} x_2$ *and* $z \preceq_{div} x_1$.

Therefore

> $z \preceq_{div} gcdplus(x_2, x_1)$,

as we wanted to show in this case.

Case: not $(x_1 = 0)$ *and not* $(x_2 < x_1)$

> Then (by the *total-asymmetry* property of $<$)
>
> $x_1 \leq x_2$.

Therefore (by the *left-addition* property of $\leq$), there exists a nonnegative integer y such that

> $x_2 = x_1 + y$.

We would like to show (‡‡), that $z \preceq_{div} gcdplus(x_1, x_2)$, that is (in this case),

> $z \preceq_{div} gcdplus(x_1, x_1 + y)$

or, equivalently (by the *addition* axiom for *gcdplus*),

> $z \preceq_{div} gcdplus(x_1, y)$.

To apply our induction hypothesis, we first establish that

> $\langle x_1, y \rangle \prec_{lex} \langle x_1, x_2 \rangle$,

that is,

> $\langle x_1, y \rangle \prec_{lex} \langle x_1, x_1 + y \rangle$.

For this purpose, it suffices to show (by the definition of the lexicographic relation, because $x_1 = x_1$) that

> $y < x_1 + y$.

But this follows (by the *left-addition* property of $<$) because *not* $(x_1 = 0)$ in this case.

By our induction hypothesis (†), taking x_1' to be x_1 and x_2' to be y, we have

> *if* $\langle x_1, y \rangle \prec_{lex} \langle x_1, x_2 \rangle$
> *then* $\mathcal{F}[x_1, y]$.

Hence (because $\langle x_1, y \rangle \prec_{lex} \langle x_1, x_2 \rangle$) we have $\mathcal{F}[x_1, y]$, that is,

$\quad$ if $\ z \preceq_{div} x_1 \ $ and $\ z \preceq_{div} y$
$\quad$ then $\ z \preceq_{div} gcdplus(x_1, y)$.

We have supposed initially (‡) that $z \preceq_{div} x_1$ and $z \preceq_{div} x_2$. Therefore (because $x_2 = x_1 + y$)

$\quad z \preceq_{div} x_1 \ $ and $\ z \preceq_{div} x_1 + y$.

Then (by the *addition* property of the divides relation $\preceq_{div}$)

$\quad z \preceq_{div} x_1 \ $ and $\ z \preceq_{div} y$.

It therefore follows that

$\quad z \preceq_{div} gcdplus(x_1, y)$,

as we wanted to show in this case. ⌡

Two other definitions of the *gcd* function are given as exercises (**Problems 12.12** and **12.13**). In **Problem 12.14**, the reader is asked to prove a property of the fibonacci function.

EXAMPLE: MERGESORT

The example in this section illustrates the use of lexicographic well-founded induction in the theory of tuples.

Consider the theory of tuples of nonnegative integers. In this theory, we provide an alternative definition of the sorting function by introducing a unary function symbol $mergesort(z)$, which sorts the elements of z by a new method. We first split the given tuple z into two subtuples x and y, where $z = x \diamond y$; the division into a "left half" x and a "right half" y is arbitrary. We sort the elements of x and y separately and then we merge the elements of the resulting tuples, so that the final result is in (weakly) increasing order.

The axioms for the *mergesort* function are as follows:

$$mergesort(\langle\,\rangle) = \langle\,\rangle \qquad\qquad\qquad (empty)$$

$$(\forall\ atom\ u)\big[mergesort(\langle u \rangle) \ = \ \langle u \rangle\big] \qquad\qquad (singleton)$$

$$(\forall\ tuple\ x,\ y)\begin{bmatrix} mergesort(x \diamond y) = \\ merge\big(mergesort(x),\ mergesort(y)\big)\end{bmatrix} \qquad (append)$$

Note that separate axioms treat the case in which the given tuple has only one element, or none at all. If we are computing the function according to these axioms, to avoid an infinite computation we should guarantee that neither half x nor y is actually the empty tuple, that is, that neither x nor y is the same as $x \diamond y$, although this is not required by the axioms.

The auxiliary function symbol $merge(x, y)$ intermixes the elements of the tuples x and y so that if x and y are ordered, the result remains in (weakly) increasing order. It is defined by the following axioms:

$$(\forall \ tuple \ y)\big[merge(\langle \ \rangle, \ y) \ = \ y\big] \qquad\qquad (left \ empty)$$

$$(\forall \ tuple \ x)\big[merge(x, \ \langle \ \rangle) \ = \ x\big] \qquad\qquad (right \ empty)$$

$$(\forall \ atom \ u, \ v) \atop (\forall \ tuple \ x, \ y) \left[{merge(u \diamond x, \ v \diamond y) \ = \atop \left\{ {if \ \ u \leq v \atop {then \ \ u \diamond merge(x, \ v \diamond y) \atop else \ \ v \diamond merge(u \diamond x, \ y)}} \right\}} \right] \quad (insertion)$$

Thus, for example,

$$merge\big(\langle 1, \ 2, \ 5 \rangle, \ \langle 2, \ 4, \ 4 \rangle\big) \ = \ \langle 1, \ 2, \ 2, \ 4, \ 4, \ 5 \rangle.$$

We would like to show that the *mergesort* axioms do indeed provide an alternative definition of sorting, that is, that

$$(\forall \ tuple \ x)\big[mergesort(x) \ = \ insort(x)\big] \qquad\qquad (insort)$$

If we regard the axioms for *mergesort* as a program describing a computational sorting method, the proof of the *insort* property can be regarded as part of the verification of the correctness of that program.

As before, it suffices to establish (by the *uniqueness* property of *insort*) two properties of the *mergesort* function: that the tuple $mergesort(x)$ is in increasing order, that is,

$$(\forall \ tuple \ x)\big[ordered\,(mergesort(x))\big] \qquad\qquad (ordered)$$

and that the elements of $mergesort(x)$ are the same as those of x, that is,

$$(\forall \ tuple \ x)\big[perm\,(x, \ mergesort(x))\big] \qquad\qquad (permutation)$$

The sorting function is the only function with these two properties. Recall that $ordered(x)$ holds if the elements of the tuple x are in (weakly) increasing order and that $perm(x, y)$ holds if the tuple y can be obtained from the tuple x by rearranging its elements (but preserving their multiplicity).

We shall require the following two properties of the auxiliary function *merge*. It is the proofs of these properties that require lexicographic well-founded induction.

The sentences

$$(\forall \ tuple \ x, \ y) \begin{bmatrix} if \ \ ordered(x) \ \ and \ \ ordered(y) \\ then \ \ ordered\,(merge(x, \ y)) \end{bmatrix} \qquad (ordered)$$

$$(\forall \ tuple \ x, \ y) \Big[perm \,(x \diamond y, \ merge(x, \ y)) \Big] \qquad (permutation)$$

are valid. ⌐

That is, if x and y are in increasing order, so is $merge(x, y)$, and the elements of $merge(x, y)$ are the same as those of x and y together.

The proof of the *permutation* property of the *merge* proposition is left as an exercise (**Problem 12.15**). The proof of the *ordered* property, which follows, depends on the *permutation* property.

In the proof, we use the *insertion* property of the *ordered* relation:

$$(\forall \ atom \ u) \\ (\forall \ tuple \ x) \begin{bmatrix} ordered\,(u \diamond x) \\ \equiv \\ \begin{bmatrix} ordered(x) \\ and \\ (\forall \ atom \ v) \begin{bmatrix} if \ \ v \in x \\ then \ \ u \le v \end{bmatrix} \end{bmatrix} \end{bmatrix} \qquad (insertion)$$

Proof (*ordered* property of *merge*).   We would like to show (renaming x to x_1 and y to x_2)

$$(\forall \ tuple \ x_1, \ x_2) \begin{bmatrix} if \ \ ordered(x_1) \ \ and \ \ ordered(x_2) \\ then \ \ ordered\,(merge(x_1, \ x_2)) \end{bmatrix}.$$

The proof is by lexicographic well-founded induction, taking both obj_1 and obj_2 to be *tuple*, and both $\prec_1$ and $\prec_2$ to be the proper-subtuple relation $\prec_{tuple}$.

We prove

$$(\forall \ tuple \ x_1, x_2)\mathcal{F}[x_1, x_2],$$

where we take the inductive sentence to be

$$\mathcal{F}[x_1, \ x_2] : \quad \begin{array}{l} if \ \ ordered(x_1) \ \ and \ \ ordered(x_2) \\ then \ \ ordered\,(merge(x_1, \ x_2)). \end{array}$$

Inductive Step

For arbitrary tuples x_1 and x_2, assume the induction hypothesis

$$(\dagger) \qquad (\forall \ tuple \ x'_1, \ x'_2) \begin{bmatrix} if \ \ \langle x'_1, \ x'_2 \rangle \prec_{lex} \langle x_1, \ x_2 \rangle \\ then \ \ \mathcal{F}[x'_1, \ x'_2] \end{bmatrix}.$$

We would like to show the desired conclusion $\mathcal{F}[x_1, x_2]$, that is,

> *if ordered(x_1) and ordered(x_2)*
> *then ordered$\big(merge(x_1, x_2)\big)$.*

We suppose that

(‡)   *ordered(x_1) and ordered(x_2)*

and show that then

(‡‡)   *ordered$\big(merge(x_1, x_2)\big)$.*

The proof distinguishes among several cases, suggested by the axioms for *merge*.

Case: $x_1 = \langle\,\rangle$

We would like to show (‡‡), that is (in this case),

> *ordered$\big(merge(\langle\,\rangle, x_2)\big)$*

or, equivalently (by the *left-empty* axiom for the *merge* function),

> *ordered(x_2).*

But this is the second conjunct of our supposition (‡).

Case: $x_2 = \langle\,\rangle$

This case is similar to the preceding one (by the *right-empty* axiom for the *merge* function).

Case: *not $\big(x_1 = \langle\,\rangle\big)$ and not $\big(x_2 = \langle\,\rangle\big)$*

Then (by the *decomposition* property of tuples), there exist atoms u_1 and u_2 and tuples y_1 and y_2 such that

(1) $x_1 = u_1 \diamond y_1$ *and* $x_2 = u_2 \diamond y_2.$

Because we have supposed (‡) that *ordered(x_1) and ordered(x_2)*, that is (in this case),

> *ordered$(u_1 \diamond y_1)$ and   ordered$(u_2 \diamond y_2)$,*

we have (by the *insertion* property of the *ordered* relation)

(2)   *ordered(y_1) and $(\forall\ atom\ v_1)$* $\begin{bmatrix} if\ \ v_1 \in y_1 \\ then\ \ u_1 \leq v_1 \end{bmatrix}$

and

(3)   *ordered(y_2) and $(\forall\ atom\ v_2)$* $\begin{bmatrix} if\ \ v_2 \in y_2 \\ then\ \ u_2 \leq v_2 \end{bmatrix}.$

We would like to show (‡‡), *ordered$\big(merge(x_1, x_2)\big)$*, that is (in this case),

(††)   *ordered$\big(merge(u_1 \diamond y_1,\ u_2 \diamond y_2)\big)$.*

We distinguish between two further subcases.

Subcase: $u_1 \leq u_2$

Then (by the *insertion* axiom for *merge*), to show (††), it suffices to show
$$ordered\left(u_1 \diamond merge(y_1,\ u_2 \diamond y_2)\right)$$
or, equivalently (by the *insertion* property of the *ordered* relation),

(4)　　　　$ordered\left(merge(y_1,\ u_2 \diamond y_2)\right)$

and

(5)　　　　$(\forall\ atom\ w)\begin{bmatrix} if\ \ w \in merge(y_1,\ u_2 \diamond y_2) \\ then\ \ u_1 \leq w \end{bmatrix}$.

Proof of (4)

We first prove (4). By our induction hypothesis (†), taking x_1' to be y_1 and x_2' to be $u_2 \diamond y_2$, we have (because, by (1), $x_1 = u_1 \diamond y_1$ and $x_2 = u_2 \diamond y_2$)

　　　　$if\ \langle y_1,\ u_2 \diamond y_2\rangle \prec_{lex} \langle u_1 \diamond y_1,\ u_2 \diamond y_2\rangle$
　　　　$then\ \ \mathcal{F}[y_1,\ u_2 \diamond y_2].$

But because (by the *insertion-adjacent* property of the subtuple relation)

　　　　$y_1 \prec_{tuple} u_1 \diamond y_1,$

we have (by the definition of the lexicographic relation)

　　　　$\langle y_1,\ u_2 \diamond y_2\rangle \prec_{lex} \langle u_1 \diamond y_1,\ u_2 \diamond y_2\rangle,$

and hence $\mathcal{F}[y_1,\ u_2 \diamond y_2]$, that is,

　　　　$if\ \ ordered(y_1)\ \ and\ \ ordered(u_2 \diamond y_2)$
　　　　$then\ \ ordered\left(merge(y_1,\ u_2 \diamond y_2)\right).$

But from our earlier conclusion (2) and supposition (‡) (because, by (1), $x_2 = u_2 \diamond y_2$), it follows that

　　　　$ordered(y_1)\ \ and\ \ ordered(u_2 \diamond y_2).$

Therefore

　　　　$ordered\left(merge(y_1,\ u_2 \diamond y_2)\right),$

which is the desired result (4).

Proof of (5)

It remains to prove (5), that is,

　　　　$(\forall\ atom\ w)\begin{bmatrix} if\ \ w \in merge(y_1,\ u_2 \diamond y_2) \\ then\ \ u_1 \leq w \end{bmatrix}$.

Consider an arbitrary atom w and suppose that

(6)　　　　$w \in merge(y_1,\ u_2 \diamond y_2).$

We would like to show that

(7)　　　　$u_1 \leq w.$

We know (by the *permutation* property of *merge*, the other part of this proposition) that

$$perm\left(y_1 \diamond (u_2 \diamond y_2), \ merge(y_1, \ u_2 \diamond y_2)\right).$$

Therefore (by the *member* axiom for the permutation relation), because, by our supposition (6), $w \in merge(y_1, \ u_2 \diamond y_2)$, we have

$$w \ \in \ y_1 \diamond (u_2 \diamond y_2)$$

or, equivalently (by the *member* property of the append function $\diamond$),

$$w \in y_1 \quad or \quad w \in (u_2 \diamond y_2)$$

or, equivalently (by the *insertion* axiom for the member relation $\in$),

$$w \in y_1 \quad or \quad w = u_2 \quad or \quad w \in y_2.$$

We treat each of these three possibilities separately.

First possibility: $w \in y_1$

We have (by our earlier conclusion (2), taking v_1 to be w)

$$if \ w \in y_1$$
$$then \ u_1 \leq w.$$

Therefore, in this case, we have the desired result (7), that

$$u_1 \leq w.$$

Second possibility: $w = u_2$

We would like to show (7), $u_1 \leq w$, that is (in this case),

$$u_1 \leq u_2.$$

But this is our subcase assumption.

Third possibility: $w \in y_2$

We have (by our earlier conclusion (3), taking v_2 to be w)

$$if \ w \in y_2$$
$$then \ u_2 \leq w.$$

Therefore, in this case, we have

$$u_2 \leq w.$$

We also know (from our subcase assumption) that

$$u_1 \leq u_2.$$

Therefore we have the desired result (7), that

$$u_1 \leq w.$$

This concludes the proof of (5).

Subcase: not $(u_1 \leq u_2)$

Then (by the *insertion* axiom for *merge*) to show (††), it suffices to show that
$$ordered\,(u_2 \diamond merge(u_1 \diamond y_1,\ y_2)).$$
The proof is similar to the proof for the previous subcase, in which $u_1 \leq u_2$. In this subcase, to apply the induction hypothesis we use the *insertion-adjacent* property of the subtuple relation,
$$y_2 \prec_{tuple} u_2 \diamond y_2,$$
to conclude (by the definition of the lexicographic relation, because $u_1 \diamond y_1 = u_1 \diamond y_1$) that
$$\langle u_1 \diamond y_1,\ y_2 \rangle \prec_{lex} \langle u_1 \diamond y_1,\ u_2 \diamond y_2 \rangle.$$
Hence (by (†), the induction hypothesis)
$$\mathcal{F}[u_1 \diamond y_1,\ y_2].$$
The remaining details of the proof are omitted.   ⌐

Once the properties of the auxiliary function *merge* are established, we can prove the required properties of the *mergesort* function.

Proposition (mergesort)
The sentences

$$(\forall\ tuple\ x)\big[ordered\,(mergesort(x))\big] \qquad\qquad (ordered)$$
$$(\forall\ tuple\ x)\big[perm\,(x,\ mergesort(x))\big] \qquad\qquad (permutation)$$
$$(\forall\ tuple\ x)\big[mergesort(x)\ =\ insort(x)\big] \qquad\qquad (insort)$$

are valid.   ⌐

The proofs of the three parts of the proposition, which do not require lexicographic well-founded induction, are left as an exercise (**Problem 12.16**). An exercise in the theory of tuples that does require a lexicographic induction is given in **Problem 12.17**.

PROBLEMS

Problem 12.1 (well-founded relations)   page 577
Which of the following relations is well-founded? Give an intuitive explanation in each case.
(a) Less-than-or-equal relation $x \leq y$ (over *integer*) in the theory of the nonnegative integers.
(b) Nonequal relation $x \neq y$ (over *integer*) in the theory of the nonnegative integers.
(c) A relation $r(x, y)$ (over *integer*) in the theory of the nonnegative integers, for which $r(0, 1)$, $r(1, 2)$, and $r(2, 0)$ are all valid.

Problem 12.2 (union relation)   page 579

(a) In a given theory, suppose that obj_1 and obj_2 are unary predicate symbols
that characterize two disjoint classes of objects, that is,

$$(\forall\, x)\big[not\, \big(obj_1(x)\ \ and\ \ obj_2(x)\big)\big]$$

is valid. Show that if $\prec_1$ and $\prec_2$ are well-founded over obj_1 and obj_2,
respectively, then $\prec_{union}$ is well-founded over obj.

(b) Part (a) requires that obj_1 and obj_2 characterize disjoint classes. Show
that if this condition is not satisfied, the union relation $\prec_{union}$ is not
necessarily well-founded.

Problem 12.3 (combinations of well-founded relations)   page 579

In a given theory, suppose that $\prec_1$ and $\prec_2$ are two binary relations that
are well-founded over obj. Which of the following relations are also necessarily
well-founded over obj? Give an intuitive explanation in each case.

(a) The conjunction relation $\prec_{and}$, defined by

$$(\forall\ obj\ x,\ y)\begin{bmatrix} x \prec_{and} y \\ \equiv \\ x \prec_1 y\ \ and\ \ x \prec_2 y \end{bmatrix}.$$

(b) The disjunction relation $\prec_{or}$, defined by

$$(\forall\ obj\ x,\ y)\begin{bmatrix} x \prec_{or} y \\ \equiv \\ x \prec_1 y\ \ or\ \ x \prec_2 y \end{bmatrix}.$$

(c) The composition relation $\prec_{comp}$, defined by

$$(\forall\ obj\ x,\ y)\begin{bmatrix} x \prec_{comp} y \\ \equiv \\ (\exists\ obj\ z)\big[x \prec_1 z\ \ and\ \ z \prec_2 y\big] \end{bmatrix}.$$

Problem 12.4 (log relation)   page 579

In the theory of the nonnegative integers, show that the log relation $\prec_{log}$,
defined by the axiom

$$(\forall\ integer\ x,y)\begin{bmatrix} x \prec_{log} y \\ \equiv \\ (\exists\ integer\ z)\big[x^z = y\ \ and\ \ not\,(x = y)\big] \end{bmatrix} \qquad (log)$$

is well-founded (over $integer$).

Hint: You may use the well-foundedness of the union relation.

Problem 12.5 (asymmetry of well-founded relations)   page 583

Use the *minimal-element* condition to prove that, in a given theory, any well-founded relation $\prec$ (over *obj*) is asymmetric (over *obj*).

Hint: Take $\mathcal{G}[x]$ in the *minimal-element* condition to be

$$(\exists \; obj \; y)[x \prec y \;\; and \;\; y \prec x].$$

Problem 12.6 (cumulative sum)   page 593

In the theory of tuples of nonnegative integers, consider the function *sumc*, defined by the following axioms:

$$sumc(\langle \; \rangle) \;=\; 0 \qquad\qquad\qquad (empty)$$

$$(\forall \; integer \; u)\big[sumc(\langle u \rangle) \;=\; u\big] \qquad\qquad (singleton)$$

$$\begin{array}{l}(\forall \; integer \; u, \; v) \\ (\forall \; tuple \; x)\end{array}\big[sumc\big(u \diamond (v \diamond x)\big) \;=\; sumc\big((u+v) \diamond x\big)\big]$$

$$(double \; insertion)$$

Prove that these axioms provide an alternative method for computing the sum of the elements of a tuple. In other words,

$$(\forall \; tuple \; x)\big[sumc(x) \;=\; sum(x)\big],$$

where the function $sum(x)$ is defined by the axioms

$$sum(\langle \; \rangle) \;=\; 0 \qquad\qquad\qquad (empty)$$

$$\begin{array}{l}(\forall \; integer \; u) \\ (\forall \; tuple \; x)\end{array}\big[sum(u \diamond x) \;=\; u + sum(x)\big] \qquad (insertion)$$

Problem 12.7 (binary-search square root)   page 594

We defined the $binsqrt(x)$ function by the axiom

$$(\forall \; integer \; x)\big[binsqrt(x) \;=\; binsqrt2(x, 1)\big] \qquad (binsqrt)$$

where the auxiliary function $binsqrt2(x)$ is defined by the axiom

$$\begin{array}{c}(\forall \; integer \; x) \\ (\forall \; positive \; u)\end{array}\left[\begin{array}{l} binsqrt2(x, u) = \\ \quad \left\{\begin{array}{l} if \;\; u \le x \\ then \;\; if \;\; \big[binsqrt2(x, 2 \cdot u) + u\big]^2 \le x \\ \qquad then \;\; binsqrt2(x, 2 \cdot u) + u \\ \qquad else \;\; binsqrt2(x, 2 \cdot u) \\ else \;\; 0 \end{array}\right. \end{array}\right]$$

$$(binsqrt2)$$

Prove that $binsqrt(x)$ computes the integer square root of the nonnegative integer x in the following three steps:

(a)　　*Tolerance*

$$(\forall \, integer \; x) \atop (\forall \, positive \; u)} \left[\begin{array}{l} \left(binsqrt2(x,u)\right)^2 \leq x \\[4pt] and \\[4pt] not \, \left[\left(binsqrt2(x,u)+u\right)^2 \leq x\right] \end{array} \right].$$

　　Hint: Use the bounded-increase relation.

(b)　*Range*

$$(\forall \, integer \; x) \left[\begin{array}{l} \left(binsqrt(x)\right)^2 \leq x \\[4pt] and \\[4pt] not \, \left[\left(binsqrt(x)+1\right)^2 \leq x\right] \end{array} \right].$$

(c)　*Square root*

$$(\forall \, integer \; x) \left[\begin{array}{l} \left(binsqrt(x)\right)^2 \leq x \\[4pt] and \\[4pt] (\forall \, integer \; y) \left[\begin{array}{l} if \;\; y^2 \leq x \\ then \;\; y \leq binsqrt(x) \end{array} \right] \end{array} \right].$$

Indicate clearly all the properties of the nonnegative integers used in your proofs; you need not prove them.

Problem 12.8 (binary-search quotient)　page 594

(a) Devise a set of axioms, analogous to those of $binsqrt(x)$ in Problem 12.7, that define the binary function $binquot(x, y)$ using binary search. This function computes the integer quotient of dividing a nonnegative integer x by a positive integer y, that is, the largest nonnegative integer z such that $y \cdot z \leq x$.

(b) Using your axioms, show that $binquot$ satisfies the property

$$(\forall \, integer \; x) \atop (\forall \, positive \; y)} \left[\begin{array}{l} y \cdot binquot(x, \, y) \leq x \\[4pt] and \\[4pt] (\forall \, integer \; z) \left[\begin{array}{l} if \;\; y \cdot z \leq x \\ then \;\; z \leq binquot(x, \, y) \end{array} \right] \end{array} \right]$$

$$(quotient)$$

Problem 12.9 (triples and tuples)　page 600

(a)　*Triples*

　　Consider a theory of triples, analogous to our theory of pairs, over three unary predicate symbols obj_1, obj_2, and obj_3. Suppose that $\prec_1$, $\prec_2$, and $\prec_3$ are well-founded over obj_1, obj_2, and obj_3, respectively. Show that the corresponding lexicographic relation $\prec_{lex}$ is well-founded over *triple*, in the theory of triples.

Hint: Use the result of the *lexicographic-relation* proposition for pairs.

(b) *Tuples*

In the theory of tuples, suppose that $\prec$ is well-founded over *atom*. Consider the relation $\prec_{lex}$ defined by the axioms

$$(\forall \ atom \ u) \atop (\forall \ tuple \ y)} \left[\langle \ \rangle \prec_{lex} u \diamond y \right] \qquad\qquad (left \ empty)$$

$$(\forall \ tuple \ x) \left[not \ (x \prec_{lex} \langle \ \rangle) \right] \qquad\qquad (right \ empty)$$

$$(\forall \ atom \ u, \ v) \atop (\forall \ tuple \ x, \ y)} \left[\begin{matrix} u \diamond x \prec_{lex} v \diamond y \\ \equiv \\ \left[\begin{matrix} u \prec v \ \ or \\ u = v \ \ and \ \ x \prec_{lex} y \end{matrix} \right] \end{matrix} \right] \qquad (insertion)$$

For example, in the theory of tuples of nonnegative integers, taking $\prec$ to be $<$, we have

$$\langle \ \rangle \prec_{lex} \langle 0 \rangle, \qquad \langle 1, \ 2, \ 3 \rangle \prec_{lex} \langle 1, \ 2, \ 4 \rangle, \qquad \langle 1, \ 2, \ 100 \rangle \prec_{lex} \langle 1, \ 3 \rangle.$$

Show, by exhibiting an infinite decreasing sequence, that $\prec_{lex}$ is not necessarily well-founded over *tuple*.

Problem 12.10 (Ackermann)   page 601

Establish the validity of the following properties of the Ackermann function:

(a) *Sort*

$$(\forall \ integer \ x, \ y) \left[integer \left(ack(x, \ y) \right) \right]$$

(b) *Right monotonicity*

$$(\forall \ integer \ x, \ y, \ z) \left[\begin{matrix} if \ x < y \\ then \ \ ack(z, \ x) < ack(z, \ y) \end{matrix} \right]$$

(c) *Left monotonicity*

$$(\forall \ integer \ x, \ y, \ z) \left[\begin{matrix} if \ x < y \\ then \ \ ack(x, \ z) < ack(y, \ z) \end{matrix} \right]$$

(d) *Exponent*

$$(\forall \ integer \ x) \left[ack(x, \ x) \ge 2^x \right].$$

Note: Not all of these require lexicographic well-founded induction.

Problem 12.11 (gcdplus)   page 605

Prove the *common-divisor* property of the *gcdplus* function, that is,

$$(\forall \ integer \ x, \ y) \left[\begin{matrix} gcdplus(x, \ y) \preceq_{div} x \\ and \\ gcdplus(x, \ y) \preceq_{div} y \end{matrix} \right].$$

Problem 12.12 (gcdbinary)   page 609

Let the *gcdbinary* function be defined by the following axioms:

$$(\forall\, integer\ x)\left[gcdbinary(x,\ 0)\ =\ x\right] \qquad\qquad (right\ zero)$$

$$(\forall\, integer\ x,\ y)\left[gcdbinary(2\cdot x,\ 2\cdot y)\ =\ 2\cdot gcdbinary(x,\ y)\right]$$
$$(even\ even)$$

$$(\forall\, integer\ x,\ y)\left[\begin{matrix}if\ \ not\ \bigl(even(x)\bigr)\\ then\ \ gcdbinary(x,\ 2\cdot y)\ =\ gcdbinary(x,\ y)\end{matrix}\right]$$
$$(odd\ even)$$

$$(\forall\, integer\ x,\ y)\left[\begin{matrix}if\ \ not\ \bigl(even(x)\bigr)\ \ and\\ \quad not\ \bigl(even(y)\bigr)\ \ and\ \ x\le y\\ then\ \ gcdbinary(x,\ y)\ =\ gcdbinary(x,\ y-x)\end{matrix}\right]$$
$$(odd\ odd)$$

$$(\forall\, integer\ x,\ y)\left[gcdbinary(x,\ y)\ =\ gcdbinary(y,\ x)\right]\quad (symmetry)$$

where the relation $even(x)$, which is true if x is even, is defined by the *two* axiom

$$(\forall\, integer\ x)\left[even(x)\ \equiv\ 2\preceq_{div} x\right]. \qquad\qquad (two)$$

(a) *Common divisor*

Show that $gcdbinary(x,\ y)$ is a common divisor of x and y, that is,

$$(\forall\, integer\ x,\ y)\left[\begin{matrix}gcdbinary(x,\ y)\preceq_{div} x\\ and\\ gcdbinary(x,\ y)\preceq_{div} y\end{matrix}\right].$$

(b) *Greatest*

Show that $gcdbinary(x,\ y)$ is the greatest of the common divisors of x and y, that is,

$$(\forall\, integer\ x,\ y,\ z)\left[\begin{matrix}if\ \ z\preceq_{div} x\ \ and\ \ z\preceq_{div} y\\ then\ \ z\preceq_{div} gcdbinary(x,\ y)\end{matrix}\right].$$

(c) *Gcd*

Show that *gcdbinary* provides an alternative definition for the *gcd* function, that is,

$$(\forall\, integer\ x,\ y)\left[gcdbinary(x,\ y)\ =\ gcd(x,\ y)\right].$$

State whatever properties of the nonnegative integers you use; you need not prove them, but use the simplest properties you can.

Problem 12.13 (revised gcdbinary)   page 609

Suppose that, in the definition of the *gcdbinary* function (defined in Problem 12.12), we replace the *odd-odd* axiom by the following two axioms:

$$(\forall \, integer \; x)\big[gcdbinary(x, \; x) = x\big] \qquad\qquad (equal)$$

$$(\forall \, integer \; x, \; y) \left[\begin{array}{l} if \quad not \; \big(even \; (x)\big) \quad and \\ \quad\quad not \; \big(even \; (y)\big) \quad and \quad x < y \\ then \quad gcdbinary(x, \; y) = gcdbinary(x, \; x + y) \end{array}\right]$$

$$(odd \; plus)$$

Show that *gcdbinary* still provides an alternative definition of the *gcd* function. (You need present only those parts of the proof that differ from the previous proof.)

Problem 12.14 (fibonacci function)   page 609

The fibonacci function $fib(x)$ was defined (in Problem 11.4) by the axioms

$$fib(0) \;=\; 0 \qquad\qquad\qquad\qquad\qquad (zero)$$

$$fib(1) \;=\; 1 \qquad\qquad\qquad\qquad\qquad (one)$$

$$(\forall \; integer \; x)\big[fib(x + 2) \;=\; fib(x + 1) + fib(x)\big] \qquad (plus \; two)$$

Prove that

$$(\forall \; integer \; x, \; y)\big[fib(x + y + 1) \;=\; fib(x + 1) \cdot fib(y + 1) \;+\; fib(x) \cdot fib(y)\big].$$

You may use basic properties of the nonnegative integers without proof.

Problem 12.15 (merge)   page 611

Prove the *permutation* property of the *merge* function, that is,

$$(\forall \, tuple \; x, \; y)\big[perm\big(x \diamond y, \; merge(x, \; y)\big)\big].$$

Problem 12.16 (mergesort)   page 615

Establish the following properties of the *mergesort* function:

(a) *Permutation*

The tuple $mergesort(x)$ is a permutation of the tuple x, that is,

$$(\forall \, tuple \; x)\big[perm\big(x, \; mergesort(x)\big)\big].$$

(b) *Ordered*

The tuple $mergesort(x)$ is in (weakly) increasing order, that is,

$$(\forall \, tuple \; x)\big[ordered\big(mergesort(x)\big)\big].$$

(c) *Insort*

The *mergesort* function is identical to the function *insort*, that is,

$$(\forall \, tuple \; x)\big[mergesort(x) \;=\; inssort(x)\big].$$

These problems do not require lexicographic well-founded induction.

Problem 12.17 (ones)   page 615

In the theory of tuples of nonnegative integers, suppose that the unary *ones* function is defined by the following axioms:

$$ones(\langle\,\rangle) = \langle\,\rangle \qquad\qquad (empty)$$

$$(\forall\ tuple\ x)\big[ones(0 \diamond x) = ones(x)\big] \qquad\qquad (zero)$$

$$\begin{matrix}(\forall\ integer\ u)\\ (\forall\ tuple\ x)\end{matrix}\big[ones((u+1) \diamond x) = 1 \diamond ones(u \diamond x)\big] \qquad (successor)$$

For each nonnegative integer n in the given tuple x, the function $ones(x)$ inserts n copies of the integer 1 into the resulting tuple. For example,

$$ones(\langle 2,\ 1\rangle) = \langle 1,\ 1,\ 1\rangle \quad \text{and} \quad ones(\langle 2,\ 0,\ 3\rangle) = \langle 1,\ 1,\ 1,\ 1,\ 1\rangle.$$

Suppose further that the unary *sum* function is defined (as in Problem 12.6) by the axioms

$$sum(\langle\,\rangle) = 0 \qquad\qquad (empty)$$

$$\begin{matrix}(\forall\ integer\ u)\\ (\forall\ tuple\ x)\end{matrix}\big[sum(u \diamond x) = u + sum(x)\big] \qquad\qquad (insertion)$$

Thus $sum(x)$ is the sum of the nonnegative integers in the tuple x.

Finally, let $\prec_{\ell\text{-}s}$ be the binary relation defined by the axiom

$$(\forall\ tuple\ x,\ y)\ \begin{bmatrix} x \prec_{\ell\text{-}s} y \\ \equiv \\ \begin{bmatrix} length(x) < length(y) \ \ or \\ length(x) = length(y) \ \ and \ \ sum(x) < sum(y) \end{bmatrix} \end{bmatrix}$$

$$(length\text{-}sum)$$

(a) Show that $\prec_{\ell\text{-}s}$ is well-founded over *tuple*.

(b) Prove that

$$(\forall\ tuple\ x)\big[sum(x) = sum(ones(x))\big].$$

You may use any properties of the nonnegative integers you wish without proof.

Hint: Use well-founded induction with respect to $\prec_{\ell\text{-}s}$.

13

Deductive
Tableaux

We have presented a deductive-tableau system to prove the validity of sentences in theories with induction, introducing various forms of stepwise induction into the deductive-tableau framework. In this chapter, we introduce a tableau form of the *well-founded induction* principle described in the previous chapter.

13.1   THE WELL-FOUNDED INDUCTION RULE

The *well-founded induction* proposition implies that:

In a given theory, suppose the binary relation $\prec$ is well-founded over *obj*.

Then, for each sentence $\mathcal{F}[x]$, without free occurrences of u, the universal closure of the sentence

$$if \ (\forall \ obj \ x) \ \begin{bmatrix} if \ (\forall \ obj \ u) \begin{bmatrix} if \ \ u \prec x \\ then \ \ \mathcal{F}[u] \end{bmatrix} \\ then \ \ \mathcal{F}[x] \end{bmatrix}$$

$$then \ \ (\forall \ obj \ x)\mathcal{F}[x]$$

(*well-founded induction principle*)

is valid (in the given theory).

This principle is represented in the tableau system as a deduction rule.

THE RULE

We include among the deduction rules of our tableau the following general induction rule.

Rule (well-founded induction)

In a theory, for a closed sentence

$$(\forall \, obj \; x)\mathcal{F}[x]$$

and an arbitrary relation $\prec$ that is known to be well-founded over obj,

assertions	goals
	$(\forall \, obj \; x)\mathcal{F}[x]$
$obj(a)$	
if $obj(u)$ *then* *if* $u \prec a$ *then* $\mathcal{F}[u]$	
	$\mathcal{F}[a]$

where a is a new constant. ◢

There is a clear correspondence between the generated assertions and goal and an intuitive proof by well-founded induction. Here, the first generated assertion corresponds to the assumption that a is an object, the second generated assertion to the induction hypothesis, and the generated goal to the desired conclusion of the inductive step.

Let us justify the new rule.

Justification. The *well-founded induction* rule, like the other induction rules, preserves validity, not equivalence. Let us show that, if the required goal

assertions	goals
	$(\forall \, obj \; x)\mathcal{F}[x]$

appears in the tableau, then we may derive the generated rows without affecting the validity of the tableau.

If the relation $\prec$ is well-founded, we know that the corresponding instance of the *well-founded induction* principle is valid, that is, the universal closure of

$$\begin{array}{l} if \ (\forall obj \ y) \left[\begin{array}{l} if \ (\forall obj \ u) \left[\begin{array}{l} if \ u \prec y \\ then \ \mathcal{F}[u] \end{array} \right] \\ then \ \mathcal{F}[y] \end{array} \right] \\ then \ (\forall obj \ x)\mathcal{F}[x] \end{array}$$

is valid.

It therefore suffices (by the *implied-row* property, because $(\forall obj \ x)\mathcal{F}[x]$ is closed) to show as a new goal the antecedent of this instance, that is,

	$(\forall \ obj \ y) \left[\begin{array}{l} if \ (\forall obj \ u) \left[\begin{array}{l} if \ u \prec y \\ then \ \mathcal{F}[u] \end{array} \right] \\ then \ \mathcal{F}[y] \end{array} \right]$

which we can rephrase without the relative-quantifier notation as

	$(\forall y)^\forall \left[\begin{array}{l} if \ obj(y) \\ then \ if \ (\forall u)^\exists \left[\begin{array}{l} if \ obj(u) \\ then \ if \ u \prec y \\ \quad then \ \mathcal{F}[u] \end{array} \right] \\ then \ \mathcal{F}[y] \end{array} \right]$

By the $\forall$- and $\exists$-*elimination* rules, we could drop the quantifiers from the goal, obtaining

	$\begin{array}{l} if \ obj(a) \\ then \ if \ if \ obj(u) \\ \qquad\quad then \ if \ u \prec a \\ \qquad\qquad\quad then \ \mathcal{F}[u] \\ \quad then \ \mathcal{F}[a] \end{array}$

Recall that by our assumption, $\mathcal{F}[u]$ and $\mathcal{F}[y]$ have no free variables other than u and y, respectively. Here the variable y, whose quantifier has strict universal force, has been replaced by the skolem constant a.

By two applications of the *if-split* rule, we can break down the goal to obtain

$obj(a)$	
if $obj(u)$ *then if* $u \prec a$ *then* $\mathcal{F}[u]$	
	$\mathcal{F}[a]$

These are precisely the three rows we obtain by application of the *well-founded induction* rule. By the *intermediate-tableau* property, we do not need to include the intermediate rows. This concludes the justification of the rule. ◢

We have remarked that the *well-founded induction* principle is actually a generalization of the *complete induction* principles for the nonnegative integers, tuples, and trees. If we apply the *well-founded induction* rule taking the well-founded relation $\prec$ to be the less-than relation $<$, the proper-subtuple relation $\prec_{tuple}$, or the proper-subtree relation $\prec_{tree}$, the rule will represent the *complete induction* principle in the nonnegative integers, tuples, or trees, respectively.

EXAMPLES

We illustrate several applications of the *well-founded induction* rule. In the first example we apply the rule to any well-founded relation $\prec$. That is, we consider a theory defined by a single axiom schema, the *well-founded induction* principle over $\prec$.

Example (asymmetry of a well-founded relation).   Now let us show that any well-founded relation $\prec$ is asymmetric, i.e., that

$$(\forall \, obj \; x, \; y) \begin{bmatrix} if \; x \prec y \\ then \; not \; (y \prec x) \end{bmatrix} \qquad (asymmetry)$$

Let $\prec$ be an arbitrary well-founded relation.

Our initial tableau (writing the quantifiers separately) is

assertions	goals
	G1. $(\forall \, obj \; x) \left[(\forall \, obj \; y) \begin{bmatrix} if \; x \prec y \\ then \; not \; (y \prec x) \end{bmatrix} \right]$

Applying the *well-founded induction* rule, on x, to goal G1, we may assume the assertion

A2. $obj(a)$	

and the induction hypothesis

A3. $if\ obj(u)$ $\quad then\ if\ u \prec a$ $\qquad then\ (\forall\ obj\ y) \begin{bmatrix} if\ u \prec y \\ then\ not\ (y \prec u) \end{bmatrix}$	

and attempt to establish the conclusion

	G4. $(\forall\ obj\ y) \begin{bmatrix} if\ a \prec y \\ then\ not\ (y \prec a) \end{bmatrix}$

Applying now the $\exists$-*elimination* rule to assertion A3 and the $\forall$-*elimination* rule to goal G4, we may drop the quantifiers from these rows, to obtain

A5. $if\ obj(u)$ $\quad then\ if\ u \prec a$ $\qquad then\ if\ obj(y)$ $\qquad\quad then\ if\ \boxed{u \prec y}\ +$ $\qquad\qquad then\ not\ (y \prec u)$	

and

	G6. $if\ obj(b)$ $\quad then\ if\ a \prec b$ $\qquad then\ not\ (b \prec a)$

Note that we implicitly abandon the relative-quantifier notation prior to eliminating quantifiers. Also the variable y of goal G4 is replaced by the skolem constant b in goal G6, while the skolemized induction hypothesis, assertion A5, retains the variable y.

By two applications of the *if-split* rule, we may decompose goal G6 into

A7. $obj(b)$	
A8. $a \prec b$	
	G9. $not\ \boxed{b \prec a}^{\,-}$

By the *resolution* rule applied to our goal G9 and the skolemized induction hypothesis (assertion A5), with $\{u \leftarrow b,\ y \leftarrow a\}$, we obtain

$$not\ false$$
$$and$$
$$not\ \begin{bmatrix} if\ \ obj(b) \\ then\ \ if\ \ true \\ \qquad then\ \ if\ \ obj(a) \\ \qquad\qquad then\ \ if\ \ true \\ \qquad\qquad\qquad then\ \ not\ (a \prec b) \end{bmatrix},$$

which simplifies to the goal

	G10. not	$\begin{bmatrix} if\ \boxed{obj(b)}^{\,+} \\ then\ \ if\ \boxed{obj(a)}^{\,+} \\ \qquad then\ \ not\ (a \prec b) \end{bmatrix}$

Because the sort conditions here are a little unusual, we spell out the details. By the *resolution* rule applied twice in succession, to assertions A7 and A2

A7. $\boxed{obj(b)}^{\,-}$	
A2. $\boxed{obj(a)}^{\,-}$	

and goal G10, we obtain

	G11. $\boxed{a \prec b}^{\,+}$

Finally, by the *resolution* rule applied to assertion A8

A8. $\boxed{a \prec b}^{\,-}$	

and goal G11, we obtain the final goal

	G12. *true*

Note that we did not apply the ∀-*elimination* rule to remove the second quantifier (∀ *obj y*) in the goal until after we had applied the induction principle. As it is, the induction hypothesis, assertion A5, contains the variable *y*, which was then replaced by the constant *a* in resolution with goal G9. Had we removed the quantifier first, the induction hypothesis would have contained a skolem constant, say *c*, instead of the variable *y*, and this step would have been impossible. ◣

In **Problem 13.1** the reader is requested to prove in the same way that any well-founded relation is irreflexive.

The next example illustrates a proof by well-founded induction in a combination of three theories.

Example (tips).   We consider a theory that combines the nonnegative integers with the tuples of trees. In this theory, the elements of the tuples are trees rather than atoms. We construct the theory by replacing the symbol *atom* with *tree* in all the axioms and properties of the theory of tuples. We also include, of course, the usual axioms and properties of the theories of trees and the nonnegative integers. In the theory of trees, the symbol *atom* is permitted to remain because our trees will be built from atoms.

In the theory of trees, we can define the function $tips(t)$, the number of atoms ("leaves") in the tree t, by the axioms (see Problem 10.5)

$(\forall\ atom\ u)\big[tips(u)\ =\ 1\big]$	(*atom*)
$(\forall\ tree\ x,\ y)\big[tips(x \bullet y)\ =\ tips(x) + tips(y)\big]$	(*construction*)

Here • is the construction function for trees.

The *tips* function can be shown to satisfy the *sort* property

$$(\forall\ tree\ x)\big[integer\,(tips(x))\big] \qquad\qquad (sort)$$

In this theory, we would like to formulate an alternative definition for the *tips* function. We introduce a function *tipstuple*; if t is a tuple of trees, $tipstuple(t)$ is the sum of the number of atoms in all the trees in t. We define *tipstuple* by the following axioms:

$$tipstuple(\langle\,\rangle) = 0 \qquad\qquad (empty)$$

$$(\forall\ atom\ u)\ \begin{bmatrix} tipstuple(u \diamond w) = \\ 1 + tipstuple(w) \end{bmatrix} \qquad (atom\ insertion)$$
$$(\forall\ tuple\ w)$$

$$(\forall\ tree\ x,\ y)\ \begin{bmatrix} tipstuple((x \bullet y) \diamond w) = \\ tipstuple(x \diamond (y \diamond w)) \end{bmatrix} \qquad (construction\ insertion)$$
$$(\forall\ tuple\ w)$$

Here $\diamond$ is the insertion function for tuples.

The argument of the *tipstuple* function can be viewed computationally as a stack of trees. If an atom is at the head of the stack, it is counted and removed from the stack. If a nonatom is at the head, it is decomposed into its left and right components, which are replaced on the stack. The computation continues until the stack is empty.

We would like to show that the preceding axioms actually provide an alternative definition for the *tips* function, in the sense that

$$(\forall\ tree\ x)\big[tips(x) = tipstuple(\langle x\rangle)\big] \qquad (special\ tips)$$

where $\langle x\rangle$ denotes the singleton tuple whose sole element is the tree x.

We first prove the more general property

$$\begin{matrix}(\forall\ tree\ x)\\(\forall\ tuple\ w)\end{matrix}\big[tipstuple(x \diamond w) = tips(x) + tipstuple(w)\big]$$
$$(general\ tips)$$

This *general-tips* property establishes that the *tipstuple* function indeed behaves as we expect. Once we have proved it, we may use it as an assertion in the proof of the desired *special-tips* property.

In our presentation, we shall first assume that we have already proved the *general-tips* property, and use it in proving the *special-tips* property. Only then do we actually prove the *general-tips* property.

Proof of the Special-Tips Property

The proof is straightforward and does not require induction.

We begin with the initial tableau. The initial goal G1 is the desired *special-tips* property.

assertions	goals
	G1. $(\forall\ tree\ x)\big[tips(x) = tipstuple(\langle x\rangle)\big]$

We include the *general-tips* property as an assertion in our initial tableau because we are assuming that this sentence has already been proved to be valid.

A2. $(\forall\,tree\ x)\ \begin{bmatrix} tipstuple(x \diamond w)\ = \\ tips(x) + tipstuple(w) \end{bmatrix}$ $(\forall\,tuple\ w)$	

We would like to remove the quantifiers in our initial tableau. By the $\forall$- and $\exists$-*elimination* rules, replacing x with the new constant r in G1, we obtain

	G3. *if* *tree* (r) *then* $tips(r) = tipstuple\,(\langle r \rangle)$

and

A4. *if* *tree* (x) *and* $tuple(w)$ *then* $\begin{bmatrix} tipstuple(x \diamond w)\ = \\ tips(x) + tipstuple(w) \end{bmatrix}$	

Applying the *if-split* rule to goal G3, we obtain

A5. *tree* (r)	
	G6. $tips(r)\ =\ tipstuple\left(\boxed{\langle\,r\,\rangle}\right)$

Recall the *singleton* axiom for tuples:

if *tree* (x) *then* $\left[\boxed{\langle x \rangle}\ =\ x \diamond \langle\,\rangle\right]^{-}$	

Note that, in our combined theory, the elements of tuples are trees, not atoms.

By the *equality* rule, applied to the axiom and goal G6, with $\{x \leftarrow r\}$, and removal of sort conditions, we obtain

	G7. $tips(r)\ =\ \boxed{tipstuple\,(r \diamond \langle\,\rangle)}$

Recall the *general-tips* property (after quantifier elimination):

| A4.   *if* $tree\,(x)$ *and* $tuple(w)$

      then $\left[\dfrac{\boxed{tipstuple(x \diamond w)} \;=}{tips(x) + tipstuple(w)} \right]^{-}$ | |

By the *equality* rule, applied to goal G7, with $\{x \leftarrow r,\ w \leftarrow \langle\,\rangle\}$, and removal of sort conditions:

| | G8. $tips(r) \;=\; tips(r) + \boxed{tipstuple(\langle\,\rangle)}$ |

Recall the *empty* axiom for *tipstuple*:

| $\left[\boxed{tipstuple(\langle\,\rangle)} \;=\; 0\right]^{-}$ | |

By the *equality* rule:

| | G9. $tips(r) \;=\; \boxed{tips(r) + 0}$ |

Recall the *right-zero* axiom for addition:

| *if* $integer(v)$

      then $\left[\boxed{v + 0} \;=\; v\right]^{-}$ | |

By the *equality* rule, with $\{v \leftarrow tips(r)\}$:

| | G10. $\boxed{tips(r) = tips(r)}^{+}$ |

By the reflexivity of equality, we obtain the final goal

| | G11.   *true* |

This concludes the proof of the *special-tips* property.

Proof of the General-Tips Property

We have shown that, once we have proved the *general-tips* property, we can prove the desired *special-tips* property. Now let us prove the *general-tips* property.

We begin with the initial tableau:

$$\text{G1.} \quad (\forall \, tree \,\, x)\left[(\forall \, tuple \,\, w)\left[\begin{array}{l} tipstuple(x \diamond w) \,\, = \\ tips(x) + tipstuple(w) \end{array}\right]\right]$$

We shall use the *well-founded induction* rule with respect to the proper-subtree relation $\prec_{tree}$, which is well-founded over *tree*. In other words, this is actually the tableau form of a complete induction proof. The only property of the subtree relation we shall use in the proof is the following *left-right* property of the proper subtree relation $\prec_{tree}$.

$$(\forall \, tree \,\, x)\left[\begin{array}{l} if \quad not \,\, atom(x) \\ then \quad left(x) \prec_{tree} x \,\, and \,\, right(x) \prec_{tree} x \end{array}\right] \quad (\textit{left-right})$$

By the *well-founded induction* rule, on x, we obtain the assertions

A2. *tree* (a)	
A3. *if tree* (y) *then if* $y \prec_{tree} a$ *then* $(\forall \, tuple \,\, w)^{\exists}\left[\begin{array}{l} tipstuple(y \diamond w) \,\, = \\ tips(y) + tipstuple(w) \end{array}\right]$	

and the goal

	G4. $(\forall \, tuple \,\, w)^{\forall}\left[\begin{array}{l} tipstuple(a \diamond w) \,\, = \\ tips(a) + tipstuple(w) \end{array}\right]$

Applying the $\exists$-*elimination* rule to assertion A3, we obtain

A5. *if tree* (y) *then if* $y \prec_{tree} a$ *then if* $tuple(w)$ *then* $\left[\begin{array}{l} tipstuple(y \diamond w) \,\, = \\ tips(y) + tipstuple(w) \end{array}\right]$	

Applying the $\forall$-*elimination* rule to goal G4, replacing w with the new constant t, followed by the *if-split* rule:

A6. *tuple*(t)	
	G7. $tipstuple(a \diamond t) \,\, =$ $tips(a) + tipstuple(t)$

Intuitively, we now treat separately the case in which a is atomic.

- *Atomic Case*

Recall the *atom-insertion* axiom for *tipstuple* and goal G7 :

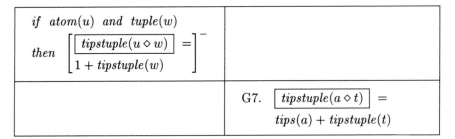

if $atom(u)$ and $tuple(w)$ then $\left[\dfrac{\boxed{tipstuple(u \diamond w)}}{1 + tipstuple(w)} =\right]^{-}$	
	G7. $\boxed{tipstuple(a \diamond t)} = $ $tips(a) + tipstuple(t)$

By the *equality* rule, with $\{u \leftarrow a,\ w \leftarrow t\}$, and removing a sort condition:

	G8. $atom(a)$ and $\left[\dfrac{1 + tipstuple(t) = }{\boxed{tips(a)} + tipstuple(t)}\right]$

The condition $atom(a)$ that the rule introduces into the goal column corresponds to the case assumption that a is atomic.

Recall the *atom* axiom for *tips*:

if $atom(u)$ then $\left[\boxed{tips(u)} = 1\right]^{-}$	

By the *equality* rule, applied to the axiom and goal G8, with $\{u \leftarrow a\}$, and the associativity of *and*:

	G9. $atom(a)$ and $\left[\dfrac{1 + tipstuple(t) = }{1 + tipstuple(t)}\right]^{+}$

By the reflexivity of equality, we obtain from goal G9:

	G10. $\boxed{atom(a)}^{+}$

Intuitively, in developing goal G10, we have completed the proof for the case in which a is atomic. By duality, the goal can be regarded as an assertion *not atom(a)*. Intuitively, we henceforth treat separately the case in which a is nonatomic.

- *The Decomposition of the Tree*

Recall the *decomposition* property of trees and goal G7:

if tree (x) *then if not atom(x)* $\quad\quad$ *then* $\left[\boxed{x} = \mathit{left}(x) \bullet \mathit{right}(x)\right]^{-}$	
	G7. $\mathit{tipstuple}\!\left(\boxed{a}\diamond t\right) =$ $\quad\quad \mathit{tips}(a) + \mathit{tipstuple}(t)$

By the *equality* rule, with $\{x \leftarrow a\}$, and removal of a sort condition:

	G11. *not atom(a) and* $\left[\dfrac{\boxed{\mathit{tipstuple}\big((\mathit{left}(a) \bullet \mathit{right}(a)) \diamond t\big)}}{\mathit{tips}(a) + \mathit{tipstuple}(t)} =\right]$

Recall the *construction-insertion* axiom for *tipstuple*:

if tree (x) *and tree* (y) *and tuple(w)* *then* $\left[\dfrac{\boxed{\mathit{tipstuple}((x \bullet y) \diamond w)}}{\mathit{tipstuple}(x \diamond (y \diamond w))} =\right]^{-}$	

By the *equality* rule, with $\{x \leftarrow \mathit{left}(a),\ y \leftarrow \mathit{right}(a),\ w \leftarrow t\}$, and removal of sort conditions:

	G12. *not atom(a) and* $\left[\dfrac{\boxed{\mathit{tipstuple}(\mathit{left}(a) \diamond (\mathit{right}(a) \diamond t))}}{\mathit{tips}(a) + \mathit{tipstuple}(t)} =\right]$

At this stage we invoke the induction hypothesis twice in succession.

- *Use of the Induction Hypothesis*

Recall assertion A5 (the skolemized induction hypothesis):

A5.   *if* $tree\,(y)$
     then if $y \prec_{tree} a$
        then if $tuple(w)$
          then $\left[\,\boxed{tipstuple(y \diamond w)} = \atop tips(y) + tipstuple(w)\,\right]^{-}$	

By the *equality* rule, with $\{y \leftarrow left(a),\ w \leftarrow right(a) \diamond t\}$, applied to goal G12, and removal of sort conditions:

	G13. $left(a) \prec_{tree} a$ *and*
	      $not\ atom(a)$ *and*
	      $\left[\,tips\,(left(a)) + \boxed{tipstuple\,(right(a) \diamond t)} = \atop tips(a) + tipstuple(t)\,\right]^{-}$

By the *equality* rule, applied to assertion A5 (again) and goal G13, with $\{y \leftarrow right(a),\ w \leftarrow t\}$, the associativity of $+$, and the associativity and commutativity of *and*:

	G14. $left(a) \prec_{tree} a$ *and* $right(a) \prec_{tree} a$ *and*
	      $not\ atom(a)$ *and*
	      $\left[\,\boxed{tips\,(left(a)) + tips\,(right(a))} + tipstuple(t) = \atop tips(a) + tipstuple(t)\,\right]$

Recall the *construction* axiom for the *tips* function:

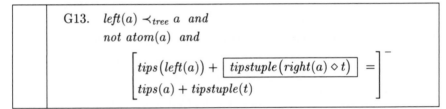

By the *equality* rule (right-to-left), with $\{x \leftarrow left(a),\ y \leftarrow right(a)\}$, and removing sort conditions:

> G15. $left(a) \prec_{tree} a$ and $right(a) \prec_{tree} a$ and
> $not\ atom(a)$ and
> $$\left[\frac{tips\left(\boxed{left(a) \bullet right(a)}\right) + tipstuple(t) =}{tips(a) + tipstuple(t)}\right]$$

Recall the *decomposition* property of trees:

> *if* tree (x)
> *then if* $not\ atom(x)$
>   *then* $\left[x = \boxed{left(x) \bullet right(x)}\right]^{-}$

By the *equality* rule (right-to-left), with $\{x \leftarrow a\}$, and the associativity and commutativity of *and*, removing a sort condition:

> G16. $left(a) \prec_{tree} a$ and $right(a) \prec_{tree} a$ and
> $not\ atom(a)$ and
> $$\boxed{\frac{tips(a) + tipstuple(t) =}{tips(a) + tipstuple(t)}}^{+}$$

By the reflexivity of equality:

> G17. $\boxed{left(a) \prec_{tree} a\ \text{and}\ right(a) \prec_{tree} a}^{+}$
>
> *and* $not\ atom(a)$

At this stage we turn our attention to the conditions associated with the well-founded relation.

- *Establishing the Well-founded Relation*

Recall the *left-right* property of the proper-subtree relation $\prec_{tree}$:

> *if* tree (x)
> *then if* $not\ atom(x)$
>   *then* $\boxed{left(x) \prec_{tree} x\ \text{and}\ right(x) \prec_{tree} x}^{-}$

By the *resolution* rule, with $\{x \leftarrow a\}$, and removing a sort condition:

> G18. $not\ \boxed{atom(a)}^{-}$

By the *resolution* rule, applied to goals G18 and G10:

	G19. *true*

This completes the proof of the *general-tips* property. ⏺

In **Problems 13.2–13.4**, the reader is requested to use the *well-founded induction* rule in the deductive-tableau framework to prove the validity of various properties. **Problem 13.5** requires a proof in the combined theory of nonnegative integers and tuples. **Problem 13.6** uses the combined theory of tuples and trees.

A-FORM

The *well-founded induction* rule applies to goals; there is a dual version that applies to assertions.

Rule (well-founded induction, A-form)

In a theory, for a closed sentence

$$(\exists \ obj \ x)\mathcal{F}[x]$$

and an arbitrary relation $\prec$ that is known to be well-founded over obj,

assertions	goals
$(\exists \ obj \ x)\mathcal{F}[x]$	
$obj(a)$	
if $obj(u)$ *then if* $u \prec a$ *then* $(not \ \mathcal{F}[u])$	
$\mathcal{F}[a]$	

where a is a new constant. ⏺

This version is actually a statement of the *minimal-element* condition (Section 12.2). Roughly, it says that if there is an object x for which $\mathcal{F}[x]$ is true, there is a minimal object a for which $\mathcal{F}[a]$ is true. The justification is left as an exercise (**Problem 13.7**).

13.2 WELL-FOUNDED INDUCTION OVER PAIRS

As discussed and illustrated in the previous chapter, sometimes it is convenient to use well-founded induction over pairs of objects, rather than over the objects themselves. In Section 12.4 we stated the following *well-founded induction over pairs* proposition:

> In the theory of pairs over obj_1 and obj_2, suppose the binary relation $\prec$ is well-founded over *pair*.
>
> Then, for each sentence $\mathcal{F}[x_1, x_2]$ without free occurrences of x_1' and x_2', the universal closure of
>
> $$if\ \begin{matrix}(\forall\ obj_1\ x_1)\\ (\forall\ obj_2\ x_2)\end{matrix} \left[if\ \begin{matrix}(\forall\ obj_1\ x_1')\\ (\forall\ obj_2\ x_2')\end{matrix} \begin{bmatrix} if\ \langle x_1',\ x_2'\rangle \prec \langle x_1,\ x_2\rangle \\ then\ \ \mathcal{F}[x_1',\ x_2'] \end{bmatrix} \right.$$
> $$\left. then\ \ \mathcal{F}[x_1,\ x_2] \right]$$
> $$then\ \begin{matrix}(\forall\ obj_1\ x_1)\\ (\forall\ obj_2\ x_2)\end{matrix}\mathcal{F}[x_1,\ x_2]$$
>
> is valid (in the theory).

We therefore include among the deduction rules of our tableau the following rule, which is a tableau form of this proposition.

Rule (well-founded induction over pairs)

In the theory of pairs over obj_1 and obj_2, for a closed sentence

$$\begin{matrix}(\forall\ obj_1\ x_1)\\ (\forall\ obj_2\ x_2)\end{matrix}\mathcal{F}[x_1,\ x_2]$$

and an arbitrary relation $\prec$ that is known to be well-founded over *pair*

assertions	goals
	$\begin{matrix}(\forall\ obj_1\ x_1)\\ (\forall\ obj_2\ x_2)\end{matrix}\mathcal{F}[x_1,\ x_2]$
$obj_1(a_1)\ \ and\ \ obj_2(a_2)$	
$if\ \ obj_1(u_1)\ \ and\ \ obj_2(u_2)$ $then\ \ if\ \ \langle u_1, u_2\rangle \prec \langle a_1, a_2\rangle$ $then\ \ \mathcal{F}[u_1, u_2]$	
	$\mathcal{F}[a_1,\ a_2]$

where a_1, a_2 are new constants. ◢

As before, the second generated assertion corresponds to the induction hypothesis, and the generated goal to the desired conclusion of an intuitive proof.

In particular, we can take $\prec$ to be $\prec_{lex}$, the lexicographic relation corresponding to the binary relations $\prec_1$ and $\prec_2$, provided that $\prec_1$ and $\prec_2$ are well-founded over obj_1 and obj_2, respectively. In that case, we know (by the *lexicographic-relation* proposition) that $\prec_{lex}$ is well-founded over *pair*. We call this instance of the rule the *lexicographic well-founded induction* rule.

The justification for this rule, which we omit, resembles the justification for the ordinary *well-founded induction* rule for tableaux.

The *well-founded induction* rule over pairs allows us to do induction on two variables at once. The rule can clearly be extended to allow us to do induction on three, four, and more variables at once in an appropriate theory of triples, quadruples, and so forth, respectively.

EXAMPLE

The following example illustrates not only the application of the *well-founded induction* rule over pairs, but also the proof that the *mergesort* "program," expressed as a collection of axioms, does satisfy certain properties we expect of it. An intuitive proof of this was given in Section 12.5.

Example (mergesort).   Recall that, in the theory of tuples of nonnegative integers, we defined the function $mergesort(z)$, which sorts the nonnegative integers in a tuple z. To sort a given tuple $x \diamond y$, where the division into a "left half" x and a "right half" y is arbitrary, we simply sort the two "halves" x and y separately, and merge the results.

The auxiliary function $merge(x, y)$ intermixes, in (weakly) increasing order, the integers in two ordered tuples x and y.

To show that the *mergesort* function does indeed yield a sorted version of the tuple x, one must prove

$$(\forall\, tuple\ x)\big[perm\big(x,\ mergesort(x)\big)\big] \qquad\qquad (permutation)$$

that is, the elements of $mergesort(x)$ are the same as those of x, in some order, and

$$(\forall\, tuple\ x)\big[ordered\big(mergesort(x)\big)\big] \qquad\qquad (ordered)$$

that is, the elements of $mergesort(x)$ are in (weakly) increasing order.

The proofs of these properties of the function *mergesort* depend on the following properties of the auxiliary function *merge*:

$$(\forall\, tuple\ x,\ y)\big[perm\big(x \diamond y,\ merge(x,\ y)\big)\big] \qquad\qquad (permutation)$$

that is, the elements of $merge(x, y)$ are the same as those of x and y together, in some order, and

$$(\forall \, tuple \ x, y) \left[\begin{array}{l} if \ \ ordered(x) \ \ and \ \ ordered(y) \\ then \ \ ordered(merge \, (x, y)) \end{array} \right] \qquad (ordered)$$

that is, the elements of $merge(x, y)$ are in increasing order, provided the elements of x and y are in increasing order.

The reader has already been requested (in Problem 12.15) to provide an intuitive proof of the *permutation* property of *merge*; we present a tableau proof here. In this proof we use the *well-founded induction* principle over pairs.

An intuitive proof of the *ordered* property of *merge* appears in Section 12.5. The reader is requested (in **Problem 13.8**) to provide a tableau proof. Tableau proofs of the *permutation*, *ordered*, and *insert* properties of *mergesort* itself are also requested in this problem.

Applying the Induction Rule

To prove the *permutation* property of the *merge* function,

$$(\forall \, tuple \ x, y)[perm(x \diamond y, \, merge(x, \, y))],$$

we begin with the initial tableau

assertions	goals
	G1. $(\forall \, tuple \ x_1, \, x_2)\big[perm\big(x_1 \diamond x_2, \, merge(x_1, \, x_2)\big)\big]$

The proof is by lexicographic well-founded induction. In other words, we are applying the *well-founded induction* rule over pairs, taking obj_1 and obj_2 each to be *tuple*. The well-founded relation will be $\prec_{lex}$, where $\prec_1$ and $\prec_2$ are each taken to be the proper-subtuple relation $\prec_{tuple}$.

Rather than use the definition of $\prec_{lex}$ directly, it will be convenient to invoke the *first* and *second* properties of $\prec_{lex}$,

$$(\forall \, tuple \ x_1, \, x_2, \, y_1, \, y_2) \left[\begin{array}{l} if \ \ x_1 \prec_{tuple} y_1 \\ then \ \ \langle x_1, \, x_2 \rangle \prec_{lex} \langle y_1, \, y_2 \rangle \end{array} \right] \qquad (first)$$

$$(\forall \, tuple \ x_1, \, x_2, \, y_1, \, y_2) \left[\begin{array}{l} if \ \ x_1 = y_1 \ \ and \ \ x_2 \prec_{tuple} y_2 \\ then \ \ \langle x_1, \, x_2 \rangle \prec_{lex} \langle y_1, \, y_2 \rangle \end{array} \right] \qquad (second)$$

These follow from the definition of the $\prec_{lex}$ relation by propositional logic.

We shall also invoke the *tail* property of the proper-subtuple relation,

$$(\forall \, tuple \ x) \left[\begin{array}{l} if \ \ not \, (x = \langle \rangle) \\ then \ \ tail(x) \prec_{tuple} x \end{array} \right] \qquad (tail)$$

By the *lexicographic well-founded induction* rule:

A2. $tuple(r_1)$ *and* $tuple(r_2)$	

A3.   *if* $tuple(y_1)$ *and* $tuple(y_2)$
     then if $\langle y_1, y_2 \rangle \prec_{lex} \langle r_1, r_2 \rangle$
        then $perm\big(y_1 \diamond y_2,\ merge(y_1, y_2)\big)$	

and

	G4. $perm\big(r_1 \diamond r_2,\ merge(r_1, r_2)\big)$

Here assertion A3 corresponds to our induction hypothesis, and goal G4 to our desired conclusion.

Intuitively, we now treat separately the case in which the constants r_1 and r_2 are nonatomic.

Decomposing the Arguments

We decompose the arguments r_1 and r_2 into their heads and tails.

Recall the *decomposition* property of *head* and *tail*:

if $tuple(x)$ *then if* $not\ (x = \langle\,\rangle)$ *then* $\left[\boxed{x} = head(x) \diamond tail(x)\right]^{-}$	

Also recall goal G4:

	G4. $perm\left(\boxed{r_1} \diamond \boxed{r_2},\ merge\left(\boxed{r_1}, \boxed{r_2}\right)\right)$

Applying the *equality* rule twice, once with $\{x \leftarrow r_1\}$ and once with $\{x \leftarrow r_2\}$, removing a sort condition:

	G5. $not\ (r_1 = \langle\,\rangle)$ *and* $not\ (r_2 = \langle\,\rangle)$ *and* $perm \left(\begin{array}{l} \big(head(r_1) \diamond tail(r_1)\big) \diamond \big(head(r_2) \diamond tail(r_2)\big), \\ merge\big(head(r_1) \diamond tail(r_1),\ head(r_2) \diamond tail(r_2)\big) \end{array} \right)$

Let us henceforth abbreviate $head(r_1)$ and $tail(r_1)$ as h_1 and t_1, respectively, and $head(r_2)$ and $tail(r_2)$ as h_2 and t_2, respectively. Thus, goal G5 may be written

> G5. $not\ (r_1 = \langle\,\rangle)\ \ and\ \ not\ (r_2 = \langle\,\rangle)\ \ and$
>
> $\qquad perm\Big((h_1 \diamond t_1) \diamond (h_2 \diamond t_2),\ \boxed{merge(h_1 \diamond t_1,\ h_2 \diamond t_2)}\,\Big)$

The Case Split

In the next few steps, we distinguish between two subcases, according to whether or not $h_1 \le h_2$.

Recall the *insertion* axiom for *merge*:

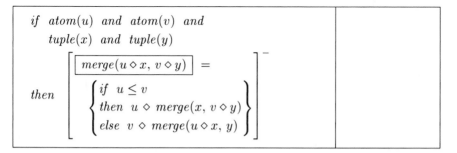

By the *equality* rule, with $\{u \leftarrow h_1,\ x \leftarrow t_1,\ v \leftarrow h_2,\ y \leftarrow t_2\}$, applied to goal G5, removing sort conditions:

> G6. $not\ (r_1 = \langle\,\rangle)\ \ and\ \ not\ (r_2 = \langle\,\rangle)\ \ and$
>
> $\qquad perm\left(\left(\begin{array}{c} h_1 \diamond t_1 \\ \diamond \\ h_2 \diamond t_2 \end{array} \right),\ \left(\begin{array}{l} if\ \ h_1 \le h_2 \\ then\ \ h_1 \diamond merge(t_1,\ h_2 \diamond t_2) \\ else\ \ h_2 \diamond merge(h_1 \diamond t_1,\ t_2) \end{array} \right) \right)$

Applying the rewriting rule, with the *predicate* conditional manipulation

$$p(\bar{r},\ if\ \mathcal{F}\ then\ t_1\ else\ t_2,\ \bar{s})\quad \Leftrightarrow\quad if\ \mathcal{F}\ then\ p(\bar{r}, t_1, \bar{s})\ else\ p(\bar{r}, t_2, \bar{s}),$$

the *cond-or* elimination

$$if\ \mathcal{F}\ then\ \mathcal{G}\ else\ \mathcal{H}\quad \Leftrightarrow\quad (\mathcal{F}\ and\ \mathcal{G})\ or\ \big((not\ \mathcal{F})\ and\ \mathcal{H}\big),$$

and the *and-or* distributivity

$$\mathcal{F}\ and\ (\mathcal{G}\ or\ \mathcal{H})\quad \Leftrightarrow\quad (\mathcal{F}\ and\ \mathcal{G})\ or\ (\mathcal{F}\ and\ \mathcal{H}),$$

followed by the *or-split* rule, we obtain

G7.	$not \left(r_1 = \langle \, \rangle\right)$ and $not \left(r_2 = \langle \, \rangle\right)$ and $h_1 \leq h_2$ and $perm\left(\boxed{(h_1 \diamond t_1) \diamondsuit (h_2 \diamond t_2)}, \; h_1 \diamond merge(t_1, \, h_2 \diamond t_2)\right)$
G8.	$not \left(r_1 = \langle \, \rangle\right)$ and $not \left(r_2 = \langle \, \rangle\right)$ and $not \left(h_1 \leq h_2\right)$ and $perm\left((h_1 \diamond t_1) \diamondsuit (h_2 \diamond t_2), \; h_2 \diamond merge(h_1 \diamond t_1, \, t_2)\right)$

These two goals correspond to two distinct subcases, according to whether or not $h_1 \leq h_2$.

The First Subcase

Recall the *left-insertion* axiom for append:

if $atom(u)$ and $tuple(x)$ and $tuple(y)$ *then* $\boxed{(u \diamond x) \diamondsuit y}^{\;-} = u \diamond (x \diamondsuit y)$	

By the *equality* rule, with $\{u \leftarrow h_1, \, x \leftarrow t_1, \, y \leftarrow h_2 \diamond t_2\}$, applied to goal G7, removing sort conditions:

	G9. $not \left(r_1 = \langle \, \rangle\right)$ and $not \left(r_2 = \langle \, \rangle\right)$ and $h_1 \leq h_2$ and $\boxed{perm\left(h_1 \diamond \left(t_1 \diamondsuit (h_2 \diamond t_2)\right), \; h_1 \diamond merge(t_1, \, h_2 \diamond t_2)\right)}$

Recall the *equal-insertion* property of *perm*:

if $atom(u)$ and $tuple(x)$ and $tuple(y)$ *then* $\boxed{perm(u \diamond x, \, u \diamond y)}^{\;-} \equiv perm(x, \, y)$	

By the *equivalence* rule, with $\{u \leftarrow h_1, \, x \leftarrow t_1 \diamondsuit (h_2 \diamond t_2), \, y \leftarrow merge(t_1, \, h_2 \diamond t_2)\}$, removing sort conditions:

	G10. $not \left(r_1 = \langle \, \rangle\right)$ and $not \left(r_2 = \langle \, \rangle\right)$ and $h_1 \leq h_2$ and $\boxed{perm\left(t_1 \diamondsuit (h_2 \diamond t_2), \; merge(t_1, \, h_2 \diamond t_2)\right)}^{\;+}$

We are now ready to use the induction hypothesis. The induction hypothesis is actually used twice in this proof, once in each subcase.

First Use of the Induction Hypothesis

Recall our induction hypothesis, assertion A3:

A3. *if* $tuple(y_1)$ *and* $tuple(y_2)$	
then if $\langle y_1, y_2 \rangle \prec_{lex} \langle r_1, r_2 \rangle$	
then $\boxed{perm\big(y_1 \diamond y_2, \ merge(y_1, y_2)\big)}^{-}$	

By the *resolution* rule, with $\{y_1 \leftarrow t_1, y_2 \leftarrow h_2 \diamond t_2\}$, applied to goal G10, removing sort conditions:

	G11. $\boxed{\langle t_1, h_2 \diamond t_2 \rangle \prec_{lex} \langle r_1, r_2 \rangle}^{+}$ *and*
	$not\ \big(r_1 = \langle\,\rangle\big)$ *and* $not\ \big(r_2 = \langle\,\rangle\big)$
	and $h_1 \leq h_2$

Recall the *first* property of the lexicographic relation $\prec_{lex}$:

if $tuple(x_1)$ *and* $tuple(x_2)$ *and*	
$tuple(y_1)$ *and* $tuple(y_2)$	
then if $x_1 \prec_{tuple} y_1$	
then $\boxed{\langle x_1, x_2 \rangle \prec_{lex} \langle y_1, y_2 \rangle}^{-}$	

By the *resolution* rule, with $\{x_1 \leftarrow t_1, x_2 \leftarrow h_2 \diamond t_2, y_1 \leftarrow r_1, y_2 \leftarrow r_2\}$, removing sort conditions:

	G12. $t_1 \prec_{tuple} r_1$ *and*
	$not\ \big(r_1 = \langle\,\rangle\big)$ *and* $not\ \big(r_2 = \langle\,\rangle\big)$
	and $h_1 \leq h_2$

At this point it is convenient to abandon our abbreviation for t_1:

	G12′. $\boxed{tail(r_1) \prec_{tuple} r_1}^{+}$ *and*
	$not\ \big(r_1 = \langle\,\rangle\big)$ *and* $not\ \big(r_2 = \langle\,\rangle\big)$
	and $h_1 \leq h_2$

Recall the *tail* property of the proper-subtuple relation:

if $tuple(x)$
  then if not $(x = \langle \, \rangle)$
      then $\boxed{tail(x) \prec_{tuple} x}$
	${}^-$

By the *resolution* rule, with $\{x \leftarrow r_1\}$, removing sort conditions:

	G13. $not \, \left(r_1 = \langle \, \rangle \right)$ *and* $not \, \left(r_2 = \langle \, \rangle \right)$ *and* $h_1 \leq h_2$

Let us set this subcase aside for a while.

The Second Subcase

The second subcase deals with the case in which $not \, (h_1 \leq h_2)$. To deal with this possibility, we return our attention to the earlier goal G8, which we have neglected until now:

	G8. $not \, \left(r_1 = \langle \, \rangle \right)$ *and* $not \, (r_2 = \langle \, \rangle)$ *and*
	     $not \, (h_1 \leq h_2)$ *and*
	     $\boxed{perm\Big((h_1 \diamond t_1) \diamond (h_2 \diamond t_2), \; h_2 \diamond merge(h_1 \diamond t_1, t_2)\Big)}$

Recall the *append-insertion* property of *perm*:

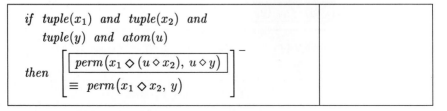

if $tuple(x_1)$ *and* $tuple(x_2)$ *and* $tuple(y)$ *and* $atom(u)$ *then* $\left[\begin{array}{l} \boxed{perm\big(x_1 \diamond (u \diamond x_2), \; u \diamond y\big)} \\ \equiv \; perm\big(x_1 \diamond x_2, \; y\big) \end{array} \right]$	${}^-$

By the *equivalence* rule applied to the goal G8, with $\{x_1 \leftarrow (h_1 \diamond t_1), \; u \leftarrow h_2,$ $x_2 \leftarrow t_2, \; y \leftarrow merge(h_1 \diamond t_1, t_2)\}$, removing sort conditions:

	G14. $not \, \left(r_1 = \langle \, \rangle \right)$ *and* $not \, \left(r_2 = \langle \, \rangle \right)$ *and*
	     $not \, (h_1 \leq h_2)$ *and*
	     $\boxed{perm\big((h_1 \diamond t_1) \diamond t_2, \; merge(h_1 \diamond t_1, t_2)\big)}^+$

Second Use of the Induction Hypothesis

Recall our induction hypothesis, assertion A3:

> A3. *if tuple*(y_1) *and tuple*(y_2)
>   *then if* $\langle y_1, y_2 \rangle \prec_{lex} \langle r_1, r_2 \rangle$
>   *then* $\boxed{perm\left(y_1 \diamond y_2, \ merge(y_1, y_2)\right)}^{-}$

By the *resolution* rule, with $\{y_1 \leftarrow h_1 \diamond t_1, \ y_2 \leftarrow t_2\}$, removing sort conditions:

>   G15. $\boxed{\langle h_1 \diamond t_1, t_2 \rangle \prec_{lex} \langle r_1, r_2 \rangle}^{+}$
>   *and not* $\left(r_1 = \langle \ \rangle\right)$ *and not* $\left(r_2 = \langle \ \rangle\right)$
>   *and not* $(h_1 \leq h_2)$

Recall the *second* property of the lexicographic relation $\prec_{lex}$:

> *if tuple*(x_1) *and tuple*(x_2) *and*
>   *tuple*(y_1) *and tuple*(y_2)
> *then if* $x_1 = y_1$ *and* $x_2 \prec_{tuple} y_2$
>   *then* $\boxed{\langle x_1, x_2 \rangle \prec_{lex} \langle y_1, y_2 \rangle}^{-}$

By the *resolution* rule, with $\{x_1 \leftarrow h_1 \diamond t_1, \ x_2 \leftarrow t_2, \ y_1 \leftarrow r_1, \ y_2 \leftarrow r_2\}$, removing sort conditions:

>   G16. $h_1 \diamond t_1 = r_1$ *and* $t_2 \prec_{tuple} r_2$ *and*
>   *not* $\left(r_1 = \langle \ \rangle\right)$ *and not* $\left(r_2 = \langle \ \rangle\right)$
>   *and not* $(h_1 \leq h_2)$

In anticipation of the next step, it is again convenient to abandon some occurrences of our abbreviation:

>   G16. $\boxed{head(r_1) \diamond tail(r_1)} = r_1$ *and*
> $tail(r_2) \prec_{tuple} r_2$ *and*
>   *not* $\left(r_1 = \langle \ \rangle\right)$ *and not* $\left(r_2 = \langle \ \rangle\right)$
>   *and not* $(h_1 \leq h_2)$

Recall again the *decomposition* property of *head* and *tail*:

> *if tuple*(x)
> *then if not* $\left(x = \langle \ \rangle\right)$
>   *then* $\left[x = \boxed{head(x) \diamond tail(x)}\right]^{-}$

By the *equality* rule (right-to-left), with $\{x \leftarrow r_1\}$, removing a sort condition, and the reflexivity of equality, and the associativity and commutativity of *and*:

	G17. $\boxed{tail(r_2) \prec_{tuple} r_2}^{+}$ *and* $not\ (r_1 = \langle\ \rangle)$ *and* $not\ (r_2 = \langle\ \rangle)$ *and* $not\ (h_1 \leq h_2)$

Recall the *tail* property of the subtuple relation:

if $tuple(x)$ *then if* $not\ (x = \langle\ \rangle)$ *then* $\boxed{tail(x) \prec_{tuple} x}^{-}$	

By the *resolution* rule, with $\{x \leftarrow r_2\}$, removing a sort condition:

	G18. $not\ (r_1 = \langle\ \rangle)$ *and* $not\ (r_2 = \langle\ \rangle)$ *and* $not\ \left(\boxed{h_1 \leq h_2}^{-}\right)$

We can now combine the results of the two cases.

Recall goal G13, at the end of the first subcase:

	G13. $not\ (r_1 = \langle\ \rangle)$ *and* $not\ (r_2 = \langle\ \rangle)$ *and* $\boxed{h_1 \leq h_2}^{+}$

By the *resolution* rule:

	G19. $not\ \left[\boxed{r_1} = \langle\ \rangle\right]^{-}$ *and* $not\ (r_2 = \langle\ \rangle)$

This concludes our treatment of the case in which r_1 and r_2 are both nonempty. By duality, goal G19 may be thought of as an assertion

$$r_1 = \langle\ \rangle \quad or \quad r_2 = \langle\ \rangle,$$

that r_1 is empty or r_2 is empty. These are the cases that remain to be treated.

Atomic Case: r_1 *is empty*

Recall our desired conclusion, goal G4:

$$G4. \quad perm\left(\boxed{r_1}\diamond r_2, \; merge\left(\boxed{r_1}, r_2\right)\right)$$

By the *equality* rule, applied to goal G19:

$$G20. \quad not \left(r_2 = \langle \, \rangle\right) \; and$$
$$perm\left(\boxed{\langle \, \rangle \diamond r_2}, \; \boxed{merge\left(\langle \, \rangle, r_2\right)}\right)$$

Recall the *left-empty* axioms for append and merge:

$$if \; tuple(y)$$
$$then \; \left[\boxed{\langle \, \rangle \diamond y} \; = \; y\right]^{-}$$

$$if \; tuple(y)$$
$$then \; \left[\boxed{merge\left(\langle \, \rangle, y\right)} \; = \; y\right]^{-}$$

By two successive applications of the *equality* rule, applied to the axioms and goal G20, with $\{y \leftarrow r_2\}$, removing sort conditions:

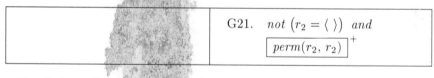

$$G21. \quad not \left(r_2 = \langle \, \rangle\right) \; and$$
$$\boxed{perm(r_2, r_2)}^{+}$$

Recall the *reflexivity property* of *perm*:

$$if \; tuple(x)$$
$$then \; \boxed{perm(x, x)}^{-}$$

By the *resolution* rule, with $\{x \leftarrow r_2\}$, removing a sort condition:

$$G22. \quad not \; \left[\boxed{r_2} \; = \; \langle \, \rangle\right]^{-}$$

We have thus disposed of the case in which r_1 is empty. By duality, goal G22 corresponds to an assertion

$$r_2 = \langle \, \rangle,$$

that r_2 is empty. This is the remaining case we must consider.

Atomic Case: r_2 is empty

Recall again the desired conclusion, goal G4:

	G4. $perm\left(r_1 \diamond \boxed{r_2}\,,\; merge\left(r_1,\, \boxed{r_2}\right)\right)$

By the *equality* rule, applied to goals G22 and G4:

	G23. $perm\left(\boxed{r_1 \diamond \langle\,\rangle}\,,\; \boxed{merge\left(r_1,\langle\,\rangle\right)}\right)^+$

The rest of the proof resembles the proof for the previous case, so we will treat it briskly.

Recall the *right-empty* property of append, the *right-empty* axiom for merge, and the *reflexivity* property of *perm*:

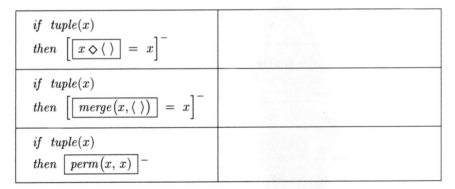

if $tuple(x)$ *then* $\left[\boxed{x \diamond \langle\,\rangle} = x\right]^-$	
if $tuple(x)$ *then* $\left[\boxed{merge\left(x,\langle\,\rangle\right)} = x\right]^-$	
if $tuple(x)$ *then* $\boxed{perm\left(x,\,x\right)}^-$	

By two successive applications of the *equality* rule and one application of the *resolution* rule, removing sort conditions, we derive the final goal

	G24. *true*

The reader is given another opportunity to use the *lexicographic well-founded induction* rule in **Problem 13.9**.

PROBLEMS

Proofs for the problems in this chapter should use the deductive-tableau technique. Follow the guidelines given for the problems in Chapter 11.

Problem 13.1 (irreflexivity of a well-founded relation)   page 629

Use the *well-founded induction* rule of deductive tableaux to prove that, in a given theory, any well-founded relation $\prec$ is irreflexive, that is,

$$(\forall \, obj \; x)\big[not \; (x \prec x)\big].$$

Problem 13.2 (evolution)   page 638

Consider a theory of animals. In the "evolution" interpretation we have in mind, the domain includes the set of all animals, and, intuitively,

$$animal(u) \quad \text{means } u \text{ is an animal}$$
$$mon(u) \qquad \text{means } u \text{ is a monkey}$$
$$u \prec_{par} v \quad \text{means } u \text{ is a parent of } v$$
$$anc(u, v) \quad \text{means } u \text{ is an ancestor of } v.$$

The only axiom you may use is

$$(\forall \, animal \; u, \, v)\Big[anc(u, v) \; \equiv \; \big[u \prec_{par} v \; \; or \; \; (\exists w)\big[anc(u, w) \; \; and \; \; w \prec_{par} v\big]\big]\Big].$$

Assuming that the *parent* relation $\prec_{par}$ is well-founded over *animal*, prove that

$$(\forall \, animal \; x, \, y) \begin{bmatrix} if \; anc(x, y) \; and \\ \quad mon(x) \; and \; not \; mon(y) \\ \\ then \; (\exists \, animal \; x', \, y') \begin{bmatrix} x' \prec_{par} y' \; and \\ mon(x') \; and \; not \; \big(mon(y')\big) \end{bmatrix} \end{bmatrix}.$$

In other words, if someone who is not a monkey has an ancestor who is, then someone who is not a monkey has a parent who is.

Problem 13.3 (quotient-remainder)   page 638

Prove the *quotient-remainder* property

$$\begin{matrix} (\forall \, integer \; x) \\ (\forall \, positive \; y) \end{matrix} \begin{bmatrix} x \; = \; y \cdot quot(x, y) + rem(x, y) \\ and \\ rem(x, y) < y \end{bmatrix}.$$

Hint: Follow the informal proof in Section 8.7. You may use any of the properties invoked in that proof.

Problem 13.4 (greatest common divisor)   page 638

Prove that $gcd(x, y)$ is indeed a common divisor of x and y, that is,

$$(\forall \, integer \; x, \, y) \begin{bmatrix} gcd(x, y) \; \preceq_{div} x \\ and \\ gcd(x, y) \; \preceq_{div} y \end{bmatrix} \qquad (common \; divisor)$$

Hint: Follow the proof in Section 8.9. You may use any of the properties invoked in that proof.

Problem 13.5 (cumulative sum)   page 638

In the theory of tuples of nonnegative integers, we define the function $sum(x)$ to compute the sum of the elements of a tuple x, by the axioms

$$sum(\langle\,\rangle) \;=\; 0 \qquad\qquad (empty)$$

$$\begin{array}{l}(\forall\ integer\ u)\\(\forall\ tuple\ x)\end{array}\bigl[sum(u \diamond x) \;=\; u + sum(x)\bigr] \qquad (insertion)$$

We also define (Problem 12.6) the function $sumc(x)$ for the same purpose by the axioms

$$sumc(\langle\,\rangle) \;=\; 0 \qquad\qquad (empty)$$

$$(\forall\ integer\ u)\bigl[sumc(\langle u\rangle) \;=\; u\bigr] \qquad (singleton)$$

$$\begin{array}{l}(\forall\ integer\ u,\ v)\\(\forall\ tuple\ x)\end{array}\bigl[sumc\bigl(u \diamond (v \diamond x)\bigr) \;=\; sumc\bigl((u + v) \diamond x\bigr)\bigr]$$
$$(double\ insertion)$$

Show that these axioms do indeed define the same function, that is,

$$(\forall\ tuple\ x)\bigl[sumc(x) \;=\; sum(x)\bigr] \qquad (alternative\ definition)$$

Problem 13.6 (flattree)   page 638

Consider a theory that combines the theories of the tuples and the trees. In the combined theory we identify the atoms of the tuples with the atoms of the trees, and therefore they are expressed by a single predicate symbol $atom(x)$.

Recall that, in Section 10.4, we defined a function $flattree(x)$, which, for any tree x, yields the tuple whose atoms are the atoms of x, in left-to-right order. We also defined a function $flattree2(x,\ z)$, which, for any tree x and tuple z, flattens x and appends the resulting tuple with the tuple z.

Prove that $flattree2$ gives an alternative definition of the $flattree$ function, that is,

$$(\forall\ tree\ x)\bigl[flattree(x) \;=\; flattree2(x,\ \langle\,\rangle)\bigr] \qquad (special\ flattree2)$$

Hint: First prove the more general property

$$\begin{array}{l}(\forall\ tree\ x)\\(\forall\ tuple\ z)\end{array}\bigl[flattree2(x,\ z) \;=\; flattree(x) \diamond z\bigr] \qquad (general\ flattree2)$$

You may follow the intuitive proof in Section 10.4, using either stepwise or well-founded induction.

Problem 13.7 (dual version)   page 638

Justify the A-form of the *well-founded induction* rule.

Problem 13.8 (mergesort)   page 641

Prove the following properties of the *merge* and *mergesort* functions:

(a) *Ordered* property of *merge*

$$(\forall\ tuple\ x,\ y)\ \begin{bmatrix} if\ \ ordered(x)\ \ and\ \ ordered(y) \\ then\ \ ordered\,(merge(x,\ y)) \end{bmatrix}$$

Hint: See the intuitive proof in Section 12.5.

(b) *Permutation* property of *mergesort*

$$(\forall\ tuple\ x)\big[perm\,(x,\ mergesort(x))\big]$$

(c) *Ordered* property of *mergesort*

$$(\forall\ tuple\ x)\big[ordered\,(mergesort(x))\big]$$

(d) *Insorting* property of *mergesort*

$$(\forall\ tuple\ x)\big[mergesort(x)\ =\ insort(x)\big].$$

You may use the sort property $tuple(mergesort(x))$ without proof.

Problem 13.9 (gcdplus)   page 650

Prove that $gcdplus(x,\ y)$, defined in Section 12.5, is a common divisor of x and y, that is,

$$(\forall\ integer\ x,\ y)\ \begin{bmatrix} gcdplus(x,\ y)\ \preceq_{div}\ x \\ and \\ gcdplus(x,\ y)\ \preceq_{div}\ y \end{bmatrix} \qquad (common\ divisor)$$

An intuitive proof was requested in Problem 12.11.

VI

Theoretical

Issues

14

Decidability and Completeness

Until now, we have avoided certain natural questions concerning the power of a deductive system. We mean such questions as "Can we prove any valid sentence?" or "Can we detect when a sentence is not valid?" We do not have the space to give detailed treatment of such questions in this book. In this chapter, we survey the results. For proofs, the reader should consult the list of references.

14.1 DEDUCTION PROCEDURES

A *deduction procedure* is a computational method that attempts to test the validity of sentences in a particular logic, such as propositional logic, predicate logic, predicate logic with equality, or the theory of nonnegative integers. Given a (closed) sentence S of the logic, a deduction procedure may respond in one of several ways:

- It may terminate and return "yes," to indicate that S is valid.
- It may terminate and return "no," to indicate that S is not valid.
- It may terminate without deciding whether or not S is valid.
- It may fail to terminate (i.e., continue to run forever) without deciding whether or not S is valid.

It is desirable that a deduction procedure have certain properties, which we introduce here. For a given theory,

- A deduction procedure is *sound* if

  > if the procedure returns "yes,"
  > then the sentence S is indeed valid
  > > and
  >
  > if the procedure returns "no,"
  > then S is indeed not valid.

- A deduction procedure is *complete (for validity)* if

  > if the sentence S is valid,
  > then the procedure returns "yes."

- A deduction procedure is *complete for nonvalidity* if

  > if the sentence S is nonvalid,
  > then the procedure returns "no."

- A deduction procedure is a *decision procedure* if

  > it is complete for both validity and nonvalidity.

If we speak about completeness without mentioning validity or nonvalidity, we shall mean completeness for validity.

Note that a sound procedure may not be a decision procedure because it may run forever on some sentences. In fact, even a sound, complete procedure may not be a decision procedure because it may run forever on some nonvalid sentences.

A decision procedure clearly must terminate. It must also be sound. For if the procedure returns "yes," it does not return "no," and hence S cannot be nonvalid, that is, S must be valid. Similarly, if the procedure returns "no," it does not return "yes," and hence S cannot be valid, that is, S must be nonvalid.

Conversely, any procedure that is sound and that always terminates and returns "yes" or "no" must be a decision procedure. It is complete because if the given sentence is valid, a sound procedure cannot return "no," and hence it must return "yes." Similarly, it is complete for nonvalidity, because if the given sentence is nonvalid, a sound procedure cannot return "yes," and hence it must return "no."

The logics we deal with impose limitations on what kinds of deduction procedures we can hope to build. For propositional logic, we can construct a decision procedure. For predicate logic, and for predicate logic with equality, we can construct a sound, complete procedure but not a decision procedure: any sound procedure will run forever on some nonvalid sentences. For the theory of the nonnegative integers and the other theories with induction, we can construct a sound procedure but, in a certain sense, there do not exist sound, complete procedures. These limitations can be established with great generality; they do not apply only to deductive-tableau procedures, but to deduction procedures based on any methods.

14.2   PROPOSITIONAL LOGIC

The truth-table and proof-by-falsification methods are both decision procedures for propositional logic. Let us design a decision procedure based on the deductive-tableau framework.

A DECISION PROCEDURE

Procedure $prove(S)$

> To determine whether a given sentence S of propositional logic is valid, form the following tableau T_0:

assertions	goals
	S_0

> The goal S_0 is the result of simplifying S. Execute the procedure $provetab(T_0)$. ⌐

Procedure $provetab(T)$

> To determine whether the tableau T consisting entirely of a (simplified) goal G is valid,
>
> - If G is the truth symbol *true*, return "yes."
> - If G is the truth symbol *false*, return "no."
> - Otherwise, G contains some propositional symbol P.
>   - Apply the *resolution* rule to G and itself, matching P.
>   - Simplify the resulting sentence, obtaining G'.
>   - Form the tableau T' containing only the goal G'.
>   - Execute the procedure $provetab(T')$. ⌐

Note that, in executing the procedure *provetab*, we are always dealing with a tableau containing a single goal (and no assertions). Contrary to our usual practice, after applying the *resolution* rule, we discard the original goal and form a new tableau for the new goal. We also disregard the *polarity* strategy in applying this procedure. This is only for simplicity of exposition; we can formulate a similar decision procedure in which no goals are discarded and the *polarity* strategy is observed.

Before we establish that $prove(S)$ is a decision procedure, let us illustrate its application with two examples.

Example (valid sentence).   Let us apply the decision procedure to the valid sentence

$$\mathcal{S}: \quad \begin{array}{l} (P \ \ and \ \ Q) \ \ or \ \ false \\ or \\ (not \ P) \ \ or \ \ (not \ Q). \end{array}$$

We form a tableau $\mathcal{T}_0$ consisting entirely of the simplified goal $\mathcal{S}_0$:

assertions	goals
	$\mathcal{S}_0:$ $\boxed{P} \ \ and \ \ Q$ or $\left(not \ \boxed{P} \right) \ \ or \ \ (not \ Q)$

We execute the procedure $provetab(\mathcal{T}_0)$.

The goal is neither *true* nor *false*, but it contains the propositional symbol P. Applying the *resolution* rule to $\mathcal{S}_0$ and itself, matching P, we obtain the sentence

$$\begin{bmatrix} false \ \ and \ \ Q \\ or \\ (not \ false) \ \ or \ \ (not \ Q) \end{bmatrix} \quad and \quad \begin{bmatrix} true \ \ and \ \ Q \\ or \\ (not \ true) \ \ or \ \ (not \ Q) \end{bmatrix}.$$

We simplify this sentence and introduce the result as the goal of the new tableau $\mathcal{T}_1$:

assertions	goals
	$\mathcal{S}_1:$ $\boxed{Q} \ \ or \ \ \left(not \ \boxed{Q} \right)$

We execute the procedure $provetab(\mathcal{T}_1)$.

The goal is again neither *true* nor *false*, but it contains the propositional symbol Q. Applying the *resolution* rule to $\mathcal{S}_1$ and itself, matching Q, we obtain the sentence

$$\begin{array}{l} false \ \ or \ \ (not \ false) \\ \quad and \\ true \ \ or \ \ (not \ true). \end{array}$$

We simplify the sentence and enter the result $\mathcal{S}_2$ as the goal of a new tableau $\mathcal{T}_2$:

	$\mathcal{S}_2:$ $true$

We execute the procedure $provetab(\mathcal{T}_2)$.

The goal $\mathcal{S}_2$ is the truth symbol *true*. Therefore we return "yes," indicating that the original sentence $\mathcal{S}$ is valid.   ◢

Example (nonvalid sentence). Let us apply the decision procedure to the nonvalid sentence

$$\mathcal{S}: \quad P.$$

We form the tableau $\mathcal{T}_0$ whose sole goal is the simplified sentence

	$\mathcal{S}_0: \quad P$

We execute the procedure $provetab(\mathcal{T}_0)$.

The goal is neither *true* nor *false*, but it contains the propositional symbol P. Applying the *resolution* rule to P and itself, matching P, we obtain the sentence

$$false \quad and \quad true.$$

We simplify this sentence and introduce the result as the goal of the new tableau $\mathcal{T}_1$:

	$\mathcal{S}_1: \quad false$

We execute the procedure $provetab(\mathcal{T}_1)$.

The goal is the truth symbol *false*. Therefore we return "no," indicating that the original sentence $\mathcal{S}$ is not valid. ◢

JUSTIFICATION OF THE DECISION PROCEDURE

It is not immediately obvious that the procedure we have outlined is indeed a decision procedure for propositional logic. To show this, we show separately that the procedure terminates and is sound; this will imply that it is a decision procedure. The proof is informal.

Termination

We first observe that, whenever we execute $provetab(\mathcal{T})$, if the goal $\mathcal{G}$ in the tableau $\mathcal{T}$ is neither *true* nor *false*, it cannot (since it is simplified) contain any occurrence of *true* or *false*, and hence must contain some propositional symbol, $\mathcal{P}$. (If we had not provided a full set of *true-false* simplification rules, this would not be the case.)

We next observe that, each time we apply the *resolution* rule to goal $\mathcal{G}$ and itself, matching $\mathcal{P}$, we remove the propositional symbol $\mathcal{P}$ from the goal and do not introduce any new propositional symbols. In the subsequent simplification, we do not introduce any new propositional symbols either. Consequently, the new tableau $\mathcal{T}'$ has strictly fewer distinct propositional symbols than the given tableau $\mathcal{T}$. Since the original tableau has only finitely many distinct propositional symbols, we cannot continue to do this forever. That is, every execution of $provetab(\mathcal{T})$ terminates.

An execution of $prove(\mathcal{S})$ consists of only a single execution of $provetab(\mathcal{T}_0)$. Hence each execution of $prove(\mathcal{S})$ also terminates.

Soundness

To show soundness, we show that if the procedure *prove(S)* returns "yes," then the original sentence *S* is valid, and that if the procedure *prove(S)* returns "no," then the original sentence *S* is not valid. To show this, we must show a *soundness* lemma concerning the procedure *provetab(T)*.

Lemma (soundness)

With each execution of the procedure *provetab(T)*,

> the tableau *T* is valid
> if and only if
> the original sentence *S* is valid. ◢

Let us see why this is enough to establish soundness.

Soundness Lemma ⇒ Soundness

We must show that if the procedure *prove(S)* returns "yes" (or "no," respectively), then *S* is indeed valid (or not, respectively).

Suppose that *prove(S)* returns "yes." This means that, at some point, we have executed *provetab(T)*, where the tableau *T* consists of the goal *true*. That is, *T* is valid, and hence (by the lemma) *S* is also valid.

Similarly, suppose that *prove(S)* returns "no." This means that, at some point, we have executed *provetab(T)*, where *T* consists of the goal *false*. Therefore *T* is not valid, and hence (by the lemma) *S* is not valid either.

It remains to prove the soundness lemma.

Proof (soundness).   We actually show an equivalent condition, that, at every execution of the procedure *provetab(T)*,

> the original sentence *S* is false under some interpretation $\mathcal{I}$
> if and only if
> the tableau *T* is false under some interpretation $\mathcal{J}$.

This implies the desired lemma because if either *S* or *T* is valid, there is no interpretation under which it is false, hence (by the preceding condition) there is no interpretation under which the other is false, and hence the other must be valid, too.

The condition holds at the first execution of *provetab(T_0)* because then the sole goal of T_0 is S_0, the simplification of *S*, which is equivalent to *S*.

If the condition holds at some execution of *provetab(T)*, it also holds for the subsequent execution of *provetab(T')*. To show this, it suffices to show that

> the tableau *T* is false under some interpretation $\mathcal{J}$
> if and only if
> the subsequent tableau *T'* is false under some interpretation $\mathcal{J}'$.

In the forward direction, this follows from the justification of the *resolution* rule itself. After all, the goal $\mathcal{G}'$ of $\mathcal{T}'$ is obtained from the goal $\mathcal{G}$ of $\mathcal{T}$ by applying the *resolution* rule and simplifying. Suppose, to the contrary, that $\mathcal{T}$ is false under some interpretation $\mathcal{J}$, that is, the goal $\mathcal{G}$ of $\mathcal{T}$ is not valid, but that $\mathcal{T}'$ is not false under any interpretation $\mathcal{J}'$, that is, $\mathcal{T}'$ is valid and therefore the goal $\mathcal{G}'$ of $\mathcal{T}'$ is valid. Thus we have obtained a valid goal $\mathcal{G}'$ by applying the *resolution* rule to a goal $\mathcal{G}$ that is not valid and simplifying, contradicting the soundness of the *resolution* rule .

To show the reverse direction, let us write the goal $\mathcal{G}$ of $\mathcal{T}$ as $\mathcal{G}[\mathcal{P}]$. We suppose that the goal $\mathcal{G}'$ of $\mathcal{T}'$ is false under some interpretation $\mathcal{J}'$, and show that then $\mathcal{G}[\mathcal{P}]$ is false under some interpretation $\mathcal{J}$. We know that $\mathcal{G}'$ is the result of simplifying the sentence

$$\mathcal{G}[false] \ \ and \ \ \mathcal{G}[true].$$

Hence one of the two conjuncts is false under $\mathcal{J}'$. We treat each possibility separately.

Case: $\mathcal{G}[false]$ is false under $\mathcal{J}'$

We take $\mathcal{J}$ to be the modified interpretation $\langle \mathcal{P} \leftarrow false \rangle \circ \mathcal{J}'$. Because $\mathcal{P}$ does not occur in $\mathcal{G}[false]$, we know that $\mathcal{G}[false]$ has the same truth-value under $\mathcal{J}$ and $\mathcal{J}'$, that is, $\mathcal{G}[false]$ is false under $\mathcal{J}$. Because $\mathcal{P}$ and *false* have the same truth-value under $\mathcal{J}$, we know $\mathcal{G}[\mathcal{P}]$ and $\mathcal{G}[false]$ have the same truth-value under $\mathcal{J}$, that is, $\mathcal{G}[\mathcal{P}]$ is false under $\mathcal{J}$, as we wanted to show.

Case: $\mathcal{G}[true]$ is false under $\mathcal{J}'$

This case is treated similarly. We take $\mathcal{J}$ to be the modified interpretation $\langle \mathcal{P} \leftarrow true \rangle \circ \mathcal{J}'$ and show that $\mathcal{G}[\mathcal{P}]$ is false under $\mathcal{J}$, as before.

This concludes the proof of the soundness lemma and the justification of the decision procedure for propositional logic. ⌐

Propositional logic is an ideal logic, in that we can test its sentences for validity. We do not have this luxury for the other logics in our repertoire.

14.3 PREDICATE LOGIC

According to Church's theorem, there is no decision procedure for predicate logic (see our references). We can nevertheless develop a sound, complete procedure. Such a procedure will return "yes" if and only if given a valid sentence of predicate logic. On the other hand, if the sentence is not valid, the procedure will sometimes return "no," but at other times will run on forever. The difficulty in using such a procedure is that if after several hours it continues to run, we do not know whether the sentence is valid and the procedure will ultimately return "yes," or whether the sentence is not valid and the procedure will run on forever.

A SOUND, COMPLETE PROCEDURE

The procedure we present, based on the deductive-tableau framework, is not efficient enough to be used in practice for any but the simplest examples, but it does have the desired properties of soundness and completeness.

Procedure $prove(\mathcal{S})$

To attempt to determine whether a sentence $\mathcal{S}$ of predicate logic is valid, form the following initial tableau $\mathcal{T}_0$:

assertions	goals
	$\mathcal{S}_0$

Here $\mathcal{S}_0$ is the result of simplifying $\mathcal{S}$. Then execute the procedure $provetab(\mathcal{T}_0)$. ⏎

Procedure $provetab(\mathcal{T})$

To attempt to determine whether the tableau $\mathcal{T}$ is valid,

- If $\mathcal{T}$ contains a final row, either the final goal *true* or the final assertion *false*, return "yes."
- Otherwise, let $\mathcal{T}'$ be the tableau obtained by adding to $\mathcal{T}$ every possible row derived from $\mathcal{T}$ by the application of a single predicate-logic deduction rule (after simplification).
  - If no new rows can be derived, that is, $\mathcal{T}'$ has the same rows as $\mathcal{T}$, return "no." This situation is known as a *stalemate.*
  - Otherwise, execute the procedure $provetab(\mathcal{T}')$. ⏎

This procedure will systematically apply all possible deduction rules to the initial tableau and will ultimately discover a proof of $\mathcal{S}$ if one exists. To simplify the exposition, we disregard the *polarity* strategy, but completeness would still be maintained if we observed it.

JUSTIFICATION OF THE PROCEDURE

The soundness of this procedure follows from the soundness of the deduction rules for predicate logic. If the procedure returns "yes," we must have derived a final row. That is, we have discovered a proof of the given sentence S, indicating that S is valid.

We shall not show the completeness of the procedure. It can be shown that if S is a valid sentence of predicate logic, it has a deductive-tableau proof. In this case, the procedure will ultimately derive a final row and return "yes."

If S is not valid, the procedure may discover a stalemate and return "no," but it may continue to derive more and more new rows, without ever obtaining a final row. We illustrate each of these possibilities with an example.

Example (stalemate). Let us apply the procedure $prove(S)$ to the nonvalid sentence

$$S : \ p(a).$$

We form the initial tableau $\mathcal{T}_0$:

assertions	goals
	$p(a)$

We then execute the procedure $provetab(\mathcal{T}_0)$.

No deduction rules apply to the tableau. Therefore a stalemate has occurred, and we return "no." ◢

In this example, a stalemate has occurred immediately. Often a stalemate will occur after several rows have been derived but no new rows can be obtained.

Now let us consider an example in which the procedure fails to terminate.

Example (runs forever). Let us apply the procedure $prove(S)$ to the nonvalid sentence

$$S : \ (\exists x)\big[p(x) \ \text{and} \ not \ p(f(x))\big].$$

We form the initial tableau $\mathcal{T}_0$:

assertions	goals
	$(\exists x)^\exists \big[p(x) \ \text{and} \ not \ p(f(x))\big]$

We then execute the procedure $provetab(\mathcal{T}_0)$.

By the $\exists$-*elimination* rule, we may drop the quantifier from the goal, obtaining the new row

	$p(x) \ \text{and} \ not \ \boxed{p(f(x))}^{\,-}$

This row is added to the tableau T_0 to form the tableau T_1. We execute the procedure $provetab(T_1)$.

In preparation for applying the *resolution* rule to the preceding goal, let us make another copy of the row, renaming the variable:

	$\boxed{p(x')}^{+}$ *and not* $p\big(f(x')\big)$

By application of the *resolution* rule, taking $\{x' \leftarrow f(x)\}$, we obtain (after simplification) the row

	$p(x)$ *and not* $p\big(f\big(f(x)\big)\big)$

By other applications of the resolution rule, it is possible to obtain other new rows. All of these rows are added to the tableau T_1 to form the tableau T_2. We execute the procedure $provetab(T_2)$.

Applying the *resolution* rule to the new row and itself as before, we may obtain the row

	$p(x)$ *and not* $p\big(f\big(f\big(f\big(f(x)\big)\big)\big)\big)$

This row is included (among others) in the tableau T_3. We execute the procedure $provetab(T_3)$.

The reader can see that stalemate is impossible; we can continue the process indefinitely, always obtaining a new row. Also, since the sentence S is not valid and the procedure is sound, we can never obtain a final row and can never return "yes." Therefore the procedure will run forever in this case. ⏌

PROOF STRATEGIES

The preceding procedure is far too expensive to be of practical value. Typically, in executing the procedure $provetab(T)$ for a tableau T of any size, there are many ways to apply deduction rules, yielding many new rows, so that the tableau T' is considerably larger than the tableau T. We quickly exhaust the available space and time before we discover a proof. It is necessary to apply strategies that restrict the application of deduction rules, so that fewer new rows are added. The *polarity* strategy is one such restriction, but it is far from sufficient to make the procedure useful.

It is desirable that strategies retain completeness, that is, that the procedure with the strategy is still complete for predicate logic. This is the case for the *polarity* strategy. The efficiency problem is sufficiently severe, however, that strategies that destroy completeness are still worthy of consideration. A procedure employing such a strategy will fail to prove some valid sentences, but perhaps it can still prove an important class of theorems.

14.4   AXIOMATIC THEORIES

The completeness problem for an axiomatic theory is simplified if there are only finitely many axioms.

FINITE THEORIES

If a theory is defined by giving a finite set of axioms $\mathcal{A}_1, \ldots, \mathcal{A}_m$, we can easily adapt the procedure *prove*($\mathcal{S}$) for predicate logic to provide a sound, complete procedure for the axiomatic theory, but not necessarily a decision procedure.

Procedure *prove*($\mathcal{S}$)

To attempt to determine whether a sentence $\mathcal{S}$ is valid in a finite theory whose axioms are (after simplification) $\mathcal{A}_1, \ldots, \mathcal{A}_m$, form the initial tableau $\mathcal{T}_0$:

assertions	goals
$\mathcal{A}_1$	
$\vdots$	
$\mathcal{A}_m$	
	$\mathcal{S}_0$

Here $\mathcal{S}_0$ is the result of simplifying $\mathcal{S}$. Then execute the procedure *provetab*($\mathcal{T}_0$). ◢

Procedure *provetab*($\mathcal{T}$)

The procedure *provetab*($\mathcal{T}$) is the same as for predicate logic. ◢

Many of our theories, including the theory of equality and the inductive theories, are defined with the help of an axiom schema, which stands for an infinite set of axioms. We cannot treat such theories as before, because we can only include a finite number of assertions in any tableau. What we have done in such cases is to provide additional deduction rules (e.g., the *equality* rule or the *induction* rule) to take the place of these axioms.

THEORY OF EQUALITY

In the case of the theory of equality, we can obtain a sound, complete procedure, but not a decision procedure.

Procedure *prove*($\mathcal{S}$)

To attempt to determine whether a sentence $\mathcal{S}$ is valid in the theory of equality, form the initial tableau $\mathcal{T}_0$:

$x = x$	
	$\mathcal{S}_0$

Here $\mathcal{S}_0$ is the result of simplifying $\mathcal{S}$. Then execute the procedure *provetab*($\mathcal{T}_0$). ◢

Procedure *provetab*($\mathcal{T}$)

This is the same as the procedure *provetab*($\mathcal{T}$) for predicate logic, except that here we apply the *equality* rule, as well as the predicate-logic deduction rules, to $\mathcal{T}$ in forming the rows of the new tableau $\mathcal{T}'$. ◢

The procedure *prove*($\mathcal{S}$) may be shown to be sound and complete, but it may run forever if given a nonvalid sentence of the theory. Again, even for valid sentences it is grossly inefficient.

This procedure can be extended to any theory with equality defined by a finite number of axioms $\mathcal{A}_1, \ldots, \mathcal{A}_m$ simply by taking the initial tableau to be $\mathcal{T}_0$:

assertions	goals
$\mathcal{A}_1$	
$\vdots$	
$\mathcal{A}_m$	
$x = x$	
	$\mathcal{S}_0$

The resulting procedure, although again sound and complete, will not be a decision procedure.

THEORY OF THE NONNEGATIVE INTEGERS

The situation is more complex in formulating deduction procedures for our theories with induction. We will talk about the theory of the nonnegative integers with addition, multiplication, and exponentiation here, but similar remarks apply to the theories of tuples, trees, and other theories with induction.

The axioms for the theory of nonnegative integers fail to describe only the intended models; there are other, *nonstandard* models, under which the axioms are true even though these models do not correspond to our intuitive notion of the nonnegative integers.

The domains of our intended models contain elements

$$0 \ \rightarrow \ 1 \ \rightarrow \ 2 \ \rightarrow \ \ldots \ .$$

Here, $0, 1, 2, \ldots$ are the ordinary nonnegative integers, and the arrow $\rightarrow$ indicates the action of the successor function. These domain elements are finite nonnegative integers.

In contrast, the domain of one of the nonstandard models contains not only the ordinary nonnegative integers

$$0 \ \rightarrow \ 1 \ \rightarrow \ 2 \ \rightarrow \ \ldots$$

but also an infinite number of "chains" of infinite elements

$$\ldots \ \rightarrow \ d{-}2 \ \rightarrow \ d{-}1 \ \rightarrow \ d \ \rightarrow \ d{+}1 \ \rightarrow \ d{+}2 \ \rightarrow \ \ldots \ .$$

The infinite elements $d, d \pm 1, d \pm 2, \ldots$ are distinct from any of the finite nonnegative integers $0, 1, 2, \ldots$. The basic axioms for the nonnegative integers all hold under these models.

According to the *Gödel incompleteness* theorem, there are some sentences in the theory of the nonnegative integers that are true under all the intended models but that do not follow from the axioms. These sentences are false under some of the nonstandard models and thus are not valid in the theory.

The flaw is not with our particular set of axioms. Any (finitely many) axioms or axiom schemata that hold under the intended models also hold under some nonstandard models. In the corresponding theory, there will be some sentences that are true under the intended models but false under some of the nonstandard models; naturally, we shall be unable to prove such sentences.

Let us say that a (closed) sentence is *i-valid* if it is true under all the intended models for a theory. Thus all valid sentences are i-valid, but a sentence may be i-valid without being valid. For the theory of the nonnegative integers, we are more interested in i-validity than in ordinary validity. As a further consequence of *Gödel's incompleteness* theorem, we cannot develop a deduction procedure for the nonnegative integers that is *i-sound* and *i-complete*, in the sense that it can prove precisely the i-valid sentences. The best we can do is to develop a procedure that is complete and i-sound. Given a valid sentence, such a procedure must return "yes." Given an i-valid sentence, it may return "yes" or may run on forever. Given a non-i-valid sentence, it may return "no" or may run on forever.

For the theory of the nonnegative integers, here is a simple procedure with these properties.

Procedure *prove*$(\mathcal{S})$

To attempt to determine whether a sentence $\mathcal{S}$ of the basic theory of the nonnegative integers is i-valid, form the initial tableau $\mathcal{T}_0$:

$\mathcal{A}_1$	
$\vdots$	
$\mathcal{A}_m$	
$x = x$	
	$\mathcal{S}_0$

where $\mathcal{A}_1, \mathcal{A}_2, \ldots, \mathcal{A}_m$ are the axioms for the nonnegative integers, and $\mathcal{S}_0$ is the result of simplifying $\mathcal{S}$. Execute the procedure *provetab*$(\mathcal{T}_0)$. ◢

Procedure *provetab*$(\mathcal{T})$

This is the same as the procedure for predicate logic, except that we apply to $\mathcal{T}$ the *stepwise induction* rule and the *equality* rule, as well as the deduction rules of predicate logic, in forming the rows of the new tableau $\mathcal{T}'$. ◢

This procedure is complete and i-sound but is neither i-complete nor a decision procedure. In fact, as it stands, the procedure will never be able to establish that a given sentence is non-i-valid; that is, it will never return "no." The only way for *provetab*$(\mathcal{T})$ to return "no" is to produce a stalemate, in which no new rows are generated. In the preceding tableau, however, unless a strategy is imposed, it is always possible to derive the endless sequence of assertions

$integer(0^+)$	
$integer((0^+)^+)$	
$integer(((0^+)^+)^+)$	
$\vdots$	

That is, stalemate cannot occur.

A similar complete and i-sound deduction procedure can be constructed for the other theories with induction.

Annotated Bibliography

We make no attempt to give a complete survey of the literature. Rather, we include a selection of text and reference books and a few technical papers, which will provide further information on the topics included in this volume.

Introductions to logic from a mathematical point of view, with no computational emphasis:

J. BARWISE and J. ETCHEMENDY, *The Language of First-Order Logic.* Center for the Study of Language and Information, Stanford, California, 1990. The text for a first course in logic; includes a disk for the educational system TARSKI'S WORLD.

J. BELL and M. MACHOVER, *A Course in Mathematical Logic.* North-Holland Publishing Company, Amsterdam, 1977. A very comprehensive introduction to logic based on analytic tableaux, which are different from deductive tableaux.

A. CHURCH, *Introduction to Mathematical Logic.* Princeton University Press, Princeton, New Jersey, 1956. An especially detailed treatment of propositional and pure predicate logic.

H. B. ENDERTON, *A Mathematical Introduction to Logic.* Academic Press, New York, 1972. An elementary introduction to first-order logic, including the completeness and incompleteness theorems.

H. B. ENDERTON, *Elements of Set Theory.* Academic Press, New York, 1977. Includes a discussion of well-founded relations and well-founded induction.

S. C. KLEENE, *Mathematical Logic.* John Wiley and Sons, New York, 1967. Covers the relationship between logic and computability.

E. MENDELSON, *Introduction to Mathematical Logic.* D. Van Nostrand, Monterey, California, 1987. Includes formal number theory, formal set theory, and computability.

J. R. SCHOENFIELD, *Mathematical Logic.* Addison–Wesley, Reading, Massachusetts, 1967. A more advanced view of logic, including model theory, recursion theory, and set theory.

D. VAN DALEN, *Logic and Structure*. Springer-Verlag, Berlin, 1989. A relatively informal introduction to propositional and pure predicate logic that emphasizes the notion of proof.

More popular and informal introductions to logic, and especially Gödel's incompleteness theorem:

D. R. HOFSTADTER, *Gödel, Escher, Bach: An Eternal Golden Braid*. Basic Books, New York, 1979. A discussion of the notion of self-reference in logic and art.

R. SMULLYAN, *What Is the Name of This Book?* Prentice-Hall, Englewood Cliffs, New Jersey, 1978. An introduction to logic, including Gödel's theorem, in the form of a sequence of puzzles.

Introductions to mathematical logic that are oriented toward automated deduction or associated topics:

P. B. ANDREWS, *An Introduction to Mathematical Logic and Type Theory: To Truth through Proof.* Academic Press, Orlando, Florida, 1986. Includes higher-order logic, in which one can quantify over relations and functions as well as over domain elements.

K. H. BLÄSIUS and HANS-JÜRGEN BÜRCKERT (editors), *Deduction Systems in Artificial Intelligence.* Ellis Horwood Limited, Chichester, 1989. Includes resolution, term-rewriting systems, and well-founded induction.

D. DUFFY, *Principles of Automated Theorem Proving.* John Wiley and Sons, Chichester, 1991. Discusses resolution, term-rewriting systems, PROLOG, and the theorem prover of Boyer and Moore.

M. FITTING, *First-Order Logic and Automated Theorem Proving*, Springer-Verlag, New York, 1990. Relates resolution and analytic tableaux. Equality but no theories with induction.

J. H. GALLIER, *Logic for Computer Science: Foundations of Automatic Theorem Proving.* Harper and Row, New York, 1986. Especially good on the relation between theorem proving and conventional deduction systems.

V. SPERSCHNEIDER and G. ANTONIOU, *Logic: A Foundation for Computer Science*, Addison–Wesley, Wokingham, 1991.

Introductions to automated reasoning that emphasize the resolution rule:

C. L. CHANG and R. C. T. LEE, *Symbolic Logic and Mechanical Theorem Proving.* Academic Press, New York, 1973. A clear, classical treatment of resolution theorem proving and its extensions.

D. W. LOVELAND, *Automated Theorem Proving: A Logical Basis*. North-Holland, New York, 1978. A thorough treatment of (primarily) resolution theorem proving.

J. A. ROBINSON, *Logic: Form and Function. The Mechanization of Deductive Reasoning*. North-Holland, New York, 1979. An elegant, informal introduction to automated deduction emphasizing resolution and its extensions.

L. WOS, R. OVERBEEK, E. LUSK, and J. BOYLE, *Automated Reasoning: Introduction and Applications*. Prentice-Hall, Englewood Cliffs, New Jersey, 1984. Special emphasis on the implementation and strategic aspects of resolution theorem proving.

Introductions to automated reasoning that emphasize nonresolution approaches:

W. BIBEL, *Automated Theorem Proving*. Friedr. Vieweg und Sohn, Braunschweig, Germany, 1987. A novel approach to theorem proving in predicate logic.

R. S. BOYER and J S. MOORE, *A Computational Logic*. Academic Press, New York, 1979. A complete description of a well-known theorem-proving system, which focuses on proofs using mathematical induction.

A. BUNDY, *The Computer Modelling of Mathematical Reasoning*. Academic Press, London, 1983. Focuses on mimicking the procedures of a human mathematician.

R. L. CONSTABLE et al., *Implementing Mathematics with the Nuprl Proof Development System*. Prentice-Hall, Englewood Cliffs, New Jersey, 1986. A description of a system for interactive theorem proving in a "constructive" logic.

M. J. C. GORDON, HOL: A Proof Generating System for Higher-Order Logic. In G. Birtwistle and P. A. Subrahmanyam (editors), VLSI *Specification, Verification, and Synthesis*, Kluwer Academic Publishers, Dordrecht, 1988, 73–128. Describes a widely used interactive theorem prover.

L. C. PAULSON, *Logic and Computation: Interactive Proof with Cambridge LCF*. Cambridge Univesity Press, Cambridge, 1987. Emphasizes interactive methods for theorem proving in higher-order logic.

Application of automated deduction to artificial intelligence, program synthesis, and logic programming:

M. R. GENESERETH and N. J. NILSSON, *Logical Foundations of Artificial Intelligence*. Morgan Kaufmann, Los Altos, California, 1987. Includes reasoning about knowledge and belief and probabilistic reasoning.

R. KOWALSKI, *Logic for Problem Solving*. North Holland, New York, 1979. Discusses the relation between theorem proving and logic programming.

Z. MANNA and R. WALDINGER, A Deductive Approach to Program Synthesis. *ACM Transactions on Programming Languages and Systems* 2 (1980) 90–121. Extension of the deductive-tableau framework to the derivation of programs.

Z. MANNA and R. WALDINGER, Fundamentals of Deductive Program Synthesis. *IEEE Transactions on Software Engineering* 18 (1992) 674–704. An introductory treatment of the deductive-tableau approach to program derivation.

L. S. STERLING and E. SHAPIRO, *The Art of Prolog*. MIT Press, 1986. Prolog programs are logical sentences; a Prolog interpreter is a kind of theorem prover.

Texts relating logic to the theory of computation:

N. J. CUTLAND, *Computability*. Cambridge University Press, Cambridge, 1980. An introduction to computability.

H. R. LEWIS and C. H. PAPADIMITRIOU, *Elements of the Theory of Computation*. Prentice-Hall, Englewood Cliffs, New Jersey, 1981. Automata theory, computability, and logic.

Z. MANNA, *Mathematical Theory of Computation*. McGraw-Hill, New York, 1974. The relationship beween logic and program correctness.

H. ROGERS, JR., *Theory of Recursive Functions and Effective Computability*. McGraw-Hill, New York, 1967. A classic and rich introduction to computability.

Books applying logic to the construction of correct computer programs:

E. W. DIJKSTRA, *A Discipline of Programming*. Prentice-Hall, Englewood Cliffs, New Jersey, 1976. Systematic program construction, based on logical ideas, with many examples.

D. GRIES, *The Science of Programming*. Springer-Verlag, New York, 1981. A logical method for program development.

S. HAYASHI and H. NAKANO, *PX: A Computational Logic*. MIT Press, Cambridge, Massachusetts, 1988. A theoretical development of a logic PX (Program eXtractor) for exatracting programs from proofs.

C. MORGAN, *Programming from Specifications*. Prentice-Hall, New York, 1990. A logic that intermixes programs with specifications; programs are developed by the systematic application of refinement laws.

J. C. REYNOLDS, *The Craft of Programming*. Prentice-Hall International, Englewood Cliffs, New Jersey, 1981. An introduction to programming based on program verification notions.

Historical references:

T. SKOLEM, Logisch-kombinatorische Untersuchungen über die Erfüllbárkeit oder Beweisbarkeit Mathematischer Sätze nebst einem Theorem über Dichte Mengen.

Videnskopsselskapits skifter, I. *Matematik-Naturvidenskabelig Klasse* 4 (1920). English translation, Logico-Combinatorial Investigations in the Satisfiability or Provability of Mathematical Propositions: A Simplified Proof of a Theorem by L. Löwenheim and Generalizations of the Theorem. In van Heijenoort [1967]. Introduces the notion of skolemization.

J. HERBRAND, *Recherches sur la Théorie de la Démonstration*. Ph.D. dissertation, University of Paris, Paris, 1930. Introduces the notion of unification and several other ideas influential in theorem proving.

K. GÖDEL, Über Formal Unentscheidbare Sätze der Principia Mathematica und Verwandter Systeme I. *Monatschefte für Mathematik und Physik* 38 (1931), 173–198. English translation, On Formally Undecidable Propositions of Principia Mathematica and Related Systems. In van Heijenoort [1967]. Establishes the incompleteness of the theory of the nonnegative integers.

E. ZERMELO, Grundlagen einer Allgemeinen Theorie der Mathematischen Satzsysteme. *Fundamenta Mathematicae* 25 (1935) 136–146. Introduces the notion of a well-founded relation.

A. CHURCH, A Note on the Entscheidungsproblem. *Journal of Symbolic Logic* 1 (1936) 40–41. Correction 101–102. Establishes the undecidability of predicate logic.

J. VAN HEIJENOORT (editor), *From Frege to Gödel*. Harvard University Press, Cambridge, Massachusetts, 1967. A collection of classical papers in mathematical logic.

J. SIEKMANN and G. WRIGHTSON, *Automation of Reasoning 1: Classical Papers on Computational Logic 1957–1966*. Springer-Verlag, Berlin, 1983. A collection of early theorem-proving papers.

J. A. ROBINSON, A Machine-oriented Logic based on the Resolution Principle. *Journal of the ACM* 12 (1965) 23–41. Introduces the resolution rule.

Papers that provide theoretical background for this book:

N. MURRAY, Completely Nonclausal Theorem Proving. *Artificial Intelligence* 18 (1) 1982, 67–85. Introduces nonclausal resolution independently from Manna and Waldinger [1980] and establishes its completeness for predicate logic.

J. HSIANG and M. RUSINOWITCH, A New Method for Establishing Refutational Completeness in Theorem Proving. *Eighth International Conference on Automated Deduction*. Springer-Verlag, Berlin, 1986, 141–152. Establishes the completeness of the resolution and equality rules for the theory of equality.

Index of Symbols

General Index

We use the following abbreviations throughout the index:

PROP — propositional logic
PRED — predicate logic
INTEGER — theory of the nonnegative integers
TUPLE — theory of tuples
TREE — theory of trees

A

A-form,
  of *∃-elimination* [rule], 290.
  of *stepwise induction* [rule], 551.
  of *∀-elimination* [rule], 286.
  of *well-founded induction* [rule], 638, 652.

AA-form,
  of *equality* (in theory with equality) [rule], 354, 355.
  of *equivalence* (in PRED) [rule], 274, 276.
  of *equivalence* (in PROP) [rule], 104, 105.
  of *resolution* (in PRED) [rule], 259, 267.
  of *resolution* (in PROP) [rule], 75.

abelian group, 333.

abstract sentence, 3, 122.

ack (in INTEGER) [function], 600.
  double successor for [axiom], 600.
  exponent of [property], 600, 619.
  greater than of [property], 600.
  left monotonicity of [property], 600, 619.
  left zero for [axiom], 600.
  problems, 619.
  rapid growth of, 600.

right monotonicity of [property], 600, 619.
right zero for [axiom], 600.
sort of [property], 600, 619.

Ackermann function:
  see *ack* (in INTEGER) [function].

Adam (in family theory) [axiom], 310.

addition $x + y$ (in INTEGER) [function], 382.
  annihilation of [property], 392, 429.
  associativity of [property], 392, 429.
  commutativity of [property], 383, 390, 547.
  computation of, 386.
  left cancellation of [property], 392, 429.
  left functional substitutivity for [axiom], 382.
  left successor of [property], 383, 388, 543.
  left zero of [property], 383, 387, 539.
  problems, 429.
  right cancellation of [property], 392, 429.
  right functional substitutivity for [axiom], 382.
  right one of [property], 383.
  right successor for [axiom], 382, 539.
  right zero for [axiom], 382, 539.